Christian  :holars

Or, Sketches of Education from the Christian Era to the Council of Trent

Augusta Theodosia Drane

Alpha Editions

This edition published in 2024

ISBN : 9789367247648

Design and Setting By
Alpha Editions
www.alphaedis.com
Email - info@alphaedis.com

Contents

PREFACE. ....- 1 -

CHAPTER I. ....- 3 -

CHAPTER II. ....- 30 -

CHAPTER III. ....- 47 -

CHAPTER IV. ....- 73 -

CHAPTER V. ....- 93 -

CHAPTER VI. ....- 117 -

CHAPTER VII. ....- 158 -

CHAPTER VIII. ....- 172 -

CHAPTER IX. ....- 183 -

CHAPTER X. ....- 207 -

CHAPTER XI. ....- 244 -

CHAPTER XII. ....- 264 -

CHAPTER XIII. ....- 298 -

CHAPTER XIV. ....- 334 -

CHAPTER XV. ....- 366 -

CHAPTER XVI. ....- 387 -

CHAPTER XVII. ....- 413 -

CHAPTER XVIII. ....- 430 -

CHAPTER XIX. ....- 464 -

CHAPTER XX. ....- 490 -

CHAPTER XXI. ....- 514 -

CHAPTER XXII. ....- 536 -

CHAPTER XXIII. ....- 549 -

CHAPTER XXIV. ....- 574 -

FOOTNOTES: ....- 592 -

PREFACE.

THE following pages have been written with the view of presenting a general and connected sketch of the history of Christian Education down to the period of the Council of Trent, illustrated from the lives of those who have, in successive ages, taken part in that great work. A subject extending over so wide a field could of necessity be only partially treated, and it seems desirable, therefore, to explain certain omissions which might otherwise cause disappointment. It was believed that the object aimed at would, in most cases, be better accomplished by introducing the reader to the teachers themselves, than by undertaking to give a complete account and critical examination of their writings. Such an examination would properly enter into a history of Christian Literature, a grand *desideratum* indeed, but one which the present volumes makes no pretensions to supply. Again, for obvious reasons, the philosophical and theological controversies connected with the lives of the great men who form the subjects of the following studies, have been designedly touched on with the greatest possible brevity: the history of such controversies seeming to belong to Ecclesiastical History, and to be unsuitable in a work like the present.

It has been the wish of the writer to treat the subject from a purely historical point of view, and to increase the value of the narrative by, as far as possible, preserving the colouring, and sometimes even the very language, of the original historians.

The notes appended to the text will give a general idea of the authorities whence the matter has been derived. The Ecclesiastical Histories of Fleury and Rohrbacher have furnished the groundwork of the general narrative. In the account of the Irish schools, the chronology and the main facts have been drawn from Lanigan's Ecclesiastical History of Ireland. The sketch of the restoration of letters under Charlemagne has been chiefly taken from Crevier's *Histoire de l'Université de Paris*, Launoy's Treatise *De Scholis Celebrioribus*, and the various lives, both ancient and modern, of Charlemagne. In the chapters referring to the subsequent history of the Dark Ages, constant use has been made of the *Acta Sanctorum Ord. S. Benedicti*, by D'Achery and Mabillon, and of the collections of the Lives of the Saints by Surius and the Bollandists; also of the *Vetera Analecta* of Mabillon, the *Spicilegium* of D'Achery, the *Amplissima Collectio* of Martene, and the *Histoire Litteraire de la France*, by the Benedictines of St. Maur. Much valuable matter has also been derived from the *Monumenta Germaniæ Historica* of Pertz, and the collection of ancient German Chronicles by Meibomius; the account of the school and scholars of St. Gall's being taken from Ekkehard's History *De Casibus S. Galli*, printed in the first volume of Goldasti's collection, and from the Benedictine Life of B. Notker. The notices of the foreign universities are chiefly drawn from Crevier, and from Tiraboschi's *Storia della Letteratura Italiana*, which latter work has been almost exclusively used in the chapters on the Renaissance in Italy. The chapter on the Dominicans and the Universities is compiled from a considerable number of authorities; chiefly, Touron's *Vies des Hommes Illustres*, the *Scriptores Ordinis Prædicatorum* by Echard and Quetil, the French translation of Dr. Sighart's *Life of Albert the Great*, and the *Constitutions of the Order*.

The sketches of our English schools and universities are mostly derived from Wood's *Antiquities of Oxford*, Ayliffe's *Ancient and Present State of the University of Oxford*, and Dugdale's *Monasticon*; whilst various notices of early English scholars have been gathered from Wright's *Biographia Britannica*, Warton's *History of English Poetry*, and the original lives of the English Saints, as given in the three collections already named. Hallam's *Literary History of Europe*, and Ranke's *History of the Popes*, have also been made considerable use of in treating of the period of the Renaissance, while the sketches of Colet and Pole have been drawn from their respective lives by Knight and Philipps. Pallavicini's *History of the Council of Trent*, and Touron's *Life of St. Charles Borromeo*, have furnished the chief materials for the concluding chapter of the work.

ST. DOMINIC'S CONVENT, STONE,
May 1867.

CHAPTER I.

THE RISE OF THE CHRISTIAN SCHOOLS.

A.D. 60 to 543.

IN the seventh year of the Emperor Nero, and the sixtieth of the Christian era, a little ship entered the harbour of Alexandria, and after rounding the great Pharos that stood at its northern extremity, cast anchor by that granite quay, round which was grouped, as in an amphitheatre, six miles in span, a city of palaces and temples. It bore on its decks one of whom that proud city as yet knew nothing, but who had come to erect his patriarchal throne in the midst of her sea girt walls, bringing with him his Gospel and the sovereignty of St. Peter's keys. It was St. Mark, the interpreter and spiritual son of the Prince of the Apostles, sent in his name and by his authority to plant the Church in the southern capital of the Empire. Descending from the ship, and crossing the crowded quay overshadowed by its plane-trees, he made his way towards the great Moon-gate which opened into the street of the Seven Stadia. He was partially bald, and his hair and beard were sprinkled with grey hairs; but his beautiful eyes flashed beneath their high arched eyebrows, and there was a quickness in his step and a grace in his movements which bespoke him not yet past the middle age.[1] So at least he has been described by the historian Simeon Metaphrastes, who, though writing in the tenth century, has embodied in his narrative the account of far earlier authors, who have minutely recorded the circumstances which attended the entry into Alexandria of her first patriarch.

We need not describe the world in which he found himself. It was the fairest city of the East; Greek in its aspect and population though planted on Egyptian soil, with a clearer sky than even that of Athens; a nobler harbour than Corinth could boast of; and that which was denied to Rome and Carthage, the command of a mighty river, which brought down to the port the corn and rose-coloured granite of Upper Egypt, the ivory of Ethiopia, the spices and gold-dust of Arabia, and the gems of Eastern lands. Like that other more ancient city on whose site she was reared, she "dwelt in the midst of the rivers; the sea was her riches, the waters were her walls."[2] Then as now the highway to India lay through Egypt, and her seaport of Arsinoe on the Arabian Gulf communicated by a canal with the Nile, the western branch of which flowed out into the Mediterranean just north of the Alexandrian harbour. Thus the capital of the Ptolemies became the central point between East and West, and into her markets flowed the costly Oriental luxuries which were carried by her merchants into every European port. She was rich and she was populous; all nations met to traffic in her harbour, all tongues were spoken in her "many-peopled" streets. Yet her trading pre-eminence formed but a small part of her glory. It is not often that a great commercial emporium becomes the haunt of the Muses; but Alexandria united graces and attractions of the most opposite character, and her fame for learning eclipsed even that of her wealth. Three hundred years before the time of which we are speaking, one of Alexander's royal successors, after erecting the temple of Serapis and the great Pharos, which last was numbered among the wonders of the world, bethought him of another way of rendering his name immortal, and gathered together a society of learned men whose duty was to consist in studying and teaching every known science. He built schools for them to lecture in, halls in which they ate in common, and marble porticoes, where, after the fashion of the Greek philosophers, they could walk and converse with their disciples. A noble library, which was enlarged by successive princes till it consisted of seven hundred thousand volumes, completed the Musæum or University of Ptolemy Soter, and the whole was joined to his own palace and delicious gardens by stately marble colonnades. Royal patronage was scarcely needed to foster the intellectual life of a city which had been designed by its founder to be the capital of the world; but with such encouragement the schools of Alexandria grew apace, and in the Apostolic age ranked as the first within the wide dominions that owned the Roman sway.

Here then the Blessed Peter came in the person of his chosen disciple, to claim for Christ the southern capital of the Empire, as he had already in his own person taken possession of East and West—of Antioch and Rome. Solitary and unknown, the Evangelist came there bent on conquests vaster than those of Alexander, for he had but enslaved a base material world; but St. Mark, as he stood at the Mendion, or Moon-gate, that led from the harbour into the busy streets, was deliberating on the conquest of a million of souls. How was he to begin? Where should he first bear his message of good tidings? Should he bend his steps to the porticoes of the Musæum, or try to find a listener in the crowded exchange which met his eye through that open gate? Providence itself was to give the reply, and neither wealth nor science was to yield him his first convert. The thong of his sandal snapped in two, and to get it mended he entered the shop of a cobbler that stood close at hand. The cobbler, whose name was Anianus, gave him hospitality that night; and questioning him as to who he was, heard in reply that he was the servant of Jesus Christ, declared in the Scriptures to be the Son of God. "Of what Scriptures do you speak?" he inquired; "I have never heard of any writings but the Iliad and the Odyssey, and other such things as are taught to the sons of the Egyptians." Then St. Mark sat down and unfolded to him the Gospel; through the long hours of the night, in the midst of that heaving world of idolatry and sin—the teacher spoke, and the disciple listened; and when morning dawned the first fruits of Alexandria had been laid up in the garner of Christ.[3]

It was meet that an Evangelist should deliver his first message to the poor; but it was not with the poor alone that he had to do. The Church of Alexandria was to receive into her embrace the philosopher of the Musæum as well as the despised Egyptian slave. She was to address herself to the wise and prudent of this world as well as to little ones. So St. Mark, as we are told, surrounded his see with learned men, and became the founder of a catechetical school. Although its chief celebrity dates only from the end of the second century, yet its first foundation is universally attributed to St. Mark.

It rose under the shadow of the temple of Serapis, near those marble porticoes where the Neo-Platonists, who despised such vulgar idolatry, were dreaming of some misty impersonal abstraction to which they gave the name of God; where Pyrrhonists took refuge in a system of universal doubt; where many were content to know nothing at all about the soul, and concerned themselves rather with mathematics and material prosperity; where Greek Epicureans talked of a world that had made itself by chance, and set up sense as the standard of certainty, and enjoyment as the end of life; while Roman freethinkers quoted the witty atheisms of Lucretius, and then went to burn incense before the statue of the Emperor. What new elements of knowledge could a Christian Evangelist contribute to such a world as this? There was no need for him to bring it the literature of Greece and Rome; and as to the sciences of figures and numbers, Egypt was their native soil. Even the Hebrew Scriptures had long ago been translated into Greek and laid up in the library of Ptolemy. But he brought the Gospel—his own Gospel in particular;[4] the one Book out of which for long ages the faithful of Alexandria were exclusively instructed, and which the teacher of the catechetical school was required to hold in his hand when he stood before his hearers. He brought the traditions of St. Paul and of St. Peter, for he had been the disciple of both. He brought the Creed, the Apostolic symbol, which in the brief compass of its twelve articles contains more truths than Plato or Cicero had ever known, and which discovered in the certainty of faith that *Eureka* which every system of human philosophy had sought in vain. He brought his Liturgy too; if not that which bears his name, at least some earlier form which served as its groundwork. And lastly, he brought that Liturgy's musical voice—the eight ancient tones, which, like so many things that belong to the Church, when first we meet with them in history, are already clothed with venerable antiquity: those tones to which the Jewish Church had for centuries chanted the Psalms of David; which must so often have fallen on the ears of Jesus, and in whose melody, it may be, His Divine Voice had sometimes mingled; the sweet songs of Sion which Jewish captives had sung by the rivers of Babylon, and whose echoes now floated from

Christian lips over the dark waters of the Nile.[5] The Holy Gospels, the Creed, the Liturgy, and the Ecclesiastical Chant, these were the contributions which were offered by the Patriarch of Alexandria to her learned stores, and which formed the first class-books of the Christian schools. But St. Mark did something more than this. All early writers agree in declaring that he established among his clergy that canonical rule of life which was a copy of the community life of the first Christians; while at the same time, as St. Jerome and Cassian[6] inform us, some of his disciples retiring into the neighbourhood of the city, and there giving themselves up to prayer and the study of the Scriptures, laid the first foundations of the cœnobitical, or monastic life.

To St. Mark, therefore, and through him to the Prince of the Apostles, may be traced up every one of those institutions which were the nurseries of the Christian schools. For, as will hereafter be seen, the Christian seminaries took their origin in the episcopal and monastic schools, and these again grew out of that system of community life which, being first embraced by the faithful at Jerusalem, was afterwards elsewhere established by the Apostles, who lived with their immediate followers as they themselves had lived with their Divine Master. The Apostolic origin of the canonical rule of life has never been denied. When St. Augustine was accused by Petilianus the Donatist of introducing a novelty into the Church by establishing his community of regular clergy, he defended himself by appealing to the example of the first Christians, and showing that, if the name of monastery were new, the manner of life which he and his brethren followed was as old as Christianity itself. It is thus that the author of the ancient book called the "Recognitions" describes St. Peter as living, with a chosen number of disciples, among whom were St. Mark, St. Clement, St. Evodius, and St. Linus; so St. Paul was accompanied by St. Luke and St. Timothy, and St. John the Evangelist by St. Polycarp and St. Papias. St. Irenæus, a disciple of the last-named saints, carried into Gaul the discipline of the school in which he had been nurtured, and, writing in after years to the heresiarch Florinus, reminds him how, when yet a child, he had been accustomed to meet him in the house of Polycarp. "Early recollections," he says, "grow with the soul, and entwine themselves about it, so that I could tell of the very place where the blessed Polycarp sat when he spoke, of his employments and his external appearance."[7]

Out of this manner of life, as we shall presently show, sprang up the episcopal seminaries, which were designed for the training of the younger clerics, whilst the catechetical schools were intended for the religious instruction of the neophytes. But though this last-named institution was, of course, *sui generis*, and exclusively belonged to those primitive ages when adult converts from Paganism had to be prepared for baptism by at least a two years' course of instruction, yet their history, and specially that of the Alexandrian school, helps us in a convenient manner to watch the absorption into the Christian system of education of every branch of learning afterwards cultivated in the schools.

In the absence of more particular details of the kind of instruction which prevailed at Alexandria before the time of St. Pantænus, we may reasonably suppose that the same system was adopted in that city as we find established at Jerusalem under St. Cyril. There the *Hearers* or Catechumens assembled in the porch of the church; the men and women sat separate from one another, and the master stood to deliver his instruction. The catecheses of St. Cyril that are preserved are twenty-three in number, eighteen being a summary of the chief articles of the Faith, given in the form of an exposition of the Creed, and the five others intended for the *competent*, or those preparing to receive the Sacraments of Baptism, Confirmation, and the Holy Eucharist. The last-named subject is treated in an explanation of the Liturgy of St. James. This, of course, was the sort of teaching for which the catechetical schools were primarily intended, and up to the year 179 the teachers of Alexandria do not appear to have aimed at anything of a higher character. But about that time Pantænus, a former stoic, whose eloquence earned him the title of *the Sicilian Bee*, became master of the school, and introduced a wider range of studies. He made use of his old learning to illustrate and defend his new faith. Clement of Alexandria, his earliest disciple, speaks of his "transcendent powers," and St. Alexander, Bishop of Jerusalem, gloried in calling him his lord and blessed father.

The renown of St. Pantænus passed into the Indies, carried thither by some of the swarthy Hindoos, who were no strangers in the busy streets of Alexandria, and who had managed to find their way to that school where Jew and Gentile, bond and free, met together without distinction. The Indians invited him to come among them, and St. Pantænus accordingly exchanged his mastership for an apostolic life, and went to preach the faith to the Brahmins. Clement, his former disciple and assistant, succeeded him. He had visited all lands and studied in all schools in search of truth, and had found it at last on the humble bench of the Catechumen. No one understood better than he the emptiness of human learning when pursued as an end, or its serviceableness when used as a means. His end was to win souls to Christ; and to reach it, he laid hands indifferently on all the intellectual weapons that fell within his reach; poetry and philosophy, science and even satire;—he neglected nothing that would serve his turn. He did not disdain to give a Christian interpretation to Pagan fables, and took occasion from the stories of Orpheus and Amphion, who, as the poets pretended, had moved the stones and tamed the wild beasts with the music of their lyres, to present to his hearers the Word made Flesh, conquering the stony and ferocious heart of fallen man, and restoring that universe which he beautifully calls "a lyre whose harmony has been destroyed by sin." He could use with equal ease the phraseology of the Neo-Platonists whilst engaged in dispersing their transcendentalism into thinnest air, or the plainer language of the Gospel when he had to put heretics to silence. Nor was he too deep or profound for the comprehension of the simple-hearted faithful; he could write hymns for little children to sing in church, and when he spoke to exclusively Christian hearers set forth no other wisdom, no other model for their imitation, than "Jesus Christ and Him Crucified."

The result of all this may be imagined. While the first neophytes of St. Mark and his immediate followers had been chiefly gained from the ranks of the Jews, to whom Alexandria was a second home, Gentile converts now flowed into the Church in ever-increasing numbers. The philosophers found in the Christian teachers those who could beat them with their own weapons, and human learning became elevated and ennobled by its marriage with the faith. It may be taken as a proof how thoroughly it was now recognised that Christians were men who could think and reason like other men, had as fair a knowledge of books and as great a command of what the Roman world valued far more than mere book-knowledge—eloquence; in short, that they were men of whom a university city need not be ashamed, and who might even be capable one day or other of setting up a university of their own— that it was becoming possible for Christians to gain a livelihood by teaching grammar and profane letters. There was one who so began his career, and who, at the age of eighteen, succeeded Clement in the direction of the catechetical school. The child of a martyr, Origen had been the pupil of saints. He had been taught not only by Clement, but also by St. Hyppolitus the martyr, commonly called Bishop of Porto, the disciple of Irenæus, the disciple of Polycarp, the spiritual son of the Apostle St. John. Hyppolitus was a man of many sciences, a philosopher, a poet, and a mathematician. He was one of the earliest who comes before us as attaining eminence in that distinctively Christian science, which will often appear in these pages under the name of the *Computum*. The computum was in fact the art of calculating the time of Easter, and included so much astronomical and arithmetical knowledge as was necessary for that purpose.[8] Hence it was a science indispensable in the education of clerics; for in those days the *Tabula Paschalis* did not as now figure at the beginning of every Prayer-book; nor did the invention of almanacs bring home much science in a simple form to the fireside of the most unlettered layman. The calculation of Easter, therefore, had to be painfully gone through year after year, to the sore travail of many heads; and he was a benefactor to his species who first thought of lightening the labour. Hyppolitus, who is supposed to have been an Alexandrian by birth, and to whom, therefore, astronomy and arithmetic were second nature, composed two cycles which determined the Easter for a hundred and twelve years to come; and after his death a statue was erected representing the bishop, with the cycles engraved on his chair, which is still preserved in the Christian Museum of the Lateran.[9]

Under Hyppolitus and the other masters provided for him by his father's care, Origen had made progress in every human science; but on becoming chief catechist of Alexandria he had to make a sacrifice. He was forced to resign his grammar-school and to sell his books. Not, indeed, that he had no further need of these treasures, but they were his solitary riches; and as even he could not absolutely live on nothing, he parted from them and lived on the small pension of four oboli a day, which was paid him by the purchaser. And having thus wedded himself to poverty, alike the spouse of the scholar and the saint, he began to study Hebrew, and entered on those vast labours which had for their object the production of a correct version of the Sacred Text. And all the time the business of the school went on, and persecution raged with small intermission. Seven of his disciples suffered under Severus—a glorious crown for the master who envied them their palms. But we are only concerned with the history of Origen in so far as it exhibits the expansion of the Christian studies. So passing over twenty years of his life, we shall follow him to Cæsarea, where in 231 he retired from the storm that had driven him from Alexandria, and accepted the direction of another school entrusted him by the two bishops, Theoctistus of Cæsarea and Alexander of Jerusalem. It appears to have been a combination of the episcopal seminary and the catechetical school, for scholars of all classes resorted to it. Among them were Theodore, better known by his Christian name of St. Gregory Thaumaturgus, and his brother Athenodorus, who were then studying in the famous law-schools of Berytus. The conversation of Origen, however, soon put Roman jurisprudence out of their heads, and determined them to apply exclusively to philosophy under the guidance of their new friend. Both were at this time pagans, and Origen had to prepare their minds to receive the truth in a very gradual manner. He began by mercilessly rooting out the weeds and briars of bad habits and false maxims which he found choking up the soil, a process which at first, as his pupils acknowledged, cost them not a little. Then he taught them in succession the different branches of philosophy: logic, in order to exercise their minds and enable them to discern true reasoning from sophistry; physics, that they might understand and admire the works of God; geometry, which by its clear and indisputable demonstrations serves as a basis to the science of thought; astronomy, to lift their hearts from earth to heaven; and finally, philosophy, which was not limited like that taught in the pagan schools to empty speculations, but was conveyed in such a way as to lead to practical results. All these were but steps to ascend to that higher science which teaches us the existence and nature of God. He permitted his pupils freely to read whatever the poets and philosophers had written on this subject, himself watching and directing their studies, and opening their eyes to distinguish those sparks of truth which are to be found scattered in the writings of the pagans, however overlaid by a mass of fable. And then at last he presented them with the Sacred Scriptures, in which alone the true knowledge of God is to be found. In one of his letters to St. Gregory he explains in what way he wishes him to regard the profane sciences. "They are to be used," he says, "so that they may contribute to the understanding of the Scriptures; for just as philosophers are accustomed to say that geometry, music, grammar, rhetoric, and astronomy all dispose us to the study of philosophy, so we may say that philosophy, rightly studied, disposes us to the study of Christianity. We are permitted when we go out of Egypt to carry with us the riches of the Egyptians wherewith to adorn the tabernacle; only let us beware how we reverse the process, and leave Israel to go down into Egypt and seek for treasure: that is what Jeroboam did in old time, and what heretics do in our own."

In addition, therefore, to the elements of education which have been named before, we see that, at the beginning of the third century, Christians were expected to teach and study the liberal arts, profane literature, philosophy, and the Biblical languages. Their teachers commented on the Scriptures, and devoted themselves to a critical study of its text; positive theology, as it is called, had established itself in the schools, together with a certain systematic science of Christian ethics, and, we may add, many branches of physical science also. It matters very little that these latter were but imperfectly known; the real point worth observing is, that every branch of human knowledge, in so far as it had been cultivated at that time, was included in the studies of the Christian schools; and, considering that this had been the work of scarcely more than two centuries, and those centuries of bloody persecution, it must be acknowledged to have been a tolerably expansive growth.

We have now to consider the gradual development of the episcopal seminaries, which in their early stage formed but a part of the bishop's household. I have already spoken of the sort of community life established among the bishops and their clergy in apostolic times. During the first four centuries of the Church this manner of life was the more easily carried out, as the clergy were to be found only in towns. The establishment of rural parishes and the appointment of parochial priests to country villages, is first spoken of in the Council of Vaison, held in 528. The community life of the city clergy had many obvious advantages, and afforded singular facilities for training younger aspirants to the ecclesiastical state under the eye of the chief pastor. Accordingly, we very early find notices of the schools for younger clerics, which sprang up in the episcopal households. Thus, the martyr St. Vincent is stated to have been educated in sacred letters, even from his childhood, by Valerius, Bishop of Saragossa. St. John Chrysostom studied for three years as lector in the household of Meletius, Bishop of Antioch, St. Cyril in that of his uncle Theophilus, and St. Athanasius with Alexander of Alexandria. Towards the close of the second century we read how Pope St. Eleutherius placed the future martyr St. Felicianus in the school which was then presided over by his archdeacon, St. Victor,[10] his successor in the Apostolic Chair; and all the early annals of the Roman Church represent her clergy as for the most part educated in this manner, under the eye of her Pontiffs. The author of the *Philosophumena* acquaints us with the fact that Pope Calixtus I. established a school of theology at Rome, which appears from his account to have been crowded with disciples. When, after the conversion of Constantine, the imperial palace of the Lateran became the residence of the popes, their ecclesiastical school was maintained within the *Patriarchium*, as the papal palace was called, and in it not a few of the greatest popes of the first nine centuries received their education. It possessed a noble library, and the names of its librarians are preserved in unbroken order from the fifth century. Here, ecclesiastical students were received at an early age, and admitted to the successive degrees of holy orders only at long intervals and after careful preparation. The very first Decretal that exists of known authenticity, that of Pope St. Siricius, addressed, in 385, to Himerius, Bishop of Tarragona, lays down the rules to be observed in promoting clerics to holy orders, and indicates the existence of such episcopal seminaries as we have described. *Those who have been devoted to the service of the Church from childhood* are to be first placed in the rank of lectors. Then, if they have persevered to the age of thirty, they may be advanced through the inferior orders to the subdiaconate, and thence to the diaconate, in which they must pass five years before being admitted to the priesthood.[11] A few years later we find St. Zozimus ordaining that the young clerics should remain in the rank of lectors till their twentieth year, and that they should not be raised to the priesthood until after many years of trial. St. Leo I. writes to the African bishops, about the middle of the fifth century, appealing to the venerable ordinances of the holy fathers on the ordination of those *who have lived from childhood subject to ecclesiastical discipline*, by which expression we must certainly understand the young lectors of the episcopal seminaries. And, glancing on to the eighth and ninth centuries, we find exactly the same discipline kept up in the school of the Patriarchium as had existed in the seventh. Pope Gregory II. is spoken of as brought up from childhood in the Lateran palace, "under the eye and discipline of the Blessed Pontiff Sergius,"[12] as being promoted by him to the subdiaconate, and after having for some years discharged the offices of treasurer and librarian, being advanced to the rank of deacon and, subsequently, of priest. So, too, Pope Leo III. is described as "educated from infancy in all ecclesiastical and divine discipline in the *vestiarium* of the Lateran Palace." In most cases the Lateran seminary was presided over by the Roman archdeacon, and, as we shall see, the superintendence of the cathedral schools continued, in after ages, to form one of the duties commonly attached to the archdiaconate.

In the fourth century, when the monastic institute spread from the East into the West, the community life of the bishops and their clergy assumed, in many places, a yet more regular form. St. Eusebius of Vercelli, who had himself been committed by his mother in early youth to the care of Pope Eusebius, and had been instructed and baptized by him, was the first to erect an episcopal monastery in his own city, which became a nursery of illustrious prelates. This was in 354, and forty years later St. Augustine established a similar monastery at Hippo, which is regarded as the parent of all houses of canons regular. Yet, though these establishments are sometimes called *monasteries*, the rule of life observed in them is ordinarily designated the *Apostolic* rule,[13] and the monasteries or colleges of a similar kind established in Gaul and Britain are said to be "of the Apostolic Order." From this time the community life of the clergy became subject to fixed rules or canons. In 398 the fourth Council of Carthage, whilst prescribing the laws for the administration of holy orders, regulates the manner of life to be observed by the bishops with their clergy in very precise terms. The bishop is to have his residence near the church; he is to commit the care of temporalities to his archdeacon, and to occupy himself exclusively with prayer, study and preaching. In the church he is to have a higher seat than his clergy, but in the house he must recognise them as in all respects his colleagues, and never to suffer them to remain standing while he is seated.[14] Similar canons were passed in the first Council of Toledo, held two years later.

In all this there is no distinct reference to the education of the younger clerics as forming one of the duties of the cathedral clergy. The Council of Vaison, held in 528, speaks, indeed, of the parish priests, who are required, according to the practice of the priests of Italy, to bring up young lectors in their houses, who may succeed them in their cure; and the establishment of similar schools was solemnly ordered, in 680, by the General Council of Constantinople; but the institution, of which we here see the germ, was not the episcopal, but the priest's or parochial school. However, in 531, the second Council of Toledo passed several canons, which bear distinct reference to the bishop's seminary, which by this time is evidently supposed to be attached to the cathedral church. Those children who are destined by their parents for the ecclesiastical state are to receive the tonsure, and to be placed in the rank of lectors in order to be instructed *in the house of the church under the eyes of the bishop, by him who shall be appointed over them.* At the age of eighteen their vocation is to be publicly examined, that no one may embrace the ecclesiastical state save with his own free consent. If this be given, they may be ordained sub-deacons at twenty and deacons at twenty-five. And clerics so educated cannot pass to any other diocese, but owe canonical obedience to the bishop at whose charge they have been brought up.[15]

Here, then, is the cathedral seminary fairly established, and a few years later we find it expanding into a noble public school. It was St. Leander, of Seville, who first conceived the idea of establishing a staff of professors for teaching the liberal arts in connection with his cathedral. He directed their labours in person, and received among his first scholars his own brother Isidore, who afterwards succeeded him in his see. Isidore greatly extended the range of studies, which included the Latin, Greek, and Hebrew tongues, and all the liberal arts, besides law and medicine. His famous *Origines* drawn up for the use of this school present an encyclopedia of every known subject, and embody several fragments of ancient authors which would otherwise have been lost to us. The first five books treat of Grammar, Rhetoric, Philosophy, Dialectics, Music, Geometry, Mechanics, Astronomy, Jurisprudence, Chronology, and History. The sixth is on the Holy Scriptures, the seventh and eighth are on God and the Angels, the ninth on the various nations and languages of the earth, and the remaining books treat of Etymology. But his efforts for the promotion of Christian education did not stop here. In 633 he presided over the fourth Council of Toledo, at which all the bishops of Spain were required to establish seminaries in their cathedral cities on the model of that of Seville, the study of the three learned languages being specially enjoined. This decree was carried into effect, and hence it is commonly said that the system of cathedral schools took its origin in Spain.

Besides the catechetical and episcopal schools, instances occur, even in the age of martyrdom, of private schools kept by Christian teachers. Such was the school of Imola, presided over by the martyr Cassian; and the story of his martyrdom exhibits to us the light in which the brutal pagan school-boy regarded his master. Yet there were cases when the hearts even of Gentile scholars were softened by the influence of a sanctity which they comprehended not. The exquisite story of the Eight Martyrs of Carthage, as related in their authentic Acts, exhibits to us the pagan scholars of the deacon Flavian obtaining his reprieve from the judge by vehemently denying his ecclesiastical character; and when he at last succeeds in proving a fact which brings with it the joyful death-warrant, his Christian disciples follow him to the place of execution to gather up the last words of instruction from their master's lips.[16] We have a yet more particular account of the school established at Cæsarea by the martyr St. Pamphilius. He had been educated, as a Gentile, in the public schools of Berytus, where he attained to great proficiency in profane science. But, on his conversion, he became desirous of acquiring a knowledge of the Sacred Scriptures, and for this purpose placed himself under the tuition of Pierius, the successor of Origen in the catechetical school of Alexandria. On his return to Syria he was ordained priest, and devoted the rest of his life, and his wealth, to the creation of a Christian school and library. No Florentine scholar in the age of the Renaissance had a more passionate love of books than he. He caused them to be sent to him from every quarter, and his library numbered no fewer than thirty thousand volumes, many of which had been copied by his own hand. They included the best works of the ancients, besides those of Christian writers. Pamphilius spent the greater part of his life in transcribing books, and both bought and wrote out an amazing number of copies of the Holy Scriptures, which he distributed gratis to all who desired to have them. He applied himself with unwearied diligence to obtain a correct edition of the whole of the Sacred Text; and, in the midst of these labours, he directed a school of sacred learning, wherein was reared more than one martyr.

The public schools of the Empire were not generally resorted to by the faithful until after the conversion of Constantine, when Christians were permitted to aspire to the professor's chair. But this privilege, great as it was, did not produce any material change in the character of the State academies; they continued to flourish under the Christian Cæsars as they had done under their pagan predecessors, but they never merited to be regarded as Christian institutions. Though both Constantine and Gratian did much to provide excellent rhetoricians and grammarians to instruct their subjects, and though Valentinian I. made some laudable efforts, to correct the worst abuses of the schools, they continued to bear the stamp of their origin; and it is a significant fact that, long after the establishment of a nominal Christianity in the institutions of the Empire, the saint whose children were destined to hold in their hands the future education of Europe is introduced to us in the first incident of his life, flying into the wilderness to escape the corruption of the semi-pagan schools of Rome.[17] St. Augustine has told us something of the condition of the schools of Carthage in his time, which may probably be taken as a fair specimen of the State gymnasia in other parts of the Empire. The masters exercised an excessive severity with their pupils, so that, as the saint confesses, he first began the use of prayer when yet a child, to beg of God that He would save him from a school flogging. His elders, and even his parents, were so used to the idea of these punishments, "whereby labour and sorrow are multiplied to the sons of Adam," that they only made a jest of his sufferings. All the sweets of Greek poetry were, he says, sprinkled with gall to him, he being forced to learn them by "cruel terrors and stripes." He lets us know moreover that the wholesome admonitions of Quinctilian were altogether neglected, and that the worst writings of the pagan authors were placed in the hands of the scholars. In academies where the professorial system reigned supreme, moral training was neither given nor expected; the professors were paid for teaching their pupils grammar and rhetoric, and, as St. Augustine remarks, would have treated it as a greater fault to pronounce *homo* without the aspirate than to hate a man. Many were pagans, like

Libanius, the master of St. Chrysostom; others were content with the smallest possible seasoning of Christianity. They were, in short, the *sophists* by profession—a pragmatical race of beings whose mental horizon hardly extended beyond the logic of Aristotle and the rules of rhetoric. Honourable exceptions of course were to be found, such as Marius Victorinus, who in the Julian persecution resigned his school rather than renounce the Divine Word who maketh eloquent the tongues of children.[18] But as a general rule the professors troubled themselves very little about questions of Christian faith or ethics. Absolute dictators of a petty circle, they were devoured by a vanity which tainted their very eloquence, and expressed itself in such a turgid and affected style, that, as Cicero said of one of their class, if you wanted to be dumb for the rest of your life you had nothing to do but to study their lectures. This vanity showed itself moreover in perpetual squabbles and rivalries, in which the disciples took part with their masters. New-comers were laid violent hands on by the scholastic jackals, who would endeavour by all manner of insolence to press them into the school of their own particular sophist, initiating them by burlesque and uproarious ceremonies. Thus it was that they prepared to seize St. Basil on his first coming to Athens, when St. Gregory of Nazianzen, who well knew how offensive such riotous scenes would prove to one of his grave and reserved character, interfered to protect him, and thus laid the foundation of a friendship which has inspired some of the most exquisite pages of Christian literature. I need not quote the well-known passage that describes their university life: it is often cited as a model for Christian students; yet St. Gregory does not forget to inform us that it was as difficult for a youth to preserve his innocence in the midst of such an atmosphere as it would be for an animal to live in the midst of fire, or for a river to preserve its sweetness when flowing through the briny ocean.

Nevertheless, the circumstances of the times compelled the faithful to resort to these academies. Many had done so even when the professorships were exclusively in the hands of the pagans. Tertullian, in his treatise on Idolatry, examines the lawfulness of the practice, and decides that though it would be impossible for Christians to *teach* in schools wherein the masters were obliged to recommend the worship of false gods, and to take part in pagan sacrifices and ceremonies, they might properly attend them as students, because they could not otherwise acquire that necessary knowledge of letters which he calls "the key of life," and because they were perfectly free to reject the fables to which they listened. Such an argument of course implies the existence of very powerful safeguards on the side of faith; and he seems to take it for granted that Christian students will imbibe only the honey from the flowers of eloquence, and reject the poison. The general feeling certainly was that human learning was sufficiently necessary to justify some risks being incurred in its acquisition. After the triumph of the Church, the most religious parents, such as those of St. Basil, hesitated not to send their sons to the public schools; and when the crafty attempt was made by Julian the Apostate to close them to the Christians, and to prohibit even their private study of pagan literature, we know how strenuously the bishops protested against his edict, as a cruel and unheard-of tyranny. So long as it remained in force they exerted themselves to supply the want of the old class-books, the use of which was interdicted, by imitations of the poets from their own pens. No one was more active in this work than St. Gregory Nazianzen, who took up the cudgels against his imperial schoolfellow in good earnest. "For my part," he exclaims, in his fourth discourse, "I trust that every one who cares for learning will take part in my indignation. I leave to others fortune, birth, and every other fancied good which can flatter the imagination of man. I value only science and letters, and regret no labour that I have spent in their acquisition. I have preferred, and shall ever prefer, learning to all earthly riches, and hold nothing dearer on earth, next to the joys of heaven and the hopes of eternity." The decree was revoked by Valentinian at the request of St. Ambrose, so unanimous were the Christian prelates in regarding human learning as a treasure the possession of which the faithful were jealously to vindicate. Even in those passages which occur in the writings of the Fathers wherein they appear to undervalue polite studies, it is evident that they only do so relatively, and the scholar is pretty sure to peep out before you have turned the page. "You ask me for my books," writes St. Gregory to his friend Adamanthus; "have you then turned a boy again that you are going to study rhetoric? I have long ago laid aside such follies, for one cannot spend all one's life in child's play. We must cease to lisp when we aspire to the true science, and sacrifice to the Divine Word that frivolous eloquence which formerly so charmed our youth. However, take my books, my dear Adamanthus—all at least that are not devoured by the worms, or blackened with the smoke, on the shelves where they have lain so long. Take them, and use them well. Study the sophists thoroughly, and both acquire and teach to others all the learning you can, provided the fear of God reign paramount over these vanities." But though the Fathers, both by word and example, authorised the study of the pagan literature, they required that it should be read with certain restrictions, and according to what may be termed the Christian method. This is explained by St. Basil, in a treatise he wrote on the subject for the guidance of some young relations. He advocates the right use of human learning, comparing the soul to a tree, which bears not only fruit but leaves also. The fruit is truth, to be found only in the Sacred Scriptures, but the leaves are the ornaments of literature which cover truth and adorn it. Moses and Daniel both became skilled in the Gentile learning before they devoted themselves to the study of sacred science. And it is not to be doubted that the poets and philosophers have many wise and virtuous precepts, which cannot be too deeply engraved on our minds. Christians are engaged in a mighty struggle, in which they should make use of everything that can help them—poetry, philosophy, rhetoric, or the arts. They should contemplate the Sun of Truth as it is reflected in the waters of human literature, and then lift their eyes to gaze on it in its full effulgence in the heavens.

He then goes on to cite many passages from Homer, Hesiod, and Socrates, and other ancient writers, showing that they abound in excellent maxims, which a Christian may very well apply to his own benefit. A Christian student, he says, should follow the example of the bees, who draw out honey from flowers which seem only proper to charm the eye, or gratify the smell. But then they must also imitate them, in only selecting those flowers that yield honey; and when they extract the sweet juices, let them be careful to leave the poison behind. In like manner we should gather together from the heathen literature whatever may be useful, and leave what is pernicious to morals behind.[19] This was but saying what Plato and Cicero had said before him, and it cannot be charged to the account of a Christian prelate as narrow bigotry, that he should insist on at least as much reserve in the use of profane writers as had been required by the pagan moralists themselves.

It cannot be supposed that the Christian prelates were insensible to the dangers incurred by students in the State academies. St. Chrysostom, indeed, who knew what they were by experience, and who was certainly the last man to undervalue a knowledge of letters, was induced to weigh the arguments for and against a public school education, and decides that the risk is too great to be compensated for by any intellectual advantage. He declares that he knows of no school in his neighbourhood where the study of profane literature can be found united to the teaching of virtue; and this being the case, he considers that Christian parents will generously sacrifice the superior tuition given in the State gymnasia, and send their children to be brought up in a monastery. His words are the more remarkable from the extreme moderation of their tone, and the evident reluctance with which he advocates a course of conduct which must needs place the faithful at a disadvantage. They are also important as showing how very early the monasteries began to be regarded as places of education, for seculars as well as religious. "If you have masters among you," he writes,[20] "who can answer for the virtue of your children, I should be very far from advocating your sending them to a monastery; on the contrary, I should strongly insist on their remaining where they are. But if no one can give such a guarantee, we ought not to send children to schools where they will learn vice before they learn science, and where in acquiring learning of relatively small value, they will lose what is far more precious, their integrity of soul. Are we then to give up literature? you will exclaim. I do not say that; but I do say that we must not kill souls.... When the foundations of a building are sapped, we should seek rather for architects to reconstruct the whole edifice, than for artists to adorn the walls. In fact, the choice lies between two alternatives; a liberal education which you may get by sending your children to the public schools, or the salvation of their souls, which you secure by sending them to the monks. Which is to gain the day, science or the soul? If you can unite both advantages, do so by all means; but if not, choose the most precious."[21]

It will be apparent from what has been said, that the State academies of the Empire are not to be numbered among the nurseries of the Christian schools. The only imperial foundation which had a distinctly Christian character about it, appears to have been that which grew up at Constantinople, under the patronage of the Greek emperors. It was established in the Basilica of the Octagon, built by Constantine the Great, where an immense library was collected, which in Zeno's time amounted to 120,000 volumes. Seven librarians and twelve professors were maintained at the public expense, and the college was presided over by a president, called the Œcumenicus, because he was supposed to be a sort of university in himself. The church attached to this academy was served by sixteen monks, and prelates were often chosen from the ranks of the professors to fill the first sees of the Empire. This noble foundation perished in 730, by the hands of Leo the Isaurian, who, finding that the academicians would not enter into his Iconoclastic views, and fearing their learning and their influence, caused fire to be applied to the building by night, so that the Basilica, the vast library, and the professors themselves, were all pitilessly consumed together.

But the parentage of the Christian schools is to be traced to less splendid sources than the Greek universities or the palace of the Cæsars. What these were has been indicated at the beginning of the chapter; the catechetical and the episcopal schools have been already spoken of, and we have now to examine how the work of education came to be embraced by the fathers of that monastic life which, like the canonical life of the clergy, found its first development among the followers of St. Mark. St. Chrysostom's words, above quoted, show that in his time the monks of the East were already in the habit of receiving and training children. In the West, the work of education did not fall into the hands of the Church until the dissolution of the Roman Empire, when she saw herself obliged to open the doors of her episcopal and monastic schools to secular students. But one thing is evident, that from the first, the Western cœnobites had a certain organised system among them for the education of their own younger members and that the germ of the monastic school is to be found even in the deserts of Egypt. In the rule of St. Pachomius, special directions are given for the instruction of all those who shall come to the monastery. If ignorant of letters, they are to have the rule explained to them, and shall be sent to one who can teach them, and standing before him, shall diligently learn from him, with all thankfulness. After that they shall write for him letters, syllables, words, and names, and they shall be compelled to read, even if unwilling; there shall be no one in the monastery who shall not learn letters, and know something of the Scriptures, at least the New Testament and the Psalter.[22] Twice a week there were to be disputations; that is, spiritual conferences or catechisms. Here is evidently the origin of the interior or claustral school for the instruction of the younger or more ignorant of the monks; and the object of such very stringent regulations is better understood when we study the rest of the rule, and observe the great importance attached to the exercise of spiritual reading, which occupied almost as large a place in the horarium of St. Pachomius as prayer or manual labour.

Nor was this all. The rule of this great monastic legislator distinctly proves that children were received, and that at a very early age, to be educated among the monks. He felt great compassion, we are told, for the young, and was accustomed to say, that in the soil of their minds good seed might be sown more easily than in more advanced years. He considered them particularly capable of being trained to acquire the habit of the presence of God; by which they might afterwards advance to great perfection. Accordingly, his rule is full of provisions for the proper care of these young disciples. The monks are warned not to scandalise them, even by an incautious word: they are to have the recreation and food proper to their age, but the monks are not to sport or laugh with them; and if any boy be too much given to play and idleness, he is to receive sharp correction. They are to eat in the refectory with the brethren, and join them at their work, but at other times a sort of separation is to be observed between them and the community.[23] The terms on which the Fathers lived with their little disciples exhibit that character of paternal tenderness which was one of the distinctive features of the early Christian schools, offering a striking contrast to the state of things existing in the pagan academies. There is, indeed, frequent mention of the rod, but strict discipline was never held incompatible with affectionate familiarity. The Fathers of the Desert had received their traditions on this head from the immediate followers of Him who took the young children in His arms, and willingly suffered them to approach Him; and so it seemed but natural that they who sought to imitate their Master, should surround themselves with little ones, and permit them a certain holy familiarity which constantly reappears in the intercourse between monks and children. Every one will remember the anecdote that is told of St. Pachomius, who, in his extreme humility, did not disdain to be set right by a little boy. As he sat at work with his brethren, making mats, one of the children said to him, "My father, you are not working in the right way; the abbot Theodore does it quite differently." "Then sit down, my child," replied the saint, "and show me how I ought to do it;" and having received his lesson, he untwisted his osiers, and began his work all over again. Another time, the saint having returned to the monastery after an absence of some weeks, one of the children ran out to meet him, saying, "I am glad you have come back, my father; since you have been away they have given us neither soup nor vegetables for dinner." "Well, my child," was the kind reply, "I will take care that you do not want them for the future;" and calling the cook, he administered to him a sharp rebuke.

Sometimes, even solitaries were induced to undertake the care of children not intended for the religious state. Thus St. Chrysostom relates the example of a Christian lady living at Antioch, who was very desirous to procure for her son the blessings of a holy education, and induced a certain solitary to leave his retreat among the mountains, and undertake the care of the youth: and he adds, the boy made great progress in the sciences, but yet more in piety, and by his example won many of his playfellows to embrace a life of virtue. When, therefore, the great father of the monastic life in the Western world received his two disciples, Placidus and Maurus, with a view to their education, and so gave his followers an example which resulted in the foundation of the great Benedictine schools, he was not departing from the earlier monastic tradition, as Mabillon is careful to show.[24] Nor must the decrees of certain councils which prohibit monks from receiving any children, save those "offered" by their parents to the religious state, be understood as implying more than that such children could not be received into the *interior* or claustral school; for, as the same writer proves, seculars were always freely admitted into the *exterior* schools of monasteries.

St. Pachomius was not the only monastic legislator of ancient times who in his rule provided for the admission and education of children. St. Basil permitted them to be received into his monasteries at a very early age, especially if they had lost their parents, because monks should be the fathers of orphans. Their education, he says, should be strictly religious; they are to have a separate portion of the monastery assigned them, and are to be governed by one of the elder monks who shall be both mild and learned, and experienced in the care of children. He is very precise on the point which proves the *crux* in most systems of education, namely, the method to be observed in inflicting punishment; and though he does not prohibit the use of the rod, he recommends in preference the adoption of such penances as may correct the fault, as well as punish the offender. "Let every fault have its own remedy," he says, "so that while the offence is punished the soul may be exercised to conquer its passions. For example, has a child been angry with his companion? Oblige him to beg pardon of the other and to do him some humble service, for it is only by accustoming them to humility that you will eradicate anger, which is always the offspring of pride. Has he eaten out of meals? Let him remain fasting for a good part of the day. Has he eaten to excess, and in an unbecoming manner? At the hour of repast, let him, without eating himself, watch others taking their food in a modest manner, and so he will be learning how to behave at the same time that he is being punished by his abstinence. And if he has offended by idle words, by rudeness, or by telling lies, let him be corrected by diet and silence."

After this he passes on to the studies of the children, and desires that instead of learning the fables of the poets they should be taught the wonderful events narrated in Scripture History. They are to learn by heart sentences chosen from the Book of Proverbs, and little prizes are to be given them in reward for their exercises of memory, "to the end that they may learn with the less reluctance, nay rather with pleasure, and as though engaging in agreeable recreation." The masters are particularly enjoined to train them to recall their wandering thoughts and fix their attention on their work, by frequently interrogating them as to what they are thinking about. And whilst acquiring a knowledge of letters, they are likewise to be taught some useful art or trade.[25]

In most of the rules drawn up by the early Gallican prelates we see that stringent regulations were introduced for obliging all the brethren to acquire a certain knowledge of letters. "Literas omnes discant," is the thirty-second brief and emphatic rule of St. Aurelian, Bishop of Arles in the sixth century. What is more remarkable, we find exactly the same provisions in rules drawn up for religious women, as in those of St. Donatus and St. Cæsarius of Arles.[26] The sixth chapter of the rule of St. Leander of Seville, is headed thus: *Ut jugiter virgo oret et legat.* "Let your time and occupation be so divided," he says, "that after reading you pray, and after prayer you read; and let these two good works perpetually alternate, so that no part of your time be wholly without them. And when you do any manual work or refresh your body with needful food, then let another read, that when the hands and the eyes are intent on work the ear may be fed with the Divine Word. For if even when we read and pray we are hardly able to withdraw our minds from the temptations of the devil, how much more prone will not the soul be to vice, if it be not held back by the chain of prayer and assiduous reading."[27] And in the chapter that follows he gives directions for the proper manner of studying the books of the Old Testament.

Before bringing these remarks to a close we cannot omit all notice of the education received in primitive times by the children of the faithful, in the bosoms of their own families. Fleury points out to his readers as one proof of the care taken by Christian parents in the instruction of their children, that in all antiquity we do not find the least notice of any public catechism for children, or any public instruction for those who had been baptized before they came to the use of reason. It was not needed, he says, for in those days, to use the words of St. Chrysostom, "every house was a Church."[28]

The office of religious instruction generally devolved on the mother. Even in Scripture there is evidence of this, for St. Paul, writing to St. Timothy, reminds him of what he owed to the "faith unfeigned" of his grandmother Lois and his mother Eunice.[29] St. Basil, and his brother St. Gregory of Nyssa, gloried in preserving the faith in which they had been trained by their grandmother St. Macrina the elder. Their other brother, St. Peter of Sebaste, was chiefly brought up by his sister of the same name. St. Gregory thus describes the extraordinary care bestowed by his mother on the education of her daughter. "My mother," he says, "took extreme pains with her instruction, not after the manner customary with those of her age, who are ordinarily taught the fables of the poets.... Instead of these she made her learn such portions of Scripture as were easiest to understand. She began with the book of Wisdom, and thence went on to the Psalms."[30] St. Fulgentius owed his education, not merely in sacred science, but also in polite literature, to the care of his mother Mariana, the *religiosa mater* as she is called in his life, who was so solicitous about the purity of his Greek accent that she made him learn by heart the poems of Homer and Menander before he studied his Latin rudiments.[31] The early education, both liberal and religious, of St. John Chrysostom was in like manner directed by his admirable mother Anthusa, whose conduct in this particular drew from the lips of the pagan sophist, Libanius, the exclamation, "Ye gods of Greece! how wonderful are the women of the Christians!" In fact it is remarkable how many Christian women of early times are spoken of as being learned. Not to mention St. Catherine of Alexandria, whose case was possibly exceptional, we know that St. Thecla, the disciple of St. Paul, was versed in philosophy, poetry, and rhetoric; St. Olympia, the holy widow of Constantinople, not only corresponded with St. Chrysostom, seventeen of whose letters are addressed to her, but received the dedication of several of St. Gregory of Nazianzen's poems. St. Jerome, again, dedicated his commentaries on Isaias and Ezechiel to his pupil St. Eustochium, who, he assures us, wrote, spoke, and recited Hebrew without the least trace of a Latin accent. And, not to multiply examples, we may just refer to that passage in his epistles where he speaks of St. Marcella, "the glory of the Roman ladies," as showing that the learned accomplishments of these illustrious women were not acquired at any sacrifice of qualities more peculiarly becoming their sex. "What virtues did I not find in her?" he says, writing to her spiritual daughter, Principia; "what penetration, what purity, what holiness! She became so learned that after my departure from Rome, when difficulties were found in any obscure passage of Scripture, people applied to her as to a judge; yet she possessed in a sovereign degree that delicate discernment which always perceives what is becoming; and used always to communicate her ideas as if they had been suggested by somebody else, so that while instructing others, she appeared herself to be a pupil."[32]

Never, surely, was there a greater error than that into which one of our most learned critics has fallen, when he asserts that "the idea and place of woman has been *slowly and laboriously* elevated by the Gospel."[33] He could not have written thus had he been as familiar with the records of the Christian Church as with those of pagan antiquity. The most perfect exemplars of Christian womanhood appear in the history of the primitive ages. The grand ideal of the Roman virgin or matron, softened, purified, and elevated by the Gospel precepts and the Apostolic teaching, retaining all its former strength, but acquiring a new element of tenderness, produced those exquisite flowers of sanctity whom the Church appears in some sort to regard as her children of predilection. They were not the growth of one Church or province, but simultaneously, wherever the Christian faith was preached, they expanded their beautiful petals to the Sun of Justice; and we have in Rome an Agnes and a Cecilia; in Sicily a Lucy and an Agatha; in Carthage a Felicitas; in Alexandria a Catherine; a Blandina in Gaul, and in barbarous Britain, an Ursula.

Whence arose this instantaneous regeneration of the womanly character? The Catholic hardly needs to ask himself the question, for the form on which it was modelled is so obvious that it requires not to be indicated. It grew out of no dead code of precepts, but out of the living memory of her, the Mother *par excellence*, the Virgin-Mother of God, and the model of all Christian virgins and mothers; she whose countenance St. Isidore describes as "gravely sweet and sweetly grave;" whose tranquil gait and gentle voice St. Ambrose has dwelt on, as well as her modesty and reverence, "rising up in the presence of her elders." And it was she of whom he also says, gathering up the precious fragments of ancient tradition, that she was "diligent in reading," *legendi studiosior*, a trait which reappears in the character of the holy women of early times, and which we are thus able to link on to the source whence they derived their ideal of womanly perfection.

It cannot be doubted that the influence of such women, and specially of such mothers, was a powerful means of preserving the Roman youth from the infection which hung over the public academies, even after the establishment of a nominal Christianity in the institutions of the State. But of these academies I need speak no further. They formed a part of the old Roman civilisation, and perished in its wreck, swallowed up in those waves of barbarism which, as they poured over Europe, ground to pieces every monument of the Empire, and swept their fragments into oblivion. In the midst of the deluge, however, the Ark of God floated over the waters, and accepted the mission of reconstructing a ruined world. The Church alone preserved so much as the memory of letters, though in the inconceivable troubles of the crisis her utmost efforts for a time only sufficed to keep up schools in which the clergy received the instruction necessary for their state; and secular learning for the most part fell into decay. But the want was felt and lamented by the clergy themselves, a proof that learning, at any rate, never lost its value in their eyes. Thus, in his letter to the Council of Constantinople in 680, Pope Agatho excuses the simplicity of his legates; "for how," he says, "can we look for great erudition among men living in the midst of barbarous nations, forced with difficulty to earn their daily bread by the labour of their hands? Nevertheless," he adds, "they will expound to you the faith of the Apostolic Church, not with human eloquence, for they have none; but with the simplicity of the faith which we have held from our cradles." The synodal letter of the Western bishops to the same council is couched in similar terms. "As to secular eloquence," they say, "we think no one in our time will boast of possessing it. Our countries are continually agitated by the fury of different nations; there is nothing around us but war, invasion, and plunder. In the midst of the barbarians our life is full of disturbance, the patrimony of our churches has been seized, and we have to live by the labour of our hands. The faith is all that is left us, and our solitary glory is to preserve it during life, and to be ready to die in its defence."

These two documents, often quoted, have perhaps given rise to somewhat exaggerated notions regarding the extent of the ignorance complained of. It is certain that there were periods of comparative tranquillity during which liberal studies were at least partially preserved. The schools of Gaul did not begin to decay till the end of the fifth century, and even then some were found who exerted themselves to keep alive the ancient learning; such as St. Sidonius Apollinaris, who received his education in the public schools of Lyons before his elevation to the Episcopate in 471, and Claudian Mamertus, a monk by profession and education, who was declared by his friend Sidonius to be equally incomparable in every science to which he applied. Besides being an amazing reader, he was an original thinker. His great work on "The Nature of the Soul" is said to display the precision and method of the latter scholastics, and contains proofs of the existence and immateriality of the soul drawn from its capacity of thought, which appear like anticipations of the famous Cartesian formula *Cogito, ergo sum*. In his arguments he appeals not only to the authority of Scripture and the Fathers, but also to that of Plato and other Greek philosophers, and shows himself not unacquainted with the systems of Zoroaster and the Brahmins. To him we owe the arrangement of a great part of the Breviary office, and the beautiful hymn for Passion Sunday, *Pange lingua gloriosi prœlium certamina*. For poetry, no less than philosophy, found votaries in the Gallican schools. The lyre, which had fallen from the hands of Prudentius, was still touched by St. Prosper of Aquitaine and St. Avitus of Vienne, the former of whom may be called the poet of Divine grace, whilst the latter, eleven centuries before the time of Milton, chose for the theme of his verses the Fall of Man.

Down to the beginning of the seventh century the schools of Gaul still taught Virgil and the Roman law, and in them the sons of the barbarous Visigoths received some tincture of polite letters. The Gallo-Roman nobility showed the utmost solicitude to obtain such education for their children as the times afforded; and we find notices of schools wherein grammar, rhetoric, and law were taught in separate courses after the Roman fashion. The Gallican orators, as in the time of St. Jerome, betrayed their Celtic origin by a certain verbose eloquence, which had to be pruned according to the severer rules of Roman rhetoric. The mother of Rufinus had sent him to the imperial capital, that the Roman gravity might temper the too great fecundity of the Gallic speech, and St. Desiderius of Cahors was made to go through a course of Roman jurisprudence with the same intention.

Nor, whilst noticing these evidences of a love of letters, surviving even in the period of decay, must I neglect to mention that notable academy of Toulouse, which at one time did its best to involve all Europe in a fog of learned perplexity. Its eccentricities would scarcely merit to be recorded, had they not left very distinct traces both in the Irish and Anglo-Saxon literature. The history of this academy has been written by one of its members, the false Virgil, as he is called, who has contrived to mystify both the date and whereabouts of its foundation. It is presumed, however, to have flourished at Toulouse sometime in the sixth century. Holding to the principle that pearls must not be cast before swine, certain enthusiasts of Aquitaine formed among themselves a secret scholastic society, the members of which spoke a language understood only by the initiated, and conferred on men and places the nomenclature of ancient Greece and Rome. The grand, I might almost say the exclusive, study of these illuminati was grammar. An assembly of thirty of their number had gravely determined that the subject most worthy of a wise man's meditation was the conjugation of the Latin verb, and on this momentous theme they split into two sects, which rivalled Guelph and Ghibelline in the ardour of their mutual animosities. The heads of these two parties, whose academic names were Terence and Galbungus, spent fourteen days and nights discussing the question whether the pronoun *Ego* had a vocative case: at last the difficulty was referred to Eneas, who decided that it might be allowed to possess one when employed in the interrogative phrase. These grammatical debates took place when Virgil was but a youth, but in his riper years he thoroughly maintained the reputation of his masters. It was the exact government of words which left him no repose, and he tells us how one night, having retired to rest, he was awaked by a knocking at his door, and found that the disturbance was caused by the arrival of a certain Spanish grammarian, named Mitterius, whom he honoured neither more nor less than if he had been a prophet of God. Mitterius begged for a night's lodging, promising in return to answer any question which his entertainer might put to him. The opportunity was not to be lost; there was but one thing just then that Virgil desired to know, and, springing from his bed, he at once required, as the price of his hospitality, a direct rule by which he could determine when the word *hic* was an adverb and when it was a pronoun. These anecdotes, however, give us but a faint notion of the labours of the Toulouse grammarians. The difficulties of the Latin syntax were not sufficient to satisfy their thirst for obscurity, and they therefore expended their ingenuity on inventing new means of perplexing their own brains and those of their scholars. "Was it to be supposed," they asked, "that this noble tongue was so poor and barren, that its words could be used in one sense only? On the contrary, the true grammarian knew very well that, besides the vulgar Latin known to the common herd, there existed eleven other kinds, each of which had a distinct grammar of its own." According to this system of "the twelve Latinities," everything had twelve names, any one of which might be used according to pleasure. New vocabularies had to be invented, either by the Latinising of Greek roots, or transposing the letters of the original words in such a way as to form a variety of new combinations. New conjugations and declensions adorned the grammar of the initiated, and to complete their system a new prosody was added, in which the dactyls and spondees appear to have been measured, not by quantity, but by accent.[34]

Even the triumphs of the barbarians did not in all cases result in the immediate extinction of letters. In Italy a second Augustan age bid fair at one time to arise under the rule of Theodoric, the Ostrogoth. His court was adorned by the genius of two great men—Boethius, the Christian philosopher, and the last of the classic writers; and Cassiodorus, in whom closed the long line of Roman consuls. Both of them exerted a powerful influence over the studies of succeeding generations. The original Latin works of Boethius supplied the schools with a series of Christian classics which were naturally held in extraordinary esteem by teachers who, as time went on, felt with increasing force the difficulty of training Christian youth exclusively out of pagan class-books. And it was chiefly by his translations from the Greek that the mediæval scholars acquired their knowledge of the Greek philosophy, at a time when the study of that tongue had ceased to be generally pursued. A yet further addition to scholastic literature was contributed by Cassiodorus. He was not indeed the only statesman who had distinguished himself in this line. Towards the close of the fifth century Marcian Capella, an African pro-consul, had produced his celebrated work on the Espousals of Mercury and Philology, which he chooses to personify as a goddess; the seven liberal sciences, into which all known learning had been classified since the days of Philo, being represented as the handmaidens presented by the bridegroom to the bride. His *Satiricon*, written in nine books, continued to be one of the most popular text-books in use during the middle ages, and was at an early period translated into the vernacular.

But Cassiodorus was not merely a writer of schoolbooks; he was the founder of a monastic school, which, for the variety of sciences which it cultivated, has not unfrequently been given the title of a university. And indeed it was not undeserving of the name. Its noble founder, when still in the service of Theodoric, had attempted, in conjunction with Pope St. Agapetus, to found a catechetical school at Rome, on the model of those which formerly flourished at Jerusalem, Alexandria, and Nisibis, in which he proposed to maintain a staff of professors at his own expense. This magnificent design having failed, in consequence of the troubles of the time, Cassiodorus retired from a world in which he had nobly toiled for seventy years, and devoted his old age to the creation of a seminary of Christian learning on his own estate of Vivaria, at the very extremity of the Calabrian peninsula. He collected a rich library, which he increased by the labours of his monks, on whom he enjoined the transcription of books as their principal manual labour. It was to ensure their accuracy in this employment that, at the age of eighty-three, he undertook the composition of his treatise *De Orthographia*. He drew up a plan of studies for his scholars, and wrote for their use two treatises, one "On the Teaching of Sacred Letters," and the other "On the Seven Liberal Arts." This latter was a kind of encyclopædia, including separate treatises on each subject, which formed some of the favourite elementary class-books in use during the middle ages. Hallam remarks of this encyclopædia and of others undertaken on a similar plan, that they themselves furnish significant indications of a decadence of letters. Such collections must necessarily include only the most meagre sketches of the sciences of which they profess to treat, and their multiplication at this period indicates that men were beginning to be content with a very superficial description of knowledge. So also the numerous translations from the Greek undertaken by Boethius and Cassiodorus are sufficient evidence that the knowledge of that language was becoming rare. Nor will the praises bestowed by Cassiodorus on his friend's versions, which he declares superior to the originals, probably raise his character as a critic in the judgment of scholars. But the fact that his labours were undertaken at a period of literary decay, when the inconceivable disorders of the time seemed to present an insuperable obstacle to the pursuit of learning, increases our admiration of the energy and zeal displayed by the old Roman, which enabled him in spite of every discouragement to create a school of sacred and profane learning, where strangers were encouraged to seek that hospitality the exercise of which was regarded as one of the most sacred duties of the brethren. There, under porticoes and gardens adorned with every beauty that could charm the eye or soothe the heart, pilgrims, weary with those scenes of violence and devastation that were turning many a fair district of Gaul and Italy into a howling wilderness, found all that remained of Roman learning and civilisation linked with the higher attractions of Christian devotion; and were able, amid the monastic shades of Vivaria, to enjoy at one and the same time the calm of retirement and the solace of prayer.

The foundation of Cassiodorus took place in the year 540. Eighteen years previously—in 522—the two Roman senators, Equitius and Tertullus, had taken their sons Maurus and Placidus to the grotto of Subiaco, and committed them to the care of a solitary named Benedict. Maurus was twelve years old and Placidus seven, and they were soon joined by other children of the same age. They were humble beginnings indeed of a mighty edifice, the first fruits of the Benedictine schools.[35] In 543 St. Maurus carried the rule of St. Benedict into Gaul, where monasteries soon multiplied, in which were cultivated letters both sacred and profane.[36] But they were not the earliest monastic schools which had sprung up on the Gallican soil. I need not here remind the reader of that famous abbey of Marmoutier, erected by St. Martin of Tours in the fourth century, and formed on the model of those episcopal monasteries founded by St. Eusebius of Vercelli and St. Ambrose of Milan. Yet more celebrated, and more closely associated with the history of letters in our own country, was the school of Lerins, a rocky isle off the coast of Gaul, where, about the year 400, St. Honoratus fixed his abode, peopling it with a race of monks who united the labours of the scholar to the penitential practices of the recluse. Its rule, though strictly monastic, aimed at making its disciples apostolic men, "thoroughly furnished to all good works." Hence the brethren were not required to renounce the pursuit of letters. St. Honoratus himself did not disdain the flowers of eloquence, and the sweetness of his style drew from St. Eucher the graceful remark, that "he restored the honey to the wax."[37] St. Hilary of Arles, another of the Lerins scholars, is represented by his biographer sitting among his clergy with a table before him, whereon lay his book and the materials of his manual work, and while his fingers were busy making nets, dictating to a cleric, who took down his notes in shorthand. It would take us too long to enumerate the distinguished prelates who were sent forth from the school of Lerins during the sixth century. The names of St. Cesarius of Arles and St. Vincent of Lerins; of Salvian, the master of bishops as he was called; of St. Eucher, the purity of whose Latin eloquence even Erasmus has praised; and of St. Lupus of Troyes, whom Sidonius Apollinaris hesitated not to call the first bishop in the Christian world—may suffice to show what sort of scholars were produced by this holy congregation.

Such then was the state of letters at the opening of the sixth century, an epoch when Europe was covered with the shattered remains of an expiring civilisation, and when whatever literary activity lingered about the old academies of Italy and Gaul must be regarded as the parting rays of a light, fast sinking below the horizon. Yet, as it sank, another luminary was sending forth its rising beams, and the essentially Christian institution of the monastic schools was acquiring shape and solidity. Such an epoch stood in need of a master to harmonise its disordered elements, and such a master it found in St. Gregory. But before speaking of him and of his Anglo-Saxon converts we must glance at the state of letters among that earlier Celtic population which sent students from Britain to the schools of Rome in the days of St. Jerome and St. Damasus. Nor whilst doing so, can we forget that sister-isle which never felt the tread of the Roman legions, and which, sharing with Britain the glorious title of the "Isle of Saints," merited by its extraordinary devotion to learning to be designated also the "Isle of Scholars."

CHAPTER II.

SCHOOLS OF BRITAIN AND IRELAND.

A.D. 380 TO 590.

ALTHOUGH the monastic institute existed in Britain almost from the period of her first conversion to the faith, yet the seminaries which produced her most illustrious scholars were only founded at a comparatively later date. Whatever schools may have existed in connection with the British episcopal monasteries of earlier times, had fallen into decay by the beginning of the fifth century, when fresh foundations of learning began to spring up, the origin of which must be traced to three distinct sources. I say *three* distinct sources, because the apostolic labours of St. Ninian among the Picts, of St. Palladius in North Britain, and of St. Germanus and St. Lupus in the southern portion of the island, were undertaken among different races, and on different occasions; nevertheless, in reality these three streams flowed forth from one common fountain, which was no other than the Holy and Apostolic See of Rome.

The mission of St. Ninian was the first in order of time. The son of a petty prince of Cumberland, he travelled to Rome for the purpose of study, about the year 380, and being introduced to the notice of Pope Damasus, was placed by him under the care of teachers, and in all probability received into the school of the Patriarchium. There he was thoroughly instructed, *regulariter edoctus*, in all the mysteries of the faith, and after spending fifteen years in Rome he at last received consecration from the hands of Pope St. Siricius, by whom he was sent back to exercise the episcopal functions in his own country. The fifth century, which was then just opening, was precisely that in which the discipline of the Church received its fullest development. Ninian, who had so long studied the ecclesiastical system at its fountain-head, and who on his homeward journey had visited Tours, and conversed with St. Martin, then drawing near his end, was fully prepared to introduce into his northern diocese the rule and manner of life which he had seen carried out in the churches of Italy and Gaul. At Whitherne in Galloway, where he fixed his see, he built a stone church, after the Roman fashion, and lived in a house adjoining it, together with his cathedral clergy, in strict observance of the ecclesiastical canons. In this episcopal college the younger clerics followed their ecclesiastical studies, whilst a school was likewise opened for the children of the neighbourhood, as appears from the anecdote related by St. Ælred of one little rebel who ran away to escape a flogging, and was nearly drowned when attempting to put to sea in a coracle, or wicker boat, which chanced to be without its usual covering of hides.[38] The great school, as St. Ninian's seminary is often styled, was resorted to both by British and Irish scholars, and among the works left written by the founder was a Book of Sentences, or selections from the Fathers, which seems to have been intended for the use of his students.

The death of Ninian took place at the time when the churches of South Britain were suffering from the ravages of the Pelagian heresy. Pelagius, himself a Briton by birth, had nowhere found more ready recipients of his doctrines than among his own countrymen, and the infection spread with such alarming rapidity that at the solicitation of Palladius, deacon of the Church of Rome, Pope St. Celestine commissioned the two Gallican bishops, St. Germanus of Auxerre and St. Lupus of Troyes, to visit Britain in the quality of Papal legates, and take the necessary steps for putting a stop to the troubles caused by the heretics. Their first visit took place in 429, on which occasion they introduced many reforms of discipline. One of the chief measures which they adopted in order to check the progress of error was the foundation of schools of learning both for clergy and laity. At Caerleon, then the British capital, they themselves began the good work by lecturing on the Holy Scriptures and the liberal arts. Their scholars appear to have done them credit, for some, we read, became profound astronomers, able to observe the course of the stars and to foretell prodigies (that is, to calculate eclipses), whilst others wholly devoted themselves to the study of the Scriptures.

Under these disciples a vast number of monastic schools soon sprang up in various parts of Britain. Indeed so undoubted is the claim of Germanus to be considered as the founder of the ancient British colleges, that some imaginative writers have assigned to him the origin of our two Universities of Oxford and Cambridge. His most celebrated followers were Dubricius and Iltutus, the first of whom established two great schools of sacred letters on the banks of the Wye, one of which, situated at Hentland, was attended by a thousand students. But this was surpassed by the monastery of Lantwit in Glamorganshire, where St. Iltutus presided over a community of two thousand four hundred members, including many scholars of note, such as the historian Gildas, the bard Taliesin, and the famous prelates, St. Sampson and St. Paul of Leon. Here, according to the Triads, the praises of God never ceased, but one hundred monks were employed each hour in chanting the divine office, which was kept up both by day and night. Iltutus was also the founder, or restorer, of the school of Bangor on the Dee, where had been a college of Christian philosophers in the days of King Lucius, and where, according to Bede, there were seven houses or colleges, each containing, at least, three hundred students; and this, says William of Malmesbury, "we may well believe by what we see; for so many half-ruined walls of churches, so many windings of porticoes, and so great a heap of ruins you may scarce see elsewhere."

Another Bangor, the same that still retains the name which was indeed common to all these foundations, owed its origin to Daniel, the fellow disciple of St. Iltutus, who, we are assured, received under his care all the most hopeful youths of West Britain. Paulinus, one of his scholars, founded the college of the White House, in Caermarthenshire, afterwards known as Whitland Abbey, or Alba Landa; receiving among other pupils St. David, who began his studies at Bangor under Iltutus. This celebrated man, whose name in our days is often regarded as almost as legendary as that of his contemporary, King Arthur, completed the extirpation of the Pelagian heresy, and by his apostolic labours merited the title bestowed on him by British historians of "the father of his country." He was the founder of no fewer than twelve monasteries, in all of which he contrived to combine the hard work of the scholar and the equally hard labour of the monk. Ploughing and grammar-learning succeeded each other by turns. "Knowing," says Capgrave, "that secure rest is the nourisher of all vices, he subjected the shoulders of his monks to hard wearisomeness.... They detested riches, and they had no cattle to till their ground, but each one was instead of an ox to himself and his brethren. When they had done their field-work, returning to the cloisters of their monastery, they spent the rest of the day till evening in reading and writing. And in the evening at the sound of the bell, presently laying aside their work, and leaving even a letter unfinished, they went to the church and remained there till the stars appeared, and then all went together to table to eat, but not to fulness. Their food was bread with roots or herbs, seasoned with salt, and they quenched their thirst with milk mingled with water. Supper being ended they persevered about three hours in watching, prayer, and genuflections. After this they went to rest, and at cock-crowing rose again, and abode in prayer till the dawn of day. Their only clothing was the skins of beasts." Yet these austere cœnobites cultivated all the liberal arts, and the monastery of the Rosy Valley, near Menevia, founded in the year 519, was no less a school of polite learning than it was a nursery of saints.

To St. Dubricius, St. Daniel, and St. David, the three dioceses of Llandaff, Bangor, and Menevia owe their origin; the fourth of the ancient sees, that of St. Asaph, sprang out of a monastic foundation which must be traced to a different source. It has been already said that the mission of St. Germanus and St. Lupus had been conferred on them by St. Celestine at the solicitation of the deacon Palladius, who by some writers is said to have been himself a Briton by birth. However that may be, his interest in the affairs of our northern islands induced St. Celestine, in the year 430, to send him to Ireland, after having first consecrated him bishop "over the Scots believing in Christ." The Christian faith had, in fact, already penetrated into Ireland, either from Gaul or Britain, but the faithful were as yet few in number, and possessed no regular hierarchy. Palladius at first met with such success, that St. Prosper, in his book against Cassian, written about this time, was able to say that St.

Celestine, after preserving the *Roman* island Catholic, had made the *barbarous* island Christian. He baptized many persons, and erected three churches in which he deposited the sacred books, some relics of SS. Peter and Paul, and his own writing-tablets. But soon afterwards the hostility of the native princes obliged him to withdraw from the country, in order not to expose his followers to persecution. As his mission was to the Scottish people, and not to any particular province or kingdom, he crossed over to North Britain, where several colonies of the Scots had already settled, and there pursued his apostolic labours with more prosperous results. His subsequent history is differently related by different authors. Some represent him as surviving for many years, and firmly establishing the ecclesiastical discipline of the North British Church. Others, with more appearance of probability, represent his death as taking place very shortly after his arrival in Scotland. It is certain, however, that regular discipline was established by him among his clergy, and that episcopal colleges were founded either by him or his immediate successors, in which young children were received and trained for the ecclesiastical state. Here the Scottish Christians of Hibernia would naturally repair, before the establishment of similar seminaries had begun in their own island, and among those who acquired the first seeds of learning in the Bishop's school was Cœlius Sedulius, whose Irish name is said to have been Sheil. His history is obscure, but, according to Trithemius, he passed over from Ireland into Britain about the year 430, and afterwards perfected his studies in the best schools of Gaul and Italy. Having embraced the ecclesiastical state, he thenceforward devoted himself exclusively to sacred letters; but his "Carmen Paschale," a Latin poem on the life of our Lord, betrays his familiarity with the poetry of Virgil. From another smaller poem on the same subject are taken two of the hymns used by the Church on the festivals of Christmas and the Epiphany.[39] St. Servanus, the first bishop of Orkney, is represented by some as a disciple of St. Palladius, but it is probable that he lived some years later. He was the founder of the monastery of Culross, where he brought up many youths from childhood, and educated them for the sacred ministry. Among these was one named Kentigern, so beautiful in person, and so innocent in manners, that his companions bestowed on him the title of *Mungo*, or the dearly beloved, by which name he is still best known in Scotland. When only twenty-five years of age the people demanded him for their bishop; he was accordingly consecrated by an Irish prelate, and chose for his residence a certain solitary place at the mouth of the river Clyde, the site of the present city of Glasgow. Here he erected a church and monastery, where he lived with his clergy according to the apostolic rule, his diocese extending from the Atlantic to the shores of the German Ocean; and over its vast extent he constantly journeyed on foot, preaching and administering baptism. The throne of the Scottish prince Rydderch the Liberal having been seized by one of his rebellious nobles, St.

Kentigern was forced by the usurper to quit the country, and took refuge in Wales, where, after visiting St. David at Menevia, he received from one of the Welsh princes a grant of the tract of land lying between the rivers Elwy and Clywd, where he erected the monastery and school of Llan-Elwy. Local tradition affirms that the name of Clywd was bestowed by him on the stream that bounded his domain, in memory of his old home on the banks of the Clyde. Here he was joined by a great number of followers, among whom he established regular monastic discipline. His rule, however, had some peculiarities in it. He divided his community into three companies, two of them, who were unlearned, were employed in agriculture and the domestic offices, the third, which was formed of the learned, devoted their time to study and apostolic labours; and this last class numbered upwards of three hundred. These again were divided into two choirs, one of whom entered the church as the others left, so that the praises of God at all hours resounded in their mouths. From this college a great number of apostolic missionaries went forth, not only into different parts of Britain, but also to Norway, Iceland, and the Orkney Islands St. Kentigern himself continued to journey about, preaching the faith, silencing the Pelagian heretics, and founding churches. On the restoration of Rydderch, in 544, St. Kentigern was recalled to his see, and left the government of his monastery and school at Llan-Elwy to St. Asaph, his favourite scholar, whose name was afterwards conferred upon the church and diocese.

One other British school must be named before passing on to the nurseries of sacred science established in the sister isle, it is that of Llancarvan, whose founder was indeed a British saint and prince, but one who had received his early education in the seminary of an Irish recluse. Few names in the ecclesiastical annals of Britain are more illustrious than that of St. Cadoc; the son of a prince of Brecknockshire, he was placed at the age of seven years under the care of Tathai, an Irish teacher, who had been induced to leave his mountain hermitage, and to take the government of the monastic college of Gwent in Monmouthshire. There Cadoc spent twelve years, studying the liberal arts and the Divine Scriptures. The times were simple, and the habits of the Irish doctor, as he is called, were somewhat austere. The young prince lighted his master's fire and cooked his frugal repast, whilst in the interval of such homely duties he conned his Latin grammar, and construed Virgil. This sort of school discipline, however, far from disgusting him with learning, inspired him with such a passion for letters, that when his father retired from the world to embrace an eremitical life, Cadoc would not accept of the dignity of chief thus left vacant, but chose to travel to various schools in Britain and Ireland, in order to perfect his studies. At last he fixed on a rural solitude in Glamorganshire, about three miles from the present town of Cowbridge, and there laid the foundation of a church and monastery, which became one of the most famous of all the British schools. It obtained the name of

Llancarvan, or the Church of the Stags, because, according to the ancient legend, whilst it was in course of building, some stags from the neighbouring forest, forgetting their natural wildness, came and offered themselves to the service of the saint, suffering him to yoke them to the cart which two weary or discontented monks had refused to draw.

Gildas the Wise, the pupil of St. Iltutus, was invited by Cadoc to deliver lectures in his college, which he did for the space of one year, desiring no other stipend than the prayers of his scholars; and during this time, says John of Tinmouth, he with his own hand copied out a book of the Gospels long preserved in the monastery of Llancarvan. At last the troubles caused by the advancing arms of "the dragons of Germany," as the Saxons were sometimes termed, obliged Cadoc and Gildas to quit Llancarvan, and take refuge in some small islands lying at the mouth of the Severn called the Holmes. Tradition still points to the Steep Holmes as the place of their retreat; and the wild peony and onion, which blossom there in profusion, but are not to be found on any part of the neighbouring coast, are commonly said to have sprung from those which grew in the garden of Gildas. He did not, however, long remain there, but in company with Cadoc joined some bands of British emigrant who had crossed over to Armorica. The two saints chose for their residence a cave in the little island of Ronech, where their fame attracted a crowd of disciples, who were accustomed twice a day to pass over from the mainland in little boats in order to enjoy their instruction. Cadoc was touched by their perseverance, and at last employed his mechanical genius in the contrivance of a bridge for their use, and did not refuse to deal out to them the bread of science. He made them learn Virgil by heart as well as the Scriptures; indeed his love for the old Mantuan was so enthusiastic that he generally carried the Æneid under his arm, and was accustomed to express his regrets to Gildas that one who on earth had sung so sweetly should be for ever shut out from the joys of heaven. St. Cadoc is said by some to have returned to Britain and found a martyr's crown at the hands of the pagan Saxons. According to the Glastonbury historians, St. Gildas also returned to his own country, and lies buried among the unnumbered saints of the isle of Avalon.

We have now to turn to the shores of that island which, if termed barbarous by St. Prosper from the circumstance of its never having formed any portion of the Roman Empire, was soon to become the means of enlightening many a land of more ancient civilisation. The history of the mission of St. Patrick has found too many narrators to need repetition in this place, and we shall only advert therefore to such points as have a particular interest in connection with the Irish schools. Whatever disputes have arisen as to the birthplace of St. Patrick, there has never been any difference of opinion as to the sources whence he derived his education. It seems certain that after his return from his second captivity in Ireland he studied for four years at Tours under St. Martin, whose nephew he is commonly said to have been; after which, in the thirtieth year of his age—that is to say, about the year 418—he placed himself under the direction of St. Germanus of Auxerre, with whom he continued his studies. Hence in the hymn attributed to Fiech it is said of him that "he read his canons under Germanus." The chronology of the next twelve years of his life is exceedingly confused, but he is stated to have been sent by Germanus to study in an island in the Mediterranean Sea, *in mari Tyrrheno*, which was evidently Lerins. Nennius adds that he also visited Rome, and spent nearly eight years there, "reading and searching into the mysteries of God, and studying the books of Holy Scripture." The length of time spent by him in Rome appears uncertain, but most writers agree on the point of his having visited the city, and of his being *Romanis eruditus disciplinis*. Having returned to Germanus, he is said to have accompanied him in his first visit to Britain, and was afterwards sent back to Rome by that holy prelate, who recommended him to Pope St. Celestine as a fit person to be employed in the Irish mission. The endless differences to be found in the various versions of his life do not affect the main facts here established, namely, that he acquired his ecclesiastical training in the first schools then existing in Christendom—those of Tours Auxerre, Lerins, and Rome—and that his institution to the apostolic office was received from the hands of the Vicar of Christ.

On his journey through Gaul we are told by Jocelin that he turned out of his road in order to pay a farewell visit to "his nurse and teacher," St. Germanus, who furnished him with a welcome supply of chalices, priestly vestments, and books. The same writer adds that he was accompanied into Ireland by twenty Roman clerics, but it appears probable that his companions were chiefly gathered in Gaul and Britain, and Lanigan mercilessly reduces their number from twenty to two. Passing over the circumstances of his first arrival on the Irish coast, and his ineffectual efforts to convert his old master Milcho, we next find the saint in the neighbourhood of Down Patrick, where he instructed, baptized, and tonsured a young disciple named Mochoe, to whom he also taught the Roman alphabet. This last-named incident is one of very frequent recurrence in the life of St. Patrick. Nennius indeed affirms that he wrote no less than 365 alphabets;[40] but, as Bishop Lloyd quaintly remarks, "the writers of those times, when they were upon the pin of multiplying, used generally to say that things were as many as the days of the year." It is quite certain, however, that this teaching of the Roman alphabet, the first step necessary for acquiring a knowledge of Latin, formed a very common item in the instruction of the Irish converts. We are not to conclude from this with the Bollandists, that previous to the arrival of St. Patrick the Irish possessed no knowledge of written characters, but it is at least clear that the apostle of Ireland considered it a part of his office to diffuse among the people committed to his pastoral care a knowledge of the letters, as well as of the faith of Rome. He also received into his company a number of young disciples, who, after being instructed in the faith, were gradually admitted to holy orders, and given the care of the newly-formed congregation. Thus, on his road to the great festival of Tara, which fills so conspicuous a place in the history of the saint, he preached the faith to a certain man whose young son Benan, or Benignus, fell at his feet weeping, and desiring ever to be in his company; and the saint, with the consent of his parents, received him as his disciple, or, as he is elsewhere called, his *alumnus*. This event took place on Good Friday; on the following Easter Sunday, when St. Patrick was invited to Tara to hold a conference with the pagan priests in presence of the king, the young neophyte, robed in white, carried the book of the gospels before his master, who advanced with his clergy in solemn procession, chanting an Irish hymn which he had composed for the occasion.

At another time a pious mother brought him her son Lananus, whom St. Patrick delivered to St. Cassan to be instructed in all good learning; and such was the ardour with which the boy applied himself to study, that in fifteen days he had learned the entire Psalter.[41] Again, Enda of Westmeath is represented entrusting his son Cormac to the care of the saint, to be educated by him; and he himself, in his confession, alludes to the sons of the kings who journeyed about with him (*qui mecum ambulant*). For this first seminary was not fixed in any college or monastery, but, as the above words imply, was formed of those who accompanied the apostle of Ireland in his ceaseless wanderings over the country. Popular accounts, indeed, generally represent him as founding at least a hundred monasteries, and even those who consider that the greater number of the Irish colleges were raised by his followers after his death, admit the fact of his having established an episcopal monastery and school at Armagh, where he and his clergy carried out the same rule of life that he had seen followed in the churches of Gaul. The government of this monastery was committed in the first instance to Benignus, who afterwards succeeded St. Patrick in the primacy.

The school, which formed a portion of the Cathedral establishment, soon rose in importance. Gildas taught here for some years before joining St. Cadoc at Llancarvan; and in process of time the number of students, both native and foreign, so increased that the university, as we may justly call it, was divided into three parts, one of which was devoted entirely to students of the Anglo-Saxon race. Grants for the support of the schools were made by the Irish kings in the eighth century; and all through the troublous times of the ninth and tenth centuries, when Ireland was overrun by the Danes, and so many of her sanctuaries were given to the flames, the succession of divinity professors at Armagh remained unbroken, and has been carefully traced by Usher. We need not stop to determine how many other establishments similar to those of Armagh were really founded in the lifetime of St. Patrick. In any case the rapid extension of the monastic institute in Ireland, and the extraordinary ardour with which the Irish cœnobites applied themselves to the cultivation of letters remain undisputed facts. "Within a century after the death of St. Patrick," says Bishop Nicholson, "the Irish seminaries had so increased that most parts of Europe sent their children to be educated here, and drew thence their bishops and teachers." The whole country for miles round Leighlin was denominated the "land of saints and scholars." By the ninth century Armagh could boast of 7000 students, and the schools of Cashel, Dindaleathglass, and Lismore vied with it in renown. This extraordinary multiplication of monastic seminaries and scholars may be explained partly by the constant immigration of British refugees who brought with them the learning and religious observances of their native cloisters, and partly by that sacred and irresistible impulse which animates a newly converted people to heroic acts of sacrifice. In Ireland the infant church was not, as elsewhere, watered with the blood of martyrs; it was, perhaps, the only European country in which Christianity was firmly established without the faithful having to pass through the crucible of persecution. And hence the burning devotion which elsewhere swelled the white-robed army of martyrs, but which here found no such vent, sent its thousands to people the deserts and the rocky islands of the west, and filled the newly raised cloisters of Ireland with a countless throng who gave themselves to the slower martyrdom of penance and love. The bards, who were to be found in great numbers among the early converts of St. Patrick, had also a considerable share in directing the energies of their countrymen to intellectual labour. They formed the learned class, and on their conversion to Christianity were readily disposed to devote themselves to the culture of sacred letters. At the Easter festival at Tara, already alluded to, the first convert gained by St. Patrick was Dubtach, the arch-priest and poet of the country. His conversion took place in 433, and after that time he devoted his talents to the service of the faith, and taught whatever science he possessed to a school of Christian disciples.

It would be impossible, within the limits of a single chapter, to notice even the names of all the Irish seats of learning, or of their most celebrated teachers, every one of whom has his own legend in which sacred and poetic beauties are to be found blended together. One of the earliest monastic schools was that erected by Enda, prince of Orgiel, in that western island called from the wild flowers which even still cover its rocky soil, Aran-of-the-Flowers, a name it afterwards exchanged for that of *Ara-na-naomh*, or Aran-of-the Saints. There may yet be seen the rude stone church of the sixth century within which rest the bodies of the 127 saints of Aran, and at no great distance the remains of small beehive houses which served as the abode of the monks. According to Lanigan, who is seldom disposed to assign a very early date to the monastic establishments of Ireland, the foundation of Enda cannot be fixed later than the year 480. It became the nursery of some of the greatest Irish teachers, and was also the resort of students from beyond the sea. Hither came St. Carthag the elder, St. Kieran, and St. Brendan. Here too St. Fursey spent many years in solitude before going forth to found his monasteries in England and France, and here he at last returned from his splendid cloisters of Lagne on the Marne to end his days and be laid to rest in the rude sanctuary of the "Four beautiful Saints." Nor does the holy soil of Aran fail to cherish a remembrance of St. Columba the Great. He came here before undertaking his mission to North Britain, and his admiration for the Isle of Saints is commemorated in verses wherein he declares that to sleep on the dust of Aran and within the sound of her church-bells is as desirable as to be laid to rest on the threshold of the Apostles.

A little later St. Finian founded his great school of Clonard, whence, says Usher, issued forth a stream of saints and doctors, like the Greek warriors from the wooden horse. Finian was baptized and instructed by one of the immediate disciples of St. Patrick, and after studying under various Irish masters he passed over into Britain, and there formed an intimate friendship with St. David, St. Gildas, and St. Cadoc. He remained for several years in Britain, and on returning to his own country founded several religious houses, in one of which he lectured on the Holy Scriptures for seven years. At last, about the year 530, he fixed his residence in the desert of Clonard in Westmeath, which had up to that time been the resort of a huge wild boar. This desolate wilderness was soon peopled by his disciples, who are said to have numbered 3000, of whom the twelve most eminent are often termed the Twelve Apostles of Ireland. Finian himself is commonly spoken of as the Master of Saints, and is esteemed, next to St. Patrick, as the greatest doctor of the Irish Church. "He was," says the writer of his life, "replenished with all science as a learned scribe to teach the law of God; and he was most compassionate and charitable, weeping with those that wept and mildly healing the bodies and souls of all who applied to him. He slept on the bare ground with a stone under his head, and ate nothing but bread and herbs," and his disciples followed the same severe manner of life. Among them none were more famous than St. Columba, St. Kieran, and St. Brendan. The first of these is known to every English reader as the founder of Iona; and Kieran, the carpenter's son, as he is called, is scarcely less renowned among his own countrymen. Some anecdotes are told of the school life of these two great men, in which the youthful infirmities[42] so frankly recorded of both will certainly not prejudice our opinion of their future sanctity. A school in those days was not exactly arranged after the fashion of Eton or Rugby: the scholars worked for their own maintenance and that of the house; and under monastic masters this initiation into the holy law of labour was never spared even to those of princely blood. The prince and the peasant were accustomed to work and study side by side; and so it was in the school of Clonard. Columba was of royal extraction, while Kieran was of humble birth. The first task assigned the young prince was to sift the corn that was to serve for next day's provision, and to the surprise of his more plebeian associates he accomplished it so neatly and with such rapidity that they all declared he must have been helped by an angel. Royal and noble scholars, however, are seldom popular in public schools, and Columba had not a little to endure from his companions on the score of his gentle blood. He exacted a deference from them which Kieran in particular would not submit to, and the result was a continual bickering. But at last, says the old legend, an angel appeared to Kieran, and laying before him a carpenter's rule and other instruments of his trade, said to him, "Behold what thou hast renounced in giving up the world, but Columba has forsaken a royal sceptre." The good heart of the carpenter's son was touched with this reproach, and from that time he and Columba only contended in the generous rivalry of the saints.

Of St. Columba's apostolic mission to North Britain we shall presently have occasion to speak; but first we must trace the fortunes of his schoolfellow, Kieran, who became the founder of another of the most renowned schools of Ireland. Kieran's future sanctity had been detected by the quick eye of St. Finian before he left Clonard. One day as he was studying St. Matthew's Gospel, having come upon the sentence, "All things that ye would that men should do unto you, do ye to them also," he closed the book, saying, "This is enough for me." One of his comrades, jesting with him, observed, "Then we shall call you not Kieran, but *Leth-Matha* (half-Matthew), for you have stopped in the middle of the Gospel." "No," said Finian, who overheard the remark, "call him rather *Leth-Nerion* (half-Ireland), for one-half of this island shall be his,"—a prophecy which was fulfilled when half the Irish monasteries accepted his rule. After leaving Clonard, Kieran, having received his master's blessing and license, repaired to an island in the lake of Erne, where he spent some time studying under St. Nennidius, another of the Clonard scholars. At last he found his way to Aran, where Enda, who was still living, received him joyfully, and employed him during the intervals of study in threshing out the corn for the use of the other monks. After remaining there seven years he founded two great monasteries, one of which was situated on the west bank of the Shannon, at a spot called Cluain-Mac-Nois,[43] or the Retreat of the Sons of the Noble. This foundation took place about the year 548, and thence the austere rule or law of Kieran spread into a vast number of other religious houses.

It is indeed worthy of note that all the great masters of the Irish schools were followers of the most severe monastic discipline. The nurseries of science were often enough the rude cave, or forest hut of some holy hermit, such as St. Fintan, the founder of Cluain-Ednech, or the Ivy Cave, near Mount

Bladin in Queen's County; whose disciples lived on herbs and roots, laboured in the fields, and, like the monks of Menevia, renounced the assistance of cattle. Yet Abbot Fintan was a polished scholar, and particularly noted for his skill as a logician; and learned men came in crowds to the Ivy Cave to perfect themselves in sacred science and the rules of a holy life. One of Fintan's most celebrated scholars was St. Comgall, who in 559 became the founder of Benchor, near the bay of Carrickfergus. The fame of this great school of learning and religion has been celebrated by St. Bernard, who, in his "Life of St. Malachi," speaks of the swarm of saints who came forth from Benchor, and spread themselves like an inundation into foreign lands. In the Latin hymn of its old Antiphonary it is extolled as the ship beaten with the waves, the house founded on the rock, the true vine transplanted out of Egypt whose rule is at once holy and learned, *simplex simul atque docta*. The most famous of its scholars was St. Columbanus, the founder of Luxeuil in Burgundy and of Bobbio in Italy, whose rule spread over most European countries, and promised at one time to rival that of St. Benedict. The letters of Columbanus prove him to have been "a man of three tongues," to use the ordinary term applied in old times to one who added to his Greek, Hebrew. His acquaintance with the Latin poets is evident in his letter to Hunaldus, and his familiarity with those of Greece in his poetical epistle to Fedolius. And as he was fifty years of age before he left his native land, it is certain that his learning must have been entirely gained in her native seminaries. Another of the Benchor scholars was Molua, or Luanus, as he is called by St. Bernard, who tells us that he founded at least a hundred monasteries. The story of his first introduction to St. Comgall has been often told, but is one of those that can scarcely be told too often. He was keeping his flocks on the mountain-side, when Comgall, attracted by his appearance, wrote out the alphabet for him on a slate, and seeing his eagerness to learn, took him to Benchor and placed him in the school. Luanus conceived such a thirst for the waters of science that he prayed night and day that he might become learned. The prudent abbot, while he admired the zeal of his new scholar, was not without some anxiety lest his craving after human learning might sully the purity of his soul. One day he beheld the boy seated at the feet of an angel, who was showing him his letters and encouraging him to study. Calling Luanus to him, he said, "My child, thou hast asked a perilous gift from God; many, out of undue love of knowledge, have made shipwreck of their souls." "My father," replied Luanus, with the utmost humility, "if I learn to know God I shall never offend Him, for those only offend Him who know him not." "Go, my son," said the abbot, charmed with his reply, "remain firm in the faith, and the true science shall conduct thee on the road to heaven."

Luanus was the founder of the monastery of Clonfert, in Leinster, and the author of another religious rule highly prized by his countrymen. The no less celebrated school of Clonfert, in Connaught, owed its foundation to St.

Brendan, the fellow-student of Kieran and Columba. Having passed some years under the direction of St. Jarlath at Tuam, and St. Finian at Clonard, and become as familiar with Greek as he was with Latin, he is declared by his historians to have set sail on a voyage in search of the Land of Promise, which lasted seven years. In the course of these wanderings by sea he discovered a vast tract of land lying far to the west of Ireland, where he beheld wonderful birds, and trees of unknown foliage, which gave forth the perfumes of such excellent spices, that the fragrance thereof still clung to the garments of the travellers when they returned to their native shores.

But it is time to speak of the Irish monastic patriot, whose name is known in our own time, as it was probably revered in his own, beyond any of those that have hitherto been mentioned. It was in the year 563 that St. Columba,[44] after founding the monasteries of Doire-Calgaich and Dair-magh in his native land, and incurring the enmity of one of the Irish kings, determined on crossing over into Scotland in order to preach the faith to the Northern Picts. Accompanied by twelve companions, he passed the Channel in a rude wicker boat covered with skins, and landed at Port-na Currachan, on a spot now marked by a heap of huge conical stones. Conall, king of the Albanian Scots, granted him the island of I, Hi, or Ai, hitherto occupied by the Druids, and there he erected the monastery which, in time, became the mother of three hundred religious houses. If Johnson felt his piety grow warmer amid the ruins of Iona, we surely cannot be indifferent while contemplating the site of that missionary college which educated so many of our early apostles, and diffused the light of faith from Lindisfarne to the Hebrides. The life led by its inmates was at once apostolic and contemplative. If at one time the monks of Iona were to be met with travelling through the islands and highlands of Scotland, preaching the faith and administering baptism where no Christian missionaries had hitherto penetrated, at others they were to be seen tilling the soil, teaching in their schools, and transcribing manuscripts. In whatever labours they engaged, Columba himself was the first to lead the way. "He suffered no space of time," says Adamnan, "no, not an hour, to pass in which he was not employed either in prayer, or in reading, or writing, or manual work. And so unwearied was his labour both by day and night, that it seemed as if the weight of every particular work of his seemed to exceed the power of man." He penetrated into the Hebrides, and twice revisited his native shores, but on his return from such expeditions he loved to take part in the agricultural or scholastic pursuits of his brethren. He would hear them read or himself read to them, and overlook their work in the Scriptorium, where he required the most scrupulous exactitude. He himself was a skilful penman, and the magnificent Codex of Kells, still preserved in the library of Trinity College, is known to have been written by his hand. Iona, or I-Colum-kil, as it was called by the Irish, came to be looked on as the chief seat of learning, not only in Britain, but in the whole Western world.

"Thither, as from a nest," says Odonellus, playing on the Latin name of the founder, "these sacred doves took their flight to every quarter." They studied the classics, the mechanical arts, law, history, and physic. They improved the arts of husbandry and horticulture, supplied the rude people whom they had undertaken to civilise with ploughshares and other utensils of labour, and taught them the use of the forge, in the mysteries of which every Irish monk was instructed from his boyhood. They transferred to their new homes all the learning of Armagh or Clonard. Of St. Munn, one of the pupils of Columba, it is said that he spent eighteen years in uninterrupted study, yet this devotion to intellectual pursuits was accompanied by a singular simplicity and love of poverty. Wherever the apostles of Iona appeared, they carried with them the reputation of frugality and self-devotion. Thus Bede remarks on the extreme simplicity of life observed by Bishop Colman and his disciples, how they were content with the simple fare, "because it was the study of their teachers to feed the soul rather than the body." "And for that reason," he continues, "the religious habit was then held in great veneration, and wherever any monk appeared, he was joyfully received as God's servant; and if men chanced to meet him on the way they ran to him bowing, glad to be signed with his hand and blessed by his mouth. And when a priest came to any village the inhabitants immediately flocked to hear from him the Word of Life, for they went about on no other account than to preach, baptize, visit the sick, and take care of souls."

In every college of Irish origin, by whomsoever they were founded or on whatever soil they flourished, we thus see study blended with the duties of the missionary and the cœnobite. They were religious houses, no doubt, in which the celebration of the Church office was often kept up without intermission by day and night; but they were also seminaries of learning, wherein sacred and profane studies were cultivated with equal success. Not only their own monasteries but those of every European country were enriched with their manuscripts, and the researches of modern bibliopolists are continually disinterring from German or Italian libraries a Horace, or an Ovid, or a Sacred Codex whose Irish gloss betrays the hand which traced its delicate letters. The Hibernian scholars were remarkable for combining acuteness of the reasoning powers with the gifts of the musician and the poet. There were no more accurate mathematicians and no keener logicians than the sons of Erin, whose love of syllogism is spoken of in the ninth century by St. Benedict of Anian. They are admitted to have been the precursors of the mediæval schoolmen, and to have been the first to apply the subtleties of Greek philosophy to Christian dogma. Their love of Greek was, perhaps, excessive, for they evinced it by Hellenising their Latin, and occasionally writing even their Latin missals in the Greek character. In the disputes that arose on the subject of the Paschal computation, they astonished their adversaries with their arithmetical science and their linguistic erudition. St.

Cummian, in the Paschal epistle wherein he so ably defends the Roman system, examines all the various cycles in use among the Jews, Greeks, Latins, and Egyptians; quotes passages from Greek and Latin fathers, and manifestly proves how well the libraries of Ireland were furnished, and how competent her scholars were to use them. Nor whilst cultivating the exact sciences did they abandon the muses. Both St. Columbia and St. Columbanus enjoyed a reputation as poets. St. Ængus, the martyrologist, began life as a professional bard, and did not lay aside his harp when he assumed the cowl of the cœnobite; while Ruman, the son of Colman, was called "the Virgil of Ireland," and is described as an "adept in chronology, history, and poetry." Rhyme, if not invented in Ireland, was at least adopted by her versifiers so generally, and at so early a period, as sometimes to be designated "the art of the Irish;" and, as Moore observes, the peculiar structure of their verse shows that it belonged to a people of strong musical feeling. Hence they soon became famous for their skill in psalmody, and were esteemed both at home and abroad as first-rate choir-masters; and the legends of the Irish saints are full of passages which describe the kind of ecstasy produced in the minds of this people, so susceptible to the beautiful in every form, by the melody of the ecclesiastical chant. We will give one of these stories, because it introduces us to the founder of the school of Lismore, the last of the great Irish seminaries which we shall notice in this place. Though said to be of noble extraction, Mochuda was employed by a chief in the humble capacity of swineherd. One day as he tended his herd by the banks of the river Mang, he was rapt out of himself by a sight and a sound of beauty altogether new to him. It was the holy bishop St. Carthag the elder, accompanied by a procession of his clergy, who as they went along made the hills of Kerry re-echo to the Psalm-tones, ever ancient and ever new, of the Gregorian chant. St. Augustine has confessed to their power over his heart, and the poor Irish swineherd was not less enraptured by their beauty than the African rhetorician had been. Drawn along, as it were, by the charm of the melody, he left his herd in the fields and followed the singers to their monastery. All night he remained outside the gates, catching at intervals the distant sound of the night office, till when morning dawned he was found there by his master Moelthuili, who desired to know why he had not returned home in the evening as was usual. "Because I was charmed with the holy songs of the servants of God," replied Mochuda, "and I desire nothing else on earth than that I also may learn to sing those songs." Moelthuili, who loved the boy, made him large promises of favour if he would remain in his service, but finding his words unheeded, he at last took him to the bishop and begged him to receive the youth among his disciples. St. Carthag bestowed his own name upon him, and admitted him among his scholars, and in process of time the fame of the pupil surpassed even that of his master. In 630 St.

Carthag the younger, as he is called, became the founder of Lismore, the fame of whose schools extended into Italy.

"One-half of this holy city," says an ancient writer, "is a sanctuary into which no woman may enter; it is full of cells and monasteries, and religious men resort thither from all parts of Ireland and England."[45] One of the most famous masters of Lismore was St. Cathal or Cataldus, the patron saint of Tarentum in Italy, and his numerous biographies in prose and verse never fail to commemorate the glories of his Alma Mater.

Whatever exaggeration may have been committed by the national annalists when they speak of the foreign students who resorted to the Irish schools, it is impossible to doubt that they were eagerly sought by nations of the most distant lands, who, in an age when the rest of Europe was sunk in illiterate barbarism, found in the cloisters of Armagh, Lismore, Clonard, and Clonmacnois, masters of philosophy and sacred science whose learning had passed into a proverb. Camden remarks how common a thing it is to read in the lives of our English saints that they were sent to study in Ireland, and the same expression occurs quite as frequently in the Gallican histories. The prodigious Litany of the Saints, composed in the eighth century by St. Ængus, includes the names not only of Britons, Picts, and Saxons, but also of Gauls, Germans, Romans, and Egyptians, all buried in Ireland. The tomb of the "Seven Romans" may still be seen in the churchyard of St. Brecan in the Isle of Aran, and a church at Meath was commonly known as the Greek Church, so called from having been served by Greek ecclesiastics. Even in the eleventh century the fame of the Irish schools was undiminished, and Sulgenus, bishop of St. David's, spent ten years studying under their best masters.

Great as was the learning of the Irish scholars, it had in it a certain character of its own. Their theology was deeply tinged with a metaphysical spirit, and in their grammar, no less than their poetry, they displayed a taste for the mystic and the obscure. This is partly to be attributed to the influence of the Toulouse academicians, with whom the Irish scholars eagerly fraternised. They seem to have found something unspeakably attractive in the bizarre language of the twelve Latinities and the novelties of the Toulouse prosody. The strange jargon in which some of their professors were accustomed to indulge occasionally steals into the Hibernian hymns and antiphons; and the Anglo-Saxons who flocked in such multitudes to the Irish seminaries, were not slow in catching the infection. They soon learnt to disfigure their pages with a jumble of Greek, Latin, and Anglo-Saxon syllables, and to expend their patience and ingenuity over compositions in which the great achievement was to produce fifteen consecutive words beginning with a P.

If Ireland gave hospitality in these remote ages to men of all tongues and races, she in her turn sent forth her swarms of saints who have left their traces in countless churches founded by them in Gaul, Germany, Switzerland, and Italy. The children of St. Columbanus reformed the Austrasian clergy, and were the first apostles of the Rhetian wildernesses. At Fiesole, in Tuscany, we find the Irish St. Donatus, compelled by the people to accept the office of bishop, and restoring, at one and the same time, sacred studies and ecclesiastical discipline. The myrtle bowers of Ausonia, however, did not make him forget his native land, for in some Latin verses which Moore has thought worthy of translation, he dwells like a true patriot on the praises of that remote western island, so rich in gems and precious metals, where the fields flow with milk and honey, and the lowing herds and golden harvests supply all the wants of man. At Lucca the English traveller is still startled to find the relics of his own Anglo-Saxon countrymen, St. Richard and St. Winibald, preserved and venerated in a church dedicated to the Irish bishop, St. Frigidian. And whilst the southern shores of Italy were welcoming the coming of St. Cataldus, Iceland and the distant Orcades were receiving missionaries of the same Celtic race.[46]

Hereafter we shall see the scholars of Ireland taking part in the Carlovingian revival of learning, and making it their boast that the two first universities of Europe, those of Paris and Pavia, owed their foundation in no small degree to Hibernian professors. But before that era dawned, they had found rivals, both in their literary and apostolic labours, in the Anglo-Saxon race. The "sea-dragons of Germany," who had extinguished faith and civilisation in the British provinces which they had overrun and conquered, had received anew those precious gifts from the hands of a great pope, whose instinctive genius led him to transfer to this remote corner of the world the sciences which were fast dying out of the Italian and Gallican schools. The story has been often told, but the course of our history obliges us to tell it over again in the following chapter.

CHAPTER III.

THE ANGLO-SAXON SCHOOLS.

A.D. 590 TO 875.

THE Donatist heresy was still raging in Africa; the Arians were triumphant in Spain and Northern Italy; a miserable schism arising out of the affair of the Three Chapters was vexing the Istrian provinces; France was torn by intestine wars, and the imperial power which nominally held rule in Italy was fast crumbling to pieces; the almost civilised dominion of the Ostrogoths had been exchanged for the wild barbarism of the half pagan, half Arian Lombards; floods, plague, and famine were rapidly depopulating the southern peninsula, when, in the year 590, St. Gregory the Great was placed in the chair of St. Peter, and received into his hands the destinies of the Western world.

"There are," says the German philosopher, Frederic Schlegel, "grand and pregnant epochs in the history of the world, in which all existing relations assume a new and unexpected form. At such junctures, God Himself seems, as it were, to interfere, and establish a theocracy." Such was the epoch of which we speak. All the power of human government had come to nought, and while men's hearts were failing them for fear, the reins were falling into the hands of a frail and feeble monk, worn out with sickness and austerity, and so little conscious of possessing in himself the capacity of ruling, that, when the unanimous voice of clergy and people raised him to the pontifical dignity, he fled in terror to the woods, and was brought back weeping, and giving vent to his anguish in accents almost of despair. It will suffice very briefly to remind the reader what kind of pontificate it was that was thus begun. During the fourteen years that St. Gregory governed the Church, he achieved greatness enough to furnish fame to a dozen autocrats. He defended Rome from the Lombards, and the Lombards themselves from the treachery of the Eastern emperors; he won them from Arianism, extirpated Donatism from Africa, and put an end to the Istrian schism. Whilst providing for the necessities of the Italian provinces, desolated by the cruel calamities of the times, he firmly resisted the exactions of the Byzantine court, and maintained the independence of the Church against the Cæsars. From the effete civilisation of the corrupt East, he turned to the new and semi-barbarous races of the West,—taught the Frankish kings the duties of Christian sovereignty, and urged their bishops to wage war against ecclesiastical abuses. His prodigious correspondence carried his paternal care into the most distant provinces. He condemned slavery, defended the peasants, and protected even the Jews. And in the midst of these multifarious labours, he found time to preach and write for future ages also. Thirty-five books of "Morals," thirteen volumes of Epistles, forty Homilies on the gospels, twenty-two on the prophet Ezechiel, an immortal treatise on the Pastoral care, four books of Dialogues, and the reformation of the Sacramentary or ritual of the Church, are the chief works left us by the Fourth Latin Doctor. Nevertheless, as most readers must be aware, there exists a certain tradition which represents this great pope as the enemy of learning, a tradition elaborated out of the rebuke administered by him to Didier, Bishop of Vienne, on occasion of that prelate having delivered lectures on the profane poets, and the supposed fact of his having burnt the Palatine Library, a fact which, however, remained without record until six centuries had elapsed.[47] We need not pause to examine charges which, however often refuted or explained, will always find credence among a certain class of writers and readers, who cling to a time-honoured *mumpsimus*. But it was necessary to recognise the existence of this view of his character before presenting the supposed destroyer of the Palatine Library as the undoubted founder of a Palatine school. And first we will hear how his biographer, John the Deacon, describes his manner of life. After naming several of the ecclesiastics, whom he chose as his chief councillors, among whom occur the names of Paul the Deacon, and our English apostles, Augustine and Mellitus, he goes on to relate how, in company with these, St. Gregory contrived to carry out monastical perfection within the walls of his own palace. "Learned clerks and religious monks," he says, "lived there in common with their pontiff, so that the same rule was exhibited in Rome in the time of St. Gregory as St. Luke describes as existing in Jerusalem under the Apostles, and Philo records as established by St. Mark at Alexandria."

These clerks assisted St. Gregory in his learned labours. Some were notaries, who wrote out his Homilies under his direction; and Paul the Deacon is introduced as the interlocutor in his Dialogues. And the historian goes on to tell us, that out of the canonical life established in the pontifical palace, there sprang a school. "Then did wisdom visibly fabricate to herself a temple," he continues, "supporting the porticoes of the apostolic see by the seven liberal arts as by columns formed of the most precious stones. In the family of the pontiff, no one from the least to the greatest, dared utter a barbarous word; the purest Latinity, such as had been spoken in the time of the best Roman writers, was alone permitted to find another Latium in his palace. There, the study of all the liberal arts once more flourished, and he who was conscious to himself that he was wanting either in holiness or learning, dared not show his face in presence of the pontiff." He goes on to speak of the number of learned men constantly to be found in the company of the pope, who encouraged poor philosophy rather than rich idleness. But he confesses that one thing was wanting: the "Cecropian muse" was absent; in other words, there was no one skilful in the interpretation of Greek.

In addition to this Palatine academy, if I should not rather say in connection with it, St. Gregory founded a school destined to have a more world-wide influence and more lasting fame. The extraordinary diligence bestowed by the holy pontiff on the reformation of the ecclesiastical chant gave rise in after times to a graceful legend, which represented him as visited in his sleep by a tenth Muse, who appeared to him with her mantle covered with the mystic notes and neumas, and inspired him with that skill in science of sacred melody, which he ever afterwards possessed. The legend, like most legends, only embalms and beautifies a fact. The Church was the real Muse who inspired her pontiff to give to her order of sacred chant the same perfection he had already bestowed upon her Liturgy. Other popes and prelates had laboured before him at the same work, and indeed the very name of *Centon*, which is given to his Antiphonary, shows that it was a compilation of those ancient melodies which passed from the Temple to the Church, and which may be traced through St. Mark at Alexandria, and through St. Ignatius at Antioch, up to St. Peter himself.[48] In process of time the Eastern churches introduced a more pompous and florid style, but in Africa, thanks to the exertions of St. Athanasius, the ancient severity was preserved, and made matter of reproach against the Catholics by the Donatist heretics, who attributed it to the natural heaviness and stupidity of the African character. Baronius observes that, according to the most ancient monuments, the Roman Church appears to have taken the middle course, between the extreme simplicity of the Africans and the florid ornamentation of the Orientals, and thus united gravity with sweetness.

St. Ambrose, who introduced the chant into Milan, permitted women to join in the chanting of the Psalms, a custom which degenerated in some churches into the establishment of female choirs; though this abuse was prohibited by many popes and councils. Everywhere the bishops encouraged the cultivation of the chant, and Fortunatus describes St. Germanus of Paris presiding in the apse of the Golden Church, and directing the singing of his two choirs. But, as St. Augustine remarks in one of his letters, no uniformity existed among the different churches, and both variations and corruptions were introduced according to the genius of different nations. Hence, the reformation of the Cantus, and the establishment of some uniform standard based on the ancient models, had engaged the attention of several popes before the time of St. Gregory, and particularly of St. Gelasius and St. Damasus. St. Gregory completed their work: he collected in his Centon, or Antiphonary, all the ancient fragments still existing, corrected and arranged them with his own pen, and added some original compositions, bearing the same character of majestic simplicity with the venerable melodies on which they were formed. And finally, to secure the permanence of these reforms, and to extend the use of the ecclesiastical chant throughout the Church, he founded a school which, three centuries later, still survived and flourished.

"After the manner of a wise Solomon," says John the Deacon, "being touched by the sweetness of music, he carefully compiled his *Centon* or Antiphonary of chants, and established a school of those chants which had hitherto been sung in the Roman Church, and built for this purpose two houses, one attached to the Church of St. Peter the Apostle, and the other near the Lateran Patriarchium, where, up to this day, are preserved, with becoming veneration, the couch whereon he was accustomed to rest when singing, and the rod with which he was wont to threaten the boys, together with the authentic copy of his Antiphonary."

The important place which the Roman school of chant occupied in the history of Christian education will be seen in the following pages. Its value in our own day can hardly be appreciated, for the training of Christendom has long since ceased to be liturgical. But an era was about to open on the world during which the human intellect was no longer to receive its shape and colouring from the forms, however beautiful, of pagan antiquity, but from that Christian Muse whom our English poet has invoked. St. Gregory lived at a time when the old empire, with its letters and civilisation, was fast passing away. The little stone had struck the statue, and the iron, the clay, the brass, the silver, and the gold, had been carried away by the wind, and become as the chaff on the summer's threshing-floor. He beheld new races rising out of the dust of fallen empires. What now are Homer and Horace to the grim Goth or savage Lombard who has spent his life in beating to pieces with his battle-axe the fairest monuments of Greece and Rome? To him no inspiration will flow from Castaly or Parnassus.

The mossy fountains and the sylvan shades,

The dreams of Pindus and the Aonian maids

Delight no more,

and the name of Woden is far more venerable in his eyes than that of Apollo. But there is *One* Power that has caught him in its golden nets and holds his soul a willing captive. When the waters of baptism flowed over his brow he was brought face to face with that mighty Mother from whose hands he was to receive the knowledge of letters, and a far vaster education than the knowledge of letters alone can ever give. Heart, will, imagination, and understanding, all found their teacher in the Church of the Living God. Her sacred offices appealed to his soul through a thousand avenues, by their inspired ceremonial, their matchless poetry, their solemn melody, and their pictured art. The following pages will sadly fail of their main object if they do not succeed in conveying to the reader a faint notion of that marvellous education which the Church supplied to countless populations who, it may be, never learnt to read. Her Liturgy became the class-book of the barbaric races: it was to them all, and far more than all, that Homer or Ossian had been to the children of a darker age. What wonder, then, that the study of its musical language should be erected by them into a liberal art, and that those who were receiving their civilisation from the Rome, not of the Cæsars, but of the Popes, should welcome among them the teachers of the Roman music with as great enthusiasm as ever Florence in the fifteenth century, welcomed her professors of Greek?

The importance of St. Gregory's foundation regarded from this point of view will readily appear. It was in some sort the mother of those grand liturgical schools which were afterwards to cover the face of Europe, the erection of which in any country serves as an epoch to mark the introduction or restoration of Christian letters. Henceforth, for nine centuries at least, grammar and the Cantus, the Latin tongue and the Roman music, were to take their places side by side as the two indispensables of education. Up to this time even the Christian learning had been coloured by a civilisation of pagan growth; but a new era had now begun: the Holy Scriptures and the Liturgy of the Church were to become to Christian Europe what the profane poets had been to the ancient world—the fountains of inspiration and the intellectual moulds wherein a new generation was to be cast; and though scholars were far from abandoning Virgil, yet for long ages the Muse of Solyma was to hold the mastery in the schools.

This new era of letters may be said to commence with St. Gregory, for the schools of Christian origin which existed before his time were fast becoming extinct, and it was chiefly from the new foundation, planted by him on English soil, that the torch of science was relit. How truly was he termed the Great, this pontiff, prince, and tutor of a barbarous world! Yet to conceive aright of his greatness we must remember that his work was painfully wrought out in the midst of continual bodily sufferings and mental troubles yet harder to bear. He who may be said to have founded the temporal sovereignty of the Roman Pontiffs had his throne in the midst of ruins. He delivered his discourses on Ezechiel while the barbarous Lombards were marching against his capital. He had to witness the Roman nobles dragged off into slavery with ropes about their necks, to be sold like dogs in the markets of Gaul. Then came the news that Monte Cassino was in flames and its monks cast out as houseless wanderers. "Woe is me!" he exclaims, "all Europe is in the hands of the barbarians. Cities are cast down, villages in ruins, whole provinces depopulated; the land has no longer men to cultivate it; and the idolaters pursue us even to death." Yet in this awful crisis his mind was bent on effecting new conquests for the faith, and he was planning the conversion of the Anglo-Saxons with the Lombards at his gates. Many writers have not hesitated to ascribe the pertinacity with which he carried out this, his favourite enterprise, to the profound sagacity of an ecclesiastical politician, who foresaw that the loyal devotion of the new converts to the Holy See would repair the losses inflicted by the barbarians on the rest of Christendom. But it may safely be affirmed that no mere natural acuteness could possibly have predicted anything favourable from the dispositions which had hitherto been manifested by the Anglo-Saxons. Ancient writers are unanimous in classing them among the most savage of the northern tribes. They slaughtered their captives taken in war, and drove a lucrative trade by the sale of their countrymen, and even of their own children, to foreign merchants. The courage which formed their solitary virtue too often degenerated into a brutal ferocity, and their notions of a future state were exceedingly faint. In Gaul they were regarded with terror as barbarians of uncouth speech and aspect, and strange stories were told of their reckless deeds of bloodshed and cruelty. Gregory himself would probably have found it difficult to explain the hold they had gained on his heart ever since he first beheld the blue-eyed and golden-haired Angles in the market-place of Rome. But from that moment the thought of them never left him; and though frustrated in his purpose of himself becoming their apostle, he made it a labour of love to provide for their conversion by other hands.

His first plan had been a sort of anticipation of the system since so successfully carried out by the Roman Propaganda. He conceived the idea of redeeming a certain number of the Anglo-Saxon youths annually brought into the slave-markets of Gaul, educating them in some monastery school, and then sending them back as missionaries to their own country. We are not told why this scheme was abandoned, but in 596 the English mission was at last opened, and a band of Roman monks, headed by St. Augustine, the former prior of St. Gregory's monastery set out for the barbarous and unknown island. Never was any mission more amply cared for. St. Gregory had poured out his whole heart upon it; he multiplied letters to the bishops and Sovereigns of Gaul to secure his monks hospitality on the road; his letters cheered them on their way, and when the welcome tidings came that their work had begun under prosperous auspices, he sent them a reinforcement of labourers under the abbot Mellitus, bringing everything necessary for the celebration of the Divine offices—sacred vessels, vestments, church ornaments, holy relics, and "many books."

A catalogue of the library which St. Augustine and his companions brought with them into England is preserved at Trinity College, Cambridge. It consisted of a Bible in two volumes, a Psalter and a book of the Gospels, a Martyrology, the Apocryphal Lives of the Apostles, and the Exposition of certain Epistles and Gospels. The brief catalogue closes with these words: "These are the foundation or beginning of the library of the whole English Church, A.D. 601." These were the books sent to us by a Pope to be the beginning of our national library, and from them did St. Augustine and his companions begin to teach the English.

The manner of life to be adopted by the missionaries was plainly laid down by St. Gregory in his instructions to St. Augustine. "You, my brother," he writes, "who have been brought up under monastic rules, are not to live apart from your clergy in the English Church; you are to follow that course of life which our forefathers did in the time of the primitive church, when none of them said that anything he possessed was his own, but they had all things in common."[49] The ancient canonical life was to be the rule of the new clergy, and measures were at once taken for carrying this precept into effect. A monastery dedicated to SS. Peter and Paul was speedily founded at Canterbury. In after years it bore the title of St. Augustine's, and obtained rare privileges as the first-born of our religious houses, being designated "the Roman Chapel in England." The abbot took his place in general councils next to the abbot of Monte Cassino, and the monastery was recognised as under the immediate jurisdiction of the Holy See. Here, then, at one and the same time, began the apostolic and scholastic labours of the missionaries. It was not, indeed, until some years later, that the school of Canterbury attained its full celebrity under the abbot Adrian, but thirty years before his time it had become the model of other seminaries founded in different parts of England. When Sigebert, King of the East Angles, who had been baptized and instructed in France, wished to set up a school for youth to be instructed in literature, "after the good fashions he had seen in that country," he sent to Canterbury for his schoolmaster, and obtained one in the person of Felix the Burgundian, who became the apostle of the East of England. At this time the liberal sciences are said to have been cultivated at Canterbury, and some writers persuade themselves that the school of Bishop Felix was the germ of Cambridge University.

Northumbria was meanwhile receiving the light of faith from the monks of Iona, who, being invited into his kingdom by St. Oswald, in 635, despatched thither the holy bishop Aidan. He chose for the site of his cathedral monastery the island of Lindisfarne, which soon became the ecclesiastical capital of the north of England. This celebrated spot, which is an island only at high tide, and is connected with the mainland when the sea retires by a firm neck of sand, doubtless bears at the present day an aspect very different from that which it presented when the monks raised their first cathedral of oak-planks thatched with reed. The ruins of a far statelier pile may now be seen, built of dark-red sandstone, to which time has given a melancholy hue not out of character with the scene. But there are some features which time itself can never quite efface; the bold promontories of the coast visible to the north and south, the wide expanse of that tossing sea so often ploughed by the keels of the Vikings, and those ruddy golden sands, are unchanged since the days when the brethren of Lindisfarne raised their eyes, weary with the labours of the Scriptorium, to rest them on that beautiful line of wooded coast, or on the sparkling waves beyond it. Their manner of life differed in no degree from that of their brethren at Iona. "It was very different," says Bede, "from the slothfulness of our times, for all who bore company with Aidan, whether monks or laymen, were employed either in studying the Scriptures or in singing Psalms. This was his own daily employment wherever he went and if it happened that he was invited to eat with the king, he went with one or two clerks, and having taken a small repast, he made haste to be gone with them either to read or write." All the money that came into his hands he employed in relieving the poor or ransoming slaves, and many of the latter he made his disciples, instructing them and advancing them to the ecclesiastical state.

Whilst the north was being thus evangelised by the disciples of St. Columba, the south also had received a foundation of Hibernian origin. In the wilds of Wiltshire a school had arisen round the cell of Maidulf, an Irish recluse, who had been tempted to settle there by the sylvan beauty of the spot, which was then surrounded by thick luxuriant woods. To procure the means of support he received scholars from the neighbourhood who supplied his scanty wants and as his pupils increased his school became famous; and the name of its teacher is preserved in that of the modern town of Malmsbury. But it is remarkable how very soon both the Scottish and Irish foundations became *Romanised*.[50] One of the first scholars of Lindisfarne was St. Wilfrid, who, not satisfied with the ecclesiastical discipline of the Scottish monks, found his way to Canterbury, and there learnt the whole Psalter over again, according to the Roman version, which differed from that used in the Northern schools. He was joined by another North Country scholar, St. Bennet Biscop, and the two set out together on a pilgrimage to Rome.

The after history of these two saints was full of momentous results to the Anglo-Saxon schools. At Rome Wilfrid studied the Scriptures, the rules of ecclesiastical discipline, and the system of Paschal computation under the Archdeacon Boniface, secretary to Pope Martin I., and Scholasticus of the Lateran school. He returned to England to found the Abbey of Ripon, into which he introduced the Benedictine rule, and whither he invited Eddi, the chanter of Canterbury, to come and teach his monks the Roman chant. Then he set himself to reform the errors of the Northern churches, and thirty years after the foundation of Lindisfarne, the Scottish discipline was, by his vigorous exertions, exchanged for that of Rome. Biscop, meanwhile, was not less busy. After his first visit to the Holy City, he returned there a second time, and devoted himself not only to ecclesiastical studies, but also to the acquisition of many useful arts which he was resolved to plant in his native land. Next he went to Lerins, where he received the habit of a monk, and spent two years learning and practising the monastic rule; and then he returned a third time to Rome, at the very moment when the death of Deusdedit, sixth archbishop of Canterbury, had induced Pope Vitalian to nominate as his successor the Greek scholar, Theodore. He was a native of St. Paul's city of Tarsus, and well skilled in all human and divine literature. So says St. Bede, and so the Western bishops seem to have thought, when they delayed drawing up their synodal letter to the Third Council of Constantinople until "the philosopher Theodore" should be able to take part in their deliberations. Vitalian had the prosperity of the English mission scarcely less at heart than St. Gregory, and discerned the full importance of providing the infant Church with men who should be capable of laying a solid foundation of sacred learning in her schools. With this view he sent together with Theodore, the abbot Adrian, whom William of Malmsbury calls "a fountain of letters, and a river of arts." At the same time Benedict Biscop received orders to join the company of the new archbishop and to him was committed the direction of the monastery and school of Canterbury. But Benedict had one purpose fixed in his heart; it was to devote his life and extraordinary energies to the foundation of a great seat of learning and religion in his own land, and to fit himself thoroughly for the work before he began it. The weald of Kent might have richer pastures, the sky of Italy a softer glow, but the brown moors of Northumbria were ever present to his mind's eye, and it was there that he desired to spend and be spent for Christ. He was not long before he found out that Adrian's acquirements were far beyond his own; so resigning the abbacy into his hands, from a master he became a scholar, and spent two years more studying under him, and acting as interpreter to him and to the archbishop. Theodore had brought with him a large addition to the English library, and among his books were a copy of Homer (which, in Archbishop Parker's days, was still preserved at Canterbury), the works of Josephus, and the homilies of St. Chrysostom. Bede's account of the new life infused into the English schools by these two illustrious foreigners is doubtless familiar to all readers. Yet it is too much to the purpose to be omitted here. "Assisted by Adrian," he says, "the archbishop everywhere taught the right rule of life and the canonical custom of celebrating Easter. And forasmuch as both of them were well read in sacred and secular literature, they gathered a crowd of disciples, and there daily flowed from them rivers of knowledge to water the hearts of their hearers: and together with the books of Holy Writ, they also taught the arts of ecclesiastical poetry, astronomy, and arithmetic. So that there are still living to this day some of their scholars who are as well versed in the Greek and Latin tongues as in their own wherein they were born. Never were there happier times since the English came to Britain, for their kings being brave men and good Christians, were a terror to barbarous nations, and the minds of all men were bent upon the joys of the heavenly kingdom of which they had heard; and all who desired to be instructed in sacred literature had masters at hand to teach them."

Adrian had many good pupils, among whom was Albinus, who succeeded him in the government of his abbey, and greatly assisted Bede in collecting the materials of his history, and who was besides an excellent Greek scholar; and St. John of Beverley, whom Oxford historians fondly believe to have been the first master of liberal arts in their university. For, according to some authorities, the Oxford schools grew out of those founded at Cricklade, which place is said to have derived its original name of "Greeklade" from the good Greek which was there taught by Adrian's disciples. Another student drawn to Canterbury by the fame of its classical learning was St. Aldhelm, one of Maidulf's early pupils, who very soon resolved upon migrating from Malmsbury to the archiepiscopal seminary. Ill-health did not permit him to remain there long, but a letter from the young collegian is preserved, addressed to his own diocesan, Hedda, Bishop of Wessex, which gives very ample information as to the nature and extent of the studies on which he was engaged. Some suspicion of exaggeration may naturally attach to such general notices of the English learning as that given by Bede, but the more minute account of Aldhelm is open to no such objection. "I confess, most reverend father," he says, "that I had resolved, if circumstances had permitted, to have spent the approaching Christmas in the company of my relations, and to have enjoyed for some time the pleasure of your society. But as I find it impossible to do so for various reasons, I hope you will excuse my not waiting on you as I had intended. The truth is that there is a necessity for spending a great deal of time in this seat of learning, specially if one be inflamed with the love of study, and desirous, as I am, of becoming acquainted with all the secrets of the Roman jurisprudence. And I am engaged also on another study still more tedious and perplexing." Here he enters at some length on the subject of Latin versification, and describes the various classical metres, all of which were taught in Adrian's school; and in the intricacies of which the Anglo-Saxon scholars singularly delighted to exercise their ingenuity. He then continues in a tone of less satisfaction; "but what shall I say of arithmetic, the long and intricate calculations of which are sufficient to overwhelm the mind, and cast it into despair? For my own part all the labours of my former studies are trifling in comparison with this. So that I may say with St. Jerome on a like occasion, 'before I entered on that study I thought myself a master, but now I find I was but a learner.' However, by the blessing of God, and assiduous reading, I have at length overcome the chief difficulties, and have found out the method of calculating suppositions, which are called the parts of a number. I believe it will be better to say nothing of astronomy, the Zodiac and its twelve signs revolving in the heavens, which require a long illustration, rather than to disgrace that noble art by too short and imperfect an account, especially as there are some parts of it—as astrology and the perplexing calculation of horoscopes—which require a master's hand to do them justice."[51]

It must be borne in mind that at the time when Aldhelm wrote, every problem in arithmetic had to be worked by means of the seven Roman letters C. D. I. L. M. V. and X., and the decimal system was unknown. Very often the student was compelled to abandon their use and *write* the numbers he was employed on in words. And in default of more convenient numerals, recourse was had to what might be called a duodecimal system, by which every number was divided into twelve parts, the different combinations of which were named and computed according to the divisions of the Roman money. And lastly, there was the system of "indigitation," wherein the ten fingers were made to serve the purpose of a modern arithmeticon.

St. Aldhelm elsewhere enumerates the studies pursued in the school of Canterbury as consisting of grammar, that is the Latin and Greek tongues, geometry, arithmetic, music, mechanics, astronomy, and astrology: he himself is also said to have studied the Hebrew Scriptures in their original text, and his works both in prose and poetry bear witness to his familiarity with the chief Latin poets, such as Virgil, Juvenal, Lucan, and Persius, whom he frequently quotes. He was the first Englishman who appeared before the world in the character of an author; his chief poems being a Treatise on the Eight Virtues, and one in praise of Virginity. His Latin versification is of the most artificial structure; in one of his poetical prefaces the initial letters of each line read downwards, the terminal letters read upwards, and the last line read backwards, all repeat the words of the first line read straightforwards; and this he pleasantly denominates "a square poem." I will give but one couplet as a sample of the kind of brain-puzzles which afforded such solace to the Anglo-Saxon students. The reader will observe that the lines may be read equally well backwards or forwards, still forming the same succession of letters:—

Roma tibi subito motibus ibit amor

Sole medere pede, ede, perede melos.

All the writings of Aldhelm exhibit instances of the same misplaced ingenuity, as well as that love of enigma which was general among his countrymen. In spite of these faults, however, and of a certain pompous and pedantic style which treats very ordinary subjects in very big words, and is an anticipation by eleven centuries of the Johnsonian dialect, it is impossible to deny that our first English author was a man of genius and erudition. In his poems, which are redundant with imagery, he gathers his similitudes now from the household arts of the smith and the weaver, now from the natural beauties of hill and field. You see that you are reading the thoughts of one who does not owe everything to books, but who has observed and reasoned for himself. Thus, desiring to show that perfection does not consist in chastity alone, but in a combination of all the virtues in their proper order, he compares it to "a web, not of one uniform colour and texture, but woven with purple threads and many colours into a variety of figures by the shuttles flying from side to side." Describing a well-stored memory, he compares it to the work of the sagacious bees, "who, when the dewy dawn appears and the beams of the limpid sun arise, pour the thick armies of their dancing swarms over the open fields; and, now lying in the honied leaves of the marigold or the purple tops of the heather, suck the nectar drop by drop, and carry home their plunder on burdened thighs." A copy of his treatise on Virginity is preserved in the Lambeth library, in which a highly finished illumination represents him seated in his chair surrounded by a group of nuns. The book was in fact written for the use of the Abbess Hildelitha and her religious daughters of Wimbourne; for the Anglo-Saxon nuns very early vied with the monks in their application to letters.

On leaving Canterbury Aldhelm returned to Malmsbury and soon raised the reputation of the school. Pupils flocked to him even from France and Scotland, for, says William of Malmsbury, "some admired the sanctity of the man, and others the depth of his learning. He was as simple in piety as he was multifarious in knowledge, having imbibed the seven liberal arts so perfectly that he was wonderful in each, and unrivalled in all." One of his pupils was Ethilwald, afterwards Bishop of Lindisfarne, to whom, as to his "most beloved son and disciple," he addressed a letter, preserved among his other works. After warning him against the vain pleasures of the world, "such as the custom of daily junketings, indulgence in immoderate feasting, and continued riding and racing," he admonishes him to be on his guard against the love of money and silly parade, and exhorts him rather to apply himself to the study of the Scriptures; and inasmuch as the meaning of almost every part of them depends on the rules of grammar, to perfect himself in that art, that so he may dive into the signification of the text. Ethilwald was a devoted admirer of the saint, and left some verses in praise of his illustrious master whom he is too good a scholar to call by his barbarous Saxon name, preferring to translate it into the more classic appellation of *Cassis prisca*, or *old helmet*. Another of Aldhelm's pupils and correspondents was Eadfrid, who, after the fashion of the times, passed over into the sister isle to profit by the learning of the Irish schools. He remained there six years, and was heartily congratulated by Aldhelm on his return from what he calls the "land of fog." "Nowadays," says the scholar of Malmsbury, "the renown of the Irish is so great that one daily sees them going or returning; and crowds flock to their island to gather up the liberal arts and physical sciences. But if the sky of Ireland has its stars, has not that of England its sun in Theodore the philosopher, and its mild moon in Adrian, gifted with an inexpressible urbanity?"

In 675 Malmsbury became an abbey, and Aldhelm was chosen its first abbot. When the diocese of Wessex was divided into two parts he was named Bishop of Sherburne, whence the episcopal see was afterwards removed to Salisbury. A well-known anecdote represents him to us instructing the rude peasantry of Malmsbury who would not stay to listen to the Sunday sermon, by singing his verses to them, harp in hand, after the fashion of a wandering gleeman. We read also of the pains he took in forming a library in his abbey, and how, being on a visit to Bretwald, Archbishop of Canterbury (an old companion and former schoolfellow), he heard of the arrival at Dover of a foreign ship, and at once hastened down to the coast to see if there were any *books* among its cargo. As he was walking on the seashore intently examining the merchandise that was unlading, he espied a heap of books, and among them a volume containing the entire Bible. This was a treasure indeed, and a very rare one, for the books of Scripture were generally written out separately, and had to be procured and copied one by one. He determined at once to secure the Bible for his library, and turning over the pages with a knowing air, began to bargain with the owners and to beat them down somewhat in the price. The sailors grumbled at this, and said he might undervalue his own goods if he liked, but not those of others. At last they turned him away with very abusive language, and, refusing all his offers, pulled off with the Bible to their ship. But a terrible tempest arose, which made them repent of their churlish conduct, and returning to the shore they entreated the good bishop to pardon their rudeness and accept the book as a gift, for it seems they considered that they had only been saved from shipwreck by his prayers. Aldhelm, however, laid down the half of their original demand, and returned with his prize to his convent, where the book was still preserved in the time of William of Malmsbury.

We must now return to St. Bennet Biscop, who, after completing his studies at Canterbury, was planning a fourth expedition to Rome, chiefly for the purpose of collecting books. His bibliographical tour was crowned with complete success. He travelled along purchasing, and also begging books in all directions, which when procured were deposited in the keeping of trusty friends, from whom he gathered them up again on his homeward journey. He returned to England laden with his treasures, and obtained a grant of land from Egfrid, king of Northumbria, for the erection of his long-contemplated monastery. It was dedicated to St. Peter, and situated at the mouth of the Wear—a spot, says William of Malmsbury, "which once glittered with a multitude of towns built by the Romans," and which in our own days also is a busy scene of trade. Though the Roman towns had disappeared in Biscop's time, his monastery was far from standing in the midst of a solitude. In fact, he sought, not shunned, the haunts of men, for his main object was their instruction. He had no intention of being merely "the man wise for himself;" his books and his learning had been acquired to profit other souls besides his own. So he did not choose a lonesome wilderness, or a marsh, or a desert island, but a spot conveniently situated within reach of what, even in the seventh century, was a tolerably busy port. "The broad and ample river running into the sea," says the old historian already quoted, "received vessels borne by gentle gales on the calm bosom of its haven;" and the parish of Monk-Wearmouth in the now smoky town of Sunderland marks the ground occupied by St. Bennet's first foundation.

It was commenced in the year 674, the monastery being at first only built of wood, but the church was planned on a more magnificent scale. Bennet, who thought nothing of a long journey in pursuit of his cherished designs, crossed over to France to seek out good masons, and brought them back with him to Wearmouth, where they built him a very handsome church of hewn stone. The fame of this noble structure spread far and wide, and Naitan, king of the Picts, sent ambassadors imploring that the French masons might be sent to build an exactly similar church in his dominions. As soon as the walls of his church were up, Bennet sent over once more to France for glass-makers, who glazed all the windows both of the church and monastery. Bede tells us that these were the first artificers in glass who had been seen in England. "It is an art," he says, "not to be despised, because of its use in furnishing lamps for the cloisters and other kinds of vessels." The church being now finished and furnished, the books were stored up in the library, and four years were spent by the abbot in collecting the spiritual stones of his edifice. The result of his labours was so satisfactory that King Egfrid desired to see another monastery of similar character founded in his kingdom, and in 682 the saint obtained a second grant of land at Jarrow-on-the-Tyne, about five miles from Wearmouth. "The spot has no claim to beauty," says a modern writer, "yet it is calculated to produce an impression of solemn quiet. The church and crumbling walls of the old monastery standing on a green hill sloping to the bay, the long silvery expanse of water, the gentle ripple of the advancing tide, the sea-birds perpetually hovering on the wing or dipping in the wave, and the distant view of Shields harbour with its clouds of smoke and forests of masts, form no ordinary combination."[52] And we may add that no ordinary feelings stir in the heart of the visitor who sees in those grey crumbling walls, with their vestiges of Norman and Saxon ornament, the remains of that monastic seminary which nurtured the genius and the sanctity of the Venerable Bede. Here arose the monastery of St. Paul's; and if you look in the eastern wall of the church you may still see the inscription, of unquestioned antiquity, which preserves the memory of its dedication. It is cut on a small tablet in good Roman letters, and tells you that the church was dedicated on the eighth of the kalends of May, in the fifteenth year of Egfrid the king, and during the abbacy of Ceolfrid.

This Ceolfrid deserves a few words to himself. He was originally a monk of Ripon, where he became master of the school and the novices. His pupils, who were mostly high-born youths, showed some disdain for those menial employments that formed part of a monk's daily life, and which they associated with the idea of servitude; but Ceolfrid, himself an earl's son, overcame their repugnance by his own example. He undertook the care of the bakehouse, and might daily be seen cleaning the oven, bolting the meal, and baking the bread for the use of the brethren. From labours such as these he passed to the school, and there made his scholars understand that a man may make a very good baker without losing his taste for the liberal arts. Ceolfrid's fame at last reached the ears of St. Bennet, who, it must be owned, was covetous of learned monks and good books. So he begged him of the abbot of Ripon, and, having obtained him, placed the new monastery of Jarrow under his government. The two houses, however, continued to be so closely united as to form but one community; they were like one monastery, says Bede, built in two places. Ceolfrid held the abbacy of St. Paul's for seven years, during which time the dreadful pestilence of 686 broke out, which swept away all the choir monks, with the exception of the abbot himself and one little boy, with whose aid he still contrived to chant the canonical hours, though their voices were often enough choked with their tears. This little boy could be no other than St. Bede himself, who had accompanied the monks from Wearmouth to Jarrow, and was then seven years of age.

St. Bennet's journeys were not yet over. As soon as the foundation of Jarrow was completed he set out on a fifth expedition to Rome accompanied by Ceolfrid, and this time brought back, not only books and relics, but also pictures. These last he placed in his two churches: at the west end of the Church of St. Peter he placed pictures of our Lady and the twelve Apostles; on the south wall were scenes from the Gospels, and on the north the visions of the Apocalypse. The pictures placed in St. Paul's were intended to show the connection between the Old and New Testaments. There you saw representations of Isaac bearing the wood of the sacrifice, and of our Lord bearing His Cross: of the brazen serpent, and the Crucifixion. "Those, therefore, who knew not how to read," says Bede, "entering these churches, found on all sides agreeable and instructive objects, representing Christ and His saints, and recalling to their memory the grace of His Incarnation and the terrors of the last judgment." But Bennet had brought from Rome something even more precious than his pictures. It was not to be supposed that in his solicitude to provide his monks with the best instruction that books or teachers could afford he should overlook the necessity of providing them with masters of the ecclesiastical chant. The Roman chant had already been introduced into Northumbria by James the Deacon, the fellow-labourer of St. Paulinus, who, says Bede, was extraordinarily skilful in singing, and taught the same to many, after the custom of the Romans. But he was now an old man, and does not seem to have formed any disciples qualified to succeed him in his office. Benedict therefore entreated Pope Agatho to allow him to take back into England no less a personage than John the Venerable, abbot of St. Martin's, and arch-chanter of St. Peter's, that he might teach in his monastery the method of singing throughout the year as it was practised in St. Peter's Church. It argues much the importance which was attached at Rome to Benedict's foundations, that his petition was granted. Abbot John received orders to set out for the barbarous north, and, taking up his residence at Wearmouth, he taught the chanters of that monastery the whole order and manner of singing and reading aloud, and committed to writing all that was requisite throughout the whole course of the year for the celebration of festivals; "all which rules," adds St. Bede, "are still observed there, and have been copied by many other monasteries. And the said John not only taught the brethren of that monastery, but such as had skill in singing resorted from almost all the monasteries of the same province to hear him, and many invited him to teach in other places."[53]

Such, then, was the provision made by St. Bennet for the instruction of his monks and the establishment among them of a school of sacred learning. And his enterprise was a grand success. His twin houses became centres of human and divine science, as well as of regular discipline. The life led within their walls has been made familiar to us by the pen of Bede, who, with that simplicity which forms the charm of his writing, describes it in all its homely features. The men who were engaged in rearing, on the barbarous shores of England, a seminary of learning which had not its equal north of the Alps, might every day be seen taking part in the duties of the farmyard and the kitchen. Abbot Easterwine, a former courtier of King Egfrid's, who was chosen to fill the place of abbot during the absence of St. Bennet, delighted in winnowing the corn, giving milk to the young calves, working at the mill or forge, and helping in the bakehouse. It is thus that Bede describes him; but he dwells also on the spiritual beauty of the abbot's "transparent countenance," his musical voice and gentle temper, and tells us how, being seized with his last illness, "coming out into the open air, and sitting down, he called for his weeping brethren, and, after the manner of his tender nature, gave them all the kiss of peace, and died at night as they were singing lauds."

As St. Bennet was still absent, the monks chose in his room the deacon Sigfrid, who continued to share the government with Bennet after his return. Both of them were afflicted with grievous infirmity during the three last years of their lives, St. Bennet being almost entirely paralysed, while Sigfrid was wasted with a slow consumption. The last hours of the saint were in harmony with his life. His monks read the Scriptures aloud to him during his sleepless nights, and he often charged them to remember the two things that he most earnestly recommended to his children, the preservation of regular discipline, and the care of his books. When unable to leave his bed, and too weak to recite the Divine Office, he caused some of the brethren to recite it in his chamber, divided into two choirs, and joined with them as well as he could. The two venerable abbots, who were both hourly expecting death, had a great wish to meet once more in this life, and to satisfy their desire, the monks carried Sigfrid on a litter to St. Bennet's cell, and laid them side by side, their heads resting on the same pillow, that they might give each other a farewell kiss; but so extreme was their weakness, that even this they were not able to do without assistance. After their departure Ceolfrid continued to govern both houses for twenty-eight years, during which time he did much to advance the studies of the brethren, and sent several of them to Rome to complete their education. He increased the library, and caused three copies of the entire Bible to be written out, one of which he sent as a present to the Pope, whilst the other two were placed in the two churches, "to the end that all who wished to read any passage in either Testament might at once find what they wanted." Naitan, king of the Picts, applied to him for church ornaments, as he had applied to St. Bennet for masons. The abbot's reply may be quoted as giving some notion of his scholarship. "A certain worldly ruler," he wrote, "most truly said that the world would be happy if either philosophers were kings, or kings philosophers. Now if a worldly man could judge thus truly of the philosophy of this world, how much more were it to be desired that the more powerful men are in this world the more they would labour to be acquainted with the commandments of God." In this passage the Anglo-Saxon monk is quoting from the Republic of Plato.

St. Bede, who has preserved these records of the Fathers of Wearmouth and Jarrow, dwells with delight on the memory of the many happy years he himself passed within those walls, and on the thought that none of them had been spent in idleness. "All my life," he says, "I have spent in this monastery, giving my whole attention to the study of the Holy Scriptures; and in the intervals between the hours of regular discipline, and the duties of church psalmody, I ever took delight in either learning, teaching, or writing." It was his love of study that made him decline the office of abbot, "for that office demands thoughtfulness, and thoughtfulness brings distraction of mind, which is an impediment to learning." Though invited to Rome by Pope Sergius, it appears certain that he never left his own country, and that all he knew was derived from native teachers, principally, as he tells us, from the abbots Bennet and Ceolfrid. The science of music, indeed, in which he excelled, and on which he wrote several treatises, he had studied under John of St. Martin's; Trumhere, a monk of Lestingham, was his master in divinity, and his Greek scholarship was probably acquired from Archbishop

Theodore himself. But the varied character of Bede's erudition must be principally explained by his free use of Biscop's noble libraries. It was at the command of his abbot, and of St. John of Beverley, who ordained him priest, that he began, at thirty years of age, to write for the instruction of his countrymen. For his greater convenience a little building was erected apart from the monastery, which Simeon of Durham speaks of as yet standing in the twelfth century, "where, free from all distraction, he could sit, meditate, read, write, or dictate." The original building must have been swept away at the time of the destruction of the monastery by the Danes in 794, yet Leland describes what he calls St. Bede's oratory, as remaining, even in his time.

His studies, however, were not suffered to interfere with his other duties, for he was most exact in the minute observance of his rule, and specially in the discharge of the choral office, though, as he owns in a letter to Bishop Acca, these necessary demands on his time, the *monasticæ servitutis retinacula*, as he calls them, proved no small hindrance to his work. Yet he never sought exemption of any kind, and least of all from attendance in choir. "If the angels did not find me there among my brethren," he would say, "would they not say, Where is Bede? why comes he not to worship at the appointed time with the others?"[54] It was thus he found the secret of keeping alive the spirit of fervour in the midst of continued labour of the head. Printed among his theological and philosophical works, is a little manual, drawn up, as it would seem, for his own private use, and consisting of a selection of favourite verses from the Psalms. His disciple, Cuthbert, says of him. "I can declare with truth, that never saw I with my eyes, or heard I with my ears, of any man so indefatigable in giving thanks to God." Besides the requirements of his monastic rule, and his own private studies, Bede had other duties which engaged a large portion of his time. He was both mass priest and scholasticus. In the first capacity, he had to administer the sacraments, visit the sick, and preach on Sundays and festivals; in the second, to communicate to others the learning he had himself acquired. Even before his ordination, the direction of the monastic school was placed in his hands, and here he taught sacred and humane letters to the 600 monks of Jarrow, as well as to the pupils who flocked to him from all parts of England. The character of his teaching is beautifully noticed in the breviary lessons for his feast. "He was easily kindled and moved to compunction by study, and whether reading or teaching, often wept abundantly. And after study he always applied himself to prayer, well knowing that the knowledge of the Sacred Scriptures is to be gained rather by the grace of God than by our own efforts. He had many scholars, all of whom he inspired with extraordinary love of learning; and what is more, he infused into them the holy virtue of religion; he was most affable to the good, but terrible to the proud and negligent; sweet in countenance, with a musical voice, and an aspect at once cheerful and grave."

The writings of Bede bear witness to the extent of his learning. He himself gives a list of forty-five works of which he was the author, including, besides his homilies and commentaries on Holy Scripture, treatises on grammar, astronomy, the logic of Aristotle, music, geography, arithmetic, orthography, versification, the computum, and natural philosophy. His Ecclesiastical History and Lives of the Fathers must always be admired as models of unaffected simplicity of style. He was well skilled in the Latin, Greek, and Hebrew tongues.[55] His Greek erudition is proved by the fact of his having translated the life of St. Athanasius out of Greek into Latin, and also by the Retractations, which, with characteristic candour, he published in his old age, to correct some errors into which he had fallen in his earlier commentaries on the Acts of the Apostles, and which he became aware of after meeting with a Greek manuscript of that portion of the Scriptures which varied from the Latin text. His treatises on grammar and versification betray an acquaintance with Latin literature which shows us that St. Bennet's libraries must have been well stored with classics.[56] In his scientific views, he of course followed the generally received theories of the time in which he lived; though in some points he corrected the errors of former writers by the result of his own observations. "Bede's works," observes Mr. Turner, "are evidence that the establishment of the Teutonic nations on the ruins of the Roman Empire did not *barbarise* knowledge. He collected and taught more natural truths than any Roman writer had yet accomplished; and his works display an advance, not a retrogression, in science." Thus, he taught that the stars derived their light from the sun; that the true shape of the earth was globular,[57] to which he attributes the irregularity of our days and nights. He explains the ebb and flow of the tide, by the attractive power of the moon, and points out the error of supposing that all the waters of the ocean rise at the same moment, instancing observations which he has taken himself on different parts of the English coast in support of his statement. He shows that the sun is eclipsed by the intervention of the moon, and the moon by that of the earth. He also gives simple and intelligent explanations of various natural phenomena, such as the rainbow, and the formation of rain and hail. He had the good sense to condemn judicial astrology as equally false and pernicious, and applied his scientific knowledge to useful purposes, constructing tables to serve the place of a modern ephemeris.

By far the greater part of his writings, however, consist of commentaries on the Holy Scriptures, in which his design is less to indulge in original speculation, than to resume the teaching of the Fathers. After the fashion of the early writers, he reproduces their metaphysical arguments, and even their words and imagery, his love of science occasionally appearing in his selections. Thus, in speaking of the Holy Trinity, he embodies in his text the beautiful illustration repeated before him by St. John Chrysostom, and other early Fathers, wherein the Three Divine Persons in one essence are compared to the form, the light, and the heat of the sun. The globular body of the sun, he says, never leaves the heavens, but its light (which he compares to the person of the Son), and its heat (to that of the Holy Ghost) descend to earth and diffuse themselves everywhere, animating the mind and kindling the heart. Yet though universally present, light never really quits the sun, for we behold it there; and heat, too, is never separated from it; and the whole is one sun, comprised within a circle, which has no end and no beginning. He shows the same analogies in other forms of nature, as in water, wherein we see the fountain, the flowing river, and the lake—all different in form, yet one in substance, and inseparable one from the other. In his treatise, *De Natura Rerum*, he not only exhibits vast erudition but often expresses himself with a certain unadorned eloquence. "Observe," he says, "how all things are made to suit and to govern one another. See how heaven and earth are respectively adorned; heaven, by the sun, moon, and stars, and earth by its beautiful flowers, its herbs, trees, and fruits. From these men derive their food, their shining jewels, the various pictures so pleasantly woven in their hangings, their variegated colours, the sweet melody of strings and organs, the splendour of gold and silver, and the pleasant streams of water which bring us ships and set in motion our mills, together with the fragrant aroma of myrrh, and the sweet form of the human countenance." Bede's love of music reveals itself in a thousand passages. "Among all the sciences," he says, "this one is most commendable, pleasing, mirthful, and lovely. It makes a man liberal, cheerful, courteous, and amiable. It rouses him to battle, enables him to bear fatigue, comforts him under labour, refreshes the disturbed mind, takes away headaches, and soothes the desponding heart."

There is one subject which engaged his attention that deserves a more particular notice, I mean the labours he directed to the grammatical formation of his native language, a work of vast importance, which, in every country where the barbarous races had established themselves, had to be undertaken by the monastic scholars. Rohrbacher observes that St. Bede did much by his treatises on grammar and orthography, to impress a character of regularity on the modern languages which, in the eighth and ninth centuries, were beginning to be formed out of the Latin and Germanic dialects. Much more was his influence felt on the Anglo-Saxon dialect, in which he both preached and wrote. A curious poetical fragment of the twelfth century, discovered some years since in Worcester Cathedral, names him among other saints "who taught our people in English," and praises him in particular, for having "wisely translated" for the instruction of his flock. This is not mere tradition. Besides commenting on nearly the whole Bible, Bede is known to have translated into English both the Psalter and the four Gospels. But this involved a labour the character and amount of which is not easily appreciated, unless we bear in mind what the state of the vernacular tongue was at that time. Before their conversion to Christianity the Anglo-

Saxons possessed no literature, that is to say, no *written* compositions of any kind, and their language had not therefore assumed a regular grammatical form. In this they resembled most of the other barbarous nations, of whom St. Irenæus observes,[58] that they held the faith by tradition, "without the help of pen and ink;" meaning, as he himself explains, that for want of letters they could have no use of the Scriptures. The Anglo-Saxons were indeed acquainted with the Runic letters; but there is every reason to believe that these were exclusively used for monumental inscriptions or magic spells. The Runic letters were indeed so closely associated in the mind of the people with magical practices that the Christian missionaries found it necessary to avoid their use,[59] and introduced the letters commonly called Anglo-Saxon, which are, however, nothing more than corruptions of the Roman alphabet. Although the Saxons had no written literature, they had, however, a body of native poetry consisting of songs and fragmentary narratives which, like the poems of Homer or Ossian, were preserved solely in the memory of the bards, who occasionally made additions or enlargements of the story, as their genius prompted. Together with the change of religion appeared a change in the character of the popular minstrelsy. Tales from the Scriptures took the place of legends of pagan heroes, and the Christian missionaries made use of these for the purpose of instilling into their rude hearers some knowledge of the mysteries of faith.

But the Saxon poetry, even in its Christianised form, does not appear to have been *written down* until the time of Alfred. Before any steps could be taken to form a literature, the language itself had to be laboriously reduced to grammatical rules. The Anglo-Saxon language, as it exists in the literature of a later period, is of extremely complex construction, far richer in grammatical inflexion than our modern English. But in its barbarous state, as we read it in the early fragments of the bardic poems, it was a barren combination of verbs, nouns, and pronouns, and nouns freely used in an adjective and verbal sense, and entirely destitute of all the smaller particles. The change it underwent during the two centuries that preceded the time of Alfred was the transformation of a barbarous dialect into a finished grammatical language, and this change was mainly effected by the labours of the monks. Nor is it mere matter of conjecture that Bede had a considerable share in this great work. He was probably the first who applied himself to it, and has himself let us know the reasons which induced him to undertake the translation of certain familiar forms of prayer into the native dialect. In 734, Archbishop Egbert, who then presided over the school of York, having invited him thither, Bede accepted the invitation, as he says, "for the sake of reading," the York library offering temptations not to be resisted. He stayed there some months, teaching in the archbishop's school; and would have repeated his visit in the following year had not his declining health rendered this impossible. To excuse the failure of his promise, he addressed a long and interesting letter to Egbert, in which, among other things, he suggests the appointment of priests to the rural districts, who should be diligent in instructing the peasantry, and who should teach them the Creed and the Our Father in their own tongue, "which," he adds, "I have myself translated into English for the benefit of those priests who are not familiar with the vernacular."[60] But the translation of these prayers was a very small part of his labours; he had, as we have already said, made an Anglo-Saxon version of the Psalter and the Gospels, and on this latter work he was engaged up to the day of his death. This we learn from the beautiful letter written by his pupil Cuthbert to a fellow reader and schoolfellow Cuthwin, which, often as it has been quoted, we cannot here omit. After speaking of the way in which his beloved master had spent the whole of his life, cheerful and joyful, and giving thanks to God day and night; and how he daily read lessons to his disciples even to within a fortnight of his death, he relates how the saint admonished them to prepare for death, "and being learned in our poetry," quoted some things in the English tongue; how, according to his custom, he often sung antiphons, specially that belonging to the season of the Ascension which then drew nigh, beginning "O Rex gloriæ." "And when he came to those words 'leave us not orphans,' he burst into tears and wept much, and we also wept with him. By turns we read, and by turns we wept; nay, we wept continually while we read." ... During this time he laboured to compose two works well worthy to be remembered, besides the lessons that we had of him, and the singing of the Psalms; namely, he translated the Gospel of St. John, as far as the words "But what are these among so many?" into our own tongue for the benefit of the Church, and some collections out of St. Isidore's works; for he said, I will not have my scholars read falsehoods after my death, or labour in that book without profit.... When the Tuesday before the Ascension of our Lord came, he passed all that day dictating cheerfully, for, he said, I know not how long I shall last, or what time my Maker will take me. And yet to us he seemed to know very well the time of his departure. And so he spent the night; and when the morning appeared, that is, Wednesday, he ordered us to write with all speed what he had begun, and this done, we walked till the third hour with the relics of saints, according to the custom of that day. There was one of us with him who said to him, "Dear Master, there is still one chapter wanting, will it fatigue you to be asked any more questions?" He answered, "It is no trouble. Take your pen and mend it, and write quickly." He then took farewell of them all, and so continued cheerfully to speak till about sunset, when the youth before mentioned said again, "Beloved master, there is still one sentence unwritten." "Then write it quickly," he replied. In a few moments the youth said, "Now it is finished." "You have spoken true," said the dying saint. "It is finished. Now, therefore, take my head into your hands, for it is a great delight to sit opposite to that holy place where I have been wont to pray, and there let me sit once more, and call upon my Father." So sitting thus on the floor of his cell, and repeating the ejaculation "Glory be to the Father, and to the Son, and to the Holy Ghost," he breathed his last, on May 26, 735.

The school of York was rising into celebrity just as Bede was withdrawn from the scene of his useful labours. Egbert, who may be considered as its founder, was himself a pupil of Bishop Eata's, but had completed his studies in Rome. He was brother to the reigning King of Northumbria, and succeeded to the see of York at a time when the affairs of the diocese had fallen into some disorder. One of his great works was the collection of a body of canons, and the publication of his famous Penitential, which furnished the Anglo-Saxon Church with fixed laws of discipline, gathered from the early fathers and canonists. While thus engaged, however, the archbishop applied himself with no less fervour to the encouragement of learning. He committed the mastership of the school he founded to his relation Albert, but himself continued to overlook the studies, and charged himself with the explanation of the Scriptures of the New Testament, leaving to Albert the other departments of literature. Under their united care the fame of the York seminary soon extended beyond the shores of Britain, and it is said to have embraced a larger course of instruction than was to be found at the same period in any school either of Gaul or Spain. Alcuin, a pupil of the academy over which he afterwards presided, enumerates among the studies there pursued, the seven liberal arts, as well as chronology, natural history, jurisprudence, and mathematics. Attached to the school was a library, which, under the munificent care of Egbert, became rich in all the works both of Christian and heathen antiquity. Alcuin, who filled the office of librarian, has given a list of its contents; he enumerates the works of SS. Jerome, Hilary, Ambrose, Augustine, Athanasius, Gregory the Great, Leo, Basil, Fulgentius and Chrysostom; of Orosius, Boethius, Pliny, Aristotle, and Cicero; of the poets Virgil and Lucan, of Prosper, Lactantius, and many others, together with the writings of Bede and Aldhelm, the two English writers who had already acquired a literary fame. These books were chiefly collected by Albert, whose custom it was to pass over to the Continent on book-hunting expeditions, in which he was generally accompanied by Alcuin.

The librarian of York afterwards composed a poem on the subject of the saints and archbishops of that city, in which he celebrates the virtues of the two illustrious prelates under whom he studied, and the treasures of science stored up by their praiseworthy care. Egbert, as he tells us, presided personally over the studies of the younger clergy, for this was then reckoned one of the chief duties of a bishop. As soon as he was at leisure in the morning he sent for some of his young clerks, and, sitting on his couch, taught them in succession till about noon, when he said mass in his private chapel. After a frugal dinner he had them with him again, and entertained himself by hearing them discuss literary questions in his presence. Towards evening he recited Compline with them, and then, calling them to him one by one, gave his blessing to each as they knelt at his feet.

In the collection of canons already mentioned Egbert provided for the religious instruction of the poor as well as the rich. The teaching of the common people is one of the duties specially enjoined on the clergy, every priest being required to "instil with great exactness into the people committed to his charge the Creed and the Lord's Prayer, as well as the whole doctrine and practice of Christianity." In the absence of books this was done orally, much use being made of instructions cast into a metrical form, and so committed to memory. Thus the multitude, if ignorant of letters, were certainly not uninstructed, as we see in the case of St. Cædmon whom Bede calls *illiteratus*, that is, unable to read; but who was nevertheless perfectly familiar with sacred history, which he had learnt by oral instruction, and was thus able to sing of the creation, the Deluge, the journeys of the Israelites, and the last judgment.

Albert, the master of the school, and the successor of Egbert in the see of York, is described by Alcuin in one of his poems as "a pattern of goodness, justice, and piety, teaching the Catholic faith in the spirit of love, stern to the stubborn, but pitiful and gentle to the good." If he marked any youths among his pupils who showed peculiar signs of promise, like a good master, he made them his friends. "He observed the natural dispositions of each with wonderful skill, and, drawing them to him, taught and lovingly cherished them. Some he dexterously imbued with the grammatical art, whilst into the minds of others he instilled the sweetness of rhetoric. These he endeavoured to polish with the juridical grindstone, those he taught to cultivate the songs of the muses, and to tread the hill of Parnassus with lyric steps. To others, again, he made known the harmony of the heavens, the motions of the sun and moon, the five zones, the seven wandering stars; the laws of the heavenly bodies, their rising and setting; the aerial movements of the sea, and the quaking of the earth; the nature of man, cattle, birds, and wild beasts; the diversities of numbers and varieties of figures." He taught also how to calculate the return of the Paschal solemnity, and above all expounded the mysteries of the Sacred Scriptures. He often travelled into Gaul and Italy in quest of books and new methods of instruction. The noblest families of Northumbria placed their sons under his care, not only those who were training for the ecclesiastical state, but those intended for the world. Indeed it is certain that the pupils of the episcopal and monastic schools were by no means exclusively ecclesiastics. Eddi tells us that St. Wilfrid received many youths to educate, who on reaching man's estate, if they chose to embrace a secular life, were presented *in armour* to the king. Alfred, the son of king Egfrid of Northumbria, was himself a pupil of St. Wilfrid, and spent some years in Ireland that he might pursue his studies with greater advantage. He became a great patron of learning, and corresponded with St. Aldhelm on philosophical subjects and the difficulties of Latin prosody; and it was to his son Ceolwulf that St. Bede addressed the dedication of his Ecclesiastical History.

On the death of Egbert in 766 the unanimous voice of the people called Albert to the vacant see. He showed himself worthy of their choice, "feeding his flock with the food of the Divine Word, and guarding the lambs of Christ from the wolf." He governed the Church of York for thirteen years, during which time he never abandoned his care of the school. The mastership, however, devolved on Alcuin, and such was the fame of his scholarship as to draw students not only from all parts of England and Ireland, but also from France and Germany. Among the latter was St. Luidger, a native of Friesland, afterwards known as the Apostle of Saxony, of whom we shall have more to say in the following chapter.

The extent and character of Alcuin's learning will be more properly studied when we come to speak of his labours at the court of Charlemagne; it will be sufficient here to notice the fact that he was a scholar of exclusively English growth, and drew all the materials with which he worked in his after career from the library and the schools of York. In his writings he often alludes to the want he feels of "those invaluable books of scholastic erudition" which were there placed at his command, through the affectionate industry of his master, Albert, who continued, after his elevation to the episcopate, to add to the treasures already collected. Two years before his death Albert resolved on resigning his pastoral charge that he might spend his last days as a simple monk, and devote himself exclusively to the affairs of his salvation. Calling to him, therefore, his two favourite pupils, Eanbald and Alcuin, he committed to the first the care of his diocese, and to the other that of his books, "the dearest of all his treasures."[61] Alcuin was despatched to Rome to obtain the sanction of the Holy See for the appointment of Eanbald and it was at Parma on his homeward journey that the solicitations of Charlemagne won his promise to settle at the court of that monarch, and transfer to a foreign soil the learning he had acquired on the shores of Saxon England.

With the death of Albert the prosperity of the Early English schools may be said to have closed. Five years later the Danish keels appeared for the first time off the Northumbrian coast: it seemed only a passing alarm, but in 793 another armament effected a landing at Lindisfarne, and after slaughtering the monks, gave to the flames the most venerable of the English sanctuaries. This was but the beginning of sorrows. The following year the twin monasteries of Wearmouth and Jarrow shared a similar fate, and all the treasures of art and literature collected by St. Biscop were ruthlessly destroyed. For seventy years these scenes of carnage and plunder went on without interruption in every part of England, and the riches laid up in the churches everywhere pointed them out as the first objects of attack. The finishing-blow came in 867, when "a great heathen army," as they are called by the Saxon chronicler, having wintered in East Anglia, and there supplied themselves with horses, marched northwards and made themselves masters of the city of York. Thence they overran the kingdom of Northumbria, carrying fire and sword wherever they appeared, till the whole country between the Ouse and the Tyne presented only the smoking ruins of what had once been cities and abbeys. Beverley, Ripon, Whitby, and Lastingham, all seats of learning and civilisation, were swept away, and in 875 the sea-king Halden crossed the Tyne and destroyed the last remains of the monastic institute in Northumbria. After burning Jarrow for the second time, he directed his course to Lindisfarne, where the episcopal see was still fixed, and where a new monastery had sprung up on the ruins of that formerly destroyed by the Danes. Eardulf was then bishop, and on learning the approach of the pagans he determined to save the holy relics of St. Cuthbert by a timely flight. Calling his monks around him, therefore, he communicated to them his resolve, and having disinterred the body of the saint, together with those of St. Oswald and St. Aidan, they prepared to bid farewell to the holy island, whence the light of Christianity had shone forth over all the north of England for two hundred and forty years. This closing scene in the history of northern monasticism exhibits to us the monks of Lindisfarne in the hour of their sorest trial, surrounded by their school. There were in the monastery, says Simeon of Durham, a certain number of youths, brought up there from their infancy, who had been taught by the monks and trained in the singing of the Divine Office. These boys entreated Eardulf to suffer them to follow him. They set out, therefore, monks and children together, carrying the bier with the holy relics, their sacred vessels, the Holy Book of the Gospels, and their other books, and commenced that melancholy journey which, after seven years of wandering, was to bring them at last to the "grassy plain, on every side thickly wooded, but not easy to be made habitable," where afterwards grew up, on the site of their wattled oratory, the princely city of Durham.

By these and similar calamities, extending not over one district, but over every part of the country, England was plunged back into the barbarism out of which she was but just emerging: her seats of learning were all swept away, and during the century that elapsed from the first landing of the Danes to the accession of Alfred, a night of gloomy darkness settled over the land.

CHAPTER IV.

ST. BONIFACE AND HIS COMPANIONS.

A.D. 686 TO 755.

THE prominent importance attaching to the schools of Kent and Northumbria must not lead us to regard them as the only learned foundations existing in England during the early period of which we have hitherto been speaking. The spread of the monastic institute among the Anglo-Saxons was so rapid and so universal, that we are sometimes led to wonder how a country so thinly populated as England must have been in the seventh century, could have furnished those crowds of religious men and women who hastened to people her newly-erected cloisters. And wherever those cloisters were reared a knowledge of letters and the civilised arts was soon introduced, and pursued with as much ardour at Selsey as at Lindisfarne, among the nuns of St. Mildred or St. Hildelitha as among the brethren of Jarrow.

If the bold and mountainous scenery of Northumbria has become indelibly associated in our mind with the lives of those saintly scholars who have been made known to us by the pen of Bede, far away at the other extremity of England there is a province which still claims as its patron saint one whose learning was as great as theirs, and whose action on the Church was even yet more important. St Boniface, or Winfrid, as he was called before he entered on his apostolic labours, was born in the same year that witnessed the entrance of Bede into the monastery of Jarrow. They were therefore contemporaries, though widely different in character, as in the career which awaited them. The simple-hearted scholar whose holy happy life flowed calmly on from childhood to old age within his convent walls, like some quiet stream that never overpasses its verdant banks, is a contrast indeed to the great apostle who, after having evangelised half Europe, and ruled the churches of France and Germany, as Vicar of the Vicar of Christ, with a spiritual sway larger than any ever exercised save by the successors of St. Peter, died, as was fitting, a martyr's death, saluting with his parting words the joy and glory of that "long-expected day."[62] Yet both in different ways exhibit to us the noblest features of the Anglo-Saxon race, whose simple piety and strong good sense are as apparent in Bede, as the ardour of its active charity is in Boniface.

He was a native then, not of the bleak and hardy north, but of the softer climate of that southern province,

Where the salt sea innocuously breaks,

And the sea-breeze as innocently plays

- 73 -

On Devon's leafy shores.

It took its name from the deep hollows where the apple-blossoms clustered as thickly then as now, and the clematis wove its tangled wreaths in as wild profusion over bank and wood. Still covered with those grand primeval forests which made perpetual shadow in its pathless valleys, and, fearless of the billows that lost their fierceness as they broke upon that gentle shore, clothed even the purple rocks themselves with verdure, and bent their branches into the briny waves, it merited to receive from St. Aldhelm the title of *dire Dumnonia*. Perhaps he could not resist the tempting alliteration, or perhaps the wooded hollows of Devonshire oppressed with their leafy gloom the senses of the traveller who, as he tells us, had just passed over the barren hills of "Cornwall, void of flowery turf." It formed the border-land of English Saxony, and touched on that unfriendly territory still inhabited by the Britons, who saw in the newly converted Saxons only a race of giants and savages, with whom they refused to hold any intercourse.

The Dumnonians, however, from the first era of their conversion, showed the same readiness to welcome the establishment among them of monks and schools as was elsewhere exhibited, and the city of Exeter is said to have received the name of Monkton from the number of religious which it contained. It was probably some of the Exeter monks who, in the course of a journey which they had undertaken for the purpose of preaching to the inhabitants of the wild Western districts, were hospitably received and entertained at Crediton by the father of Winfrid. The passing visit left an indelible impression on the boy's heart, and he grew up with the fixed desire of becoming a monk and a scholar. His father did what he could to turn him from his purpose, but finding himself forced at last to yield to his son's entreaties, he committed him to the care of Wulphard, abbot of Exeter. Winfrid was at that time thirteen years of age. His education had not been neglected in his father's house, and he now threw himself into his studies with an ardour which made it evident that he deserved some higher kind of teaching than the monks of Exeter could supply. The school of Nutscell, in Hampshire, a monastery afterwards destroyed by the Danes, possessed as high a reputation as any in Wessex, so thither Winfrid was transferred, and placed under the direction of the learned abbot Winbert. In this monastery Winfrid was able to satisfy his thirst for grammar, poetry, and the sacred sciences, and at last, being appointed to the care of the school, he drew students to hear him from all the southern provinces. In short, the scholasticus of Nutscell became a famous man; he taught not only the monks but even the nuns of that part of the world to study grammar and write hexameter verse; he attended royal councils and episcopal synods, and he even appeared in the character of an author, and composed a treatise on the Eight Parts of Speech. "Yet, though indued with such excellent knowledge," says his biographer, "he was nothing puffed up in mind, nor did he despise any who were of meaner abilities, but the more his learning increased so much also did he increase in virtue, only showing himself the more humble, devout, pitiful and obedient." Both King Ina, of Wessex, and Archbishop Bretwald, of Canterbury, knew his worth, and desired nothing better than to raise him to the highest dignities; but neither the charms of a studious life in his own cloister, nor the certain prospect of court preferment, sufficed to satisfy his ambition. He had within him in its fullest measure the apostolic fervour which animated so many of his countrymen, and led them to carry back to the old Germanic soil from whence they sprang the new faith which they had learnt in Britain. Year after year there came the news of English missionaries who had passed over into that huge province which then extended between the Elbe and the Rhine, the greater part of which was swallowed up in the inundation of 1287, and now forms the bed of the Zuyder Zee. It was called Friesland, and was the chief seat of the English missions. The first man who gave a certain sort of shape and system to these missions was an English priest named Egbert, who had been educated at Lindisfarne by Bishop Colman, and afterwards passed over to Ireland to improve himself in her schools. The Anglo-Saxon scholars were accustomed at this time to resort in great numbers to the sister isle, going about from one master's cell to another, to gather from each the science for which he was most renowned. The Irish received them hospitably, and furnished them with food, books, and teaching, gratis.

Egbert and his friend Edilhun were studying in the monastery of Rathmelsigi, in Connaught, when the great pestilence of 664 broke out, which caused such terrible ravages both in England and Ireland. It was on this occasion that St. Ultan, bishop of Ardbraccan, collected all the children who were left orphans, and had them brought up in a hospital or asylum at his own charge. The two English students were attacked by the plague, and Egbert, believing his last hour was at hand, went out in the morning, and sitting alone in a solitary place thought over his past life, and being full of compunction at the thought of his sins, watered his face with his tears, praying to God that he might yet have time granted him to do penance. He also made a vow that should it please God to spare his life, he would never return to his native land, but live abroad as a stranger; and that besides the Divine Office of the Church he would every day recite the entire Psalter, and every week pass one whole day and night fasting. Edilhun died the next night, gently reproaching his friend for having thus prevented their entering into everlasting life together; and Egbert kept his vow and remained in Ireland, doing good service as well to the Scots and Picts as to his countrymen, for it was through his influence that the former at last conformed to the Roman method of observing Easter, and his school was resorted to by every Anglo-Saxon student who crossed the sea in search of Divine wisdom. In his heart, however, Egbert nursed a great design, which he was never suffered to carry out in person. He desired to carry the Gospel among the races of Germany whence the English were originally descended, and Wicbert, one of his companions, being filled with the like desire, did actually proceed to Frisia, and there preached for two whole years among the heathen, but without much fruit. Egbert, understanding that it was not the will of God that he should himself embrace a missionary life, and being warned that his vocation lay rather among his own people, cherished the hope of at least inspiring some of his scholars with the apostolic spirit. Among these was Wilibrord, who, after receiving his early education among the monks of Ripon, had passed over into Ireland in his twentieth year, attracted by the excellent science which then flourished in her schools, and the fame of his learned countryman. It appears probable that the two Ewalds, martyred in Friesland in 695, were likewise pupils or friends of Egbert's, for Bede tells us that they were living strangers in Ireland for the sake of the eternal kingdom; that both were pious, but that Black Ewald was the more learned of the two. Wilibrord departed for Friesland in 696, accompanied by twelve fellow-missionaries; and the protection of Pepin, who then ruled the Franks as mayor of the palace to the Merovingian monarch, enabled him to pursue his apostolic career in spite of the opposition of Radbod, the Pagan duke of the country. It would be pleasant, did space permit it, to say something of his labours;— to relate how he found his way into Denmark and brought away thirty young Danes, whom he sent to be instructed in the schools which he had founded at Treves and Utrecht; how on his voyage back to Friesland he landed at Heligoland, the holy island of the Saxons, but which then bore the name of Fosetesland, from the hideous idol to whose worship it was dedicated. It was a wild, mysterious spot. No animals that had once grazed on its sacred herbage were suffered to be molested, and near the altar of the god a clear stream bubbled up of which the natives never drank save in awful silence, for the utterance of a single word would, as they believed, bring down on them the vengeance of the dreaded Fosete. Wilibrord caused some of the cattle to be killed for food, and baptized three converts in the fountain, over the waters of which he broke the mystic silence by pronouncing the invocation of the Holy Trinity. This daring act excited the direful wrath of Radbod, and on the death of Pepin, in 714, Wilibrord found himself forced to leave the country. He was, however, reinstated in his bishopric of Utrecht by Charles Martel, and in 717 we find him engaged in destroying another Frisian idol in the isle of Walcheren.

Tales like these fired the heart of Winfrid with the desire of sharing in such glorious enterprises. After a journey to Rome, whither he went to obtain the authority and blessing of Pope Gregory II., he joined Wilibrord at Utrecht, and for some time laboured under his direction. But finding that the bishop intended to have him appointed his successor, he fled away in alarm, and took refuge in the heart of Germany, where he continued until 723, preaching among the Saxons and Hessians. According to the old writer, Adam of Bremen, "Winfrid, the philosopher of Christ," as he calls him, is undoubtedly to be regarded as the first apostle of that part of the country. It was at this time that he gained a young disciple, whose story is sufficiently connected with the subject which we wish to illustrate to justify its insertion here. Adela, the daughter of King Dagobert II., had founded a monastery at Treves, where, on his journey from Friesland into Hesse, Winfrid was hospitably received and entertained. After he had said mass, he sat down to table with the abbess and her family; and her young grandson, Gregory, a boy of fifteen, who had just come from the court school, was summoned to read aloud the Latin Scriptures, according to custom, during the repast. Having knelt and received the holy missionary's blessing, he took the book, and acquitted himself of his task with sufficient success. "You read very well, my son," said Winfrid, "that is, if you understand what you are reading." Gregory replied that he did, and was about to continue the lecture, when Winfrid interrupted him. "What I wish to know, my son, is whether you can explain what you are reading in your native tongue." The youth confessed that he could not do this, but begged the missionary to do so himself. "Begin again then," said Winfrid, "and read distinctly;" and this being done, he took occasion to deliver to the abbess and the rest of the community, a discourse so sublime and touching, that when they rose from table Gregory sought his grandmother, and announced his determination of following their guest, that he might learn the Scriptures from him, and become his disciple. "How foolish!" said the abbess; "he is a man of whom we know nothing: I cannot tell you whence he comes, or whither he goes." "I care nothing for that," replied Gregory; "and if you will not give me a horse, I will follow him on foot." His importunity prevailed, and he was permitted to join the company of Winfrid, and journey with him into Thuringia.

The prodigious success that accompanied the labours of Winfrid, having reached the ears of Pope Gregory II. he was summoned to Rome, and there consecrated bishop of the German nation. At the same time he received his new name of Boniface, and solemnly signed an oath of fidelity to the Holy See, which he placed on the tomb of the Apostles. Then returning to Germany he pursued his apostolic career along the banks of the Rhine and the Danube; he penetrated into the wild fastnesses of Hesse, cut down in the ancient Hercynian forest the huge *Donner Eiche*, or thunder oak, sacred to Jupiter, and erected a wooden chapel out of its timbers, on the spot where now stands the town of Geismar. Within the space of twenty years one hundred thousand converts had abjured their idols and received baptism, but the work as it grew on his hands required additional labourers. The eloquence which in old time had earned for the monk Winfrid a scholar's fame, was now employed to rouse the apostolic spirit in the hearts of his countrymen, and a circular letter addressed to the bishops and abbots of England, painted the wants of the German mission in such moving terms that his appeal was quickly responded to, and he soon found himself surrounded by a noble band of missioners, among whom were Burchard, Lullus, Wilibald, and Winibald, the two last named being nephews of the saint.

We find from the lives of these great men, written by their immediate followers, that the same form of community life was adopted among them which we have seen had been already established in the English dioceses. The bishop and his clergy formed a kind of college;[63] and, in this episcopal monastery, as it may be called, the younger clerics were trained in letters and ecclesiastical discipline. The college thus founded by St. Wilibald at Ordorp, became so famous as to draw learned men from all parts of Europe to take part in his labours among the populations of Hesse and Thuringia. Yet more renowned was the episcopal seminary, founded at Utrecht by St. Gregory, the young disciple of St. Boniface already named, who, after completing his studies at Ordorp, and following the saint through the long course of his missions, was sent by him a little before his death to administer the see of Utrecht, then vacant by the death of Wilibrord. Gregory formed his clergy into a community, which he governed in person, and was joined by many illustrious Englishmen, among whom was St. Lebwin, the apostle of Overyssel, and the patron saint of Deventer. The seminary of Utrecht produced some famous *alumni*, of whom I will name but one whose history cannot be altogether passed over in a narrative of schools and schoolboys. Luidger was the son of a Friesian noble, who confided him to St. Gregory's care at a very early age. In fact, Luidger's somewhat premature commencement of his school life was the result of his own entreaties. He was a precocious child, who cared nothing at all for play, and so soon as he could walk and talk gave signs of a passion for books and reading. Whilst his companions were engaged in the sports of the age he would gather together pieces of bark off the trees and busy himself in making little books out of these materials. Then he would imitate writing with whatever fluid he could find, and running to his nurse with these fine treasures, bid her take care of them, as though they had been the most precious codices. If any one asked him what he had been doing all day, he would reply that he had been making books; and if further questioned as to who had taught him to read and write, he would answer "God taught me." It will not seem astonishing that a child of this temper should be possessed with a strong desire to learn how to read and write in good earnest. Yielding to his persevering request his parents accordingly sent him to Utrecht, where Gregory placed him in his school and gave him the tonsure. The Monk of Werden, who wrote his life, records his sweetness with his companions, and his devotion in church. He was always reading, singing, or praying; and always to be seen with a bright and smiling countenance, though seldom moved to laughter. And there was something about him so winning and amiable, that master and schoolfellows all loved him alike. In course of time he was sent to England to receive deacon's orders, Gregory himself not having received episcopal consecration; and here, for the first time, he became acquainted with Alcuin, whose scholastic career was just then commencing. Luidger returned to Utrecht, but an unfortunate blunder which he made in the public reading of a lesson, and which drew down on him a severe reproof from his abbot, suggested to him the desirableness of a further course of study, under the great English master. Gregory reluctantly consented to his plan, and Luidger undertook a second voyage to England, and spent three years and a half in the school of York. Here he was as popular as he had formerly been at Utrecht, and his biographer seems half disposed to think that the extraordinary signs of affection lavished on him by his masters and fellow-students require some excuse, for he tells us they really could not help it, and that any one who had known him must have done the same. To none, however, was he so dear as to Alcuin, who always bestowed on him the title of "son." During his residence in York, Luidger read through the whole of the Old and New Testaments besides a great many books of secular literature, and thoroughly studied the monastic rule as it was carried out in the English monasteries; and at the end of that time he returned to Utrecht, laden with books, and well fitted to instruct others. Alberic, the successor of Gregory, ordained him priest, and sent him to preach in his own country, till the Saxons drove him out, and then he became the apostle of that people also. Charlemagne heard of his merit from Alcuin, who by that time was fixed at the imperial court, and by his orders, sorely against the will of the missioner, Luidger was consecrated first bishop of Mimigardford in Saxony. He immediately founded a great monastery of regular canons to serve his cathedral, from which circumstance the name of the place was changed to Minster, or Münster, which it still bears. But his favourite foundation was at Werden, a spot which he had chosen in the midst of the huge virgin forests which clothed the banks of the river Rura. The old legend makes us understand what sort of work was involved in these foundations, when it tells us that the bishop and his companions, having pitched their tents, prepared to cut down the trees and clear a space large enough to contain a few rude huts; but they were dismayed when they beheld the massive trunks of the growth of centuries, with their branches so thickly interlaced that they could catch no glimpse of the sky, while the summits of the mighty oaks seemed to touch the clouds. They determined to wait till morning to commence their task; and meanwhile Luidger knelt down beneath one of the largest oaks, and was soon absorbed in his devotions. It was then a clear and beautiful night, the moon and stars shining unclouded in the heavens. Gradually, however, the clouds gathered, the wind arose, and a furious tempest burst over the forest. The monks heard the crash of falling trunks and trembled with fear; they guessed not that the stormy elements were being forced to do them service. When morning dawned there was an open space around them, the trees lay prostrate on all sides, and a sufficient space was cleared for the foundation of the monastery. One tree alone remained untouched, it was that beneath which St. Luidger had prayed, and which was long reverentially preserved. When at last it was cut down, a stone was placed on the site in memory of the event.

In these episcopal monasteries Luidger established a course of sacred studies, over which he personally presided. Such was, in fact, the universal discipline observed by the German missionaries, and hence the institution of cathedral schools spread over every province from Denmark to the mountains of the Tyrol. There we find the same class of foundations established by St. Virgil, Bishop of Saltzburg, concerning whom it will be necessary to speak a little more particularly. He was a native of Ireland, and held to be one of the most learned men of his time. It appears probable, though it is by no means certain, that he is the same Virgil who, when still a simple priest, was sent into Bavaria, together with Sidonius, and was there reported to have given expression to certain scientific theories of doubtful orthodoxy. It is not easy at the present day to determine precisely what the supposed errors were, as the only notice of them that remains occurs in a letter from St. Boniface to Pope Zachary, wherein Virgil is charged with teaching "that there is another world, and other men under the earth, another sun and another moon." The reply of the Pope was to the effect that if on examination by a council Virgil should be convicted of teaching this "perverse doctrine," he should be degraded; and the matter was finally settled by his being summoned to Rome, where inquiry was made into the facts of the case. It would seem that his explanation of his own doctrine must have proved satisfactory, if the priest Virgil here spoken of were the same who was shortly afterwards raised to the see of Saltzburg, and who in 1233 was solemnly canonised by Pope Gregory IX. These facts have, however, furnished the groundwork of a story which has been repeated by D'Alembert, and adopted with all its crowd of attendant blunders by a host of modern imitators. According to this version, Virgil, Bishop of Saltzburg, was excommunicated by St. Boniface for teaching the existence of the antipodes, and this sentence is represented to have been confirmed by Pope Zachary.[64] It will be seen, however, that the person of whose doctrines Boniface complained was not a bishop, but a priest; that the opinions attributed to him bore no reference to the antipodes; that he was not excommunicated; and that so far from either passing or confirming such a sentence, the Holy See examined, and it is to be presumed approved his doctrine, since it raised him to a bishopric, and at a subsequent period canonised him. St. Boniface reported the supposed errors of Virgil as they were reported to him, and whatever may be understood by the expressions which he quotes, they cannot be held to signify a belief in the antipodes. They rather seem to point to some theory of the existence of another race of men, distinct in origin from the sons of Adam, who therefore shared neither in original sin nor the benefits of redemption, errors which, as Baronius shows, might reasonably be styled 'perverse.' It is indeed true that Bede, and other early writers on natural philosophy, did not believe in the antipodes; not, as Mr. Turner remarks, from "any superstitious scruple," but because they followed the geographical system of Pliny, who imagined the climate of the southern hemisphere to be incapable of supporting human life. Yet this history of Virgil and his condemned propositions has been made the occasion of impeaching St. Bede, St. Boniface, and the whole race of monastic scholars, not only of considering a belief in the antipodes as heretical, but of denying the spherical form of the earth, a point which was certainly never involved in the controversy.[65]

Next to the foundation of churches and monasteries, St. Boniface trusted to the establishment of public schools for the consolidation of the faith in the newly converted countries. In every place where he planted a monastic colony a school was opened, not merely for the instruction of the younger monks, but in order that the rude population by whom they were surrounded might be trained in holy discipline, and that their uncivilised manners might be softened by the influence of humane learning. At Fritislar and at Utrecht, as afterwards at Fulda, public schools were therefore opened, and how nearly the maintenance and prosperity of these schools lay at the heart of their founder, may be gathered from the epistle which he wrote shortly before his martyrdom to Fulrad, the councillor of King Pepin, in which he implores the protection of that monarch for such of his disciples as were engaged in the work of educating children. We also find incidental notices in his letters of certain monks appointed by him to the post of schoolmasters (*magistri infantium*).

St. Lullus, who has been named above among the companions of St. Boniface, and who was destined in after years to become his successor, had been educated at Malmsbury, whence he removed to Jarrow and finished his studies under Bede. Nine of his letters are preserved among those of St. Boniface, and in one of them, addressed to Cuthbert, abbot of Wearmouth, he entreats that copies of the works of his venerable master may be sent to him without delay. Cuthbert's reply shows in what esteem Bede was already held as a writer, both at home and abroad, and how great was the demand for his works, which the copyists could not multiply fast enough. He begs for a little indulgence, seeing that the terrible cold of the past winter has disabled the hands of his best writers. "Since you have asked me for some works of the Blessed Bede," he says, "I have prepared, with the help of my boys, what I now send you, namely, his books in prose and verse on the man of God, Cuthbert. I would have sent you more had I been able. But this winter the frost in our island has been so severe, with terrible winds, that the fingers of our transcribers have been unable to execute any more books." Here is a glimpse into what one may call the real life of the scriptorium, which we are sometimes disposed to regard in a certain picturesque and sentimental light. Incessant labour and chapped hands formed part of the business, and the severities of climate made themselves felt in rooms entirely destitute of the appliances of modern comfort. Cuthbert goes on to entreat St. Lullus to send him if possible some foreign artificers skilled in the art of making glass vessels, and also a *harper.* "I have a harp," he says, "but no one who knows how to play on it." The whole correspondence of St. Boniface and St. Lullus bears witness to the deep interest felt by their countrymen in the work on which they were engaged. Their letters are addressed to bishops, abbots, monks, and nuns, and show how close an intercourse was kept up with England in spite of the difficulties of communication. Presents are exchanged between the absent missionaries and their friends at home. While the English kings and prelates send contributions of books and altar-plate, and the English nuns despatch a welcome supply of clothing, Boniface sends back a chasuble, "not all of silk, but mingled with goats' hair," and some linen cloths, which, before the linen manufactory had been introduced into England, were highly prized luxuries. To another friend he presents some fine German falcons. Some of the letters preserved are of peculiar interest, as showing us what kind of learning was then pursued in the religious houses of England, and specially in those of the English nuns, whom Mabillon calls, "the peculiar glory of the Order." Boniface in former years had directed the studies of several convents of religious women, and kept up an active correspondence with his old pupils, who entered heartily into all his interests, and forwarded them to the best of their power. Naturally enough, their talk is often of books. In one of his earliest letters, addressed to the Kentish abbess Eadburga, he begs her to send him the "Acts of the Martyrs;" and in her reply, which is written in Latin, she informs him that, together with the literary offering, she has sent him fifty pieces of gold and an altar carpet. Her liberality encourages him to beg for new favours; and whilst he thanks her for her present, he petitions that she will get written out for him, either by herself or her scholars, the Epistles of St. Paul in *letters of gold,* in order to inspire his neophytes with greater reverence for the Holy Scriptures. In his next epistle he rewards her diligence with the appropriate present of a silver pen.

Eadburga removed to Rome, whence many of her letters to Boniface were afterwards addressed. But the correspondence continued to be carried on by some of the pupils whom she had left behind her in England, and specially by a relation of the saint's named Lioba, then a religious in the convent of Wimbourne.

Of this convent and its learned inmates I must say a few words, as they deserve a place in our catalogue of English scholars. The present collegiate church of Wimbourne, ancient as it is—and the architecture of its tower bears out its claim to have been founded by the Confessor—does but mark the site of that far more ancient minster which owed its erection to the two sisters of good King Ina, Cuthburga and Guenburga by name. This was one of the very earliest convents of women founded in England, and is noticed by St. Aldhelm in a letter written in 705, wherein he declares that he has purposed, in the hidden recesses of his soul, to grant the privilege of free election to certain monasteries in his diocese; among others, that which lieth by the river Wimburnia, presided over by Cuthburga, sister to the king. Perhaps he was moved to this act of favour by the fact that Cuthburga and Guenburga were pupils of his old friend the abbess Hildelitha, the first of English virgins who had consecrated herself to Christ. Hildelitha received her education at Chelles, in France, and brought into the cloisters of Barking all the learning of that famous school. This she increased by her intercourse with St. Aldhelm; and her disciples, as we have seen, were rather profoundly versed in sacred letters. Neither did the Wimbourne scholars decline in learning under the good abbess Tetta, who was governing a community of five hundred nuns with admirable wisdom at the time when Lioba first introduced herself to the notice of St. Boniface in the following graceful letter:—

"To the most noble lord, decorated with the pontifical dignity, Boniface, most dear to me in Christ, and, what is more, united to me by the ties of blood, Leobgitha, the last of the handmaids of Christ, health and salvation.

"I beg your clemency to condescend to recollect the friendship which you had some time ago for my father. His name was Tinne; he lived in the western parts, and died about eight years ago. My mother also desires to be remembered by you; her name is Ebba, she is related to you, and suffers much from infirmity. I am their only daughter, and desire, though unworthy, to claim you as my brother, for there are none of my relations in whom I have so much confidence as in you. I send you a little present, not as being worthy of your greatness, but that you may preserve the memory of my littleness, and may not forget me on account of the distance which separates us. What I chiefly ask of you, dearest brother, is that you will defend me by the buckler of your prayers from the hidden snares of the enemy. I beg you to excuse the rustic style of this letter, and not to refuse me a few words from your affability which may serve me as a model, and which I shall be eager to receive. As to the little verses you will find written below, I have endeavoured to compose them according to the rules of poetry, not out of presumption, but as a first attempt of my weak little genius, desiring the help of your elegant mind. I learnt this art from Eadburga, who ceased not to meditate on the Divine law day and night. Farewell; live long and happy, and pray for me."

Then follow four rhymed hexameters in Latin, wherein she not inelegantly commends him to the protection of Heaven. This was a common way of concluding a letter in the eighth century, and St. Boniface, in his epistles to his friends, frequently relieves the graver subjects of which he treats by a Latin distich or acrostic; sometimes also by a scrap of Saxon verse. He responded very heartily to Lioba's appeal, and a familiar correspondence was at once opened between them. It is supposed, with every show of probability, that the *lady* to whom St. Boniface afterwards dedicated his poem on the Virtues was no other than the Anglo-Saxon nun. In the dedication to this poem he says, "I send to my sister ten golden apples gathered on the tree of life, where they hung amid the flowers." These golden apples are ten enigmas, each containing the definition of some virtue, the name of which, in true Saxon taste, is formed by the initial letters of the lines.

Another of the most constant correspondents and advisers of Boniface was his old diocesan, Daniel of Winchester, whom he frequently consulted in the difficulties with which he was beset. Ozanam observes that the former grammarian and scholasticus peeps out in one of the questions he sends for solution; namely, if the baptism were valid, administered by a certain priest who was in the habit of using the form, *In nomine Patria et Filia, et Spiritui Sancta?*[66] But we may, I think, acquit our great apostle of the charge of pedantry, founded on this passage. He was engaged in planting the Church on a new soil, and a scrupulous exactness, in preserving the sacramental forms of words from corruption, need not be taken as a sign of scholastic priggishness. There is no saying where the "Patria et Filia" might have ended, or what more extensive variations might not have been added by the *il*-literati of Thuringia. Bishop Daniel gave him a great deal of excellent advice, and was of considerable service to Boniface by supplying him with books. On one occasion we find the missionary writing to his good friend, begging him to send the book of the Prophets "which the abbot Wimbert, my master, left at his death. It is written in large and very distinct letters; I could not have a greater consolation in my old age, for there is no book like it in this country, and as my sight grows weak I cannot distinguish the small letters which run together in the volumes I now have."

In 732, Boniface received the pallium from the hands of Pope Gregory III., together with the authority of Papal Legate and Vicar over the bishops of France and Germany. This office empowered him to take every step necessary for the firm establishment of the faith in the newly converted countries, and at the same time he was charged with the far more difficult task of restoring Church discipline in the Gallican provinces, where, owing to the barbarism of the times, a frightful state of anarchy prevailed. We shall chiefly follow him in his apostolic career in Germany, where his first care was to provide for the necessities of the infant Church by the erection of several new sees. Burchard was consecrated Bishop of Wurtzburg, and Wilibald was appointed to the see of Eichstadt, a woody district overspread with oaks, which as yet contained but one small church. Other prelates were named to fill the sees of Erfurt, Ratisbon, and Friesingen. The care of the Archbishop was next directed to providing a succession of clergy for the new dioceses, and with this view he founded several monasteries, one of which became in after-times the greatest monastic school in Germany. In the year 730, when Boniface travelled into Bavaria, to re-establish ecclesiastical discipline in that country, many Bavarian nobles committed their sons to his care, and among these was Sturm, who was offered by his parents to the service of God. Boniface placed him in the monastery he had recently founded at Fritzlar, under the care of Wigbert, one of his English disciples, and took great care of his education. The innocence and humility of the youth made him dear to all his masters, and he quickly learnt the Psalter by heart, and studied the hidden sense of the sacred Scriptures. Being ordained priest, he preached among the neighbouring population for three years, but at the end of that time he was seized with the desire to seek out some solitude where he might found a religious house; and Boniface, approving his design, sent him into the forest of Buchonia to choose a fitting site. Taking two companions with him, they travelled on for two days, seeing nothing but the earth and the sky, and the huge trees through which they made their way. At the end of the third day they reached Hirsfield, where they built themselves some rude huts with the bark of the trees which they felled, and began the practices of a religious life. Boniface, however, was not satisfied with their choice of a situation, and at his desire, Sturm, after exploring the upper course of the river Fulda without success, set out alone, mounted on an ass, on a journey into the wilderness, through which he travelled for days, seeing nothing but the huge trees, the birds, and the wild beasts that roamed at large in the forest glades. At night he cut down wood enough with his axe to make a little enclosure, within which he fastened his beast to save it from the wolves; but for himself he feared nothing, and after tranquilly making the sign of the cross on his forehead, he lay down and slept till morning. At last he reached a vast and woody solitude, which Prince Carloman, the owner, bestowed on him as a free gift, and here, in the year 744, nine years after their settlement at Hirsfield, Sturm, with seven companions, laid the foundation of the Abbey of Fulda. St. Boniface gave them the necessary instructions, and visited them every year; but being desirous to establish among them the rule of St. Benedict in its perfection, he sent Sturm into Italy to visit the monastery of Monte Cassino, and others most renowned for their strict observance, that he might be the better able to form his own community in regular discipline. After a year thus spent in studying the monastic rule, Sturm returned to Fulda, where, before he died, he had the consolation of seeing a zealous community of 400 monks serving God in what had before been a desolate wilderness, and the abbey, like all those founded by St. Boniface, became quickly renowned for the sanctity of its inmates, and the good scholars whom it nurtured within its walls.

To complete the conversion and civilisation of the country, Boniface conceived the plan of bringing over some religious women from England, and establishing them in various parts, that they might provide the means of education to their own sex. Othlonus, in his history, names Chunihilt and her daughter Berathgilt as the first Englishwomen who passed over into Germany at the invitation of Boniface, and calls them *valde eruditæ in liberali scientia*. But their renown has been eclipsed by that of St. Lioba, to whom the archbishop naturally turned as the likeliest of his English friends to aid him in his great designs. In fact, there were many at Wimbourne disposed to enter heart and soul into the interests of the German mission. Lioba and her cousin Thecla were nearly related to the archbishop, and Walburga was sister to his two companions, Winibald and Wilibald. He knew that their acquirements qualified them to teach others. They had all been carefully trained by the abbess Tetta, and were skilful, not merely in the womanly art of the needle, but likewise in sacred literature. Lioba's accomplishments may be truly called surprising, when we remember that their owner was a nun, living in the middle of the eighth century in a remote abbey of a half-barbarous land. Instructed from her childhood in grammar, poetry, and the liberal arts, she had increased her treasure of learning by assiduous reading. She had attentively studied the Old and New Testaments, and committed a great part of them to memory. She was familiar with the writings of the Fathers, and with the decrees and canons of the Church—grave sort of reading for so fair a student—(and I do not use the epithet in a conventional sense, for her biographer tells us she was named Lioba, or the *beloved one*, because of her exceeding beauty); but in those days lighter literature there was none. As we have seen, she could write in the Latin tongue with a graceful simplicity, both in prose and verse. When not engaged in study she worked with her hands, as was enjoined by the rule, but she greatly preferred reading, or hearing others read, to manual employments. Indeed, it was not easy to satisfy her in this respect. When abbess, she insisted on all those under her charge taking that midday repose allowed by the rule of St. Benedict, chiefly, as she said, because the want of sleep takes away the love of reading. But when she herself lay down at these times to rest, she had some of her pupils to read the Scriptures by the side of her couch, and they could not omit or mispronounce a word without her correcting it, though apparently she might be asleep. Yet all this learning was accompanied with a modesty and humility that made her seek in all things to be regarded as the least in the house. There was nothing of arrogance in her behaviour, nothing of bitterness in her words, says her biographer, Ralph of Fulda. "She was as admirable in her understanding as she was boundless in her charity. She liked to wash the feet of her spiritual children, and to serve them at table, and she did this when she herself was fasting. Her countenance was truly angelic, always sweet and joyful, though she never indulged in laughter. No one ever saw her angry, and her aspect agreed with her name, which in Saxon signifies the Beloved, and in Greek, Philomena."[67]

It was in 748 that the letters from St. Boniface reached Wimbourne, requesting that Lioba, Thecla, and Walburga might be sent over to him, together with as many of their companions as might be willing to share in their enterprise. Thirty nuns at once offered themselves, and the little colony, after a stormy passage across the sea to Antwerp,[68] was met at Mentz by the archbishop, who proceeded to establish Lioba in a monastery he had built for her at Bischoffsheim, where she very soon collected a numerous congregation of holy virgins. Walburga went on to Thuringia, where her brother, Winibald, was superior of seven houses of monks. He had long purposed retiring to some greater solitude, and, with the advice of his brother, he chose a wild valley in the diocese, clothed with majestic forests and watered by mountain streams. It bore the name of Heidensheim; and here, in 752, Winibald, having cleared the ground, erected a church and two monasteries, one for himself and his monks, the other for Walburga's community. The savage natives beheld with jealous eyes this intrusion into their solitudes, and the destruction of their sacred oaks; but ere a few years had passed, the minster of Heidensheim stood in the centre of a Christian population, and the wild pagan forest had been converted into a smiling land of woods and pastures, where all the arts of civilised life were taught and practised in a society over which the abbot presided with something like paternal sway.

Walburga and her nuns seem to have cultivated letters as diligently in their forest home as by the banks of the Wimburnia. The travels of St. Wilibald, who had made the pilgrimage to Jerusalem, and often related what he had seen to his sister and her nuns, were afterwards written by them, not certainly in very classical Latin, but with a lucidity and truthfulness of style which appears in all the Anglo-Saxon writers, and which contrasts very remarkably with the marvellous narrations of Sir John Mandeville. St. Walburga appears also to have been the author of the "Life of St. Winibald," and it is quite clear that the singular taste for literature existing among German nuns in the tenth century formed part of the tradition which they had received from their Anglo-Saxon foundresses. Mabillon praises not merely their erudition, but the zeal they displayed in employing it for the good of their neighbours, and says that, moved by a laudable emulation, they devoted themselves to study and the transcription of books with no less energy than the monks. He particularly praises the nuns of Eiken, who employed their time in reading, meditating, transcribing, and painting; specially the two abbesses Harlinda and Renilda, who wrote out the Psalter, the four Gospels, and many other books of Holy Scripture, adorning them with liquid gold, gems, and pearls.

The after-career of St. Boniface exhibits him to us reforming the Frankish Church, long vexed with schism and other frightful disorders, which had grown out of a century of treasons and civil distractions unequalled in any history. The enemies of discipline were naturally enough enemies also to the authority of the Holy See. They had taken advantage of the chaotic state to which society had returned to reject the law of clerical celibacy, and to establish the practice of simony on a gigantic scale. St. Boniface struck at the root of the evil by enforcing obedience to the Roman pontiff, and, happily for the future destinies of the French Church, his efforts were heartily supported by the brothers Carloman and Pepin, the two mayors of the palace, and the real sovereigns of Gaul. His canons of reform were promulgated in a grand national council, and in 748 Pope Zachary established the authority of the see of Mentz over all the German provinces from Utrecht to the Rhetian Alps. One would have thought that the government of such a province would have sufficed to employ the energies of one man; but Boniface kept a place in his thoughts for the necessities of his native land. Exile as he was, he never forgot that he was an Englishman, and though it does not appear that he ever revisited his own country, he took a very active part in some of her affairs. It is rather puzzling to make out how in those days of rude civilization the German missionaries contrived to carry on their voluminous correspondence with friends at home, for the transmission of letters was certainly not provided for by any international postage regulations. It appears, however, from many passages in the letters of St. Boniface that his mails were brought to him by the Anglo-Saxon pilgrims who were continually streaming from England to Rome. Some of these were students, going to make their studies in the Saxon school, lately established in the holy city by King Ina; others were devout monks; and others, unhappily, rather indevout and disedifying characters, who made their pilgrimage a pretext for gadding about the world, and casting off the restraints of respectability. The see of Canterbury was at that time filled by a great friend of St. Boniface, named Cuthbert, who applied to him for help and advice in the sore troubles which surrounded him. The evil example of Ethelbald, King of Mercia, was causing a grievous relaxation of discipline among the clergy, whereby many grave scandals were brought on the Church, and St. Boniface did not hesitate to address the king a letter of remonstrance, which seems to have produced its effect. In 747, the Council of Cloveshoe was summoned for the reform of abuses by command of Pope Zachary, Ethelbald also giving it the weight of his presence and authority.

The Fathers of this Council owed much to the advice of Boniface, and their decrees, which are exceedingly interesting, have a good deal to say on the subject of education. They ordain that priests should constantly teach and explain the Creed and the "Our Father" in the vulgar tongue; that bishops, abbots, and abbesses do by all means diligently provide that all their people incessantly apply their minds to reading; that boys be brought up in the ecclesiastical schools, so as to be useful to the Church of God, and that their masters do not employ them in bodily labour. Sunday is to be strictly observed, and no man is to dare to do any servile work on that day, save for the preparing of his meat; but if it be necessary for him to journey on that day he may ride, row, or travel by any conveyance he chooses, provided he first hear mass. It is only fitting that every man should honour that day, on which God created light, sent manna to the Israelites, rose from the dead, and sent down the Holy Ghost, and it is also fitting that Christian men should prepare for its celebration by coming to church on Saturday, bringing a light with them, and then hearing evensong, and after midnight, prime also; being careful whilst there to keep a peaceful mind, and not to dispute or quarrel. Our forefathers were not left in uncertainty as to what was comprised under the head of servile work, for on this point Archbishop Theodore had laid down rules of great exactness. He divided it into two heads, man's work, and woman's work; the first of which comprised husbandry, garden work, the felling of trees, the building of houses and walls, the quarrying of stone, and the digging of ditches; while to the gentler sex belonged weaving, washing, sewing, baking, brewing, wool-combing, the beating of flax and the shearing of sheep. The feeling with which the observance of the Sunday was regarded is best expressed by the beautiful Saxon word by which it was called, the *freolsday*, or day of *freedom*, on which even serfs did not do serfs' work. The *freolsung*, or Sunday freedom, lasted from noontide on Saturday to the dawn of light on Monday morning—other similar seasons of freedom being established at the greater festivals. The council likewise enjoined the exercise of private prayer after the accustomed formula, wherein prayer to the saints and intercession for the dead are specially named. In church schools every one is to learn the psalter by heart, even if he cannot master the art of chanting it, and the chant itself, as well as the ritual for the administration of the Sacraments, the order of feasts, and everything else appertaining to divine worship, is ordered to be exactly conformed to the custom of the Roman Church.[69]

It may be asked what are the schools to which reference is made in these decrees? Chiefly, no doubt, the Episcopal and monastic seminaries; but it would seem that the mass priest's school is also intended, of which mention is often made in the Anglo-Saxon councils. Among our Saxon forefathers the education of the children of his parishioners was recognised as one of the chief duties of the parish priest. "Mass-priests shall always have in their houses a school of learners; and if any good man will trust his little ones to them for lore, they shall right gladly receive and kindly teach them. For ye shall remember that it is written: 'They that be learned shall shine as heaven's brightness; and they that instruct many to justice shall shine as stars for ever.' They shall not however, for such lore, demand anything of the parents, besides that which the latter may give of their own will."[70] This decree, the parentage of which is to be traced to the Council of Vaison, reappears in the acts of several councils of England, France, and Italy, the very language being preserved in the Carlovingian Council of Orleans, and in the Constitutions of Atto of Vercelli. And here we see the origin of our parochial schools, which are as emphatically the priest's schools, as the seminaries are the schools of the bishop.

The career of Boniface was now drawing to its close, and he seized the occasion of Pepin's coronation to obtain the sanction of the new monarch to a design he had long secretly cherished. It was that of resigning his dignities, and ending his life, as he had begun it, in humble missionary labours. He accordingly wrote, entreating the king's protection for his churches, clergy, and scholars. "I beg his highness," he says, "in the name of Christ, to let me know, while I live, in what way he will deal with my disciples after my death. For they are, almost all of them, foreigners; some are priests established in distant places, others monks *employed in their different cloisters in the education of youth*, some of them are old men, who have been for years the companions and sharers of my labours. Therefore I am most anxious that they should not be disturbed after my death, but should remain under the protection of the king." Pepin having fully granted all his wishes, and recognised Lullus, whom, by permission of Pope Zachary, Boniface had named as his successor, the archbishop published the charter granted by the Holy See to the abbots of Fulda, which exempted it from episcopal jurisdiction, and made over to Lullus the church of St. Martin at Utrecht, the ancient see of his predecessor and countryman, St. Wilibrord. When all these arrangements had been made, St. Boniface joyfully prepared for his fourth and last expedition to Frisia, where he seems to have already anticipated receiving the martyr's crown. He wrote to Lullus early in 755 telling him that the end of his life was approaching, and bidding him finish the church of Fulda, in which he desired that his body might be laid. "Prepare all things for my journey," he says, "and do not forget to enclose with my books a shroud, to contain my mortal remains."

He would not depart without bidding farewell to St. Lioba, whom he recommended to his successor, giving orders that at her death she also might be buried in the church of Fulda, that together they might await the resurrection. Having nothing of greater value to bestow on her, he gave her, as his parting gift, his monk's cowl, a precious token of his fatherly regard, and of the absolute poverty which he professed. He then set out, attended by Eoban, an Anglo-Saxon monk, whom he had consecrated Bishop of the Frisians, and fifty-one companions, of whom ten only were priests; and, sailing down the Rhine, made his way into Eastern Friesland. A great number of the pagans were induced by his preaching to embrace the faith; and June 5, being the vigil of Pentecost, was fixed for the administration of Holy Baptism. A tent was erected on a plain near the banks of a little river, not far from the modern town of Dokkum. But whilst the saint awaited his converts, the tidings reached him that a band of pagans were approaching, armed with shields and spears. The laymen in his company would have offered resistance, but Boniface forbade them to draw their swords. "Forbear, my sons," he said, "for the Scripture teaches us to return not evil for evil, but rather good. To me the long-expected day has at last arrived: the time of my departure is at hand. Be comforted, and fear not them who can destroy the body, for they cannot touch the immortal soul. Trust in God and rejoice in Him, and fix the anchor of your hope in Him who will give you a place in His glorious mansion together with the angels."

Whilst he was yet speaking, the barbarians rushed on him and struck him to the ground. As he fell, with the instinct of self-preservation, he raised the hand which held the Book of the Gospels, in order to protect his head. A sword-stroke from one ruffian cut through the book, while at the same time the dagger of another pierced his heart; and the rest of the band turned on his companions who stood around, and slaughtered them every one. They then seized the baggage of the archbishop, which they hoped would prove a rich booty, but to their disappointment found nothing but books and holy relics, which they scattered about the surrounding fields, casting some of the books into a neighbouring marsh, whence they were afterwards rescued by the Frisian Christians. Three of them are still preserved at Fulda; they consist of the copy of the Gospel already mentioned, which had been written out by the saint's own hand, and which, though cut through with the sword which took his life, has not so much as a letter destroyed; a Harmony of the Gospels or Canons of the New Testament, and a Book containing various Treatises and Letters, the pages of which are stained with his blood.

The body of St. Boniface was carried to Mentz, and thence translated to Fulda, when the church of that monastery was consecrated by St. Lullus, the whole history of the event being related by the monk Candidus, in his metrical Life of Abbot Eigil. St. Lioba survived her friend for twenty-four years, during which time she founded a great number of convents, all of which she governed as superior. She received special marks of respect from Charlemagne and his queen Hildegardis, who often sent for her to Aix-la-

Chapelle, and loved her as her own soul. She frequently visited Fulda, and on her death, which took place in 779, her body was carried thither for burial. The elder monks remembered the wish that had been expressed by St. Boniface, that their bones should be laid together, but, fearing to open the sepulchre of the holy martyr, they buried St. Lioba at the north side of the altar, which he had himself consecrated in honour of the twelve Apostles. There the two saints still repose, for though the church of Fulda has been rebuilt four times since the day of its first dedication, the ancient crypt has always been preserved, and there the English pilgrim may still revere the relics of his great countryman which are preserved in their antique shrine, together with two memorials of him, the ivory crosier which he was accustomed to use, and the dagger that shed his blood.

CHAPTER V.

CHARLEMAGNE AND ALCUIN.

A.D. 747 TO 804.

AT the moment when the nascent civilisation of Saxon England was being doomed to extinction, and the Danish hordes were everywhere making havoc of those religious houses which for 160 years had been the chief nurseries of learning in the West, light was beginning once more to dawn over the schools of France, where under the barbarism of the Merovingian kings liberal studies had all but entirely decayed. At an earlier period indeed, as we have seen, the Church of Gaul, far from deserving the charge of barbarism, had produced a crowd of illustrious writers, by whom the Christian dogmas were clothed in a classic dress. Down to the end of the sixth century remains of the old Roman municipal schools continued to exist, wherein Christian students disdained not "to hold the harp with Orpheus, or the rule with Archimedes; to perceive with Pythagoras, to explain with Plato, to imply with Aristotle, to rage with Demosthenes, or to persuade with Tully"[71]—in other words, they followed the ordinary course of studies provided in the Roman schools. Even when these disappeared, the episcopal and monastic schools continued to preserve some knowledge of letters. The multiplication of monasteries, even before the arrival of the Benedictines in 543, had progressed with extraordinary rapidity. We read of one bishop establishing forty communities in his own diocese; and during the century that succeeded the first foundation made by St. Maurus, as many as 238 Benedictine monasteries are known to have arisen in different provinces of Gaul. It is probable that most of these monasteries, to whatever rule they belonged, possessed a school. The monastic rules which sprung up previous to the arrival of St. Maurus—such as those established by St. Martin, St. Eugendus, St. Yrieix, and St. Columbanus—all enjoined study and the transcription of books, as well as manual labour. Nor can it be doubted that secular as well as religious pupils were received in the monastic schools, and that the education given was not exclusively ecclesiastical. It even appears as though the Gallo-Roman nobility of this period were more solicitous to give their sons a liberal education than their chivalric descendants of six centuries' later date. I will give but two examples. At the monastery of Condat it is expressly stated that noble secular youths were educated in all the learning of the times; and what this term implies is explained in the life of St. Eugendus, who received his entire training there, and never once left the monastery from his seventh to his sixtieth year. He was as familiar with the Greek as with the Latin orators, says his biographer, and was besides a great promoter of sacred studies. The other example is even more to the point, as showing up to what age secular youths were then expected to continue students. St.

Aicard received his education in the monastic school of Soissons, about the middle of the seventh century, and remained there until his seventeenth year, when he was summoned home by his father to be introduced at court and to commence his military career—a career, be it remembered, into which the aspirant to chivalry in the twelfth century would have been initiated at seven. He afterwards embraced the religious state, and did much to improve the studies in his monastery of Jumièges. Then there were the episcopal schools, in which the learning given was far from being superficial. St. Gregory of Tours tells us that when King Guntram entered Orleans in 540 he was met by a band of scholars from the bishop's school, who welcomed him in Latin, Greek, Hebrew, and Syriac verses of their own composition. St. Gregory had himself received his education in the episcopal schools of Clermont and Vienne, and informs us that even ecclesiastical students, before entering on their sacred studies, went through a course of the seven liberal arts, together with one of poetry and the Cantus.[72] M. Guizot gives a list of the principal monastic and episcopal schools of which a distant notice is to be found in the histories of the seventh century. Twenty of them are in Neustria alone, and their multiplication forms the subject of repeated decrees of provincial councils.

We need not, however, dwell on their history more particularly, for whatever may have been their number or their excellence, it is certain that before the accession of Charlemagne, the Gallican schools had fallen into general decay. The decline was progressive, but it ended in something like total extinction. "At the end of the fourth century," says M. Guizot, "profane and sacred literature flourished side by side: pagan letters were indeed dying, but they were not entirely dead. They soon, however, disappeared, and sacred literature alone was cultivated. But if we go on a little further, we find that the cultivation of Christian literature has itself vanished,"[73]—the decay had, in fact, become universal.

Tennemann, in his history of philosophy, does not hesitate to attribute this deplorable state of things to the tyranny of the Church, and the triumph of the principle of faith and authority over that of liberty and reason. But from the sixth to the eighth century, the ecclesiastical powers in Gaul had not the strength to exercise tyranny, even had they possessed the will. The slightest acquaintance with the history of those centuries and their horrible social disorders will suffice to show that submission to the principle of Church authority had not at that time assumed any very alarming proportions north of the Alps. The Church of Gaul was torn with petty schisms, and disgraced by scandals arising mainly from the absence of any authority at all strong enough to repress them, and the supremacy of the Holy See had to be firmly re-asserted by St. Boniface before any adequate remedy of these disorders could be applied. The intellectual sterility of this epoch may rather be traced to the want of that principle, than to its excess; it was in fact an unavoidable result of the anarchy and dissolution of all social ties which followed on the fall of the Roman Empire. Had ecclesiastical discipline been preserved, we might yet at least have found the theological studies flourishing; but what could be expected from bishops who had either simoniacally obtained their dignities, or had been appointed by barbarian rulers from the ranks of their own soldiers or courtiers? Destitute themselves of all knowledge of sacred letters, they were not likely to cherish them in others; and in many cases they held their sees as baronies might be held by lay proprietors. The incessant civil commotions that prevailed perpetuated the reign of darkness, for, as the writer just quoted remarks, when the state of society becomes rude and difficult, studies necessarily languish. "The taste for truth and the appreciation of the beautiful are delicate plants, needing a pure sky and a kindly atmosphere:—in the midst of storms they droop their heads and perish." So far from the Church being held answerable for the decay of literature, it was she alone that provided it any asylum in those dismal times, and it was in her monastic houses that learning, "proscribed and beaten down by the tempest that raged around, took refuge under the shelter of the altar, till happier times should suffer it to reappear in the world."[74]

The dawn of a better state of things began to show itself under the rule of Pepin. That monarch appears to have contemplated something of the same plan of reform afterwards carried out by the vaster genius of his son. His first step was to renew those close relations with the Holy See, the interruption of which had so largely contributed to disorganise the Church of France. In 747, being then mayor of the palace, he despatched an embassy to Pope Zachary, imploring his assistance and advice in the reformation of the episcopal order. It has been shown in the foregoing chapter, that a similar reformation had been set on foot in Austrasia by his brother Carloman, where, by the assistance of St. Boniface acting as apostolic vicar, the bishops and secular clergy had solemnly engaged to observe the ecclesiastical canons, and the abbots, to receive the rule of St. Benedict. The subsequent change of dynasty was affected by the will, it is true, of the Frankish people, but not until it had received the sanction of the Pope, who decided that he who held the power of king should likewise assume the royal title. This appeal of the Franks to the authority of the Holy See in the election of their sovereign is a fact of immense political importance, and from that hour the tide of barbarism began to ebb. The councils held under Pepin ceased not to labour at the correction of abuses; and the journey of Pope Stephen III. into France in 748, if it exhibits him on one hand as a fugitive from the Lombards, displays him to us no less as receiving from kings and people the homage due to him as Father of the Christian Church.

Together with the restoration of ecclesiastical discipline and the legitimate authority of the Holy See, appear the first indications of an approaching revival of learning. One of the ambassadors despatched by Pepin to conduct the Pope into France was Chrodegang, Bishop of Metz, a German by birth, and learned for the times in which he lived. In 762 he had done his best to restore discipline and letters in his own diocese, by establishing canonical life among his cathedral clergy, and giving them a rule in which provision was made for the maintenance of the episcopal seminary. Previously to this he had founded several monasteries, with the view of promoting sacred studies, among others the great abbey of Gorze, the school of which became afterwards so famous. At the same time Pepin was directing his attention to the correction of the liturgical books. He obtained from Pope Stephen an Antiphonary and Responsory, together with copies of the works of St. Denys, the dialectics of Aristotle, some treatises on geometry and orthography, and a grammar. The movement was inaugurated by an attempted reform in the ecclesiastical chant. During the stay of Pope Stephen at the Frankish court, Pepin was struck by the majesty of the Roman tones, and entreated that some of the Papal singers might instruct the choristers of his own chapel. Simeon, the Pope's chapel-master, therefore remained in France, and gave lessons there for some years; but the reform thus effected was only partial, and was not finally established in Charlemagne's time without a struggle.

Pepin's further plans were cut short by his death, which took place in 768, and was followed in 771 by that of his son Carloman, Charlemagne, the surviving son of Pepin, being thus left master of all the Frankish territories. We need not follow the course of his conquests, which gradually extended the boundaries of his empire, from the shores of the Baltic to the banks of the Ebro, and from the Danube to the Atlantic Ocean. During the forty-six years that he ruled the destinies of Europe, he was engaged in incessant wars, which seemed to leave little leisure for literary pursuits, and was organising a vast political system which, even in peaceable times, would have demanded the undivided attention of any ordinary sovereign. But if there ever was a man who by his mere natural endowments soared above other men, it was Charlemagne. His life, like his stature, was colossal. Time never seemed wanting to him for anything that he willed to accomplish, and during his ten years campaign against the Saxons and Lombards, he contrived to get leisure enough to study grammar, and render himself tolerably proficient as a Latin writer in prose and verse. He found his tutors in the cities that he conquered. When he became master of Pisa, he gained the services of Peter of Pisa, whom he set over the Palatine school, which had existed even under the Merovingian kings, though as yet it was far from enjoying the fame to which it was afterwards raised by the teaching of Alcuin. He possessed the art of turning enemies into friends, and thus drew to his court the famous historian,

Paul Warnefrid, deacon of the Church of Rome, who had previously acted as secretary to Didier, king of the Lombards. When Charlemagne set the crown of Lombardy on his own head, in 744, Paul resisted the new order of things, and made three attempts to restore his country's independence. The Frankish judges condemned him to lose his eyes and his hands, but Charlemagne interfered. "We shall not easily find another hand that can write history," he said, and Paul, conquered by his generosity, went back with him to France, and accepted the charge of teaching Greek to the young princess Richtrude, who had been affianced to the Greek emperor, Constantine. The Lombard scholar appeared nothing less than a prodigy in the eyes of the Frankish courtiers, and Peter of Pisa poured out his admiration in a poetical epistle, in which he calls him, "in Greek, a Homer; in Latin, a Virgil; in Hebrew, another Philo." It speaks well for the real scholarship of Paul that he declined swallowing all the flattery conveyed in this pompous address, and plainly stated in his reply that though he could read Greek, he could not speak it, and that he knew no more of Hebrew than a few words he had picked up at school. As to his being a second Homer or Virgil, he seems to have considered the insinuation anything but a compliment, and declared rather bluntly that he wished to have nothing in common with two heathens. He was afterwards employed in establishing the schools of Metz, and finally became a monk at Monte Cassino, where he wrote his life of St. Gregory the Great, and the well-known hymn "Ut queant laxis."[75]

Another Italian scholar, St. Paulinus, of Aquileja, was coaxed into the service of the Frankish sovereign after his conquest of Friuli; I will not say that he was *bought*, but he was certainly paid for by a large grant of confiscated territory made over by diploma to "the Venerable Paulinus, master of the art of grammar." But none of these learned personages were destined to take so large a part in that revival of learning which made the glory of Charlemagne's reign, as our own countryman Alcuin. It was in 781, on occasion of the king's second visit to Italy, that the meeting took place at Parma, the result of which was to fix the English scholar at the Frankish court. Having obtained the consent of his own bishop and sovereign to this arrangement, Alcuin came over to France in 782, bringing with him several of the best scholars of York, among whom were Wizo, Fredegis, and Sigulf. Charlemagne received him with joy, and assigned him three abbeys for the maintenance of himself and his disciples, those namely, of Ferrières, St. Lupus of Troyes, and St. Josse in Ponthieu. From this time Alcuin held the first place in the literary society that surrounded the Frankish sovereign, and filled an office the duties of which were as vast as they were various. Three great works at once claimed his attention, the correction of the liturgical books, the direction of the court academy, and the establishment of other public schools throughout the empire. Alcuin began with the task first on the list, for until the books at his command were themselves rendered readable, it was of small avail to talk of opening schools. In the hands of ignorant copyists the text of Scripture had become so corrupt as to be hardly intelligible. The Book of Gospels and Epistles for Sundays and festivals was first corrected, and such a system of punctuation and accentuation adopted as might enable even the unlearned to read them without making any gross error. The more arduous undertaking of correcting the whole Bible was not completed till the year 800, when on the occasion of Charlemagne's coronation at Rome as Emperor of the West, Alcuin forwarded to him, as the best present he could offer, a copy of the sacred volume, carefully freed from error.[76]

But it was as head of the Palatine school that Alcuin's influence was chiefly to be felt in the restoration of letters. Charlemagne presented himself as his first pupil, together with the three princes, Pepin, Charles, and Louis, his sister Gisla and his daughter Richtrude, his councillors Adalard and Angilbert, and Eginhard his secretary. Such illustrious scholars soon found plenty to imitate their example, and Alcuin saw himself called on to lecture daily to a goodly crowd of bishops, nobles, and courtiers. The king wished to transform his court into a new Athens preferable to that of ancient Greece, in so far as the doctrine of Christ is to be preferred to that of Plato. All the liberal arts were to be taught there, but in such a way as that each should bear reference to religion, for this was regarded as the final end of all learning. Grammar was studied in order better to understand the Holy Scriptures and to transcribe them more correctly; music, to which much attention was given, was chiefly confined to the ecclesiastical chant; and it was principally to explain the Fathers and refute errors contrary to the faith that rhetoric and dialectics were studied. "In short," says Crevier, "the thought both of the king and of the scholar who laboured with him was to refer all things to religion, nothing being considered as truly useful which did not bear some relation to that end."[77]

At first Alcuin allowed the study of the classic poets, and in his boyhood, as we know, he had been a greater reader of Virgil than of the Scriptures. His writings evince a perfect familiarity with the ancient poets and philosophers, whom he continually quotes, and though in his old age he discouraged his monastic pupils from following this study, it is certain that he allowed and even advocated it while presiding over the Palatine school. This appears from one of his familiar epistles to Charlemagne, in which he gives a lively picture of the labours carried on there by the students and their masters. One he describes as teaching the lectors of the royal chapel to read without misplacing their accents; another is training the boys in sacred chant; Eginhard, who is pronounced "learned in prosody," seems to have been idling his time, but Gisla had been contemplating the stars in the silent night. *"But what crime,"* he continues, *"has harmonious Virgil committed? Is not the father of poets worthy of finding a master who shall teach the children of the palace to admire his verse?*" And he concludes with the hope that two, whom he names Thyrsis and Menalcas, may long survive to keep the cooks in order, and supply the writer with large goblets of Greek wine, and smoking dishes.

In this little *jeu-d'esprit* we see, in the midst of its playful allusions to their familiar intercourse, what was the serious work of the Palatine scholars, and when Alcuin thus wrote he was certainly far from entertaining those severe views regarding classical studies which are generally attributed to him. It is true that at a later period he endeavoured to dissuade his disciple, Sigulf, from studying what he called, "the impure eloquence of Virgil," telling him that the Sacred Scriptures should be enough for him. He also rebuked Rigbod, Archbishop of Mentz, for carrying Virgil in his bosom, and wished he would carry in its place the Book of the Gospels; but it is probable that most ecclesiastics would think with him that an archbishop might spend his time more profitably over the Gospels than over the Æneid. Sigulf did not certainly feel himself obliged literally to carry out the advice of his master, for in the school of Ferrières, which he afterwards governed, the Latin poets were very generally studied. He established such a classical taste among his scholars, that in the next reign we find Lupus of Ferrières correcting the works of Pliny, and sending to Rome copies of Suetonius and Quintus Curtius. It is clear, therefore, that the classics were not absolutely excluded from Alcuin's system of education, though in the main Crevier's account must be allowed to be correct, and gives a fair statement of the views that prevailed during the whole of the monastic period. The authors whose study Charlemagne and Alcuin desired to promote, were not so much Virgil and Cicero, as St. Jerome and St. Augustine; and Charlemagne, in his excessive admiration of those Fathers, gave utterance to the wish that he had a dozen such men at his court. The *City of God* was read at the royal table, and the questions addressed by the court students to their master turned rather on the obscurities of Holy Writ than the difficulties of prosody. In one thing, however, they betrayed a classic taste, and that was in their selection of names. The Royal Academicians all rejoiced in some literary soubriquet; Alcuin was Flaccus; Angilbert, Homer; but Charlemagne himself adopted the more scriptural appellation of David.

The eagerness with which this extraordinary man applied himself to acquire learning for himself, and to extend it throughout his dominions, is truly admirable, when we remember the enormous labours in which he was constantly engaged. Hincmar, Bishop of Rheims, has left us an interesting account of the business of all kinds which he every day personally investigated. Yet, while the "King of Europe," as he was fitly called, was regulating with his own hands the affairs of a mighty empire, he was patiently pursuing a course of studies which might have befitted a university student. He spoke and wrote Latin with facility, and read Greek well, though he was not equally successful in speaking it. He had some knowledge of Syriac, and towards the end of his life corrected a Latin copy of the Gospels, after comparing it with the Greek and Syriac text. He studied all the liberal arts under Alcuin, and was a true German in his love of music. He completed the reform of the Church chant, which his father had attempted, an undertaking rendered somewhat difficult by the obstinacy of his own singers. It was during the Easter festival of 787, that Charlemagne, being then at Rome, was called on to decide a dispute which had broken out between the Gallican and Roman chanters. The Gallicans maintained that their tones were the most beautiful, whilst the Romans appealed to the teaching of St. Gregory, which had been jealously preserved in his school, but which, as they affirmed, the Gallicans had corrupted. The dispute grew warm, for whilst the fiery Franks, trusting in the king's protection, loaded their opponents with abusive epithets, the more refined Romans took refuge in sarcasm, and affected to pity the rusticity of such ignorant barbarians. Charlemagne listened to what both parties had to say, and then addressed his own chanters. "Tell me," he said, "where is the stream the purest, at its source or in its channel?" "In its source, of course," was the reply. "Well, then," said the king, "do you return to the source, for by your own showing, the corruption lies with you." This was an argument *ad hominem*, and the crestfallen Franks were fain to own themselves vanquished. To set the question at rest for ever, Charlemagne requested Pope Adrian to give him two chanters from the Gregorian school, and an authentic copy of the Roman Antiphonary, which Adrian had himself noted according to the system then established at Rome. The two chanters, Theodore and Benedict, accordingly accompanied the king back to France, and were employed to teach the correct chant; and to purge the Gallican Antiphonaries of their corruptions, Charlemagne established two schools of music, one at Metz, for Austrasia, and the other at Soissons, for Neustria, which were each presided over by one of the Roman teachers; all choir masters were commanded to resort thither and study under their direction, and to send in their books for correction, which, up to that time, says the monk of Angoulême, every one had spoiled after his own fancy.[78]

John the Deacon, who wrote in the following century, and who evidently exceedingly relished the defeat of the Gallicans, introduces the whole story of the dispute into his life of St. Gregory. He observes that the Frankish organs were unable to express certain tremblings and delicacies of the Italian chant. "The barbarous harshness of their cracked throats," he says, "when, by inflections and reverberations, they endeavoured to emit a gentle psalmody, out of a certain natural hoarseness sent forth grating sounds like that of carts on a high road; and thus, instead of delighting the souls of their hearers, their singing, on the contrary, rather troubled them, by provoking distractions."[79] This is bad enough; but the Monk of Angoulême would have us know that it was not merely through their ears that the Frankish congregations had to suffer distractions. The sore distress which one inexperienced singer endured in his attempt to produce the required "tremblings" must certainly have severely tried the self-command of those who witnessed it. "It chanced," says the historian, "that a certain clerk, ignorant of the accustomed rules, was called on to figure in the royal chapel, when, agitating his head in a circular manner, and opening an enormous mouth, he painfully endeavoured to imitate those around him." The choir, of course, was in a suppressed titter, but Charlemagne, without betraying the slightest token of annoyance or ridicule, called the unfortunate performer to him after the office was over, and rewarded his good-will with a handsome present. This great king often assisted at matins, and indicated with his hand the clerk who was to sing the lessons, or responsory. It is also said that he used to mark the end of the motetts with a certain guttural sound (a *grunt*, his historian calls it), which became the diapason for the recommencement of the phrase. The use of organs began to be introduced during his reign, and Walafrid Strabo tells us of a woman who died of the ecstacy occasioned by first hearing one of these instruments.

It has been repeatedly asserted that Charlemagne, with all his learning, never knew how to write. The supposition rests on the words of his secretary, Eginhard, who says, "He tried to write, and constantly carried little tablets about him, that in his leisure moments he might accustom his hand to the drawing (*effigiendis*) of letters, but he succeeded badly, having applied himself to the art too late." Even if this passage is to be understood of the use of pen and ink, it only informs us that the emperor wrote a schoolboy's scrawl, a circumstance not altogether without a parallel in the history of great men. But the expression of *drawing* or *delineating* letters seems rather to apply to the art of illumination and *ornamental writing*, which properly forms the art of caligraphy: and this explanation derives additional support from the fact that Charlemagne was a passionate admirer of painting, and caused innumerable manuscripts to be adorned with miniatures and ornaments, many of which are still preserved, the portrait of the emperor being often introduced. His very camp oratory was painted, and one of the offices of the envoys, whom he sent at stated periods through his dominions, was to inspect and report on the state of the paintings in the churches. His warlike hand very probably wielded the sword with more address than the pen, and, it may easily be believed, made sad results with the paint-brush, but that he knew how to write is sufficiently proved by the copy of the Gospels corrected by his hand, after he had compared it with the Greek and Syriac text, which is still preserved at Vienna, and by the direct testimony of Hincmar.[80]

This prelate, in his account of the Council of Nismes, remarks: "We have often heard the courtiers of King Charles say that this prince, who excelled all the other kings of France in knowledge of the Scriptures and of the civil and ecclesiastical law, always had at his bed's head *tablets and pens*, to note down, whether by day or night, any thoughts that occurred to him that might be useful to Church or State." He also presented to the Church of Strasburg a Psalter, in which his name was written with his own hand;[81] and it is to be presumed that he himself transcribed his numerous letters to Alcuin. Among the works of that scholar we find thirty letters addressed to the king, containing answers to his questions on theological and scientific subjects. These letters show that Alcuin had no easy task in satisfying the intellectual requirements of a man who thought of everything, and busied himself equally with history, chronology, morals, astronomy, grammar, theology, and law. He took a very special delight in the study of astronomy, and on serene nights was fond of observing the stars from the roof of his palace. In the year 798 considerable anxiety was felt both by the king and his academicians, in consequence of the erratic movements of the planet Mars, whose disappearance for a whole year it passed their powers to account for. Alcuin was written to, and entreated to explain the phenomenon, and his reply shows that he had tested the statements found in his books by careful astronomical observations. "What has now happened to Mars," he says, "is frequently observed of all the other planets, viz., that they remain longer under the horizon than is stated in the books of the ancients. The rising and setting of the stars vary from the observations of those who live in the southern and eastern parts of the world, where the masters chiefly flourished who have set forth the laws of the universe." From these words it may be gathered that Alcuin was acquainted with the globular form of the earth, and comprehended the phenomena depending on it. Charlemagne had some claims to the reputation of a poet, and nine pieces of Latin poetry from his pen are printed in his works, which are given in the collection of the Abbé Migne.[82] One of these was an epitaph on his friend Pope Adrian I., which he desired to have placed over the tomb of that pontiff, and caused it therefore to be engraved in letters of gold on a marble tablet, and sent to Rome. These verses, thirty-eight in number, have attained a singular kind of immortality. The tablet has been preserved in the portico of St. Peter's Basilica, where it may still be seen by the pious visitor, together with another inscription containing the ancient grant from Pope Gregory II. of a wood of olives to supply the oil for the lamps burning round the Apostle's tomb. All ancient writers are unanimous in declaring these verses to have been the genuine composition of the emperor, and not of Alcuin, as some pretend. They bear the title, *Epitaphium Adriani I., Papæ, quo Carolus Magnus sepulchrum ipsius decoravit*.

But one of the most interesting features in Charlemagne's intellectual labours was the attempt he made to perfect his native language, and give it a grammatical form. He began the composition of a German grammar, which was afterwards continued by Raban Maur; the other Palatine scholars joined him in the task, and assigned to the months and days of the week the names which they still bear in German. In pursuance of the same design, the emperor made a collection of old Tudesque songs, some of which he took down from the lips of his soldiers; but after his death Louis the Debonnaire found the manuscript, and perceiving the names of Scandinavian deities, with little appreciation of the importance of the work on which his great father had been engaged, tossed it into the fire. There was nothing which Charlemagne had more at heart than the completion of this undertaking, and he was accustomed to say that he hoped to see the day when the laws should be written in the Frankish tongue, comparing the shutting them up in a language of which the common people were ignorant to the conduct of Caligula, who caused his edicts to be written in illegible characters, and placed out of sight, that the people might unconsciously break them and so incur sentence of death. Alcuin no doubt assisted in this work, which was one that ever found favour with the English monks. Even before leaving his native country he is said to have made an Anglo-Saxon version of the Pentateuch, which was preserved and used so late as the twelfth century; and he would naturally be disposed to enter into the king's designs, and specially to provide for the religious instruction of the people in their own language. Something in this direction had already been done in Germany by the followers of St. Boniface; and early in the eighth century we find formulas of confession, brief confessions of faith, and portions of psalms and hymns translated for popular use into the rude Tudesque dialect. Some of the early German hymns appear to have been written by the monks of St. Gall, and were used as valuable means of instructing the people in the elements of religion. Specimens of these are given by Noth in his history of the German language, and among them is a fragment of the 138th Psalm. It will of course be borne in mind that the language spoken by the people of Germany was essentially the same as that of the English missionaries, who thus possessed peculiar facilities in preaching and instructing their converts. Thus the form of abjuration and the confession of faith drawn up by St. Boniface and his followers, for the use of their German catechumens, is equally akin to the Anglo-Saxon and to the Tudesque idioms:—"Forsachister Diabolæ? Ec forsachs Diabolæ. Gelobistu in Got Almehtigan, Fadaer? Ec Gelobo in Got, Almehtigan Fadaer. Gelobistu in Crist, Godes suno? Gelobistu in Halsgan Gast?" And when we speak of Charlemagne as cultivating the Tudesque or old German dialect, it will also be remembered that the Franks were a German race, and that what we now call *French* is not formed from their language, but from the Romanesque, or corrupt Latin, which prevailed in the southern provinces of Gaul, as well as in Spain and the north of Italy. As in course of time the Gallo-Roman element prevailed in France, the Romance language became universally used, while the Tudesque remained, as before, the language of the Germans. Hence Verstigan was not dealing in paradox when he asserted that in old times the English people all talked French, the Frankish and Saxon dialects being substantially the same language.

The graver studies of the Palatine scholars were enlivened, after the fashion of the Anglo Saxon schools, by dialogues, in which enigmas and a play of words are introduced in tiresome profusion. A curious fragment exists bearing the title of a disputation between Alcuin and Pepin, wherein the wits of the pupil are stimulated by the questions of the master. These exercises, *ad acuendos pueros*, as they were called, were much used by the English teachers, and specimens of a similar description are to be found which appear to have been used so late as the fourteenth century. "What is writing?" asks Alcuin. "The keeper of history." "What is speaking?" "The interpreter of the soul." "What is the liberty of man?" "Innocence." "What is the day?" "The call to labour." "What is the sun?" "The splendour of the universe." "What is winter?" "The exile of spring." "What is spring?" "The painter of the earth." Alcuin says, "I saw the other day a man standing, a dead man walking, a man walking who had never breathed." Pepin. "How can that have been? explain yourself." Alcuin. "It was my image reflected in the water." Pepin. "How could I fail to understand you? I have often seen the same thing."

In his letters to the young princes Alcuin freely points out their faults, and gives them excellent advice. "Seek," he writes, "to adorn your noble rank with noble deeds; let humility be in your heart, and truth on your lips; and let your life be a pattern of integrity, that so God may be pleased to prosper your days." The court school, however, was not intended exclusively for princes and nobles; children of an inferior rank were also admitted, in order to receive such an education as might hereafter fit them to fill various offices in church and state. Charlemagne took this charge on himself, and afterwards promoted his scholars according to their merits and ability. We learn this from the following charming narrative related by the Monk of St. Gall.

"The glorious King Charles," he says, "returning into Gaul after a prolonged absence, ordered that all the children whom he caused to be educated should be brought before him, that they might present him their compositions in prose and verse. Those of an inferior and obscure rank had succeeded best, whereas the sons of the nobles brought nothing of any value. Then the wise prince, separating the good scholars from the negligent ones, and putting the first on his right hand, said to them, 'My children, you may rely on my friendship and protection, since you have done your best to execute my orders, and have worked hard according to the best of your abilities. Try to do yet better, and depend upon it you will receive the most honourable offices I have to give, and that you will always be precious in my eyes.' Then turning to those on his left hand; 'As to you,' he said, 'born of noble blood, and children of the first houses in my kingdom, vainly confident in your birth and riches you have neglected to obey my orders, and have preferred play and idleness to study, which is the proper glory of your age. But I swear to you, your noble birth shall find no consideration from me; and if you do not make up for your indolence by earnest study, you will obtain no favour from Charles.'"

Some writers, and among them M. Ampère, have considered that after all that has been said and written about the Palatine school, there was in reality no school, but only a literary academy. The probability is that there was both a school and an academy, and that the two institutions, though not identical, were directed by the same masters. According to this view, the Palatine *Academy* was formed of the friends and courtiers of Charlemagne, while the *School* was for the education of youths, chiefly, if not exclusively, intended for the ecclesiastical state, and chosen from all ranks, noble and simple. The Monk of St. Gall is decisive on this last point, and mentions two scholars, the sons of millers, who, after leaving the emperor's school, in which they do not seem greatly to have distinguished themselves, obtained admission into the monastery of Bobbio. The proofs of the actual existence of this school are in fact too overwhelming to admit of a doubt. M. Ampère appears to have been staggered at the notion of a crowd of schoolboys accompanying the emperor wherever he sojourned. However strange and inconvenient such a system appears to our notions, the historical evidence is very strong in proof that it really existed. In the life of St. Adalard, there are allusions to the *turba clericorum palatii*. Alcuin in his letters complains not a little of the fatigue occasioned by this constant journeying. And we know that Otho the Great, whose revival of a Palatine school was undertaken in avowed imitation of Charlemagne, always required his scholars to accompany him; and that his brother Bruno, who superintended their studies, followed the court, and carried his books with him.

It was then, as we must believe, a real school over which Alcuin presided, and most French writers claim it as the germ of the university of Paris. The court of the Frankish monarch was indeed fixed, not at Paris, but at Aix-la-Chapelle, but it seems to have been removed to Paris in the reign of Charles the Bald, and there the Palatine school continued to flourish under a succession of famous masters, and possibly formed the nucleus of that great institution which fills so large a place in the history of education.

Meanwhile, his scholastic labours did not so occupy the time of Alcuin, as to hinder him from devoting himself to the correction of manuscripts, and the multiplication of books went on apace. A staff of skilful copyists was gradually formed, and so soon as any work had been revised by Alcuin and his fellow labourers, it was delivered over to the hands of the monastic scribes. Particular abbeys, as that of Fontanelles, acquired renown for the extraordinary accuracy of their transcribers, and the beauty of their writing. At Rheims and Corby, also, the monks greatly excelled, and laying aside the corrupt character which had till then been in use, they adopted the smaller Roman letters. Rules were made forbidding any man to be employed as a copyist who had not the knowledge of grammar requisite for enabling him to avoid errors; and treatises on orthography and punctuation were drawn up by Alcuin for the special use of his scribes. Libraries were gradually collected in all the principal monasteries, including the chief works of the Fathers and the Latin classics. In the library of St. Riquier, of which abbey Angilbert became superior, we find a few years later copies of Homer, Virgil, and Cicero; in that of Rheims, Cæsar, Livy, and Lucan; Dijon possessed a Horace, and at Montierendes there were the works of Cicero and Terence. The text of the last-named author was revised and corrected by Alcuin himself, a fact which confirms what has been before said of his toleration of the poets. From this time the transcription of books came to be regarded as one of the ordinary branches of monastic manual work, in a great degree taking the place of that agricultural labour on which, in earlier ages, the monks were so generally employed. The real hard work of head, eyes, and hand, which it involved, was pithily expressed in the well-known couplet:—

Tres digiti scribunt, totum corpusque laborat,

Scribere qui nesciunt, nullum putant esse laborem.

If the hope of gain stimulated those outside to follow it as a trade, more spiritual motives were laid before the children of the cloister. As a work of charity done for the love of God and man, it was promised an eternal reward, and the persevering toils of a long life were, it was thought, capable of being offered as an acceptable work of penance. Meanwhile, the spirit of improvement was diffusing itself from the court through the whole country. The Capitulars of Charlemagne—so called because arranged in heads, or chapters—included amongst various laws for the regulation of the civil government others which regarded the encouragement of learning. A circular letter addressed by Charlemagne on his return from Rome in 787 to all the bishops and abbots of the kingdom, after thanking them for their letters and pious prayers, proceeded to criticise the grammar in which these had been expressed. "They who endeavour to please God by a good life," writes the king, "should not neglect to please Him by correct phraseology, and it is well that monasteries and episcopal seminaries should pay attention to literature as well as to the practices of religion. It is better indeed to lead a good life than to become learned; nevertheless knowledge precedes action. Each one, then, should understand what he is about, and the mind better comprehends its duty when the tongue in praising God is free from mistakes of language." The writer then goes on to notice that the excellent sentiments of his clergy had been expressed in a rude and uncouth style; they had been inspired by true devotion, but the tongue had failed for want of culture. "But if errors in words are dangerous, much more so are errors in their signification. We exhort you therefore that you fail not to cultivate learning with the humble intention of pleasing God, so as more surely to penetrate the mysteries of the Holy Scriptures. We wish, in short, to see you what the soldiers of Christ ought to be—devout in heart, learned in intercourse with the world, chaste in life, and scholars in conversation—so that all who approach you may be as much enlightened by your wisdom as they are edified by your holy life." This was not allowed to remain an empty recommendation; it was followed by ordinances for reviving the old monastic and cathedral schools, and for founding other public schools, the establishment of which forms the most important feature in Charlemagne's revival of learning. In the Benedictine monasteries two kinds of schools had always existed, or been supposed to exist—the greater and the less. In the minor schools, according to Trithemius, were taught "the Catholic faith and prayers, grammar, church music, the psalter, and the *Computum*, or method of calculating Easter," while in the major schools the liberal sciences were also taught. In the Capitular of Aix-la-Chapelle, published in 789, Charlemagne required that minor schools should be attached to all monasteries and cathedral churches without exception, and that children of all ranks, both noble and servile, should be received into them. At the same time the larger and more important monasteries were to open major schools, in which mathematics, astronomy, arithmetic, geography, music, rhetoric, and dialectics were taught; and these again were of two descriptions.[83] Some were interior, or claustral, intended only for the junior monks, while others were exterior, or public, and intended for pupils as well secular as ecclesiastic. Some monk, qualified by his learning, was appointed scholasticus, and if none such were to be found in the community, it was not an uncommon practice to invite a monk from some other religious house to take charge of the school. A claustral and an exterior school often existed attached to the same monastery or cathedral, governed by separate masters, the scholars of the claustral school forming part of the community, while those of the exterior school, though subject to a certain claustral discipline, did not follow the same religious exercises. Lay students were received in these exterior schools, and that far more extensively than is commonly supposed, most popular writers having represented the monastic schools as exclusively intended for those in training for the religious life, thus confusing together the interior and exterior schools. Public schools of this kind were erected at Fulda, St. Gall's, Tours, Hirsauge, Hirsfield, Gorze, Fleury, L'Isle Barbe, Fontanelles, and Ferrières, as well as at many other monasteries and cathedrals, a list of which is given by Mabillon.[84] Bulæus, indeed, endeavours to show that Charlemagne limited the studies of the ecclesiastical schools to grammar and sacred learning, and only permitted the monasteries and episcopal churches to retain the *minor* schools, "from the clear view that a variety of sciences, sacred and profane, is inconsistent with the profession of ascetics." He even ventures to put forth the notion that the higher schools were confined to certain central spots, such as Pavia, Bologna, and Paris. But Bulæus wrote with an object, which was to magnify his university at the expense of the monastic schools. We ask ourselves with surprise where he could have found evidence even for the existence of any schools at all at Paris and Bologna in the reign of Charlemagne?[85] And as to limiting the monastics to minor schools, it may be safely affirmed that the idea of limitation of any kind was the very last that ever suggested itself to the mind of the emperor. As Theodulph of Orleans says, he did nothing all his life but urge forward his monks and bishops in the pursuit of learning. During the whole Carlovingian period the schools of most repute were certainly not those of Bologna, Paris, and Pavia. They were the episcopal and monastic schools of Tours, Fulda, Rheims, St. Gall, and Hirsfield, the teachers of which were all either monks or canons. The ordinance of 789 must be clearly understood, not as forbidding ecclesiastics to study anything but theology, grammar, and church music, but as rendering it obligatory on them to study *at least* so much; whilst, to use the words of Trithemius, "where temporal means were more abundant, and by reason of the number of the monks, more likelihood existed of finding one skilled in the teaching of sacred letters," the other liberal arts were also required. The monks of those monasteries in which the higher studies were not taught travelled to other religious houses, and studied in their public schools; and we certainly find no trace, however faint, of the principle that the higher studies were considered unsuitable to ascetics, for, in point of fact, the ascetics were all but the only scholars of the age. If lay students were also to be met with—and even, as I think we shall see, more frequently than is ordinarily acknowledged by modern historians—yet they were still exceptional cases, and the vast majority of those who studied, as of those who taught, continued for centuries to be drawn from the monastic body.

The establishment or revival of the ecclesiastical schools scattered the seeds of learning broadcast over the Frankish empire. All the great men whom Charlemagne gathered around him took part in one way or other in this work. Theodulph, Bishop of Orleans, a Goth by nation, and an Italian by birth, specially distinguished himself by his zeal in the establishment of schools throughout his diocese. He published a Capitular on the duties of priests, in which he permitted them to send their nephews or other relations to certain schools in the diocese which were not then regarded as public. He also enjoined that priests should open schools in villages and rural districts, "and if any of the faithful should wish to confide their little ones to him in order to study letters, let him not refuse to receive and instruct them, but charitably teach them." This was to be done gratis, no remuneration being accepted save what might be willingly offered by the parents. One would gladly know more of the kind of teaching given in these parochial schools, and specially how far the children of the peasantry were admitted into them. That village rustics really went to school and learnt something in the days of Charlemagne seems, however, past dispute; and among the Capitulars of the King of Europe we find one which requires the peasants, as they drive their cattle to pasture and home again, to *sing the canticles of the Church*, that all men may recognise them as Christians. This command obviously implied that the Latin canticles were well known to the peasantry, and probably the conning of church hymns and antiphons formed a very large portion of their school instruction. Theodulph was one of the *missi dominici*, or envoys sent by Charlemagne through the provinces of his empire to inquire into and reform abuses. On his return from one of these expeditions he published a poem entitled, "An Exhortation to Judges," in which he gives a very remarkable account of his progress through the Narbonnese provinces, and describes the difficulty he found in resisting the attempts that were made to bribe him. The proffered bribes were of all kinds—gold and precious stones, delicately chased vases—which, from the classic subjects they represented, were doubtless relics of ancient Grecian art—horses, mules, furs, woollen stuffs, and candles. He refused everything, however, except food for himself and hay for his horses, and advises all judges to do in like manner. This was the same Theodulph whose name is familiar to us as author of the Responsory, *Gloria, laus et honor.* Having incurred the displeasure of the Emperor Louis, he was imprisoned by order of that prince at Angers; but on Palm Sunday as the emperor passed in the solemn procession of the day by the bishop's prison walls, Theodulph sang from the window the words which he had composed, and thereby so touched the heart of the Debonnaire monarch that he gave him his liberty, and caused the same anthem to be thenceforth introduced into the office of the day, of which it still forms a part.

The name of Theodulph is to be had in remembrance not only as a founder of schools, but also as a writer of school-books. He felt compassion for young and tender minds condemned to gather all their knowledge from the dry and unattractive treatises of Priscian, and Martian Capella, and hit on a plan of his own for rendering them a little more popular. He composed in easy Latin verse the description of a supposed tree of science, which he caused moreover to be drawn and painted, on the trunk and branches of which appeared the seven liberal arts. At the foot of the tree sat Grammar, the basis of all human knowledge holding in her hand a mighty rod; Philosophy was at the summit: Rhetoric stood on the right with outstretched hand, and on the left the grave and thoughtful form of Dialectics; and so of the rest. The whole was explained in the *Carmina de septem artibus*, wherein the good bishop endeavoured with all his might to scatter the thorny path of learning with the flowers of imagination. The attempt was at least commendable, and in so great a scholar it had the gracefulness of condescension, for Theodulph is reported to have pursued some rare branches of study, and to have had at least a tincture of Greek and Hebrew.

Other ministers of Charlemagne are also named as actively sharing in the labours of the Renaissance. Smaragdus, abbot of St. Michael's, in the diocese of Verdun, and one of the emperor's prime councillors, not only established schools in every part of the diocese, and specially in his own abbey, but wrote a large Latin grammar for the use of his scholars. The copy which Mabillon saw preserved in the abbey of Corby bore on the title-page the words: *In Christi nomine incipit Grammatici Smaragdi Abbatis mirificus Tractatus.* Then follows a prologue in which the abbot declares that having, according to his capacity, taught grammar to his monks, they had been accustomed to transfer the pith of his lectures to their tablets, that what they took in with their ears they might retain by dint of frequent reading. And from this they took occasion to conjure him to write this treatise, which he has done, adorning his little book with sentences not from Maro or Cicero, but from the Divine Scriptures, that his readers may at one and the same time be refreshed with the pleasant drink of the grammatical art and also of the Word of God. And his reason for doing so has been that many defend their ignorance by saying that in grammar God is not named, but only pagan names and examples, and that therefore it is an art rightly and justly neglected. But he is rather of opinion that we should do as the Israelites did when they spoiled the Egyptians, and offer to God the treasures taken from the heathen. He appears to have devoted some attention to the vulgar dialects, and gives lists of Frank and Gothic patronymics with their Latin interpretations.[86]

St. Benedict of Anian, the cupbearer of Charlemagne, and afterwards the great reformer of the Benedictine order, was almost as zealous in restoring studies as in bringing back regular discipline. "Everywhere," says his disciple St. Ardo, "he appointed cantors, taught readers, established grammar-masters, and those skilled in sacred letters; also he collected a great multitude of books." Nor must we omit to notice the labours of Leidrade, the emperor's librarian, and one of the "missi dominici," who, being appointed Archbishop of Lyons, addressed a curious letter to his imperial master, in which he describes the result of his various labours. He has, by God's grace, established regular psalmody in his church; he has schools of singers, and schools of readers, who cannot only read the Scriptures correctly, but who understand the spiritual sense of the gospels and the prophecies; some even have attained to the mystical signification of the books of Solomon and of Job. He has also done what in him lay to promote the copying of books, and has built, repaired, and decorated an incredible number of churches and monasteries. Besides these there was Angilbert, the favourite minister both of Pepin and Charlemagne, who retiring from court became abbot of St. Riquier and founder of a noble library; and Adalhard, the emperor's cousin, created by him count of the royal palace, who, out of a holy fear of offending God, and losing His grace in the seductions of a court atmosphere, took refuge in the abbey of Corby, where he was eventually chosen abbot. In this capacity he greatly raised the reputation of the Corby schools. Paschasius, who wrote his life, says that Adalhard was a most elegant scholar, having been carefully educated in the Palatine school, and that he was equally eloquent in the Tudesque and Romanesque dialects as in Latin, and instructed the common people in their own barbarous tongues. His literary friends gave him the double surname of Antony Augustine—Antony from his love of that saint, and Augustine, because like him he studied to imitate the virtues of all those around him.

Meanwhile Alcuin, who had been master to most of these illustrious men, ceased not to cherish the hope that he might be suffered to return to his native land. "The searcher of hearts knows," he writes, "that I neither came thither, nor do I continue here for the love of gold, but only for the necessities of the Church." Like a true Englishman his heart clung to his old home, to the memory of his quiet cell at York, where he had studied Horace and Homer, undisturbed by other sound than the waving of the branches as they were shaken by the genial morning breeze, a sound which, he says, did but stir his mind the more to meditation. The flowery meadows and murmuring streams of England, the smiling garden of his monastery full of its May apple blossoms or its July roses, and the abundance of birds singing in the Yorkshire woods, all these find a place in the sweet verses in which the English exile paints the beloved scenes in the midst of which he had passed his childish days;[87] and all the brilliancy of Charles's court could not compensate to his mind for the loss of home. In 790 he was, therefore, permitted to revisit England, but two years later he was recalled by urgent messages from the emperor, who desired that he should attend the Council of Frankfort held to condemn the heresy of Elipandus. Alcuin felt himself obliged to obey the summons, but he did not bid farewell to York without testifying the regret with which he tore himself from its peaceful retirement. "I am yours in life and in death," he writes to his brethren, "and it may be that God will have pity on me, and suffer that you should bury in his old age, him whom in his infancy you brought up and nourished." Charlemagne, however, having regained possession of his favourite scholar, was not to be induced a second time to give him up; the utmost that poor Alcuin could obtain was permission to retire from the court to some monastery within the Frankish dominions. Fulda was too far distant from the royal residence, and the death of Ithier, abbot of St. Martin's of Tours, in 796, enabled the emperor to appoint Alcuin as his successor.

Tours at that time held the first rank among the religious houses of France, and what with the task of reforming its discipline and establishing a first-rate school within its walls, Alcuin enjoyed little of the leisure after which he yearned. He found himself in fact in possession of a great abbatial lordship, to which were attached vast revenues and 20,000 serfs. The revenues were expended by him in foundations of charity, such as hospitals, which earned for him the gratitude of the people of Tours. He applied himself to his new duties with unabated energy, enriched his library with the precious manuscripts he had brought from York, and by his own teaching raised the school of Tours to a renown which was shared by none of its contemporaries. In the hall of studies a distinct place was set apart for the copyists, who were exhorted by certain verses of their master, set up in a conspicuous place, to mind their stops, and not to leave out letters. Here were trained most of those scholars whom we shall have to notice in the following reigns, such as Rabanus Maurus, the celebrated abbot of Fulda. A letter addressed by Alcuin to the emperor soon after his establishment at Tours gives a somewhat bombastical account of his labours, but the reader will pardon the pedantry of one who had spent all his life as a schoolmaster. "The employments of your Flaccus in his retreat," he says, "are suited to his humble sphere, but they are neither inglorious nor unprofitable. I spend my time in the halls of St. Martin, teaching the noble youths under my care: to some I serve out the honey of the Holy Scriptures; others I essay to intoxicate with the wine of ancient literature: one class I nourish with the apples of grammatical studies, and to the eyes of others I display the order of the shining orbs that adorn the azure heavens. To others again I explain the mysteries contained in the Holy Scriptures, suiting my instructions to the capacity of my scholars, that I may train up many to be useful to the Church of God and to be an ornament to your kingdom. But I am constantly in want of those excellent books of erudition which I had collected around me in my own country, both by the devoted zeal of my master Albert and my own labour. I therefore entreat your majesty to permit me to send some of my people into Britain that they may bring thence flowers into France...." After some lengthy praises of the utility of learning, he proceeds: "Exhort then, my lord the king, the youth of your palace to learn with all diligence, that they may make such progress in the bloom of their youth as will bring honour on their old age. I also, according to my measure, will not cease to scatter in this soil the seed of wisdom among your servants, remembering the words, 'In the morning sow thy seed, and in the evening withhold not thy hand.' To do this has been the most delightful employment of my whole life. In my youth I sowed the seeds of learning in the flourishing seminaries of my native soil. Now in the evening of my life, though my blood is less warm within me, I do not cease to do the same in France, praying to God that they may spring up and flourish in both countries." In consequence of this suggestion, a commission was despatched to England for the purpose of transcribing some of the treasures of the York library. The French scribes made copies of the English service books, and that so exactly, that they took no heed of the geographical distinctions of the two countries, but copied the pontifical of Archbishop Egbert, and its form for the anointing and coronation of kings, exactly word for word. Hence in a Rheims pontifical of the ninth century, still preserved in Cologne cathedral, the emperor of the Franks is addressed as King of the Saxons, Mercians, and Northumbrians—a circumstance which has induced some modern critics to speculate as to the exact time when the North of England was subject to the Frankish sceptre. The copies procured through the industry of these scribes were multiplied at Tours, and thence dispersed throughout the kingdom. Alcuin's own works were also in great demand, specially his elementary treatises on the different sciences. His other works, which are very numerous, consist chiefly of theological treatises and commentaries on the Scriptures, some metaphysical and philosophical writings, and a collection of poems, among which are the *Eulogium on the Archbishops and the Church of York*, and the *Elegy on the Destruction of Lindisfarne*, the latter of which is perhaps the happiest production of his pen, and evinces the real feeling of a poet. The news of the sad event which it commemorates excited consternation throughout Europe, but by none was it received with bitterer sorrow than by the abbot of Tours. "The man," he says, "who can think of that calamity without terror, and who does not cry to God in behalf of his country, has a heart not of flesh but of stone." He at once wrote letters of sympathy to Ethelred, King of Northumbria, and the monks who had escaped from the sword, which would be sufficient to evince how fondly his heart still clung to his native land even without the touching apostrophe which he introduces to his cell at York. What view was taken by Alcuin of the work of education, to which his whole life was devoted may be gathered from his treatise on the seven liberal arts, the introduction to which is cast in the form of dialogue between the master and his disciples. I will give an extract which may suffice to show the noble and elevated sentiments which these early scholars entertained on the subject of learning:—

Dis. "O, wise master, we have often heard you repeat that true philosophy was the science that taught all the virtues, and the only earthly riches that never left their possessor in want. Your words have excited in us a great desire to possess this treasure. We wish to know where the teaching of philosophy will lead us, and by what steps we may attain to it. But our age is weak and without your help we shall not be able to mount these steps."

Master. "It will be easy to show you the way of wisdom, provided you seek it purely for God's sake to preserve the purity of your own soul, and for the love of virtue; if you love it for its own sake, and do not seek in it any worldly honour and glory or, still less, riches or pleasure."

Dis. "Master, raise us up from the earth where our ignorance now detains us, lead us to those heights of science where you passed your own early years. For if we may listen to the fables of the poets, they would seem to tell us that the sciences are the true banquets of the gods."

Master. "We read of Wisdom, which is spoken of by the mouth of Solomon, that she built herself a house and hewed out seven pillars. Now, although these pillars represent the seven gifts of the Holy Ghost and the seven Sacraments of the Church, we may also discern in them the *seven liberal arts*, grammar, rhetoric, dialects, arithmetic, geometry, music, and astronomy, which are like so many steps on which philosophers expend their labours, and have obtained the honours of eternal renown."

As the school of St. Martin rose in celebrity, it became the resort of a crowd both of foreigners and natives. Alcuin's own countrymen in particular flocked around him, and it would seem that the number of English scholars who constantly arrived, at last excited the jealousy of the clergy of Tours. One day as four Frankish priests were standing at the gate of the monastery, a newly arrived Englishman, Aigulf by name, passed in, and supposing him to be ignorant of their language, one of them exclaimed, "There goes another of them! When shall we be free from these swarms of Britons? They gather round the old fellow like so many bees!" Aigulf hung his head and blushed; but when Alcuin heard what had passed he sent for the Frenchmen, and courteously requested them to sit down, and drink the health of the young scholar in his best wine. "The old Saxon," as they called him, ceased not in his retirement to watch over the interests of learning, even in the remotest provinces. There was hardly a bishop or abbot of any distinction who had not at one time or other been his pupil, and he continued to enjoy and exercise among them the privileged freedom of an old and honoured master. His letters bear evidence of the immense range over which his influence extended. In his ninety-fourth epistle he conjures a young missionary to be always reminding the parish priests to keep up their schools. Another time he addresses a bishop, and advises him to return to his own country that he may set in order good grammar lessons for the children of his diocese. His fifty-sixth letter is to the English Archbishop of York; and in it he enters into several useful details; and advises him to have his school divided into different classes—one for reading, one for writing, and one for chanting, so as to preserve good order. Then comes a letter to the Emperor, reminding him to have the Palatine scholars daily exercised in their learning; arithmetical subtleties accompany another letter, and some sage observations on the utility of punctuation, which commendable branch of grammar has, he regrets to say, been of late much lost sight of. In short, his active mind, thoroughly Anglo-Saxon in its temper, worked on to the end; labouring at a sublime end by homely practical details. One sees he is of the same race with

Bede, who wrote and dictated to the last hour of his life, and when his work was finished, calmly closed his book and died.

It was after the retirement of Alcuin from court, that we must date the arrival in France of the Irish scholars, Dungal and Clement, concerning whom the monk of St. Gall relates a story which is treated as apocryphal by Tiraboschi, though it has found a place in most earlier histories. He tells us, that having landed on the coast of France, they excited the curiosity of the people by crying aloud, "Wisdom to sell! who'll buy?" The rumour of their arrival reaching Charlemagne's ears, he caused them to be brought before him, and finding them well skilled in letters, retained them both in his service. Clement remained at Paris and received the direction of the Palatine school, whilst Dungal was sent to Pavia, where he opened an academy in the monastery of St. Augustine. Whatever may be thought of the incident connected with their first appearance in France, there is no doubt as to their historic identity. Tiraboschi quotes an edict of the Emperor Lothaire published in 823, for the re-establishment of public schools in nine of the chief cities of Italy, from which it appears that Dungal was at the time still presiding over the school of Pavia. He seems to be the same who, in 811, addressed a long letter to Charlemagne on the subject of two solar eclipses, which were expected to take place in the following year, and may be yet further identified with the *Dungalus Scotorum præcipuus*, who is noticed in the catalogue of the library of Bobbio, where he at last retired, bringing with him a great store of books, which he presented to the monastery. Among them were four books of Virgil, two of Ovid, one of Lucretius, and a considerable number of the Greek and Latin fathers.

As to Clement, there is no difficulty in tracing his career. He seems to have been deeply imbued with the learned mysticism of the school of Toulouse, and in a treatise on the eight parts of speech, which is still preserved, quotes the rules of the grammarian Virgil, and the writings of the noble doctors Glengus, Galbungus, Eneas, and the rest. Alcuin complained much of the disorder introduced into the Studies of the court school after his departures. "I left them Latins," he exclaimed, "and now I find them Egyptians." This was a double hit at the gibberish of the twelve Latinites, which Alcuin could not abide, and at the hankering which the Irish professors always displayed, both in science and theology, for the teaching of the school of Alexandria, many of them having embraced the peculiar views of the Neo-Platonists. The Egyptians, however, found a welcome at the court of Charlemagne in spite of their eccentricities; for there no one was ever coldly received who could calculate eclipses, or charm the ears of the learned monarch with Latin hexameters. And it is perhaps to one of these Irish professors that we must attribute those verses preserved by Martene, and professing to be written by an "Irish exile," which contain such agreeable flattery of the Frankish sovereign and of his people, and which were presented to the emperor as he held one of those solemn New-year courts, at which his subjects vied one with another in offering him jewels, tissues, horses, and bags of money. And perhaps, to his mind, the graceful lines that celebrated the Frankish people as "a race of kings come forth from the walls of Troy, into whose hands God had delivered the empire of the world," were more acceptable than even the glittering heaps of the precious metals.

Charlemagne did his utmost to draw Alcuin once more to his side, and specially pressed him to accompany him on his visit to Rome, in the year 800, when he received the imperial crown. But Alcuin was not to be moved by his arguments and entreaties, though he did not refuse to quit his retirement at the call of real duty. In 799 he attended the council of Aix-la-Chapelle, to oppose in person the heretical teacher, Felix of Urgel, who, together with Elipandus, had revived the Nestorian heresy in a new shape. After a disputation of six days, Felix owned himself vanquished, and frankly renounced his errors. This was perhaps the most glorious moment in Alcuin's life; but he only used the credit which he had thus obtained with his sovereign to solicit permission to resign all his preferments into the hands of his disciples, that he might spend the remainder of his life in retirement. Frèdegise, therefore, succeeded him in the abbacy of St. Martin's, and Sigulf in that of Ferrières. "I have made all things over into the hands of my sons," writes the old man, rejoicing in his late-earned freedom, "and laying down the burden of the pastoral care, I wait quietly at St. Martin's until my change shall come."

The short remainder of his life was spent in the humblest exercises of charity and devotion. He chose the place of his interment and often visited it with disciples, and his letters show him to have been incessantly occupied with the great thought of his approaching end. It came at last, and on the morning of Whitsunday, May 19, 804, the great scholar passed gently and happily to the eternity he had so long contemplated. Charlemagne mourned his death as that of a friend and master, and before his final departure addressed him some Latin verses, which, if not distinguished for much poetical merit, at least do justice to the honest affection that dictated them. He survived Alcuin ten years, and was buried in the royal "chapel"[88] that he had erected as the place of his sepulture, not reclining in a coffin, but seated on his throne, with the crown on his brow, the sceptre in his hand, his good sword Joyeuse by his side, and the book of the Gospels resting on his knees. And a brief inscription marked the spot where rested all that was mortal of "the great and orthodox emperor."

CHAPTER VI.

THE CARLOVINGIAN SCHOOLS.

A.D. 804 TO 900.

THE death of Alcuin in no degree checked the intellectual movement to which he had communicated the first impulse. He had fairly done his work; and even after his death his influence survived in the disciples whom he had so carefully trained and who long supplied the public schools of the empire with a succession of excellent masters. St. Martin's of Tours, indeed, declined under the government of Fredegise, and the Palatine scholars themselves did not pass into the best hands. After Alcuin's withdrawal from court the school of the palace fell, as we have seen, first under the management of the Irishman Clement, who had a fancy for changing the whole method of instruction, and then under that of Claud, Bishop of Turin, a man of audacious opinions, the only one of the Western bishops who declared in favour of the Iconoclasts, and who likewise took up the heretical tenets of Felix of Urgel. The school continued to decline during the whole reign of Louis le Debonnaire; but it revived under his son and successor Charles the Bald, who followed the example of his illustrious grandfather, and gathered around him learned men from all countries, especially from England and Ireland. The crowds of scholars who flocked from the latter island is noticed by Henry of Auxerre, who says, that it seemed as if Ireland herself were about to pass over into Gaul, and it became a proverb during the reign of this monarch, that instead of speaking of the school of the palace, one should rather call the royal residence the palace of the schools. Charles was not merely an encourager of humane letters; he possessed a certain philosophical turn of mind which led him to indulge in abstruse speculations, and to encourage similar tastes in those around him. He addressed a capitular to the bishops of his kingdom, questioning them on their opinions as to the immateriality of the soul; and he placed at the head of his royal school a scholar more famous for the subtlety of his intellect than the orthodoxy of his views. John Scotus Erigena, an Irishman by birth, had early applied himself to the study of the Greek language and philosophy, and had embraced the chief doctrines of the Neo-Platonic school. He astonished the Western world by his translation of the works of St. Denys the Areopagite, an achievement which the Roman scholars, who still regarded their Transalpine neighbours as essentially barbarians, could hardly be brought to credit, and which exhorted compliments from Anastasius, the papal librarian, and some complaints from Pope Nicholas I., who would have been better pleased had the work been first submitted to ecclesiastical approval. Erigena's free opinions won him no disfavour with Charles the Bald; nevertheless certain controversies, of which we shall have to speak hereafter, and in which he took an active part, drew from him the expression of heterodox sentiments which excited no little scandal. This was increased by the publication of his philosophical treatise, "*De Natura Rerum*," in which he plainly put forth the doctrines of the Greek Platonists, and represented the Creator and the creature as essentially one and the same. Besides this radical Pantheistic error, which runs through all his works, his views on the subject of the supremacy of reason over authority are liberal in the extreme.[89] "Authority," he says, "emanates from reason, not reason from authority; true reason has no need to be supported by any authority. We must use reason first in our investigations and authority afterwards." He also affirmed that the substance of man was his will. The only punishment of sin, he says, is sin; there is no eternal fire; even the lost enjoy a certain happiness, for they are not deprived of truth. These, and a thousand equally unsound passages, raised him a crowd of adversaries, all of whom he treated with that supercilious contempt which would seem necessarily to enter into the character of the scholastic heretic. "They are all deceived," he writes, "owing to their ignorance of liberal studies; they have none of them studied Greek, and with a knowledge of the Latin language alone it is impossible for them to understand the distinctions of science."

In 855 the Council of Valence, nothing dismayed at having to deal with a foe who was acquainted with Greek, examined his writings, declared certain propositions extracted from his treatise on Predestination to be the invention of the devil, and everywhere interdicted them from being read. Nevertheless, Erigena was not removed from his post at court; nor was it until ten years later, in 865, that he found himself obliged to retire, in consequence of the remonstrances addressed to the king by Pope Nicholas I., who required his removal from the Palatine academy, "where he was giving poison instead of bread, and mingling his tares with the wheat." All authorities agree in regarding him as intellectually superior to any man of his age, though it is possible that his heterodox principles have had some share in winning him the extraordinary favour which he has found at the hands of Hallam and Guizot, who are willing, naturally enough, to make the most of one who in the Dark Ages set at nought the claims of authority, and raised the standard of independent reason. In spite, however, of the prominent position which he holds among men of letters, and the noisy eulogiums which have been heaped on him at the expense of his more orthodox contemporaries, I shall say no more of him in this place than that he withdrew from Gaul,[90] and was succeeded in his office as Palatine scholasticus by the monk Mannon, who, after teaching with success for some years, returned to his monastery at Condat; after which we hear no more of the Palatine school till its revival, at the beginning of the tenth century, under the famous Remigius of Auxerre.

But the Palatine school by no means held the most important place in the educational institutions bequeathed by Charlemagne to the empire. The work begun by Alcuin was being far more successfully carried out in the monastic schools, especially those of Fulda, Rheims, and the two Corbys. The abbey of Fulda, mindful of its great origin, was one of the first to enter heartily into the revival of letters initiated by Charlemagne; and in order to fit the monks for the work to which they were called, it was resolved to send two of the younger brethren to study under Alcuin himself at Tours, that after being there imbued with all the liberal arts, they might return to their own monastery as teachers. The two chosen for this purpose were Hatto and Rabanus, and they accordingly began their studies at St. Martin's in 802. The name of Maurus was bestowed by Alcuin on his favourite disciple, and was afterwards retained by Rabanus in addition to his own. He studied both sacred and profane sciences, as appears from the letter he addressed many years later to his old schoolfellow, Haimo, Bishop of Halberstadt, in which he reminds him of the pleasant days they had spent together in studious exercises, reading, not only the Sacred books, and the expositions of the Fathers, but also investigating all the seven liberal arts. In 813, being then twenty-five years of age, Rabanus was recalled to Fulda, by the abbot Ratgar, and placed at the head of the school, with the strict injunction that he was to follow in all things the method of his master Alcuin. The latter was still alive, and addressed a letter to the young preceptor, which is printed among his other works, and is addressed to "the boy Maurus," in which he wishes him good luck with his scholars. His success was so extraordinary that the abbots of other monasteries sent their monks to study under him, and were eager to obtain his pupils as professors in their own schools. The German nobles also gladly confided their sons to his care, and he taught them with wonderful gentleness and patience. He carried out the system which had been adopted by Alcuin of thoroughly exercising his scholars in grammar before entering on the study of the other liberal arts. "All the generations of Germany," says Trithemius, "are bound to celebrate the praise of Rabanus, who first taught them to articulate the sound of Greek and Latin." At his lectures every one was trained to write equally well in prose or verse on any subject placed before him, and was afterwards taken through a course of rhetoric, logic, and natural philosophy, according to the capacities of each. From this time the school of Fulda came to be regarded as one of the first monastic seminaries of Europe, and held a rank at least equal to that of St. Gall. It had inherited the fullest share of the Anglo-Saxon spirit, and exhibited the same spectacle of intellectual activity which we have already seen working in the foundations of St. Bennet Biscop. Every variety of useful occupation was embraced by the monks; while some were at work hewing down the old forest which a few years before had given shelter to the mysteries of Pagan worship, or tilling the soil on those numerous farms which to this day perpetuate the memory of the great abbey in the names of the towns and villages which have sprung up on their site,[91] other kinds of industry were kept up within doors, where the visitor might have beheld a huge range of workshops in which cunning hands were kept constantly busy on every description of useful and ornamental work in wood, stone, and metal. It was a scene, not of artistic *dilettanteism*, but of earnest, honest labour, and the treasurer of the abbey was charged to take care that the sculptors, engravers, and carvers in wood, were always furnished with plenty to do. Passing on to the interior of the building the stranger would have been introduced to the scriptorium, over the door of which was an inscription warning the copyists to abstain from idle words, to be diligent in copying good books, and to take care not to alter the text by careless mistakes. Twelve monks always sat here employed in the labour of transcription, as was also the custom at Hirsauge, a colony sent out from Fulda in 830; and the huge library which was thus gradually formed, survived till the beginning of the seventeenth century, when it was destroyed in the troubles of the thirty years' war. Not far from the scriptorium was the interior school, where the studies were carried on with an ardour and a largeness of views, which might have been little expected from an academy of the ninth century. Our visitor, were he from the more civilised south, might well have stood in mute surprise in the midst of these fancied barbarians, whom he would have found engaged in pursuits not unworthy of the schools of Rome. The monk Probus is perhaps lecturing on Virgil and Cicero, and that with such hearty enthusiasm that his brother professors accuse him, in good-natured jesting, of ranking them with the saints. Elsewhere disputations are being carried on over the Categories of Aristotle, and an attentive ear will discover that the controversy which made such a noise in the twelfth century, and divided the philosophers of Europe into the rival sects of the Nominalists and Realists, is perfectly well understood at Fulda, though it does not seem to have disturbed the peace of the school. To your delight, if you be not altogether wedded to the dead languages, you may find some engaged on the uncouth language of their father-land, and, looking over their shoulders, you may smile to see the barbarous words which they are cataloguing in their glossaries; words, nevertheless, destined to reappear centuries hence in the most philosophic literature of Europe. The monks of Fulda derive their scholastic traditions from Alcuin and Bede, and cannot, therefore, neglect a study of the vernacular. Yet they are, I am sorry to say, beset with one weakness common to the scholars of the time, and are ashamed of their Frankish and Saxon names; and Hatto, Bruno, and Rechi, three of the best pupils of Rabanus, are known in his academy under the Latin soubriquets of Bonosus, Candidus, and Modestus. Brower, in his "Antiquities of Fulda," has depicted the two last-named scholars from an illuminated manuscript of their monastery in which their portraits are introduced. Candidus, the assistant of Rabanus in the school, holds a book in one hand while with the other he points out to Modestus a passage on the page before him. From the open lips and extended hand of his pupil we surmise that he is reciting the words thus indicated. Both are clothed in the tunic without sleeves, scapular, and large capuce which then formed the Benedictine habit. It may be added that the school of Fulda would have been found ordered with admirable discipline. Twelve of the best professors were chosen and formed a council of seniors or doctors, presided over by one who bore the title of Principal, and who assigned to each one the lectures he was to deliver to the pupils.

In the midst of this world of intellectual life and labour, Rabanus continued for some years to train the first minds of Germany, and counted among his pupils the most celebrated men of the age, such as Lupus of Ferrières, Walafrid Strabo, and Ruthard of Hirsauge, the latter of whom was the first who read profane letters to the brethren of his convent "after the manner of Fulda." Lupus was a monk of Ferrières, where he had been carefully educated by the abbot Aldric, who was a pupil of Sigulf, and had acted for some time as assistant to Alcuin in the school of Tours. Aldric afterwards became Archbishop of Sens, and sent Lupus to complete his education at Fulda, under Rabanus. Like all the scholars of Ferrières, Lupus had a decided taste for classical literature; the love of letters had been, to use his own expression, innate in him from a child, and he was considered the best Latinist of his time. His studies at Fulda were chiefly theological, and he applied to them with great ardour, without, however, forgetting "his dear humanities." It would even seem that he taught them at Fulda, thus returning one benefit for another. The monastery was not far from that of Seligenstadt, where Eginhard, the secretary and biographer of Charlemagne, was their abbot. A friendship, based on similarity of tastes, sprang up between him and Lupus, and was maintained by a correspondence, much of which is still preserved. Lupus always reckoned Eginhard as one of his masters; not that he directly received any lessons from him, but on account of the assistance which the abbot rendered him by the loan of valuable books. In one of his earliest letters to this good friend he begs for a copy of Cicero's "Rhetoric," his own being imperfect, as well as for the "Attic Nights" of Aulus Gellius, which were not then to be found in the Fulda library. In another letter, he consults him on the exact prosody of certain Latin words, and begs him to send the proper size of the Uncial letters used in manuscripts of that century.

Among the fellow-students of Lupus at this time was Walafrid Strabo, a man of very humble birth, whose precocious genius had early made him known in the world of letters. In spite of the unfortunate personal defect which earned him his surname of Strabo, (or the lame), Walafrid's Latin verses had gained him respect among learned men at the age of fifteen, and they are favourably noticed even by critics of our own time. He had received his early training in the monastery of Reichnau, the situation of which was well fitted to nurture a poetic genius. His masters had been Tetto and Wettin, the latter of whom was author of that terrible "Vision of Purgatory" which left an indelible impress on the popular devotion of Christendom. From Reichnau he was sent by his superiors to study at Fulda, where he acquired a taste for historical pursuits, and is said to have assisted in the compilation of the annals of the monastery. It was out of the Fulda library that he collected the materials for his great work, the Gloss, or Commentary on the Text of Scripture, gathered from the writings of the Fathers. It received many additions and improvements from subsequent writers, and, for more than six hundred years, continued to be the most popular explanation of the Sacred text in use among theologians. Returning to Reichnau, Walafrid was appointed to the office of scholasticus, and filled it with such success as fairly to establish the reputation of that monastic school. Ermanric, one of his pupils, says of him, that to the end of his life he continued to exhibit the same delightful union of learning and simplicity which had endeared him to his masters and school-fellows. Even after he was appoined abbot, he found his chief pleasure in study, teaching, and writing verses, and would steal away from the weightier cares of his office to take a class in his old school and expound to them a passage of Virgil. Neither old age nor busy practical duties dried up the fount of Abbot Walafrid's inspiration, and we find him in his declining years writing his poems entitled "*Hortulus*," wherein he describes with charming freshness of imagery, the little garden blooming beneath the window of his cell, and the beauty and virtue of the different flowers which he loved to cultivate with his own hands.

Another of the Fulda scholars contemporary with those named above, was Otfried, a monk of Weissemburg, who entered with singular ardour into the study of the Tudesque dialect. Rabanus himself devoted much attention to this subject, and composed a Latin and German glossary on the books of Scripture, together with some other etymological works, among which is a curious treatise on the origin of languages. Otfried took up his master's favourite pursuits with great warmth, and the completion of Charlemagne's German grammar is thought to be in reality his work, though generally assigned to Rabanus. On retiring to his own monastery, where he was charged with the direction of the school, he continued to make the improvement of his native language the chief object of his study. A noble zeal prompted him to produce something in the vernacular idiom which should take the place of those profane songs, often of heathen origin, which had hitherto been the only production of the German muse. Encouraged by a certain noble lady named Judith, to whom he confided his ideas, he conceived the plan of rendering into Tudesque verse the most remarkable passages from the Life of Our Lord, which he chose so happily, and wove together with so skilful a hand, that his work may be regarded as a Harmony of the Gospel narrative. It was accompanied with four dedicatory epistles, in one of which, addressed to Luitbert, Archbishop of Mentz, he complains of the neglect with which the Franks have hitherto treated their own language. Prudentius, Juvencus, and other Latin writers had written the Acts of the Lord in Latin verse, wherefore he now desired to attempt the same in his mother tongue. "I wish," he says, "to write the Gospels, the history of our salvation, in the Frankish tongue. Now, therefore, let all men of good-will rejoice, and let those of the Frankish tongue also rejoice, and be glad, since we have lived to celebrate the praises of Christ in the language of our fathers." The other epistles were addressed to the Emperor Louis, and to some of the monks of St. Gall, who were celebrated for the labour which they bestowed on the cultivation of the Tudesque dialect, and could therefore appreciate Otfried's work at its full value. It had the effect which he anticipated; his verses became familiar in the mouths of those who had hitherto been acquainted only with the rude songs of their pagan ancestors, and dispelled much of the prejudice which existed against the use of the barbarous dialects for the purpose of religious instruction. And in 847, three months after Rabanus was raised to the see of Mentz, a decree was published by the provincial council, requiring every bishop to provide himself with homilies for the instruction of the people, translated out of Latin into Tudesque or Romanesque (as the Rustic Latin was sometimes called), that they might be understood by rude and ignorant persons.

The character of Rabanus may be gathered from that of his pupils. He was in every respect a true example of the monastic scholar, and took St. Bede for the model on which his own life was formed. All the time not taken up with religious duties he devoted to reading, teaching, writing, or "feeding himself on the Divine Scriptures." The best lesson he gave his scholars was the example of his own life, as Eginhard indicates in a letter written to his son, then studying as a novice at Fulda. "I would have you apply to literary exercises," he says, "and try as far as you can to acquire the learning of your master, whose lessons are so clear and solid. But specially imitate his holy life.... For grammar and rhetoric and all human sciences are vain and even injurious to the servants of God, unless by Divine grace they know how to follow the law of God; for science puffeth up, but charity buildeth up. I would rather see you dead than inflated with vice."

Nevertheless, the career of Rabanus was far from being one of unruffled repose, and the history of his troubles presents us with a singular episode in monastic annals. The abbot Ratgar was one of those men whose activity of mind and body was a cross to every one about him. He could neither rest himself nor suffer anybody else to be quiet. The ordinary routine of life at Fulda, with its prodigious amount of daily labour, both mental and physical, did not satisfy the requirements of his peculiar organisation. He had a fancy for rearranging the whole discipline of the monastery, and was specially desirous of providing himself with more splendid buildings than those which had been raised by the followers of the humble Sturm. Every one knows that the passion for building has in it a directly revolutionary element; it is synonymous with a passion for upsetting, destroying, and reducing everything to chaos. Hence, the monks of Fulda had but an uncomfortable time of it, and what was worse, Ratgar was so eager to get his fine buildings completed, that he not only compelled his monks to work as masons, but shortened their prayers and masses, and obliged them to labour on festivals. Rabanus himself could claim no exemption; he had to exchange the pen for the trowel; and to take away all possibility of excuse, Ratgar deprived him of his books, and even of the private notes which he had made of Alcuin's lectures. Rabanus was too good a monk to protest against his change of employment, and carried his bricks and mortar as cheerfully as ever he had applied himself to a copy of Cicero; but he did not conceive it contrary to religious obedience humbly to protest against the confiscation of his papers, and attempted to soften the hard heart of his abbot with a copy of verses. "O sweet father!" he exclaims, "most excellent shepherd of monks! I thy servant pray thee to be propitious, and to let thy tender pity hear me, who cry to thee though unworthy. O ever-compassionate Ruler! thy kindness in old time permitted me to study books, but the poverty of my understanding was a hindrance to me; and lest my wandering mind should lose all that my master taught me by word of mouth, I committed everything to writing. These writings in time formed little books, which I pray thee command to be returned to thy unworthy client. Whatever slaves possess is held by right of their masters, therefore all that I have written is thine by right. Nor do I petulantly claim these papers as my own, but defer all things to thy judgment; and whether thou grantest my petition or not, I pray God to grant thee all good things, and help thee to finish the good fight by an honourable course."

Such a petition, so just, so modest, and so free from the least tinge of insubordination might have been thought capable of touching the hardest heart, but, says Rudolf his biographer, "he sang to a stone." The building grievance at last grew to such a pitch, that the monks in despair appealed to Charlemagne, who summoned Ratgar to court to answer their charges, and appointed a commission of bishops and abbots to inquire into the whole matter. Their decision allayed the discord for a time, and so long as the emperor lived, Ratgar showed his monks some consideration. But no sooner was he dead than the persecution recommenced, and Rabanus, again deprived of his books and papers, seems to have consoled himself by making a pilgrimage to Jerusalem. He describes the unhappy state of Fulda at this time, in some very doleful verses addressed to one of the exiled monks; for, not content with overwhelming his brethren with fresh labours, Ratgar had turned many out of the monastery, chiefly the aged ones, whose temperate remonstrances annoyed him. We have in these verses a touching account of the farewell visit paid by the exiles before their departure to the tomb of St. Boniface, whom they conjured to intercede in their favour. Some of them did not rest content with a course of passive submission, but repaired once more to court and implored the Emperor Louis to apply some remedy to the abuses, which threatened to end in the disruption of the first religious house in his dominions. A new commission was therefore appointed, and the result was that Ratgar was deposed from office and banished from the monastery, while in his place was elected the holy and gentle St. Eigil, a disciple of St. Sturm, whose government presented a singular contrast to that of the harsh and haughty Ratgar. He did nothing without consulting his brethren, and made it his aim to heal the wounds which a long course of ill-treatment had opened in the community. To set his children an example of humility and paternal concord, he often served them at table, and especially during the feast of Christmas. In his overflowing love and charity, he petitioned, as a personal favour, that they would consent to the recall of poor Ratgar, and on his return it appeared that his humiliation had not been without a beneficial effect. He showed no disposition to disturb the peace of the community again, but as the twofold desire of commanding and of building was not wholly eradicted from his soul, they let him satisfy it in moderation, by constructing a small monastery on an adjoining hill, to which he afterwards removed himself. He seems to have made a good end, asking pardon of all those whom he had offended, and Fulda very soon recovered its former flourishing condition. Rabanus was restored to his books and his school immediately on the election of St. Eigil, and in 822, on the death of the good abbot, whose life was written by the monk Candidus, Rabanus was chosen his successor. To him this was a very sorrowful business, for, with the government of a community of one hundred and fifty monks on his hands, he was necessarily obliged to give up his scholars. He resigned them to the care of Candidus, in all that concerned the humane letters, reserving to himself, however, the interpretation of the Holy Scriptures. Singularly enough, however, the man whose whole life had been passed in literary labour, evinced a talent for business not always found united to great scholarship. He kept up regular discipline, and put all the offices of the abbey in a state of thorough efficiency, completing many of the half-finished buildings of Ratgar, and enriching his treasury with a vast quantity of holy relics. He also looked so well after the farms and dependencies of the abbey as greatly to increase its revenues. Still the school was not neglected, and the lectures he delivered there were destined to be the seeds of a work important in the history of ecclesiastical literature. His pupils had been accustomed from time to time to ask him questions on the chief duties of ecclesiastics and their signification, and the proper manner of administering the Rites of Holy Church. His answers they noted down on their tablets, without, however, observing much method, and as the matter constantly increased in bulk and value, they begged him at length to revise their notes and arrange them in better order. The result was his celebrated Treatise *De Institutione Clericorum*, an invaluable monument of the faith and practice of the Church in the ninth century. It treats in three books of the Sacraments, the Divine office, the feasts and fasts of the Church, and the learning necessary for ecclesiastics, concluding with instructions and rules for the guidance of preachers. On the last subject he observes that three things are necessary in order to become a good preacher; first, to be a good man yourself, that you may be able to teach others to be so; secondly, to be skilled in the Holy Scriptures and the interpretations of the Fathers; thirdly, and above all, to prepare for the work of preaching by that of prayer. As to the studies proper to ecclesiastics, he distinctly requires them to be learned not only in the Scriptures, but also in the seven liberal arts, provided only that these are treated as the handmaids of theology, and he explains his views on this subject much in the same way as Bede had done before him. For the rest, he was an enemy to anything like narrowness of intellectual training. His own works, in prose and verse, embraced a large variety of subjects, some of them belonging to mystic theology, such as his book on the Vision of God and his poem on the Holy Cross, which, in spite of its inaccurate prosody, still raises the admiration of the reader from the elevation of its sentiments. He is also commonly reputed the author of the "Veni Creator."

In 847, Rabanus was raised to the archiepiscopal see of Mentz, in which office he was called on to examine the errors of Gotteschalk, a man who, beginning life as a monk of Fulda, had quitted that monastery in disgust, and subsequently led a wandering and not very reputable life, though he appears to have considered himself attached to the monastery of Orbais. The opinions he broached on the subject of predestination being condemned by the council of Mentz, Rabanus sent him to his own metropolitan, Hincmar, Archbishop of Rheims. The severity with which he was treated was disapproved even by many who condemned his doctrines, and a warm controversy arose, in the course of which Hincmar, who was far more a man of action than of the pen, bethought himself of employing on his side of the argument the genius of Scotus Erigena, then at the head of the Palatine school. Erigena was as yet only known to the learned world as a Greek, Hebrew, and Arabic scholar, and a man of surpassing wit and power of argument. His heterodox tendencies were not even suspected, and Hincmar congratulated himself on having engaged the services of one confessedly without a rival in the arena of letters. But his choice of an ally proved most unfortunate. Erigena opened fire on the opposite party with the assertion, characteristic enough of the self-sufficient sophist, that every question, on every imaginable subject, was capable of solution when submitted to the four philosophic rules of division, definition, demonstration, and analysis. To work he went, therefore, with his four rules, and while combating the ultra-predestination of Gottischalk, gave utterance to such free opinions on the subject of Divine Grace as raised against him all the theologians of France. Among these were St. Prudentius of Troyes, Amolan, Archbishop of Lyons, a Hebrew scholar whose wise and moderate manner of dealing with the subject aimed at refuting the errors of both the opposite partisans, and his successor, St. Remigius. The opinions put forth by Scotus had increased the difficulties of the question, and writers thickened on both sides. It is needless to say that neither Rabanus nor Hincmar were any way responsible for the errors broached by Scotus; nevertheless, the line of argument which they took did not satisfy the theologians of Valence and Lyons, and in the course of the controversy which troubled his declining years, Rabanus found himself opposed by his former pupil, Lupus of Ferrières. He died in 856, leaving his books to be equally divided between the abbeys of Fulda and St. Alban's, of Mentz.

Meanwhile, Lupus of Ferrières had become abbot of his monastery, for Sigulf in his old age resigned his dignity, and chose to become the disciple of his former pupil. Lupus continued after his promotion to carry on his labours in the monastic school. The favour with which he was regarded by Charles the Bald was the occasion of much trouble to the poor scholar, who was constantly summoned to act as royal ambassador, and sometimes even to join the army and take part in active war. His monastery happened to be one of those which owed the king military service, and in an action fought in Angoumois between Charles and his nephew Pepin, Lupus, who had no taste at all for the life of a soldier, lost all his baggage and found himself a prisoner. So soon as he recovered his liberty he addressed a moving letter to the king, imploring him to set him free henceforth from his military engagements at any price. "Most willingly," he says, "will I resume the office of professor in my monastery, for I desire nothing better than all my life to teach what I have learnt." Charles appears to have seen that by persisting in his feudal claims he would only be making a very bad soldier out of an admirable scholar, so he suffered him to return to Ferrières, where he set about collecting a noble library, as well sacred as profane. As he wrote himself to Einard, he never grew weary of books; he took extraordinary pains in seeking for his treasures even in distant countries, in causing them to be transcribed, and sometimes in lovingly transcribing them himself. His interesting correspondence contains frequent allusions to these Bibliographical researches. At one time he asks a friend to bring him the "Wars of Catiline and of Jugurtha" by Sallust, and the "Verrines of Cicero." At another, he writes to Pope Benedict III., begging him to send by two of his monks, about to journey to Rome, certain books which he could not obtain in his own country, and which he promises to have speedily copied and faithfully returned. They are, the "Commentaries of St. Jerome on Jeremias," "Cicero de Oratore," the twelve books of Quinctilian's Institutes, and the "Commentary of Donatus on Terence." With all his taste for the classics, however, Lupus had too much good sense not to see the importance of cultivating the barbarous dialects, and sent his nephew with two other noble youths to Prom, to learn the Tudesque idiom.[92] In his school he made it his chief aim to train his pupils, not only in grammar and rhetoric, but also in the higher art of a holy life. The monastic seminaries were proverbially schools of good living as well as good learning, *recte faciendi et bene dicendi*, as Mabillon expresses it; and there was nothing that Lupus had more at heart than the inculcation of this principle, that the cultivation of head and heart must go together. "We too often seek in study," he writes in his epistle to the monk Ebradus, "nothing but ornament of style; few are found who desire to acquire by its means purity of manners, which is of far greater value. We are very much afraid of vices of language, and use every effort to correct them, but we regard with indifference the vices of the heart." His favourite Cicero had before his time lifted a warning voice against the capital error of disjoining mental from moral culture, and in the Christian system of the earlier centuries they were never regarded apart.

Lupus was not too great a scholar to condescend to labour for beginners, and drew up, for the benefit of his pupils, an abridgment of Roman history, in which he proposes the characters of Traian and Theodosius for the study of Christian princes. He was wont to boast of his double descent from Alcuin, as being a pupil of Sigulf and Rabanus, both of them disciples of the great master. His own favourite scholar Heiric, or Henry of Auxerre, indulged in a similar morsel of scholastic pride. He had studied under both Lupus and Haimo of Halberstadt, the former school-fellow of Rabanus, at St. Martin of Tours. Haimo seems to have lectured for some time at Ferrières, and Heiric tells us in some not inelegant verses that it was the custom of the two pedagogues to give their pupils a very pleasant sort of recreation, relating to them whatever they had found in the course of their reading that was worthy of remembrance, whether in Christian or Pagan authors. Heiric, who was somewhat of an intellectual glutton, and had a craving for learning of all sorts and on all imaginable subjects, made for himself a little book, in which he diligently noted down every scrap that fell from the lips of his masters. This book he subsequently published, and dedicated to Hildebold, Bishop of Auxerre. Heiric himself afterwards became a man of letters; he was appointed scholasticus of St. Germain's of Auxerre, and was intrusted with the education of Lothaire, son of Charles the Bald, as we learn from the epistle addressed to that monarch which he prefixed to his life of St. Germanus, in which he speaks of the young prince, recently dead, as in years a boy, but in mind a philosopher. Another of his pupils was the famous Remigius of Auxerre, who, towards the end of the ninth century, was summoned to Rheims by Archbishop Fulk, to re-establish sacred studies in that city, and worked there in concert with his former schoolfellow, Hucbald of St. Amand, who attained a curious sort of reputation by his poem on bald men, each line of which began with the letter C, the whole being intended as a compliment to Charles the Bald. Fulk himself became their first pupil, and after thoroughly restoring the school of Rheims, Remigius passed on to Paris, where we shall have occasion to notice him among the teachers of the tenth century. From his time the schools of Paris continued to increase in reputation and importance, till they developed into the great university which may thus be distinctly traced through a pedigree of learned men up to the great Alcuin himself. This genealogy of pedagogues is of no small interest, as showing the efforts made in the worst of times to keep alive the spark of science and the persistence with which, in spite of civil wars and Norman invasions, the scholastic traditions of Alcuin were maintained.

We must not take leave of abbot Lupus without noticing one other pupil of his, more celebrated than any yet named, the great St. Ado of Vienne. He studied in the school of Ferrières under Sigulf, Aldric and Lupus, and from his school life his masters predicted his future sanctity. The jealousy of his companions obliging him to leave Ferrières, he removed to Prom, and placed himself under the discipline of the good abbot Marcward, and there taught the sacred sciences for some years, after which he found himself able to return to Ferrières. During the course of a journey into Italy he met with an ancient martyrology, which served as the basis on which he compiled his own, which was published in 858. Two years later he became Archbishop of Vienne, and in that office did much for the promotion of letters. The scholars of these dark ages were often bound together in ties of very close friendship, founded on mutual tastes, the recollection of early school days spent together under some wise and well-loved master, and the exchange of good offices in the shape of manuscripts lent and borrowed. If Ado's intellectual superiority had made him enemies among a few of the more churlish spirits of Ferrières, his sweet and amiable disposition elsewhere earned him many friends. Among these was the Deacon Wandalbert, a monk of Prom, and the learned Florus of Lyons. When Ado left Prom, Wandalbert succeeded him as scholasticus, and a famous one he made. His peculiar line was natural philosophy, and in pursuing it he was not content with gathering up other men's ideas, but observed and experimentalised for himself. He greatly excelled in poetry, and produced a martyrology written in verse, in which, besides hymns in honour of the different saints whom he commemorates, he contrives to introduce short poems descriptive of the seasons, the different rustic labours proper to each month, the beauties of nature under her different aspects, seed-time and harvest, the vintage and the chase; together with other more learned subjects, such as the movements of the heavenly bodies by which we regulate our time. He gives rules for telling the time by the length of shadow cast by the sun, though he is careful to remind the reader that these rules will not be the same in all countries, inasmuch as in those that lie more to the south the shadows will necessarily be shorter, the earth being then more directly under the solar rays.

We must now turn to the great abbey of Old Corby, where, as we have already seen, Adalhard, a Palatine scholar, and a prince of the blood-royal, had retired from the perils of a courtier's life, and become abbot. Unusual importance attached to its monastic school, from the circumstance of its having been chosen by Charlemagne as the academy to which the youth of Saxony were sent for education, in order that on their return to their own country they might assist in planting the Church on a solid foundation. The master chosen for the task of rearing these future missionaries was Paschasius Radpert, one of the most remarkable men of his time. Originally of very humble birth, he owed his education to the charity of the nuns of Soissons, who first received the desolate child into their own out-quarters, and then sent him to some monks in the same city, under whose tuition he acquired a fair amount of learning, and addicted himself to the study of Virgil, Horace, Cicero, and Terence. He never forgot the kindness of his early benefactresses, and in after years dedicated his Treatise on the Virginity of the Blessed Virgin to the good nuns, styling himself therein their *alumnus*, or foster-son. The deep humility of this great scholar is spoken of by all his biographers as his characteristic virtue, and is apparent in a passage which occurs in his exposition of the 44th Psalm, which he dedicates to these same nuns. In it he refers to the fact of his having received the clerical tonsure in their Church, and, as it would seem, in their presence. After expressing the reverence he feels for those whose names are written in heaven, and whom he regards not only as the spouses of Christ, but as the choicest flowers in the garden of the Church, he goes on to say: "When I behold you I sigh bitterly to think that this sacred crown, which as a boy I received before the holy altar of the Mother of God, in the midst of your prayers and offices of praise, I lost long ago, exiled in the world's wilderness, and stained by many worldly actions.... I pray you, therefore, when you lift up your hearts on high, be mindful of me also, and implore for me the divine grace, that the most clement Judge may restore to me my lost crown." In fact, after receiving the tonsure in early youth, Paschasius, whose tastes for Terence and Cicero rather predominated at that time over his relish for more sacred studies, abandoned his first inclination for the cloister, and lived for some years a secular life. Touched at last by divine grace, he entered the abbey of Old Corby, and there made his profession under the abbot Adalhard. All the ardour he had previously shown in the pursuit of profane literature he now applied to the study of the Divine Scriptures. Yet he only devoted to study of any kind those "furtive hours," as he calls them, which he was able to steal from the duties of regular discipline, and was never seen so happy as when engaged in the choral office or the meaner occupations of community life.

Such, then, was the master chosen by Adalhard for the responsible office of scholasticus, and a very minute account is left us of his manner of discharging its duties. Every day he delivered lectures on the sacred sciences, besides preaching to the monks on Sundays and Festivals. His thorough familiarity with the best Latin authors appears from the frequent allusions to them which occur in his writings. Quotations from the classic poets drop from his pen, as it were, half unconsciously, and we are told that he continued to keep up his acquaintance with them, so far as was necessary for teaching others. But his own study was now chiefly confined to the Holy Scriptures and the Fathers;[93] and among the latter, his favourites were St. Augustine, St. Jerome, St. Ambrose, St. John Chrysostom, St. Bede, and St. Gregory the Great. "He did not approve," says his biographer, "of the diligence displayed by some men of the time in explaining and meditating on profane authors." In a passage which occurs in the preface to his exposition of St. Matthew's Gospel, he blames those lovers of secular learning, "who seek various and divers expounders, that so they may attain to the understanding of beautiful lies concerning shameful things, and who will not pass over—I do not say a single page, but a single line or syllable, without thoroughly investigating it, with the utmost labour and vigilance, while at the same time they utterly neglect the Sacred Scriptures. I wonder," he continues, "that the Divine words can be so distasteful to them, and that they can refuse to scrutinise the mysteries of God with the same diligence they so unweariedly bestow on the follies of profane tragedies and the foolish fables of the poets. Who can doubt that such labour is altogether thrown away, being bestowed on a thing undeserving of reward?" This was not the utterance of a narrow-minded bigot, who condemned pursuits and tastes to which he was himself a stranger. Few were more keenly alive than he to the charms of polite literature, neither did he at all condemn its use within proper limits, even among cloistered students. It would, indeed, have been a difficult matter to have eradicated the love of the beautiful from the heart of Paschasius. He possessed it in every shape, and was not merely a poet, but a musician also. In one of his writings he lets fall an observation which might be taken for a prose rendering of a verse of Shelley's, although the Christian scholar goes beyond the infidel poet, and does not merely describe the sentiment which all have felt, but traces it to its proper source. Shelley complains that—

Our sincerest laughter

With some pain is fraught;

Our sweetest songs are those that tell of saddest thought.

Paschasius explains the mystery: "There is no song to be found," he says, "without a tone of sadness in it; even as here below there are no joys without a mixture of sorrow; for songs of pure joy belong only to the heavenly Sion, but lamentation is the property of our earthly pilgrimage." His musical tastes were perfectly shared and understood by his master St. Adalhard, whose sensibility to the influence of melodious sounds is spoken of by his biographer Gerard. Even during his residence at the court of Charlemagne, it is said of him that "he was always so full of a sweet intention towards God, that if while assisting at the royal council he heard the sound of some chance melody, he had it not in his power to refrain from tears, for all sweet music seemed to remind him of his heavenly country." The importance attached to the study of music by the Christian scholastics of these times is not a little remarkable. They inherited the traditions of the ancients, and with them regarded music as a science intimately associated with the knowledge of divine things. They were the true descendants of those holy fathers of old, who, as the son of Sirach tells us, "sought out musical tunes and published canticles, and were rich in virtue, studying beautifulness, and living at peace in their houses." The narratives of our early English schools will sufficiently have illustrated the fact that music held a very prominent place in the system of education which held sway in the early centuries; and the theory on which this high esteem was based will nowhere be found better explained than in the writings of Rabanus. "Musical discipline," he says, "is so noble and useful a thing, that without it no one can properly discharge the ecclesiastical office. For whatsoever in reading is correctly pronounced, and whatsoever in chanting is sweetly modulated, is regulated by a knowledge of this discipline; and by it we not only learn how to read and sing in the church, but also rightly perform every rite in the divine service. Moreover, the discipline of music is diffused through all the acts of our life. For when we keep the commandments of God, and observe His law, it is certain that our words and acts are associated by musical rhythm with the virtues of harmony. If we observe a good conversation, we prove ourselves associated with this discipline; but when we act sinfully, we have in us no music."[94]

Paschasius, then, was a poet and a musician, but he was also a scientific theologian, and one who was in some degree in advance of his age in the philosophic method he adopted when analysing the dogmas of faith. In the year 831 he wrote his famous treatise on the "Sacrament of the Altar," which was specially intended for the instruction of his Saxon pupils, who required a plain and comprehensive exposition of that mystery. He composed it, therefore, in a very simple style, comparing it to "milk for babes;" and it is evident that in a treatise drawn up under such circumstances, for the instruction of young converts, the author would necessarily seek, not the setting forth of theological subtleties or private views, but the simple, straightforward statement of the Church's doctrine as universally taught and believed by all the faithful. He declares in very express and distinct terms that "the *substance of bread* is not to be found in the Sacrament, and that there is present only the Real Body of Jesus Christ, the same that was born of the B. Virgin, and was crucified, and rose again, and ascended into Heaven."[95] The treatise was dedicated to Warin, abbot of New Corby, and excited no controversy until fifteen years later, when a second edition, dedicated to Charles the Bald, fell into the hands of Scotus Erigena, whose captious mind found matter of offence in the expressions used by Paschasius. He, accordingly, wrote in reply *his* treatise on the "Holy Eucharist," of which no copy now exists; for, after being condemned by several Councils, all the copies that could be found were ordered to be burnt in 1059, in consequence of the use made of them by the Berengarian heretics. Paschasius defended his words by a simple appeal to the universal sense of Christendom, which, since the days of the Apostles, had never ceased to believe and confess this salutary doctrine.

At the time when this vexatious controversy broke out he was abbot of his monastery, and soon after retired from office, and joyfully returned to his cell and his studies, spending his last days in the completion of his greatest work, the "Commentary on St. Matthew's Gospel." Whether in public or private life, his lowliness of spirit was equally remarkable, while the self-sufficient presumption of his opponent Erigena exhibits an ugly example of that knowledge which puffeth up. In Paschasius we see the opposite virtue, which faileth not "when tongues shall cease and knowledge shall be destroyed." He styled himself by no more honourable title than the "Monachorum Peripsema," and in his last sickness imposed so strict an injunction on his brethren never to write his life, that they dared not disobey him, and thus many interesting particulars concerning him have necessarily been lost.

He left many disciples, among whom was Anscharius, who succeeded him in the government of his school, and of whom we must now say something. He had begun his school life very early, being sent to the monastery after his mother's death, when a child of only five; and, says his biographer, Rembert, after the manner of young children, he showed at first a much greater liking for childish sports than for learning of any kind. At five this may perhaps be thought excusable, but there are those whom wisdom preventeth, and when they go forth they find her "sitting at their door." And to Anscharius the love of wisdom was brought by Her who is herself "the Mother of fair love, and of fear, and of knowledge, and of holy hope; in whom is all grace of the way and of the truth, all hope of life and of virtue." One night he seemed to find himself in a dark and gloomy place, out of which, when he sought to find some way of escape, he perceived a delightful path wherein Our Lady appeared to him surrounded by a crowd of saints clothed in white garments, among whom he recognised his mother. He ran towards her, stretching out his childish hands; whereupon the Blessed Virgin addressed him, saying: "My son, do you wish to come to your mother? Know that if you would share in her happiness you must fly from vanity, lay aside childish follies, and abide in holiness of life. For we detest all vice and idleness; neither can they who delight in such things be joined to our company."

From this time Anscharius changed his conduct: he applied himself to his tasks, and spent his whole time in reading and meditation, and acquiring useful arts; so that his companions wondered at a change the cause of which was unknown to them. As he grew in years he was favoured with other heavenly visions, which I notice here, because it is often said, and doubtless with much truth, that the occupations of study and teaching have in them a direct tendency to dry up the sources of devotion. When, therefore, in studying the history of these ancient Christian schools we find among their teachers a succession of saints, and even of contemplatives, who enjoyed the most intimate communications with God, and were distinguished by the highest supernatural gifts, one cannot but ask wherein the difference lay; what divine secret they possessed enabling them to keep the sweet fountain of holy tears from drying up, so that they seem to have been wholly unconscious of the existence of any danger to the spiritual life in the occupations of study or teaching, and regarded such duties as in themselves spiritual. Possibly their safeguard lay in those happy *retinacula* of religious life of which St. Bede speaks, and which, as we have seen, were regarded as their first object even by scholars like Rabanus and Paschasius, who devoted to study only the "furtive hours" not claimed by prayer and obedience. And hence they created a tradition which was kept up in the Christian schools down to a far later period, the grand principle of which was to interweave spiritual with intellectual employment, and by timely interruptions, prevent the whole nature from being poured out over its mental work. In what manner this was effected in the collegiate foundations of the Middle Ages we shall have occasion to show hereafter; it is sufficient here to remind the reader that such a system was naturally supplied by the discipline of religious life in those cloistered schools which were the nurseries of Christian education. And the result was that the monastic teachers were something very unlike the modern notion of schoolmasters; they were not mere men of the rod and the grammar; and it cannot but strike us as remarkable how almost universally they are spoken of as enjoying, in a very special degree, the gift of prayer. This was preeminently the case with St. Anscharius, and some of his visions are related by his biographer, Rembert, who had heard them in confidence from his own lips. He mentions one remarkable revelation received by the saint in the early part of his religious life, whence he understood that he was to be called to preach the faith to heathen nations. Some of these supernatural incidents are related as mixed up with ordinary details of his life in the schools. While he was scholasticus of Old Corby it was his invariable custom, says Rembert, when going to and returning from the school, to turn aside into a little oratory dedicated to St. John the Baptist, and there pray awhile in secret. On one such occasion when he rose from his knees he saw standing at the entrance One clothed after the Jewish fashion, beautiful in countenance, from whose eyes went forth a Divine light. Recognising it to be our Lord Anscharius prostrated at His feet, but in a sweet voice He bid him rise, saying, "Confess thy sins, Anscharius, that thou mayst receive pardon." "What need is there, O Lord," said Anscharius, "that I should tell them to Thee, seeing that Thou knowest them all?" But he replied, "I know them, indeed, nevertheless I would have thee confess them that thou mayst be justified." Anscharius accordingly declared all the sins he had ever committed since his childhood, and was consoled by the assurance that he had received their full remission. About the same time, continues Rembert, it happened that one of his little scholars, named Fulbert, received a blow with a slate from another lad, of so serious a nature that within a few days he died. When the accident was made known to Anscharius, the good master was overwhelmed with anguish at the thought of such a mischance having befallen a child committed to his care. During the time that Fulbert continued to linger, Anscharius never left his bedside, till at last, wearied out with sorrow and long watching, they persuaded him to take some repose. He fell into a heavy slumber, in which he was consoled by a gracious vision. He seemed to see the dear child carried up to heaven by the hands of the angels, and placed in the company of the martyrs; and, wondering at the sight, it was explained to him that because Fulbert had borne his wound with great patience, and had heartily loved and forgiven him from whom he had received the injury, and had prayed much for him, accepting his own premature death with loving submission to the Divine will, his sweetness and resignation had deserved from the Divine compassion so great a reward as to be placed among the holy martyrs. Anscharius was still absorbed in the joy of this revelation when he was roused by Witmar, a younger monk associated with him in the government of the school, who came to tell him that even at that very moment Fulbert had expired. He found that Anscharius already knew it, and doubtless, adds Rembert, this comfort had been given him by God that he might not grieve overmuch for the death of the child, but might rather rejoice at the happy state of his soul.

Anscharius was one of those chosen to colonise the monastery of New Corby, the mention of which requires a few words of explanation. The foundation of this daughter-house was the great work of St. Adalhard, who so soon as his young Saxons were sufficiently trained in learning and monastic discipline, consulted them on the possibility of their obtaining a suitable site for a foundation in their native land. After many difficulties had been raised and overcome, ground was procured, and the building of the abbey was begun. Adalhard repaired thither to superintend operations in company with Paschasius and his own brother Wala, who, brought up like himself as a soldier and a courtier, had in former years held military command in Saxony and won the affections of the people by his wise and gentle rule. When the Saxons saw their old governor among them again in the monastic habit, nothing could exceed their wonder and delight: they ran after him in crowds, looking at him, and feeling him with their hands to satisfy themselves that it was really he, paying no attention whatever to the presence of the abbot or any other of his companions. The first stone of the new abbey was laid on September 26, 822; Old Corby made over to the new colony all the lands held by the community in Saxony; the Emperor Louis gave them a charter, and some precious relics from his private chapel, and in a few years that great seminary was completed which was destined to carry the light of faith and science to the pagan natives of the farther North. It would be hard to say which of the two Corbies held the highest place in monastic history; a noble emulation existed between them, each trying to outstrip the other in the perfection of monastic discipline. New Corby, in her turn became the mother-house of a vast number of German colonies, over all of which she continued to maintain a certain superiority. A law was made obliging every abbot of these branch-houses to keep a chronicle of his monastery and send a copy of it to the Corby library; and by another law, every novice on the day of his profession was bound to present to the library some useful book. The library of new Corby grew to be one of great value and importance, and its catalogue, still preserved, exhibits the names of not a few Arabic and Hebrew works. It was here also that in the days of Leo X. was disinterred the famous manuscript of Tacitus, which may still be seen at Florence.

A monastery that cared so much for the formation of its library was not likely to be indifferent to its school. It was the boast of both Corbies in turns to possess Anscharius as their scholasticus, "that great preceptor," as Mabillon calls him, for his reputation as a master was spread over all Germany. He was at the same time appointed to preach to the people, an office particularly agreeable to that apostolic spirit which he had never ceased to nurture in his heart. The time was approaching when the prophetic vision of former years, and the secret instincts of his own soul, were to be accomplished. In 826 Harold, king of Denmark, having embraced the faith, and been baptized with great pomp at Mentz, petitioned the Emperor Louis to give him some holy missionaries, who might accompany him home to Denmark, and plant the Church in that country. Wala, then abbot of New Corby, fixed on Anscharius, and he, mindful of the revelation which had long before assured to him the glory of an apostolic career, joyfully accepted the mission, heedless alike of the criticism of friends and enemies, who all found something to say against it. Anscharius turned a deaf ear to their reasonings and remonstrances, and withdrew to a certain vineyard in the neighbourhood of Aix-la-Chapelle, where he prepared for his new duties by a kind of spiritual retreat. Here he was sought out and discovered by a monk of Old Corby, named Aubert, and thinking that his visitor had only come to pester him with more advice, Anscharius bade him spare himself the trouble of arguing the question, as he had irrevocably made up his mind. "You have nothing to fear from me," said Aubert, "my only reason for coming to you, is to beg you to accept me as your companion, if the abbot Wala can be brought to give his consent." Anscharius joyfully welcomed him as a fellow labourer, and they soon after set out in company with the king. His majesty, however, was more than half a barbarian, and the equipment he provided for his missioners was not luxurious. The royal and ecclesiastical retinue embarked on board a very dirty boat, the only accommodation on board consisting of two miserable cabins in which king and missioners were packed together with very little ceremony. However, they arrived at last at their journey's end, and began their labours by opening a little school in Friesland, where they received twelve children, among whom were the two sons of king Harold himself. A little later we find them passing on to Sweden, attacked on the way by pirates, and robbed of all their baggage, containing their library of forty books. Such were the humble beginnings of a great apostolate, which at its close found Anscharius Archbishop of Hamburgh, and papal legate, not only over the Scandinavian kingdoms, but also over Iceland and the distant shores of Greenland, which are expressly named in the Bull of Pope Gregory IV. One of the most successful means adopted by the saint for the propagation of the faith, was the purchase of young Danes who were offered for sale as slaves, and whom he then sent to Corby, whence, after receiving a Christian education, they returned to their own country as zealous missionaries.

It would take us too long, and probably prove but wearisome to the reader, were we to examine in detail the foundation and history of all the monastic schools of this period. Glance where we will, we shall find indications of the same intellectual activity struggling to make head against the darkness of a semi-barbarous age. The schools of Hirschau, Hirsfield, Fleury, and Prom, might all be made to furnish illustrations of the ardour with which scientific and literary pursuits were carried on by their scholars. But while passing over these and others, which have almost equal claims on our interest, it is impossible to leave without notice two houses whose preeminent importance in the history of monastic studies has made their names especially venerable: I mean the abbeys of Reichnau, and St. Gall. The first foundation of St. Gall's belongs indeed to a date far earlier than that of which we are now treating: it owed its origin to St. Gall, the Irish disciple of St. Columbanus, who, in the seventh century, penetrated into the recesses of the Helvetian mountains and there fixed his abode in the midst of a pagan population. Under the famous abbot St. Othmar, who flourished in the time of Pepin, the monks received the Benedictine rule, and from that time the monastery rapidly grew in fame and prosperity, so that in the ninth century it was regarded as the first religious house north of the Alps. It is with a sigh of that irrepressible regret called forth by the remembrance of a form of beauty that is dead and gone for ever, that the monastic historian hangs over the early chronicles of St. Gall. It lay in the midst of the savage Helvetian wilderness, an oasis of piety and civilisation. Looking down from the craggy mountains, the passes of which open upon the southern extremity of the lake of Constance, the traveller would have stood amazed at the sudden apparition of that vast range of stately buildings which almost filled up the valley at his feet. Churches and cloisters, the offices of a great abbey, buildings set apart for students and guests, workshops of every description, the forge, the bakehouse, and the mill, or rather mills, for there were ten of them, all in such active operation, that they every year required ten new millstones; and then the house occupied by the vast numbers of artisans and workmen attached to the monastery gardens too, and vineyards creeping up the mountain slopes, and beyond them fields of waving corn, and sheep speckling the green meadows, and far away boats busily plying on the lake and carrying goods and passengers— what a world it was of life and activity; yet how unlike the activity of a town! It was, in fact, not a town, but a house,—a family presided over by a father, whose members were all knit together in the bonds of common fraternity. I know not whether the spiritual or the social side of such a religious colony were most fitted to rivet the attention. Descend into the valley, and visit all these nurseries of useful toil, see the crowds of rude peasants transformed into intelligent artisans, and you will carry away the impression that the monks of St. Gall had found out the secret of creating a world of happy Christian factories. Enter their church and listen to the exquisite modulations of those chants and sequences peculiar to the abbey which boasted of possessing the most scientific school of music in all Europe; visit their scriptorium, their library, and their school, or the workshop where the monk Tutilo is putting the finishing touch to his wonderful copper images, and his fine altar frontals of gold and jewels, and you will think yourself in some intellectual and artistic academy. But look into the choir, and behold the hundred monks who form the community at their midnight office and you will forget everything, save the saintly aspect of those servants of God who shed abroad over the desert around them the good odour of Christ, and are the apostles of the provinces which own their gentle sway. You may quit the circuit of the abbey and plunge once more into the mountain region which rises beyond, but you will have to wander far before you find yourself beyond the reach of its softening, humanising influence. Here are distant cells and hermitages with their chapels, where the shepherds come for early mass; or it may be that there meets you, winding over the mountain paths of which they sing so sweetly,[96] going up and down among the hills into the thick forests and the rocky hollows, a procession of the monks carrying their relics, and followed by a peasant crowd. In the schools you may have been listening to lectures in the learned, and even in the Eastern tongues; but in the churches, and here among the mountains, you will hear these fine classical scholars preaching plain truths, in barbarous idioms, to a rude race, who before the monks came among them sacrificed to the Evil One, and worshipped stocks and stones.

Yet, hidden away as it was among its crags and deserts, the abbey of St. Gall's was almost as much a place of resort as Rome or Athens—at least to the learned world of the ninth century. Her schools were a kind of university, frequented by men of all nations, who came hither to fit themselves for all professions. You would have found here not monks alone and future scholastics, but courtiers, soldiers, and the sons of kings. The education given was very far from being exclusively intended for those aspiring to the ecclesiastical state; it had a large admixture of the secular element, at any rate in the exterior school. Not only were the Sacred sciences taught with the utmost care, but the classic authors were likewise explained; Cicero, Horace, Virgil, Lucan, and Terence were read by the scholars, and none but the very little boys presumed to speak in any tongue but Latin. The subjects for their original compositions were mostly taken from Scripture and Church history, and having written their exercises they were expected to recite them, the proper tones being indicated by musical notes. Many of the monks excelled as poets, others cultivated painting and sculpture, and other exquisite cloistral arts; all diligently applied to the grammatical formation of the Tudesque dialect and rendered it capable of producing a literature of its own. Their library in the eighth century was only in its infancy, but gradually became one of the richest in the world. They were in correspondence with all the learned monastic houses of France and Italy, from whom they received the precious codex, now of a Virgil or a Livy, now of the Sacred Books and sometimes of some rare treatise on medicine or astronomy. They were Greek students, moreover, and those most addicted to the cultivation of the "Cecropian Muse" were denominated the "fratres Ellenici." The beauty of their early manuscripts is praised by all authors, and the names of their best transcribers find honourable mention in their annals. They manufactured their own parchment out of the hides of the wild beasts that roamed through the mountains and forests around them, and prepared it with such skill that it acquired a peculiar delicacy. Many hands were employed on a single manuscript. Some made the parchment, others drew the fair red lines, others wrote on the pages thus prepared; more skilful hands put in the gold and the initial letters, and more learned heads compared the copy with the original text, this duty being generally discharged during the interval between matins and lauds, the daylight hours being reserved for actual transcription. Erasure, when necessary, was rarely made with the knife, but an erroneous word was delicately drawn through by the pen, so as not to spoil the beauty of the codex. Lastly came the binders, who enclosed the whole in boards of wood cramped with ivory or iron, the Sacred Volumes being covered with plates of gold and adorned with jewels.

In such a school it was no wonder that the pupils of St. Gall, like those of Eton, became famous for their good writing. Ekhehard I. had a method in this as in everything else; if he found a boy dull over his grammar he set him to copy; arguing that nature was an economist in her gifts, and did not dispense all to all; and that often where the head was somewhat slow in learning, the deficiency was made up by an extra dexterity with the fingers. But boys were never employed on the Gospels, or Church service books, these being reserved for men of perfect age, who would bring greater care to their responsible task. We have even the copy ordinarily set for beginners in the monastic scriptorium, a doggerel line, introducing every letter of the alphabet:

"Adnexique globum Zephyrique Kanna secabant."

That the labour of transcription was often exceedingly irksome, is evident from sundry notes scattered over these manuscripts. "As the sick man desireth health," writes one, "even so doth the transcriber desire the end of his volume." Another contents himself with the laconic observation, "written with great trouble;" but a third, who may be supposed to have been employed over a very tough copy, breaks out into verse, and exclaims at his last page:

"Libro completo

Saltat scriptor pede læto."

The monks of St. Gall were no less famous for their music than for their painting. Their musical tastes were inherited probably from their Irish founders, and were further improved by the teaching of those Roman cantors, whom we have seen in a former page sent into France, at Charlemagne's request, to civilise the barbarous singing of his Frankish cantors. On their way back into Italy, one of them, to whom the St. Gall historians give the name of Romanus, was attacked by fever, and stopping at the Swiss monastery, was there charitably entertained and nursed by the brethren, who had excellent doctors among them. In return, he taught them the Roman chant, and bestowed on them the identical antiphonarium he had brought from Rome, making a certain case or instrument to contain it. "And to this day," writes Ekhehard, "if there is any dispute about the singing, the error may be detected by consulting this book." Moreover, this Romanus was the first who thought of assigning the letters of the alphabet to the musical notes, a system which Notker Balbulus afterwards explained, and which, being further elucidated by a certain friend of his named Lambert, was adopted throughout Germany.[97]

Leaving a more particular notice of the studies and students of this great abbey for a future chapter, I must here add a few words on another religious house, the history of which is closely associated with that of St. Gall, and where the sciences flourished in equal perfection under the shelter of those lofty mountains which shut out the tumult of the world and the incursions of the barbarians. At the western extremity of the lake of Constance, just where it narrows towards the outlet of the Rhine, lies a green island sparkling like an emerald gem on the unruffled surface of the waters. There, half hidden amid the luxuriant foliage, you may still see the grey minster of that famous abbey called Augia by its Latin historians, but better known by its German name of Reichnau. Walafrid Strabo, the pupil of Rabanus and the chief chronicler of his time, was abbot of Reichnau in the ninth century, and in one of his poems has painted its situation in very exact terms. He gives the succession of abbots from St. Pirminius, who first established himself in the island in the reign of Pepin, and shows that the school was one of the very earliest which had at that time attained celebrity. I have already spoken of Walafrid's fame as a master, but I cannot here omit mentioning his pupil and biographer, Ermenric, who has made himself known to us by a letter which he wrote after paying what seems to have been a very pleasant visit at St. Gall's. Walafrid had sent him there for a holiday, and on his return he expressed the enjoyment it had given him, in an epistle addressed to abbot Grimoald. As soon as he crossed the lake, he says, he found himself welcomed by a group of illustrious men. "There," he continues, "I found each one humbler and more patient than his fellow. I saw neither envy nor jealousy, but all were bound together with the triple chord of charity, simplicity, and concord. How shall I speak of the generosity of Engilbert, or the kindness of that most clever brother Hartmod? It would be impossible for me to do justice to the excellence which these servants of God had attained in so many of the arts, but you may judge of the birds by looking at the nests which they inhabit. Examine their cloister and you will agree with what I say. What else can I call Winhart but a second Dædalus? or Isenric but another Beseleel? for indeed the graving tool is never out of his hand, save when he stands at the altar to exercise his sacred ministry. And yet there is such humility among them that no one disdains the humblest employment, remembering those words of Scripture, 'the prayer of the humble shall pierce the clouds.'"

Reichnau, however, had its own line of great masters, among whom Ermenric, who could do such generous justice to the excellence of others, was himself worthy to be reckoned. The most illustrious was, perhaps, the cripple Hermann Contractus, originally a pupil of St. Gall's, who is said to have prayed that he might not regain the use of his limbs, but that he might receive instead a knowledge of the Scriptures. He was master of Latin, Greek, Hebrew, and Arabic; he wrote treatises on history, poetry, ethics, astronomy, and mathematics; he calculated eclipses, and explained Aristotle, and, in spite of an impediment in his speech, his lectures were so learned that he had pupils from the most distant provinces of Italy. He set his own poems to music, made clocks and organs, and was as much revered for his sanctity as his universal genius. Many hymns and antiphons used by the Church are attributed to his pen, among others the *Alma Redemptoris*. But if Hermann was the most famous scholar of Reichnau, a yet greater celebrity, though of a different kind, attaches to the name of Meinrad. The story of his vocation to the eremitical life affords an apt illustration of the contemplative character already noticed as so frequently belonging to the early pedagogues: and as it presents us with an agreeable picture of a "whole play-day" in the Dark Ages, we will give it as it stands in the pages of the monk Berno. Meinrad was the son of a Swabian nobleman of the house of Hollenzollern, and had studied in the monastic school under abbot Hatto and his own uncle Erlebald. When the latter became abbot he appointed Meinrad to the care of the school which was attached to a smaller house dependent on Reichnau, and situated at a spot called Bollingen, on the lake of Zurich. He accordingly removed thither, and had singular success with his scholars, whom he inspired with great affection by reason of his gentle discipline. He used to take them out for walking parties and fishing parties, into what Berno, his biographer, calls "the wilderness," a wilderness, however, which was adorned with a majestic beauty to which Meinrad was not insensible. One day he and his boys crossed the lake in a small boat, and landing on the opposite shore sought for some quiet spot where they might cast their fishing lines. Finding a little stream which flowed into the lake and gave good promise of trout, Meinrad left them to pursue their sport and strolled about, meditating on the joys of that solitary life after which he secretly pined. After a while, returning to his scholars, he found that their fishing had been unusually successful, and taking up their baskets, they retraced their steps to the village of Altendorf, where they entered the house of a certain matron to rest and refresh themselves with food. Whilst the boys ate and drank, and enjoyed themselves in their own way, Meinrad and their hostess engaged in conversation, and Meinrad, who was full of the thoughts to which his mountain walk had given rise, opened his whole heart to her. "Beyond all riches," he said, "I desire to dwell alone in this solitude that so I might wholly give myself to prayer, could I but find some one who would minister to me in temporal things." The good lady immediately offered to provide him with whatever he wanted, in order to carry out his design; and the result of that day's fishing-party was the establishment of the former scholasticus of Bollingen in a little hermitage which he constructed for himself out of the wattled boughs of trees. But he found himself in one way disappointed; he had sought the desert to fly from the world, and the world followed him thither in greater throngs than he had ever encountered at Reichnau. The saints possess a strange power of attraction, and neither mountains nor forests are able to hide them. In his own day men compared St. Meinrad to the Baptist, because the multitudes went out into the wilderness to hear him preach penance and remission of sins. For seven years he continued to dispense the Word of Life to the pilgrims who gathered about him from all parts of Europe. But one day unable to resist his longing for retreat, he took his image of Our Lady, a missal, a copy of St. Benedict's rule, and the works of Cassian, and laden with these, his only treasures, he plunged into the forest, and choosing a remote and secluded spot erected a rude chapel which he dedicated to Our Lady, and a yet ruder dwelling for himself. There he lived for thirty years, and at the end of that time he was assassinated in his hermitage by some ruffians who hoped to find some hidden treasure in his cell. His body was carried back to Reichnau, and in after years the great sanctuary of Einsidlen rose over the site of his hermitage, where is still venerated the image of Our Lady which he had formerly carried thither with his own hands.

We are now in a position to form some idea of the real character of these early monastic schools, and of the teaching which they conveyed. From the eighth to the twelfth century, the scholastic system underwent so little change, that we may select our illustrations indifferently from any part of that period, without risk of inaccuracy.

First, then, as to the schoolroom itself. In most cases the interior or claustral schools of monasteries and cathedrals were held in the cloisters. A strange contrast, indeed, to the luxurious requirements of modern times; but boarded floors, patent stoves, and easy-backed forms were luxuries undreamt of by the hardy Frankish or Gothic students who studied under Walafrid or Rabanus. It is not until the fifteenth century that we meet with a document hinting at the novelty of providing schoolrooms with boarded floors.[98] The cloisters of York and Worcester, now so desolate and deserted, were once peopled with a busy race of scholars, who probably suffered often enough, like the pupils of Bede, from stiffened fingers and bleeding cracks. Even so late as the twelfth century, the schools of Paris were held in the cloisters of Nôtre Dame, and only removed thence when the repose of the canons was disturbed by the unruly crowds who rushed to listen to the lectures of Abelard. The number of scholars received into a monastery varied according to its size. At St. Riquier, where there were 300 monks, abbot Angilbert wished never to have less than a hundred children, the sons of dukes, counts, and kings.[99] They were seldom or never left alone, and in the cloister or schoolroom the master's seat was so arranged, that all were under his eye. It does not seem, however, that the surveillance in school-hours was carried out with any excessive rigidity, for we find frequent notice of the pranks and surreptitious consumption of good things perpetrated by the school boys in the temporary absence of their masters. In the dormitories, however, the discipline was more strict; there the lamp was kept constantly burning, and though there are no traces of an odious espionage, there is evidence of a constant, ever present vigilance. Awaked in the morning by the wooden signal board of the master, the children were conducted to the lavatory by the "pedagogues" or junior assistants of the school. These pedagogues were very numerous, and their duties were various. Among other things it belonged to them to see to the cleanliness and neatness of dress and person, a thing not at all despised in the Dark Ages. At Cluny, where in the twelfth century all the older monastic traditions of school discipline were resumed and perfected, it was not permitted for the children to sit together on benches, but each one had his own little box, in which he kept his writing materials, and which also served him for a seat. A midday siesta was allowed at Cluny, but no one was permitted to read or write on his bed.[100] In all these regulations may plainly be seen a solicitude for order and good morals, together with a certain tone of refinement, which is more than we should expect, and which satisfies us how profoundly the whole subject of education had been studied by the medieval masters. Their ideas on the subject of punishment were in more simple accordance with those of Solomon than our fastidious age would approve. The rod, in fact, was so very generally used, that under the form of the ferule it afterwards became the badge of the bachelor in arts, and was solemnly delivered to him when he took his degree. Medieval schoolboys were not more fond of a flogging than those of later growth, and to escape it the scholars of St. Gall once adopted the extraordinary expedient of setting fire to the monastery. Yet with all this austerity of discipline, nothing is more certain than that the monastic masters possessed the secret of making themselves beloved, and that the love which they inspired was not the less familiar because mingled with respect. I may add, that at Cluny, though flogging was permitted, boxing on the ears was strictly prohibited, apparently with the view of allowing no indulgence to the irritated feelings of the master. Punishment, like everything else at Cluny, was administered in an orderly and methodical manner; in fact, the peculiar excellence of the Cluniacs lay in their manner of systematising everything, whether homely or sublime.

The masters in most large schools were very numerous, but none were allowed to hold any office until of mature age. At Fulda there were twelve professors and a principal (*Principalis*), besides assistants.[101] In the cathedral schools, in like manner, there was the *Archischolus* and his assistants, and the *Proscholus*, or prefect of discipline.[102] The reader will perhaps smile when he hears that one of the duties of the *Proscholus* was to teach the children how to walk, bow, and behave in presence of superiors. This, however, was a speciality of the Canons Regular. Learning was not the only qualification required in a master. He was to be of tried virtue. The office of teacher was a cure of souls, and so great was the honour in which it was held, that bishops even, who had formerly filled the post of scholasticus, not unfrequently affixed their old to their new title, when signing their names.

The education of the scholars began at a very early age, sometimes at five or six. The first task consisted in learning by heart certain portions of Holy Scripture, and specially of the Psalter. Even those who very early abandoned their books for the more congenial exercises of the tilt-yard, seldom did so till they had run through their Psalter: "*decurso psalterio,*" is a common expression used in speaking of a youth who had left school with the least possible smattering of an education. As for those who stayed a more reasonable time at school, they acquired, besides their profane learning, a familiarity with the Church office and with the words of Holy Writ, not certainly possessed by all scholars of the present day. This is abundantly illustrated by the histories of the times. Thus Einold of Toul, sitting at the window of his cell, hears a voice chanting the words, "I will give you the heritage of your father Jacob," and at once concludes that it must be a schoolboy conning his morning's task. How beautiful is that story which we find in the chronicle of Monte Cassino, of the monk Levitius, who, returning from Jerusalem, came to Mount Albaneta, where he proposed to build a monastery. As he was inspecting the site of his new foundation, he saw approaching him a little school boy, carrying his bag of books on his shoulders, and the thought came into his head that he would ask him if he could sing. The boy replying that he could, Levitius told him to sing the first thing he could remember, secretly resolving that he would place the church under the dedication of any saint the boy might happen to name. The little scholar thought a moment, and then intoned the Antiphon, *Veni electa mea*, which he sang with much sweetness. Levitius listened with delight, and the monastery which afterwards rose on the spot was dedicated to the Ever Blessed Virgin. Scholars of all ages were very largely exercised in what one old monk calls "the holy memory." Learning by rote was used more generally than among ourselves, partly because books were rare, and all could not enjoy the luxury of a Psalter or Breviary for private use; and partly, because the teachers of old time sought to sanctify this power of the soul, by thoroughly informing it with holy words. Besides the Psalter, the novices of a religious house were expected to know the New Testament at least by heart, half-an-hour a day being assigned for the purpose.

The liberal arts were, as is well known, classed under two heads, the *trivium*, which included grammar, logic, and rhetoric; and the *quadrivium*, which embraced arithmetic, geometry, music, and astronomy. This division is expressed in the well-known distich:—

Gram: loquitur. Dia. vera docet. Rhet. verba colorat.

Mus. canit. Ar. numerat. Geo. ponderat. Ast. colit astra.

The trivium, with the Ecclesiastical chant, and so much of arithmetic as was required for the computation of the calendar, was taught in all schools; the quadrivium only in those which embraced the higher studies. Music was divided into two kinds, the *cantus*, which formed part of the routine of studies even in the lower schools, and *musica*, properly so called, which included the theory of music, a knowledge of the laws of sound, and the connection of harmony with numbers. And this explains how it was that a knowledge of music was in those days considered a proof that its possessor was a well-educated man: it evidenced that he had not only gone through the elementary studies of the trivium, but that he had completed his education in one of those higher schools in which the quadrivium also was taught. And these higher schools were frequented not only by ecclesiastics but by laics, whose inferiority to the clergy in point of mental culture has been greatly overstated, and where it existed, was the effect of accident rather than of system. Men who by force of necessity were called into the field at a very early age, and engaged in active military service during the greater part of their lives, had seldom much time to devote to study; but there was no sort of prejudice against their becoming as learned as they chose. Abbot Philip, of Good Hope, who lived in the time of St. Bernard, when the institution of Chivalry had certainly not tended to render the lay-nobles more studious, protests against the notion that learning is the exclusive apanage of the clergy. "Many laymen," he says, "are well instructed in letters. When a prince can withdraw from the tumult of arms and business he should study himself in books just as he contemplates his face in a mirror." And he proceeds to speak in commendation of the noble Count Charles who was "as prompt in meditating the Psalms as in drawing the sword to avenge outraged justice," and Count Adolph "who ceased not to bless his parents for the good education they had given him." Of Henry, Count of Champagne, it is said that between his warlike expeditions, when not engaged in the judicial duties of his rank, he delighted in withdrawing to some retired part of his castle and entertaining himself with a classic author or a volume of the Fathers. And in the Imperial library is still to be seen a fine copy of Valerius Maximus, written out for him by the monks of Provins. Every one is familiar with the name of Fulk the Good, Count of Anjou, against whose learning Hallam has directed so uncourteous a sneer. The story, threadbare as it is, affords too good an illustration of the subject to be omitted. He was accustomed to sing in choir with the canons of St. Martin's of Tours, and when ridiculed by king Louis IV. of France, for the habit, sent to that monarch a pithy epistle to the following effect: "Know, sir, that an illiterate king is a crowned ass." "It seems, then," observes Hallam, "that with the monkish historians a knowledge of music passed for literature. The same writer calls Geoffrey Plantagenet *optime literatus*, which perhaps imports little more learning than was possessed by his ancestor, Fulk."[103] The monkish biographer here alluded to meant nothing of the kind, but he knew, as both Fulk and Louis also knew, that at that time a knowledge of music might be taken as a tolerably satisfactory token that the musician had studied at one of the higher schools, and completed the full course of the quadrivium. And such, indeed, was the case with Fulk, who, as the same biographer tells us a few pages further on, was well read in Cicero and Aristotle.

A methodical idea of the system of education which prevailed in the higher monastic schools, is given in a little manual called the "Doctrinale Puerorum," the authority of which is beyond dispute. Though the production of the twelfth century, so little change took place in the system of studies from the time of Charlemagne to that of Lanfranc that it may be taken as equally descriptive of the method followed in the ninth and tenth. According to the writer of this manual a child as soon as he had learnt to read and write, set to work on the Latin Grammar of Donatus or Priscian, if he were so fortunate as to be able to provide himself with a book. The larger number of pupils probably had to depend on the oral instructions dictated by their master, and their own notes of his lessons. We know for certain that not only grammar, but rhetoric and the explanation of classic authors were taught orally, rules and examples being thus dictated and learnt by frequent repetition. From their ninth to their twelfth year the boys studied elementary Latin books, specially the Fables of Esop, and the poems of Christian authors, such as Theodulus, who, in the tenth century, wrote in verse the miracles of the Old and New Testaments, with the view of providing young children with suitable class-books. The *Distichia Moralia*, commonly attributed to Cato, a very old class-book, was probably the authorship of some Christian writer of the seventh century; and has found a home even in the Eastern languages. As the boys advanced in years, select portions from the works of Seneca, Ovid, Virgil, Persius, and Horace, but specially of Lucan and Statius were placed in their hands, explained and committed to memory, and these were followed by Cicero, Quinctilian, and the Latin version of Aristotle.[104]

Some readers will, doubtless, be tempted to regard such an account of the ancient course of classical studies as a work of the imagination. They will call to mind the scruples of Alcuin and the condemnation passed by Paschasius on those who spent their time in the explanation of the profane poets. But it may be observed, that the very examples so often quoted to prove that the monks disapproved of the study of the classics, show us that at any rate they knew a good deal about them. Alcuin had studied Virgil himself before he forbade Sigulf to do so, and so had St. Odo, who prohibited the reading of the Mantuan bard, after he had seen in a vision a vessel full of serpents, which he understood to represent his works. And the strictures of Paschasius on those who neglected the Scriptures, while they weighed every line and syllable of Pagan authors, shows at least how extensively those authors were read. But it must strike every impartial reader that these prohibitions do, in fact, prove nothing at all as to the state of school studies. They apply entirely to the use of the classics, not among students, but among the monks themselves. Because it was thought undesirable that young ecclesiastics should spend their time in the study of the profane poets, and because their attention was rather directed by their superiors to the cultivation of sacred science, we must not, certainly, conclude in the face of evidence that the classics were excluded from the schools. Teachers in the ninth century were no less solicitous than those of the nineteenth to form the mind and the style of their scholars; their compositions are perhaps not quite so full of the *membra disjecta* of Tully as a scholar of the Renaissance might have desired, yet he was certainly read, and though the imitations of Virgil and Ovid attempted by these obscure writers may be very indifferent, they could only have been produced by men who were perfectly familiar with the original writings of the Latin poets. Mabillon has not failed to draw the distinction between the studies pursued by monks and bishops, and those of masters and scholars.[105] He quotes two passages very much to the point, in one of which Lanfranc declines entering into certain questions appertaining to secular literature, submitted to him by the monk Domnoald, because he says, "though in my youth I delighted in such things, I determined wholly to renounce them when I accepted the pastoral charge." In the other passage St. Anselm writes to his old pupil, Maurice, and advises him to read Virgil, and the other good Latin authors, as much as he can, excepting always such passages as offend good morals.

This last condition is often insisted on; nor was it until the period of the classic Renaissance that the *indiscriminate* use of the classics by the young was tolerated. Rabanus in his book *De Institutione Clericorum*, while permitting the study of profane literature, even to clerics, stipulates that it be read for edification, and that whatever has a contrary tendency be put aside. The monastic scholars even recognised that reflection of primeval tradition which gleams through the pagan authors, and which, as Ozanam says, opened to Virgil the schools of the Middle Ages. What they did not allow was that the exclusive study of these models should be suffered to paganise the Christian mind, and they contrived, therefore, in explaining the works of Cicero or Plato to weave a Christian tone into the lessons by connecting them or comparing them with passages from the Holy Scriptures.

Latin was the only language universally cultivated, though the other learned tongues were not entirely neglected. Bede and Alcuin certainly possessed a knowledge of Greek and Hebrew, and, no doubt, communicated their learning to some of their pupils. Greek, as we have seen, was studied at St. Gaul's, and Charlemagne, who himself had some knowledge of that tongue, founded a Greek college at Osnaburgh, chiefly with a view to providing ecclesiastics whose familiarity with the language of the Eastern empire might be of service to him in his constant intercourse with Constantinople. Some writers whose aim it is to represent the learning of these centuries as altogether unworthy of notice, affect to doubt whether the Greek college, if proposed, were ever really founded; but the evidence of contemporary historians is positive on the point. "Do not wonder," writes the chronicler of Ottberg, "that the abbot of Hermann should always have carried with him a Greek Testament, that learned man was well skilled in the Greek tongue, which he had learnt in the Caroline college at Osnaburgh, for in that foundation all the clergy were skilled in Greek as well as in Latin." Louis the Debonnaire and Charles the Bald were both Greek scholars, and the latter monarch had a Greek and Latin glossary compiled for the use of the Church of Laon, which he would hardly have had done had there been none capable of using it. Florus, the learned deacon of the Church of Lyons, was well versed not only in Greek but Hebrew, as we learn from the following circumstance. A certain abbot, Hyldrade, sent him a Latin Psalter, begging him to correct it carefully, that it might serve as a copy for his monks to transcribe from. Among the many curious and valuable monuments of antiquity discovered by the late Cardinal Mai, is the reply of Florus to this request. From it we find that he had compared the Latin version of St. Jerome with the Septuagint, and suspecting that the text of St. Jerome had itself become corrupted by careless copying, had likewise collated it with the original Hebrew. He quotes what he calls "the well-known" letter of St. Jerome to two learned Celts, pointing out the errors in the vulgar copies; but Rohrbacher remarks that this letter was well-known only in the ninth century, for in ours it no longer exists. The whole letter of Floras is exceedingly valuable as evidence of the extraordinary learning and diligence bestowed on the correction of the Sacred Text.[106]

Nevertheless, an examination of the catalogues of early monastic libraries, makes it clear that the study of Greek, if not wholly neglected, was exceptional, and certainly did not include any extensive acquaintance with ancient Greek literature. Among the books named as the favourites of St. Paschasius, we find the works of St. John Chrysostom; but in general the book collections are only rich in the Latin Fathers. Scotus Erigena evidently introduced a novelty when he translated the works of St. Denys the Areopagite, and the eagerness displayed by Louis the Debonnaire to possess a Latin version of the works of this author arose, perhaps, less from an interest in Greek letters, than from the opinion, then finding favour with Gallican scholars, which identified him with the Apostle of France.[107] The mention, however, of any Greek poets or philosophers is exceedingly rare. Homer, as has been said, had been brought into England by Archbishop Theodore, and the St. Gall library contained the works of Sophocles, but these are certainly exceptions, and we may conclude that a knowledge of the Greek language was a rare accomplishment, from the extreme complacency with which the possession of a very superficial smattering of it was often regarded. Hincmar, of Rheims, warns his nephew to avoid the foolish affectation of some, who pick a handful of Greek words out of their glossaries to adorn their pages and give them a learned look; a folly too common also with our native scholars.

The sciences of arithmetic and geometry were probably taught in rather a meagre form, until the genius of Gerbert, in the tenth century, gave fresh impulse to these branches of learning. We have seen what difficulties attended their study in the days of St. Aldhelm; nevertheless the path of the young student was somewhat smoothed by pleasant devices, and the Anglo-Saxon masters quickened the brains of their pupils by problems and questions, some of which, such is the power of tradition, have kept their places in our own school-books. Arithmetical problems, such as the following, were propounded to the schoolboys of Alcuin and Rabanus: "The swallow once invited the snail to dinner; he lived just a league from the spot, and the snail travelled at the rate of one inch a day: how long was he before he dined?" Or, again: "An old man met a child; 'Good day, my son,' he said, 'may you live as long as you have lived and as much more, and thrice as much as all that put together, and then if God give you one year more, you will be just a century old;' how old was the boy?"

Besides the sciences above enumerated, some schools, and particularly those of England, taught a certain amount of natural philosophy, very imperfect, if compared with our own larger and more accurate knowledge of these subjects, yet valuable in its way, as directing the mind to a branch of learning where improvement could only be hoped for by patient and persevering observation. Geography, again, though in its infancy, was a favourite study with the Anglo-Saxons, and from none did it receive greater extension than from king Alfred, who added whole chapters to the science as it existed before his time. This, in common with a great many other branches of knowledge, was sometimes taught to tardy scholars by the help of verses. Several versified summaries of grammatical rules and geographical definitions are in existence in very early English, but for the credit of the geographers, I will not say in what quarter of the globe they place the land of Egypt.

We have yet to speak, however, of a far more important subject connected with the early monastic schools, the religious training of their pupils, and the sacred studies which they pursued. In nothing, probably, did the ancient system of education differ more widely from our own, than in the amount of vocal prayer in which children were expected to take a part. Of course we must bear in mind when reading of children assisting at all the Canonical Hours of the monastery in which they were educated, that in most cases the children spoken of were those "offered" by their parents and intended for the monastic state. They were the pupils of the interior or claustral schools; and it is probable that those belonging to the exterior school were subject to a less rigorous discipline. Still, in either case, they were children, with the propensities common to all children, whether of the ninth or nineteenth centuries; yet we find nothing to indicate that the choral attendance described by the Anglo-Saxon schoolboy in the dialogues of Ælfric, was found by experience to be excessive. "To-day," says the boy, "I have done many things; this night, when I heard the knell, I arose from my bed and went to the church and sang Night-song with the brethren; after that we sang the service of All Saints and the morning Lauds; then followed Prime and the Seven Psalms, and the Litanies, and the first Mass; then Tierce, and the Mass of the day; then Sext; and then we ate and drank and went to sleep, and rose again and sang None; and now we are here before thee ready to hear what thou hast to say to us." "Who awakens you for Night-song?" asks the interlocutor. "Sometimes," answers the scholar, "I hear the knell, and rise of myself; but ofttimes the master arouseth me with his rod."

If this attendance in choir surprise us as being daily required from young children, we must remember that the habits of the grown-up laity in early ages would be equally at variance with our own. The Divine Office of the Church was not then exclusively recited by priests and religious; the faithful assisted even at the Night-hours, and were constantly urged to do so. In the days of Charlemagne, as in those of St. John Chrysostom, rich and poor, men and women, took part in that sublime worship, and so eager were they in their desire to join in the chant, that it became necessary for abbots to issue injunctions, forbidding their monks to cut up their Psalters in order to distribute the leaves to seculars who solicited the precious fragments, certain devout women being foremost among the beggars. Without some knowledge of the habits of the time, we can form no tolerably fair judgment on the education which was of course fitted and adapted to those habits. The spirit of these early ages was pre-eminently *Liturgical*. The world was as yet too little civilised to furnish her children with those countless elegant methods of killing time which later ages have so marvellously multiplied; theatres had no existence, and even the superabundant games and pastimes so popular in the Middle Ages, were as yet unthought of. The people sought not merely their instruction, but their recreation also in the Church, and their education thoroughly fitted them to join in her ceremonies and ritual, which it is to be feared, by more cultivated intellects of a later generation, are too often but very imperfectly understood. The education of children partook, of course, of the character of the age; it was more or less ecclesiastical, even for those not intended for the religious or clerical state; and this has given rise to the very hasty conclusion that in the centuries of which we speak, education was given to none save those who aspired to the priesthood. But in point of fact the whole atmosphere of society was then so permeated with the Christian, and what we have ventured to denominate the *Liturgical* spirit, that children of seculars then received a training which, to modern eyes, appears exclusively suited to ecclesiastics.

The one branch of learning, therefore, which, in the judgment of the monastic teachers, exceeded in importance all the rest, was undoubtedly the study of the Scriptures. "In the study of the Scriptures," says Mabillon, "consisted the whole science of the monks." Scholastic theology was as yet unknown, and the Holy Scriptures and the commentaries of the Fathers formed the exclusive study of theologians. That alliance between faith and reason, wherein reason, exercising itself on revealed truth under the control and guidance of faith, built up the dogmas of the Church into a compact and well-ordered system, was the work of later centuries; the monastic scholars of the age of Charlemagne knew nothing about it. They had the Scriptures, interpreted by the Fathers, and the decrees of the Church, for their guides in dogma; and for discipline, the sacred Canons. With these they were abundantly satisfied. Placed in green pastures and by the side of running waters, they enjoyed the inheritance that had fallen to them, and sought for nothing more. Their divines, therefore, hardly aimed at the merit of original composition, and were content to study, to copy, and to compile the teaching, and often the very phraseology of St. Augustine, St. Ambrose, or St. Gregory. Hence the complaint not unjustly brought against them, is that, though tolerably acquainted with books, they were for the most part deficient in original argument. In fact, they sought to hand on the traditions of the Church pure and uncorrupted, rather than to earn for themselves a fame as original thinkers; and one of the marks of the age is an absence of the disputatious spirit which, if it diminishes their rank in the world of letters, forms the charm of their characters as men. There was nothing of the sophist or logician in those sweet and venerable countenances, the unruffled beauty of which is so often dwelt on by their biographers. True, indeed, controversies did arise, as we have seen in the beginning of this chapter, but they were out of harmony with the time. The character of Scotus Erigena, like his learning, was that of a man born out of due time; he belonged to the twelfth rather than to the ninth century, and his wrangling must have sounded strangely discordant in the ears of his contemporaries. The real spirit of the age was one of reverence for Tradition; and the large and active intellects of a Bede, a Boniface and a Paschasius, found all they sought and all they desired in the Positive Theology of the Church.

So much has been done in our time to dispel the vulgar illusion that the Scriptures were unknown and uncared for in the Dark Ages, that I need not here enter into any proof of what is now, or at least ought to be, an uncontroverted fact. Mr. Maitland's "Essays" have convincingly proved that if the monks read nothing else they at least read the Bible. But what he has not shown with equal power, is the love, the enthusiasm with which, to use the expression of the biographer of Rabanus, they "fed themselves on the Divine Scriptures." Like the Jews of old, they meditated on them, "sitting in the house or walking on a journey;" they were written "on the entry and on the doorposts."[108] At the tables of bishops and abbots, of nobles and of kings, the Scriptures were daily read aloud: the little child learnt from them his first lesson, and the old man died with their accent on his lips. What need had they of the fables of the poets, when the beauties of the inspired writers were graven on their memories, familiar as household words? How could they care to listen to what Ovid had to tell them of the Golden Age, they to whom the glowing imagery of the Prophet had painted the kingdom of the Son of Jesse, where the wolf was to dwell with the lamb, and the kid with the leopard, and a little child should lead them? And what great wonder was it if the degrading tales of heathen deities, even when sung by the Muse of Virgil, should fall somewhat flat and profitless on their ears, accustomed as they were to the sublime marvels of God's dealings with His ancient people, and the history of the Incarnate Word?

It was not merely as the inspired Word of God that the Holy Scriptures were thus valued; but in the schools of which we are speaking they held the place of the great Christian classic. They were not a mere dry repertory of texts illustrative of doctrine, but they formed at once the favourite book of prayer, of meditation, of spiritual reading, and of recreative delight. Pondered on day and night, with all their hidden meaning laid open by the comments of the Fathers, what a treasury of wisdom, what a fountain of poesy was there! The very language of Scripture wonderfully harmonised with the daily monastic life, so patriarchal in its simplicity, its noble toils, and its humble duties of the shepherd, the husbandman, and the vinedresser. It harmonised with the scenes in the midst of which they lived, the mountains, and the wooded valleys, the fields standing thick with corn, the wilderness in its untrampled beauty, where rose up "the verdure of the reed and the bulrush," and where the myrtle and the olive-tree grew by the running waters. It harmonised with their deep sympathy with the Beautiful, their intimate acquaintance with Nature in all her aspects, by day or by night, so familiar to the eyes of those who sanctified all hours by prayer, and to whom "the outgoings of the morning and of the evening were made joyful," by the Matins and Vesper psalmody. But chiefly and above all, it harmonised with that thirst that devoured their souls for the true and living God; a thirst which made them weary of all things in which He was not to be found, which made all things sweet in which He had His part; which led them by a strange inspired ingenuity to turn all things to Him, to Christianise every study, to divinise every act; which taught them to create new arts to deck His sanctuary, new sciences to minister to His praise—a thirst which, unslaked by the choicest fountains of Gentile antiquity, drank deep and refreshing draughts at those streams of sacred poetry, out of which they framed the language of their daily Office, and which moulded the very fashion of their daily speech.

The Scriptures, then, were the Christian classics of the monks and their pupils. Their study was not confined to ecclesiastical students, but formed one of the chief branches of every Christian man's education.[109] And by their study we must understand, of course, not a mere familiarity with the dead letter, but an intimate knowledge of their spiritual sense. We may gather some idea of what was implied in the monastic study of the Scriptures, from a letter written by a certain monk of Citeaux to one of his friends, in which he draws out a compendious method for his guidance. Together with the different divisions of his subject, he advises him to read appropriate commentaries. Thus Josephus and Hegesippus are to be read with the Pentateuch and the Historical Books, and if any words occur of doubtful signification, the student is to consult the "Etymologies" of St. Isidore, and St. Jerome on the "Explanation of Hebrew Names;" and that other book on "Derivations," "which is to be found in most large libraries," and finally the "Gloss." Certain passages of more importance, and summaries of the principal facts, are to be written out and committed to memory; and the writer proceeds to give directions on this point, adding, that on all the subjects he names it will be useful to consult St. Augustine "De Quæstionibus." When the Historical Books have been carefully studied, the Prophetical Books may be begun. We are to note which prophecies are fulfilled, and which unfulfilled, and the exact time and circumstances under which each was written. After these the Books of instruction, and then the Gospels. In reading the Gospels, it will be necessary to have St. Jerome's description of the "Holy Places of Palestine," and the "Harmony of the Gospels." And we must carefully observe where, when, and before whom our Lord's Sermons were delivered, and His miracles worked. The rest of the New Testament is afterwards to be read. The student is then directed to read certain works on the Sacraments, on the reason for assigning different portions of Scripture to different seasons, and some of the works of St. Augustine. And when the literal sense of the Holy Books has been thus carefully studied, and not before, he may pass on to their allegorical and mystic interpretation, and read both Testaments through in the same order a second time, special authors being recommended to assist his comprehension of their spiritual sense.[110]

This double method of study, in which the literal meaning of the Scriptures was made the basis of interpreting their spiritual signification, was begun very early, and even young children were considered capable of being introduced by degrees to the spiritual comprehension of the Sacred Books. So far from these being a treasure sealed up to all save the clergy, they formed the foundation stone of all education. Thus Thegan writes of the Emperor Louis le Debonnaire, that he had been perfectly instructed in the allegorical and mystical interpretation of the Scriptures, and we learn from St. Aldhelm's treatise, "*De Laudibus Virginitatis*," that the nuns for whom he intended it were not only accustomed to read the Old and New Testaments, together with the Commentaries of the Fathers, but that they also studied the historical, allegorical, and analogical senses of different passages. Nor is this by any means an exceptional case, for in the religious houses of women sacred studies were pursued with hardly less eagerness than in those of men.

And here the temptation presents itself to say something of the schools provided in the Dark Ages for the education of women, such as the royal house of Chelles, where the wise Bertilla presided over scores of English scholars sent by their parents to France, as we must needs suppose, for fashion's sake, for there were certainly plenty of good schools to be found in England. Fashion, however, has much to do with the selection of a school, and Chelles was naturally popular with the English, having been founded in the seventh century by a princess of Anglo-Saxon blood.

Queen Bathildis, indeed, was not of royal birth; she was a poor maiden who had been sold as a slave into France, and attracting the attention of Clovis II., was raised by him to share his throne. Her first thought in her new position was to procure the abolition of slavery, or at least the amelioration of the condition of slaves. "She was," says her biographer, "of a beautiful and cheerful countenance, to her husband an obedient wife, to the princes a mother, to boys and youths the best of counsellors; to all an amiable and gracious friend," and he adds that among her other good deeds, "she was always exhorting and encouraging the youth around her to religious studies." So soon as her son Clothaire was old enough to govern, Bathildis, who during his minority had acted as regent, retired to Chelles and spent the remainder of her days in the humble office of infirmarian. But her foundation had meanwhile acquired a great reputation for learning, which was yet further increased when Gisella, the sister of Charlemagne, and the pupil of Alcuin, assumed its government in the ninth century.

Nor must it be supposed that these examples of learning in the cloisters of nuns were confined to those communities which had caught their tone from the little knot of literary women educated by St. Boniface. It was the natural and universal development of religious life. We have but to glance back a century or two, and we shall find foundations of purely French origin, those of St. Cesarius of Arles, in which the nuns were to be seen reading even over their work, and busy at the transcription of the Sacred Books. And we might quote the account of St. Cesaria's death, written by one of her devout children, which M. Guizot hesitates not to rank among the gems of literature. Or we might turn to the Latin poems of St. Radegundes, the Queen of Clothaire I., and the friend of Venantius Fortunatus, who composed his celebrated hymn "Vexilla regis" on occasion of the translation to her monastery at Poitiers of a relic of the true Cross. This royal nun of the sixth century was accustomed to read the Greek and Latin Fathers, and as her biographer tells us, was not only *vultu elegans*, but *litteris erudita*. She liked her disciples to be as learned as herself, insisted that all should be able to read, and should learn the Psalter by heart, and gathered together more than two hundred daughters of noble families, in whose company and instruction she took such passing great delight, that, says Baudoniva, one of them whom she had educated from a child and who afterwards wrote her life, she would address them in the tenderest terms, calling them her light, her life, and her chosen little plants.[111]

The picture of St. Cesaria in the sixth century, and of St. Lioba in the eighth, is reproduced in that of St. Adelaide of Gueldres, abbess of Cologne in the tenth. She had enjoyed a learned education, and took great delight in collecting around her young virgins to whom she communicated her lessons with a truly maternal care. Every day she showed herself in the school, and propounded grammatical subtleties to her disciples; rewarding the diligent with caresses, and punishing the slothful with a severity for which her tender heart was wont afterwards often to reproach her. In fact, were I to repeat all that her biographer relates of her zeal in the matter of correction, I might convey the impression that the pupils of the abbess Adelaide lived under a rather terrible taskmistress. She sometimes visited the offenders with rods, and sometimes with a good box on the ear. The latter chastisement was even inflicted in choir when her pupils sang out of tune; but her biographer adds, it was never found necessary to administer it a second time, for the touch of her saintly hand had such power in it, as to cure all defects of voice and ear for the future.[112] But yet she was a tender and a loving mother, and when she had punished any one, would conjure some of her sisters to go and console the poor victim whom she immediately began to compassionate. Nay, her love went so far, that besides the incessant thought she bestowed on providing her children with good food and raiment, she would steal into their dormitory in the winter nights, to find out if any were suffering from cold feet, and would warm them by rubbing them with her hands.

These examples are all of religious women; but we have direct evidence that even those who embraced a secular life were expected to receive a certain amount of education. Amalarius, of Metz, whose great work on the "Ecclesiastical Offices" appeared in the year 820, requires that young girls should learn the Psalter, the Books of Job and Proverbs, the Four Gospels, and the Acts of the Apostles. Perhaps there is no more interesting and decisive testimony as to the amount of learning to be found among the laity in the Dark Ages, than the curious will of Count Eberhard, of Terouanne, who died in 860, and left behind him a precious library, equalling in extent many of those possessed by religious houses. He directed that this library should, after his death, be divided among his children in the manner prescribed by his will. The four sons and four daughters each received their share, though the boys, naturally enough, obtained the lion's share. Among the books named in the catalogue are treatises on law, military affairs, history, and natural philosophy, besides religious works.[113] One of the books bequeathed to Gisla, is the "Enchiridion" of St. Augustine. We have besides incidental notices occurring in the biographies of the time, which represent mothers writing to their sons and conveying to them sound practical advice, and noble ladies keeping up a correspondence with learned ecclesiastics, who seem to have directed their studies. There was certainly no difficulty in the way of ladies obtaining an education if they chose, for the convents of Chelles, Farmoutier, Brie, and Andelys, all had excellent schools, and often enough English mistresses, whose teaching was held in special esteem. And Theodulph, of Orleans, does not seem to have been giving the princess Gisella a piece of advice at all out of harmony with the manners and ideas of the age, when he counselled her to divide her time equally between reading and the homely cares of the household, concluding his admonitions with the two following lines:

Assidue si ores, tibi si sit lectio crebra,

Ipsa Deo loqueris, et Deus ipse tibi.

An attentive study of the history of the following centuries will convince us that if the dames and spinsters of the Middle Ages were not exactly blue-stockings, they perfectly understood the value of Theodulph's counsels, and that they were often not only learned themselves, but the cause of learning in others. For not a few of the learned foundations in England owe their existence to the munificence of noble ladies, who, in this country at least, have ever shown themselves the nursing mothers of polite letters. But of this there will be more to say in its proper place.

CHAPTER VII.

KING ALFRED.

A.D. 873 TO 900.

THE history of King Alfred, and his noble efforts in the cause of learning, are so familiar to all readers that it may seem unnecessary to say much of the restoration of letters which took place in England during his reign. From our childhood, the stories of his life have been as familiar to us as those of Scripture, and it is probable that the illuminated manuscript which first tempted him to learn his alphabet has encouraged not a few of us in our childish love of picture-books. Every one knows that at the time of his accession England was plunged in her darkest night of ignorance; and every one who has studied Hume, Hallam, and other standard writers, knows that the illiteracy of the English clergy at that precise period is commonly cited as a sample of the state of things which prevailed throughout Europe during the Dark Ages. Hallam, indeed, in a note appended to his remarks on the subject, admits that before the Danish Invasion, the churches were well furnished with books, but adds that "the priests got little good from them, being written in a foreign language they could not understand."[114] The fact that the state of things complained of was not normal, but accidental, is uniformly ignored by these writers; they beheld the waters of an inundation, and would have their readers believe them to be the ocean in its natural bed. However, far from wishing to deny the ignorance which existed in England at the time of Alfred's accession, I will add to the colouring of the picture by quoting Dr. Lingard's brief but emphatic summary of the grievances under which the kingdom then groaned. "At the close of this calamitous period," he says, after a graphic sketch of the devastations perpetrated by the Danes, "the Anglo-Saxon church presented a melancholy spectacle; the laity had resumed the ferocious manners of their pagan forefathers; the clergy had grown indolent, dissolute, and illiterate; the monastic order was apparently annihilated, and it devolved on Alfred, now victorious over his enemies, to apply remedies to all these evils."

The Whitsuntide of the year 873 had been signalised by the great battle of Ethandun, gained by Alfred over the Danes; and this was followed by a short but brilliant campaign, at the close of which the "heathen men" retired into East Anglia and made their submission to the crown of Wessex. This final success was succeeded by fifteen years of comparative tranquillity, which were employed by Alfred in those multifarious acts of wise legislation which restored order to his distracted kingdom, and gained for himself the well-merited title of "the Great." No work, however, lay closer to his heart than the restoration of learning, for though at this time quite as illiterate as the rest of his people, Alfred's desire to become learned had very early evinced itself. He had learned to read and write at twelve years old, in spite of many obstacles, no good masters being then to be obtained in all Wessex. His reading, however, was not extensive; it seems to have been confined to a little book in which were collected the day hours of the church, and a few psalms and collects, and which he always carried about him. The manuscript which by its brilliant illuminations had first excited his curiosity was a collection of Anglo-Saxon poetry, and there is no reason for supposing that Alfred was at this time possessed of any other books.

But an intellect like his finds other food than that which can merely be extracted from books. In company with his father, Ethelwulf, Alfred had made the pilgrimage to Rome, where Ethelwulf rebuilt the Saxon school which had been founded by King Ina.[115] On their homeward journey he had visited the court of Charles the Bald, and seen and talked with learned men; he had assisted at his father's second marriage with the Princess Judith, which was celebrated by Hincmar of Rheims; and at St. Omer's he had made acquaintance with the Provost Grimbald, whose conversation left a lasting impression on his mind. All this had been a kind of education to him, and by showing him the superior enlightenment of other countries, made him more bitterly regret the rudeness of his own. The first step he took in order to begin a reform was to search out the few learned men still to be found among the Anglo-Saxon clergy. How few they were he lets us know in that oft-quoted passage from the Preface to his translation of St. Gregory, and which, after speaking of the "blessed times" formerly existing in England, when there were holy kings and a zealous clergy, and people came hither from foreign countries in quest of instruction, he laments over the change that has fallen on the land, and declares that knowledge has now so escaped from the English people, that few priests south of the Humber can be found who understand the divine service, or can explain a Latin epistle in English. "They are so few," he adds, "that I cannot remember one, south of the Thames, when I began to reign."

And yet, says Hallam, the district south of the Thames was "the best part of England." This, however, is clearly a mistake, for every one of the surviving Saxon scholars whom Alfred succeeded in hunting out and drawing to his court were Mercians. They were Werefrith, Bishop of Worcester; Plegmund, who when the Danes were ravaging the country had fled into Cheshire and there became a hermit; and two other Mercian priests, named Ethelstan and Werwulf. Plegmund was drawn out of the solitude called from him Plegmundesham, and in 890 was chosen by God and the people to be Archbishop of Canterbury, says the Saxon Chronicle, of great part of which he is supposed to have been the compiler. Werefrith, whom Asser calls most erudite in the divine Scriptures, was sufficiently a Latin scholar to undertake the translation of St. Gregory's dialogues. Ethelstan and Werwulf were appointed royal chaplains, and had no light office, for they were required by the king to read to him at every leisure moment, "both by day and by night," that so he might become acquainted with books which he could not read for himself. In Wessex Alfred found no one fitted to take part in the proposed reform, with the exception of a poor swineherd named Denewulf, whom he fell in with whilst hunting in the forest of Selwood; and, charmed with the native genius he betrayed in his conversation, had him educated, and eventually raised him to the see of Winchester. These, however, were not sufficient for the work which the king contemplated, and his thoughts turned to the foreign monks whose acquaintance he had formed on his journey from Rome. He specially desired to obtain possession of Grimbald, who was renowned for his knowledge of the Scriptures and his proficiency in the musical science, and for this purpose despatched an embassy to Fulk, Archbishop of Rheims, begging that the learned provost might be sent to him without delay. Mr. Turner, in his interesting account of the literary labours of Alfred, informs us that Fulk addressed the king a very singular letter in reply, wherein he calls both Grimbald and the English prelates who formed the embassy by the name of *dogs*. "You have sent me some noble generous dogs to drive away the irreligious wolves, and they came desiring other dogs, not dumb dogs like those spoken of by the prophet, but good noisy dogs that can bark and make themselves heard." Reference to the original letter of Fulk however, which is printed at the end of Asser's Life of Alfred,[116] will show that this is a very free translation of a passage capable of simple explanation. The neighbourhood of Rheims was, it seems, infested with wolves, no uncommon thing even in the suburbs of great cities in those wild times; and Alfred, among the costly presents which he sent to the archbishop, had included a pack of English wolf-hounds. Fulk in his letter thanks him for the welcome gift. "You have sent us," he says, "noble and generous, although mortal and corporal dogs, to drive away the visible wolves with which, among other scourges of God's justice, our country abounds; and you have asked of us, other dogs, not corporal, but spiritual ones; not such as those of whom the Psalmist speaks, saying, 'Dumb dogs not able to bark,' but such as may guard their master's house by their barking, and wisely keep his flock from the wolves of the unclean spirit, which are the devourers of souls, of which number one is Grimbald the priest and monk," whose learning and sanctity he then proceeds to extol. Grimbald arrived in England in 884, and, after being honourably received by Alfred and Archbishop Ethelred, is said to have made an excellent oration to the clergy and nobility in a Synod held at London, calling on them, one and all, to embrace a devout life, and to lend their aid in remedying the disorders which had followed on the Danish invasions. According to most writers, he began to teach sacred letters in the schools opened by Alfred at Oxford, and afterwards became abbot of the monastery which the king had founded at Winchester. Another of Alfred's foreign scholars was John of Old Saxony, a monk of Corby, who has been erroneously confused with John Scotus Erigena. He appears to have brought with him a small community of French monks who were placed by Alfred in the monastery newly erected in the Isle of Athelney.

But none of these rendered Alfred such effectual help in his literary labours as the British scholar Asser, a monk of St. David's monastery, whose fame having reached the King's ears, he was invited to the royal "vill" of Dene, in Sussex, and travelled thither "through many wide intervening ways," under the conduct of some Saxon guides, in the same year that witnessed the arrival of Grimbald. Asser, who has told us much concerning his royal patron, and has traced his genealogy through Woden up to Bedwig, the grandson of Noe, has been provokingly concise in his account of himself, and the history of his first introduction to the Saxon court. We only know that Alfred vainly endeavoured to induce him to give up his own country, and devote himself entirely to his service; and that Asser steadily refused to do so, thinking, as he says, that it was not right to forsake the holy place where he had been nurtured and consecrated for the prospect of earthly gain and honour. A compromise was, therefore, agreed to, by which Alfred secured his services for six months in every year; and the direction of the court school was delivered into his hands. The plan of this school was the same as that of Charlemagne's Palatine academy; and in it not only the princes and sons of the nobility, but many also of humbler rank, received their education. They read both Saxon and Latin books, and wrote in both languages, so that before they were strong enough to take part in the chase and other manly sports, they were fully instructed in what Asser calls the liberal arts. Ethelward, Alfred's youngest son, is specially commended for his diligence and love of learning; and his elder brother, Edward, and their sister, Ethelswitha, continued their studies even after they were grown up. We have not the same accurate information with regard to the nature of their acquirements as we have of those of Alcuin's scholars; but Asser says they pursued all the liberal sciences, learnt the Psalter, and read Saxon books very frequently, especially Saxon poems. Another school was opened at Athelney, which seems to have been exclusively intended to educate future monks and clergy, and among its scholars the greater number were foreigners. Asser speaks of having seen one of the pagan youths studying there, by which expression he probably means a Dane. He himself had no reason to complain of not being well paid for his services, for Alfred had the merit, so highly prized among his nation, of possessing an open hand. He conferred on his favourite scholar the monasteries of Congresbury and Banwell in one day; and another time gave him Exeter and all the parishes annexed to it in Wessex and Cornwall, as well as a silk pallium and a man's load of incense, with promises of more at a future time. These liberal grants of land and possessions were possibly made with the covert design of eventually fixing Asser altogether on the Saxon side of the Severn, and not without success, if, as seems probable, he afterwards became Bishop of Sherborne.

It was Alfred's own desire to extend the blessing of education to all his free-born subjects; and he even made it a law that every freeman possessed of two hides of land should keep his sons at school till they were fifteen, "because a man born free, who is unlettered, is to be regarded no otherwise than as a beast, having, like them, no understanding." If they had no sons of their own, he encouraged them to choose among the sons of their vassals those of most promise, who might at their expense be trained in good learning, and fitted to fill offices in church and state. He was literally dismayed at the amount of ignorance which he found among his judges, and by his reproofs shamed some of them into seeking in their old age for the instruction they had neglected in their youth. "I marvel," he would say, "that you who have been intrusted with the office of the Wise (Witan) should have neglected the studies of the wise. Therefore, either at once resign your offices, or apply yourselves to gain wisdom." Many, urged by words like these, placed themselves under the court teachers, and those who considered the labour of learning to read too gigantic to be undertaken at their age, had their sons and freed men educated, and employed them to read to them, lamenting their own ignorance, and extolling the superior advantages enjoyed by the youth of the present times.

But though the good work was begun, Alfred knew well enough that the only way to perpetuate it was the foundation of monastic schools; and here lay his great difficulty, for not only were all the old monasteries destroyed by the Danes, but the religious spirit that had formerly peopled the cloisters of Malmsbury, and Jarrow, and Croyland, and Lindisfarne with communities numbering their hundreds, were now entirely extinct. Asser informs us that the monastic institute was held in such contempt at that time, that no freeman was to be found in all Wessex willing to embrace it, and those from other provinces who had embraced it neglected all its rules. A gross sensuality had taken possession of the English people, and resulted in a wide-spread neglect on the part of the secular clergy of the sacred canons which bound them to a single life. Their example was ruinous to the morals of the laity, and the practice of divorce was becoming common among all ranks; and to complete the moral degradation of the English, drunkenness was frightfully on the increase among them, that vice the progress of which St. Boniface had so often lamented in his letters to the English prelates, saying that he blushed to find England alone disfigured by a brutal habit to which the very pagans were strangers. In such a state of society we are not surprised to find that the monastic profession was generally regarded with dislike. Athelney had to be peopled with foreign monks, and the murderous attempts they made on the life of their abbot seems to show that the community was made up of worthless members. The only other religious house of any importance which owed its foundation to Alfred was that at Winchester, and in consequence of the support it received from the king it seems to have enjoyed a larger share of prosperity. Still, it must be admitted that Alfred's efforts to restore monasticism in England were a failure; and in this respect his restoration of learning differed from that of Charlemagne. The Frankish monarch found himself surrounded by institutions which only needed encouragement to become the fit instruments for his work. The monastic spirit was vigorous in France in the eighth century, and he had but to speak the word to see schools and libraries starting up in connection with the cathedrals and monasteries. But in England the case was far different, and hence the real good achieved by Alfred was effected less by the schools that he founded than by the books that he wrote.

It is truly astonishing to think that we should number among our authors a king who, when he came to the throne, could barely read and write, and who during the whole of his reign was overwhelmed with business of all kinds, and worn down by constant bodily sickness. If Charlemagne's greatness had a more brilliant character, that of Alfred is perhaps more admirable when we remember how very few he had to assist him in his toils. He had to regenerate every branch of government, and to see to each department with his own eye. If Asser's statement is to be received as literally correct, the king found himself called on to teach his officers even their most homely duties. In the midst of Danish incursions and daily infirmities, he had not only to guide the rudder of the State, but to instruct his goldsmiths and other artificers, his huntsmen, falconers, fowlers, and dog-keepers. Many useful arts he himself taught his people; they were so barbarised and discouraged by their long continued sufferings that agriculture was becoming neglected in many parts, and the king was forced to offer premiums to those who would apply themselves to it, and to distribute seed from the royal storehouses. He was likewise a great builder, and introduced the fashion of building brick and stone houses instead of wooden hovels, himself furnishing the necessary directions and designs. I need not speak of what he did as a lawgiver, or of the numberless social and political institutions which he created. He was at once head, eye, and hand to the kingdom, and found so few among his nobles capable of seconding him in his efforts for the good of his people, that we are told he had to hang forty-five of his judges for gross crimes in the execution of their duty. How in the midst of all these multifarious cares he contrived to find time for the liberal arts, is only to be explained when we remember that he was pre-eminently a good manager and an economist of time; not an economist in that sense of the word in which we understand one who sacrifices everything to business, for according to this practical view Alfred might certainly have made more of his time than he did; and his method of disposing of the eight hours a day which he devoted to prayer and study, would probably by some be regarded as anything but economical. A man who was in the habit of hearing mass and reciting the divine office daily, and of satisfying his devotion by frequent and stealthy visits to the church, at such times as he judged himself least likely to be observed by his attendants, seemed to be expending his few and precious leisure moments on duties not of obligation. But this holy prodigality of the time given to God is a speciality in our early Christian scholars on which it is profitable to dwell. It formed a part of their system, and was as remarkable in Alfred as it was in Bede. And however familiar the reader may be with the anecdotes of his life, some, perhaps, will not be equally familiar with them as they stand in their original garb, from which the religious element has been carefully pared away by each successive story-teller. I shall, therefore, make no apology for introducing so threadbare a subject as King Alfred and his horn lanthorns, persuaded that comparatively few of those who have heard of him as their inventor, have ever dreamt that they had any sort of connection with the spiritual side of our great king's character. Here, then, is the story as it appears in the pages of Asser. After telling us of the many undertakings happily brought to completion by the king, and his incessant activity in the government of the realm, he continues: "Having set all these things in order, mindful of that saying of Holy Writ, 'Let him who would give an alms begin with himself,' he reflected on what he could offer to God of the service of his own mind and body, wishing to consecrate these to God as well as his exterior riches. So he promised, as far as infirmity, possibility, and means would permit, willingly and with all his might to give to God one-half of the service of his mind and body, both by day and night. However, as he could not any way reckon the night hours, by reason of the darkness, nor equally divide those of the day, because of the frequent rain and clouds, he began to think how he might, with God's help, observe the tenor of his vow even until death. At last he hit on a useful and clever device. He ordered his chaplains to provide a sufficient quantity of wax, which when brought he caused to be weighed out in pennyweights. When seventy-two pennyweights of it had been measured out, he ordered his chaplains to make thereof six candles, all of equal dimensions, each candle being marked out into twelve inches of length. This being done the six candles were burnt day and night without intermission through the twenty-four hours before the holy relics of many saints, which he took with him wherever he went. But as sometimes the candle would not burn through a whole night and day up to the same hour at which they had been lighted the preceding evening (doubtless because of the violence of the winds, which often blew through the doors and windows of the church, or through the many chinks in the walls and roofs, and their hangings), and as thus they burnt out more quickly than they should have done, Alfred began to consider how he might prevent this effect of the wind, and caused a lanthorn to be beautifully constructed of wood and cow's horn (for white cows' horns carefully scraped are no less transparent than glass), and the candle, being placed in this lanthorn, shone as brightly without as it did within, unimpeded by the blasts of wind."[117]

So, then, it was in fulfilment of a religious vow that King Alfred cast about to discover how he might accurately measure out his time, and his horn lanthorns were but the means he hit on to help him how to give the half of his service of mind and body, day and night, to God. Truly a vow worthy of a Christian hero, and right faithfully and heroically kept. Of course, in the time thus consecrated to God, he included those hours he devoted to study, for this with him was a religious exercise. How, indeed, he contrived to secure his eight hours a day of prayer and reading, is a mystery of the same nature with those marvellous facts which we meet with in the lives of the saints, whose days and nights seem to have had forty-eight hours in them, if we measure them by the amount of prayer and work they accomplished during their course. Alfred, whilst thus disposing of his time by vow, had, as it might seem, no time to himself. However, he made the most of what with most men are idle moments, and when not actually engaged in business was always reading or hearing others read. In his chamber he always had a book open before him, and never travelled without carrying his books with him. The attainment of wisdom, both human and Divine, was his absorbing desire; and Asser, after speaking of his incomparable affability and cheerfulness with others, and the great love and honour he showed to all those whom he drew around him, as well foreigners as natives, and his exceeding tenderness for his own children, and for the other youths whom he caused to be bred up in his palace, as though they were all members of his own family, goes on to say that he had no real consolation in any of these things, but that day and night he was devoured with one thought, and with what he calls an anxious sadness, which he poured out to his familiar friends; and this was his ceaseless desire that Almighty God would make him skilled in divine wisdom and in the liberal arts; so that he sought for wisdom even as did King Solomon, esteeming it to be preferable to glory and riches, and, like him, found them also together with her; according as it is written, "Seek ye first the kingdom of God and His justice, and all other things shall be added to you." This coupling together of divine wisdom and the liberal arts, as equal objects of solicitude, is easily understood when we remember the plan according to which human knowledge was then pursued, always in subordination to that which is divine, and mainly in connection with it. Intellectual pursuits not having yet been set free from their holy servitude to the faith, were not recognised as possessing any peculiar dangers; nay, rather, they seem invariably to have been regarded as something meritorious; and knowledge, far from being preached against as perilous to the soul, was ranked among those better gifts which a good man might earnestly covet.

Asser has related to us the circumstances which led to the king's first applying himself to earnest study. Hitherto, as we have seen, he had been content with making his chaplains read to him, and when Asser first took up his residence at the Court of Leonaford, he also was employed to read to his royal master all the books he desired to become acquainted with, or that could be at that time procured. "One day, as we were sitting together," he says, "conversing as was our wont, I chanced to recite to him a passage out of a certain book. He listened with great delight, and showing me the little book containing his prayers, which he always carried about with him, asked me to transcribe in it the passage I had quoted." But every corner was found to be filled up, and Asser suggested writing out the quotation on a separate leaf. "We cannot tell," he said, "whether we may not meet with other passages which you may like, and if so we should be glad to collect them." Some fresh sheets were accordingly procured, and the same day three more quotations were entered, and so it went on till at last the new book was filled as completely as the old one; and this very day, being the feast of St. Martin, 885, Alfred, then thirty-six years of age, resolved without delay to commence the study of Latin, that he might himself be able to read and translate books into English for the benefit of his people.

His first work, of which unhappily nothing has been preserved but a few fragments, was the very collection alluded to above, and which Asser and William of Malmsbury speak of as his "Enchiridion" or manual. But there yet remain his more important translations from St. Gregory, Orosius, Boethius, and Bede, the first of which contains that admirable preface which explains so modestly and simply the intention of the writer, and the way in which he executed his work. In the mere verbal translation he was assisted by the learning of others, for he tells us with regard to his version of the "Regula Pastoris" of St. Gregory, that it was done by him into English, sometimes word for word, and sometimes sense for sense, "as I learnt it from Plegmund, my archbishop, and Asser, my bishop, and John and Grimbald, my mass-priests." But both in this and his other works, he was far more than a translator, and continually expands the ideas of his authors, introducing new matter of his own; sometimes even he substitutes whole chapters for those which he omits, so as to make his translation almost an original work. In the passages which are from his own pen, we admire at once the philosophic lucidity of his thoughts and the noble simplicity with which he expresses them. A brief sentence of Boethius is thus expanded. "Then, said Reason, Dost thou like fair lands? and Mind answered to Reason, and said, Why should I not like fair lands? How? Is not that the fairest part of God's creation? Full oft we rejoice at the mild sea, and admire also the beauty of sun, moon, and stars. Then answered Wisdom and Reason to the Mind, and said, How belongeth Heaven's fairness to thee? Desirest thou to glory as though its beauty were thine? It is not, it is not. Knowest thou not that thou madest none of these things? If thou wilt glory, glory in God.... Wherefore now dost thou rejoice in the fair blossoms of Easter, as if thou hadst made them; canst thou make any of such things? Not so, not so. Or is it now in thy power that the harvest is so rich in fruits? I know that this also is not in thy power." Boethius says, "Survey the space, the firmness, and the rapidity of the heavens, and cease to admire vile things." This is enlarged by Alfred as follows: "Behold now the spaciousness, the firmness, and the swiftness of the heavens. Yet all this is not to be compared to its Creator and Governor. Why do ye not let yourselves be weary of admiring and praising, that which is unprofitable? That is, worldly riches. For as heaven is better, and fairer, and more precious than all within it, excepting only man, so is man's body better and more precious than all his possessions. But much more bethink thee that his soul is better and more precious than his body. Every being is to be honoured in fit proportion, and always the highest, most. And therefore the Divine Power is to be honoured, adored, and worshipped above all other things." The following remarkable passage on free-will is entirely his own. "I said, I am sometimes very much disturbed. Quoth he, at what? I answered, It is at this, that thou sayest, that God gives to every one freedom to do evil as well as good, whichsoever he will. Now I wonder much at this. Then, quoth he, I may very easily answer thee this remark. How now would it look to thee if there were any very powerful king, and he had no freemen in all his kingdom, but only slaves? Then, said I, it would not be thought by me right or reasonable if servile men only were to wait on him. Then said he, *It would be more unnatural if God, in all His kingdom, had no free creatures under His power*; therefore he made two kinds of rational creatures free, angels and men, and he gave them thus this great gift of freedom." Mr. Turner, in quoting this passage, remarks that Alfred's solution of the difficulty shows him to have been a true king of the English people. He felt from his own great heart that the Divine Sovereign must prefer to govern freemen rather than slaves, because this was his own sentiment as a king. If it were derogatory to the dignity of an earthly ruler to have none but slaves for his subjects, far more so would it be for the King of Heaven to have no creatures endowed with free-will.

But perhaps the most interesting of all these interpolated passages is that which occurs in his paraphrase of Boethius, where, treating of the duties of a king, he speaks thus in his own person: "I never well liked or strongly desired this earthly kingdom; yet when I was in possession of it I desired materials for the work I was commanded to do, that I might fitly steer the vessel, and rule the realm committed to my keeping. There are tools for every craft, without which a man cannot work at his craft; and a king also must have his materials and his tools. And what are these? First, he must have his land well peopled, and he must have prayer-men, and army-men, and work-men. Without these tools no king can show his skill. His materials are provision for these three brotherhoods; land to dwell in, gifts, and weapons, and meat, and ale, and clothes, and whatever else they need. Without these he cannot keep his tools, and without his tools he cannot work. Therefore I desired materials that my craft and power might not be given up and lost. But all craft and power will soon be worn out and put to silence if they be without wisdom. Therefore I desired wisdom. This is now what I can truly say. I have desired while I lived to live worthily, and after my death to leave to men that should be after me a remembrance in good deeds."

In his version of the Chronicle of the World, by Orosius, he followed the same plan, and took occasion to insert a great many corrections and additions, specially in those parts relating to geography, a study for which, like most Anglo-Saxon scholars, Alfred evinced a special liking. His most important additions are a description of Germany, and an account of the voyages of Wulfstan and Othere, the latter of whom was a Norwegian whale-fisher, who sailed round the North Cape into the White Sea, and also entered the mouth of the river Dwina. The narrative was taken down from the lips of the adventurers by the king himself, and is given with the brief biblical simplicity which marks all the compositions of the writer. A considerable portion of the coasts of Prussia and the Baltic are here described for the first time; neither Wulfstan nor Othere removed the impression then prevalent that the Scandinavian peninsula was an island, nevertheless, their discoveries added considerably to the existing geographical knowledge, and the industry shown by the king in collecting and publishing these important facts is well deserving of praise.

The treatise of St. Gregory on the pastoral office was translated by Alfred with peculiar care, and his object in selecting such a work is sufficiently obvious. It contained the instructions of that great Pope whose name was venerated in England as that of her first apostle, on the duties of the pastoral office, and the good king doubtless trusted that its study would revive a better spirit among his clergy. It had in fact a very special degree of authority, and in all the Synods held under Charlemagne was commonly referred to as the standard of ecclesiastical discipline, and would naturally have a special claim on the interest of English readers, as being one of the books bestowed on St. Augustine by the author, and laid up in the Canterbury Library. So highly did Alfred value the translation of the "Hirde-boc," as he calls it, that he caused a copy to be sent to every cathedral church in his dominions, with strict injunctions that they should never be removed thence except for the purpose of transcription, or for the bishop's own reading. Three of these copies are still preserved, with the names of the bishops inserted in the prefatory letters; they are those belonging to Wulfsige of Sherborne, Werferth of Worcester, and Plegmund of Canterbury.

Many other writings and translations are attributed to Alfred by Malmsbury and other historians, and we are assured by the former that he was engaged on an Anglo-Saxon version of the Psalter when attacked with his last sickness. An Anglo-Saxon translation of the New Testament also exists bearing his name, and was printed at London in 1571. Indeed the literary reputation of their "darling," as the Anglo-Saxons popularly termed him, induced them to ascribe to his pen any English writing of uncertain authorship. The real part to be assigned to him in the history of learning is, in fact, that of the founder of Anglo-Saxon literature. Up to this time few books had appeared in the native idiom, with the exception of the national ballads. But it was his wish to substitute that noble tongue, which none knew better how to write than himself, in place of the incorrect Latin which had been used by earlier scholars; his own translations and paraphrases were the first attempts at anything like extensive prose works in the vernacular, but from that time the number of Anglo-Saxon writers rapidly increased.

I have said that the good achieved by Alfred was accomplished rather by his writings than his schools. Mr. Craik, in his history of English literature, speaks of it indeed as "probable" that Alfred restored many of the old episcopal and monastic schools, though he admits there is no satisfactory evidence of his having done so. We may safely affirm, from the absence of all historic evidence, that no such restorations took place, and the reason is obvious; to effect them he must first have restored the monastic institute, and however ardently he desired to do so, it is quite clear that his efforts were crowned with very imperfect success. But his claim to be regarded as the founder of Oxford University rests on more respectable tradition, which, to use the words of Hallam, "if it cannot be maintained as a certain truth, at least bears no intrinsic marks of error." It is assumed by most historians that the schools to the support of which Alfred devoted one-fourth part of the moiety of his revenues, were those which he founded or restored at Oxford, by the advice, as it is said, of St. Neot, and where it is further stated that Grimbald taught theology on first coming to England. Hardyng, the historian, tells us that these schools were founded in virtue of a brief from Pope Martin II.

In the yere Eight hundred four score and tweyne

The Pope Marteyne graunte to Kynge Alwerede

To founde and mak a studye then ageyne,

And an universitie for clerkes in to rede,

The whiche he mad in Oxenforde, in dede,

To that intent that clerkes by sapience

Agayn heretiks suld mak resistence.

The passage, indeed, which occurs in one manuscript of Asser's history, giving an account of certain dissensions between Grimbald and the old scholastics whom he found already established at Oxford, is now very generally held to be an interpolation of later writers, who were anxious by this means to stretch back the antiquity of their university to a date of indefinite remoteness.

For the Cambridge professors having, in Queen Elizabeth's time, unblushingly claimed for their founder, Eneas, the son of Brute, those of Oxford cast about for some way of lengthening their own pedigree to "prehistoric" times, and not content with the reputation of having Alfred for their founder, boldly asserted that Oxford had been a place of study for at least a thousand years before the Christian era; and appealed to the "old scholastics" whom Grimbald is said to have found in possession, in support of their statement. But though the disputed passage is not to be found in the more authentic manuscripts of Asser, yet in them he makes mention of certain schools founded by Alfred, the locality of which he does not name, and there seems no solid ground for rejecting the tradition that fixes them at Oxford, and represents Grimbald as exercising there the office of teacher. The same tradition assigns St. Peter's Church as the scene of his labours, and the Saxon crypt of that church, which is beyond all doubt one of the highest antiquity, is commonly called St. Grimbald's crypt, and is said to have been built by him and intended as his own place of sepulture. But even granting thus much to the Oxford antiquarians it is evident that the circumstantial account which represents the university as founded by Alfred in the same regular form which it assumed in the thirteenth century is altogether fabulous. And it must be allowed that national pride has considerably overstated the work achieved by Alfred as a reviver of learning, and a reformer of discipline. How small an improvement had taken place in the general tone of the Anglo-Saxon clergy may be gathered from the severe reproof addressed to them in the following reign by Pope Formosus, in which it is declared that the impieties of paganism had been suffered to revive in England, while the bishops "remained silent like dogs unable to bark." Such a deplorable state of things can in no way be attributed to any negligence on the part of Alfred, but as he himself has told us, "without tools no man can do his work," and in his day the right tools were wanting. Hence, though several of his successors inherited his learned tastes, they were able to accomplish but little for the promotion of letters. Edward the Elder is said to have founded or restored some schools at Cambridge, and Athelstan is not only styled a *doctarum artium amator*, but is even to be numbered in our list of royal authors, some of his books being discovered by Leland in the library of Bath abbey. But the renewed incursions of the Danes, and the continued wars in which these princes were engaged, prevented their devoting much attention to the encouragement of literature, and, as Wood expresses it, the drum of Mars forced Minerva into a corner. The dearth at this time of monastic houses, and consequently of schools, is proved by the fact that the very few Englishmen who were attracted to a religious life either chose the eremitical state, or emigrated to the foreign cloisters of Fleury or Montfaucon. But in England the old sanctuaries of learning and piety were suffered to lie desolate. The collegiate clergy formerly attached to the cathedrals were exchanged for secular canons, and in the reign of Edgar the Peaceable, that monarch was able to affirm, as a fact known to all men, that, under the rule of his predecessors, monastic institutes had entirely decayed.

The only surviving establishment that still kept up something like a monastic school was the little colony of Irish clergy who served the church of Glastonbury, and it was here that the rudiments of education were received by that extraordinary man who was destined to restore the monastic institute in England, and thus to become the author of a revival of learning more real and lasting than that which Alfred had attempted. This was a work demanding something more than royal power and human greatness for its accomplishment; it implied a struggle with the corrupt sensualism of the world, and a conquest of those powers of evil which are not to be cast forth save by prayer and fasting. A spirit had to be breathed into the dry bones, and the dead, in a certain sense, to be raised to life; and all this called for nothing less than the ministry of a *saint*. And in the hour of the darkest need, a saint was granted to the English Church, which had for more than a century borne the curse of sterility. Or rather not one, but a cluster of glorious stars suddenly illuminated her clouded heavens, whose labours, if they were primarily directed to the reform of ecclesiastical discipline, embraced at the same time, and as a necessary means for accomplishing that end, the establishment of monasteries and schools.

CHAPTER VIII.

ST. DUNSTAN AND HIS COMPANIONS.

A.D. 924 TO 992.

If there be any spot in England consecrated alike by sacred and poetic traditions, it is surely the "thrice famous isle" of Glastonbury, where, according to common belief, the faith was first planted in Britain by St. Joseph of Arimathea, and which was regarded by the inhabitants of this island with a veneration which induced a vast number of the British saints who flourished before the Saxon conquest to retire before their death to the Glassy Isle, that their dust might mingle with its sacred soil. Still surrounded by the marshy waters which once formed a glassy lake around it; still made beautiful in spring by the apple blossoms to which it owes its poetic name of Avallon; still preserving that mysterious hawthorn-tree which, like the roses of Pœstum, "boasts its double bloom," and marks the spot where our first apostle struck his staff into the ground; and still covered with the ruins of that noble abbey which kings vied with one another in beautifying and enriching as "the fountain and origin of all religion in the realm of Britain,"—Glastonbury might well claim, even in its present desolation, to draw pilgrims to its ruined shrines. The poet wanders there to weave new Idylls over the grave of Arthur, whilst the devout client of our native saints kneels to kiss the soil which was the cradle of St. Dunstan. And some may even recall the thought of days long since fled away into the haze of the past, when those two names, so rich in legendary lore, were first cast like golden grains into the storehouse of their memory, as they stood rapt in childish wonder amid those venerable walls, and there taking root, gave birth in their souls to a new idea, so that they passed out of the ruins of Glastonbury, believers, for the first happy moment of their lives, in the possibility of an heroic life.

Glastonbury was at once the birthplace of St. Dunstan and the nursery of his greatness in riper years. There as an infant he was offered by his parents at the altar of Our Lady, and so soon as he could prattle, was given over by them to the care of some Irish monks who had settled in the deserted abbey, and earned a scanty subsistence by educating the children of the neighbourhood. His extraordinary genius soon displayed itself, not merely by a rapid acquisition of grammar, but by the excellence he attained in music, poetry, and the arts. Having been introduced to the notice of the king by his uncle Athelm, Archbishop of Canterbury, his superior talents excited the jealousy of the courtiers, who accused him of magic, a charge which they chiefly grounded on his musical skill, by which they declared that he bewitched the king, and his familiarity with the old bardic poetry of the Anglo-Saxons. Obliged to withdraw from court, he returned to Glastonbury, and for some time led an eremitical life in a small cell adjoining the church. We need neither the testimony of the old legend, nor the suggestions of romance, to understand how it was that a mind like Dunstan's had to pass through much tribulation ere it could utterly resign itself to the guidance of grace. The noblest natures have the hardest combats to undergo, and are not crowned till they have striven and overcome. So it was in the midst of many trials that Dunstan spent his solitary noviciate, chasing away the tempter now with prayer, and now with manual labour. He did not lay aside his artistic tastes, but toiled away at his smith's forge, producing those exquisite works in gold and other metals long preserved with reverence in many English churches, or carving in wood, or painting, engraving, and moulding in wax and clay. He used his musical skill, too, to soothe his weary spirit, by reminding himself of the heavenly harmonies, and once, having hung his harp against the wall, the wind, it is said, swept over the strings, and brought out from them a plaintive strain in which he recognised one of the antiphons sung in the Common of Martyrs, *Gaudent in cœlis animæ sanctorum qui Christi vestigia secuti sunt.* At last King Edmund, the brother and successor of Athelstan, recalled him to court, made him his chief councillor, and bestowed on him the territory of Glastonbury, that he might restore the abbey to its former splendour. Dunstan therefore collected a community, to whom he gave the rule of St. Benedict, and according to many writers he is to be regarded as the first real founder of the Benedictine order in this country. Even if this be an historical error, and the early Anglo-Saxon monks may likewise be claimed as Benedictines (a warmly controverted point on which it is needless here to enter), St. Dunstan's work as the restorer of the order is of no less importance than if we consider him the first English founder, for the firm establishment of the monastic rule in England at this particular juncture was the means by which, under God, the Church itself was preserved in this land.

The corruption of the secular clergy had become so general that the total decay of religion must soon have been the inevitable result, had not sacred letters and ecclesiastical discipline been revived by the monks. Happily, St. Dunstan was not alone; he found a band of great souls, able and willing to second him in his efforts, and among these were the three saints, Odo, Oswald, and Ethelwold. Odo was the son of Danish and heathen parents, who, disgusted at their son's interest in everything connected with the Christian worship, turned him adrift, while still a child, to shift for himself. Athelm, one of King Alfred's thanes, took compassion on him, and sent him to be educated at the court school, where, we are told, he acquired so thorough a knowledge both of Greek and Latin as to be able to write in both languages with great facility. Being promoted to the priesthood, Athelm chose him for his confessor, and, according to the custom of the more pious laity of early times, recited the divine Office with him daily. After that he became chaplain to the good king Athelstan, in which capacity he was present at the great battle of Brunanburgh. Athelstan procured his election to the see of Sherburne, whence, in 942, he was translated to the archbishopric of Canterbury. He hesitated to accept the primacy, however, on the ground that he was not a monk, as all those had been who had preceded him in that see. But the king overruled the objection by sending to the abbot of Fleury, who himself brought over the monastic cowl with which he invested the archbishop elect. Odo at once addressed himself to the Augean task of reform, and appointed his nephew, Oswald, to the deanery of Winchester, hoping thereby to introduce more regular discipline among the canons of that cathedral. But Oswald found his efforts so utterly fruitless that he withdrew to Fleury, whence, however, he was compelled to return at the command of his uncle, who could ill spare labourers from the English vineyard. The archbishop's canons, together with the pastoral letter which accompanied them, bear evidence alike of his zeal and his learning. But something more than a paper reform was required to heal the terrible wounds of the English Church. The only real hope of remedy lay in the formation of an entirely new body of clergy, who should from their youth have been trained in sacred letters, holy living, and ecclesiastical discipline. Church seminaries were needed; and where could these be established save in the newly-founded abbeys now springing up under the government of St. Dunstan?

The destruction of the monastic schools had been one chief cause of the existing evils, and in their restoration Odo saw the only hope of remedy. And, marvellous to say, they were being restored. At Glastonbury St. Dunstan had already founded the first regular monastic school which had been seen in England since the destruction of her old seminaries; and here some of the most famous ecclesiastics who flourished during the tenth century received their education. Dunstan allowed the reading of the Latin poets, because, as he said, it polished the mind and improved the style; he also encouraged the study of Anglo-Saxon poetry, as it would seem with a view of rendering his clergy eloquent in the vernacular tongue, and more powerful preachers. Neither was science forgotten; and the study of arithmetic, geometry, astronomy, and music were carefully cultivated by his pupils, many of whom likewise excelled in those artistic pursuits in which their master was an adept. Nor was Glastonbury the only scene of this revived intellectual activity. The combined influence of great genius and great sanctity was effecting that reaction in favour of monasticism which Alfred had vainly attempted to bring about, and to which he also had looked as the only means of establishing a real reform. In his time monks had sunk so low in the estimation of the Anglo-Saxon people, that none but churls could be found willing to wear the cowl. But St. Dunstan's example had turned the tide, and Glastonbury was soon able to send out colonies and found other houses, whose abbots were supplied from the ranks of the saint's chosen disciples.

Among these, by far the most distinguished was St. Ethelwold, who, after for some years filling the office of dean in the monastery of Glastonbury, formed the design of passing over to Fleury in order to perfect himself more thoroughly in religious discipline and sacred science. King Edred, who was then reigning during the minority of his two nephews, heard of his purpose and forbade him to leave the kingdom, but, to sweeten his disappointment, offered him the old ruined abbey of Abingdon, that he might restore the monastic rule within its walls. He was right in thinking that such an offer was likely to reconcile Ethelwold to his detention on the English soil, and the saint at once applied himself to his labour of love. He began by sending over to Corby for some monks well-skilled in monastic discipline, whom he desired to have as foundation stones of his community; and, not content with this, he despatched one of his brethren from Glastonbury to study all the ways and fashions of that celebrated seminary of learning. Ethelwold had nothing more at heart than the restoration of sacred studies, and was resolved that his monastic school should be the best of its kind. Wolstan, his biographer, tells us that he had been the companion of St. Dunstan in his studies, and not only distinguished himself by his proficiency in grammar, poetry, and the mechanical arts, but had also spent several years in the work of teaching others. "He taught the art of grammar with great skill," says his disciple, "and that of poetical metre with most mellifluous sweetness; and like the prudent bee which is used to seek for pleasant scents flying about among the trees and flowers, and agreeably loading itself with the odoriferous juices, even so did he pluck the blossoms of the sacred volumes, and studiously apply himself to the study of the Catholic Fathers." He was, moreover, like his master Dunstan, an enthusiastic lover of science, and a great adept in architecture and bell-founding; and thus the restoration of the old abbey was one of those undertakings in which his piety and his taste were able to work in concert. The new abbey church was adorned with four large bells, two cast by the hand of its abbot, and two yet larger ones, the handiwork of St. Dunstan. Nor was Ethelwold less renowned as a musician and mathematician, and one of his mathematical treatises, addressed to the celebrated Gerbert, is still preserved in the Bodleian Library. He had, moreover, that yet more excellent gift, the power of engaging the affections of those whom he taught. The young were irresistibly attracted to him, and this was one cause of the influx of youths who soon filled the schools of Abingdon. The account has been preserved of the death of one of his scholars, an innocent boy named Ædmer, who was greatly loved both by the abbot and his schoolfellows, on account of his holy simplicity and angelic virtue. Whilst still in the happy state of baptismal grace he was attacked by mortal sickness. As his death drew on he was rapt in ecstasy, and beheld the

Blessed Virgin seated on a glorious throne surrounded by many saints. With a kind and loving countenance, she asked him whether he would prefer remaining amid that heavenly company, or continuing in his mortal life. And he, seeing no sadness among those on whom he gazed, said he would far rather abide there with them; whereupon Our Lady promised that he should have his wish. And so, returning to himself, he made known to the abbot what he had seen and heard; and presently his happy soul departed to its rest.

In the reign of the dissolute Edwy, a storm arose which for a time threatened to overthrow the new foundations, and put a stop to the good work so happily begun. The courageous reproof administered to that prince by the abbot of Glastonbury having exposed him to the royal displeasure, he was obliged to withdraw to Flanders, and the two abbeys of Glastonbury and Abingdon were dissolved by the king's command, and the monks dispersed through the country. The vices of Edwy, however, brought their own punishment with them: the provinces north of the Thames threw off his authority, and chose for their king his brother Edgar, who at once recalled St. Dunstan, and promoted him to the same post of confidence he had filled under Edmund and Edred. The see of Worcester falling vacant, Edgar, who by the death of Edwy was now king of all England, insisted on his accepting the episcopal charge, and he was accordingly consecrated by St. Odo, in 957. Two years later, on the death of the primate, Dunstan was chosen his successor, and going to Rome to receive the Pall, was sent back to England invested with the authority of Apostolic Legate.

He was now in a position effectually to carry out those great measures of reform for which he had so long been preparing the instruments. He found himself surrounded by a band of faithful and carefully-trained ecclesiastics, animated with his own devoted spirit; and his first step was to procure the election of Oswald, the nephew of Odo, to the see of Worcester. Ten years later, St. Oswald became Archbishop of York, being allowed, by extraordinary dispensation, to hold both sees together; Dunstan being unwilling that the good discipline he had established at Worcester should suffer by his removal. Ethelwold was placed over the see of Winchester, and, with the help of these two holy coadjutors, the archbishop entered on the task of enforcing the observance of the sacred canons. The royal sanction to his plan was formally granted at a great council, for Edgar entered heart and soul into all the plans of his primate. "I hold the sword of Constantine," he said, "and you that of St. Peter; together we will purify the sanctuary." The choice was everywhere offered to the secular clergy of promising obedience to the laws of the Church, or resigning their benefices. In some places the secular canons accepted the reform, but where they refused to do so they were summarily ejected. St. Oswald was fortunate enough to succeed in winning his Worcester canons, not merely to promise a regular life, but to embrace the monastic rule; and, under his wise and gentle government, they in time became excellent religious. St. Ethelwold was less happy; and finding it impossible to convert his canons from their life of lawless indulgence, he replaced them with a body of Benedictine monks.

At the same time that many cathedrals and collegiate churches were receiving these monastic colonies, new foundations were everywhere springing up. Ely, Peterborough, Malmsbury and Thorney abbeys rose once more out of their ruins; and such was the eagerness of the king and his nobles to promote the ecclesiastical reform, that more than forty abbeys were founded or restored during the primacy of St. Dunstan. With these events, however, so important in the Church history of England, we are only concerned in so far as they affected the restoration of learning; and, in fact, the revival of the monastic institute was one and the same thing with the revival of the English schools. From this time, in spite of many corruptions and abuses, which resisted even the efforts of Dunstan to remove them, the Dark Age, *par excellence*, of English history began to disappear. A new race of scholars sprang up in the restored cloisters, some of whom were not unworthy to be ranked with the disciples of Alcuin and Bede. St. Dunstan himself, during the remainder of his primacy, was occupied with measures rather of practical, than of educational reform; nevertheless, we find from his canons that his solicitude was directed in a very special way to providing for the religious instruction of the common people. He revived the old parochial schools, and obliged his parish priests to preach every Sunday to their flocks, requiring them also in their schools to teach the children of their parishioners grammar, the church-chant, and some useful handicraft trade.

It was St. Ethelwold, however, who exhibited the greatest zeal for the restoration of sacred studies. He loved the work of teaching for its own sake, and had no sooner got possession of his own cathedral, and banished the canons who had so long disgraced it, than he applied all his care to collect and educate a staff of young clergy, who, he trusted, would prove worthy to fill the vacant benefices. "It was ever sweet to him," says his charming biographer Wolstan, "to teach youths and little ones, to explain their Latin books to them in English, to instruct them in the rules of grammar and prosody, and allure them by cheerful words to study and improvement. And so it came to pass that many of his disciples became priests and abbots, some also bishops and archbishops, in the realm of England." Among these was St. Elphege, who afterwards became Archbishop of Canterbury, and was martyred by the Danes, and Cynewulf, abbot of Peterborough, an apt and gentle teacher, whose monastic school was so celebrated that, as Hugo Candidus says, scholars flocked to it from all countries as to the court of a second Solomon. He wrote some Anglo-Saxon poems, still preserved; their authorship being detected by the curious insertion here and there of a Runic letter, which, when put together, spell the writer's name.

It will be observed that the new race of scholars did not exclusively cultivate Latin literature. The labours of Alfred had given a powerful stimulus to the study of English, and this was yet further encouraged both by St. Dunstan and St. Ethelwold, who desired nothing more than to facilitate the instruction of the common people in their own tongue. Ethelwold translated the rule of St. Benedict into Anglo-Saxon for the use of his monks, and a copy of this work may still be seen in the Cottonian Library, the Latin text being accompanied with an interlinear Anglo-Saxon version. Elfric, one of Ethelwold's scholars, devoted himself with particular energy to the cultivation of English literature. Besides translating a considerable number of the books of Scripture, at the request of his friend, the ealderman Ethelward, he composed a Latin and English grammar, and other school books, such as a Latin and English glossary, and his well-known "Colloquies," written in both languages, for the use of beginners. The grammar has a Latin and English preface, in which he tells us that he undertook the work for the promotion of sacred studies, specially among the young, for, he observes, "it is the duty of ecclesiastics to guard against such a want of learning in our day as was to be found in England but a very few years ago, when not a priest could be found to translate a Latin epistle, till Archbishop Dunstan and Bishop Ethelwold encouraged learning in their monasteries."

His most celebrated work was his collection of Homilies[118] for the use of parish priests. None are original compositions; they are selections and translations from the early Latin Fathers, as well as from Bede and a few other French and German homilists. The Anglo-Saxon into which they are rendered is considered the fairest specimen that can be cited of our ancient national tongue, and raises a regret that so noble a language should ever have been allowed to corrupt into our modern hybrid English. The compiler subscribes his name to the work as, "Ælfric, the scholar of Ethelwold," a title he evidently regarded as no small honour. I may add, that many of his writings are addressed to his friend Ethelward and another English thane, Sigwerd of East Heolen, and seems to intimate that the laity as well as the clergy were now beginning to cultivate letters.

Ethelwold's zeal for the restoration of the monastic institute moved him to petition King Edgar for a grant of all the minsters that had been laid waste in old time by the "heathen men." It would be too long to notice all the restoration effected by "the father of monks" as he was called, or the many works of active benevolence which earned for him, from his grateful people, his other beautiful title of "the well-willing bishop." He exercised his engineering talents in supplying his cathedral city with water, and in time of dearth broke up his altar plate to feed the multitudes. He rebuilt his cathedral church with great splendour, as we learn from the poem in which Wolstan has dwelt with loving minuteness on every detail from the crypt to the tower, which last was surmounted by a gilded weathercock, which says the poet, "stands proudly superior to the whole population of Winton, and brazen as he is, rules all the other cocks of the city." There was likewise an organ of marvellous construction, and a certain wheel full of bells, called "the golden wheel," only brought out on solemn occasions, both of these being the workmanship of the bishop.

Meanwhile, St. Oswald was pursuing much the same course in his northern dioceses. He restored the abbeys of Pershore, Winchecombe, and St. Alban's, and founded several others, particularly that of Ramsey, which long maintained the reputation of being the most learned of the English monasteries. The history of its foundation is given at length by the monk of Ramsey. A certain ealderman, named Aylwin, having offered to devote his wealth to some work of piety, St. Oswald asked him if he had any lands suited for the building of a monastery. He replied that he had some land, surrounded with marshes, and free from resort of men, and there was a forest near it full of various kinds of trees, and having several spots of good turf and fine grass for pasturage. They went together to view the spot, which was so solitary and yet possessed of so many conveniences for subsistence and secluded devotion, that the bishop decided on accepting it. Artificers of all kinds were at once collected, and the neighbours willingly offered their services. Twelve monks from another cloister came to form the new foundation; their cells and a temporary chapel were first raised, and by the next winter they had provided iron and timber enough for a handsome church. In the spring a firm foundation was made in the fenny soil, the workmen labouring as much from devotion as for profit. Some brought the stones, others made the cement, and others worked the wheel-machinery that raised the stones to their places, and so in a short time the sacred edifice, with two fair towers, appeared in what had before been a desolate wilderness.

The monks mentioned in this account as having been brought from "another cloister," were a colony from Fleury, and among them was the celebrated Abbo of Fleury, of whom there will be occasion to speak in another chapter. He remained two years at Ramsey, and thoroughly established its school. His most distinguished pupil was Bridferth, originally a monk of Thorney, who migrated to Ramsey soon after its foundation, and was probably one of the first scientific scholars of his time. He had received his early education from St. Dunstan, and imbibed all his tastes. In his Commentary on Bede he incidentally notices a scientific observation which he had made when a student at Thionville in France, whence it appears that he had enlarged his stock of knowledge by visits to foreign academies. His Commentaries on the treatises De Rerum Natura and De Tempore, consist of notes of lectures delivered in the Ramsey schools. Whilst explaining his author he frequently introduces original illustrations, sometimes supporting Bede's statements by numerical calculations of his own, sometimes amplifying the text and clearing up doubtful expressions. He quotes St. Clement, St. Augustine, Eusebius, St. Ambrose, St. Jerome, and St. Isidore, also Pliny, Macrobius, Priscian, and Martian Capella, and continually refers to the Latin poets as familiar to his hearers. He was also the author of a treatise "De Principiis Mathematicis," and a life of his old master. St. Dunstan, the last of which he dedicated to Ælfric, and extols him in his preface for the "enormity of his well-known learning."

The later annals of Ramsey abbey are full of interest, and how that the school thus brilliantly founded was not suffered to fall into decay. Some of these will reappear in a later portion of our narrative; but, before bidding adieu to the old Saxon abbey, I must notice one little narrative which shows that all the scholars there educated were not destined for the ecclesiastical state. Four little boys named Oswald, Etheric, Ædnoth, and Athelstan had been placed in the school by St. Oswald, all being sons of powerful Saxon thanes. They were received before they were seven years old, and were of innocent manners and beautiful countenances. At certain times they were suffered by their master to go and play outside the cloister walls. One day, being thus sent out by themselves, they ran to the great west tower, and laying hold of the bell rope, rang with all their might, but so unskilfully that one of the bells was cracked by the unequal motion. The mischief becoming known, the culprits were threatened with a sound flogging; a threat which occasioned abundance of tears. At last remembering the sentence they had so often heard read from the rule of St. Benedict, "If any one shall lose or break anything, let him hasten without delay to accuse himself of it," they ran to the abbot and, weeping bitterly, told him all that had happened. The good abbot pitied their distress, and calling the brethren together who were disposed to treat the matter rather severely, he said to them, "These innocents have committed a fault, but with no evil intention; they ought, therefore, to be spared, and when they grow up to be men it will be easy for them to make good the damage they have done." Then, dismissing the monks, he secretly admonished the boys, how to disarm their anger, and they, following his directions, entered the church with bare feet, and there made their vow; and when they grew up to manhood and were raised to wealth and honour they remembered what they had promised, and bestowed great benefits on the church.[119]

Not the least benefit conferred by the monks on their countrymen by the foundation of these abbeys was the improvement of the lands which they drained and cultivated. This, indeed, does not properly enter into our present subject; but the graphic pictures which monkish historians have left of the spots which they thus tamed and beautified, must be referred to as showing that their minds and tastes were no less richly cultivated. It is thus that William of Malmsbury speaks of Thorney abbey after its restoration by St. Ethelwold, who took great pains in planting it with forest and fruit trees: "Thorney," says the historian, "is indeed a picture of paradise, and for pleasantness may be compared to heaven itself, bearing trees even in the very fens, which tower with their lofty tops to the clouds; while below, the smooth surface of the water attracts the eye and reflects the verdant scene. Not the smallest spot is here unimproved—all is covered with fruit trees or vines, which creep along the ground, and in some places are supported on poles."

But it remains for us to speak of the death of those great men, whose successful labours had effected so much for the real civilisation of their country. Ethelwold was the first to depart; and four years later, in 988, St. Dunstan terminated his grand career, rapt, as it would seem, in an ecstasy of love; for, after receiving the Holy Viaticum, he poured out a sublime prayer, and expired with its accents on his lips. St. Oswald survived his two friends until the February of 992; and among all the beautiful narrations of the deaths of the saints, "precious in the sight of the Lord," few can be found more touching than that which describes his end. On the day previously, coming out of his oratory into the open air, he stood for a while gazing up into the sky, as though fixedly contemplating some glorious sight. Being asked what he saw, he only smiled, and said he was looking at the place whither he was going. He then returned to his oratory and desired them to give him the Holy Unction and the last Viaticum, although, indeed, he had no appearance of illness. That evening he assisted at the night office in his cathedral, and when morning came, according to his custom, he washed the feet of twelve poor men, reciting as he did so the Gradual Psalms. At their close, still kneeling, he pronounced the *Gloria Patri*, and then, bending gently forward, expired at the feet of the poor. When his holy body was carried to the grave, a milk-white dove, with wings extended, hovered over the bier all the way. He had been granted the satisfaction of witnessing the completion of his favourite abbey of Ramsey, which he consecrated just three months before his death.[120]

The English restoration of letters, inaugurated by St. Dunstan and his companions, took place at a critical period, when fresh tides of barbarism were overwhelming the continental territories, and reducing the monastic institute in France to its very lowest ebb. This tenth century was, in fact, the famous "Age of Iron," which, in spite of its celebrity as the very midnight of the Dark Ages, fills, strange to say, a very important place in the history of monastic literature. It will, therefore, be necessary to consider its various bearings at some length; and we will begin with the ungracious task of painting it in its blackest aspect.

CHAPTER IX.

THE IRON AGE.

A.D. 900 TO 1000.

BARONIUS, when about to enter on the history of the tenth century, thinks it necessary to prepare his readers for what is coming by a sentence which, in spite of the wildness of its metaphors, has obtained an odd kind of immortality. "We are now entering on a period," he says, "which for its sterility of every excellence may be denominated *iron*; for its luxuriant growth of vice, *leaden*; and for its dearth of writers, *dark*." Why iron should be chosen as most fit to typify the sterility of virtue, and lead to figure forth the luxuriance of vice, is not perhaps at first sight obvious; but these words, which are certainly not remarkable for the appropriateness of their imagery, have formed the text for many commentators; from one of whom, as being a professedly Catholic writer, I select a passage which claims to explain at least one of the phenomena of this period—the darkness, namely, that succeeded the establishment of the Carlovingian schools.

"The want of success in the excellent establishments of Charlemagne," observes Mr. Berington, in his "Literary History of the Middle Ages," "may be traced to various causes:—to the inaptitude of the teachers, who, though endowed with the natural powers of intellect, knew not how to excite attention or interest curiosity; to the subjects called sciences, or the seven liberal arts, which were so taught as to disgust by their barbarous elements, and of which the emaciated and haggard skeleton was alike unfit for ornament or use; to the absence of the first rudiments of education, as of reading and writing, in the higher orders of society, and their habitual devotion to martial exercises; to the oblivion in which the classical productions of former ages were held; to a want of capacity in the bishops and clergy and monks, upon whom the weighty charge of education had devolved; to a selfish reflection in the same order of men that, *in proportion to the decline of learning and the spread of ignorance, their churches and monasteries had prospered*, whilst the revival of letters was likely to direct the copious streams of benevolence into a channel less favourable to the interests of the clergy and monks; to a marked aversion in the Bishop of Rome to any scheme by which the minds of churchmen or others might be turned to the study of antiquity, and of those documents which would disclose on what futile reasons and sandy foundations the exclusive prerogatives of his see were established; and *to the genius of the Christian system* itself, which, when it expelled the Pagan Deities from their seats, too successfully fixed a reproach on many things connected with them, and thus contributed to banish from the schools, and consign to oblivion those works on the study and prevalence of which will ever depend the progress of the arts, of the sciences, and of literary taste."[121]

The above passage has been somewhat of the longest, and I shall therefore do no more than allude to the terms in which another historian of the Middle Ages, of yet greater repute, speaks of "the inconceivable ignorance which overspread the face of the Church, broken only by a few glimmering lights which owe almost all their distinction to the surrounding darkness;" to his unqualified and unsupported declaration, that "the cathedral and monastic schools were exclusively designed for religious purposes, and afforded no opportunities to the laity;" that "for centuries it was rare for a layman, of whatever rank, to know how to sign his name;" that "with the monks a knowledge of church-music passed for literature;" and that as to the religion which prevailed during the same period, "it is *an extremely complex question whether it were not more injurious to public morals and the welfare of society than the entire absence of all religious notions.*"[122]

"One of the later Greek schools," says Bacon, "is at a standstill to think what should be in it that men should so love lies;" yet he presently adds, "the mixture thereof doth ever give pleasure." Charity, then, obliges us to believe that the fictitious element which appears in these passages has only been added to stimulate the pleasure of the reader. In perusing them, and scores of others which might easily be accumulated from writers both great and petty, we are, of course, left with the impression on our minds, that not only was the ignorance most dense, gross, and universal, but that it found its cause in the low cunning of the clergy, and especially of the monks, who had just wit enough to keep the rest of the world in darkness. And as the first writer has expressly told us that their object in doing this was to maintain that flourishing state of monastic prosperity which, we are assured, existed in proportion to the spread of ignorance, we are logically bound to suppose that the countries and the times wherein darkness thus prevailed were the Elysium and the golden age of monkhood. No one certainly would be led to suppose that the iron, leaden, and pitch-dark state of society in the tenth century, could be accounted for by any particular circumstances in the history of the times, which, far from favouring the monastic institute, all but destroyed it, and did totally eradicate it in the districts most subject to their influence. No,—our historians do not so much as allude to such insignificant episodes in history as the irruptions of three new races of barbarians, but complacently refer us to the superstition and selfishness of the Bishop of Rome and his clergy, which they regard, as a certain astronomer regarded the spots in the sun, as being "large enough to account for anything."

The prospect before us looks but dreary; and in candour it must be confessed that a nearer acquaintance with this unhappy period will not set it in a more advantageous light. It was indeed a time as dark and terrible as the imagination can well depict, though whether the human mind were altogether in a state of ruin, and whether the darkness were exclusively the work of the monks, and whether monasteries grew and prospered as ignorance increased, or whether some other possible causes may not be assigned for the state of things so universally deplored, are questions which cannot be resolved without a glance at the current history of the times.

Enough has been said in a former chapter of the restoration of letters which took place under Charlemagne. If any work ever had fair promise of success, it was surely this, and yet in a certain sense it was a failure. The century that followed his decease was precisely the iron century which all historians have agreed to vilify, and it is undoubtedly true that in some respects the state of Europe under the Carlovingian monarchs was even worse than under their Merovingian predecessors. The dream of a restoration of the Roman Empire, which had been realised only so long as the European sceptre was grasped in the mighty hand of Charlemagne, fell to pieces after his death like a child's house of cards. The fatal step taken by Louis the Debonnaire, of dividing his dominions among his sons during his lifetime, plunged the whole empire into a civil war, which resulted in his own deposition, and which did not cease on his death. The various subdivisions into which the empire then split were indeed reunited under Charles the Fat, but his cowardice and incapacity having rendered him contemptible to those great feudal vassals who were gradually assuming all the real power in the realm, he also was deposed, and the imperial dignity ceased to find a representative till it was revived under Otho the Great. For a century after the death of Charles, France was nominally governed by princes of the Carlovingian race, appointed or removed at the will of the dukes of France. On the death of Duke Hugh the Great, his son, Hugh Capet, contented himself for a time with the system adopted by his predecessors, but in 987 he assumed the royal title, the powers of which he had long exercised, and became the founder of the Capetian dynasty. During the progress of these events, the firmly-knit and centralised government of Charlemagne totally disappeared; the territories of his empire were divided first into three, then into seven kingdoms; and were finally dismembered into more than fifty feudal sovereignties. Florus, the deacon of Lyons, mentioned in a former chapter, in a poem entitled *Querela de divisione Imperii*, describes the disorders consequent on these changes with an eloquent pen. "A beautiful empire," he says, "once flourished under a glorious crown. Then there was one prince and one people, and every town had judges and laws. The word of salvation was preached to nobles and peasants, and youth everywhere studied the Sacred Scriptures and the liberal arts.... Now, instead of a king, we see everywhere a kinglet, instead of an empire, its fragments. The bishops can no longer hold their synods, there are no assemblies, no laws; and if an embassy arrive, there is no court to receive it."[123]

By the end of the tenth century feudalism had fairly established itself on the ruins of the empire. The new system brought in its train many evils and some social benefits, but whilst in process of development its immediate effect was to throw the whole governing power into the hands of a number of petty lords, who were responsible to no superior for their exercise of it. In spite, however, of the turbulence of the times, we shall find, on comparing them with the Merovingian period, that there was a decided advance in point of civilisation, which shows that the labours of Charlemagne and his bishops had not been entirely thrown away. The century which preceded the coronation of Hugh Capet, with all its intrigues and bloody contests, does not present us with a single political murder; whereas the Merovingian annals consist of little else than a catalogue of such crimes. Nay, after the great battle of Fontenay, fought in 841, in which it is said that a hundred thousand of the noblest warriors of France were slain, and which for ever established the preponderance in that country of the Romanesque over the Tudesque race and dialect,[124] the victorious combatants submitted to the severe penance imposed on them by the bishops of the realm; and the same singular spectacle was exhibited in 923, when, after the battle of Soissons, the bishops assembled in council imposed very severe penances on all concerned, thus protesting in the name of humanity and religion against these miserable civil broils.

In the midst of such contests, however, the scholastic system established by Charlemagne was entirely deprived of that support which it had received from him and his immediate successors. The monastic and cathedral schools were left to flourish or decay according as the ruling abbot or bishop chanced to foster or neglect them. The withdrawal of imperial patronage was not probably in every respect a misfortune, but in cases where schools had only been kept up by state support they would naturally not long survive the break up of the government. This, however, though one, was not the main cause of the decline of letters in the tenth century. Schools disappeared for the simple reason that the churches and monasteries to which they were attached had disappeared also. It is inconceivable how any author who has read the most meagre abridgments of European history can be found to advance the monstrous assertion that monasticism flourished after the death of Charlemagne in proportion as ignorance increased. The tenth century, this very century of lead and iron ignorance, witnessed the all but total extinction of the monastic institute in France; and in Germany, where it survived and flourished, schools and letters continued to flourish likewise. If any spots are discoverable west of the Rhine where sparks of learning were still kept alive, we shall find them in those remote retreats where the monks took shelter from the storm which was elsewhere laying waste all the fairest sanctuaries of the land. In short, the iron age was an age of darkness because it witnessed a return of those barbaric incursions which had already swept away the

Roman civilisation, and which were now attacking the Christian civilisation which had sprung up in its place. The calamities that were already hanging over Europe before the death of Charlemagne had not been unforeseen by his eagle glance. So early as 810 the Norman keels had appeared off the shores of Friesland, and the powerful marine force which then guarded the coasts of the empire proved but a vain protection. He himself beheld them in the offing from the windows of his palace in one of the Narbonnese cities, and sorrowfully predicted the evils they would bring on his people after his death. And his words were only too soon fulfilled. In the reign of Louis the Debonnaire the Normans sailed up the Loire and laid siege to Tours, reducing the whole country as far as the Cher to a desert. In the following reign they showed themselves yet bolder. Entering the Seine they proceeded up that river to Paris, which they sacked, after massacring all the inhabitants who had not saved themselves by flight. Treves, Cologne, Rouen, Nantes, Orleans, and Amiens, shared a similar fate. At Aix-la-Chapelle they turned the chapel of Charlemagne into a stable: Angers was twice given to the flames; and in 885 took place that terrible siege of Paris, by an army of thirty thousand Normans, which has been rendered famous by the historic poem on the subject written by the monk Abbo, and which lasted for thirteen months. In the course of this siege the Normans filled up the ditch which separated them from the walls by the bodies of their slaughtered prisoners.

The mode of warfare adopted by the invaders was entirely novel. Their fleets entered the estuaries of rivers and ascended them almost to their source, predatory bands landing on either bank to ravage the surrounding country. From the great rivers they proceeded up the lesser streams, which led them into the heart of fertile districts. They would seize on some island suited for their purpose, where they fortified themselves and spent the winter. In this way whole provinces, even those most remote from the sea-coast, were devastated, and that so entirely that, says one writer, "not a dog was left to bark in them." The inhabitants deserted their villages and fields at the first alarm, and fled to the woods; towns were sacked and given to the flames, and the churches and monasteries which were supposed to contain the greatest treasures were the first objects of attack. "What else is now to be seen," says the author of the "Romaunt of the Rose," "but churches burnt and people slain? The Normans do as they please, and from Blois to Senlis there is not an acre of wheat left standing." Another monkish historian thus describes what was passing under his own eyes: "Not a city, not a town, not a village but has in its turn felt the barbarity of the heathen men. They overrun the whole country, and their cabins form great villages where they keep their miserable captives in chains." The desolate tracts of country thus laid waste became the resort of packs of wolves, which prowled about unmolested; it seemed, says one historian, as if France were abandoned to the wild animals.

The Carlovingian princes offered but a feeble resistance to these terrible invasions. The Normans themselves were surprised at the supineness of their victims. "The country is good," said Ragnar Lodbrog to the Danish monarch, after returning from the sack of Paris, "but the people are tremblers. The dead there have more courage than the living, for the only resistance I met with was from an old man named Germanus, who had been dead many years, and whose house I entered." He spoke of the Church of St. Germain d'Auxerre, where his sacrilegious marauders had been miraculously put to flight. In the reign of Charles the Bald the only opposition to the invaders was offered by Robert the Strong, who in reward of his exertions received the dukedom of France, by which name was then designated the country lying between the Seine and the Loire. As to the king himself he was content to buy off the sea-king Hasting by the payment of forty thousand livres of silver, promising either to give up as prisoners, or to ransom at a fixed sum, every Frenchman who had escaped from the Normans' hands, and to pay a composition for every Norman who should be slain; a stipulation which probably exceeds in infamy any other ever agreed upon by a Christian prince. A few years later the cowardice exhibited by Charles the Fat, at the second siege of Paris, moved his indignant subjects to deprive him of the crown; an heroic defence was indeed offered by Eudes, son of Robert the Strong, but his chief supporters were three priests, Gauzlin, Bishop of Paris, his nephew Ebbo, and Anchesius, abbot of St. Germain-des-Pres. In 912, the devastations committed by Rollo and his followers obliged Charles the Simple to make peace with them, on terms which made over to the Norman chieftain the feudal sovereignty of Neustria. The wild sea-king received baptism, and became the first duke of Normandy but though a stop was thus put to the attacks on Paris and the northern coast, the Northmen continued their ravages in the provinces south of the Loire.

Terrible as they were, however, these barbarians were only one out of the many savage swarms let loose on Europe at this unhappy time. In 836, the Saracens, who were the masters of the Mediterranean, attacked the coasts of Provence. Marseilles, the only city of Septimania where Roman letters still partially lingered, was surprised and pillaged, and the monks and clergy carried into slavery. The Saracens established themselves at Frassinet, a port between Toulon and Frejus, and held possession of it for more than a century. From these head-quarters they were able at their pleasure to ascend the Rhone as far as Arles, and to overrun all the south of France. About the same time they sailed up the Tiber, and advancing as far as Rome, burnt a great part of that city. "How many and great are the things we are suffering from the Saracens!" wrote Pope John VIII. to Charles the Bald; "why should I attempt to describe them with the tongue, when all the leaves of the forest, were they turned into pens, would not suffice. Behold cities, walled towns, and villages bereft of inhabitants! Wild beasts usurp the sanctuaries once filled with the chair of doctrine. Instead of breaking the bread of life to their flocks there, bishops have to buy their own. Rome herself is left desolate. Last year we sowed, but could not reap our harvests by reason of the Saracens; this year we can hope for none, for in seed-time we could not till the ground." Every part of the Italian peninsula was wasted by these barbarians, who established themselves at Benevento, and were not driven thence till the end of the century. They even had the audacity to seize and hold possession of fortified posts in Provence, Dauphiny, Savoy, and Piedmont, which gave them the command of the Alpine passes, so that they could stop and levy tribute on all the pilgrims travelling from the north to Rome.

But this was not all. The last and worst of the plagues poured out on Christendom yet remains to be noticed. Towards the close of the ninth century, the Magyars or Huns, driven westward by the advance of other Asiatic tribes, crossed the Carpathian mountains, and descended into the plains of Dacia. Thence they spread like a torrent over Germany, which they ravaged as far as the Black Forest. Crossing the Alps, they laid waste the plain of Lombardy, and thence poured into Aquitaine, which they overran as far as the Pyrenees. Some bands proceeded as far as the southern extremity of Italy, others found their way into Greece, and advanced to the walls of Constantinople. In 926, they appeared on the frontiers of Lorraine, and laid the German princes under tribute. Their wild habits and ferocious appearance inspired such universal terror, that it was commonly believed that the sun turned blood red at their approach. "They live not as men, but as savage beasts," says one chronicler, "eating raw flesh and drinking blood. It is even reported that they devour the hearts of their prisoners, and they are never known to be moved to pity." Filled with the bitterest hatred of the Christian name, their track was marked by the smoking ruins of churches and monasteries, and the panic which they spread has survived even to our own time in the popular tales of the savage Ogres, a corruption of the name *Ungren*, by which they were known in the Tudesque dialect. The incursions of the Hungarians lasted, at intervals, for the space of eighty years, nor did they entirely cease until the death of their great chief Tatsong, in 972.

Events such as these will, probably, be thought sufficient to account for any amount of social disorder and literary decay. As to the supposed prosperity enjoyed by the monasteries in this darkest of all the dark ages, it might be illustrated by a catalogue of their sacked and smoking ruins. Fontanelles, with its noble library, St. Ouen and Jumièges, were all burnt by the Norman sea-king Hasting in 851. Marmoutier was pillaged two years later, one hundred and sixteen of the monks being slain. St. Martin's of Tours was burnt in 854, and most of the seats of learning founded in the former century—such as the abbeys of Corby, Liege, Stavelo, Prom, and Malmedy—were destroyed about the same time. By the beginning of the tenth century hardly one of the great French abbeys was left standing; and the monks being slaughtered or dispersed, their houses and lands were in many cases seized by laymen, who lived there with their wives, children, and hunting-dogs, a scandal complained of in 909 by the fathers of the council of Troli. Italy presented much the same spectacle. The abbey of Nomantula was plundered no less than seven times over—"first by Christians in the civil wars; next by the Vandals; a third time by the Saracens in 831; a fourth time by the Normans, which was *desolatio desolationum*; the sixth, and seventh time by the Huns," who in 899 slaughtered all the monks, together with their abbot Gregory. A page might be filled with the names of French bishops massacred with their clergy. It could hardly be expected that schools and letters would greatly flourish at a time when the whole country was lit up by the flames which were destroying the only sanctuaries of learning; and when the libraries which had cost years of persevering toil in their collection were destroyed in one hour of ruthless barbarism. Mezeray, in his history of France, particularly notices the destruction of books among the calamities of the period. "Books," he says, "were becoming scarce at this time, the wars had almost destroyed them all by burning, tearing, and other such like barbarities; and as there were none but monks who transcribed the copies, *and as monasteries were now for the most part deserted*, the number of learned men was but small." Odericus Vitalis in like manner speaks of the irreparable loss occasioned by the destruction of those manuscripts, which furnished the only materials for compiling the history of the times, all of which had perished with the monastic libraries in which they were preserved. Hallam, however, while noticing the destruction of the monasteries and the incursions of the barbarians, sees nothing in these facts to explain that prevailing ignorance of which he elsewhere so loudly complains. In one passage only does he so much as connect the two ideas together, and then it is only in order to direct a sneer against the monks. "As the Normans were unchecked by religious awe," he says, "the rich monasteries were overwhelmed in the storm. *Perhaps* they may have sustained some irrecoverable losses of ancient learning; but their complaints are of monuments disfigured, bones of saints and kings dispersed, and treasures carried away."[125]

There is no doubt that the monks did attach a very great value to the holy relics preserved in their churches, and that they rarely notice the destruction of any sanctuary without saying something of their loss, or the efforts made to preserve them. But it is puzzling to think how Mr. Hallam could have become aware of this fact without also informing himself of their kindred lamentations over the loss of their books. The monastic chroniclers generally couple the two subjects so closely together, that we know not what term to bestow on that singular organisation which enables a reader to acquaint himself with one without knowing anything at all about the other. A very few instances given at random may suffice to show what we are to think of the innuendo conveyed in the sentence above quoted. When the Normans burnt Hamburgh, they destroyed not only the city, but the church and monastery which St. Anscharius had built with such extreme care, together with the library containing a collection of books presented to him by Louis the Debonnaire, all beautifully transcribed. None were saved, excepting so many as each monk was able to carry with him. They went out of the city, therefore, bearing *their books and their relics*, not knowing whither to bend their steps; but Anscharius, who saw the labours of a lifetime destroyed in a moment, uttered no complaint, repeating only the words of Job: "The Lord gave, and the Lord hath taken away; blessed be the name of the Lord!"[126] Pingonio again gives the following narrative from the ancient chronicles of the monastery of Novalesa. In 906 the monks of that house flying on the approach of the Saracens, took with them *their treasure and their library*, which last numbered upwards of 6000 volumes. They found their way safely to Turin, where, not being able to procure a house in which to stow away so many books, Riculf, Bishop of Turin, took 500 volumes off their hands, in part discharge of the cost of their maintenance. Erelong, however, the Saracens entered Turin also, plundered their treasure, and *burnt their library*; and the books which Riculf had taken were unhappily lost after his death, so that the poor monks were never able to recover them. Again, in 842, when the Normans sacked the town of Nantes, and slaughtered the bishops and clergy in the cathedral, the historian of Armorica tells us that, having loaded their vessels with plunder and captives, the heathen men proceeded to a certain island to divide the spoil. A quarrel ensued over the division, and some of the captives profited by the confusion to make their escape. One man, bolder than the rest, thought he might as well secure some of the valuables. And on what does the reader suppose he pitched? Neither on jewelled reliquary, nor church-plate, but on the great Bible which had been used in the cathedral, and which he took on his back and ran off with to the mines, where he remained concealed with some of his companions, until the Normans took their departure. "The fugitives then issued from their hiding place, and returned to Nantes," says the chronicler, having lost much in *books*, silver and gold, and having saved nothing but their Bible.

Sometimes, again, we read of the strange expedients used by the owners of books to conceal them from plunderers. In the abbey of Pfeffers, the books and the church-plate were always hidden together, and on more than one occasion unexpected discoveries were made in aftertimes, of the deposits thus contrived. In the twelfth century one of these secret stores was accidentally brought to light, and contained, besides church plate and vestments, a rich library. Its catalogue included, besides missals and choral books, the works of most of the Latin fathers, and those of Virgil, Lucan, Statius, Sallust, Cicero, and many others. When the great abbey of St. Gall's was threatened by the Huns, the first thought of the abbot was to send the books across the lake to Reichnau. In some of the Italian convents it was always the custom to bury the books on the approach of the Saracens; and several manuscripts may still be seen in the Library of Florence, bearing traces on their covers of having been so dealt with. Not unfrequently the relics are spoken of as being kept in the library, of which an instance occurs in an anecdote preserved by Martene, concerning the monks of St. Florent. When their monastery was threatened by the Normans, they fled to Tournus, taking with them the body of their patron saint. The danger being past, they prepared to return, but their ungenerous hosts, the monks of Tournus, refused to let them take the body with them. Very disconsolately they bent their steps back to St. Florent without their treasure: but one of their number, named Absalon, devised a scheme for its recovery. "He was," says the historian, "a very skilful youth, very fond of law-studies, and much given to letters." His law-studies had possibly sharpened his wits, but the reader must forgive his wiliness, remembering that it was put forth in a just cause. He feigned illness, and remained behind at Tournus, where the monks entrusted him with the offices of scholasticus, librarian, and cantor, and one night, having the keys of the library he effected a quiet entrance, and taking the body of St. Florent from the place where it was deposited, lost no time in finding his way with it back to his own monastery.

One other story may suffice on this subject, which I purposely select as having more to do with relics than books, because it shows that even the narratives more specially devoted to chronicling the loss of saints' bones often indicate the loss of books also; and because, moreover, it gives us to understand that monks could sometimes act as village schoolmasters. It is from the pages of Odericus Vitalis, and will assist us in forming some notion of the sort of violence to which monasteries were exposed, not only from Huns and Saracens, but even from their Christian neighbours.

For many years after the conversion of the Normans, and their peaceable establishment in the north of France, they continued to be objects of jealous fear to the French sovereigns, and particularly to Louis l'Outremer, who, in 943, treacherously got possession of the young Duke Richard, and detained him prisoner. He then proceeded to lay plans for recovering possession of the duchy. He offered Hugh the Great, duke of France, the grant of an enormous territory on condition of his reducing the strong places of the Normans, and Hugh, nothing loth, overran the duchy with a powerful army, and sent some of his men under command of his chancellor, Herluin, to Ouche, where they were hospitably entertained at the monastery of St. Evroult. The simple monks, who thought they had nothing to fear from Christians and Frenchmen, showed them all over the house, and exhibited their oratories and the secret recesses where the bones of the saints were deposited. For this act of confidence they soon paid dearly.

Bernard the Dane, uncle to the young duke, finding himself unable to resist the superior force of the French, had recourse to stratagem, and persuaded the king that the Normans would at once own his sovereignty, if the army of Duke Hugh were withdrawn. Louis accordingly sent orders to Hugh to retire; but the fiery duke, enraged at this breach of faith on the part of a monarch whose crown depended on his good will, commanded his soldiers to withdraw indeed from Normandy, but not till they had wasted the country, burnt the towns, and driven off the cattle. The savage soldiery executed his orders with delight, and the band that had been quartered at St. Evroult, remembering the treasures which had been displayed to them, hastened thither without delay, and bursting into the church, laid hands on the body of St. Evroult, with other holy relics, and after ransacking the house of "everything serviceable to human existence," together with books, vestments, and even furniture, they took their departure, and marched back to their own country laden with their spoils. The poor monks were left very disconsolate; stripped of their all, they knew not what to do, but after a while they came to the resolution of abandoning their ruined monastery, and following the body of their holy founder into exile. They considered themselves the guardians of this treasure, and would not desert their trust: perhaps, too, they hoped to soften the hearts of their enemies, and move them at least to restore the relics. All therefore prepared to depart, with the exception of Ascelin, the prior, who refused to quit the monastery. "Go in God's name," he said, "but as for me, I will never forsake the place where I have received so many blessings: I shall remain as the guardian of these solitudes, till through the mercy of the King of kings, a better day shall dawn upon us." Finding he was not to be moved, the others took leave of him, and set out on their melancholy journey. They reached the duke's camp, and told their tale, and Hugh, touched by the recital, promised to protect them and provide for their maintenance, if they would follow him to his own city of Orleans. There they had the mortification, however, of seeing the chiefs dividing their spoils. Herluin took for his share the head of St. Evroult, a portable altar plated with silver, and one of the books. Ralph de Tracy, who had commanded the plundering party, obtained the remainder of the saint's body, which he very devoutly presented to another abbey, but the poor monks of Ouche recovered nothing. However, they were treated with tolerable kindness by the men of Orleans, who provided them with a habitation, and plenty of fish, bread, and wine, and so ended their days in France in comparative prosperity.

Meanwhile Ascelin, whom we left in the deserted abbey, did not waste his time in barren regrets. He set himself to consider what he could do to provide for the continuance of God's service in that place, and at last resolved on a step which must be acknowledged as not a little creditable in a monk of the Age of Iron: he opened a school. He sought out and assembled together the youths of the neighbourhood, and among them his own nephew, and taught them to read. There is something both picturesque and touching in the idea thus presented to us, of the old man keeping school among his ruins, and acting as the faithful guardian of the holy spot, doing what good he could whilst time and strength remained to him, and with too much quiet confidence in God to lose heart and courage because all else was lost. At last, however, he died, persevering to the last in the observance of his monastic rule, and then his scholars were scattered, the forest thickets grew up round the ruins, and gradually the ancient solitude recovered its former wildness, and became the resort of wild animals. In the next generation, the names of Ouche and St. Evroult had passed utterly out of mind, till one day a peasant in search of a strayed bullock, followed him into the deserted valley, and making his way through bushes and brambles, found his beast couched on a little plot of soft green grass, before what seemed a ruined altar, surrounded by grey walls held together by ivy roots. And then grey-headed men were found who had heard their fathers talk of the time when St. Evroult, who despised the world, had made himself a dwelling in these wilds, and how his brethren had been driven away by the soldiers of Hugh the Great. The good knight Gaston de Montfort rebuilt the church, and the abbey was afterwards restored and colonised from Jumièges; and at last, in 1130, two hundred years after the forcible translation of the relics from Ouche to Orleans, they were brought back to their rightful home, in consequence of the eloquent entreaties of St. Bernard.[127]

We have said enough of the disorders of the ninth and tenth centuries to show that, whatever were the intellectual sterility of the Iron Age, there was cause enough to account for it. Let us now reverse the picture, and inquire whether the clergy resigned themselves contentedly to this lamentable state of things, or what means they took for amending it. Our wonder is, not that the age was one of literary decay, but that learning was not wholly extinguished; and the exertions made by a few to preserve a knowledge of letters in the midst of such unparalleled discouragements, strike us as more justly meriting admiration than all the magnificent institutions founded in more prosperous times. And such efforts were certainly made. In the ninth century the attention paid to the establishment of schools and the cultivation of learning under Charles the Bald and his successors, led Henry of Rheims to declare that it seemed as if the Grecian muses had migrated to France. This is, perhaps, a rhetorical flourish; yet most of the episcopal schools, the names of which are given by Mabillon, were founded during forty years of incessant civil distraction. Even when the ravages of the barbarians swept away the fruits of so many labours, how wonderful is the patient, hopeful perseverance displayed by the bishops in reconstructing their shattered work! Give them but a few years' respite, a short interval of comparative tranquillity in any province, and you will invariably find the schools restored and the old discipline beginning over again. Thus Egidius, in his "History of the Bishops of Liège," tells us of the extraordinary efforts made by Bishop Heraclius to re-establish studies in his diocese. It had borne the brunt of the Norman invasions in the ninth century; all the existing schools had been destroyed, and the ecclesiastics had grown so indifferent to the subject that, when Heraclius began his administration, he found no one to support him in his attempts to organise a fresh staff of teachers. And yet in a few years he succeeded in restoring monastic schools throughout the whole province, and reviving a love of learning among all classes. He accomplished this not so much by his exhortations as his example; for, says his biographer, "he did not think it beneath him to frequent these schools by turns, taking on himself the office of teacher, giving lectures to the elder students, and patiently explaining and repeating his lessons to those who did not understand him. When he travelled to any distance he always corresponded with his scholars, sporting with them in pleasant verse. Even from Italy and Calabria he remembered to send them agreeable letters to provoke them to the love of study, and he generally took some of them with him on his journeys, that he might beguile the tediousness of the way by conferring with them on the Holy Scriptures." His successor, Notger, carried on the good work with even greater ardour. Like Heraclius, he always taught in his own cathedral school, and a great many of his pupils afterwards became bishops. They were so many, and so remarkable for their good scholarship, that their names and their various excellences were thought worthy by a certain scholasticus named Adelman, of being made the subject of some verses, which are still preserved.[128] Notger had originally been a monk of St. Gall's, and had been called thence to direct the school of Stavelot. He naturally, therefore, had a taste for teaching, and, like Heraclius, he never travelled without a troop of scholars, abundance of books, and what his biographer calls *arma scholaria*. Nor were all of his scholars clerks, for we are expressly told that he had numerous young laics entrusted to him that he might train them in a manner suitable to their state of life. He did so much for his cathedral city, that he has been called its second founder, and not a few of the churches and pious institutions existing there at the present day owe their erection to his munificent zeal.[129]

At Rheims, which from its geographical position enjoyed a longer immunity from pillage than cities situated on the great rivers, schools and teachers found a safe retreat and ample encouragement from Archbishop Hincmar. However, the Normans at last made their way thither; and when Fulk succeeded to the archiepiscopal dignity, he found both the cathedral school, and that established for the rural clergy, ruined and deserted. He restored them both, and invited the two monks, Remigius of Auxerre and Hucbald of St. Amand, to come and take charge of them. Their scholastic pedigree has been given in a former chapter, and they are commonly regarded as the chief restorers of learning in France. Fulk, who knew their value, encouraged his clergy to profit from their instructions by himself taking his seat as a scholar among the youngest of his clerks. The Rheims pupils included many men of note, such as Flodoard the historian, whom Fleury calls the ornament of his age. The old epitaph on his tomb praises him as "a good monk, a good clerk, and a better abbot," and concludes with two lines somewhat hyperbolical in their expression:—

Per sen histoire maintes nouvelles sauras

Et en ille toutes antiquité auras.

Hucbald was famous as a poet, musician, and philosopher; but his colleague, Remigius, was great in grammar, and wrote comments on Priscian, Donatus, and Marcian Capella. He taught humane letters and theology, and was extraordinarily learned in Scripture and the Fathers. After the death of Fulk he proceeded to Paris, and opened the first public school which we know with any certainty to have been established in that city. This, according to the Paris historians, was the real germ of the university; at any rate it was the first of those celebrated schools out of which the university subsequently developed. Nevertheless, half a century earlier, in the midst of the great siege of Paris, there had been both schools and scholars, for Abbo of St. Germain apologises for the incomplete state of his poem before mentioned, "on account of the multitude of his pupils." Whence we gather that even famine and massacre had never entirely extinguished the Parisian thirst for letters.

Remigius continued to teach at Paris for several years, pupils coming to him from all parts of France. Among them was one whose story deserves to be told a little more at length, inasmuch as it exhibits, in a striking manner, the utter ruin which had fallen on the monastic institute in the French provinces, and at the same time shows us that in the tenth century laymen were to be found who were possessed of a respectable education, and were capable of collecting libraries. There lived at that time, in the province of Maine, a certain noble named Abbo, who had been fortunate enough in his youth to find some school where he not only learnt how to sign his name, but acquired a great taste for reading. His reading, too, was of a solid kind, for his favourite studies were the histories of the ancients, and the "Novellæ" of Justinian, the latter of which he knew by heart, using his legal erudition when called on to dispense justice to his feudal subjects, and to act as umpire in the disputes which arose among his neighbours. The Gospels were always read aloud at his table, and on the Vigils of solemn feasts he and his family spent the night in prayer and watching. Nor are we to draw the hasty conclusion that Abbo's household, and his way of life, was at all an extraordinary exception from the common rule. He had friends as learned and as holy as himself, such as Duke William of Aquitaine, whose religious habits earned him the surname of "the Pious," while his love of letters gained him that of "the Grammarian." This good prince had a number of books in his castle, and during the long winter evenings he amused himself by reading them, never leaving his studies till fairly overcome by sleep. Abbo had one son named Odo, born in 879, and whilst yet an infant, his father going to see him in his cradle, by a devout impulse took him in his arms and offered him to St. Martin. As he grew up he was given in charge to a priest to be taught his letters, but it does not appear that there was any idea of bringing him up to the ecclesiastical state: on the contrary, his father placed him in the household of Duke William, that he might acquire the martial exercises becoming a knight. Odo, however, had no taste for these pursuits, and the chase and the tilt-yard were insupportably wearisome to him. Praying to Our Lady that he might be guided in the choice of a state of life, he was for three years attacked by inveterate headaches, which obliged him to return home, and which obstinately resisted every remedy. His father at last became persuaded that it was not the will of God that his son should pursue a secular calling. Remembering his former promise to St. Martin, and finding that Odo's own wishes pointed in the same direction, he took him to Tours, and placed him, in his nineteenth year, among the canons of that city. There was a very solemn reception of the noble postulant, and among those who assisted at the ceremony was the brave Count Fulk of Anjou, the same who has before been mentioned as himself holding a canon's stall, and scandalising king Louis by his proficiency in music.

No sooner did Odo find himself in quiet possession of his new retreat than he applied himself to his books with an ardour that quite astounded his brother canons. They perpetually asked him what he meant by all this reading, and where could possibly be the good of it. Odo let them talk as they would, and made no change in his habits. He often spent the whole day in study, and the whole night in prayer. He finished his course of grammar, and was about to commence Virgil, when he was deterred by a vision, in which he seemed to see a beautiful vessel filled with serpents, which he understood to indicate the poison to be found in the charms of profane literature. Putting it aside, therefore, he devoted himself exclusively to the study of the Scriptures, and to obtain the more freedom from interruption, he shut himself up in a little cell which Count Fulk had given him, and distributing all his money to the poor, lived on the moderate daily allowance of half a pound of bread and a handful of beans. However, he soon became desirous of better teaching than he had as yet been able to procure, so he set out for Paris, and entered at the school of Remigius of Auxerre. That master made him go through a course of the liberal arts, and gave him to study the treatises of Marcian Capella, and the "Dialectics" of St. Augustine.[130]

On his return to Tours he applied himself to the study of St. Gregory's "Morals," in which he took such delight that he wrote an abridgment of it, which is still preserved. His love of letters may be gathered from the fact that he gradually procured himself a library of a hundred volumes—a very large collection in those days for any private individual. Among them were some "Lives of the Holy Fathers," and the "Rule" of St. Benedict, the constant study of which filled Odo with an intense desire to embrace the monastic state. In this he was encouraged by the intimate friendship he formed about this time with a knight named Adegrim, one of the household of the good Count Fulk. At last Adegrim threw up his military employments and came to live with the young canon at Tours. The talk of the two friends was ever of monks and of monasteries, and they made many journeys into different parts of France to seek out the sites of those once famous abbeys of which they had read, and to discover if perchance one yet survived in its ancient state of discipline. But these expeditions invariably ended in disappointment. For more than sixty years the monastic institute in France had been utterly ruined. Most of the houses so renowned in the last century were now nothing but heaps of blackened ruins. The monks had either been slain or driven out as wanderers. Sometimes they were to be met with in the guise of poor vagrants; sometimes in places far from public resort you might come upon a miserable hut, where the remnants of what had once been a flourishing community were gathered together in the wilderness, striving to keep their Rule as best they might. This is not a fancy picture. It was about this very time that William Longsword, duke of Normandy, was induced to restore the abbey of Jumièges, having when hunting in the forest come upon two poor monks who were trying to construct a cell for themselves out of the ruins of the abbey. All the refreshments they could offer him were some barley bread and some water; and the spectacle of their poverty, together with the remembrance that the desolation he witnessed had been the work of his own Norman forefathers, induced the duke to undertake the work of restoration. Abbo and Adegrim, however, were not to be discouraged in their plan. Finding no house in France where they could embrace the life to which they longed to devote themselves, they resolved to carry on their search in Italy, and Adegrim accordingly set out, intending to make the pilgrimage to Rome. But as he passed through Burgundy he accidentally found his way to La Baume, a small monastery which had been recently founded by the abbot Berno, and in which the Rule of St. Benedict was strictly observed, together with the reformed Constitutions of St. Benedict d'Anian. Adegrim at once wrote to his friend, bidding him come without delay, and bring all his books with him; and Odo lost no time in obeying the summons. In the year 909 he began his noviciate, being then exactly thirty years of age. Adegrim, after three years of penitential exercises, begged leave to retire to a little cave about two miles distant from the monastery, where he spent the rest of his life as a hermit. But a very different course awaited his friend Odo. His books pointed him out to be the right sort of man for a schoolmaster, and he was therefore charged with the education of the children brought up in the monastery, and the younger monks. He had much to suffer from the jealousy of some of his brethren; but Berno, rightly appreciating both his talents and his humility, sent him to Turpion, Bishop of Limoges, to be ordained priest.

The reformed monastery of La Baume soon became the mother-house of other foundations. Those who deplored the decay of learning and religion were eager to provide for the restoration of both, by erecting houses in which the Rule and spirit of St. Benedict might be revived in their ancient vigour. Abbo's old friend, Duke William of Aquitaine, was of the number of those who desired to take part in the good work, and he invited Berno to choose a site for a new foundation in any part of his dominions. Berno selected a beautiful solitude, about four miles from Macon, on the confines of Burgundy, where the river Grosne, after passing the village of Bonnay, winds down to the Seine from the mountains of Beaujolais, through a valley girt in by high hills covered with forests. It was exactly suited for the purposes of a religious retreat, but the duke hesitated when Berno named it, for it was his favourite hunting ground, and was at that time occupied by his kennel of dogs. "Well, sir," said Berno, when the duke had explained his difficulty, "it is only to turn out the dogs, and to turn in the monks." This recommendation was accordingly followed, and in course of time there arose among those wooded hills the stately abbey of Cluny, the church of which was inferior in size to none save St. Peter's of Rome.

On the death of Berno in 927, the bishops of the province obliged St. Odo to accept the government of Cluny and two of the other five houses which had sprung under the reformed Rule. Not content with this, they likewise forced upon him the most odious and difficult of all imaginable enterprises; that, namely, of restoring monastic discipline in a vast number of other houses both in France and Italy, which had fallen into the hands of a dissolute set of men, who sometimes opposed the entrance of the abbot, sword in hand. Odo entered on this work in obedience, and accomplished it in the spirit of meekness. There is no courage like that of gentle souls, and the history of this great reformer exhibits him to us forsaken by his terrified attendants, and riding up on his ass to the gates of Fleury, where a band of armed men were awaiting his coming, having sworn to kill him if he dared set foot among them. But Odo's meekness gained the day, and among the seventeen abbeys which accepted the Cluniac reform, that of Fleury became one of the most flourishing.

In fact, the character of St. Odo had nothing of that stern austerity which we commonly associate with the notion of a reformer. Its force was its amiability. He used to tell his monks that cripples and beggars were the door-keepers of heaven, and would not endure that they should be spoken to with harshness. If he heard the porter giving a gruff answer to the crowds of poor who thronged his gate, he would go out to them and say, "My friends, when that brother comes to the gates of Paradise, answer him as he has just answered you, and see whether he will like it." On his journeys, if he met any children, he always stopped, and desired them to sing or repeat something to him, and he did this, says his biographer, that he might have an excuse for giving them something. And if he met an old woman or a cripple, nothing would prevent his getting off his beast and mounting them in his place, when he would desire his servants to hold them securely in the saddle, while he himself led them on their way. This excess of goodness made him so dear to his monks, that they would often steal behind him and indulge their affection and respect by secretly pressing to their lips the hem of his garment.

St. Odo died in 942, and in 965 Maieul or Majolus, a former canon of Macon, was elected abbot. His life, like that of his predecessor, affords an illustration of the two features in the century which I am most solicitous to bring before the reader's notice; the disordered state of society, consequent on the barbaric invasions, and the fact that in spite of such disorders, men were not wholly indifferent to letters, though they were often sadly at a loss to find the means of acquiring them. Maieul made his studies at Lyons, which his biographer, Odilo, declares was then regarded as the nurse and mother of philosophy, under a rather celebrated teacher named Anthony de l'Isle Barbe. He learnt both kinds of literature, says the monk Syrus, who also wrote his life, the divine and human, and attained to whatever was most sublime in the one, and most difficult in the other. The approach of the Saracens obliged him to leave Avignon, his native city, and retire to Macon, where he was chosen first canon and then archdeacon. But as he found that the clergy and people had it in their mind to procure his further promotion to the bishopric of Besançon, he fled to Cluny, where he was received with great affection, and in process of time was appointed schoolmaster, librarian, and syndic of the house. In this combination of the intellectual and the temporal government he managed to make himself greatly beloved, and in 948, with the consent of the whole community, Aimard, the successor of Odo, whom Syrus styles a son of innocence and simplicity, surrendered the government of the abbey and all its dependencies into his hands. Both as scholasticus and coadjutor to the abbot, Maieul superintended the studies of his monks, and it is remarkable that he had to use the bridle rather than the spur. He was obliged to exert his authority to discourage their excessive study of the profane poets, especially Virgil; not that he disapproved of a moderate use of humane literature; on the contrary, he advocated the principle that we should get all the good out of it that we can; but he would have preferred to see his monks learned in the Scriptures, the reading of which formed his own delight. Whether he walked or rode, the Sacred volume was never out of his hands, and when he travelled into distant countries he always took with him a portable library. These journeys were very frequent, for Maieul extended the Cluniac reform into a great number of abbeys, and made many pilgrimages to Rome. Returning from that city in 973, he was attacked, whilst crossing the Alps, by the Saracens of Frassinet, and carried off, together with all his retinue. His captors chained him hand and foot, and confined him in a cave among the mountains, plundering him of all his baggage, and among other things of his books. The saint recommended himself to God in the spirit of martyrdom, and then lay down on the floor of the cavern to take what rest he might. On awakening he was surprised to find lying on his breast one of his lost books, which appeared to have been overlooked by the plunderers. He opened it, and found it was a treatise on the Assumption of Our Lady, and counting the days, he found that there remained exactly twenty-four to the Feast of the Assumption; so he began to pray that through the intercession of the Queen of Heaven, he might perhaps be permitted to keep that Feast among Christians. After a while the Saracens began to treat him more kindly. They allowed him to write a letter to his brethren directing them to send the money for his ransom, and seeing that he did not eat the meat which they set before him, one man took a shield, and baring his arms, he proceeded to knead some meal in this strange dish, and produced a cake which the prisoner gratefully accepted. Another time a Saracen, wishing to clean his lance, set his foot on the great Bible which formed part of the abbot's library. Pained at the irreverence, the saint gently remonstrated with him, but without effect, and a few days afterwards the man quarrelling with his companions, they cut off the very foot that had been set on the Sacred Volume. At last the ransom arrived, and the prisoners were liberated, and Maieul spent the Feast of the Assumption among Christians, as he had prayed. Not long afterwards the Saracens were driven from Frassinet by Duke William of Arles, and the books of St. Maieul being found among their baggage, were sent back to him at Cluny to his very great joy.

The information conveyed in stories of this kind will be taken for what it is worth. It does not certainly represent the monks of the Iron Age as prodigies of erudition, but it shows that they did a little more than learn their Psalter. In some cases they certainly set themselves to overcome the difficulties which then beset the path of learning with a perseverance and success that merit all praise; and one example of this sort occurs among the monks of that very abbey of Fleury, the reformation of which was effected by St. Odo in the teeth of an armed rabble. Abbo of Fleury, as he is commonly called, a contemporary of St. Maieul, did not enter the monastery until some years after it had begun to flourish under the Cluniac rule, and the good discipline of Abbot Wulfhad. He was a native of Orleans, and a boy of such a sweet disposition and such a happy memory, that he forgot nothing of his master's lessons, and studied much in private, not merely for the sake of knowledge, says his biographer, but also because he counted application to study to be a means of subjecting the flesh to the spirit. The Fleury teachers at this time were not first-rate; however, far from being disgusted with "the haggard and emaciated skeleton of barbarous elements," the more Abbo learnt the more he desired to learn. He was appointed in time *scholasticus* to his convent, but he felt by no means satisfied as yet with his own attainments. He was tolerably well versed in grammar, logic, and arithmetic, but he had found no one at Fleury who could teach him the other liberal arts. With the permission of his abbot, therefore, he resigned his office, and went first to Paris, and then to Rheims. In these schools he acquired a knowledge of philosophy and astronomy, but not so much of the last science as he desired. So he next proceeded to Orleans, and there not only perfected himself in other branches of learning, but, by dint of expending a good sum of money, managed to get some excellent lessons in music. This, however, could only be done secretly, by reason of the opposition of envious minds. He had now studied five out of the seven liberal arts, and he could not rest till he had acquired the other two. But not being able to find any good master either in rhetoric or geometry, he endeavoured to supply the first by a careful study of Victorinus, the master of St. Jerome, and also by his own exertions gained some knowledge of mathematics. We have seen in the last chapter how he was summoned to England by St. Oswald of York, and established sacred and scientific studies in the monastery of Ramsay. So greatly was he esteemed by both St. Oswald and St. Dunstan, that an amicable quarrel arose between the two prelates as to which should keep possession of so great a treasure. The question was settled by the abbot of Fleury recalling Abbo to his own convent after a two years' absence.

His English friends took leave of him with no small regret, and loaded him with parting presents. St. Dunstan gave him a number of exquisitely-wrought silver ornaments of his own workmanship, which he requested him to present as his offerings to St. Benedict, a portion of whose body was preserved at Fleury. St. Oswald ordained him priest, and gave him a chalice, some vestments, and everything else requisite for saying mass. In 988 he became abbot, in which office he continually recommended his monks to cultivate study as the most useful exercise next to fasting and prayer. For himself he ceased not all his life to read, write, or dictate. His favourite studies, next to the Holy Scriptures, were dialectics and astronomy, and among his works were some treatises on both those subjects. Renowned for his learning throughout Europe, he was killed at last in 1004 in an affray between his servants and some Gascon monks of the monastery of Reole, whither he had been sent to effect a reform.

In fact, if the age exhibited much decay and many scandals, it found men ready to spend their lives in the weary work of restoration and reformation. And it is remarkable that the greatest prelates of the time invariably regarded the revival of monachism as the only means of restoring good discipline and learning. Such were the views of St. Dunstan and his fellow-labourers, and such was also the conviction of the excellent Adalberon, who in 933 became Bishop of Metz. He was brother to the reigning duke of Lorraine, and his talents and zeal equalled the nobility of his birth. In order to provide his diocese with a seminary of devoted and learned men, he resolved on restoring the great monastery of Gorze, which had been founded by St. Chrodegang of Metz, but which had been ruined under the combined attacks of the Normans and the Hungarians. He completed the rebuilding of the abbey, but was still uncertain whence he should procure his colony of monks, when he was informed that a little society of ecclesiastics, which had been formed in the neighbouring diocese of Toul, was about to pass into Italy, seeking some spot where they might unmolested lead a more perfect life. The way in which this society had been organised was altogether remarkable. At their head was John of Vandières, the native of a village in the diocese of Nancy, who, having been born when his father was advanced in years, had suffered from some of the disadvantages of being a spoiled child. The fond parent, however, was at last persuaded to send the boy to school, first at Metz, and then at the monastery of St. Michael's, where Master Hildebold, a pupil of Remigius, gave lessons in grammar. John, however, profited very little by his teaching, and on his father's death, his mother, marrying a second time, recalled him home, and gave him the charge of all the temporal affairs of the house. John showed considerable ability in the management of lands and revenues, and absorbed in these cares, soon forgot the little he had learnt at school. However, as time went on, he became disgusted with his secular way of life, and embracing the ecclesiastical state, received two benefices in the diocese of Toul. There he became acquainted with the learned deacon Berners, who, by no means approving of illiterate clerks, persuaded John to begin his studies over again. Divine grace quickening his powers, he did his best to make up for lost time. But he was never much of a grammarian. He contented himself with what his biographer calls a *sprinkling* of Donatus, just so much as enabled him to read and understand the Scriptures, to the study of which he then exclusively devoted himself, and in which he obtained very extraordinary light. The church which he served was dependent on a convent of nuns at Metz, where his duties called him from time to time to say mass. He became acquainted with the community, and the example of their holy and mortified life inspired him with new ardour. He began a course of reading with these good religious, which speaks in favour of his diligence and their patience, and in which, says his biographer, he persevered "with all his might."

First, then, having read through with them the whole of the Old and New Testaments, he committed both to memory, "and that so accurately that no man could do it better," also "all the lessons appointed to be read in church," which are contained in the book called *Comes*; then the rules for the computing of Easter and the canonical laws, that is, the decrees of councils, the judgments of penitents, the mode of ecclesiastical proceedings, and the secular laws, all of which he treasured up word for word. Of homilies, sermons, and treatises on the Epistles and Gospels, I will only say that he was able to repeat an alarming catalogue of them in the vernacular, "straightforward from beginning to end, as if he were reading from the book." At the same time he laboured hard to acquire a knowledge of church music, not caring for the derision of some who considered it an unsuitable enterprise for one of his age to engage in. However, his perseverance was rewarded with very fair success, and it was thus that he employed his intervals of leisure time, together with the handmaids of God.

It must be confessed that John's choice of reading, considering the gentler sex of his fellow-students, was somewhat of the driest. Nor do I at all cite him as a model of erudition, though, considering the deficiencies of his early education, his achievements in that line might have saved him from the contempt of Brucker, who notices him only to string him up among other barbarous dunces. His studies probably took their direction from the very few books which he had at his command, and it is at least clear that he made a tolerable use of those he possessed.

His intercourse with the nuns inspired him with a great desire to embrace a religious life, but, like St. Odo, he sought in vain for any religious house in his own part of the country where religious discipline still flourished. So first he joined the company of a recluse of Verdun, named Humbert, and then he passed some time with a hermit in the forest of Argonne, and at last, in company with Bernacer of Metz, who was a tolerable scholar, he set out on pilgrimage to Rome. However, even in Italy he found nothing that exactly suited him, and returning to Verdun, resumed his former exercises of prayer and study, under the direction of Humbert.

About the same time Einold, Archdeacon of Toul, had been touched with similar desires after a perfect life; and distributing all his goods to the poor, he shut himself up in a little cell adjoining the cloisters of his cathedral, together with his books and his priestly vestments, living only on what the Bishop Gauzelin sent him as an alms. The times were, indeed, dreary enough, when, one after another, these good men were to be found seeking, and seeking in vain, for some spot untouched by the spoiler's hand. As Einold prayed for guidance, what seemed a little schoolboy's voice in the street outside chanted the words, "I will give you the heritage of your father Jacob;" and half disposed to take the words as a sign of divine encouragement, he was still pondering over their meaning, when Humbert of Verdun came to ask his counsel. To be brief, the four friends, Einold, Humbert, John, and Bernacer, determined on migrating to Italy, and establishing themselves either among the solitaries of Mount Vesuvius, or in the neighbourhood of Monte Cassino. And it was this little knot of holy men, who had been drawn together by the ties of Christian sympathy, whom Adalberon proposed to detain in France for the purpose of entrusting them with the restoration of monastic life in the abbey of Gorze. They accepted his offer; a very few of the old monks who yet survived were brought back, and willingly accepted the strict reform which Adalberon desired to establish; Einold was chosen abbot, and the house soon became a model of good discipline. Sacred studies were at once instituted in the school, and after his religious profession, John of Gorze, as he was henceforth called, entered on rather a wider range of reading than he had hitherto been able to follow. We find him applying himself to St. Augustine, and working with characteristic energy at certain logical studies, which were, however, cut short by the prohibition of Einold, who desired him to leave logic for secular students, and to confine himself to more spiritual subjects, an injunction which he humbly and promptly obeyed. He became abbot of Gorze about the year 960.

Adalberon's zeal was not satisfied with the restoration of Gorze; he invited a learned body of monks over from Ireland, under a superior named Cradoc, and established them in another deserted monastery, that of St. Clement's at Metz. When Gerard, Bishop of Toul, the successor of Gauzelin, heard of the arrival of the Irishmen, he never rested till he had procured some of them for his own diocese. He had already procured a community of exiled Greek monks, among whom, in the following century, Cardinal Humbert acquired his Greek learning. A sort of holy emulation sprang up between the two prelates, which should outstrip the other in their labours at reform and revival; and Gerard was not content with setting others to work; he worked himself as hard as the humblest scholasticus. He took into his own hands the instruction of his clergy in all that appertained to ecclesiastical discipline and the ministry of preaching; and acting on the principle that he who instructs others should never cease to be a learner, he never considered that his time of study was ended; and his historian declares that even when he was in bed he appointed some of his clerks to read to him until he fell asleep.

From all that has been said, it may be seen that there was no want of solicitude on the part of the pastors of the Church to amend the disorders of the time. In fact, we might appeal to the acts of those very councils which show what the abuses of the times were, as affording proof of the strenuous exertions made to correct them.

In Spain we are told the incursions of the Saracens had left everything in ruins. The school of Palencia, established in the sixth century for the education of the clergy, had fallen into decay; the monastic institute had all but disappeared; and the sites of many monasteries, like the famous one founded near Vierzo by St. Fructuosus, had become wildernesses, overgrown with thorns and brushwood. But here, as in France and Germany, bishops were to be found stemming the strong tide of barbarism. Gennadius of Astorga restored a great number of abbeys destroyed by the Saracens, and placed them under the Benedictine Rule. And as the libraries that formerly enriched them could not be at once replaced, he introduced a custom by which the books belonging to one house were lent to a number of others in regular succession, always returning to their original owners. Among the books so lent appear the works of St. Gregory, St. Jerome, St. Ambrose, and St. Augustine.

Even the education of the poor was not wholly uncared for in the Iron Age. Witness the constitutions of Ado of Vercelli, Dado of Verden, and Heraclius of Liege, in which the establishment of "little," or parochial, schools, is ordained, wherein poor children of both sexes, about the age of seven, are to be received and taught gratis, the girls and boys being always separated from one another. The regulations, simple as they are, have a very modern sound; and so also have those other constitutions of Riculf of Soissons, who, for the improvement of his parish priests, hit on a scheme of *clerical conferences*, in order to afford them means of mutual edification, on a plan precisely similar to that adopted in later times.

But we have dwelt long enough on the aspect which the tenth century presented in France. Something remains to be said of the state of schools and monasteries during the same period on the other side of the Rhine, where the achievements of the German prelates were crowned with a much larger share of success, and well deserve a chapter to themselves.

CHAPTER X.

THE AGE OF THE OTHOS.

A.D. 911 TO 1024.

LOUIS THE FOURTH, surnamed the Child, the last of the race of Charlemagne who bore rule in Germany, died in 911, leaving the empire torn to pieces with feudal wars and the devastations of Hungarians, Sclaves and Normans. As the right of choosing his successor belonged to the nobles, they offered the crown to Otho, duke of Saxony, who with singular disinterestedness refused it, and recommended as most worthy of the royal dignity, his own feudal rival, Conrad of Franconia, who accordingly received the crown. Not to be outdone in generosity, Conrad, at his death, named the son of Otho as his successor, and thus Henry the Fowler became the first German sovereign of the house of Saxony. His victory over the Hungarians at Marsberg, in 933, gave them their first decisive check, and in 936, his son Otho the Great completed the discomfiture of the barbarians at the great battle of Leck, after which they never again showed their face in Germany. In 952, Otho was crowned king of Italy, having been called into that country to oppose the usurper Beranger. Eight years later he was invited to Rome by Pope John XII. and crowned emperor, no prince having borne that title in the West for the space of forty years. Though on some occasions he failed not to evince that tendency to despotism in Church matters which was the hereditary vice of the German emperors, yet his reign was truly glorious, and is spoken of by ancient writers as a kind of golden age. His mother Matilda, and his two wives, Editha and Adelaide, the first of whom was an English princess, together with his brother Bruno, Archbishop of Cologne, were all canonised saints. He showed himself the friend of religion and learning, and caused his son, Otho II., to receive a learned education. His grandson, Otho III., who succeeded to the crown in 983, was also a scholar, and a pupil of Gerbert's, and surnamed the Wonder of the World. At his death the crown passed to his cousin, St. Henry of Bavaria, whose brother-in-law, St. Stephen of Hungary, converted his people to Christianity, and changed those wild barbarians, so long the scourge of Europe, into a civilised and Christian nation.

Thus, for the space of a century, Germany was blessed with a succession of great Christian rulers, who, if they had some defects, were yet on the whole protectors of religion, and encouragers of learned men. Italy, indeed, is represented by most historians as presenting during the same period a scene of lamentable decay; and Tiraboschi gives the names of only two bishops as possessing any pretensions to learning, namely, Atto of Vercelli, and Ratherius of Verona. But allowance must be made for the exaggerations of party-writers, and there are facts which cannot be altogether reconciled with their sweeping statements. Studies were certainly carried on in the monasteries that escaped the rage of the Saracens, and Muratori cites a long catalogue of books, all either copied or collected at Bobbio during the tenth century. Baronius, whose strictures on the state of Italy are exceedingly severe, quotes the acts of a council held at Rheims in 992, wherein it is declared that there was scarcely one person to be found at that time in Rome who knew the first elements of learning. Considering the unhappy and scandalous factions which then held sway in the Roman capital, no picture of social disorder would seem too black for us to credit; yet bad as things were, one is staggered at the notion that no one in the city of the Popes and the Cæsars should know even how to read. A few years previously to the date assigned, Rome, as we shall see, not only possessed good masters herself, but supplied them to the German seminaries; nor is there any reason for supposing that her political disasters necessarily closed her schools. If, from the acts of a remote council, we turn to the writings of one thoroughly conversant with the state of Italy, the man of his age best qualified to judge of any matter connected with learning—I mean the famous Ratherius of Verona—we shall find a very different description of the state of things which he had witnessed with his own eyes. His testimony is the more remarkable from the fact that he was the great censor of his age, sparing neither clergy nor bishops in his caustic attacks. Yet he assures us that in his time, and he died in 974, there was no place where a man could get better instructed in sacred letters than in Rome. "What is taught elsewhere on ecclesiastical dogma," he says, "that is unknown there? It is there that we find the sovereign doctors of the whole world; it is there that the most illustrious princes of the Church have flourished. There the decrees of the pontiffs are to be found; there the canons are examined; there some are approved and others rejected; what is condemned there is nowhere else approved, nor do men elsewhere approve of what is there condemned. Where, then, could I be more sure to find wisdom than at Rome, which is its fountain-head?"[131] About the same time Gerbert, the literary wonder of his age, arrived in Rome, where his scientific acquirements were so thoroughly appreciated by Pope John XIII. as to induce that pontiff to prevent his return into Spain; and he accordingly wrote to the emperor, advising him to secure the services of a man who was thoroughly well-versed in mathematics, and able to teach them to others. But how preposterous it seems to suppose that the mathematics of Gerbert should be thus highly valued in a city where hardly a man was to be found acquainted with the first elements of letters! Again, we find from Gerbert's own correspondence that it was from Italy that he chiefly obtained his books. There is no city in that country, he says, where good writers and copyists are not to be found; a fact which conclusively proves that somebody was also to be found to buy what was written, for the book trade could not have been kept up without a fair supply of readers. And in the year 1000 only eight years after the above-named council had furnished Baronius with its dismal authority for proving Italy to be sunk in the grossest ignorance, we find a German noble named Wippo exhorting the emperor Henry II. to send the sons of the German nobles to be educated "after the manner of the Italians." Not that it at all concerns us to whitewash the history of Italy in the tenth century, confessedly the very *nadir* of her ecclesiastical annals; but there is no reason for unfairly blackening even a damaged reputation, and the united testimonies given above may at least be taken as evidence that the words of the council must not be too literally understood.

In the present chapter, however, I propose to speak only of the state of letters in Germany, where the tenth century was certainly very far from deserving to be stigmatised as an age of iron or lead. All the monastic chroniclers bear witness to the rapid extension of letters, which was encouraged by the Saxon emperors, to the extraordinary multiplication of schools, and the harvest of great men whom they produced, so that even Meiners is forced to acknowledge that at no period did Germany possess so many virtuous and learned ecclesiastics. Much of this happy state of things is to be attributed to the labours and example of St. Bruno, the younger brother of Otho the Great, and, like him, a pupil of Heraclius of Liege. His education began at Utrecht, where he was sent at the mature age of four, to commence his studies under the good abbot Baldric. Utrecht had never entirely lost its scholastic reputation since the days of St. Gregory. Only a few years before the birth of Bruno the see had been filled by St. Radbod, a great-grandson of that other Radbod, duke of Friesland, who had so fiercely opposed the preaching of St. Boniface. Radbod the bishop, however, was a very different man from his savage ancestor; he was not only a pious ecclesiastic, but an elegant scholar, for he had been educated in the Palatine school of Charles the Bald, under the learned Mannon, whose heart he won by his facility in writing verses; and the cares of the episcopate never induced him altogether to neglect the Muses. Besides a great number of poems which he wrote during his residence at Utrecht, we have a Latin epigram, which he improvised at the moment of receiving the Holy Viaticum, and which is perhaps as worthy of being preserved as the dying epigram of the Emperor Hadrian.[132]

In consequence of the encouragement given to learning by so many of its bishops, Utrecht became the fashionable place of education, and it had grown a sort of custom with the German sovereigns to send their sons thither at an early age. Little Bruno made rapid progress both in Greek and Latin literature; he particularly relished the works of Prudentius, which he learnt by heart; never let himself be disturbed by his noisy companions, and took great care of his books. Indeed, the only thing that ever moved him to anger was the sight of any one negligently handling a book. His reading included something of all sorts; historians, orators, poets and philosophers—nothing came amiss. He had native Greeks to instruct him in their language, and became so proficient in it as afterwards to act as interpreter for his brother to the Greek ambassadors who frequented the German court. With all this he did not neglect the sacred sciences, and a certain Isaac, a Scotch, or rather Irish professor, who taught at Utrecht, spoke of him as not merely a scholar, but a saint. The monk Ditmar, one of his schoolfellows, himself afterwards celebrated in the literary world by his chronicle of the royal house of Saxony, bears witness to the habits of piety which adorned the very childhood of the young prince. "Every morning," he says, "before he left his room to go to the school, he would be at his prayers, while the rest of us were at play." A certain tone of exaggeration is not unfrequently indulged in by early writers when extolling the subjects of their biographies as prodigies of every literary excellence, but the descriptions left us of Bruno's intellectual achievements do not admit of being understood as mere figures of speech. His love of reading was almost a passion. He read everything, "even comedies," says his biographer, who seems a little scandalised at the fact, but explains that he attended only to the style, and neglected the matter. To complete the picture of Bruno's school-days, it must be added that he was an excellent manager of his time, and always made the most of his morning hours, a good habit he retained through life. I will say nothing of his early career as the reformer of Lauresheim Abbey; he was still young when his brother Otho succeeded to the throne, and at once summoned Bruno to court, charging him with the task of erecting there a Palatine academy, after the model of that of Charlemagne. Nothing was better suited to Bruno's wishes and capacity, and he began at once to teach the entire curriculum of the liberal arts to a crowd of noble pupils. Whatever was most beautiful in the historians and poets of Greece or Rome, he made known to his disciples, and not content with the labour entailed on him by his own lectures, he did not allow the professors whom he chose to assist him to commence theirs till he had previously conferred with them on the subjects they were about to explain.

One of Bruno's chief assistants was that same Ratherius who has been already named. Originally a monk of Lobes, he had accompanied his patron Hilduin of Liege into Italy, and there became bishop of Verona. He was a man of great learning, and zeal too little tempered with discretion, and his life was a series of episcopal ejectments. Thrice was he turned out of the see of Verona, and once out of that of Liege, to which Bruno had procured his nomination after the death of Hilduin. His writings are of considerable value as monuments of the doctrine and discipline of the times, but I mention him here rather in the character of a benefactor to youth. For after being the second time obliged to fly from Verona, he retired, says Folcuin, in his history of the abbots of Lobes, "to that part of Burgundy which is called Provençe, where he taught the son of a certain rich man named Rostang; and for his benefit composed a little book on the grammatical art, which he called by the pleasant name of *Spara-dorsum*, or *Spare-the-back*, to the end that young children making use of the same in schools might be preserved from scourges."

In 953, Bruno, in spite of his youth, was demanded by the clergy and people of Cologne for their archbishop, and being consecrated, he at once entered on a career of gigantic labours, everywhere re-establishing ecclesiastical discipline and social order throughout a province long wasted by war and barbaric invasions. His political position, moreover, imposed on him yet more extensive cares; for Otho, who called him his second soul, when summoned into Italy, created his brother duke of Lorraine and imperial lieutenant in Germany. The dukedom of Lorraine at that time included all the country from the Alps to the Moselle, which now, therefore, acknowledged Bruno as its actual sovereign. But these multiplied dignities, and the accumulation of business which they entailed, did not quench Bruno's love of study. Whenever he travelled, whether in the visitation of his diocese, or when accompanying his brother's court, he always carried his library with him, "as if it had been the ark of the Lord," says the monk Rotger, who, moreover, remarks that this library was stored both with sacred and profane authors, for, like a good householder, he knew how to bring out of his treasury things new and old. Nothing ever prevented his finding time for reading, and he excited every one about him to cultivate similar tastes, specially his nephew Otho, who was for some time his pupil. Indeed, Rotger goes so far as to say that the archbishop felt a certain want of confidence in those who had no attraction to study; meaning probably to those unlettered clerks who cared not to acquire the learning proper to their sacred calling. Of these there was no lack in Lorraine; but Bruno effected a great change in the condition of that afflicted province, by appointing good bishops, healing feuds, reforming monasteries, and making men love one another in spite of themselves. In all these good works he was assisted by the learning and martial valour of Ansfrid, count of Lorraine, who was well read both in law and Scripture, and who used his sword exclusively to repress pillage and defend the helpless. This feudal noble of the Iron Age spent all his leisure hours in study, and when at last he embraced the ecclesiastical state, and at the entreaties of the emperor accepted a bishopric, he was able to lay his sword on the altar and render witness that it had never been drawn in an unjust cause.

Bruno's example made a great stir in Germany, and moved many bishops to exert themselves in the work of reform. Poppo, Bishop of Wurtzburg, sent to Rome for a celebrated master named Stephen, and with his help the episcopal seminary was restored, and soon boasted of a "crowd of students, and a great store of books." Among other pupils educated under Master Stephen were two friends, named Wolfgang and Henry. Wolfgang was a student of Bruno's type, possessing an avidity for all sorts of learning; and though he began his school-life at seven, he is said in a few years not only to have acquired an extensive acquaintance with the letter of the Scriptures, but to have penetrated into the pith and marrow of their mystical sense. His father had thought it sufficient to place him under a certain priest, to receive a very scanty elementary education, but Wolfgang entreated that he might be sent to Reichnau, which then enjoyed a high reputation; and here he first met with his friend Henry. Henry was the younger brother of Bishop Poppo, and easily persuaded Wolfgang to migrate with him to Wurtzburg, for the sake of studying under the famous Master Stephen. It soon appeared, however, that the disciple was more learned than the master, and when the Wurtzburg students found Master Stephen's lectures very dull, or very obscure, they were in the habit of applying to Wolfgang, who possessed that peculiar gift of perspicacity which marked him from his boyhood as called to the functions of teaching. Moreover, he was so kind and so willing to impart his knowledge, that his companions declared he made daylight out of the darkest matters; when Stephen's prosy abstruseness had fairly mystified them, five words from Wolfgang seemed like the "Fiat lux," and these observations reaching the ears of Stephen, had the proverbial fate of all comparisons. At last, one day when Wolfgang was surrounded by a knot of his schoolfellows, who entreated him to expound a passage in Marcian Capella, Master Stephen, moved to jealous anger, forbade Wolfgang any longer to attend the lectures. This ungenerous command obliged him to continue his studies alone, but he seems to have lost little by being deprived of the benefit of an instructor whom he had already far outstripped in learning.

Henry and Poppo were both of them relatives of Otho, who in 956 caused the former to be raised to the archbishopric of Treves. Henry insisted on carrying his friend with him into his new diocese, and wished to load him with benefices and honours, all of which, however, Wolfgang refused. He would accept of no other employment than that of teaching youth, for which he knew his aptitude, and which he heartily loved; and, in the true spirit of a Christian teacher, he chose to discharge this office gratuitously, not as a means of private gain, but as a work for souls, even supporting many of his scholars out of his own purse. He cared as much for their spiritual as their intellectual progress, and set them the example of a holy and mortified life. The archbishop, in despair at not being able to promote him as he desired, at last got him to accept the office of dean to a certain college of canons. Wolfgang did not allow the dignity to be a nominal one, but obliged his canons to embrace community life, and to commence a course of sacred studies, assuring them that the sustenance of the inner man is as necessary as that of the body. Archbishop Henry dying in 964, Wolfgang, who had only remained at Treves out of affection to him, prepared to return into Swabia, which was his native country. But Bruno had his eye on him, and inviting him to Cologne, offered him every dignity, even the episcopate itself, if he would only remain in his duchy. Wolfgang, though he persisted in refusing to accept any promotion, felt himself obliged to pass some time at the prince-bishop's court, and testified afterwards to the fact of his great sanctity. Finding that he could not move the resolution of his friend, Bruno at last reluctantly allowed him to return to Swabia, where he remained only just long enough formally to renounce his hereditary possessions, after which he withdrew to Einsidlen, and took the monastic habit under the English abbot Gregory.

At Einsidlen, as at Treves, he devoted himself to the office of teaching, and with the same success. It was as hopeless for him to attempt to conceal his talent, as to hide a light under a bushel. The world soon resounded with the fame of his school, and bishops travelled to Einsidlen to bargain for his possession. This time the friendly persecution was revived by St. Udalric of Augsburgh, who was himself sufficiently learned to understand the merits of the poor monk, who asked nothing of the world but a quiet hiding-place, and was never suffered to enjoy it for any length of time. Udalric was a scholar of St. Gall's, and had given marks of sanctity even during his school days. A minute account of his manner of life when archbishop is given in the beautiful life written by his friend Gerard. Let it suffice to say, that besides singing the Divine Office in the cathedral with his canons, and daily celebrating two or three masses (a privilege then permitted to priests, as we learn from Walafrid Strabo), he every day recited the entire Psalter, the Office of Our Lady, together with that of the Holy Cross, and of All Saints; that he entertained a number of poor persons at his table, exercised hospitality on a right royal scale, administered strict justice to his people, and courageously defended them against the oppression of their feudal lords; finally, that he took particular care of the education of his clergy, and directed the studies of his cathedral school in person, none being better fitted to do so than himself. When he made the visitation of his diocese, he travelled in a wagon drawn by oxen, which he preferred to riding on horseback as it enabled him to recite the Psalms with his chaplains with less interruption. In this arrangement he certainly displayed a sound discretion, for in the ancient chronicles of these times, more than one story is preserved of the disasters which befell travelling monks and bishops, owing to their habit of reading on horseback.[133] His cathedral city of Augsburgh was repeatedly attacked by the Huns; and during one of their sieges, the holy bishop, sending the able-bodied men to the walls collected a number of infants in arms, and laying them on the floor of the cathedral, before the altar, prostrated himself in prayer, hoping that their tender cries might ascend as prayer before the Throne of God. His prayers were heard, and Augsburgh was delivered. Such was the prelate who at last succeeded in drawing Wolfgang out of his retirement, and compelling him to receive priestly ordination. And in 972 the emperor Otho II., at the united entreaties of his bishops, appointed him Bishop of Ratisbon, which see he governed for twenty-two years, never, however, laying aside his monastic habit. Henry, duke of Bavaria, thoroughly understood his merits, and knowing his love of the office of teaching, entreated him to take charge of his four children, St. Henry, afterwards emperor of Germany, St. Bruno, who succeeded Udalric in the diocese of Augsburgh, and the two princesses, Gisela and Brigit, who both died in the odour of sanctity. The singular blessing which attended his labours with these and other noble children committed to his care, gave rise to a proverb which deserves remembrance: "Find saints for masters, and we shall have saints for emperors."

The emperors of the tenth century were certainly fortunate in this respect, and as I have just named Otho II., it will not be amiss to say a few words about him, and about the tutor to whom was committed the education of his son and successor. Otho II. had been brought up among the canons of Hildesheim, and had acquired from them a taste for letters, which was still further increased by his marriage with the Greek princess Theophania. At this time the court of Constantinople was the centre of all that survived of the old imperial civilisation and literature. Theophania was a woman of beauty and talent, and remarkable for her wit and eloquence, she soon infused into the Germans a rage for Greek literature, and gave such a brilliant character to the literary coteries of the imperial court, that Gerbert, who was then residing there, speaks in one of his letters of the "Socratic conversation" which he found among the learned men who thronged the company of the empress, which, he says, sufficed to console him amid all his troubles. In more peaceful times it is probable that a sovereign of Otho's character would have effected a great restoration of letters, but the ten years of his reign were occupied with continual wars, which affixed to his name the appellation of "the Sanguinary," and gave no scope for the exercise of his really great abilities. Before his death, which took place in 983, he obtained the election of his infant son, Otho III. as emperor, and left him to the guardianship of Theophania, who, during the minority of her son, governed the empire as regent.

The empress showed herself fully qualified for both offices. She had it greatly at heart to provide the young emperor with a learned education, and not unmindful of the proverb we have quoted above, was equally solicitous to secure for his tutor one who should merit the title of a saint. The priest whom she chose was a noble Saxon named Bernward; he was nephew to Folcmar, Bishop of Utrecht, who sent him when a child of seven years old to be educated in the episcopal school of Hildesheim, by the grave and holy master

Tangmar. This good old man, who afterwards wrote his life, received him kindly, and to test his capacities, set him to learn by heart some of the select passages from Holy Scripture which were usually given to beginners. Little Bernward set himself to learn and meditate on them with wonderful ardour, and associating himself to the most studious of his companions, tried with their help thoroughly to master, not only the words, but the hidden sense of his lessons. As he was not yet judged old enough to join any of the classes, he sat apart by himself, but listened attentively to the lectures of the master, and the explanations which he gave, and was afterwards found reproducing the same in a grave and sententious manner for the edification of his younger schoolfellows. Surprised and delighted at these marks of precocious genius, Tangmar spared no pains in the cultivation of so promising a scholar, and had him constantly by his side. "Whenever I went abroad on the business of the monastery," he says, "I used to take him with me, and I was always more and more struck by his excellent qualities. We often studied the whole day as we rode along on horseback, only more briefly than we were used to do in school; at one time exercising ourselves in poetry, and amusing ourselves by making verses, at another, arguing on philosophic questions. He excelled no less in the mechanical than in the liberal arts. He wrote a beautiful hand, was a good painter, and an equally good sculptor and worker in metals, and had a peculiar aptitude for all things appertaining to household and domestic affairs." Under the care of so devoted a master, the boy Bernward, as the old man always called him, grew up to be a wise and learned man. He had that singular ardour for acquiring knowledge which seems one of the gifts poured out over ages in which its pursuit is hedged about with difficulties that must necessarily discourage a more ordinary amount of zeal. Bernward always read during meal times, and when unable to read himself, he got some one to read to him. His reputation determined Theophania to choose him as tutor to her son, who made great progress under his care, and was then sent to finish his education in the school of the famous Gerbert. Bernward meanwhile was appointed Bishop of Hildesheim, and in the midst of his episcopal functions, continued to cultivate literature and the fine arts. He made time by employing the day in business and the night in prayer. He founded *scriptoria* in many monasteries, and collected a valuable library of sacred and profane authors. He tried to bring to greater perfection the arts of painting, mosaic work, and metal work, and made a valuable collection of all those curiosities of fine art which were brought to Otho's court as presents from foreign princes. This collection Bernward used as a studio, for the benefit of a number of youths whom he brought up and instructed in these pursuits. It is not to be said what he did for his own cathedral, supplying it with jewelled missals, thuribles, and chalices, a huge golden corona which hung from the centre of the roof, and other like ornaments. The walls he painted with his own hands. The visitor to Hildesheim may still admire the rich bronze gates, sixteen feet in height, placed in the cathedral by its artist-bishop, the crucifix adorned with filagree-work and jewels, made by his own hands, and the old rose-tree growing on the cloister, which tradition affirms him to have planted.

His manner of life is minutely described by his old tutor Tangmar. After high mass every morning he gave audience to any who desired to speak to him, heard causes, and administered justice with great readiness and promptitude. Then his almoner waited on him, and accompanied him to the distribution of his daily alms, for every day a hundred poor persons were fed and relieved at his palace. After this he went the round of his workshops, overlooking each one's work and directing its progress. At the hour of nine he dined with his clerks. There was no worldly pomp observable at his table, but a religious silence, all being required to listen to the reading, which was made aloud. The barbarians gave him plenty of trouble, for they had seized possession of both shores of the Elbe, and were therefore able to enter Saxony whenever they liked, and often appeared at the gates of Hildesheim. But Bernward raised troops for the defence of his diocese, and repeatedly forced them to retire; and at last built and garrisoned two strong fortresses which kept the pirates in check.

Bernward had many illustrious disciples, and among them was one destined to be known in history as the Apostle of the Sclaves. The title may puzzle those readers who have met with other and earlier narratives of the conversion of these people, but the fact is that the Sclaves absorbed almost as much Apostolic labour as China has done in later times. Twice converted they had twice apostatised, and were finally brought within the fold of the Church by the labours of Bennon, Bishop of Misnia. This remarkable man belonged to the family of the counts of Saxony, and was placed under the care of St. Bernward at the age of five years. The restored monastery of Hildesheim, dedicated to St. Michael, of course possessed its school, which was presided over by Wigger, a very skilful master, under whose careful tuition Bennon thrived apace. "*Now as the age was learned,*" writes the good canon, Jerome Enser—who little thought in what light that same age would come to be regarded—"as the age was learned, and cultivated humane letters, as may be seen by the lives and writings of so many eminent men, Wigger would not allow the child committed to his care to neglect polite letters;" so he set him to work at once to learn to write, being careful to transcribe his copies himself. And how well Bennon profited from these early lessons might yet be seen by any who chose to examine the fine specimens which were preserved in the Church of Misnia when Jerome Enser wrote his biography. After this Wigger exercised his pupil in the art of reading and that of composing verses, taking care to remove from his way everything offensive to piety or modesty. Bennon had a natural gift of versification, and soon learnt to write little hymns and poems by way of amusement. His progress and his boyish verses endeared him to his masters, and indeed, adds Jerome, "he was beloved by God and man." None showed him more affection than St. Bernward, who was now overwhelmed with the infirmities of old age, though his mind was as bright and active as ever. During the last five years of his life he was entirely confined to his bed, and all this time little Bennon proved his chief solace. Sometimes he read aloud to his beloved father. Sometimes he made verses, or held disputations to entertain him; never would he leave his side, discharging for him all the offices of which his youth was capable. When at last death drew near, Bernward called the child to him together with his master Wigger, and addressed to him a touching exhortation. "If by reason of thy tender age," he said, "thou canst not thyself be wise, promise me never to depart from the side of thy preceptor that he may be wise for thee, and that so thou mayest be preserved from the corruptions of the world whilst thy heart is yet soft and tender. Yea, if thou lovest me, love and obey him in all things, as holding the place of thy father." Then he kissed the child's little hand, and placed it in that of Wigger, and soon after departed this life, rich in good works, and secure of a heavenly reward.

The sorrow of Bennon was too great for words. He wept without ceasing, and pined away in his grief, till at last Wigger had to mingle his consolations with timely reprehension. His words in some degree restored his pupil to peace, but so deep an impression had been made on his heart of the nothingness of a world which sooner or later deprives us of all we most love, that he resolved to have nothing more to do with it, and to devote his life to God in the monastery. He never forgot his good father Bernward, and the first composition which he wrote after the death of the bishop was a poetical epitaph which his biographer inserts, and which is not a favourable specimen of his genius. Jerome probably felt that it was open to criticism, which he judiciously forestalls. "The verses," he says, "show that if not ignorant of the metrical art, he did not affect a flowery style, but was content with plain and simple language. But if some, having delicate ears, should be disposed to turn up their noses at the line,"

"Quem Deus Emmanuel diligat, et Michael."

"I would remind them of the singular devotion which the Blessed Bernward bore to St. Michael whence it will appear that this line did not escape our Bennon unwarily. They who are moved by the Spirit of God care not much for the outside shell of words, and prefer a good life to a good style of writing." He adds, "the scholastic discipline of Hildesheim was at this time extremely severe. It was reckoned a great fault not merely to be absent from choir or refectory, but even to come late. The scholars each day had to bring their Scripture to the dean, and rehearse their Psalms. And the rod was freely used." Bennon being kept under this strict discipline, passed safely through the slippery time of youth, and in his after-life proved himself not unworthy the extraordinary care bestowed on his education.

Many other great prelates of this period might be enumerated, distinguished either as the founders or the masters of schools. Of Notger of Liege we have already spoken. The school of Verdun was founded by one of his disciples, and boasted of possessing that wonder of the eleventh century, Master Herminfrid, who spoke and wrote with equal facility Latin, Greek, French, German, and Italian. Then there was St. Meinwerc, who like Bennon was a pupil of Hildesheim, where he studied along with his cousin St. Henry of Bavaria, and the prince, even after he became Emperor, remembered their schoolboy days together, and was fond of putting him in mind of them by sundry tricks that savoured of the grown-up schoolboy. Meinwerc was not much of a scholar himself, but when he became Bishop of Paderborn, he showed a laudable zeal in promoting good scholarship among his clergy. In fact, he was the founder of those famous schools of Paderborn which are described as flourishing in divine and human science, and which were perfected by his nephew and successor, Imadeus. The boys were all under strict cloistral discipline; there were professors of grammar, logic, rhetoric, and music; both the trivium and quadrivium were there taught, together with mathematics, physics, and astronomy. Horace, Virgil, and Statius were read by the students, whose ordinary recreation it was to make verses, while great attention was paid to the arts of writing and painting. Brucker treats this account as apocryphal, on the ground that Meinwerc was an *ignoramus* himself, and sometimes made blunders in reading Latin. The story of Bishop Meinwerc and his mules, the only one, be it remembered, on which this charge of ignorance is founded, together with the explanation of the same so amusingly given by Mr. Maitland in his "Dark Ages," need not here be repeated. When emperors take to playing tricks, even the wisest of bishops may be snared into a blunder. But granting the fact that Meinwerc himself possessed no more scholarship than our own Wykeham, there seems no reason for supposing it therefore impossible that he should desire to rear a race of students more learned than himself. We know that he was a strict disciplinarian in all that regarded the right discharge of the sacred offices, and that he was wont to examine and burn all incorrect copies of books used at the altar, administering very sharp correction, in the shape of stripes, to careless and negligent priests.

However, the object of the present chapter being chiefly to show something of the interior of schools in the Dark Ages, we will pass over a great many names of founders and learned bishops, and take our way to Magdeburg, where Otho I. had erected a cathedral, and Archbishop Adalbert had founded a school. Here, in 973, the yet more famous St. Adalbert of Prague was sent by his parents for education. They were of the Bohemian nation, and had vowed to offer their son to God should he recover of a dangerous sickness. Before he left his father's house he had learnt the Psalter, and under Otheric, the famous master then presiding over the school of Magdeburg, he made as much progress in sanctity as in learning. He had a habit of stealing away from the schoolroom in the midst of his studies to refresh his soul with a brief prayer in the church, after which he hastened back and was safe in his place again before the coming of the master. To conceal his acts of charity from the eyes of others, he chose the night hours for visiting the poor and dispensing his abundant alms. It often happened that when Otheric was out of the school, the boys would divert themselves with games more or less mischievous to relieve the weary hours of study. Adalbert seldom took part in these pastimes, neither would he share in those stealthy little feasts which they sometimes held in obscure corners, where they contrived to hide from Otheric's quick eye the sweets and other dainties furnished them, as we must suppose, by some medieval tart-woman.[134] However, if Adalbert was proof against this last-named temptation, it appears he was not altogether superior to the love of play, and that when his master's back was turned, he did occasionally throw aside his books and indulge in a game of ball. When such delinquencies came to the ears of Otheric, he did not spare the rod, and on these occasions, observes his biographer with cruel pleasantry, Adalbert was often known to speak in three languages. For it was a strict rule that the boys were always to talk Latin in the schoolroom, and never allow the ears of their master to catch the sound of a more barbarous dialect. When the rod was produced, therefore, Adalbert would begin by entreating indulgence in classic phraseology, but so soon as it was applied, he would call out for mercy in German, and finally in Sclavonic. After nine years' study at Magdeburg, Adalbert returned to Bohemia, with the reputation of being specially well read in philosophy, and taking with him a useful library of books, which he had collected during his college career. After his consecration as Bishop of Prague, at the early age of twenty-seven, he is said never again to have been seen to smile. Twice the hard-heartedness of his people compelled him to abandon his diocese, and after his departure the second time, he travelled as missioner into the then heathen and barbarous provinces of Prussia, where he met with his martyrdom in the year 997. A Sclavonic hymn to the Blessed Virgin, formerly wont to be sung by the Poles when going to battle, is attributed to this saint.

Hitherto we have spoken only of the episcopal seminaries of Germany; those attached to the monasteries were, if possible, more celebrated. The great school of St. Gall's attained its highest degree of splendour in this century. Something has already been said of the general character of the studies pursued there, but its succession of great masters deserves a more particular notice. Originally founded by Irish monks, the monastery owed no little of its renown to the teaching of Irish professors. In the year 840, Marx, an Irish bishop, travelling home from Rome in company with his nephew Moengall, stopped at St. Gall's, and after a few days' visit, both of them entreated the abbot to admit them into his community. Permission being granted, they dismissed their servants and horses, threw their money out of the window, and, keeping only their books and sacred vessels, vowed to spend the rest of their lives in the seclusion of the cloister. Moengall, to whom the monks gave the less barbarous name of Marcellus, was soon after appointed master of the interior or cloistral school, the exterior one being governed by the famous master, Iso. This last-named personage, whom Ekkehard styles a *doctor magnificus*, enjoyed such a reputation that all the monasteries of Gaul and Burgundy were eager to obtain his disciples, and it was commonly said that he possessed ways of his own for sharpening the dullest wits. At the precise time of which we speak, he had among his pupils Solomon, afterwards Bishop of Constance, and the three friends, Notker Balbulus, or the stammerer, Ratpert, and Tutilo, all of whom afterwards chose the monastic state, and passed, therefore, to the interior school, presided over by Marcellus.

The Irish scholar greatly improved the system of studies; he extended, if he did not first introduce, the study of Greek, and it is evident that his influence, and that of many of his countrymen, who filled subordinate professorships, may be traced in the character which distinguished the education of St. Gall's from that of most of its contemporaries. It was larger and freer, and made more of the arts and sciences; indeed, so far as regards its studies, it had a better claim to the title of a *university* than any single institution which can be named as existing before the time of Philip Augustus. Marcellus was fortunate in his pupils, but the character of the three who were most prominent among them must be given in the words of Ekkehard. Though united in one heart, he says, they were of very different dispositions. Notker was weak, not in mind but in body; in speech, but not in spirit, a stammerer. Firm in spiritual things, patient in adversity, mild to all, yet a strict disciplinarian, and timorous at any sudden alarm, except of demons, whom he combated valiantly. He was very assiduous in reading, writing and composing, and was, in short, a vessel of the Holy Ghost. Very different was Tutilo; he was a good and useful man; as to his arms and all his limbs, such as Fabius teaches us to choose for a wrestler. He was eloquent, with a fine voice, skilful in carving, and an excellent painter. He was a musician, too, like his companions, and excelled everybody in all kinds of stringed and wind instruments, and taught their use to the sons of the nobility educated in the exterior school. He was, moreover, a very wise builder, powerful in reading and singing, cheerful whether in jest or earnest, and what is more, ever diligent in choir; in secret, given to devout tears, and skilful in the composition of songs and melodies. Ratpert was something between the two:

from his youth he had been schoolmaster of the external school, where he succeeded Master Iso, and a kind, straightforward teacher he was, very strict in discipline, and so seldom given to go abroad that, he made one pair of shoes last a twelvemonth. He was very famous as a poet, and so fond of the ancients that he was known, even in chapter, to quote a verse from Virgil. He died some years before either of his friends; and forty of his former pupils, all of them priests or canons, stood around his deathbed, and promised each one to say thirty masses for the repose of his soul, a thing which gave him infinite joy and satisfaction.

Tutilo was a good classical scholar, and could preach both in Greek and Latin; but he was chiefly esteemed as an artist and a musician. He sang his own melodies to the harp, an instrument which the Irish monks had rendered very popular at St. Gall's. His magnificent statuary in bronze and stone continued to decorate the abbey church till the time of its pillage by the *soi-disant* reformers, and all the French and German prelates were eager to obtain his works. With the permission of his abbot, therefore, he travelled far and wide, executing devout carvings and paintings, much to the dissatisfaction of Ratpert, who was wont to say that this gadding about the world was the destruction of a monk. It did not, however, prove so with Tutilo, who, to all his brilliant genius and gigantic muscular strength, united in a singular degree the grace of humility. Whenever he found that his artistic skill drew on him any notable amount of admiration, he generally found some excuse for departing from the place where he was at work, and his long journeys never lessened his devotion, or deprived him of his gift of holy tears. It was his custom to adorn his sculptures and pictures with pious verses, in order to draw the thoughts of those who beheld them from the work of the artist to the divine mystery which it represented. One of his most celebrated pieces of sculpture was an image of the Blessed Virgin, which he carved for the cathedral at Metz. Whilst engaged on this masterpiece, two pilgrims came up and begged an alms of him, and having received it, asked of a clerk who was standing by, who that beautiful lady was whom they saw at his side, holding his compasses, and directing him in his work. The clerk looked, and saw the same wondrous vision, and believed it to be Our Lady herself who had come in person to assist her client. But when the rumour of the thing spread abroad, Tutilo fled away, nor could he ever be persuaded to return to the city. His verses were highly esteemed, and some of his elegies are still preserved. Besides all this, he was great in mathematics and astronomy, and constructed an astrolabe which showed the course of the stars. For it must be remembered that scientific studies were highly prized at St. Gall's, and that even geographers were to be found among the monks, such as Abbot Hartmot, who constructed a large map of the world, in those days a very rare and valuable curiosity.

Among these three famous scholars, we may select Notker as the most perfect specimen of the monastic type. Like his two friends, he was a poet and musician, and his brethren considered him a second Horace for the beauty of his songs and sequences. It was the reputation of learning enjoyed by St. Gall's which had first attracted him thither, for indeed, says Ekkehard, "he was devoured with a love of grammar." Like a true poet, he was keenly susceptible to the sights and sounds of nature, and loved to "study her beautifulness" in that enchanted region of lakes and mountains. The gentle melancholy inseparable from exalted genius, which in him was increased by his exceeding delicacy of organisation, found its expression in the wild and mystic melodies which he composed. The monotonous sound of a mill-wheel near the abbey suggested to him the music of the "Media Vita," the words being written whilst looking into a deep gulf over which some labourers were constructing a bridge. This antiphon became very popular in Germany, and was every year sung at St. Gall's during the Rogation Processions. But it was not as a poet or man of science that the Blessed Notker was best known to posterity; profoundly learned in human literature, he yet, says Ekkehard, applied more to the Psalter than to any other book. Even in his own lifetime he was revered as a saint. He was master of the interior and claustral school at the same time as Ratpert governed the exterior school, and kept up the same strict discipline, "stripes only excepted." The gentleness of his disposition peeps out in the fact that one of the faults he was hardest on in his pupils was the habit of bird's-nesting. He was always accessible; no hour of day or night was ever deemed unseasonable for a visit from any who brought a book in their hands. For the sake of maintaining regular observance, he once forbade his disciples to whisper to him in time of silence, but the abbot enjoined him under obedience to let them speak to him whenever they would. Ratpert relates a story of him, which shows the opinion of learning and sanctity in which he was held. The emperor Charles, having on one occasion come to the monastery on a visit, he brought in his suite a certain chaplain, whose pride appears to have taken offence at the consideration with which his master treated the Blessed Notker. When they were about to depart, therefore, seeing the man of God sitting, as was his custom, with his Psalter in his hand, and recognising him to be the same man who, on the previous day, had solved many hard questions proposed to him by Charles, he said to his companions, "There is he who is said to be the most learned man in the whole empire; but if you like, I will make this most excellent wiseacre a laughing-stock for you, for I will ask him a question which, with all his learning, he will not be able to answer." Curious to see what he would do, and how Notker would deal with him, they agreed to his proposal, and all went together to salute the master, who courteously rose, and asked them what they desired. Then said the unhappy man of whom we spoke, "O most learned master, we are very well aware that there is nothing you do not know. We therefore desire you to tell us, if you can, what God is now doing in heaven?" "Yes," replied Notker, "I can answer that question very well. He is doing what He always has done, and what He is shortly about to do to thee, He is exalting the humble, and humbling the proud." The scoffer moved away, while the laugh was turned against him. Nevertheless, he made light of Notker's words and the prediction of evil which they seemed to contain regarding himself. Presently the bell rang for the king's departure, and the chaplain, mounting his horse, rode off with a great air in front of his master. But before he came to the gate of the city the steed fell, and the rider being thrown on his face, broke his leg. Abbot Hartmot hearing of this accident, desired Notker to visit the sick man, and pardon him, giving him his blessing. But the foolish chaplain protested that the misfortune had nothing to do with Notker's prediction, and continued to speak of him with the greatest contempt. His leg, however, remained in a miserable state, until one night his friends besought Notker to come to him and aid him with his prayers. He complied willingly enough, and touching the leg, it was immediately restored; and by this lesson the chaplain learned to be more humble for the future.

Notker was the author of various works, amongst others of a German translation of the Psalter, which Vadianus speaks of in his treatise on the "Ancient Colleges of Germany," and which he says is scarcely intelligible by reason of the excessive harshness of the old Tudesque dialect. He gives a translation of the "Creed," and the "Our Father," from Notker's version, in which it is not difficult to trace the German idiom.[135] Notker's German studies were yet more extensively carried on by his namesake, Notker Labeo, or the Thick-Lipped, who wrote many learned works in the vernacular, and was also a great classical scholar. He translated into German the works of Aristotle, Boëthius, and Marcian Capella, and some musical treatises, all which are still preserved. His translation of St. Gregory's "Morals" is lost. He is commemorated in the chronicles of his House as "the kind and learned master," and whilst he presided over the claustral school, he educated a great many profound scholars, among whom was Ekkehard junior, the author of the chronicle "De Casibus S. Galli," and of the celebrated "Liber Benedictionum." This Ekkehard, at the request of the empress, transcribed Notker's "Paraphrase of the Psalms" for her use with his own hand, and corrected a certain poem which his predecessor Ekkehard I. had written when a schoolboy, and which was full of Tudesque barbarisms, such as the delicate ear of Ekkehard junior might not abide. He held that the barbarous idioms could not be translated into Latin without a great deal of painstaking. "*Think* in German," he would say to his scholars, "and then be careful to render your thought into correct Latin." There was yet a third Ekkehard whose memory is preserved in the annals of St. Gall under the surname of *Palatinus*. He was nephew to Ekkehard I., and presided over both the exterior and interior schools, and that with great success. He made no distinction between noble and plebeian scholars, but employed those who had less talent for learning in writing, painting, and other like arts. He was able to take down in shorthand the substance of anything he heard, and two discourses are still preserved thus noted by his hand. He was afterwards most unwillingly summoned to the Court of Otho I., who appointed him his chaplain and secretary, and tutor to his son Otho II. So venerated was this great man throughout Germany, that when he attended the council of Mentz in 976, six bishops rose up to salute their old master, all of them having been educated in the school of St. Gall. To this list of masters I must add the name of another Notker, who, from his strict observance of discipline, received the surname of "Piperis-granum," or the Peppercorn, though his pungency of temper did not prevent his brethren from commemorating him in their obituary as the "Doctor benignissimus." He was renowned as a physician, a painter, and a poet, and was also well skilled in music. Most of these great men find a place in a narrative which I will give here for the sake of its connection with the classical studies of St. Gall, and which is related by Ekkehard junior in his chronicle of the abbey.

Hedwiga, daughter to Duke Henry of Bavaria, was at that time the reigning Duchess of Swabia, having been left a widow by the death of her husband Duke Burkhard. She was a woman of wonderful beauty, but of so severe and imperious a temper as to be held in terror through all the surrounding provinces. In her youth she had been promised in marriage to the Greek prince, Constantine, who sent a cunning artist to take the portrait of his future bride, and at the same time to instruct her in Greek literature. But Hedwiga, not admiring the Greek alliance, made such terrible contortions of her fair nose and eyebrows whenever the painter applied himself to his task, that his efforts at a likeness proved fruitless, and the marriage was broken off in consequence. From the Greek painter, however, Hedwiga had acquired a very fair proportion of Greek scholarship, and on her marriage with Burkhard, she likewise applied herself to the study of Latin. She was a frequent visitor to the abbey of St. Gall, where her nephew, Burkhard, was then abbot, and in return for her splendid gifts, insisted on nothing less than that the abbot should make over to her, as tutor, the hapless Ekkehard Palatinus, who then filled the office of porter, and was known to be an excellent scholar in both languages. The abbot very unwillingly consented to her demand, and poor Ekkehard had to pay frequent visits to the castle of Dwellia, where, in spite of the beauty and talents of his fair disciple, her sharp temper and exasperating ways often made his office a hard one. Once, when out of humility he had begged that a certain canopy erected over his bed might be taken down, the wrathful duchess ordered the servant who had executed the order to be flogged, and would have cut off his head had it not been for the entreaties of the master. However, she had an open hand, though a somewhat heavy one, and bestowed liberal gifts on the monks of St. Gall, in the shape of embroidered copes and chasubles. But even in her bounty she showed the same wilful disposition, for having once given them a very rich dalmatic, cunningly worked in fine gold, and representing the espousals of Mercury and Philology, she took it away again in dudgeon at the refusal of Abbot Immo to let her have the antiphonary on which she had set her heart.

The favours which St. Gall's received at her hands, however, and the frequent visits exchanged between the abbey and Dwellia roused the jealousy of Ruodman, abbot of the neighbouring monastery of Reichnau. He was a prying, gossiping sort of a personage, and set afloat so many mischievous and ill-natured tales as greatly to distress the monks. But this was not the worst. Not content with whispering his calumnies, Ruodman conceived the plan of stealing into the convent in the absence of Abbot Burkhard, to see if he could not spy out some matter which he might turn to the disadvantage of the inmates. On a certain day, therefore, mounting his horse he set out for St. Gall, and arriving at the monastery about nightfall, stole into the cloister and cautiously crept about spying this way and that to see what he could discover. Having satisfied his curiosity by an inspection of the cloister, he proceeded on tiptoe upstairs to the dormitory, but not so softly but that the watchful ear of Dean Ekkehard, the senior, caught the sound. Quietly providing himself with the abbot's lantern, he followed the footsteps, and presently discovered the intruder. Ere long the whole community was down upon him, and I leave the reader to guess what were their sentiments when the abbot's lantern displayed the features of the trembling Ruodman. The younger part of the monks were earnest in their entreaties that he might be chastised as his impertinence merited, and some of them ran forwith to provide themselves with rods. The unhappy Ruodman, in great anguish of soul, implored their mercy: "Spare me, good youths!" he exclaimed; "I am in your hands, deal with me gently, or at least wait to hear the judgment of your dean:" for at that moment Ekkehard senior was consulting with the elder fathers what was to be done in so strange an emergency. Meanwhile Notker, the Peppercorn, appeared on the scene, and his voice was for summary measures. "O wicked man!" he exclaimed, "dost thou go about as a lion, seeking whom thou mayest devour, and like another Satan, desiring to accuse thy brethren?" But he, cunningly taking advantage of the known mildness of the good dean, threw himself entirely on his mercy. "Most prudent father," he exclaimed, "I have indeed done very wickedly; but lo! I repent, I ask pardon of everybody, and from henceforward I will utterly abstain from molesting any of you." The kind-hearted monks were touched by his speedy repentance; some indeed regretted that he should be let off without receiving a severe lesson, but the voices of the seniors prevailed, and Ruodman was conducted by Ekkehard himself to the spot where his horse awaited him, and dismissed in peace and forgiveness.

My readers will probably be of opinion that he got off very easily. So was Abbot Burkhard when he heard of the affair, though he was far from being of a pugnacious temper; and so too was the mighty duchess. The next time that Ekkehard Palatinus appeared to give his lesson, she vented her wrath in very strong language; to be candid, she swore, "by the life of Hedwiga," to have her revenge. But her anger for that day, at least, was dissipated by a pleasant incident which sets her character in a more amiable light. Ekkehard had brought with him one of his junior scholars, whose infantine beauty attracted the admiration of the duchess. "Wherefore have you brought this child?" she inquired of her tutor; who replied with his customary courtesy, "For the sake of the Greek, gracious lady, which I hope he will gather from your lips." Then the boy, who was well trained in the versifying habits of the St. Gall's scholars, spoke for himself in an extempore line of Latin:—

"Esse velim Græcus, cum sim vix, Dom'na, Latinus."[136]

Charmed with his ready wit, she drew him to her, and kissing him kindly on the forehead made him sit on the footstool at her feet, requiring him to make her some more verses immediately. The child, confused with these unwonted caresses, looked first at one and then at the other of his teachers, and then stammered out,

"Non possum prorsus dignos componere versus,

Nam nimis expavi Duce me libante suavi."[137]

The severe heart of the duchess was fairly conquered, and making the little poet stand up before her, she then and there taught him to sing the antiphon, *Maria et flumina,* which she had herself translated out of Latin into Greek, and frequently afterwards had him at her castle and taught him how to make Greek verses. Moreover, she treated him with a tenderness that went nigh to spoiling, and gave him a Horace, and some other books which one wishes Ekkehard junior had named, and which were long preserved in the library. I will not pursue the story of Ruodman, which has been chiefly introduced for the sake of this graceful ending. He had great difficulty in making his peace with the abbot and the duchess, though he tried the mollifying gift to the former of a very handsome horse, which threw its rider the very first time he mounted it, so that in spite of all the skill displayed by Notker Piperisgranum, poor Abbot Burkhard went for some time after on crutches.

The school anecdotes of these times attest the familiar and paternal relations which existed between the scholars and their masters. The sports and enjoyments of the boys were amply provided for, and we find mention of running, wrestling, swimming, country walks, and fishing parties. Sometimes, as at Eton or Harrow, a visit from royalty procured an extra play-day, and on certain high festival days it is recorded that they were regaled with wine and a choicer fare at dinner. Hartmann, one of the learned disciples of Marcellus, retained such a liking for the school that even when he became abbot he spent half his time among the boys. And Solomon, the schoolfellow of Ratpert and Tutilo, who from abbot became Bishop of Constance, in like manner never forgot his old pupils, for he, too, had in his day held the ferule, being assistant to Iso in the external school. On one occasion, paying a visit to the abbey during the Christmas festival, on the day after Holy Innocents, before going away he peeped into the school, and finding the master absent walked into the midst of the boys to bid them all good-bye. They were about him in a minute; and the knowing ones among them lost no time in demanding their rights. There was a custom of long standing in the school that when any stranger entered the schoolroom, he might be captured as a prisoner, and not released till he had ransomed himself by a gift or favour. Undismayed by the rank of their present visitor, they surrounded him with daring familiarity, and declared him their captive. Good-naturedly entering into their sport, he suffered them to do what they liked with him; whereupon they led him to the master's chair, and made him understand that he should not come out thence till he had promised them something handsome. "Very well," he said, "as you have put me in the master's chair, I shall exercise the master's authority; prepare all of you to be flogged." This was turning the tables on them with a vengeance, but the boys were quick enough to find a way of escape. "Be it so," they replied, "only we claim to be suffered to redeem ourselves as we do with our master." "And pray, how is that?" said the bishop. "By making verses, to be sure," they replied; and he agreeing to their terms, they proceeded to spout little metrical compositions of their own, improvised for the occasion, two of which are even yet preserved. Charmed with their readiness, the bishop rose and kissed them all, one after the other. "Yea, as I live," he said, "I will surely ransom myself nobly." And so he did; for, calling the masters, he commanded that from that day forward and for ever, the boys should every year have three whole play-days after the Feast of Holy Innocents, and that on each of these days they should have meat dishes for dinner from the abbot's kitchen, which custom continued uninterruptedly till the troubles occasioned by the Hungarian invasions.

This Abbot Solomon was a learned as well as a kind-hearted man. He kept up a literary correspondence with two brother bishops, Dado, of Verdun, and Waldram, of Strasburg, and most of the letters that passed between them were in verse. He was, moreover, well skilled in the arts, and no one succeeded so well as he in designing the capitals for illuminated manuscripts; nay, even after he became bishop, he did not think this occupation unworthy his episcopal hand. He always kept up the same affectionate intercourse with St. Gall's and its scholars, and loved to encourage their studies and amuse himself with their innocent freedoms. Nor was it only by ecclesiastics drawn from the ranks of the community that these marks of favour and interest were bestowed. All the great German sovereigns understood the value of St. Gall's, and frequently visited it in person. Otho the Great was accustomed to say that he would willingly break his imperial crown into fragments to preserve regular observance in that abbey. His sagacious mind discerned the vast benefits which must flow to his empire from the preservation in the midst of it of such a centre of civilisation. So very solicitous was he for the well-being of the monastery, that reports having reached him in 968 of a rumoured decay of discipline, he used his imperial authority after the fashion of Charlemagne, and appointed a commission of abbots and bishops to investigate the case. They gave a good report of the state of the monastery; but the emperor, not yet satisfied, dispatched Kebon, abbot of Lauresheim, and some others, to enforce the observance of the Rule to the very letter. The only irregularity which the commissioners could discover was, that the Sunday chant was in too high a key, and that the Friday fast was too rigorous. Otho did not fail to do justice to the monks, and paid them a visit in person to console them for the trouble he had given them by his royal commissioners. It is said that assisting with them in choir, he let his stick fall as if by accident, and was edified to see that not one head was turned to observe the cause of the disturbance.

Ekkehard relates another royal visit from King Conrad I., which took place in 912. The king being at Constance on Christmas-day, the bishop happened after dinner to speak of the processions which were celebrated at that season at St. Gall's. "Why should we not go there to-morrow?" said the king; and his courtiers eagerly assenting, the next day very early they set out in boats across the lake, and so reached the abbey, where they spent three days. They specially admired the procession of the children; and to test their discipline, the king threw an apple among them, which none of them so much as looked at, whereat he greatly wondered. He dined with them in the refectory, and took pleasure in hearing the boys read in succession. As they came down from the desk, he sent some gold to be put into their mouths, which one of them spitting out again, Conrad declared he would make an excellent monk. His visit ended pleasantly to the children, for after causing himself to be enrolled as a conscript brother, he granted the scholars three extra play-days, and discharged the expenses of a great feast, furnishing the pepper, as he said, to season their beans. When Conrad II. and his empress paid a similar visit in 1033, they contrived to coax Abbot Dietbald to give them the German Psalter and the book of Job, which had been written out by Notker

Labeo, a treasure worth more to the community than many such instalments of royal pepper.

I have lingered so long on the history of St. Gall's as to leave little space for noticing the other monastic schools of the period. Most of those in Germany were remarkable for their cultivation of the arts, in which they far outstripped their Italian contemporaries. Godeschard, the successor of St. Bernward of Hildesheim, thoroughly shared his tastes, and carried on his designs. He even founded a school of painting in his episcopal palace which propagated the art through all the German dioceses. The subjects chosen were mostly scenes from the Old and New Testaments, being professedly intended for the instruction of the unlearned. Rio fixes the latter part of the tenth century as the date of the invention of glass painting, and the first fabrication of carpets and hangings. These new branches of industry were at once taken up by the monks, and at St. Florent de Saumur, in 985, a manufactory was established for weaving tapestries adorned with flowers and figures of animals. Sometimes the love of nature, so inherent in the monkish soul, induced them to decorate their cloisters with woodland scenes, in which the figures of men, dogs, horses, and deer, appear taking part in the chase. This was, of course, a departure from the principles on which the art of religious painting rested; and in the twelfth century these artistic caprices drew down severe reproofs from St. Bernard, who particularly disliked the representation of monsters, such as centaurs, and quadrupeds with a fish's tail. He thought that they savoured of heathenism, and were unsuitable to the gravity of a religious house. Hugo, of St. Victor, objected even to the natural designs of sheep and oxen; "It may be well," he said, "that monasteries should have paintings for the edification of those who are not delighted with Scriptural subtleties, but for monks themselves a horse or an ox is more useful in the fields than in a picture." These landscape subjects were, however, exceptional; far more frequently the monastic paintings were of a character described in their annals as "solemn pictures." They were pathetic representations of the Sacred Passion, accompanied with pious verses, not without a reference to the part of the convent where they were fixed. Thus, in the lavatory, the monks were bid not to wash their hands only, but their hearts also; in the refectory, to remember the gall and vinegar which Our Lord received on the Cross; and in the cloister, to think how the fashion of this world flees past us with noiseless step. The great abbey of St. Denis, in France, was covered all over with carvings and paintings, its very doors being sculptured with the mysteries of the Passion and Resurrection; while within the cloister was a whole series of paintings, historical and mystical, some of the latter exceedingly quaint, such as that which represented St. Paul turning a mill, and all the prophets of the Old Testament bringing a sack of corn to be ground in it; figuring thereby his gift in the interpretation of the Sacred Scriptures of the Old Law.

One thing cannot be overlooked whilst studying the annals of these early monastic schools; it is the peculiar charm attaching to the character of the masters. Everywhere we see the same features of cheerful labour, and a certain tranquil activity. Turn to the newly converted land of Normandy, and hear how Oderic Vitalis describes the abbots and masters of his own monastery of St. Evroult. In one page he paints the good abbot Theodoric, a very skilful scribe, who managed to collect a fine library, partly by the diligent exercise of his own pen and the labours of his youths, and partly by "gentle solicitations." Then there was Osbern, eloquent in speech, with a lively genius for sculpture, architecture, and painting. How we seem to behold him with "his stately stature, and his head, profusely covered with black hair sprinkled with grey!" He was always urging the novices to make progress in reading, singing, and writing; and loved with his own hands to make the writing implements and waxen tablets for the use of the boys. Or shall he tell us of that most promising scholar, William, who was placed in the abbey when nine years old, and was so diligent at his books, that the monks called him Gregory the Second? Not only did he make an excellent reader and chanter, and an exceedingly skilful copyist, but he was so devoted a student of the Scriptures, that he committed to his tenacious memory the Epistles of St. Paul, the Proverbs of Solomon, and many other books of either Testament.

Of another youth, who began his education at five, and who afterwards became schoolmaster, the same historian remarks, that his special gift lay in his powers of conversation. He had a knack of making everything interesting, and told the commonest things in a way that was quite delightful; and the monks were never weary of hearing him recite the narratives of Scripture, or the histories of learned men. It is not merely as men of learning that the character of these monastic students claims our admiration. It is the union of strength with tenderness, of scholarship with humility, which renders them so dear and venerable in our eyes. How seldom in these records are we disgusted with any of those traits of pedantry and self-seeking, the offsprings of a pride which had been pruned away by the knife of religious discipline? The monks were not mere scholars, and the tendency to literary conceit was effectually corrected by the daily exercises of community life. In the best days of monasticism, labour was cultivated hand in hand with letters. The same man who at one hour was engaged in writing a commentary on the Scriptures, producing Christian imitations of Horace or Virgil, or elaborating some of the exquisite master-pieces of cloistral art, found himself at another, employed on the meanest and humblest offices for the service of his brethren. The finest glass-painter of one medieval convent had to leave his paintings to take their chance in the furnace, while he was sent on the quest; and the Pope's messengers who brought a cardinal's hat to another learned friar, found him busy in the kitchen. This was the invariable *régime* which existed wherever the monastic institute preserved its discipline uncorrupted. Thus Odericus says of Roger de Warrene, son of the famous earl of Surrey, that entering the abbey of St. Evroult at the age of forty-six, he never plumed himself on his noble birth or varied accomplishments, but chose rather base employments, "cleaning the shoes of the brethren, washing their stockings, and cheerfully doing other services which appear mean to stupid or conceited persons." Yet he was a very skilful artist; and when he had finished with the shoes and stockings, he gave the rest of his time to the labours of the scriptorium, where he ornamented a book of the Gospels with gold, silver, and precious stones. And the historian knows not how to say enough of his pleasant and musical voice, his constant attendance in choir, and his courteous manner with the other monks, "always abstemious towards himself, always generous to others, always alive for vigils, and incredibly modest."[138] What a fragrant sweetness hangs about such notices as these, coming as they do in the midst of records of bloodshed and violence! Truly, we may say of the monastic schools, that they were "as beds of flowers by the dens of lions encompassed!" Huns and Saracens raged around them, but these gentle scholars fled to the mountains and the wilderness, and building their nests amid the rocks, while the world was flooded by new forms of barbarism, they wrote, they studied, they taught, and they prayed, and perpetuated that beautiful character which even Michelet has owned to have been in all ages the appanage of monks; sweetness, goodness of heart, and innocence. It remained wholly unaffected by the stormy turbulence of the world around them. They had a world of their own apart from and above it. All Europe might be in arms, whilst at St. Gall's Tutilo was constructing his wonderful table, which showed all the courses of the stars, or Notker was composing those hymns and sequences which for centuries afterwards were to be incorporated into the Office of the Church. Whilst the barbarians were laying all things in ruins, they, heedless alike of fame or profit, were patiently laying the foundations of European civilisation. They were forming the languages of Schiller, of Bacon, and of Bossuet; they were creating arts which modern skill in vain endeavours to imitate; they were preserving the codices of ancient learning, and embalming the world, "lying in wickedness," with the sweet odour of their manifold virtues. Surely, it was of such as these that the Wise Man spoke when he described that wisdom which God has given to His chosen ones. For they had received "the true knowledge of the things that are: the revolutions of the year, and the dispositions of the stars; the natures of living creatures, the reasonings of men, the diversities of plants, and the virtues of roots,"—and in them was "the spirit of understanding, holy, one, manifold, eloquent, active, undefiled, sweet, loving that which is good, beneficent, gentle, and kind."[139]

But before closing our sketch of the tenth century, we have yet to speak of its greatest scholastic glory: one whose attainments have elicited not only the admiration of his contemporaries, but the respectful notice even of those writers least disposed to believe that anything good can come out of the Dark Ages. The scholars of whom we have hitherto spoken, if regarded as great men by their contemporaries, are spoken of by later critics with very general contempt. They do not even allow them to have been useful in their own poor way, as transcribers of volumes that they scarce knew how to read, for Mr. Berington considers that even as copyists, the monks were sadly idle. Two names, however, escape the otherwise universal oblivion to which such writers would willingly consign the scholars of the Dark Ages, they are Erigena Scotus and Gerbert. There is, I hope, no malice in supposing that the intellectual superiority of these men does not form their only claim to exemption from the obloquy so plentifully heaped on their fellow-students. The independent views of Erigena were well fitted to win him favour with all disciples of the Rationalistic school; whilst the *supposed* circumstance of Gerbert having acquired his knowledge of science in an Arabic, and not in a Christian, academy, to say nothing of his having been at one time involved in a dispute with the Holy See, may have had some share in procuring him a larger meed of indulgence. To admit his merit did not entail the necessity of giving any credit to the Christian teachers, for if Gerbert ended his days on the chair of St. Peter, it is at least a comforting reflection to our historians, that he began life in the Moorish schools of Granada.

This consolation, alas! they enjoy no longer. Modern researches, which have upset so many time-honoured traditions, have proved beyond the possibility of dispute that Gerbert owed nothing either to Moors or Pagans, that his education was exclusively Christian, and that whatever be his value as a man of science, the Christian schools of the Iron century must bear the credit of it. It is hard to dissipate fables so romantic as those which represent the young scholar Gerbert enabled, through the favour of a fair Moorish damsel, to gain possession of her wizard father's conjuring-book, the mystic Abacus—and return to Europe with the unholy treasure, which was to infuse a gleam of Saracenic light into the dull intellects of Christendom. But the recent discovery of an authentic memoir of this famous monk, whose name casts so broad a splendour over his age, written by his own disciple, Richer, of Rheims, has cleared away every obscurity which hitherto hung over his history.[140]

Few particulars of his early life are known, save that he was the son of poor parents, that he was a native of Aurillac in Auvergne, and entered the monastery of that town when still a youth, about the end of the ninth century.

He had already commenced his studies in grammar, when Borrel, count of Barcelona, came to the monastery on pilgrimage. The abbot, hearing from him of the excellent schools which then flourished in Spain, begged him to take back with him some of their young monks, and Gerbert accordingly accompanied the count into Spain, and was placed under Hatto, then Bishop of Vich, in Catalonia, where he formed an intimate friendship with Warin, abbot of Cusan, one of the most learned men of his time. From this account, the authenticity of which is beyond question, it appears that the popular notion which represents Gerbert as acquiring his learning among the Arabs is incorrect, and all the romantic stories connected with his acquisition of the mysterious Abacus vanish into thin air. Doubtless, the Christian schools of Spain profited not a little from their proximity to the Arabic universities, and the sciences of mathematics and astronomy were naturally those which were most successfully cultivated. Gerbert made extraordinary progress in both; and when he accompanied Borrel and Hatto on their next pilgrimage to Rome, Pope John XIII. was not long in discovering his talents. The liberty of the subject seems not to have been much understood in the tenth century, for when it became known that the young monk was an adept both in music and mathematics, neither of which sciences were then taught in Italy, the Pope lost no time in communicating the fact to the emperor Otho I., who conjured him not to permit his return to Spain. Gerbert was accordingly most affectionately kidnapped and sent without delay to Otho's court, where being interrogated as to the extent of his knowledge, he replied that he was tolerably acquainted with mathematics, but was ignorant of logic, which science he greatly desired to study. It happened that at that time Gerard, archdeacon of Rheims, an excellent logician, had been sent as ambassador to Otho from Lothaire, king of France, and Gerbert at last won the emperor's consent to his returning home with him, that he might teach mathematics and study logic in the schools of that city. Adalberon was then archbishop of Rheims, and he forthwith committed the studies of his cathedral school to the direction of the young professor. Richer gives a very precise account of the method he followed. He began with the "Dialectics of Aristotle," going through and thoroughly explaining the propositions of each book. He particularly explained the Introduction of Porphyry; and passed on to the "Categories" and the "Topics" of the same author, as translated out of Greek into Latin by Cicero, and commented on in six books by the Consul Manlius. In the same way he lectured on the four books of Topical differences, two of Categorical syllogisms, one book of Divisions, and one of Definitions. And here the reader will not fail to observe that these logical lectures must have been the fruit of studies pursued not in Spain, but in France, for previous to Gerbert's coming to Rheims, we have his own acknowledgment that he knew nothing of that science. After he had taken his scholars through this course, says Richer, he proceeded to initiate them into the art of rhetoric;

and he set out on the principle, that in this branch of study a knowledge of the classical poets was essential. He therefore read and explained Virgil, Statius, and Terence; then the satirists, Juvenal, Persius, and Horace, and last of all, Lucan. After this, his pupils were exercised in disputation, which he taught with such art, that the art was never apparent; a thing, observes his biographer, which is held to be the perfection of oratory. Then he popularised the science of music;[141] and as to arithmetic, mathematics, and astronomy, he made these difficult studies easy and delightful. Richer devotes several pages to the description of the various instruments which he constructed, and by which he contrived to render the science of astronomy, as it were, sensible to the eyes of his scholars. A round wooden ball, *with its poles oblique to the horizon*, figured the world, the various astronomical and geographical phenomena being represented by other circles. In fact, from the minute description of the writer, we are obliged to conclude that Gerbert exhibited at his lectures two very passable specimens of the terrestrial and celestial globes. But the great boon, which he is commonly represented as bestowing on the European schools, was the introduction of that wonderful table, "in which nine ciphers represented all the numbers, and produced in their infinite combinations all multiplications and divisions." This was the mystic *Abacus*, the foundation, no doubt, of our present system of numeration. It consisted of a tablet, on which three columns were marked out, sometimes in fixed lines, sometimes in sand sprinkled over its surface; and in these columns figures were arranged in units, tens and hundreds. The method in use for working out calculations, even with the assistance of this decimal system, as explained by Gerbert in several treatises, was, however, extremely intricate, though it was probably a vast improvement on the clumsy contrivances which had been resorted to by former scholars. How far, however, the Abacus is to be regarded as a new invention, appears more than doubtful. Its history has been made the subject of interesting modern researches, and the result seems to be that the system of numeration used and explained by Gerbert, contained nothing in it which had been unknown to Boëthius.[142] Nevertheless, he certainly seems to have elucidated and popularised the science of arithmetic, which from this epoch began to be more seriously studied.

It is not easy to convey any notion of the enthusiasm excited by Gerbert's lectures, or the tide of scholars that flocked to him not only from every part of France, but from Germany, Italy, and the British Islands. Brucker is careful to repeat the old calumny, which represents the dull heads of his contemporaries as attributing his superior science to the effect of magic. "The knowledge of nature which Gerbert possessed," he says, "so far surpassed that of his contemporaries, that they thought him possessed of magical powers; *and Benno, a cardinal who owed him a grudge for his opposition to the See of Rome*, invented a tale of his holding converse with the devil." Alas for the accurate historian! this round assertion must go to keep company with that other from the same pen touching the trial of Polydore Vergil before the Inquisition. It was, doubtless, a temptation to represent the person who charged a man of genius with being a magician as one of the dull orthodox, moved to the malicious act by his zeal on behalf of the See of Rome, but the facts are exactly the contrary. Benno, the zealous cardinal who owed Gerbert a grudge for his opposition to the Pope, happened himself to be a schismatic and a partisan of the anti-pope; and instead of being a contemporary of Gerbert's, he lived a century later, in the time of St. Gregory VII., and introduced this precious story in a writing, the express purpose of which was to defame the character of the Roman pontiffs.[143] In justice to Gerbert it must be added, that not only was he innocent of sorcery, but that he was altogether above all petty jealousy and self-seeking, and desired nothing so ardently as to communicate his discoveries to as many as wished to receive them. Not content with instructing his own scholars, he corresponded with the scholastics of Tours, Sens, Fleury, and Aurillac, and spared no pains or expense in the collection of his library. In this work he was generously assisted by his friends, scattered over the length and breadth of Europe. It is in his "Epistles" that we catch a glimpse of that prodigious activity of mind which took cognisance of all subjects, and never rested till it had sounded all to the depth. In one letter, we find him begging the loan of a Cæsar from his archbishop, and offering in exchange eight volumes of Boëthius and some excellent geometrical figures. In another, he solicits the monks of Aurillac to furnish him with a Spanish treatise on the arts of multiplication and division, and directs them in the work of correcting a manuscript of Pliny. Then, again, we find him writing on the medical science, to which he and his disciples directed a good deal of attention, and in which they followed the Greek masters. In fact, it was the diversified character of his acquirements that made Gerbert the wonder of the world in the eyes of his contemporaries. He knew all things, they said, and all things equally well. If this were an exaggeration, it is certain that he possessed the rare power of being able to direct his attention to a very wide range of studies, though natural philosophy was certainly his special attraction.

Whilst still presiding over his school, Gerbert produced several treatises on astronomy, mathematics, and geometry; on the formation of the astrolabe, the quadrant, and the sphere, as well as on rhetoric and logic. The monk Ditmar tells us that when at Magdeburg with his old pupil, Otho III., he made a clock, regulating it according to the movement of the polar star, which he observed through a kind of tube. Another writer speaks of certain hydraulic organs which he constructed, in which the wind and necessary movements were introduced by means of boiling water: and these obscure notices seem to indicate that wheeled clocks, the telescope, and the power of steam, were known by Gerbert fully three centuries before what has been considered their earliest discovery by our own Roger Bacon. Gerbert did not teach at Rheims alone. Crossing the Alps, he passed through most of the towns of Northern Italy, then subject to his great patron, Otho I. In 970 he also visited Rome in company with the bishop Adalberon, and at Pavia met the emperor, together with the celebrated Saxon, Otheric, whom we have seen filling the office of scholasticus in the episcopal school of Magdeburg. Otheric had up to that time enjoyed the reputation of being the greatest scholar of his age, and perhaps regarded himself somewhat in the light of a literary dictator. In the course of the previous year he had felt no little uneasiness at the daily increasing renown of the French professor, and had despatched one of his own Saxon pupils to Rheims to bring him an exact account of Gerbert's method of dividing the sciences. The Saxon made an unsatisfactory report. It was Gerbert's custom to represent physics and mathematics as equal and independent sciences. But Otheric's disciple, whose head was none of the clearest, made him teach that physics were subordinate to mathematics, as the species to the genus. On this, Otheric decided that he knew nothing of philosophy, and proceeding to the court of the emperor, Otho I., he spoke to that effect before an assembly of learned men. Otho, who was himself passionately fond of these studies, was not satisfied, and resolved to sift the matter to the bottom. He therefore seized the occasion of Gerbert's presence at Pavia to inaugurate a grand scientific tournament, and invited all the *savants* of his empire to witness the dispute between the first scholar of France and the first scholar of Germany. He himself presided at the conference, and opened it with a brief allocution of his own, in which he very clearly explained the question in dispute. Then Otheric began his attack, first in words, and then in writing. The conference lasted the whole day, and Gerbert, who cited the authorities of Plato, Porphyry, and Boëthius, was still speaking in reply when the emperor gave the signal for the conclusion of the debate. Gerbert's fame never appeared more illustrious, and he returned to France loaded with magnificent presents.

His after career was full of troubles; but in 990 the influence of his imperial pupil, Otho III., obtained his election to the see of Ravenna, and nine years later to the Apostolic chair. It was a great day in the annals of learning when the philosopher Gerbert became Pope Sylvester II., and one which brought no small satisfaction to the hearts of his pupils. Half the prelates and princes of Europe gloried in having called him master, and most of them did him credit. Among them were our own St. Ethelwold; Fulbert of Chartres, the oracle of his own time; and Robert, king of France, the son of Hugh Capet, and the most religious and learned sovereign of the age. King Robert was well skilled in all the humane sciences; but the love of music, which he had imbibed from his master, amounted to a passion. Even after his accession to the throne, he devoted no small part of his time to composing anthems, and motetts, to the indignation of his queen, Constance, who asked him once, if he must compose, to compose something upon *her*. Robert sat down and produced the hymn *O Constantia martyrum!* and the queen, who fortunately understood nothing of Latin, was quite satisfied, imagining that her own perfections formed the subject of the poem. He often assisted in the choir of St. Denis, dressed in his royal robes, singing with the monks and directing the chant. Robert is said by his biographer always to have had a book in his hand, and to have carried the Psalter in his bosom. He once visited Rome, and during the Pope's mass laid on the altar, as his offering, a folded packet, which from its great size and weight the attendants concluded to be gold. On opening it, however, they found it to be only a fair copy of his antiphon, *Cornelius Centurio*. Admiring the writing and the musical notes, as well as the genius and piety of the author, the Pope desired that thenceforward this antiphon should always be sung on the festival of St. Peter, of whose Office it still continues to form a part.

Not less learned was Gerbert's other royal pupil, Otho of Germany, surnamed "the Wonder of the World," whose early death prevented his making as much use of his advantages of education as was confidently expected by all who knew the singular excellence to which he had attained. Besides these illustrious disciples, Gerbert had others of every rank and calling. The great St. Ethelwold is said by many writers to have studied under him for a time, and the rapid development in England and elsewhere of mathematical studies at this period must certainly be assigned to the impulse given them by the teaching of the master of Rheims. His genius was emphatically *scientific*, and this is the character which we find impressed on the learning of most of his followers. Thus Richer, the monk from whose history most of the above particulars have been taken, was more particularly skilled in the science of medicine. As an instance of the solicitude which monks of the tenth century displayed in the pursuit of knowledge, I may refer to the very curious account which he gives us of the perilous journey he once undertook, for the purpose of perusing a single book on his favourite science. "It was in the year 951," says Richer, "when my mind, being much and deeply engaged in the study of literature, I had long entertained an ardent desire of having the opportunity of learning the logic of Hippocrates of Cos. One day I chanced to meet in the city of Rheims a horseman coming from Chartres. Asking him who he was, and wherefore he had come hither, he replied that he was a messenger from Heribrand, a clerk of Chartres, and that he wished to speak to one Richer, a monk of St. Rémi. As soon as I heard my friend's name, and the subject of his message, I told the stranger that I was the person he was in quest of; whereupon, having embraced one another, he gave me a letter, which I found was an invitation to come to Chartres and peruse the 'Aphorisms.' I was much rejoiced at this; wherefore, taking a servant with me, I determined on accompanying the horseman back to Chartres. The only assistance I received from my abbot was a loan of one of the draft horses.

Without money, or even a change of clothes, and destitute of every necessary for the journey, I set out and reached Orbais, where I was not only delighted with the conversation of the abbot, but greatly assisted by his noble gifts, so that next day I was able to get on as far as Meaux. On entering the woods, however, with my two companions, we were involved in several disasters; for, deceived by its wild and broken openings, on coming to a place where two ways met, we took the wrong turning, and were led six leagues out of our road.

"By the time we passed Château Thierry my cart-horse, which had at first seemed a sort of Bucephalus, began to lag on the road as lazily as if he had been a donkey. The sun had been sinking for some time, and the rain was falling fast. At this moment the horse, worn out with fatigue, sank under the lad who was riding him, and the poor beast expired, as though struck by lightning. This happened when we were about six miles from the city of Meaux. My agitation and anxiety at this disaster may be well conceived; the boy, quite inexperienced in such emergencies, lay helpless on the road, by the side of the dead horse. There lay the luggage also, with no one to carry it; the rain was pouring down from a dark and cloudy sky, and the sun was just on the horizon. By God's goodness a prudent thought, however, suggested itself to my mind. I left the boy on the road with the baggage, telling him what he ought to say if questioned by travellers, urging him not to yield to any inclination to sleep. Then, accompanied by the horseman from Chartres, I set out for Meaux. There was scarcely light to see the bridge; and on examining it, a new misfortune presented itself. It was so broken, and had such enormous holes in it, that even by day it could hardly have been crossed in safety. The Chartres horseman, however, here showed himself a ready man. After vainly searching for a boat, he returned to the bridge, and, with the help of God, succeeded in getting the horses over it. In some places he covered the huge holes with his shield, so as to support the feet of the animals; in others he put the separated planks close together, and what with stooping, and what with holding himself erect, and now keeping the beasts together, and now separating from them, he contrived to get over in safety. It was a dreadful night, and all around was buried in darkness when I reached the church of St. Faro, where I was hospitably received by the monks, and refreshed with kind words and abundance of food. The horseman was at once sent back with other steeds, again passed the dangerous bridge, and proceeded to search for the poor boy, whom we had left on the road. It was the second watch of the night when he came up with him. He at once brought him to the city, but fearful of attempting a third time to cross the bridge they determined on passing the night in a poor cabin, and at break of day appeared at the gates of the monastery, half dead with hunger. Food was immediately given them, and corn and straw supplied to the horses.

"Leaving the dismounted boy with Abbot Augustin (of St. Faro), I hastened on to Chartres with the horseman, whence I sent back horses, who brought the lad back from Meaux. When he was come, and my mind was thus set at rest, I sat down at once to the earnest study of the 'Aphorisms' of Hippocrates, together with Master Heribrand, a man as much distinguished for his politeness as for his great learning. But as in these 'Aphorisms' I only learnt the premonitory symptoms of diseases, and as this knowledge did not satisfy me, I desired also to study another book showing the concordance between Hippocrates, Galen, and Suranus. This also I obtained from Heribrand, who was perfectly well skilled in the science to which he devoted his time. Indeed, there was nothing in medicine, pharmacy, botany, or surgery unknown to him." Richer's appreciation of his friend's learning may possibly have been exaggerated; but who can fail to admire his perseverance in overcoming such difficulties as a journey then presented, with the simple view of increasing his stock of scientific knowledge by the perusal of one precious book?

Allusion has been made to the improvements introduced by Gerbert in the study of music. A little later a more important addition was made to the same science by Guy, a monk of Pomposa, commonly called Guy of Arezzo, from the city which gave him birth. He had been educated from the age of eight years in the monastery of Pomposa; and being well skilled in music, was employed in teaching the ecclesiastical chant to the children brought up in the house. But the immense difficulties of his task induced him to consider whether some method of facilitating the notation of music might not be devised. As yet, the sounds of the musical scale were only represented by the first seven letters of the alphabet, or by notes, as was the custom in the abbeys of Corby and St. Gall, which showed indeed the relative length and value of each tone, but did not render their succession sensible to the eye. After seeking for a long time for some easy and precise system, Guy one day recognised in the chant to which the hymn of St. John Baptist was ordinarily sung, an ascending diatonic scale, in which the first syllable of each line occupied one note: *Ut queant laxis—Resonare fibris—Mira gestorum—Famuli tuorum,—Solve polluti—Labii reatum,—Sancte Ioannes.* He applied himself to teach this chant to his pupils, and to render them familiar with the diatonic succession of the syllables, *ut, re, mi, fa, sol,* and *la.* Next, he arranged the notes on lines and intervals, and thus produced the musical staff with its proper clefs. By means of these improvements he found himself able, in a few months, to teach a child as much as a man, under the ancient system, would have had difficulty in learning in the course of many years. However, such a storm of jealousy arose against him on the score of his discovery, that he found himself obliged to leave the monastery; and accordingly, in 1024, he travelled to Rome, where Pope John XIX. warmly received both him and his newly-invented gamut.

"The Pope," he says, "having received me kindly, conversed with me for a long time, asking many questions, and turning over the leaves of my antiphonarium, seemed to think it a sort of prodigy. He conned its rules, and would not rise from his seat till he had tried to learn a verse which he had never yet heard sung, and to his great astonishment found himself able to do it." Guy was not allowed to leave Rome till he had promised to return the next winter, and give a regular course of musical instructions to the Pope and his clergy. The sunshine of Papal favour soon dissipated the storm, but the humble religious was no way puffed up by his triumph. He only rejoiced at being able to spread the knowledge of a discovery which would be useful to others. "The designs of Providence," he writes, "are obscure, and falsehood is sometimes suffered to oppress the truth; God so ordering it lest, puffed up with self-confidence, we should suffer loss. For then only is what we do good and useful when we refer all we do to Him who made us. God inspiring me with the knowledge, I have made it known to as many as I could, to the end that if I, and those who have gone before me, have learnt the *Cantus* with extreme difficulty, those who come after me, doing so with greater facility, may pray for me and my fellow-labourers, that we may obtain eternal life and the remission of our sins."

At the very time when Gerbert was astonishing the world by the marvels of his genius, a simple nun of Gandersheim had attained a degree of literary excellence, which is the more remarkable as it was exclusively acquired within the enclosure of her own convent. The foundation of this convent had taken place at the same time with that of New Corby, and its object had been specially to provide for the education of the Saxon ladies. Peculiar attention was therefore directed to maintaining its school in a due state of efficiency, and learned traditions were always kept up among the nuns. Having fallen into decay in the ninth century, it was restored by Count Lindolph, whose daughter, Hathmuda, became abbess in 856. Her life has been left, written by her brother Agius, or Egbert. Hathmuda was a great lover of letters. "From a child," says her brother, "she cared nothing at all for fine clothes, head-dresses, ribbons, combs, earrings, necklaces, bracelets, handkerchiefs, girdles, and scents, the possession and wearing of which stirs up the ambition of so many women." She preferred to pray and to study, and "the lessons to which others had to be forced by stripes she willingly applied herself to, giving herself up to them with indefatigable ardour." When she became abbess she was most desirous to keep up those sacred studies for which the monastery had ever been so famous. "She insisted on the study of the Scriptures, and those who applied themselves to reading she greatly loved, but did not admit to equal familiarity such as herein showed themselves to be slothful." Her cares were amply rewarded, and the school of Gandersheim produced a succession of excellent teachers, among whom was Hroswitha, the fourth abbess, who died in 906, and was the authoress of a treatise on logic, much esteemed among the learned of her own time.[144]

It is of a namesake of this fair logician that we are now about to speak, Hroswitha, the nun of Gandersheim, as she is called. She was born in the year 940, and was brought up in the convent school, where she studied Greek and Latin, the philosophy of Aristotle, and the other liberal arts. We are often told that expressions like these, however magnificent they look on paper, would dwindle into insignificance could we test their value by the real amount of learning which they represent. With regard to Hroswitha, however, the true nature of her erudition is not left to conjecture. She has left behind her writings which have attracted the favourable notice even of modern critics, who agree in declaring that the Latin poems of this obscure nun of the tenth century are marvels of classical taste and poetic genius. Besides a panegyric on the three Othos, she wrote eight poems on various religious subjects, some of them being taken from the life of our Lord, and some from the legends of the saints; and seven prose dramas in the style of Terence, being tales of holy women, and having for their subject the praise of chastity. While praising the delicacy of the sentiments and the correctness of the style, her critics observe that these dramas afford incidental evidence of her perfect familiarity with the sciences of music, astronomy, and dialectics, as then taught in the schools. In one of them she introduces a sort of apology for her own learning, which has a certain feminine grace about it, more charming than all her logic. It occurs in the drama of "Paphnutius," where, after a philosophic discussion on the art of music, one of the disciples of the saint is made to ask him:

"Whence do you derive all this knowledge?" and he replies, "It is but a little drop that I have gathered from the ever-flowing sources of science; and now I desire to share it with you."

Dis. "Thanks to your goodness; nevertheless that admonition of the apostle terrifies me: 'God hath chosen the foolish of this world to confound the wise.'"

Paph. "Foolish and wise will alike be confounded before God, if they do what is evil."

Dis. "That cannot be denied."

Paph. "How, I pray you, can the arts and sciences be better employed than in the praise of Him who has created all things that we can know, and who furnishes us at once both with the matter and the instruments of our knowledge?"

Dis. "Certainly, that is the best way to use science."

Paph. "It is; for the more we know of the admirable laws by which God regulates the weight, number, and proportion of all things, the more our hearts will burn with love of Him."

Where shall we find more admirable teaching than this on the vexed question of the danger of intellectual pursuits? Dangerous only, as Hroswitha justly argues, when we cease to refer them to Him, who, as she so beautifully expresses it, "furnishes us at once with the matter and the instruments of our knowledge;" but good, holy, and greatly to be desired, when, by supplying us with a more perfect knowledge of Him, they fill our hearts with His love. That this was her own case, we may gather from the modest preface which heads her first collection of poems.

"Here," she says, "is a little book, simple in style, though it has cost the writer no small trouble and application. I offer it to the criticism of those kind judges who are disposed rather to put an author right than to find fault with him. For I willingly acknowledge that it contains many errors as well against the rules of composition as those of prosody; but methinks one who frankly confesses her defects, merits to meet with a ready pardon and a friendly correction. If it be thought amiss that I have taken some of my subjects from books, considered by some to be apocryphal, I must explain that this is not the result of presumption but of ignorance, for when I began my work I was not aware that they were held as of doubtful authority. As soon as I learned that this was the case, I ceased to use them. For the rest I claim indulgence, in proportion as I feel a want of confidence in myself. Deprived of most resources of study, and still young, I have been forced to work in my rustic solitude far from the help of the learned. It has been alone and unaided that I have produced my little work, by dint of repeated compositions and corrections. The main substance I have gathered from the Holy Scriptures, which were taught me in this convent of Gandersheim, first by the wise and blessed mistress, Richardis, and the religious who succeeded her in her office: and then by the excellent Gerberga, of royal birth, under whose government I am now living. Younger than me in years, but older in knowledge, she deigned to form my mind by the reading of good authors, in which she had also been instructed by learned mistresses. Although the art of making verses is difficult, specially for a woman, I have ventured, trusting in the Divine aid, to treat the subjects of this book in heroic verse. My only object in this labour has been to prevent the feeble talent committed to my keeping from growing rusty. And I desired by the hammer of devotion to compel it to give forth some sweet sounds to the praise of God. Wherefore, dear reader, if thou thinkest according to God, thou wilt know how to supply what is wanting in this book; and if thou findest anything good in it, refer it to God only, and attribute nothing to me but the faults; without, however, reproaching me for them too severely, but excusing them with that indulgence which a frank avowal deserves."

Hroswitha's humility had to stand the test of flattery from the literary world, and it stood it well. There are phrases scattered through her writings which evince how accurately she had gauged the shallowness of intellectual vanity, and how little hold it had upon her heart. "Often enough when curiosity is satisfied," she writes, "we find nothing but sadness." In the epistle prefixed to her prose dramas, she acknowledges the approbation which she has received from the learned with an unaffected simplicity. "I cannot sufficiently wonder," she says, "that you who are so well versed in philosophy should judge the humble work of a simple woman worthy of your commendation. But when in your charity you congratulate me, it is the Dispenser of that grace which works in me that you praise, believing as you do that the little knowledge I possess is superior to the weakness of my sex. Hitherto, I have hardly ventured to show my rustic little productions to any one, but reassured by your opinion, I shall now feel more confidence in writing, if God give me the power. Yet I feel myself drawn by the two opposite sentiments of joy and fear. I rejoice from my heart to see God and His grace praised in me, but I fear lest men should think me greater than I am. I do not mean to deny that, aided by Divine grace, I have attained to a certain knowledge of the arts, for I am a creature capable of instruction as others are; but I confess that left to my own strength I should know nothing."

These extracts require no comment. They prove something more than the solid nature of the studies pursued in the convent school of Gandersheim. How skilfully had the teachers of Hroswitha contrived, whilst directing her intellectual labours, to preserve her womanly modesty, her almost childish naïveté, and her deep religious humility! Better things were included in their scheme of education than a mere knowledge of the liberal arts; the wisdom "whose beginning is the desire of discipline," and into which "no defiled thing cometh." Under their training the genius of the young poetess was guarded by the cloak of humility from the cunning moth of pride; and whilst we are amazed at her learned attainments, her modesty and candour at the same time conquer our hearts.

And with this agreeable picture we will close our present chapter, trusting that the nun of Gandersheim may be allowed to have shed something of beauty and fragrance over the rugged annals of the Iron Age.[145]

CHAPTER XI.

THE SCHOOLS OF BEC.

A.D. 1000 TO 1135.

WITH the close of the tenth century we may be said to have taken our last farewell of the Dark Ages. Already on the horizon we have seen the dawn of a period of greater intellectual light, which ere long is to usher in the blaze of a splendid era. And yet it must be owned, it is with something of regret that we take our leave of those remote centuries, and with the wish of the poet in our hearts that "their good darkness were our light." The approaching sunrise puts out the quiet stars; and in the bustle of intellectual life into which we are about to enter, our heart misgives us lest something of the charm which has hitherto hung round the history of the Christian Schools may perchance be lost. Already a new element has appeared in our studies, more easily felt than described. The career of Gerbert, however brilliant, does not leave on the mind the same impression as that of Bede; we feel a predominance of the scholastic, over the religious character; and we think of him less as a monk than as a mathematician. This element will now be far more frequently met with, and what is worse, it will in many cases be found accompanied by the ugly shapes of pride, love of novelty, and self-interest, too often finding their final result in heresy and open unbelief. The design of these pages is not to paint a series of fancy pictures, but to study past ages so as to establish in our mind a true standard of Christian Scholarship; to distinguish the precious from the vile, the false lights of the intellect from those kindled at the altar fire; and it will therefore be necessary to put forth some of these unhappy examples in a broad and honest daylight, that we may better see what those principles are, the forgetfulness of which renders intellectual culture dangerous to faith.

Hitherto we have heard but little of the perils of the intellect. Learning, in the eyes of the old monastics, was the twin sister of prayer. They would almost as soon have thought of apprehending danger in their Psalter as in their grammar, and indeed the end for which they used them both was substantially the same. Among the characters named in the foregoing pages, how few appear disfigured with the stains of vanity or self-interest! Scotus Erigena indeed, is a notable example of the self-sufficient rationalist, and Otheric of Magdeburg is said to have died of disappointment at not obtaining a bishopric; but such instances are rare exceptions; and though others doubtless existed, they do not appear on the surface of history, and give no character to the scholastic profession. As a class, the pedagogues of the Dark Ages were the most disinterested of men. Poverty was recognised, not as the accident of a student's life, but as one of its most honourable features, and it was reckoned as something monstrous and disgraceful for a man to sell his learning for gold. This, of course, arose from the religious light in which learned pursuits were regarded; they were spiritual wares, the sale of which was held almost as simoniacal as the sale of a benefice. If instances occasionally occur of any such sordid practices, they are named by historians with a kind of horror; and Launoy quotes the reproof addressed by the abbot Baldric to a certain scholar of Angers, who had gone over to England to teach grammar for the sake of "cursed gold," and whose sudden death was believed by his acquaintances to have been sent in just punishment of his sin. This tradition survived, in theory at least, for many centuries, and in 1362 the Professors of Paris University are found pleading their inability to pay the expenses of a lawsuit then pending, "it being their profession as scholars to have no wealth." In Spain there was a proverb which described a scholar as rich in letters, and ragged in everything else, and Chaucer only produced the current type of a student when he represented his Clerk of Oxenford as "full hollow and threadbare."

Now, however, a change passes over the picture; scholasticism is about to appear less as a vocation than as a profession, and a profession sought with the view of earning for him who embraces it, honour at least, and perhaps also the more solid advantages of worldly fortune and rich preferment. Some writers have supposed that the promotion of Gerbert to the Papal dignity was one cause of this change, leading others to hope that a brilliant scholastic career might chance to prove the high road to wealth and dignities. Rohrbacher recognises in the rising spirit of the age distinct traces of an infernal agency. "Hitherto," he says, "heresy had made no great progress in the West. But in the eleventh century the Spirit of Darkness, seeing its empire confirmed in the East by the great apostacy of Mahomet and the formal schism of the Greeks, seems to have transferred the war from the East to the West. From that epoch down to our own time, the great revolt against God and His Church has never ceased to appear in one form or another. Its two principal sources have been Pride and Luxury, the corruption of the intellect, and the corruption of the heart. Hence, in princes, the attempt to usurp authority over the Church: hence, among men of learning, the mania for innovation, together with that superficial vanity which urged Berengarius to his fall; which Luther and Calvin erected into a principle under the name of Reform, and to which Voltaire and Rousseau put the key-stone under the title of Philosophy."[146] Fleury also supports this view, and speaking of the swarm of heresies that sprang up suddenly in the eleventh century, sees in the fact a fulfilment of the prophecy in the Apocalypse that Satan should be loosed after being bound for a thousand years. The whole of Christendom was possessed at the time with a vague foreboding that an era had opened big with melancholy change, and this presentiment of evil naturally enough took the shape among the vulgar, of the belief that the world was about to come to an end.

It is at this precise epoch that we first begin to meet with teachers who were neither monks nor clerics. Free from the restraints of cloisteral discipline, these new scholastics were professors of grammar and rhetoric, and they were nothing more. The saintly rule of a Benedict or a Columbanus had not moulded them to habits of humility and obedience; they taught, and they made profit by their teaching; and he who taught the most attractive novelty drew most pupils, and made his teaching answer the best. It was a question in which worldly lucre, rather than the interests of souls, was at stake, and to be successful it became necessary for the teacher to adapt himself to the tastes and humours of his audience. Hence arose a race of pedants who had nothing in common with the elder scholastics, and who bore a peculiar stamp of self-sufficiency and arrogance, which impresses them all with a sort of family likeness, and carries back one's thoughts to the sophists of the pagan schools.

The first notice which we find of a scholastic who was neither monk nor canon, occurs about the year 1024, when Rodolphus Glaber, a monk of Cluny, mentions in his chronicle a certain Witgard, a grammarian by profession, who was so bewitched by the study of the Latin poets, that he fancied he beheld in a vision Virgil, Horace, and Juvenal, who thanked him for the affection he bore them, and promised him immortality. The poor man's head was so turned with this idea, that he immediately began to teach that whatever was contained in the poets, was to be believed *de fide*, and strange to say, not a few were found to listen to him. He was cited before the archbishop of Ravenna, and put to silence, after creating a good deal of disturbance. I merely name him here as an indication of the new class of men into whose hands the work of teaching was beginning to fall; a far more important illustration of the subject is to be found in the history of Berengarius. Before speaking of him, however, something must be said of his master, Fulbert, the pupil of Gerbert, and the restorer of the cathedral school of Chartres. Though reckoned among French worthies, he seems to have been a Roman by birth, and received his early education in a very humble school. However, he afterwards studied under Gerbert, and under his direction the school of Chartres rose to such an eminence, that it rivalled that of Rheims, and Fulbert may be said to have become preceptor to almost every man of letters who distinguished himself in France during the eleventh century.

We gather from the catalogue of the Chartres library, that Fulbert had inherited no inconsiderable portion of his master Gerbert's scientific tastes.

We find in it treatises on the properties of the sphere and the globe, on the astrolabe, on the measurement of superficies, and on land measurement, together with a Greek and Arabic alphabet. Fulbert himself had the rare accomplishment of Hebrew learning, as may be seen by his "Treatise against the Jews." His disciples went forth from his school to restore sacred studies all over France, and the honour of being a pupil of him whom they lovingly termed "Father Fulbert," was claimed by a long list of excellent masters, every one of whom might be described in the terms with which Adelman has sketched the character of Rainald of Tours; as "ready with the tongue, fluent with the pen, and mighty in grammar." "As to thee, Father Fulbert," he exclaims, "when I attempt to speak of thee, my words fail, my heart melts, my eyes break forth into weeping."[147] Fulbert was, in fact, worthy of any praise that could be bestowed on him, and so thoroughly convinced of the sacredness of the office of teaching, that even after he became Bishop of Chartres in 1016, he continued to direct the studies of his episcopal school. He was regarded as the prelate of his time most thoroughly versed in ecclesiastical discipline, which he caused to be exactly practised. As a writer, he is best known by his letters, which display a wonderful delicacy of thought. He was knit in bonds of close friendship with St. Odilon of Cluny, to whom he confided his fears, lest he might not have been truly called to fill an office, the solemn responsibilities of which almost overwhelmed him. "Yet," he adds, "remembering my own nothingness, and that without birth or fortune I have been raised to this chair like a beggar from the dunghill, I am forced to believe it is the will of God."

A teacher of this temper was sure to have it at heart to impress on the souls of his disciples a love of humility. It was the favourite virtue of this truly great man, who was perfectly aware that the elevation of Gerbert to the pontifical dignity had given rise to a sentiment of ambition among men of letters, from which he boded evil. He was therefore earnest in warning his pupils to avoid novelties and to walk in the old footpaths; and his keen sagacious eye rested with uneasiness on one young face among the scholars who were accustomed to gather round him in his little garden and listen to his affectionate exhortations, as children hang on the words of a venerated parent. Berengarius, for it was he, had begun his studies in the school of St. Martin of Tours, whence he passed to Chartres, in company with his friend Adelman. He had a brilliant rather than a solid genius, a ready tongue which made the most of what he knew, but withal a certain affectation in speech and manner which betrayed a fund of secret vanity. Fulbert knew him well, and often spoke to him even with tears, conjuring him never to forsake the beaten track, but to hold fast to the traditions of the fathers. In 1028 the good bishop, then lying on his death-bed, called all his disciples around him to bid them farewell, but seeing Berengarius among the rest, he motioned for him to withdraw, for, he said, "I see a dragon by his side."

His prognostics were too soon fulfilled. Berengarius returned to Tours, where his reputation for scholarship induced the canons to commit their school to his management; and even after he was appointed archdeacon of Angers, he continued to lecture at Tours, earning the reputation of immense learning, eloquence, and skill in grammar and philosophy. All, however, were not equally pleased with the character of his teaching, and some hesitated not bluntly to avow their belief that the brilliant archdeacon was somewhat shallow, and that his philosophy verged on sophistry. He had a way of mystifying the simplest subjects by a display of learned words; affected new and startling definitions, and had some tricks for practising on the minds of his audience, which gave offence to many. He chose that his chair should be raised higher than the others, had a pompous way of walking, spoke in a slow and particularly plaintive tone of voice, and would sit with his head wrapped up in his mantle, like an ancient philosopher, absorbed, as it seemed, in some very profound meditation. In short, he was one of those who aim at what Bacon calls "being wise by signs;" did trifles in a solemn way, and so imposed on the simpler sort who thought him a prodigy; a sentiment in which, it is needless to say, he himself fully concurred.

Let us leave this pompous personage for a while to enjoy the admiration of his numerous disciples, whilst we cast our eyes on the schools of law which were just then springing up at Bologna, where a young student of Pavia, Lanfranc by name, was distinguishing himself by his skill as a writer and an advocate. On leaving Bologna, he is thought to have taught jurisprudence for some time in his native city, and then crossing the Alps, he came into France, bringing with him no other riches than his learned reputation. Arriving at Tours, his name reached the ears of Berengarius, who at once sought him out and challenged him to a public disputation. The end aimed at was evidently the glorification of the archdeacon, who counted on an easy victory over the young stranger, which might help to swell his reputation. Never were expectations more completely disappointed. Berengarius was worsted in his arguments, and obliged to retire with ruffled feathers; far from increasing his renown, he had suffered a severe defeat, and in the eyes of wounded vanity, defeat is the bitterest of mortifications. His followers were astonished to find their master was not infallible, and began to transfer their admiration to his successful rival. Lanfranc, meanwhile, proceeded to Avranches, where he opened a school which was soon thronged by deserters from that of Berengarius. It was a crisis in his life, for his character was one which was as likely as not to have yielded to the perils that surrounded him. If free from the vanity which devoured his rival, his proud and impetuous temper was at that time quite as little under the restraint of religious principle; his devotion to science was perhaps more thoroughly the genuine enthusiasm of a scholar who loved learning for its own sake, rather than for the meed of human applause, but it was as yet wholly unsanctified by a higher and diviner intention. Nevertheless, there was a candour and uprightness of soul about him which the other did not possess, and when the call of grace sounded in his ear, he responded to it with noble generosity.

One day as he was journeying from Avranches to Rouen, he had to pass through a forest, where he was attacked by robbers, who having stripped him of all he possessed, tied him to a tree, wrapped his hood about his head so as to muffle his cries for help, and then abandoned him. Left thus during the entire night exposed to danger of death from the wolves, or the more lingering tortures of starvation, Lanfranc in his extremity bethought him of his prayers, but the learned advocate and philosopher found himself unable to call to his remembrance the simplest form of devotion. That one fact spoke volumes to his conscience; during the long hours of that terrible night he had time bitterly to mourn over the years lost in pursuits, the vanity of which he had never known till now; and ere morning dawned he solemnly vowed, if God should deliver him from his danger, to dedicate the remainder of his life to the task of reparation.

At break of day some passing travellers discovered and unbound him, and Lanfranc's first request was to be led to the nearest monastery. There was by this time no want of religious houses in the duchy of Normandy. The century that had elapsed since the conversion of Duke Rollo, had witnessed a very general restoration of the monastic institute in that province, and many of the great abbeys, such as Jumièges, St. Wandrille, Fécamp, and Bernai, had risen from their ashes, with even greater splendour than they had exhibited before their destruction. But it was to none of these that the good Providence of God guided the steps of Lanfranc. In the year 1039 the little house of Bec had been founded by a pious Norman knight named Herluin, who himself became the first abbot. Nothing could be ruder or simpler than the commencements of this famous abbey. Herluin was poor and unlettered, he and his monks had to live hardly by the labour of their hands, their ordinary food was bread made with bran, and vegetables, with muddy water brought from a well two miles off. At the very moment when Lanfranc presented himself, the abbot was superintending the construction of an oven, and was kneading the bread with somewhat dirty hands, for he had come fresh from the labour of the field. At another time the sight would have disgusted the refined and fastidious Lombard, but at that moment his heart felt an appetite for abasement, and he promptly offered himself, and was received as one of the little community.

He was subjected to a severe noviciate. For three years, it is said, he kept a rigorous silence, and was tested by every kind of humiliation. Once, when reading aloud in the refectory, the prior corrected his Latin accent, and desired him to pronounce the *e* in *docere* short. This was probably a hard trial to the humility of the Bolognese professor, who must have regarded his

Norman companions as little better than barbarians; but Lanfranc complied without hesitation, judging, says his biographer, that an act of disobedience was a greater evil than a false quantity in Latin. After he had passed through his probation, the abbot, who had learnt to value both his learning and his sincere humility, finding him unfit for manual labour, desired him to begin to teach, and thus were founded the famous schools of Bec. Their renown soon eclipsed that of every other existing academy. "Before that time," says Odericus, "in the reigns of six dukes of Normandy, scarce any Norman applied himself to regular studies, nor had any doctor arisen among them till, by the Providence of God, Lanfranc appeared in their province." But now a new era was inaugurated. Priests and monks came to Bec in multitudes, in order to place themselves under a master who was pronounced the best Latinist, the best theologian, and the best dialectician of his time; there were never fewer than a hundred pupils; the Norman nobles, and even the Dukes themselves, sent their sons thither for education, and made enormous grants of land to the favoured abbey.

It is not to be supposed that the fame of this new academy was long in reaching the ears of Berengarius, whose chagrin at finding his own renown eclipsed by his former rival was hard to endure. Up to that time he had addicted himself exclusively to dialectics, and had given very little study to the Scriptures, a circumstance sufficiently illustrative of the wide chasm which separated the rising school of teachers from that which immediately preceded them. But now, to support his failing credit, Berengarius began to lecture on a subject he had never studied, and to explain the Scriptures, not according to the traditions of the Fathers, but after the whims of his own imagination. His first errors were on questions connected with marriage and infant baptism, but it was not long before he broached his grand heresy, and attacked the Catholic doctrine of the Real Presence in the Most Holy Eucharist, reviving all the arguments and sophistries of Scotus Erigena. The scandal spread from Tours through France and Germany. His old friend Adelman, at that time scholasticus of Liège, heard the news and wrote to him in moving terms, conjuring him to retract his fatal errors. "I have been wont to call you my foster brother," he says, "calling to mind the happy days we passed together at the school of Chartres (though you were younger than I), under that venerable Socrates, Fulbert. Remember the conversation he used to hold with us in his garden near the chapel, how tenderly he used to speak to us, his voice sometimes choked with tears, conjuring us not to depart from the old paths, but to keep firm to the traditions of the Fathers. And now they tell me that you have separated from the unity of the Church, teaching that what we daily offer on the altar is not the true body and blood of Jesus Christ, but only a figure! God help you, my brother! let me implore you by the mercy of God, and the memory of the Blessed Fulbert, not thus to trouble the peace of our Holy Mother the Church, for whose faith so many millions of doctors and martyrs have constantly contended."

Adelman's entreaties produced no effect on him to whom they were addressed, and a controversy began in which Lanfranc took a distinguished part, assisting at the councils of Rheims, Rome and Vercelli. In all these Berengarius was successively condemned, and required to abjure his errors. But he obeyed with the lips only. As he continued to propagate his heresies in spite of repeated abjurations, Pope Victor II., in 1054, summoned two other Councils, at Florence and Tours, at the last of which Berengarius signed a solemn retractation with his own hand. But so soon as he left the presence of the assembled fathers, he set himself secretly to disseminate his former doctrines. At a second Council held at Tours, attended by 113 bishops, he again appeared, signed a profession of Catholic doctrine, and threw all his own writings into the fire, and the same farce was repeated at three other Councils, followed by the same result. It was not until 1079 that Lanfranc, then Archbishop of Canterbury, published his famous treatise "On the Body of Our Lord," and about the same time his scholar Guitmond, afterwards Bishop of Aversa, wrote an equally celebrated treatise, bearing the same title, in which he traces the errors of Berengarius to the fatal root of vanity. "Even when a youth at school," he says, "according to the account of those who then knew him, he made little account of the teaching of his master, held as nothing the opinions of his companions, and despised the books on liberal arts. He could not himself attain to the profounder parts of philosophy, for he was not of a very penetrating mind, and therefore tried to gain a learned reputation by new and unheard-of verbal definitions." There is something mournfully significant in this account, and the grievous termination of a career, the very dawn of which was marked by such prognostics, makes the character and history of Berengarius one which scholars of all ages would do well to set before them as a warning beacon. The writings of Lanfranc and Guitmond seem at last to have opened his eyes to the truth; at any rate from that time he kept silence, and is said to have spent the remaining eight years of his life in retirement and sincere penitence. William of Malmsbury says that his dying words betrayed his consciousness of the irreparable evils he had inflicted on the Church, and the terror with which he was filled at the thought of the souls whom he might have ruined. "This day will my Lord Jesus Christ appear to call me, either to glory, by His mercy, on my repentance, or, as I fear, on account of the loss of other souls, to my punishment." Yet his followers were neither numerous nor of any weight or character. We find in the letter written by Gozechinus of Liège to a brother scholastic, that every one of the great masters of the time, such as those who presided over the schools of Rheims, Paris, Spires, and Bamberg joined heart and soul with Lanfranc in condemning his doctrines.[148] Malmsbury says he had in all but three hundred disciples, while on the other hand the united voice of Christendom, and especially of the monastic order, was raised against him, and never was any heresy more universally condemned.

Meanwhile the schools of Bec grew and prospered, and the convent was soon found too small to contain its scholars. There were gathered together students of all ranks and conditions, "profound sophists," as Oderic Vitalis calls them, and a long list of ecclesiastics destined to become the shining lights of the Church. Among these were Ivo of Chartres, Fulk of Beauvais, Gundulph, afterwards bishop of Rochester, Anselm de Bagio, afterwards Pope Alexander II., and a great number of the Anglo-Norman abbots. Alexander II., in after years, gave a memorable sign of the respect with which he regarded his old preceptor. When Lanfranc visited Rome as Archbishop of Canterbury, and was introduced into the presence of the Pontiff, the latter, contrary to the usual custom, rose, and advanced to meet him. "I show this mark of respect," he said, turning to the surrounding prelates, "not to the archbishop, but to the man at whose feet I sat as a disciple in the schools of Bec." Besides these there was Guitmond, already named, the courageous monk, who, entreated by the Conqueror to accept high ecclesiastical promotion in England, not only refused the offer, but accompanied his refusal with a letter of reproof which probably spoke plainer truths to William of Normandy than he had ever before had an opportunity of hearing. Oderic calls him devout and deeply learned, and in his book on the Sacrament of the Altar, the good monk recalls with affection the teaching he had received at Bec, which he styles "that great and famous school of literature." But by far the greatest disciple of this school was a countryman of Lanfranc's, destined to surpass him in renown both as a saint and a doctor. Anselm, a native of Aosta, in Lombardy, abandoning his native land, had after three years of study in Burgundy, established himself at Avranches, where he seems to have taught for some time in the school formerly directed by Lanfranc. But in 1059, being then but twenty-five years of age, he found his way to Bec, and soon distinguished himself as the first of all the noble crowd of scholars. For a while he continued there, studying and teaching by turns, but erelong the desire of religious perfection mastered that of intellectual progress. He resolved to take the monastic habit, but was unable to determine whether it should be at Cluny or at Bec. At Cluny indeed his vast acquirements would be of small profit; at Bec the superiority of Lanfranc would, he believed, almost equally eclipse him. But what of that? it was eclipse and nothingness that he was in search of, rather than fame and distinction. He opened his heart to his master, who, reluctant to decide a point in which his own feelings would naturally colour his advice, referred him to Maurillus, Archbishop of Rouen, and the result was that Anselm remained at Bec. His profession took place in 1060, and three years later Lanfranc, being appointed by Duke William abbot of his newly-founded monastery of St. Stephen at Caen, Anselm succeeded him in the office of prior. Some of the monks murmured at this appointment, but he overcame their ill-will by the sweetness of his charity. One young monk, named Osbern, who had shown the greatest opposition to the new prior, became at last his favourite disciple, won over by the patient long-suffering of a master who showed him a mother's tenderness, mingled with a father's care. At first he gained his good-will by encouraging his talents, overlooking his childish sallies of temper, and granting him many favours; but when his confidence was secured he accustomed him to severer discipline, and showed his satisfaction at his pupil's progress by requiring him to accept very humiliating penances. He trusted to have found in this youth one destined to achieve great things for God, but Osbern was carried off by a sudden sickness, and left none to replace him in the affections of the prior.

Anselm's life at Bec was one of continual labour. Whilst directing the studies of his pupils he did not neglect his own. His deeply philosophic mind was one of those which is incapable of desisting from a course of reasoning on any subject which it has once grasped, till the final solution is reached. His genius possessed a certain metaphysical subtlety, which engaged him in speculative questions, to resolve which he gave up, not merely whole days, but whole nights also. His studies were accompanied with rigorous austerities, which were, however, very far from diminishing that sweetness of disposition which rendered him dear to God and man. To his other labours were added those entailed on him as librarian to the monastery. Lanfranc had commenced the formation of the library, and his work was carried on by his successor with unwearied zeal. The Bec library was afterwards enlarged by the donations of Philip of Harcourt, Bishop of Bayeux, and besides a rich collection of the Fathers and the Latin classics, contained the Institutes of Quinctilian and the Hortensius of Cicero, of which latter work no copy is now known to exist. The great destruction of books which had taken place during the barbaric invasions rendered them now both rare and costly. Superiors of the different religious houses were therefore glad to establish friendly relations one with another, and to make agreements by which each supplied what they possessed, and what was wanting to the others. "We are ready to give you a pledge of our affection," writes Durandus, abbot of La Chaise Dieu, to St. Anselm, "and in return we will ask one of you. Choose what you will that we possess; as to us, our choice is the Epistles of St. Paul." Anselm was not content with collecting books; he spared no pains to correct them, and spent a good part of his nights in this employment. The multifarious duties which fell on him devoured so large a portion of his day that he could only supply the requisite time for his literary labours by defrauding himself of sleep; and he would have resigned his office in order more exclusively to give himself up to meditation and study had he not been withheld by the prohibition of Maurillus.

The subject which most frequently engaged his thoughts was the Being and Attributes of God. The first work which he wrote was his *Monologion*, in which he endeavoured to state the metaphysical arguments by which the existence of God might be proved even according to mere natural reason. The work was written at the request of some of the monks, but before publishing it he sent it to Lanfranc, desiring him to correct, and even to suppress, whatever he judged proper. After producing some other philosophical treatises, the thought occurred to him to try and discover whether it were possible, by following any single course of reasoning, to prove that which in his *Monologion* he had supported by a variety of arguments. The idea took possession of his mind: sometimes he thought he had found what he was seeking for, and then again it escaped him. So utterly was he absorbed by the subject that he lost sleep and appetite, and even his attention at the Divine Office became distracted. Dreading lest it should be some dark temptation, he tried to banish the whole matter from his mind, but it was in vain; the more he fled from his own thoughts the more constantly did they pursue him. At last one night every link in the chain being complete, he seized some waxen tablets and wrote the argument as it stood clear and distinct in his mind. A copy was made on parchment by his monks, and this new work formed his *Proslogion*, which, at the desire of the legate Hugh, Archbishop of Lyons, was published with his name attached. The argument of this celebrated book is thus analysed by M. Rémusat, in his life of the saint. "He who believes in God believes that there is Something so great that a greater cannot be conceived. Does such a nature really exist? The infidel who denies it nevertheless understands what is meant by the idea, and this idea exists in his understanding, if it exist nowhere else. The mere idea of an object does not necessarily imply the belief in its existence. A painter has an *idea* of a picture which he knows does not as yet exist. But this Something which is better and greater than anything of which we can conceive cannot exist merely in our minds; for if it did exist only in our minds, we should be able to imagine it as existing in reality, that is to say, we should be able to conceive of it as being yet greater, a thing which according to our original supposition was not to be allowed as possible. Therefore, that which is so great that nothing can be greater must exist, not only in the mind, but in fact. Were the Being which is supposed to be above all that can be imagined, to be regarded as having no real existence, He would no longer be greater than we could conceive. To make Him so, He must have existence. The contradiction is evident. There is then really and truly a Being above Whom nothing can be conceived, and Who therefore cannot be thought of as though it were possible that He should not exist. And this Being, it is Thou, O my God! *Et hoc es tu, Domine Deus noster!*"[149] Many were found both in his own and later times who took alarm at reasoning so bold and original, but Anselm defended his arguments in an Apology, which established his fame as the greatest metaphysician who had appeared in the Latin Church since the days of St. Augustine.[150]

As we are here engaged rather with the history of schools than with that of literature, this passing glance at St. Anselm's studies will suffice to indicate the new direction which the awakening intellect of Europe was about to follow. Hitherto ecclesiastical writers had for the most part been content to gather up and reproduce the traditionary wisdom of the Fathers; but now, when those traditions had become firmly established, a scientific superstructure was to be raised on that broad foundation, and the theology of the Church was to be built up into a compact and well-ordered system. This was the work of the scholastic theologians, of whom St. Anselm may be considered as the first.

It is pleasant to trace in the system of education followed by so profound a thinker, the same paternal sweetness which characterised the older monastic teachers. Intellectual depth is often enough deficient in tenderness, and it would scarcely have been matter of surprise had we found the metaphysical mind of Anselm incapable of adapting itself to the simplicity and waywardness of childhood. But the problems, which intellect alone is powerless to resolve, are quickly unlocked by the key of charity. Anselm would have been no saint had not his heart been far larger than his intellect; and his heart it was that communicated to him those three graces which one of our own poets has so beautifully described as bearing up the little world of education—Love, Hope, and Patience.[151] One day he was visited by the abbot of a neighbouring monastery, who came to consult him on the proper manner of bringing up the children committed to his care. Those whom he had hitherto trained were, he said, most perverse and incorrigible. "We do our best to correct them," he added; "we beat them from morning till night, but I own I can see no improvement." "And how do they grow up?" inquired Anselm. "Just as dull and stupid as so many beasts," was the reply. "A famous system of education truly," observed the abbot of Bec, "which changes men into beasts. Now tell me, what would be the result, if, after having planted a tree in your garden you were to compress it so tightly that it should have no room to extend its branches? These poor children were given to you that you might help them to grow, and be fruitful in good thoughts; but if you allow them no liberty their minds will grow crooked. Finding no kindness on your part, they will give you no confidence, and never having been brought up to know the meaning of love and charity, they will see everything around them in a distorted aspect. You beat them, you tell me? But is a beautiful statue of gold or silver formed only by blows? The weak must be treated with gentleness, and won with love; you must invite a soul to virtue with cheerfulness, and charitably bear with its defects." He then explained his own method of education, till at last the other cast himself at his feet, owning his imprudence, and promising in future to abandon his excessive severity.

The names of Lanfranc and St. Anselm have, of course, a special interest to English readers, although it is rather as abbots of Bec than as Archbishops of Canterbury that they find a place in these pages. The Norman Conquest, which placed Lanfranc on the episcopal throne of St. Augustine, must, however, be regarded as an important era in the scholastic history of England, from the total revolution which it effected in the ecclesiastical administration of that country. Whatever may be thought of the manner in which the change was carried out, there can be little doubt that the substitution of an Anglo-Norman for an Anglo-Saxon hierarchy was on the whole beneficial to the cause both of religion and learning. Most of the ecclesiastics promoted by William were men of high character, and this was indeed one of the few consolatory thoughts which presented themselves to his mind when he lay upon his bed of death. His choice of Lanfranc for the primacy filled that prelate with dismay, nor was it until Cardinal Hubert laid on him the commands of the Apostolic See, that he could be induced to accept a charge so begirt with difficulty. His letter to his old pupil Pope Alexander II., shortly after his arrival in England, expresses the distress of his mind, at the hard heartedness, cupidity, and corruption which everywhere met his eye, and which, together with the barbarism, as he deemed it, of the inhabitants, and his total ignorance of their language, moved him to implore that he might resign the onerous dignity. As, however, this could not be permitted, he applied himself to the reform of the church of Canterbury, and the restoration in it of the monastic rule, which, since the martyrdom of St. Elphege, had fallen into utter decay. In spite of the pressing difficulties of the times, he contrived also to do something for the encouragement of letters, though far less than he would have effected under more favourable circumstances.

The schools of Peterborough and Evesham are likewise noticed as famous during the reign of the Confessor, who was himself a lover of learning, and, among his other laws, decreed that the person of a schoolmaster should be regarded as equally inviolable with that of a clerk. Winchcombe, always devoted to letters, whose scholars had been famous since the days of St. Kenelm, was still known as a place of study, and kept up its reputation so late as the fifteenth century. Old Ramsey, too, retained its celebrity, and scholars still wandered under the trees planted by St. Ethelwold, and kept up the arts which he had introduced into its scriptorium. In 1047 a certain monk of St. Edmundsbury became abbot there, whose skill in all gold and silver work was a sort of marvel. One of his monks, named Oswald, refused a bishopric on the simple ground that he could not tear himself from his books. "He chose rather," says the chronicler, "to cherish the placid cultivation of letters in the bosom of his mother, the church of Ramsey. We have still in our archives a certain versified book of his, bearing evidence of his multifarious knowledge and perspicacious wit." Nor must we forget the holy Wulstan, the last of our Anglo-Saxon saints. He had been educated in the minster school of Peterborough by the monk Ervene, who coaxed him to learn his letters by choosing for his lesson-book a fine Psalter, illuminated by his own hands. After he became prior and scholasticus of Worcester, Wulstan devoted himself to study with such ardour as often to spend two or three days in reading without so much as breaking his fast. His long night-watches seriously injured his health, and in the morning he was often found in the church fast asleep, with his worn-out head resting on the book he had been studying.

It will be seen, therefore, that the love of letters was not quite extinct in the cloisters of Saxon England; and the coming of Lanfranc blew the embers into a flame. He set himself to restore a great number of cathedral and monastic schools that had fallen into decay, and during his leisure hours liked to hear some poor scholars hold disputations in his presence on learned subjects, rewarding them with liberal gifts.

But besides his encouragement of learned men, Lanfranc did good service to the cause of letters in other ways. He often interposed his kind offices to save the ancient English foundations from the vengeance of the Conqueror. Thus, having succeeded in averting the threatened destruction of St. Alban's Abbey, which William had doomed in consequence of the brave resistance he had met with from its abbot, Frithric, Lanfranc conferred it on a relative and pupil of his own named Paulinus, who has fallen under the lash of Matthew Paris, but who nevertheless proved an excellent abbot. He introduced the "Constitutions," published by Lanfranc for the government of the English Benedictines, reformed a host of irregularities, and, with the help of subsidies liberally granted by the archbishop, built several useful offices, and established the first scriptorium attached to the abbey.

I know not what my readers will say when they hear that the mill, the bakehouse, and the scriptorium erected by Paulinus were all built out of the tiles and stones of the ancient Verulam, collected by his Saxon predecessors Ealdred and Eadmer, who had made some very curious excavations among the ruins of the Roman city, and had laid open a palace with its baths and its atrium. Moreover, they had dug up a number of books in good preservation, one of which was in a tongue unknown to all, and proved at last to be a British history of the "Acts of St. Alban." The other books were in Latin, and, relating to heathen worship, were committed to the flames. This sounds barbarous to antiquarian ears, but there is worse to tell. Eadmer ordered that all the altars, urns, coins, and glass vessels discovered by the workmen should be destroyed. The day had not yet come when relics of paganism were deemed safe or fit objects for good Christians to collect in their museums, and the Vatican collection itself would probably have fared but badly in the hands of Alcuin or St. Boniface. However, the monks of St. Alban's, though destroyers of the Verulam antiquities, were very active in setting up their scriptorium. Paulinus furnished it with twenty-eight "notable volumes," and many others were presented by Lanfranc. There is, moreover, a distinct notice of the existence of the abbey school. Abbot Richard, who succeeded Paulinus (after the Red King had contrived to keep the abbacy vacant for five years), showed a great interest in the success of this school, and invited over from Maine a certain master named Geoffrey de Gorham, to take on him its direction. Gorham however, was rather dilatory, and by the time he arrived in England the office had been given to another. So he removed to Dunstable, and there read lectures for some time, and whilst so occupied, invented a miracle-play, said to be the first that is noticed in history, the subject being the martyrdom of St. Katherine. These sacred dramas were used as means of popular instruction, and often contained a fine vein of poetry. As time went on, and they fell out of the hands of the ecclesiastics into those of a class of writers and actors whose object it was to please, rather than to instruct the multitude, they became debased by the introduction of coarse jests and buffoonery, which abound in the specimens best known to English readers, but of which there is not the slightest trace in the earlier religious dramas. The dress and getting up of the pieces, in which there was a wonderful amount of ingenuity displayed, and even of stage trickery,[152] of course enhanced their success; and Gorham borrowed from the sacristan of St. Alban's the choral copes of the abbey, to be used in the first representation of his play. Unfortunately, the very next night his house caught fire, and the borrowed copes, together with his own books, were all destroyed. It was a great disaster; and in atonement for his carelessness he assumed the monastic habit at St. Alban's; and this was the reason, says Matthew Paris, that when he became abbot he was so careful to provide the choir with new rich copes.

In the midst of his many cares and anxieties, Lanfranc found time to devote to literary toils. They were useful ones, well worthy of a monk and a bishop. He corrected the text of the entire Bible, and of several of the Fathers. He never forgot Bec, and sent several youths, and among others his own nephew and namesake, there for education; and much of his correspondence with St. Anselm turns on the progress of these young men in their studies. Anselm, on his part, frankly confesses that he gets very weary of continually teaching the younger boys their declensions; and lets us know that he required his pupils to compose often in Latin, and rather in prose than in verse; that he recommended them to read Virgil and the other classics, and to be diligent in copying manuscripts. At other times his letters, treating of literary subjects, and accompanying presents of precious books to the Canterbury scriptorium, introduce allusions to the health of his scholars, evincing that paternal tenderness which was so remarkable a feature in his character.

Anselm, who had been elected abbot of Bec on the death of Herluin, during his visits to England became personally known to the Conqueror, whose furious passions were restrained in presence of the gentle saint, who won both his love and his reverence. It was whilst at Canterbury, on a visit to his friend Lanfranc, that the abbot of Bec made his first acquaintance with his future biographer, the young Saxon Eadmer. This was the time when he so sweetly defended the memory of the Anglo-Saxon saints from the contempt with which Lanfranc was disposed to regard them; and possibly this circumstance may have had some share in securing him the confidence and affection of Eadmer, who then held the office of precentor in the cathedral of Canterbury.

Lanfranc died in 1089, having survived the great Conqueror nearly two years. The events which, four years later, placed St. Anselm on the archiepiscopal throne of Canterbury, and his heroic struggles against the usurpations of the temporal power in the reigns of William Rufus and Henry I., scarcely fall within our present subject, though they form not the least important chapter in our national Church history. But the succession to the primacy of another great scholar was an event which made itself felt in the world of letters, and kindled extraordinary ardour for learned pursuits among the English clergy. This spirit was certainly encouraged by the Norman kings, who, ferocious tyrants as they were, all more or less exhibited a taste for letters. The Conqueror took special care of the education of his children. Henry Beauclerk was educated at Abingdon Abbey, under the care of Faricius, an Italian monk of Malmsbury. The proficiency of the young prince as displayed by his version of Æsop's fables, is commonly said to have earned him his learned sobriquet; but Mr. Wright, in his "Biographia Britannica," calls his authorship in question. Both his sisters, and his two queens, Matilda of Scotland and Adeliza of Louvaine, were patrons of letters. Some epistles from Matilda to St. Anselm are preserved, which display no mean degree of scholarship, if they were really the production of her own pen. The encouragement of these two princesses quickened the imagination of a host of versifiers, who began to neglect the composition of hexameters in limping Latin, and to substitute in their room songs and romances in Norman-French. The Anglo-Saxon tongue was, of course, never heard at court; and some writers, like William of Malmsbury, went so far as to omit the Saxon names of men and places, through an over-delicate fear of distressing refined organs by such barbarous sounds. A new literature meanwhile sprang up, bearing the impress of an age of knight-errantry. Alexander, Arthur, and Charlemagne found themselves transformed from historic personages into heroes of quaint and extravagant fictions, full of hippogrifs, dragons, and enchanted castles, where distressed damsels were held captive by wicked magicians, in order to be delivered by the prowess of doughty knights—a style of composition to which we give a name borrowed from the language used by the narrators, that, namely, of the *Romance* dialect of France. Among the accumulation of rubbish written in this dialect, which was about this time poured forth into the world, one book of a higher character appears, the production of Prior Guichard of Beaulieu. It is a sermon in verse on the vices of the age, and appears to have been written to be actually recited, for he begins by telling his hearers that he is going to talk to them, not in Latin, but in the vernacular, that every one may understand what he says. De la Rue, who notices this curious poem, observes that the mention of a sermon in verse need not cause surprise, as at that epoch it was a common thing for the Anglo-Norman clergy to read to the people on Sundays and holy-days the lives of the saints in French verse. Nine such versified lives are still preserved, the production of Boson, nephew to Pope Alexander II. The mediæval preachers had sometimes recourse to strange expedients in order to rouse the slumbering attention of their hearers. Vincent of Beauvais tells us that in his time it was a common thing to lighten a dull subject by introducing one of Æsop's fables, a practice which he does not absolutely condemn, but recommends to be used sparingly.

Besides the disciples reared in our native schools, a large number of English scholars were to be found, who mingled with the graver pursuits of learning something of that spirit of knight-errantry and wild adventure which characterised the times. Arabic Spain was just then regarded as the fountain-head of science. The Moorish sovereigns of Cordova had collected an immense library in their capital, and are reported to have had seventy others in different parts of their dominions. Thither, then, wandered many an English student, attracted rather than repelled by the tales of glamour associated with a Moslem land. One of these scholar adventurers was Athelhard of Bath, the greatest man of science who appeared in England before the time of Roger Bacon. In the reign of the Red King he had left his own country to study at Tours and Laon, in which latter place he opened a school. Thence he proceeded to Salerno, Greece, Asia Minor, and Spain, increasing his stock of learning, and returned at last, after a long absence, in the reign of Henry I. After this he opened a school in Normandy, where he taught the Arabic sciences, in spite of the prejudices which many felt against learning acquired from so suspicious a source. Among those who so objected was Athelhard's own nephew; and in defence of his favourite studies the English master wrote a book, in which he reminds his nephew of an agreement formerly made between them, that one should gather all the learning taught by the Arabs, while the other should, in like manner, study the wisdom of the Franks. This book is written in the form of a colloquy, in which the nephew is made to appear as the champion of the old system of education, and the uncle of the new.

I do not know whether we should conclude that Athelhard gained very much from his Arabic masters; for if he studied at Cordova the causes of earthquakes, eclipses, and tides, we find from his *Quæstiones* that he had also devoted a considerable portion of his time to investigating the reason why plants cannot be produced in fire, why the nose is made to hang over the mouth, why the human forehead is not furnished with horns, whether the stars are animals, whether on that hypothesis they have any appetite, with other equally singular and puerile questions. In spite of these eccentricities, however, Athelhard was a really learned man. He translated Euclid and other mathematical works out of the Arabic, and is styled by Vincent of Beauvais, "the Philosopher of England." A few years later we find another Englishman, named Robert de Retines, studying at Evora in company with a certain Hermann of Dalmatia, who is called a most acute and erudite scholar. Robert had travelled in search of learning through France, Italy, Dalmatia, Greece, and Asia Minor, and finally made his way into Spain, where Peter of Cluny found the two friends studying astrology at Evora. Peter's journey into Spain was undertaken with the view of obtaining more exact information as to the Mohammedan doctrines and writings, and he induced the two scholars to give up their unprofitable pursuits, and employ their knowledge of Arabic in translating the Koran. This they did in 1143. Robert afterwards became archdeacon of Pampeluna; he did not, however, entirely forsake his own country, but returning thither, wrote a translation of the Saxon Chronicle, which is preserved in the Bodleian library, and which is dedicated to Peter of Cluny. His friend Hermann, who is styled "a most acute and profound scholastic," produced a translation of Ptolemy's "Planisphere," which he addressed to his old Spanish preceptor Theodoricus, and from the preface to this book we find that the school at which they studied was not Arabic, but Christian, a fact of some importance, as it is very generally stated that the Spanish academies resorted to at this time by European students were those of the Arabic masters, who are represented as alone possessing any knowledge of the mathematical sciences. It is clear however that now, as in the time of Gerbert, there existed Christian schools in Spain, no less efficient than those of the Moors, and that it was to these that many of the French and English scholars resorted for the purposes of study.

To the names of these learned Englishmen I must add that of Odericus Vitalis, the course of whose education is best given in his own words in that short summary of his life with which he concludes his history. "I was baptized," he says, "at Attingham, a village in England, which stands on the bank of the great river Severn. There, by the ministry of Odericus the priest, Thou didst regenerate me with water and the Holy Ghost. When I was five years old I was sent to school at Shrewsbury, and offered Thee my services in the lowest order of the clergy in the Church of SS. Peter and Paul. While there, Siward, a priest of great eminence, instructed me for five years in the letters of Carmenta Nicostrata,[153] and taught me psalms and hymns, with other necessary learning. I was ten years old when I crossed the British sea, and arrived in Normandy, an exile, unknown to all, and knowing no one. But supported by Thy goodness, I found the utmost kindness and attention from these foreigners. I was professed a monk in the monastery of St. Evroult, by the venerable abbot Mainier, in the eleventh year of my age, and he gave me the name of Vitalis, in place of that which I received in England, and which seemed barbarous to the ears of the Normans. In this monastery, through Thy goodness, I have lived fifty-six years, loved and honoured by my brethren far more than I have deserved. Bearing the heat and burden of the day in a strange land, I have laboured among Thy servants, and as Thou art faithful, I fear not but I shall receive the penny which Thou hast promised."

He elsewhere tells us that his master in this abbey was John of Rheims, a disciple of the famous school of that city, who was an author of no mean fame, and composed a great number of works both in prose and verse. It does not appear that he ever studied in any other academy, but whatever learning he afterwards attained must have been acquired within the walls of his own monastery, and he could scarcely have found his way to a better school. In the eleventh century there was no branch of learning which was not cultivated among the monks of St. Evroult; music, medicine, poetry, painting, and the mechanical arts, all found there able professors. The history of Odericus leaves us in no doubt as to the extent of his literary attainments. He quotes most of the ancient classical writers, and many of the Fathers of the Church, and the intelligence of his mind is displayed by the way in which he collected the materials of his work. Nothing escaped his notice, and from the lips of some wandering Crusader or passing pilgrim he gathered up the tales and episodes with which he enlivened his pages, giving them in many parts the lively colouring of a romance. One day a monk of Winchester who stopped at the abbey for a few hours chanced to show him a life of St. William, copies of which were then rare in Normandy. Odericus, in raptures at the sight of the treasure, longed to copy it, but the traveller was in haste, and the fingers of Odericus were benumbed with cold, for it was the depth of winter. However, the opportunity was not to be lost, and seizing his tablets he with great difficulty took such notes from the manuscript as enabled him afterwards, at his leisure, to compose a life of the founder of St. Gellone. His "Ecclesiastical History of England and Normandy," which occupied twenty years in its compilation, is the only work he has left to posterity.

Thus much may suffice as to the state of letters in England and Normandy in the time of Lanfranc and Anselm; the scholars who arose after them were not unworthy to be the disciples of a school founded by these two illustrious archbishops; and it will be seen that the University of Paris, which was soon to efface by the splendour of its fame that of every other lesser academy, owed its renown in no small degree to the learning of its English professors.

CHAPTER XII.

THE RISE OF SCHOLASTICISM.

A.D. 1049 TO 1200.

WE are sometimes disposed to think and speak of the Middle Ages, as though by that term was to be understood a period including several centuries, during the whole of which society was governed by the same laws, and made but little progress. In point of fact, however, men seldom lived faster, if such an expression be admissible, than during the five centuries to which the term mediæval is most strictly applied. There was then, as now, a continual expansion and development going on, and then, as now, the development was partly good, and partly evil. During the hundred years that elapsed from the accession of Hugh Capet in 996, to the conquest of Jerusalem in 1099, Christendom assumed an entirely new aspect. The institutions of feudalism and chivalry were becoming firmly established; the barbaric invasions had ceased, and the Crusades directed the arms of the Christians against a common enemy, and so put an end to the civil wars which had raged under the Carlovingian dynasty. If these changes cannot be said to have ushered in a period of absolute peace, they at least tended to consolidate civil government; and the comparative state of security and order which ensued, naturally encouraged greater intellectual activity. On the other hand, the Saxon emperors of Germany had been replaced by the house of Franconia, and that grievous contest had begun between the temporal and spiritual powers which, for centuries, formed the great political question of Europe; while the convulsions of the last century had let loose on the Church a flood of corruption which probably makes this period one of the saddest in her history.

The chronicles of a semi-barbarous age, however, possess one charm which does not attach in an equal degree to those of more civilised periods. Full as they are of crimes and scandals, they depict a state of society more keenly susceptible than our own to the influence of master-minds. Hence they are often enough the records of heroes, whereas our tamer annals deal less in the acts and words of great men, than in changes of ministry. The eleventh century groaned under the threefold scourge of simony, sensuality, and temporal usurpation. It had the peculiar infelicity of being an age of transition, when the children of the Church were growing weary of submitting to the canonical discipline of ancient times, whilst nothing had yet been established as its substitute. It was, therefore, a time of wild license and feeble restraint. Three men, however, arose to rule and reform their age. The first was of royal blood, a descendant of Charlemagne and Witikind, whom we first find studying at Toul about the year 1018, along with other princely and ducal cousins, for Toul was always celebrated for its noble students. Bruno of Dachsburg was the handsomest man of his time, the idol of his family, graceful, eloquent, and learned, and a skilled musician. The world was already predicting his success at the court of his imperial cousin Conrad, when a trifling accident changed his whole career. One day, the young student, after a hard morning's work, threw himself on the grass at his father's castle in Alsace, and fell asleep. An insect stung his face, and the result was a malignant fever which brought him to the gates of death. He rose from his sick bed to renounce all that the world had to offer, and to embrace the monastic state. In 1026 he became Bishop of Toul, and for two-and-twenty years devoted his energies to the reformation of manners and the revival of discipline. At the end of that time he was elected Pope, and, as St. Leo IX., struggled for five years more against simony, the Berengarian heresy, and the Greek schism. But, in the midst of his other labours, he did not neglect letters and the arts. He caused good studies to flourish at Rome, reformed her school of chant, and employed as his legates learned men, such as his old schoolfellow, Cardinal Humbert, who had acquired at Toul that Greek erudition which he used so ably against the Photians.

On the day when Pope Leo entered Rome barefoot to take possession of the Apostolic throne, he was accompanied by a Cluniac monk, whom he had met on his journey into Italy, and well-nigh compelled to join his train. Rome was no new scene to the monk Hildebrand; it was there, in St. Mary's Abbey on the Aventine Mount,[154] that the poor carpenter's son had received his education. But he returned thither now to fill a very different station, for Leo created him cardinal, and abbot of St. Paul's; and from that time up to the day of his death, thirty-six years later, the life of Hildebrand forms the history of his times. The name of him whom the Church reveres as St. Gregory VII. must suffice in this place, there remains to be noticed a third Christian hero, a friend of both those illustrious pontiffs, who struggled with them in the same cause, and against the same enemies. Born at Ravenna towards the close of the tenth century, the youngest of a large family, who only saw in him another to divide their slender inheritance, Peter Damian was all but abandoned in his infancy, and on the death of his parents was maintained by a brother, who treated him as a slave, and employed him to keep swine. The poor farm-drudge grew up without friends and without education; but the soul that was within him had instincts and aspirations which no ill-usage could stifle. One day he chanced to find a piece of money lying on the ground; it was the first time his hands had ever touched silver, and for a moment the thoughts which might occur to other boys flashed through his brain. He would purchase food, or clothes, or give himself an hour's brief enjoyment. But then came another thought: "When the food is eaten, and the enjoyment past, what will remain to me of my money? Better give it to the parish priest and have a mass said for my father's soul." The second thought was followed; and soon afterwards his elder brother Damian, the arch-priest of Ravenna, took pity on the boy, and sent him to school, first at Faenza, and then at Parma, which at that time possessed excellent masters. Peter, who in gratitude assumed his brother's name in addition to his own, became not only a good scholar, but in time a professor, and his singular capacity in this office obtained him both scholars and wealth, for, as we have seen in the last chapter, the profession of scholasticus was beginning to be one of profit. But he had never forgotten his early experience, and the money that flowed in went to feed the poor, whilst he himself persevered in the practice of rigid poverty. One day he made the acquaintance of two poor hermits belonging to a community that had established itself at a spot called Fonte-Avellano, at the foot of the Umbrian Apennines. His biographer calls it a desert, but it was a desert only in the Italian sense of he word, a solitary valley, that is, shut in between mountains clothed with evergreen oaks, and chest nuts, and the silvery olive, its thickets bright with the blossoms of the Judas-tree and the oleander, and its grass, with the starry cyclamen. To this desert, then, Peter's new friends conducted him, on a visit to their hermitage, which had been founded a few years previously by the Blessed Ludolf. He found there a community who took the same view of human life as himself. They regarded man as a being made up of two noble and immortal parts, that were to be served and cherished—the soul and the intellect; and of one base and perishable part, that was good only to be mortified—the body. Simple men as they were, they had conceived the idea of doing penance for the huge evil world that lay outside their wilderness. So they lived four days a week on bread and water, allowing themselves on the other three the indulgence of herbs, afflicted their flesh in many ways, and divided their time between psalmody and study. Peter embraced this life with hearty earnestness, and outstripped his companions alike in his austerities and in his application to sacred learning. But his light could not be hid; abbots entreated that he might be sent to instruct their religious; his own brethren elected him their superior; seven successive popes employed him in the service of the Church; and, in 1057, Stephen IX. created him cardinal bishop of Ostia. His life was spent in struggles to stem the corruption of his age and to reform the clergy. Fleury observes that we must not look in his writings for acuteness of reasoning; but he had to do with men sunk in rude gross vices, which were hardly to be remedied by metaphysics. The medicine which St. Peter Damian prescribed for the sick world was penance; and he preached it in a plain homely sort of way, which might possibly offend fastidious tastes, but which had this merit about it, that it was practical, and had results. He entered the profaned sanctuary, scourge in hand, to drive out the unclean animals, and to overthrow the tables of the money-changers. In the intervals between his incessant legations to reform churches and rebuke princes, he retired to his cell at Fonte-Avellano, and might be found there living on pulse and water, employed in making wooden spoons, or other coarse manual labour, and submitting, even to his eightieth year, to the same rule of life as the youngest novice. Yet this was the most elegant scholar of his time; nay, more, he was a poet. And we do not use the term as classing him among the crowd of versifiers who wrote their chronicles, and even their theological treatises in lines which, often enough as Hallam remarks, can only be rendered into hexameters "by careful nursing." He imitated neither Virgil nor Horace, but wrote in those rhymed trochaics which many classical purists would brand as barbarisms. Yet where shall we see richness of imagery wedded to greater harmony of numbers than in those wonderful stanzas, *De Paradisi Gloriâ*, wherein Paradise is depicted under the form of all that is fairest and brightest to the poet's eye? The sparkling of precious gems, the blossoming of early flowers, the glory of the autumn cornfields, and the long shining of a summer's day, lit by a sun that knows no setting, are painted in words that sound like the echoes of a harpsichord. And from these sensible images of earthly beauty he rises to that which is above sense, and sets before us the ineffable joys of those who see the Divine Beauty face to face, and are filled from the fountains of Eternal charity. The joys of heaven formed, in fact, the constant subject of his meditation, and in one of his prose treatises, speaking on this exhaustless theme, he gives utterance to the sentiment felt by every poet, of the insufficiency of words to express the emotions of the heart. "There is always more in the thing itself than the mind conceives, and more in what the mind conceives than the tongue can utter."

The reform of manners so vigorously set on foot by these saints and their many disciples was friendly to the growth of letters. Parma attained such celebrity as to be called *Chrysopolis*, or the golden city, in the days of the great Countess Matilda, who was herself, says Donizzo, her chaplain, more learned than many bishops, and was never without an abundance of books. At her instance Irnerius, the *Lucerna Juris*, as he was called, began to lecture at Bologna on Roman law about the year 1128. The cathedral schools were everywhere revived by St. Gregory VII., who required the bishops to found seminaries where such did not already exist, where boys should be educated for the priesthood free of cost, certain prebends being set apart for the support of the masters. This injunction was very generally obeyed, and many ancient schools were revived which had fallen into decay. Landulph tells us that at Milan, where things had been in a very bad state, but where the mingled zeal and gentleness of St. Peter Damian, and of St. Ariald, had effected a reform,[155] the schools of philosophy were held in the porch of the cathedral, where the clerics attended, the archbishop presiding in person. In fact, the Italians who, in the tenth century, are represented as having none to teach them the first rudimentary elements, had somehow contrived in the eleventh to possess themselves of academies which they considered the first in the whole world.

A document given by Mabillon illustrates in an amusing manner the jealousy existing at this time between the schools of Italy and France. A certain prior of Chiusi, named Benedict, coming to the abbey of St. Martial at Limoges, was imprudent enough to call in question the commonly-received opinion that St. Martial was an immediate disciple of our Lord. Of course a storm arose, its fury bursting over the head of the luckless and too enlightened critic. The quarrel was taken up by all the monasteries of southern Gaul; and Ademar, a monk of Angoulême, thought it his duty to address a circular to the French monasteries, warning them not to listen to the horrible scandals promulgated by Benedict, whose conceit, he says, was at the bottom of the whole affair. He attempts to pillory his antagonist, by putting in his mouth a ridiculous speech. "I am the nephew," he is made to say, "of the abbot of Chiusi. He has taken me to many cities of France and Lombardy to study grammar, and my various masters have cost him the round sum of 2000 soldi. I studied grammar nine years, and am studying it still. I am a most learned man. I have two great boxes full of books, and I have not yet read one-half of them. In fact there is not a book in all the world that I have not got. When I leave the schools there will not be such a doctor as myself under heaven.... I am prior of Chiusi, and know how to write sermons.... I am so wise I could arrange and manage an entire council. In Aquitaine there is no learning of any kind, every one there is a dunce; if a man knows a sprinkling of grammar, he is thought at once to be a second Virgil. In France (that is, the province, not the kingdom of France), there is a little more erudition, but not much. The real seat of wisdom is in Lombardy, where I have carried on my studies." In spite of the sarcastic exaggeration running through this passage, we may gather from it that Benedict had probably assumed a tone of superiority over his Gallican neighbours, and that studies must have greatly revived in Lombardy since the days of the Othos, to furnish the text for a *jeu d'esprit* of this description.

An age of such increased intellectual activity could hardly fail to be attended with many changes, bad as well as good. We have seen in the last chapter that the new class of teachers who were now springing up taught for gain or reputation, rather than with an eye to the higher ends of education, and that thus learning in their hands lost much of its Christian dress. The intellectual curiosity of students induced many to seek for knowledge in distant lands, with the same perseverance and spirit of enterprise which young knights displayed in quest of military adventure. We can hardly in our day appreciate the difficulties which had to be overcome by men like Athelhard and Robert of Retines, whose student life was the very romance of scholarship. If the stock of knowledge thus collected, surpassed in breadth and variety that which could have been gained in any single monastic school, it is evident, on the other hand, that the education of these itinerant scholars must have been sadly deficient both in mental and moral discipline, failings which were abundantly evident in the character of the new scholastics. They had picked up, it may be, a knowledge of medicine at Salerno, and of mathematics at Cordova, but the claustral rule, the strict subjection to authority, the holy atmosphere or devotion and obedience, had not entered into their intellectual life. They had gained their learning from the lips of professors, in order to become professors in their turn; but a wandering life through half the cities of Europe was but a poor exchange for the claustral discipline; and not a few were found to embrace this kind of life for the very sake of its greater license and freedom from restraint.

But though this new element was making itself perceptibly felt in the learned world, it must not be supposed that in the eleventh century the old system of education was at all superseded for the cathedral and monastic schools still continued the chief seats of learning. They even witnessed a sort of classical renaissance, which sprung up under the encouragement of a crowd of masters who directed the labours of their scholars to the imitation of ancient models, without, however, in any way abandoning the line of Christian studies traced out by Alcuin and his disciples. At Mans, the office of scholasticus was held by the Blessed Hildebert a pupil of Berengarius, and a poet and philosopher, who afterwards became bishop of the same see, and had the distinguished honour of being imprisoned by the Red King, for refusing, at his bidding, to pull down the towers of his cathedral. At Autun, the cathedral schools were directed for twenty years by Honorius, who in his treatise *De Exilio Animæ*, reprinted in the *Thesaurus Anecdotorum* of Pez, has described the course of studies followed by his pupils. To the ordinary branches of the trivium and quadrivium, he added instructions in physical science, and gave a distinct course of Holy Scripture. His lectures on rhetoric included the explanation of the best Latin classics, and the same was done in most monastic schools of the period. The notices become more frequent of scholars learned in Greek and Hebrew, and the fact of their being named as engaged in the correction of manuscripts in those languages, compels us to believe that their learning was something more real and solid than that which has been before noticed as rather foolishly displayed on the pages of certain writers of the preceding centuries. Thus, Sigebert of Gemblours, and Marbœuf of Angers, are both spoken of as Greek and Hebrew scholars. Sigebert is said by his biographer to have been learned in the Hebrew Scriptures, which he used in his controversies with the Jews. He was also a good Latin classic, and much addicted to the composition of verses in imitation of his favourite author Horace. He gave lectures on poetry and logic in Paris, but his vanity was not proof against temptation, and led him to take part with Henry IV. against the Holy See. He is the author of a chronicle and other historical works, which he made the vehicle for conveying grave calumnies against the Roman pontiffs. Dante to whom his character as a Ghibelline partisan was itself a recommendation, has placed him in Paradise and notices him as lecturing on logic in the streets of Paris, to students seated, after the custom of the time, on bundles of straw.[156]

It is difficult to determine how much the scholars of this period were really in advance of their predecessors. Hallam, who is generally so sparing of his praise when speaking of any period earlier than that of the Cinque Cento, admits that at the close of the eleventh century a good, and even elegant school of Latin writers was springing up; and notices the Latin vocabulary of Papias as evincing an amount of profane learning far superior to anything that had hitherto been known. Du Cange, however, shows that Papias drew his materials from a dictionary which had been compiled in the Dark Ages, namely, that published in the tenth century, by Solomon, abbot of St. Gall's. Still, it may be concluded that classical studies were more universally followed than they had hitherto been, and at the same time extraordinary activity was displayed in the multiplication of books and the collection of libraries. Useful results sometimes flow from human infirmities, and there is said to have mingled with the honest love of learning which encouraged this activity, a certain spirit of rivalry and emulation among the different monasteries and religious orders. The Black Monks did not like to be cut out by the new Cistercians; and Bec, as a matter of course, was not going to yield to Cluny. Mabillon says that it was the peculiar pride of the Benedictine abbots of this time, to collect large libraries, and to have their manuscripts handsomely written and adorned. Never, therefore, was there a busier time in the scriptorium; a finer character of writing, and a more convenient system of abbreviation was introduced, and many abbots are mentioned as remarkable for their skill as miniaturists. It is said, however, I know not with what truth, that the copyists, if they got through a greater amount of work, were often less accurate than their brethren of the eighth and ninth centuries, and that in this, as in other things, the proverb held good of "more haste and worse speed." Hallam, whilst complaining of the multiplication of blunders, does full justice to the prodigious industry exhibited by the monastic copyists of this particular period. As an illustration of the subject, we may quote the account which Othlonus, the scholasticus of St. Emmeran's, gives of his labours. He seems to have been a Bavarian by birth, and his first school was that of Tegernsee, in Bavaria, a monastery which had been founded in 994, and was famous for its teachers *in utrâque linguâ*, and even for its Hebrew scholars. Here, in the twelfth century, lived the good monk Metellus, whose eclogues, written in imitation of those of Virgil, describe the monastic pastures and cattle, and the labours of the monks in the fields. The library of Tegernsee was rich in classic works, and possessed a fair illuminated copy of Pliny's "Natural History," adorned with pictures of the different animals, from the cunning hand of brother Ellinger. Medicine was likewise studied here, to facilitate which, the monks had a good botanical garden. In such a school Othlonus had every opportunity of cultivating his natural taste for study, which grew by degrees to be a perfect passion. As a child he had intended to embrace the monastic state, but the persuasions of his father, and his own desire to give himself up exclusively to learned pursuits, induced him to abandon this design, and after leaving school he devoted himself for several years to classical studies, with an ardour which his biographer finds no words strong enough to express.

His only earthly desire at this time, as he himself tells us in one of his later spiritual treatises, was to have time to study, and abundance of books. It would seem, however, that this excessive devotion to human learning had its usual results in the decay of devotion. It is thus he describes himself at this period of his life, in his versified treatise *De doctrina Spirituali.* "Desiring to search into certain subtle matters, in the knowledge of which I saw that many delighted, to the end that I might be held in greater esteem by the world, I made all my profit to consist in keeping company with the Gentiles. In those days what were not to me Socrates, Plato and Aristotle, and Tully the rhetorician?... that threefold work of Maro, and Lucan, whom then I loved best of all, and on whom I was so intent, that I hardly did anything else but read him.... Yet what profit did they give me, when I could not even sign my forehead with the cross?"

However, two severe illnesses wrought a great change in his way of looking at life, and in 1032, remembering his early dedication of himself to God, he resolved to forsake the world and take the habit of religion in the monastery of St. Emmeran's, at Ratisbon, where he gave up all thoughts of secular ambition, in order to devote himself heart and soul to the duties of his state. St. Emmeran's was, like Tegernsee, possessed of an excellent school and library. In the former many good scholars were reared, such as abbot William of Hirschau, who became as learned in the liberal arts as in the study of the Scriptures, and who afterwards made his own school at Hirschau one of the most celebrated in Germany. Othlonus tells us that in this monastery he found "several men in different classes, some reading pagan authors, others the Holy Scriptures," and that he began to imitate the latter, and soon learnt to relish the Sacred Books, which he had hitherto neglected, far above the writings of Aristotle, Plato, or even Boëthius.[157]

It will be seen from this little sketch that Othlonus was not a mere transcriber, and indeed he afterwards produced several treatises on mystic theology, besides his "Life of St. Wolfgang," and was regarded by his brother monks as "a pious and austere man, possessed of an immense love of books." This love he showed not only by reading them, but by multiplying them; and his achievements in this kind are related by himself with a certain prolix eloquence which, in mercy to the reader, I will somewhat abridge.

"I think it right," he says, "to add some account of the great capacity of writing which was given me by the Lord from my childhood. When as yet a little child I was sent to school, and quickly learnt my letters; and began long before the usual time of learning, and without any order from the master, to learn the art of writing; but in a furtive and unusual way, and without any teacher, so that I got a bad habit of holding my pen in a wrong manner, nor were any of my teachers afterwards able to correct me in that point. Many who saw this, decided that I should never write well, but by the grace of God it turned out otherwise. For, even in my childhood, when, together with the other boys, the tablet was put into my hands, it appeared that I had some notion of writing. Then, after a time, I began to write so well and was so fond of it, that in the monastery of Tegernsee, where I learned, I wrote many books, and being sent into Franconia, I worked so hard as nearly to lose my sight.... Then, after I became a monk of St. Emmeran's, I was induced again to occupy myself so much in writing, that I seldom got an interval of rest except on festivals. Meantime there came more work on me, for as they saw I was generally reading, writing, or composing, they made me schoolmaster; by all which things I was, through God's grace, so fully occupied that I frequently could not allow my body the necessary rest. When I had a mind to compose anything, I could not find time for it, except on holidays or at night, being tied down to the business of teaching the boys, and transcribing what I had undertaken. Besides the books which I composed myself I wrote nineteen missals, three books of the Gospels, and two lectionaries; besides which I wrote four service books for matins. Afterwards, old age and infirmity hindered me, and the grief caused by the destruction of our monastery; but to Him who is author of all good, and who has vouchsafed to give many things to me unworthy, be praise eternal!" He then adds an account of a vast number of other books written out by him and sent as presents to the monasteries of Fulda, Hirschfeld, Lorsch, Tegernsee, and others, amounting in all to thirty volumes. His labours, so cheerfully undertaken for the improvement of his convent, were perhaps surpassed by those of the monk Jerome, who wrote out so great a number of volumes, that it is said a wagon with six horses would not have sufficed to draw them. But neither one nor the other are to be compared to Diemudis, a devout nun of the monastery of Wessobrun, who, besides writing out in clear and beautiful characters five missals, with graduals and sequences attached, and four other office books, for the use of the church, adorned the library of her convent with two entire Bibles, eight volumes of St. Gregory, seven of St. Augustine, the ecclesiastical histories of Eusebius and Cassiodorus, and a vast number of sermons, homilies, and other treatises, a list of which she left, as having all been written by her own hand, to the praise of God and of the holy apostles SS. Peter and Paul. This Diemudis was a contemporary of Othlonus, and found time in the midst of her gigantic labours to carry on a correspondence with Herluca, a nun of Eppach, to whom she is said to have indited "many very sweet letters," which were long preserved.

I have mentioned as one of the scholars of St. Emmeran's the holy William of Hirschau, who was chosen abbot of his monastery in 1070, and applied himself to make his monks as learned and as indefatigable in all useful labours as he was himself. He had about 250 monks at Hirschau, and founded no fewer than fifteen other religious houses, for the government of which he drew up a body of excellent statutes. These new foundations he carefully supplied with books, which necessitated constant work in the scriptorium. And a most stately and noble place was the scriptorium of Hirschau, wherein each one was employed according to his talent, binding, painting, gilding, writing, or correcting. The twelve best writers were reserved for transcribing the Scriptures and the Holy Fathers, and one of the twelve, most learned in the sciences, presided over the tasks of the others, chose the books to be copied, and corrected the faults of the younger scribes. The art of painting was studied in a separate school, and here, among others, was trained the good monk Thiemon, who, after decorating half the monasteries of Germany with the productions of his pencil, became archbishop of Saltzburg, and died in odour of sanctity. The statutes with which abbot William provided his monasteries, were chiefly drawn up from those in use at St. Emmeran's, but he was desirous of yet further improving them, and in particular of assimilating them to those of Cluny, which was then at the height of its renown. It was at his request that St. Ulric of Cluny wrote out his "Customary," in which, among other things, he gives a description of the manner in which the Holy Scriptures were read through in the refectory in the course of the year. This "Customary" is one of the most valuable monuments of monastic times which remains to us; it shows us the interior of the monastery, painted by the hand of one of its inmates, taking us through each office, the library, the infirmary, the sacristy, the bakehouse, the kitchen, and the school. How beautiful is the order which it displays, as observed in choir, where, on solemn days, all the singers stood vested in copes, the very seats being covered with embroidered tapestry! Three days in the week the right side of the choir communicated, and the other three the left; during Holy Week they washed the feet of as many poor as there were brethren in the house, and the abbot added others also to represent absent friends. When the Passion was sung, they had a custom of tearing a piece of stuff at the words "they parted my garments;" and the new fire of Holy Saturday was struck, not from a flint, but a precious beryl. There were numberless beautiful rites of benediction observed, as that of the ripe grapes, which were blessed on the altar during mass, on the 6th of August, and afterwards distributed in the refectory, of new beans, and of the freshly-pressed juice of the grape. The ceremonies observed in making the altar breads were also most worthy of note. The grains of wheat were chosen one by one, were carefully washed and put aside in a sack, which was carried by one known to be pure in life and conversation to the mill. There they were ground and sifted, he who performed this duty being clothed in alb and amice. Two priests and two deacons clothed in like manner prepared the breads, and a lay brother, having gloves on his hands, held the irons in which they were baked. The very wood of the fire was chosen of the best and driest. And whilst these processes were being gone through, the brethren engaged ceased not to sing psalms, or sometimes recited Our Lady's office. A separate chapter in the "Customary" is devoted to the children and their master, and the discipline under which they were trained is minutely described. We seem to see them seated in their cloister with the vigilant eye of the master presiding over their work. An open space is left between the two rows of scholars, but there is no one in the monastery who dare pass through their ranks. They go to confession twice a week, and always to the abbot or the prior. And such is the scrupulous care bestowed on their education, and the vigilance to which they are subjected, both by day and night, that, says Ulric, "I think it would be difficult for a king's son to be brought up in a palace with greater care than the humblest boy enjoys at Cluny."

This "Customary" was drawn up during the government of St. Hugh of Cluny, whose letter to William the Conqueror displays something of the independence of mind with which abbots of those days treated the great ones of the earth. William had written to him requesting him to send some of his monks to England, and offering him a hundred pounds for every monk he would send. This method of buying up his monks at so much a head offended the good abbot, who wrote back to the king declining to part with any of his community at such a price, and adding that he would himself give an equal sum for every good monk whom he could draw to Cluny. During the sixty-two years that he governed his abbey, he is said to have professed more than 10,000 subjects. Enough has been said to show that the monastic institute was still strong and vigorous in the eleventh century. Cluny, indeed, represented monasticism rather in its magnificence than in the more evangelic aspect of poverty and abasement, yet in the midst of all her lordly splendour, she continued fruitful in saints. Even the austere St. Peter Damian, whilst he disapproved of the wealth of the monks, was edified at their sanctity, and left them, marvelling how men so rich could live so holily. Their revenues were not spent on luxury; they went to feed 17,000 poor people, and to collect a library of Greek, Latin, and Hebrew authors, such as had not its equal in Europe. It contained among other treasures a certain Bible, called in the chronicle, "great, wonderful, and precious for its writing, correctness, and rich binding, adorned with beryl stones," which had been written by the single hand of the monk Albert. The following inscription inserted in the volume attests the piety as well as the industry of the writer. "This book was written by a certain monk of Cluny, named Albert, formerly of Treves. It was done by the order and at the expense of the venerable abbot Pontius, Peter being at that time the librarian, and providing all things necessary with joy and diligence. And the aforesaid monk, in company with a certain brother named Opizo, diligently read through the whole book, that he might be able to improve it according to the authority of other books; and he twice corrected it. Therefore Brother Albert a sinner, prostrating himself at the feet of the brethren of Cluny, humbly begs of them to pray to God for himself and for his father, that they may obtain the forgiveness of their sins."[158]

Elsewhere also the monastic schools continued to produce a number of excellent masters who thoroughly entered into the revival of classical studies, which we have noticed as having at this time sprung up. At Fleury the monk Raoul taught the art of versification to a crowded audience, and in his own poems advocated the study of the ancient models, especially of Horace. Quotations from the same poet, as well as from Virgil and Statius, not unfrequently appear in the lives of the saints, and even the sermons of this period, a fact not adduced as an instance of the good taste, but simply of the erudition, of the authors. In the school of Stavelot, even Greek poetry was studied. Here was trained the celebrated Wibald, successively abbot of Stavelot, Monte Cassino, and Corby.

The letters and other remains of this remarkable man have been inserted by Martene in his collection, and throw much light on the history of the times. He filled several important offices under the Emperor Conrad, who confided to him the education of his son and successor Henry; but whilst constantly immersed in public business he failed not to labour for the good cause which lay at the heart of every true monk, the multiplication of books, and the encouragement of learning. Thus among his letters we find one addressed in 1149 to the scholasticus of Corby, in which he enumerates among the writers to be studied in the school, Pythagoras, Plato, Sophocles, and Simonides, a sufficient proof that Greek literature was then cultivated in certain seminaries, and that the knowledge of that language was not confined, as Hallam suggests, to the occasional singing of a Greek *Kyrie* or *Sanctus*. There are other letters addressed to the superiors of monasteries whom he engaged to assist him in the collection of books. Among these was the abbot of Hildesheim, from whom he hoped to obtain a complete copy of the Offices of Cicero. His petition for these is in a certain sense apologetic, for, from the days of St. Jerome, religious men were wont to be a little sensitive, lest too great a love of the Latin orator should expose them to the charge of being a *Ciceronian* rather than a *Christian* student. Something of this sort had been playfully hinted at by the abbot of Hildesheim, and Wibald replies: "We do not serve the dishes of Cicero at the first or principal table; but when replenished with better food we partake of them as of sweetmeats that are served for dessert." Sometimes his letters are addressed to friends who have visited his library, and who shared in his literary tastes. "I wish," he writes to the Archbishop of Bremen, "that you would come again and remain longer with us, and, as you promised, turn over the volumes on our shelves. I wish we might have this pleasure together in peace and quiet; there is surely no greater happiness to be enjoyed in life."

It is, perhaps, superfluous to multiply illustrations of this kind, but I cannot resist adding to the names already cited that of Marianus Scotus, whom some call an Irishman, and some a Scot, while others affirm him to have been an honest Northumbrian, and a member of the family of Bede.[159] He died towards the end of the eleventh century, having been successively monk in the abbeys of Cologne, Fulda, and Mayence, and professor of theology some years in that of Ratisbon. He was a poet, and the author of a Chronicle frequently quoted as one of the best mediæval histories, and continued by later writers. His biographers say of him that his countenance was so beautiful, and his manners so simple, that no one doubted he was inspired in all he said and did by the Holy Ghost. A most indefatigable writer, he transcribed the whole Bible with sundry commentaries, and that not once but repeatedly. Moreover he drew out of the deep sea of the holy Fathers, certain sweet waters for the profit of his soul, which he collected in prolix volumes. With all this he found spare moments which he devoted to charitable labours on behalf of poor widows, clerks, and scholars, for whose benefit he multiplied psalters, manuals, and other pious little books, which he distributed to them free of cost for the remedy of his soul. Who will refuse to believe that such loving toils as these were found worthy to receive the miraculous token of favour related in the old legend? "One night," says the annalist, "the brother whose duty it was, having forgotten to give him candles, Marianus nevertheless continued his work without them; and when the brother, recollecting his omission, came late at night to his cell, he beheld a brilliant light streaming through the chinks of the door, and going in softly, found that it proceeded from the fingers of the monk's left hand, and he saw and believed."

In some writers of this time there are indications of increased attention being paid to natural phenomena, and the geographical notices introduced into the chronicle of Otto of Frisingia are praised by the authors of the *Histoire Littéraire* for their exactness and intelligence. A very singular and interesting fact is recorded in the chronicle of Marianus (or rather in its later continuation), which, though of a supernatural character, may perhaps be admitted among the scientific notices of the time. I allude to the vision seen and described by the Blessed Alpais of Cudot, who saw in rapture the earth hanging suspended in space shaped like a globe, or rather a spheroid, for she calls it not perfectly round, but egg-shaped. It was surrounded by water, and the sun appeared of a vastly greater size. Equally remarkable in another branch of science are the speculations of Ithier, a monk of Limoges, on the faculties of the mind corresponding to different parts of the brain, in which we catch a first glimpse of the modern theory of phrenology. Nor must it be supposed that the classical and scientific studies, which excited so much interest, caused the cultivation of the vulgar dialects to be forgotten. Abbots and bishops often preached in Romance, like St. Vital of Savigny and Hildebert of Mans, though the latter is said to have succeeded better in Latin. St. Bernard delivered his exhortations to his brethren not in Latin but Romance, for the benefit of the lay-brothers who were ignorant of the learned tongues, as Mabillon labours to prove. A vast number of translations were likewise made into the popular dialects, and about the end of the eleventh century the monk Grimoald published a version in Romance of the entire Bible; this translation being made nearly a century before that of the Waldenses, though the latter is very generally represented to be the earliest known version of the Scriptures in any vulgar tongue.[160]

It is evident, then, that all the learning of the eleventh and twelfth centuries was not swallowed up by the new race of scholastics, nor was every scholastic a Berengarius. Yet there is a certain change perceptible in many of those who at this time attained to literary eminence, and a greater predominance of the philosophic element, consequent in some degree from the nature of the studies rendered popular in the school of Bec. We begin more frequently to meet with tales of scholars who, in the midst of their learned pursuits, were overtaken with a dread of the perils which beset their course, and sought to escape them by flying into the desert. The cloisters were peopled with such refugees from the schools, who, like Lanfranc, often reappeared after a while to resume the weapons of human science, which they had thought to fling aside for ever, and use them in the service of their Master.

Of these converts were St. Bruno, the founder of the Carthusians, and Odo of Tournai. Bruno is said to have studied at Tours under Berengarius, though this appears doubtful. In 1056 the scholasticus of Rheims having resigned his charge, that he might devote himself exclusively to the affairs of his own salvation, Gervase, Archbishop of Rheims, promoted Bruno to the office, which by this time had become associated to that of Chancellor of the diocese, and gave its holder a certain superiority over the other diocesan schools. Bruno continued to fill this responsible post for twenty years, during which time he numbered among his pupils Odo, afterwards Pope Urban II., and many of the greatest prelates of the time. He was reckoned the first philosopher, theologian, and poet of France, and by writers of his own day is extolled as "the doctor of doctors, the glory of the Church, the model of good men, and the mirror of the whole world." The romantic story which ascribes his conversion to religion to the horror caused by the voice which came from the dead body of a certain eminent doctor, proclaiming his damnation, is now universally rejected as the production of a later age. In fact, St. Bruno has himself related the manner in which his resolution was first formed in a letter addressed to Raoul, provost of Rheims, wherein he reminds him of a certain day when they were walking with another canon named Fulcius, in the garden adjoining his house, conversing together of the vanities of the world. "Then it was," he says, "that the Holy Spirit moved us to renounce all perishable things, and embrace the monastic life that we might merit life eternal." It would also appear that a grievous case of simony, which had scandalised the diocese, powerfully wrought on Bruno's mind, and moved him to fly from a world so hedged about with temptations. He was followed into his retreat by a number of his former scholars; but it was not until 1084 that they at last determined on the way of life they should choose, and, receiving the monastic habit from the hands of St. Hugh of Grenoble, laid the foundation of the Carthusian Order, which took its name from the desert they had chosen for their abode. In after years the order continued to be largely recruited from the same class whence their first founder had been drawn. Many a fine scholar came to the wild rocks of the Chartreuse to seek in obscurity for a peace which he found by experience the world of intellect could never give; and Bulæus informs us that no order of monks received among their ranks so many members of Paris University as did these austere and penitential recluses.

Odo, or Oudart, the other convert to whom allusion has been made, first attracted notice as a teacher at Toul, a city which had always been rich in schools and schoolmasters, and which had felt a special pride in keeping up its learned reputation, since 1048, when it had sent its bishop to fill the chair of St. Peter in the person of St. Leo IX. Odo's fame reached the ears of the canons of Tournai, who entreated him to take charge of their cathedral school, which he accordingly governed for five years. A skilful teacher, and a devourer of books, Odo possessed extraordinary powers of labour, and when any literary work was in hand, he rested neither day nor night till it was accomplished. He was also a great friend of method and good moral discipline, but as yet he had been too exclusively taken up with the cares and pleasures of his profession to give much thought to spiritual things. Or perhaps we might rather say that he hardly knew of their existence. Like other busy, hard-working men, he was swept along in the tide of daily life, and thought it much to preserve a character of stainless honour and respectability. His success as a teacher was so great, that disciples came to him from all parts of France, as well as from Flanders, Italy, and Saxony. The city of Tournai became literally filled with students, who might be seen disputing together in the public streets: and as you drew near the school you would see them walking with the master, or seated around him; or, in the evening, standing with him at the church door, while he taught them the various constellations, and explained to them the course of the stars.

Odo was as remarkable for his virtue as his learning. He took all his disciples to the church with him daily. They never numbered fewer than two hundred; but he made them walk two-and-two through the streets, he himself bringing up the rear, and enforcing a discipline as strict as would have been observed in the most regular monastery. No one ventured to speak to his companion, or to look right or left, and in choir they might have been taken for monks of Cluny. He did not allow them to frequent the company of women, or to wear any kind of finery; and if they transgressed his orders in these respects, he turned them out of his school. At the hours when he gave his lectures no layman was allowed to enter the cloisters, which were at other times the resort of the public. So strict was he in this, that he did not hesitate to exclude Everard, the Castellan of Tournai, a nobleman of power and influence; for it was Odo's principle that a man must not deviate a hair's-breadth from his duty from the motive of human respect. By these means he won the love and esteem of every one: canons and people alike spoke well of him, though some were found to say that his regularity of life sprang rather from philosophy than religion.

He had directed his school for about five years, when one day, a certain clerk having brought him St. Augustine's "Treatise on Free-will," he purchased it, merely with the view of increasing his library, and threw it into a coffer among some other books without looking at it, for his taste inclined him rather to the study of Plato than of the Fathers. About two months afterwards, however, as he was explaining Boëthius to his disciples, he came to the fourth book of the "Consolations of Philosophy," in which the author treats of Free-will. Remembering the book he had lately purchased on the same subject, he sent for it, and having read two or three pages, was struck with the beauty of the style; and calling his pupils, said to them, "I own that until now I was ignorant how agreeable and eloquent are the writings of St. Augustine;" and that day and the following he read to them from this work, explaining its difficulties as he proceeded.

In this way he came to that passage in the third book, wherein St. Augustine compares the soul of the sinner to a slave condemned to some vile and disgusting labour. Odo sighed as he read the powerful words of the writer, exclaiming, "How striking is this comparison! it seems as if written expressly for us men of science. We adorn the corrupt world with the little stock of learning which we possess, and after death, perhaps, are not found worthy of eternal happiness, because we have done God no service; but have used our intellects for vanity and worldly glory!" With these words he rose from his chair, and going into the church, remained there in floods of tears, his scholars meanwhile remaining astonished and perplexed. From that day he gradually discontinued his lectures, and began to frequent the church more diligently, and to distribute in alms all the money he received from his pupils. He also fasted so rigorously that his appearance soon completely changed, and he became so thin and attenuated as scarcely to be recognised.

The rumour soon ran through the town that Odo, the famous doctor, was about to abandon the world. Four of his disciples resolved never to quit him, and made him promise to do nothing except in concert with them. Monks and abbots from every religious house in the neighbourhood of Tournai, wanted Odo to join their communities, but his disciples preferred the rule of the canons as being easier than that of the monks. Rabod, the Bishop of Tournai, accordingly made over to them an old church, part of an abbey which had been destroyed by the Normans, and they took possession of it in 1092. Two years later they resolved on embracing the monastic rule, and the bishop giving his consent, Odo was elected first abbot of the restored abbey of Tournai. Though he had fled to the cloister to escape from the pride of the schools, he did not neglect the cause of learning. Like most of the religious superiors of his day, he gave much time and trouble to the formation of a good library and scriptorium, and used to make an innocent boast of the many good writers whom the Lord had given him. Had you gone into his scriptorium, says his successor, you would have seen twelve youths, sitting in silence, most diligently engaged in copying manuscripts, at tables made for the purpose. And he enumerates among the books so transcribed the works of St. Jerome and St. Gregory, and all that he could collect of Bede, Isidore, Ambrose, Austin, and the Lord Anselm of Bec.

About this time the rival philosophical sects known as the Realists and Nominalists began to attract attention. The questions in dispute between them regarded the validity and existence of *universal ideas*. The expression requires explanation. An idea is the representation in the mind of some impression made on the senses by an external object. These ideas may be either *particular* or *universal*. They are particular when they correspond to some individual object, as *John Smith*, or *that tree*. They are universal when we separate them from any individual object, and conceive them as corresponding to something which is to be found in many individuals, whereby these may be classified together, as when we speak of *men* or *trees*. According to the scholastics, there are five kinds of such universal ideas, namely, *species, genus, difference, property* and *accident*. The species includes many individuals, as *sheep, oak*. The genus includes many species, as *animal, tree*. Difference is something which distinguishes one species from another belonging to the same genus. *Property*, or essential attribute, is what necessarily belongs to the essence of a thing; as when we say of a globe that it is *round*. Accident is some attribute to be found in a thing which is not necessary to its existence, as if we were to say of the same globe that it is *green*. We are able to hold these ideas in our mind, abstracted from any object, and so we come to have the abstract ideas of men, animals, trees, roundness, or whiteness, without connecting them with any particular individual. But the Nominalists denied the existence of such ideas, and declared the above distinctions to be mere sounds of the voice, corresponding to no external reality. They knew what was meant by a wise man, or a white horse, but professed themselves unable to comprehend what was meant by *wisdom* or *whiteness*. The Realists, on the other hand, appealing to the authority of Boëthius, contended that these ideas were real and existent.

Both parties numbered great names in their ranks. Odo of Tournai was a partisan of the Realists, as was also the Blessed Robert of Arbrisselles. At the head of the Nominalists appeared his fellow-student and professor in the Paris schools, Roscelin, a canon of Compeigne, and a man whose character too closely resembled that of Berengarius. He seems to have adopted novel and startling opinions as a means of drawing the eyes of men on himself, and the manner in which he applied his philosophical method of reasoning to revealed doctrines, specially that of the Holy Trinity, resulted in actual heresy, and brought on him in 1092 the condemnation of the Council of Soissons. Taking refuge in England, he there met with a vigorous opponent in the person of St. Anselm, who, whilst freely admitting, and even advocating the exercise of the intellectual powers on the mysteries of faith, marked out the limits between faith and reason, and severely condemned the presumption of those who would attempt to make reason the test of faith. He declares that we must seek the intelligence of those things that we already believe; that reason is not the means by which we attain to faith, but rather that by which we enjoy the evidence and contemplation of the mysteries which we already believe: and that right order demands that we should first receive the profound truths of faith before we dare to exercise our reason upon them.[161] As time went on, and both sects pushed their philosophical views to extremes, grave errors were charged against both, and the foundations were laid of many forms of modern Rationalism.

Paris was now rapidly becoming the centre of scholastic activity. The fame of her masters spread over Europe, and among them were Lambert, a disciple of Fulbert of Chartres; Manegold, whose very daughters were learned, and opened a school for the education of their own sex, Anselm of Laon and Bernard of Chartres. John of Salisbury, whose favourite master, William de Conches, had himself been a pupil of Bernard's, has left us an interesting account of the method of this last-named teacher. He explained all the best authors, not confining himself to grammar strictly so called, but making his pupils observe all the refinements of rhetoric. He pointed out the propriety of certain terms and metaphors, and the best order and arrangement of a subject; and showed the variety of styles to be used according to the different matters treated of by a writer. If any passage occurred in their reading referring to other sciences, he took pains to explain it, according to the capacity of his hearers. He was careful to cultivate their memory, making them learn and recite choice passages from the classic historians, poets, and philosophers; requiring them one day to give an exact account of what they had heard or read the day previous. He was always exhorting them to read much in private, but not indiscriminately, directing them to avoid what was only fit to feed curiosity, and to content themselves with the works of standard authors. For, he used to say, quoting Quinctilian, "it is a great weakness to read all that every miserable writer has to say on every subject, and only loads the memory with superfluous and worthless things."

As he knew that it is to very little purpose to hear or study examples unless we accustom ourselves to reproduce the treasures thus stored up in the memory, he was anxious that his pupils should every day compose something both in prose and verse, and he established conferences among them wherein they mutually questioned and answered one another, the utility of which exercise John of Salisbury speaks of very highly; "provided," as he observes, "that charity govern the emulation displayed in such encounters, so that while we make progress in letters we still preserve humility. For a man should not serve two masters so opposed one to the other as learning and vice."

This was also the rule observed by Bernard, who maintained that the first and principal key to knowledge was Humility, to which he assigned Poverty as a companion. The subjects on which he exercised his scholars were always fitted to cherish both faith and good morals. And the work of each day was finished with the recitation of the "Our Father," and a brief prayer for the dead.

Anselm of Laon was a teacher of much the same character, and, if possible, of greater renown. He and his brother Radulph were called by Guibert de Nogent the two eyes of the Latin Church, and by their knowledge of the Scriptures converted many heretics. Some of their pupils were as famous as themselves, such as Hugh Metellus, a great lover of the classics, whose flow of language was so great that he dictated to two secretaries at once, and could improvise a thousand verses, standing on one leg, and who was induced by the teaching of his pious masters to exchange a life of worldly vanity, the love of dress and delicate diet, for the austere regimen of a canon regular of Toul. Another of Anselm's scholars was William de Champeaux, under whom the Paris schools first attained that pre-eminence which they maintained in the world of letters down to the period of the Revolution. After studying successively under Manegold and Anselm, he was appointed archdeacon of the Church of Paris, and master of the Cathedral school, where he taught logic, rhetoric, and theology, with great success. And about the year 1100 his reputation attracted one disciple whose name is indelibly associated with the literary history of the period,—the celebrated Peter Abelard.

Abelard's choice of a scholar's life is said to have been influenced in the first instance by his dislike of the profession of arms. Nature, while it had given him an insatiable desire for fame and worldly glory, had denied him the gift of personal courage, and he himself made no secret of the feeling which, as he said, had moved him to enrol himself under the banners of Minerva, rather than those of Mars. His subtle mind was very early devoted to the study of logic, but not satisfied with the teaching to be found in his own diocese of Nantes, he led a wandering life for some time, passing from school to school; and at last found his way to Paris, where William de Champeaux was then at the height of his reputation as a teacher of dialectics. The brilliant qualities of his new pupil at first won the heart of his master, but erelong Abelard began to show signs of that presumption and contempt of every one's attainments except his own, which kept him at war with all his contemporaries. He came to the lecture rooms less with the view of learning than with the secret hope of outshining his fellow-students and perplexing his master. He was perpetually proposing vexatious questions, for the purpose of entrapping the latter in some logical subtlety; and affecting to consider that William had shown himself unable to answer these difficulties, he disdained any longer to be the scholar of one whom he considered his inferior, and determined on setting up a school for himself.

Unable to do this in Paris, where the influence of William de Champeaux was at that time all-powerful, he established himself first at Mélun, and then at Corbeil, which was nearer to the capital. He was but twenty-two when he first appeared before the world as an independent professor, and soon made himself talked of for his brilliancy, his fluency, and the vehemence with which he attempted to make the art of logic supersede all the other liberal arts, which he was accustomed to treat with contempt. His passion for glory soon brought him back to Paris, where William de Champeaux was now archdeacon, and head of the cathedral school. Abelard renewed his attacks on his old master, and that with such success, that the cloisteral schools became deserted, and the fickle audience flocked to the lectures of the new professor. The circumstance seems to have touched the heart of William with a contempt for intellectual renown which was so easily won and lost, and resigning his school, he retired among the canons regular of St. Victor, a religious house destined to play a great part in the history of the future university. This was in 1109, and, by the advice of Hildebert, Bishop of Mans, who wrote to the new canon, congratulating him on "the step by which he had at last become a true philosopher," William opened a school within his monastery, which afterwards produced several illustrious theologians, who are all distinguished by the surname of St. Victor.

It is unnecessary to pursue the rivalries of the two professors through all their windings; in 1113 William was raised to the see of Châlons, a circumstance which seems to have first induced Abelard to study theology, with the hope of attaining similar honours. Accordingly, we next find him at Laon, attending the school of Anselm, now dean of that church, whom, however, he very soon declared to be altogether unworthy of his great renown. "His learning was," he said, "nothing but foliage without fruit; long custom, rather than any real merit, had acquired him a name. If you consulted him on any difficulty, you came away just as wise as you went. There was nothing but abundance of fine words, without a grain of sense or reason." So, in despair of finding a master wise enough to teach one of his genius, he resolved to do without one, and, with the help of a commentary, began to give lectures on the prophet Ezechiel. His wit, his fluency, and his singular charms of voice and manner, veiled the real shallowness of his theological attainments, and, on returning to Paris, he succeeded in gaining what had been for so many years the great object of his ambition, the direction of the cathedral school. Then began the period of his extraordinary popularity; disciples flocked to him from all parts of France and Germany, as well as from Rome and England. His vanity easily persuaded him that he was not merely the greatest, but the only philosopher of his time; all the world hung on his eloquence, but amid the long catologue of his admirers, none was to be found so bewitched with his merits as he was himself.

Abelard's teaching bore the character of his own restless and impatient genius. Disdainful of anything which did not promise quick results, he aimed at presenting his disciples with a philosophy which professed to lead them to the possession of wisdom by a royal road. The trivium and quadrivium were to be consigned to oblivion; the classics and the Fathers might alike grow dusty on the shelves, logic was to be all in all, and the philosopher and the theologian might abandon every other study, provided they perfected themselves in the art which St. Bernard characterised with caustic wit, as "that of ever studying, and never reaching the truth." Abelard's condemnation of the classics is worth noticing, as showing the similarity of mind which existed between him and Berengarius, whom Guitmond describes as "making no account of the opinions of his masters, and despising the liberal arts." In neither of them did this condemnation arise from a preponderance of the Christian sense; but from their repugnance to objective realities.[162] Their philosophy was in short that of which the apostle speaks, when he condemns the "vain babblings" of those who "desire to be teachers of the law," which differed little from the "foolish questionings" of the sophists. The effect of these new doctrines was to inaugurate a scholastic revolution. One by one the fair branches of the tree of science were severed from the trunk, till at last nothing remained but the exercise of subtle and captious argumentation, wherein logic came to be used not as a means but an end, and the scholar was no longer led to seek for truth as his object, but to rest content with the search after it.

Thus passed several years, during which Abelard had earned a fame, brilliant indeed beyond that of any of his contemporaries, but unhappily one which left his moral reputation far from stainless. In 1117 we find him in the abbey of St. Denis, where he had taken refuge from the disgrace entailed on him by his connection with Heloïsa. Even here his insupportable vanity was not long before it betrayed itself in the criticisms he passed on his abbot and his brother monks, among whom he seems to have aspired to act as the reformer. The abbot longed to get rid of so troublesome a subject, and the opportunity of doing so soon presented itself. Crowds of students began to clamour at the gates of St. Denis for their old master, and to implore him to reopen his school. He therefore resumed his lectures, but unable to rest contented with teaching only what had been taught before him, he began to introduce logical subtleties into his theological views, and put forth certain explanations on the doctrine of the Holy Trinity, which raised a storm of opposition. His chief opponents were Alberic and Lotulf, two former disciples of Anselm of Laon, and William of Champeaux. They not only attacked his opinions as heterodox, but complained that he had no right to teach at all. His position as a professor was, they said, altogether irregular, for, contrary to the established usages of the Paris schools, he taught *sine magistro*.

This term requires a little explanation; and shows us the germ of what soon afterwards developed into the system of university graduation. According to established custom, no scholar could be licensed to *teach* publicly who had not previously gone through a regular course of study under some approved doctor. But Abelard had had no master in theology, except himself; for, as we have seen, he gave up his attendance in Anselm's school through contempt for his inferiority, and had at once begun to teach a science which in reality he had never studied. At a Council assembled at Soissons, his Treatise on the Holy Trinity was condemned, and he himself required to cast it into the fire, and to make public profession of the faith by reciting the creed of St. Athanasius, which he did with many tears and sighs, after which he was sent back to the monastery of St. Denys. He had not been there long, however, when a controversy which he thought fit to raise on the question of the identity of St. Denys, the Areopagite, with the patron of the abbey, got him into fresh trouble, and he fled from the monastery to the territory of the Count of Champagne, where he fixed his residence in a beautiful solitude near Nogent, which was soon found out by his disciples. "They came crowding to me," he writes, "from all parts, and leaving the towns and cities, were content to dwell in the wilderness. Instead of spacious houses, they set up for themselves little tents, and put up gladly with wild herbs instead of delicate viands. People said one to another, 'Behold the world is gone after him.' At last, as my little oratory would not hold them, they enlarged it, building it of wood and stone." To this new building he gave the name of the *Paraclete*, and it might truly have been his consolation could he have learnt wisdom from the past, and bowed his erratic genius under the yoke of faith. But the school of the Paraclete soon resounded with new errors; to the former opinions put forth regarding the Holy Trinity, were now added equally heterodox views on the subject of grace and original sin, which were at once discerned and denounced by two saints who then illuminated the church with their doctrine and their virtue—St. Norbert, and St. Bernard of Clairvaux. Abelard, whose natural cowardice shrank from the prospect of new dangers, endeavoured to escape the consequences of his own imprudence by abandoning the Paraclete, and accepting the government of St. Gildas' abbey; but the uncouth manners and language of the monks filled him with repugnance, or perhaps it would be truer to say, the monastic routine proved insufferable to one who had nothing of the real monk about him. In 1126, therefore, we find him once more teaching in the schools of St. Geneviève. He was never really at home save in the Professor's chair, but unhappily he never filled it without betraying himself into some of the audacities of unorthodox philosophy. Soon his old errors were reproduced, and called forth the zeal of St. Bernard, who protested with all the force of his nervous eloquence against the strange assemblage of heresies to be found united in the teaching of a single man. "When he speaks of the Holy Trinity," he says, "it is in the style of Arius; he is a Pelagian when he treats of grace, and a second Nestorius when he speaks of the Person of Jesus Christ. His vanity," continues the saint, "is such that he brags as if there were nothing in heaven and earth he did not know; and in truth he knows a little of everything except himself." In his 190th Epistle, addressed to Pope Innocent II., St. Bernard sums up all the errors of Abelard, who had ventured to deny, and even to ridicule, the doctrine of Redemption, which he presumptuously declared illogical, declaring that our Lord came only to instruct us by His Word and Example. His final condemnation took place at the Council of Sens, which imposed silence on him for ever, a sentence confirmed by the authority of Pope Innocent II. This condemnation might possibly have had no better result than that of Soissons, had it not been for the charity of the Venerable Peter of Cluny, at whose monastery Abelard stopped on his way to Rome, where he purposed to appeal against his sentence. The holy abbot succeeded in drawing from him a recantation of his errors; he induced him to renounce the scholastic career, which had been the source of so many temptations, and frankly to submit to the judgment of the Council and the

Pope. More than this, he exerted himself to effect a personal reconciliation between Abelard and St. Bernard, and lastly, he offered to the wounded spirit of the unhappy scholar a secure and sheltered retreat in his own community, where, under the habit of religion, the Professor of St. Geneviève spent the last years of his life in the exercise of piety and penance.

There then, let us leave him, in his poor cell with its wooden candlestick and its crucifix, with the Holy Scriptures and a few treatises of the Fathers for his only library; defeated, as some might say, put to silence, and extinguished— but with his heart, at last, at peace. Well might he have exclaimed with the Psalmist, "It is good for me that Thou hast humbled me!" A change was wrought in him so great, that, as we read the words in which his good abbot describes it, we can scarcely recognise the old Abelard of former years. "Never did I see a man more humble," writes Peter the Venerable, "whether in gesture, habit, or countenance. He read continually, prayed often, and kept silence at all times, unless when forced to speak; and after his reconciliation with the Holy See, offered the Holy Sacrifice almost daily, and occupied himself only with meditating or teaching me truths of religion or philosophy." A marvellous change indeed; and happy were it if all who incurred the same censures could follow in the same course.

We have seen that the rationalistic errors of Abelard found their ablest opponent in St. Bernard, who had conceived a distrust of the new philosophy when studying as a mere boy in the canon's school at Chatillon, where the fashionable scholasticism was just then beginning to be introduced. He seems to have felt an instinctive dread of its ultimate tendencies, and to have preserved during his whole life the sentiments resulting from his early experience of what his biographer Geoffery of Igny designates as the "wisdom of the world." Closely united to him in their theological views, were the great scholars of St. Victor's, Hugh, Richard, and Adam. Hugh of St. Victor, the third prior in succession from William de Champeaux, was styled the second Augustine, from his devoted admiration of that Father. Brought up in a house of canons regular in Saxony, he bore testimony in after life to the care they bestowed on his education. "I do not fear to certify," he says, "that they neglected no means of perfecting me in the sciences, and even instructed me in many things which might be thought trifling and extraordinary." These words occur in his *Didascalion*, or Treatise on Studies, which he drew up with the view of remedying the disorderly and unmethodical manner in which most scholars then pursued their academic labours. In it he gives an interesting account of his own early life as a scholar. "I never despised anything that belonged to erudition," he says; "when I was a scholar I studied the names of everything I saw. I committed to memory all the sentences, questions, replies, and solutions I had heard and learnt during the day; and I used to describe the figures of geometry on the floor with charcoal. I do not say this to boast of my knowledge, which is nothing, but to show that he proceeds best who proceeds with order. You will find many things in histories and other books, which taken in themselves seem of little profit, but which nevertheless are useful and necessary when taken in connection with other things." Hugh, like all the disciples of this school, advocated the old system, according to which all the parts of knowledge stood in mutual relation to one another, and theology dominated over the whole. In his Treatise *De Vanitate Mundi*, he describes an imaginary school, in which is no doubt depicted that of his own monastery. The students are described divided into groups, according to the different subjects on which they are engaged. All the liberal arts are cultivated in turn, and while the fingers of some are employed in designing or colouring an illuminated page, others are studying the nature of herbs, or the constitution of the human frame. As a spiritual writer, Hugh of St. Victor is considered to be surpassed by his disciple Richard of St. Victor, a Scotchman by birth, and one of the greatest mystic theologians of the Church. The special doctrines insisted on by this school were those which put forth faith, and not reason, as the ground of certainty, and maintained that reason was to be exercised only to demonstrate the truths that were held by faith. Abelard, in his extravagant exaltation of the claims of reason, had gone so far in his "Introduction to Theology," as to define faith as an opinion, and to depreciate a too ready belief, praising that cautious philosophy which does not yield its faith till it has subjected all things to the test of reason. To believe without doubting, according to this view of things, was the religion of women and children; to doubt all things before we believe them was alone worthy of the dignity of man. The scholars of St. Victor not only vindicated the true claims of faith, but they sought to prove that faith itself must rest on the foundation stone of charity. They loved to remind their disciples of those words of Our Lord, "If any man will do the will of God he shall know of the doctrine." Charity, they said, is then the foundation, and Humility the key, to all true science, and we can understand the Truth of God only in proportion as we obey it. They did not seek to set aside the just use of the reason, but to assign it limits, and to prohibit the search after things confessedly above the grasp of human intellect. "What is it to be wise," asks Hugo of St. Victor, "but to love God? for love is wisdom." He complains of the cavilling spirit of the dialecticians who would fain turn the simplest precepts of the Gospel into matter of dispute. If they read that we are to love our neighbour as ourselves, they begin to argue, saying, "If I love one man as myself, then I must love three or four men more than myself;" and this they style seeking truth. Again, he blames the conceit of those who, ignorant of the very first elements, will condescend to study nothing but the sublimest matters, forgetting that the beginning of all discipline is humility. Neither would he endure that presumptuous spirit which gloried in the subtlety of its own powers, but, like a true disciple of St. Augustine, desired that reliance on Divine Grace should be the foundation of the whole spiritual and intellectual edifice.

Perfectly in accordance with this teaching was that of John of Salisbury, who exposed the vain pretensions of those who ought to make philosophy consist in a barren exercise of the reasoning powers. "Philosophy," he says, "is nothing else but the love of God, and if that love be extinguished philosophy vanishes away. All studies worthy of that end must tend to the increase of charity, and he who acquires or increases charity has gained the highest object of philosophy. This, therefore, is the true rule of philosophy, that all learning and all reading should be made conducive to truth and charity, and then the choir of virtues will enter into the soul as into a temple of God. They most impudently err who think that philosophy consists in mere words, who multiply phrases and propose a thousand ridiculous little questions, endeavouring to perplex their hearers that they may seem more learned than Dædalus. But though eloquence is a useful and noble study, this loquacity of vain disputation is a most hateful thing." Truth, as all agreed, was the only object of science; but whilst Abelard and his followers sought this truth in the subjective reasonings of their own minds, the mystics of St. Victor's school declared that it was not to be sought by the understanding alone, but by the heart and will. For what is Truth, they asked, but God Himself? Who is to be sought by love rather than by science. He therefore who seeks God, seeks the highest truth, and embraces it when it finds Him. It knows all things in proportion as it knows more of God, Whom not to know is darkness. And it knows all things in Him, for, in the words of St. Gregory, "what does not he see, who sees Him Who sees all things?"

Such was the sublime teaching which St. Bernard and the contemplatives of his time opposed to the growing spirit of philosophic rationalism. The Cistercian cloisters and the disciples of the school of St. Victor everywhere propagated the same spiritual maxims, and thus provided a wholesome antidote to the baneful spirit of the age. But the very existence of the antidote bears witness how wide-spread was the poison which it sought to nullify, how greatly the mind of Christendom had broken away from the old landmarks of thought, and how rapidly it was sweeping onward to what threatened to cause the wreck of faith and philosophy together.

The actual state of the schools at the middle of the twelfth century may best be gathered from the description given by our own country man, John of Salisbury, of his own course of studies. He appears to have come to Paris for the first time in 1136, being then a youth of sixteen, and, like thousands of the same age, was launched into the world of the great capital, to complete his education under the many wise professors who were contending for popular favour. Here we catch a glimpse of the new system which was gradually establishing itself. Education was no longer given exclusively in cloistered schools, but in great cities, where the young aspirant after science, instead of being sheltered under law and discipline, was cast abroad to shift for himself, and only required to attend the lectures of some licensed master. No doubt it was an excellent way of teaching him a knowledge of the world, but this had not hitherto been included in the branches of a noble youth's early education. However, at sixteen John had to take care of himself in the great world of Paris, which exercised over him the fascination of which all were conscious who passed from the semi-barbarous isle of Britain to the brilliant capital, and beheld the gay vivacity of its citizens, the gravity of its religious ceremonials, the splendour and majesty of its many churches, and the busy life of its schools.[163] "Happy banishment," wrote the young scholar, "that is permitted here to find a home!" His first care was to choose what Professor he would attend. It was just the time when Abelard's fame was at its greatest height, and the English youth was naturally enough led to join the crowds that thronged the school of St. Geneviève. His first impression was one of delight, but soon his English good sense revolted at the shallowness which he detected under the showy outside, while the contemptuous neglect with which Abelard was wont to treat the ancient learning, was unendurable in the eyes of one who, young as he was, already had a thoroughly-formed taste for the classics. So bidding adieu to St. Geneviève, he placed himself under the two English masters, Robert de Mélun and William de Conches; by the first of whom he was initiated into the art of logic. He praises the disinterestedness shown by Robert, who, in his conduct as Professor, despised worldly gain and sought only the benefit of his scholars. Robert afterwards became Bishop of Hereford, and in that capacity acquired a very unenviable notoriety as one of the chief opponents of St. Thomas of Canterbury. Under William de Conches, John next passed three years with very great profit, studying grammar, which was then understood to include the explanation of good authors. He never regretted the time he devoted to this study. William was a disciple of the old school, a stout champion of the liberal arts, and warmly opposed to the new system introduced by Abelard. He liked to exercise his pupils in prose and verse, and required not only good prosody, but also good sense from his scholars. It was doubtless a fine thing to hear the warm-hearted, testy Englishman speak of the schools in which he had been brought up half a century ago, when boys were taught to behave like boys, and to listen to their masters in silence. Things were much altered now; and it was no longer the custom to follow the wholesome rule which Pythagoras taught his disciples, namely, to listen in silence for seven years, and only begin to ask questions in the eighth. On the contrary, these new scholars would come into your school with a supercilious air, and propose you their doubts and quibbles before they were well seated. They seemed to fancy that they knew everything when they had followed the schools for a year, and as if their business was to instruct their masters by their amazingly clever questions. On all these abuses Master William was wont to expend his honest indignation, but he certainly could not complain that John of Salisbury exhibited any of these marks of reprobation. Far from seeming to think he knew everything after a year's study, John, after spending twelve years in the schools, regarded himself as still a learner. After his three years of grammar, he spent seven years more in successive courses of rhetoric, mathematics, and theology. Among the masters whose lectures he attended were Robert Pullus, or Pulleyne, and Gilbert de la Poiree. The latter afterwards became Bishop of Poitiers, in which dignity he was accused of teaching certain heterodox opinions on the Holy Trinity, which were condemned at the Council of Rheims, in 1148. His errors, like those of Abelard, appear to have arisen out of an abuse of that scholastic method of argumentation so popular among the professors of the time, and which too often proved dangerous weapons in the hands of men whose theological studies by no means kept pace with the cultivation of dialectics. Robert Pullus, the English master of theology, and restorer of sacred studies at Oxford, was a man of far more solid learning. "He knew," says his great disciple, "how to be wise with sobriety." The soundness of his doctrine was evinced by his "Sum of Theology," and his disinterestedness, by his refusal of a bishopric offered him by Henry I. Robert declined abandoning a life of study for the precarious honours of a dignity which exposed its owner to the almost certain contingency of a struggle with the crown. He desired nothing more honourable than the life of a master; nevertheless, he was unable to avoid the dignities thrust on him by Celestine II., who created him cardinal and chancellor of the Roman Church.

During the whole time of his residence at Paris, John of Salisbury enjoyed a scholar's honourable state of poverty, and supported himself by giving lessons to younger students, much after the fashion of a modern college tutor. His tutorship was, however, by no means a very profitable post, and supplied him with little beyond the bare necessaries of life. Happily, however, the threadbare gown of the poor scholar was still regarded with respect, and his humble circumstances did not prevent him from forming many valuable friendships. Among his friends he numbered the two great masters Adam du Petit Pont, and Richard l'Évêque, the former of whom he describes as a man of undoubted learning, but so vain that he wrapped up his knowledge in a cloud of obscurity, and made himself unintelligible for the sake of appearing profound, saying to those who reproached him with this weakness, that were he only to teach in the common way, he should get no one to attend his lectures. Richard was a man of a very different temper; his pride lay rather in concealing what he knew, than in displaying it; he cared nothing at all for worldly applause, and was deemed as holy in life as he was erudite. At first he followed the excellent method of Bernard of Chartres, but by degrees he yielded to the fashion of the times, and giving up the teaching of grammar and rhetoric, confined himself entirely to lecturing on dialectics.

To these friends of John of Salisbury we must add the name of a third, an Englishman like himself, and one of Anglo-Saxon blood. He was a young law-student, who, if inferior to many of his companions in scholastic acquirements, made up for the deficiency by the brilliancy of his native gifts, and those personal graces which add so largely to the power of wit or eloquence. The large grey eyes, thin aquiline nose, and beautiful countenance, so calm, yet with a glance so full of fire, are all known to us; for if the features of St. Thomas à Becket have not been preserved chiselled in marble, they have yet been made familiar to us by the description of those who laid up in their hearts the memory of that beloved countenance. It bore the unmistakable impress of genius, and of that sensitive organisation with which genius is so frequently accompanied. But his great natural gifts had received very imperfect culture in the schools of Merton and those of the English metropolis. At Paris his studies were almost exclusively confined to law, and he afterwards regretted that he had not devoted more time during his academic career to sacred learning. The intimacy which sprang up between him and John of Salisbury was not, therefore, based on any similarity in their literary tastes. The letters of both evince a striking difference in their intellectual training; those of St. Thomas, powerful in matter, are yet abrupt, harsh, and technical in style—those of his friend, on the other hand, are conveyed in classic phraseology, and betray the careful polish, not always free from affectation, of one who has laboriously formed himself on ancient models. In fact, John of Salisbury was, beyond dispute, the first scholar of his day, and naturally enough bewailed the revolution which he witnessed taking place in the schools. The science of reasoning was now affirmed by its advocates to contain the pith of all philosophy. Rhetoric was regarded by them as altogether unnecessary, because eloquence being a gift of nature, could not be acquired by art. Those who possessed the gift needed no study of ancient authors to infuse it into them; and those who did not possess it, would study them to no purpose. The art of logic to such men was all in all, and such was the eagerness with which they indulged their taste for disputation, that some spent their whole days in argument, and carried on their tiresome wrangling in the very streets. And what arguments they were! They examined seriously and at alarming length the weighty question, whether a pig who is driven by a man to be sold at the market, is held by the man, or by the cord fastened round his leg; and whether one who buys a cloak can be held to have purchased also the hood fastened to the cloak. As two negatives are equal to one affirmative, professors were accustomed to introduce into their arguments such a number of negatives, that in order to reckon them up, and see in what sense their propositions were to be understood, the hearers had recourse to the device of dropping a bean at each negative, and reckoning up the sum total at the end of the lecture. John, in his writings, complains of all these extravagancies, and of the tiresome way in which these choppers of logic would dispute over a tuft of wool, and instantly contradict any man who opened his lips in their presence. Nor did he cease lamenting over the neglect of good literature, which was resulting from the predominance given in the schools to logical disputation. He specially attacks one of the leading scholastics whom he does not name, but speaks of him under the sobriquet of "*Cornificius*;"[164] and those who showed themselves hostile to the claims of grammar and rhetoric are denominated by him "*Cornificians*." In spite of all his wit and eloquence, the Cornificians won the day. The study of polite literature fell into neglect, and the intellectual power of the twelfth and thirteenth centuries was turned into another channel—a channel which no doubt gave rise to a good deal of barbarous Latinity, but whence was to issue, in process of time, something more precious than mere literary elegance, the scholastic philosophy of the Church.

The caustic strictures of John of Salisbury were not directed against that system of philosophy, which as yet had no existence,[165] but against the error which put forth the exercise of sophistical argumentation as itself the sum of all philosophy, and the danger which he saw too well must arise from the deification of human reason. For the scholastic method, to which the theology of the Church stands so deeply indebted, is not to be confounded with the scholasticism which was rampant in the days of Abelard. The errors and sophistries of the professors of his day, arising as they did out of an extravagant adherence to the uncorrected teaching of Aristotle, were from the first discerned and condemned by the ecclesiastical authorities; and by none were they more firmly opposed than by St. Bernard, who saw to what fatal results the unrestrained culture of human reason, under the guidance of a pagan master, must necessarily lead. We shall see further on how jealously the Church continued to regard the study of Aristotle, and in what way she sought to check the evils flowing from it to the schools, up to the time when his philosophy was finally adapted to the service of the faith by the labours of St. Thomas.

In the midst of his studies, his tutorships, and his passages of arms with the Cornificians, twelve years slipped away, at the end of which time John of Salisbury found himself possessed of a vast fund of erudition[166] and an empty purse. The latter circumstance was not one which greatly disquieted him, for his theory was that the keys which opened the door of philosophy were not of gold, but consisted of poverty, humility, silence, and a quiet life, together with that detachment from family and worldly ties which is best found in a foreign land.[167] So little had he of the spirit of worldly ambition, that when in 1148 Peter des Celles, abbot of Moutier des Celles, offered him a chaplaincy in his monastery, he gladly accepted a post, which, however humble, gave him at least the leisure and the means to study. He remained in this retreat for the space of three years. Peter des Celles was one of the most remarkable men of his time, and has made himself best known by his epistles; for, like most of the literary personages of the twelfth century, he was a great letter writer. He had received his education in the monastic school of St. Martin des Champs, and does not seem to have been one whit behind the more fashionable students of Paris. "I had," he writes, "an insatiable appetite for learning; my eyes were never tired of beholding books, or my ears of listening to them; yet with all my ardour, God was always the beginning, centre, and end of all my studies. They had but Him for their object, though indeed I studied everything, even law, without prejudice, however, to the duties of my state, attendance on the Divine Office, and my accustomed prayers." This worthy inheritor of the genuine monastic spirit acted the part of a true father to our English scholar, who at last, through the favour of St. Bernard, obtained the post of secretary to Theobald, Archbishop of Canterbury, in whose household he renewed his acquaintance with two of his former fellow-students, Peter de Blois, and Thomas à Becket. Peter de Blois had been one of his pupils; a man of versatile talent, who had studied first at Tours, then at Paris, and lastly at Bologna, and had seen something of half the courts of Europe. He was equally skilled in law, medicine, and theology, but it is by his epistles that he is chiefly known, and his ready and somewhat gossiping pen has left us graphic sketches of the manners and customs of his time. He was, in fact, the Horace Walpole of the twelfth century, curious, fluent, and volatile. Henry II. made him archdeacon, first of Bath, and then of London, and often employed him as secretary, so that he had excellent opportunities for studying the court of our first Plantagenet sovereign, which he describes in a sufficiently amusing manner. He assures us that Henry's court, from the conversation of learned men and the discussion of questions, was a daily school. The king, he says, is deeply versed in literature, and has more gifts of mind and body than he can so much as enumerate; nevertheless, he lets out the ugly fact that it is best not to go too near him when he is out of humour, as he is then more of a lion than a lamb, and is quite as likely as not to tear out your eyes. How any man of letters can ever attach himself to a court life is more than he can understand; and how any man, lettered or unlettered, could be brought to endure the daily miseries he describes, such as the eating of "mouldy bread and stale fish, wine that can only be drunk with the eyes shut, lodgings for which pigs would be ashamed to quarrel," and days spent "without order, plan, or moderation of any kind," must seem equally incomprehensible to his readers. But he has something more cheering to say of the household of Archbishop Theobald. It is crowded with learned men, who spend their time between prayers and dinner in lecturing, disputing, and examining causes. All the knotty questions of the kingdom are referred to them, and discussed in the common hall; and there is no sort of jealousy or contention, but the youngest present is listened to with courtesy and attention. In these letters Peter de Blois has a good deal to say On the subject of education. He tells us that in his youth he was trained, not in idle fables, but solid literature, and names Livy, Quintius Curtius, Tacitus, Suetonius, and Josephus among the books then most commonly used in schools. He regards the new scholasticism with undisguised contempt: it is good, he says, neither at home nor abroad, neither in the church, the cloister, the camp, the court, or the bar. In fact, in his literary tastes he showed himself a worthy disciple of John of Salisbury.

Meanwhile the latter attached himself to the rising fortunes of St. Thomas, and dedicated to him, when chancellor, his two great works, the *Polycraticon* and the *Metalogicon*, the last of which is a formal apology for humane letters, and is considered to display an amount of learning and literary elegance far exceeding anything which had been produced since the days of Boëthius. When St. Thomas became primate, his friend continued to retain the office he had held under his predecessor, and never spared the archbishop the benefit of his frank and fearless advice. Among other things, he took on him to give him some directions with regard to his studies which are worth quoting, as showing the view taken at that time by spiritual men, of the danger resulting from an excessive application to law and logic. "My counsel is," he says, "that you put off some of your other occupations, in order to give your whole mind to prayer. Laws and canons are all very well, but believe me, they nourish curiosity more than devotion.... Who ever rose from the study of law with a sentiment of compunction in his heart? Nay, I will say more, the exercises of the schools often increase knowledge till a man is puffed up with it, but they rarely inflame devotion. I would far rather that you meditated on the Psalms or read the 'Morals of St. Gregory,' than that you were learned in philosophy, after the fashion of the scholastics." St. Thomas was not slow in taking his friend's advice, and both at Canterbury and Pontigny often spent whole nights in the study of the Scriptures, and was wont always to carry a few pages in the loose sleeve of his tunic, that he might have them at hand whenever he found a leisure moment for reading.

We need not pursue further the history of John of Salisbury. The fidelity with which he adhered to the cause of St. Thomas exposed him to no small loss and personal danger, and after the martyrdom of the saint he had to fly from England, and taking refuge in France, became Bishop of Chartres in 1176, his election being entirely due to his personal merits, and the honour with which the French clergy regarded one who had been the companion of the Blessed Martyr. But before concluding our notice of the Parisian masters, it remains for us to name the three Peters, as they are called, who all illustrated the schools about the same period. The first was Peter Comestor, or the

Eater—so called from his habit of devouring books—a very famous personage in his day, who became chancellor of Paris in 1164, but resigned all his dignities to put on the habit of the canons of St. Victor's. His *Historia Scholastica*, or Epitome of Sacred History, was so much esteemed in the twelfth century, that portions of it were read in the churches. A namesake of his, called Peter the Chanter, was almost of equal fame. He too, after filling the eye of the public for several years, withdrew from their applause, and became a simple religious in the Abbey of Long-Pont, where he died in 1197.

Both were men of tried virtue, and showed themselves hostile to the sophists of the day, whose wranglings they declared to be opposed to the simplicity of the Gospel. But more renowned than either was the Italian scholar, Peter Lombard, the Master of the Sentences, as he was called, and the real Father and founder of scholastic theology. He commenced his study of civil law at Bologna, and thence passed on to Paris, where he was admitted among the canons of St. Victor's, and afterwards taught for some years in the cathedral school. In 1159 he became bishop of Paris, through the influence of his royal pupil, prince Philip, brother to the reigning king, Louis the Young. The king offered the bishopric to his brother, who was educated for the ecclesiastical state, but he nobly refused it in favour of his master. Peter Lombard's great work was the celebrated Book of Sentences, consisting of a number of passages selected from the works of the fathers, and commented on in such a manner as to present the student with a body of theological doctrines systematically arranged. The convenience of finding every point of theology treated of in a precise and methodical order, and within the compass of a single volume, was speedily recognised, and the Book of the Sentences soon became the favourite text-book used in the schools, both for the lectures of the masters and the private study of their disciples. Hence the title of *Sententiarus*, which came to be applied to those who taught or studied the Sentences. Notwithstanding the immense popularity obtained by this work, it is said to contain several important omissions, and even some theological errors, one of which was formerly condemned by Pope Alexander III. Its importance is derived from the circumstance of its being the first attempt to reduce theology to a compact and orderly scientific system; and from this period we date the real rise of the science of scholastic theology.

It will have been observed that in what has been said up to this time of the schools of Paris, they have not been designated by the title of a university. For, in fact, as yet these schools had no claim to be regarded as a corporate body; they were accidents rather than an institution, and it was only gradually that they acquired a corporate character, and became possessed of a government, a head, and a body of laws and privileges. This change was effected by no sudden act of royal or ecclesiastical legislation; it developed itself insensibly but of the very necessity of the case. The immense number of masters and pupils who flocked to the capital, gave rise to disorders, which obliged the superiors of the different schools to unite together and agree to certain rules of common discipline.

Thus in 1195 we find a certain John, abbot of St. Albans, associated to the "body of elect masters." Some years before, in the very thick of the quarrel between Henry II. and St. Thomas, occurs the first notice of that division of the scholars into *nations* or provinces, which formed one of the peculiarities of the university. Henry offered to choose as arbiters either the peers of France, the French clergy, or the heads of the different *provinces* in the school of Paris. We find also certain laws, or at least established customs having the force of laws, respecting the method to be observed in granting licenses for the opening of a school. It was the rule in all dioceses that no one could open a school without permission from the cathedral scholasticus, or chancellor of the diocese, who was bound to grant such licenses to all who were capable. Pope Alexander III., who showed a lively interest in everything that concerned the encouragement of education, ordered that such licenses should be granted gratuitously, but he afterwards permitted the Chancellor of Paris, who was at that time Peter Comestor, to exact a certain fine. It appears, also, that in Paris the chancellor or scholasticus of St. Geneviève shared this right with the chancellor of Notre Dame. There were also other laws, such as those which prohibited religious from teaching or studying in the schools of law or medicine. The two faculties, as they were called, of arts and theology, which formed the basis of the university, appear to have been already distinguished. Certain privileges, too, were already enjoyed by the students. They were beginning to claim the right of being tried only by the ecclesiastical tribunals, and this right was granted to them in 1194 by a decree of Celestine III. Alexander III. permitted clerics to retain their benefices whilst teaching or studying at Paris. Finally, in the year 1200, we find the existence of the university as a corporate body, governed by a head, acknowledged in the diploma of Philip Augustus, wherein, having confirmed the exemption of the scholars from the secular courts, he decreed that the head of the studies should, in particular, be incapable of arrest or punishment from the secular judge, and obliged every provost of the city on his entrance into office to swear to the observance of this decree.

From this time, therefore, we may properly date the formal recognition of the university of Paris, and passing over the obscurities in which its earlier commencements are involved, shall proceed to present our readers with a sketch of that institution as it existed in the palmy days of the thirteenth century.

CHAPTER XIII.

PARIS AND THE FOREIGN UNIVERSITIES.

A.D. 1150 TO 1250.

THE modern visitor to Paris who finds his way to that portion of the city lying on the southern bank of the river, which still bears the name of the *Quartier de l'Université*, sees himself surrounded by buildings, many of which bear unmistakably the character of their original destination. He stands, in fact, amid the *débris* of the old university of Paris, the schools and colleges of which were clustered for the most part about the Mont St. Geneviève, and occupied an entire suburb, which was first enclosed within the city walls by Philip Augustus. That monarch, passionately desirous to increase the splendour of his capital, and at the same time to afford larger space for the accommodation of the crowds of students, whose numbers are said to have exceeded those of the citizens themselves, added a large district, which in the year 1200 presented a fair expanse of fields and vineyards, interspersed with churches, houses, and farms, but in which you would vainly have sought for any of those magnificent and semi-monastic structures which we are accustomed to associate with the idea of a university. Colleges, in fact, had as yet no existence at Paris, and the university consisted of an assemblage, not of stately buildings, but of masters and scholars gathered out of every European land.

It is no easy matter to convey an idea of the enthusiasm with which the Paris schools were regarded at the beginning of the thirteenth century. No one, whatever might be his country, could pretend to any consideration who had not studied there in his youth; if you met a priest or doctor, whose skill in letters you desired to praise, it was enough to say, "one would think he had passed his whole life in Paris." It was, to use the expression of Gregory IX., the *Cariath-sepher*, or city of letters,[168] which drew to itself the intellectual wealth of Christendom. "Whatever a nation has that is most precious," writes William of Brittany, the chaplain of Philip Augustus, in his poem of the *Philipide*, "whatever a people has most famous, all the treasures of science and all the riches of the earth; lessons of wisdom, the glory of letters, nobility of thought, refinement of manners, all this is to be found in Paris." Others declared, in yet more pompous language, that neither Egypt nor Athens could be compared to the modern capital, which was, they said, the very fountain-head of wisdom, the tree of life in the midst of the terrestrial paradise, the torch of the house of the Lord. The exile who had once tasted of its delights no longer regretted his banishment from his own land; and, in truth, the beauty of the city, its light elastic atmosphere, the grace and gaiety of its inhabitants, and the society of all that was most choice in wit and learning, rendered it no less fascinating a residence in the thirteenth century as the capital of learning than it has since become as the metropolis of fashion.

To these attractions were added the advantages which the Parisian students enjoyed in virtue of their privileges. I have already spoken of the diploma granted by Philip Augustus, and its provisions were greatly enlarged by subsequent monarchs. Philip le Bel ordered that the goods of students should never be seized for debt, and they were also exempt from taxes. If a French scholar travelled, all farmers were obliged to supply him with horses at a reasonable rate of hire. Artisans were not allowed to annoy him with unpleasant odours or noises, and on complaint being made of such nuisances, they had to remove themselves out of his neighbourhood. The rights of citizenship were likewise enjoyed by the members of all the French universities, and in those days this involved many important exemptions. Scholarship was, in short, regarded as an honourable profession, something which almost conferred on its possessor a patent of nobility; the new master of arts had lighted flambeaux carried before him in the public streets, and the conferring of a doctor's degree was an event which caused as much stir as the dubbing of a knight. Nay, in those days, so permeated with the romantic spirit of chivalry, scholars were not unfrequently spoken of as "the knights of science," and the disputation at which some youthful aspirant contended for the doctor's cap was regarded as the intellectual tournament.

Yet, there was another side to this brilliant picture, and one plainly discerned by those whose calmer judgment would not suffer itself to be deceived as to the perils which awaited so many young and ardent minds, exposed without restraint or guidance to the manifold temptations, both moral and intellectual, that awaited them in that busy throng. "O Paris!" exclaims Peter of the Cells, in a letter to one of his monks who had been sent thither to study, "resort of every vice, source of every disorder, thou dart of hell; how dost thou pierce the heart of the unwary!" John, the young monk whom he addresses, had, it would seem, deplored the new scenes amid which he found himself as painfully out of harmony with his monastic training. "Who but yourself," replies the abbot, "would not reckon this Paris to be a very Eden, a land of first-fruits and flowers? Yet you have spoken truly, though in jest, for the place which is richest in bodily pleasures miserably enslaves the soul. So, at least, thinks my John, and rightly therefore does he call it a place of exile. May you always so esteem it, and hasten home to your true country, where in the book of life you will find, not figures and elements, but Divinity and Truth itself. O happy school of Christ! where He teaches our heart with the word of power, where the book is not purchased nor the Master paid. There life avails more than learning, and simplicity than science. There none are refuted save those who are for ever rejected; and one word of final judgment, *Ite* or *Venite*, decides all questions and all cavils for ever. Would that men would apply themselves to these studies rather than to so many vain discourses; they would find more abundant fruit and more availing honour."

In these words we see the distrust with which the representatives of the old learning regarded the rising university system, contrasting as it did so strangely with the claustral discipline in which they had themselves been reared. Nor can it be denied that the fair outside of the great city concealed a monstrous mass of deformity. James de Vitry, who had himself been a student, gives a frightful picture of the vices which were fostered in a society drawn from every rank and every country, and associated together without moral discipline of any kind, at an age when the passions were least subject to restraint. The very sense of moral rectitude, he says, seems to have been lost. A profuse extravagance was encouraged by the example of the more wealthy students, and those who lived frugally, or practised piety, were ridiculed as misers and hypocrites. There was at that time no provision for the accommodation of the students in halls or hospices; they lodged in the houses of the citizens wherever they could secure the cheapest entertainment. Not unfrequently the very schools of the masters were held in the upper story of some house, the groundfloor of which was the resort of the most abandoned characters.[169] There was no common table; but the students dined at taverns where they often associated with the worst companions, and indulged in the lowest excesses, and the jealousy between "town and gown" continually broke out in disgraceful quarrels, terminating not unfrequently in bloodshed. As most of those engaged in these affrays were clerics, and as the striking of a cleric brought on the guilty party the sentence of excommunication, the results of these disorders were exceedingly grave. It became necessary to grant extraordinary powers to the university officers, and to prohibit the scholars from bearing arms, a prohibition grounded on the atrocious crimes with which they stood charged; and which at one time threatened to bring about the total extinction of the university. For the magistrates having proceeded to revenge a certain riot which had arisen out of a tavern quarrel, by ill-judged acts of severity, both masters and scholars resolved to abandon the city; nor did they return till the wise and timely interference of Pope Gregory IX. brought about a reconciliation between the civil and academic authorities.

The university, in fact, presented the spectacle, at that time new in Christendom, of a system of education which aimed at informing the intellect without disciplining the soul. Its work was done in the lecture room, where alone the master exercised any authority, and the only tie existing between him and his disciples was the salary paid by one party and received by the other. In addition to the dangers incident to this state of uncontrolled liberty, were the more subtle temptations to pride and presumption which beset a man in the schools. Mere youths were sometimes seen promoted to the professor's chair, and seeking to win a passing popularity by the promulgation of some new extravagance, an abuse which led to the passing of an ordinance forbidding any one to teach Theology before he had attained the age of twenty-five. But the teaching of the professors was influenced by other peculiarities in their position. "The university doctors," says Fleury, "were doctors, and they were nothing more. Exclusively engaged with theoretic views, they had leisure to write at great length on the most frivolous questions; and plentiful occasions were thus ministered of quarrel and dispute." And he proceeds to notice the contrast between such a system and that of earlier ages, when the teachers of the Church were for the most part bishops, engaged in the duties of their pastoral charge, and able to support their doctrines with the weight of practical experience. The character of the new professors is drawn severely enough in the curious poem of Architrenius,[170] which was written towards the close of the twelfth century by John de Hauteville, an English monk of St. Albans. Architrenius, the hero, is supposed to travel through the world, trying various states and conditions, and finding vanity and emptiness in all of them; at last he comes to Paris, and devotes a whole book to describing the vanity of the masters, and the miseries of their disciples. He depicts the negligent and squalid appearance of the poor scholars, their ragged dress, uncombed hair, bad lodging and hard beds. After spending half the night in study, he says, they are roused at daybreak and forced to hurry to the school, where the master treats them rudely, and where they have to endure the mortification of seeing others of less merit rewarded, and themselves passed over with neglect. He goes on to describe the hill of presumption which he peoples with doctors and scholastics, gifted with far less learning than conceit, and concludes, that the schools are as full of vanity and disappointment as the rest of the world.

The sufferings of the poor scholars, which Architrenius so graphically describes, were destined, however, to bring about a most beneficial change in the university system, by being the chief occasion of the foundation of hospices and colleges, the multiplication of which, and their organisation under regular discipline, in time applied a remedy to the worst of the existing evils. From a very early date, the relief and support of poor scholars had been recognised as a meritorious work of charity; it formed one of the favourite devotions of the two kings, Robert the Pious and Lewis the Young, the former of whom attempted something in the shape of a hospital to receive them. How miserable their condition was, we may gather from the benefaction of the good knight Jocius de Londonne, who, returning from the Holy Land in 1171, found some poor scholars miserably lodged in the Hôtel-Dieu, and gave money to provide them with beds, and a small monthly alms, on condition of their carrying the Cross and Holy-water at the funeral of those who died in the hospital, and repeating the Penitential Psalms for the repose of their souls. The earliest establishment actually made for their reception appears to have been the Hospice of St. Thomas of Canterbury, founded in the twelfth century by Robert Dreux. It embraced a number of other charitable works, and was administered by canons who were under religious vows, the scholars being governed by a provost of their own. Other colleges gradually arose, some for scholars of particular nations, as those of the Danes and Swedes; others for separate dioceses. One of the earliest foundations was the College of Constantinople, founded by Baldwin of Flanders, shortly after the taking of Constantinople by the Latins, for the education of young Greeks in the orthodox faith. Chapels were opened in connection with these colleges so early as 1248, in which year we find Pope Innocent IV. granting permission for such a chapel to be attached to the college *des Bons Enfants*. But the collegiate system became more thoroughly established by the influence of the Religious Orders, who very soon found themselves obliged to open religious houses in connection with the university, for the education of their own students. These houses of studies afforded the young religious the regular discipline of the old monastic schools, combined with the advantages of university education; and their example made it a necessity to provide similar protection for the secular students.

The Trinitarian Order, founded by one of the most illustrious of the Parisian doctors, and largely recruited from the ranks of his co-professors, was naturally the first to associate itself to the university, out of whose bosom it had sprung; and so early as the year 1209, we find the friars in possession of the Church of St. Maturin, which was ordinarily used by the university as their place of assembly. Next to them came the Dominicans and Franciscans, the former of whom owed their establishment in Paris to the good will of the university authorities, who made over to them certain claims they possessed on the Hospital of St. James, which had been granted to the new comers by the good doctor, John of St. Quentin. A little later, the College of the Bernardines was founded by Stephen of Lexington, an Englishman who had been a pupil of St. Edmund, and who in 1242 became abbot of Clairvaux. Strictly contemplative as was the rule of the Cistercians, it did not exclude the cultivation of sacred studies. It aimed rather at restoring monastic life to the ancient Benedictine type, in which, as we have seen, the homely labours of husbandry were mingled with those of the scriptorium. The Cistercians, whilst they laboured to bring back religious poverty and simplicity into the cloister, always showed themselves hearty encouragers of learning. St. Stephen Harding had himself set on foot that great copy of the Bible, long preserved at Citeaux, which was corrected with the utmost precision after being collated with a vast number of manuscripts, several learned Jews being consulted by the abbot on the Hebrew text. To procure a correct version of the Gregorian Antiphonary, he sent all the way to Metz, trusting to obtain a sight of the copy laid up there by Charlemagne. The library at Citeaux was rich in the works of the Fathers, though the outside of the books exhibited nothing of that costly ornament on which the skill of monastic binders and jewellers was elsewhere expended. The early Cistercians were connected very closely with some of the best Paris scholars, such as William of Champeaux, the friend of St. Stephen, and after his elevation to the episcopate, the diocesan of St Bernard. In England their ranks had been largely recruited from the University of Oxford, and their monastery of Rievaux was famous at home and abroad for its school of learning. Stephen of Lexington was not, therefore, departing from the traditions of his order in considering that the maintenance of sacred studies was a necessity of the times. Two years after his election he obtained permission from Pope Innocent IV. to begin the erection of a college at Paris for the young monks of his order; but the proposal was very unfavourably received by the other Benedictine houses who saw in it the break-up of the old monastic system of studies. The conservative spirit which was roused among them is discernible in the complaints of Matthew Paris, who laments over the contempt with which a proud world is beginning to regard the old Benedictine monks. "This new institution of colleges," he says, "is not, that we can see, derived from the rule of St. Benedict; on the contrary, we read that *he* quitted the schools to retire into the desert."

Stephen, however, persevered in his design; he was aware that the contempt with which the monks were so frequently treated, both by the secular doctors and the new orders of friars, was grounded on the charge of their illiteracy, and he therefore believed it essential to provide his monks with better means of education than, under the altered state of things, they were now able to command in their claustral schools. His design was crowned with perfect success. Not only did the College of the Bernardines become illustrious for its good scholarship, but the conduct of its religious shed a good odour of edification over the whole university, and ten years after its foundation, Matthew Paris himself bore honourable witness to the holy example of the monks, which, he said, "gave pleasure to God and man." For Stephen there was reserved the reward of disgrace and humiliation. The Chapter-General of Citeaux deposed him from his office in 1255, instigated, says Matthew Paris, by envy for the superior merits of an Englishman. Whatever were the cause of his disgrace, it gave him an opportunity of proving that his adoption of what had seemed an innovation on established customs, sprang out of no defect in the religious spirit. He refused to accept of the protection offered him by the Pope, in favour of which he might have been reinstated in his dignity, and preferred spending the rest of his days as a private religious, entirely occupied with his own sanctification.

The example of the Bernardines was quickly followed by other religious orders. The Carmelites took up their station at the foot of Mt. St. Geneviève, the Augustinians in the Quartier Montmartre. The old Benedictines, or Black Monks, had their college near the abbey of St. Germain, and the Carthusians received from St. Louis a grant of the royal Chateau de Vauverd. The monks of the latter order were indeed prohibited by their rule from attending in the schools, but the object of their establishment so near the capital is expressly stated to have been, that they might profit by the salutary streams of doctrine which flowed forth from the city of letters. To these must be added the monks of Cluny and Marmoutier, the former of whom provided their students with lecturers within their own cloisters; and a new Institute originally founded by four doctors of theology, who in 1201 gave up their academic honours and pursuits, and, smitten with that desire of poverty and obscurity which not unfrequently overtakes men in the very zenith of their popularity and success, retired to a wild valley in the diocese of Langres, and assumed the religious habit of the Canons Regular of St. Victor. Here they were soon joined by other professors and scholars, till their numbers rendered it impossible for them to find subsistence in the desolate wildness they had chosen, exposed to the fury of the mountain torrents, and the falling of precipitous rocks. They, therefore, removed in 1224 to a more fertile valley, which obtained the name of the Val d'Ecoliers, a title afterwards bestowed on the new order itself. Five years later they opened a house of studies in Paris, and the Church of St. Catherine was built for them at the charge of a certain knight, in fulfilment of a vow he had taken at the battle of Bouvines, the young St. Louis laying the first stone with his own hand.

The bishops were not slow to follow the example set them by the monastics; and indeed they, more than others, felt the necessity of providing in some way or other for the training of their clerks. It was vain to think of competing with the university in the cathedral schools; and, on the other hand, what was to be hoped from a secular clergy, formed in no higher school of discipline than that which James of Vitry has described? Colleges, therefore, where the young clerics might be reared in ecclesiastical habits, were, strictly speaking, essential; and, accordingly, we find them established for the clergy of different dioceses, as those of Laon, Narbonne, and Bayeux. In these the scholars lived in common, celebrated the Divine Office, had appointed hours of study and recreation, and were governed and watched over by regents. In fact, says Fleury, "they were so many little seminaries;" differing in many respects, and doubtless, far inferior to those old ecclesiastical schools which had been established in the bishop's house, wherein the young clerks grew up under the eye, and were trained by the lips of their chief pastor; yet still schools of discipline, the good results of which were so apparent that, erelong, every country which followed the Latin rite adopted the system which had begun in France and Italy. The most famous of all the secular colleges was that of the Sorbonne, the founder of which, Robert of Sorbonne, was chaplain to St. Louis. Crevier calls it the greatest ornament of the university, and from very humble beginnings it came at last to be regarded as the first theological school in the Christian world. In it were afterwards founded no fewer than seven Chairs of Theology; namely, those of the Reader, of Contemplative, and Positive Theology, of the Holy Scriptures, of Casuistry, of Controversial Divinity, and of the Interpretation of the Hebrew Text.

Gradually, but surely, the university freed itself from the chaotic disorder of its first beginnings, and assumed the form of a great institution, governed by regular laws and invested with vast powers and privileges. At the period of its complete development, it was composed of seven companies; namely, the Faculties of Theology, Law, and Medicine, and the four nations of France, Picardy, Normandy, and England. These four nations together formed the Faculty of Arts, but each had a separate vote in the affairs of the university. The Rector was chosen by the nations out of the Faculty of Arts, the other faculties being governed by their deans.

An immense benefit was conferred on the University by Innocent III., who had himself studied at Paris at a time when the want of discipline was most severely felt. He was the first to supply his Alma Mater with a body of academic statutes; which were promulgated in 1215 by his legate, Robert de Courçon, an Englishman by birth, and a man of piety and learning. They embraced the whole discipline of the schools, regulating the conditions on which everyone was to be admitted to teach, the books that were to be read and those that were prohibited. No one was to profess arts before the age of twenty-one, or without having previously studied for six years under some approved master. He must bear a good reputation, and before commencing his lectures, was to undergo an examination according to certain rules. The books he was to read were to be the "Dialectics" and "Topics" of Aristotle, Priscian, and certain others, the authors of which are not named, but which seem to have been well-known popular treatises on philosophy, rhetoric, grammar, and mathematics. The physics and metaphysics of Aristotle were forbidden, together with the writings of certain heretics, such as Amauri de Bene, who had drawn their errors from the teaching of the Greek Philosopher.[171]

To teach Theology, the statutes required that a man should be at least thirty-five years of age, and that he should have studied under some approved master. We see here the germ of the system of graduation, which was perfected before the close of the century. The rule, as then established, was for a bachelor to begin by explaining the Sentences in the school of some doctor for the space of a year. At the end of that time he was presented to the Chancellor of the Cathedral of Paris, and if, on examination, he was judged worthy, he received a license and became licentiate, until he was received as doctor, when he opened a school of his own, in which he explained the Sentences for another year. At the end of that time he was allowed to receive some bachelor under him. The whole doctor's course lasted three years; nor could any one take a degree unless he had taught according to these regulations. It was supposed that before beginning his theological studies the doctor must have passed through his course of arts, the various stages in which were distinguished by the names of grammar, poetry, philosophy, &c., in each of which, according to the theory of the ancient schools, a student had to study successively for an appointed time. The plan was excellent, says Fleury, had its execution been possible; but life was too short to allow of a man's perfecting himself in every known branch of learning before entering on his theological studies. It implied that his whole life was to be spent in the schools; and, indeed, no inconsiderable portion of it was so spent, as we have seen in the case of John of Salisbury, whose academical career spread itself over the space of twelve years. But, in estimating the exact value of these statements, we must bear in mind that the university course at this time began at a very early age, and included those more elementary studies which occupy a schoolboy of our day for several years before his matriculation.

The statutes of Paris University, first promulgated by Innocent III., and enlarged under subsequent pontiffs, not only regulated all matters of study and discipline, but provided for the preservation of that religious element which must always find a place in any system of education sanctioned by the Church. The Christian schools, as we have seen, found their cradle in the monastic and episcopal seminaries, in which, as a matter of course, religious exercises were intermingled with intellectual ones, to a very large degree. The Catholic universities, in their complete form, adapted this system to their own needs, and required of their students daily attendance, not only in the lecture rooms, but also in the church or the collegiate chapel. The weekly "chapels" exacted from our Oxford and Cambridge students are fragments of the old rules, which, at Paris as in the English universities, required daily attendance at Mass and Vespers, and, at certain times also, at the Office of the Dead; and appointed public processions at different seasons of the year, and days when the public studies were suspended in order to give more time for the due celebration of feasts, and preparation for the reception of the Sacraments. If any reader be disposed to think that these demands on the time of the students must have proved an interruption to their studies, the fact is at once, and readily, admitted. But it may be suggested whether, in this interruption, there does not manifest itself a grand principle on which the Church acts wherever there is question of the exercise of the human intelligence. The problem she had to resolve was, not how to convey the greatest possible amount of knowledge with the greatest possible saving of time; but rather, how to provide that a certain amount of intellectual labour should be gone through in such a way as not to interfere injuriously with the spiritual well-being of the soul. In cases where the intellect is brought into exercise and stimulated to extraordinary activity, there is danger lest what is in itself a wholesome and necessary exercise may become vitiated by a certain natural impetuosity, which disposes a man to pour himself out into the occupation in which he is engaged; an impetuosity which opens the door to the human spirit, and which brings in along with it a host of bad company, such as pride, envy, ambition, contention, and the like. If this be allowed, study, instead of being an instrument of our sanctification, degenerates into its enemy; and hence the object aimed at in the Catholic system has ever been to supply checks and safeguards to nature, and to sanctify intellectual labour by a large admixture of prayer. Among the monastic students the regular duties of religious life supplied these necessary checks, the "*retinacula*," as they were called by Bede, who fully understood their value and importance; and the Catholic universities, to a certain degree, imitated the monastic system, by requiring fixed religious duties to be complied with by their students, as a part of their academic course. Nor need we suppose that these interruptions, so salutary in a spiritual sense, were at all injurious in an intellectual point of view. The discipline of the Church, by a beautiful harmony, provides for the well-being of our nature, at the very time that she mortifies it. Her rules of fasting and abstinence, when observed, often prove the best preservatives of health; and, in the same way, her checks on study were not always hindrances. The truest economy of time does not, obviously, consist in cramming the twelve hours of the day with excessive work, but in laying them out to the best advantage. It is possible to tax the mental powers beyond their strength, in which case nature revenges herself on those who violate her laws, and the mind itself weakens under the pressure of excessive labour. Could we compare the *horarium* of an Oxford or Paris student of the thirteenth century, with that of a modern Rugby schoolboy, and obtain an accurate statistical table, showing the proportion of exhausted brains to be found among an equal number of either class, it might appear that the Church legislated even for the mental well-being of her children when she interposed so often between them and their studies, by requiring of them the fulfilment of solemn offices at stated times.

Of course, besides the principle above alluded to, there was the more manifest object of religious training, touching which I will merely quote the words of a former Rector of the Paris University, who wrote in anything but a religious age. "Religion," says M. Rollin, in his treatise on "Education," "should be the object of all our instructions; though not perpetually in our mouths, it should always be in our minds. Whoever examines the ancient statutes of the university which relate to masters and scholars, and takes notice of the prayers, solemnities, public processions, festivals, and days set apart for preparing for the Sacraments, may easily discover that the intention of their pious Mother is to consecrate and sanctify the studies of youth by religion, and that she would not carry them so long in her bosom were it not with the view of regenerating them to Jesus Christ. It is with this design that she requires that in every class, besides their other exercises of piety, the scholars should daily repeat certain sentences from Holy Scripture, and especially from the Gospels, that their other studies may be, as it were, seasoned with salt." And he quotes passages from the ancient statutes, requiring that "the Divine Word be mingled with the eloquence of the pagans, as is fitting in Christian schools where Christ, the One Teacher of man, should not only be present, but preside."

The very slight mention made in the statutes of Robert de Courçon of Rhetoric, as included in the course of arts, is the last which we shall meet with for a considerable space of time. The Bull of Gregory IX., published in 1231, and the statutes of the Regents of Arts, which appeared in 1254, make no reference to this study. The arts are there represented by philosophy alone, and there is no allusion to the cultivation of rhetoric, or the reading of the classical authors, which from this date became very generally neglected. As a natural consequence, grammar also lamentably decayed. It was, of course, not absolutely banished, inasmuch as a certain amount of it was essential for the pursuit of any studies at all; but it became altogether barbarised and debased. Those rules of syntax and prosody, over which the old monastic masters had so lovingly lingered, were totally neglected, and although Latin poems were still produced, their Latinity was full of false quantities and grammatical solecisms. The tenth century, with all its darkness, knew far more of humane letters than the thirteenth; nor was the superiority of the earlier schools confined to a knowledge of the classics. The exaggerated prominence given to philosophy, or rather to dialectics, had caused a neglect of the Fathers, who were now chiefly studied in Sums and Sentences, which professed to present the student with the pith of theology in a single volume, forming the text-books on which the doctors delivered lectures and commentaries, coloured, naturally enough, with their own ideas. The original works of the Fathers, which had been the familiar study of the monastic students, appear at this time to have been little in request; and when St. Louis, on his return from Palestine, formed a plan for collecting a library of all the most useful and authentic ecclesiastical writings, he had to get copies made of St. Ambrose, St. Augustine, St. Jerome, St. Gregory, and other Catholic doctors, from the codices stored up in remote monastic libraries; for in the schools of Paris they were not to be found. The extreme scholastics, indeed, were accustomed to speak of the Fathers as *rhetoricians*; writers, that is, who expressed themselves according to the rules of natural eloquence, a terrible delinquency in the eyes of the new *illuminati*, who considered that a man should display his science by loading his pages with the terms of logic—assertion, proof, major, minor, and corollary. The good king, however, whose taste was superior to that of most of his contemporaries, persevered in his noble enterprise, and at great pains and cost collected a library of the best Christian authors, in which he himself studied profoundly; liberally granting its use to others also. "He read the works of the Fathers, whose authority is established," says his biographer, "more willingly than those of the new doctors;" and he gave as a reason for making new copies, in preference to buying up the old ones, that by this means he multiplied writings which he desired should be more widely known. He ordered that after his death this library should be divided among the three monasteries he had founded; those, namely, of the Franciscans, the Dominicans, and the Cistercians; and it was from this source that the Dominican, Vincent of Beauvais, who filled the office of tutor to the royal children, drew the materials of his famous work, *The Great Mirror*, of which we shall hereafter have occasion to speak.

If positive theology and the humanities began to be neglected, however, civil and canon law were better treated. The appearance in 1157 of the "Decretals" of Gratian, had been followed by the erection of a Chair of Jurisprudence at Bologna, and another at Paris. The new branch of study had one advantage which commended it to popular favour: it led to substantial profits, and scholars were found not unwilling to let Horace and Cicero drop into disuse in favour of a science which paid so well for the time spent on its acquisition. The prodigious popularity of these new pursuits at length caused grave apprehensions lest the schools of arts and theology should in time be altogether deserted, and in 1220 Honorius III. found it necessary to forbid the further study of civil law at Paris. Crevier complains of this prohibition as injurious to the university, and it was, in fact, very generally eluded; although the formal permission to include civil law in the Faculty of Right was not granted till 1679. But in point of fact, the alarm which was felt was not without foundation. At Oxford such a revolution had been brought about by the introduction of the law lectures, that it was feared both arts and theology would be utterly neglected. What was worse, the law students aspired after and obtained benefices; and this abuse was encouraged by sovereigns, who found law prelates much more easy to deal with, and to accommodate to their own political views, than theologians. Innocent III. had, at last, to prohibit the admission to benefices of those who had only graduated in law, and insisted that all who aspired to ecclesiastical benefices should also pursue a regular course of theology. The tendency of the age, however, was manifest; the universities were falling more and more away from that idea of education which the old system had, in theory at any rate, professed to carry out; namely, the presenting of knowledge as a whole, its various parts arranged under the heads of the seven liberal arts, presided over by theology. Philosophy, according to this idea, included a knowledge of truth in all its various departments, and all the arts were but branches springing from one trunk, one of which could not be struck off without injuring the proportion and harmony of the whole.

The neglect of arts, and the excessive preponderance given to law studies and dialectics, made up a grave and momentous change in the whole theory of education, which was daily losing something more of that breadth and largeness which formed one of the chief features of education as proposed by the ancients, whose traditions had been accepted by the Christian schools. This seems a fair statement of the mischievous side of the change; but there is also another view of the question, which justly claims to be recognised. There was a deeper cause for the popularity of law and logic in the European schools of this period than any sordid motive of gain, or any mere love of disputation. Both of them formed a part of that extraordinary intellectual revolution which marked the opening of the thirteenth century. Men had grown indifferent to the study of language in proportion as they had been aroused to the deeper interest of mental science. Though the immediate result was to introduce a decay of polite letters, and not a few philosophic extravagancies, it cannot be doubted that many faculties were roused into vigorous action, which, under the former system, had lain dormant. The grand defect of the old monastic scholars, as scholars, was, that they cultivated learning rather than mind; they studied other men's thoughts, but were not equally exercised in training their own. They seldom investigated for themselves either mental or physical phenomena; whatever absurdities were to be found in the natural philosophy which they received from the ancients, were generally adopted without question, and handed on to the next generation; and the instances are rare in which an appeal is made to the results of personal observation.

Even their theological works were chiefly compilations, and St. Anselm may be called the first original thinker who had appeared among divines since the close of the fifth century. When the intellectual powers of Europe again woke into action, men were not unnaturally induced to regard mere elegances of style with a certain rude indifference. Like soldiers who, when about to engage in a conflict for life or death, are careless whether or no they wear their holiday trappings, the scholastics of the thirteenth century, while they exercised their mental powers in subtle disputation, conceived a contempt for the charms of mere rhetoric, and valued language only as the vehicle for expressing the distinctions of philosophy. Under such circumstances Latinity, of course, grew barbarous; and many far graver disorders arose out of the daring and undue exercise of reason. Yet, real intellectual progress was being made, in spite of the decay of letters; and the growth of mind went on in the same way as the growth of body, when the delicate tints and graceful form of childhood disappear, whilst bone and muscle are being built up, and the feeble child is expanding into the strong-armed man. When the revival of literature took place two centuries later, it found a race of strong thinkers in place of diligent readers. The scholars of the Renaissance were forward in ridiculing the barbarism of the scholastic philosophers, but in doing so they showed that they had very superficially studied the intellectual era that preceded their own. Undoubtedly, the *excess* of legal and logical studies had many abuses, but they are not therefore to be arbitrarily condemned. Even the lawyers, with whom it is most difficult to keep charity, and whose influence was the most mischievous in the schools, had a considerable share in the education of modern Europe. Careful critics, on studying the legal documents of the Middle Ages, such, for example, as our own Magna Charta, fail not to express their wonder and admiration at the keenness of intellect which is displayed in their provisions, and the precision of language in which they are expressed. The men of the pen were cautiously and sagaciously circumventing the men of the sword. Every constitutional principle laid down in the statute-book established the sovereignty of law over that of brute force; it was a victory of mind over matter, and was therefore a mighty step in the history of intellectual progress.

These considerations must be calmly weighed before we pass any judgment on the scholastic revolution of the thirteenth century. Our sympathies, no doubt, will linger with the elder scholars, and we shall be disposed to look with a very jealous eye on the triumph of the sophists and the Cornificians; but it will suffice to reconcile us to the temporary necessity of the change, that it was accepted by the Church, and that she set her seal to the due and legitimate use of those studies which were to develope the human intellect to its full-grown strength. Nay, more, she absorbed into herself an intellectual movement which, had she opposed it, would have been directed against her authority, and so, to a great extent, neutralised its powers of mischief. The scholastic philosophy, which, without her direction, would have expanded into an infidel Rationalism, was woven into her theology itself, and made to do duty in her defence, and that wondrous spectacle was exhibited, so common in the history of the Church, when the dark and threatening thunder cloud which seemed about to send out its lightning bolts, only distils in fertilising rain.[172]

The statutes of Robert de Courçon, after regulating the studies, pass on to the manners of the students. They descend with great simplicity into various details, which are not uninteresting, as furnishing us with some idea of the usages of the times. Great banquets were forbidden to be held at the installation of new masters, who were only allowed to invite a few companions and friends. No master reading arts was to wear aught but a round black gown falling as low as his heels, "at least," adds the cardinal with much naïveté, "*when it is new.*" A cloak is allowed, but the abomination of pointed shoes is strictly prohibited. When a scholar of arts or theology died, one-half of the masters were to attend his funeral; if it were a master, all the other masters were to assist at the Office for the Dead. They were, moreover, to recite, or cause to be recited, an entire Psalter for his soul, to remain in the church where the Office was celebrated until midnight, and on the day of burial all exercises in the schools were to be suspended. He confirms to the students the free possession of those broad and delightful meadows, so dearly prized as a place of recreation, which gave their name to St. Germain des Prés, and for the protection of the scholars, fixes the rate at which the citizens shall be obliged to furnish them with lodgings.

The university thus established, redounded, it need not be said, to the profit as well as to the glory of the French capital. Not only the intellect, but the wealth also, of Europe flowed into that great centre. New branches of industry sprang up in connection with the schools; the Rue de Fouarre supplied them with straw for their seats, and the Rue des Ecrivains was entirely peopled with booksellers and book-lenders, mostly Jews, who furnished the scholars with literary wares, suffering those who were too poor to buy, to hire their volumes at a fixed rate. The bookselling trade fell at last under the jurisdiction of the university, and the booksellers were enrolled as academic officers, taking an oath on their appointment to observe the statutes and regulations. They were not suffered to open a traffic without testimonials as to character, and the tariff of prices was fixed by four of their number appointed by the university. Fines were imposed for incorrect copies, and the traders were bound to hang up a priced catalogue in their shops. If books of heretical or immoral tendency were found introduced, they were burnt by order of the university officers. The same powers were exercised over the book trade by the universities of Vienna, Toulouse, and Bologna, and the name of *Stationarii* began to be given to those who held these stores; stalls, or shops of all descriptions, being often denominated *Stations*. By degrees, however, the licensed *Stationarii* lost their monopoly of the trade, and the custom became tolerated of allowing poor scholars to sell books of low price in order to obtain the means of pursuing their studies. The *Librarii* were the copyists of new books, who dealt also in parchment and writing materials, and exercised a very important profession before the days of printing; those who transcribed old books were considered a separate branch, and styled *Antiquarii*, and by this distinction the scholar in search of a volume knew at once from which *Statio* he might obtain the object of his desires.

But as in those days of high prices and book scarcity, the poor student was sorely impeded in his progress, to provide against these disadvantages, a law was framed at Paris, compelling all public booksellers to keep books to lend out on hire. The reader will be surprised at the idea of lending libraries in the

Middle Ages, but there can be no doubt of the fact that they were established at Paris, Toulouse, Vienna, and Bologna. These public librarians, too, were obliged to write out regular catalogues of their books, and hang them up in their shops with the prices affixed, so that the student might know beforehand what he had to pay for reading each book. Some of these lists are preserved, in which we find three sous charged for the loan of Peter Lombard's Book of the Sentences, and ten sous for a Bible.

The custom began to be introduced among the scholars of expending great sums on the adornment of their books with gilt letters and fantastic illuminations, and writers of the time complain of the extravagant sums thus dissipated. Thus Odofred speaks of a certain gentleman who sent his son to Paris, giving him an annual allowance of 100 livres. "What does he do? Why, he has his books ornamented with gold initials and strange monsters, and has a new pair of boots every Saturday." The mention of these literary trades leads me to speak of what we may call the great festival day of the trades in general, and of the scholars and booksellers in particular. Who has not heard of the great fair of St. Denis, the *Landit*, as it was called, originally held to enable the Bishop of Paris to display the relics preserved in the abbey to those devout multitudes whose numbers, being too great for any church to contain them, rendered it necessary to assemble them in the open fields? A French poet describes this fair as he beheld it at the close of the twelfth century, crowded with tailors, furriers, linendrapers, leather-sellers, shoemakers, cutlers, corn-merchants, jewellers, and goldsmiths. The enumeration of all the trades at last passes his powers, and he begs his readers to excuse his completing the catalogue. And what has this to do with the university? it may be asked. Much, for thither also flocked the sellers of parchment. The rector of the university went there in state to choose the best article which the fair produced; nay, what is more, all dealers in parchment were forbidden by royal edict to purchase any on the first day of the fair, until the merchants of the king and the bishop, and the masters and scholars of the university, had laid in their yearly provision. This going of the rector to the *Landit* was the grand annual holiday. He was attended by all the masters and scholars on horseback, and not unfrequently, says Lebœuf, in his "History of the Diocese of Paris," this expedition was the occasion of many falling sick, through heat and fatigue, especially the youngsters.

The *Landit* was not the only recreation day of the scholars; besides those red-letter days which in olden time were lavishly provided for solace and refreshment of mind and body, they took part in all popular rejoicings, and on occasion of the great victory of Bouvines claimed and obtained a whole week's vacation, during which time, says Lebœuf, "they sang and danced continually." Their country walks to Chantilly and other rural villages were known as the *Ire ad Campos*, for which leave had to be asked by the inmates of colleges. James of Vitry alludes to the national characteristics apparent in the different nations represented among the students, the luxurious habits of the French, the love of fighting exhibited by the Germans, and the propensity of the English to indulge in deep potations. In the schools their habits were simple enough. The lectures were begun punctually at the first stroke of the bells of Notre Dame, as they rung out the hour of Prime. Clocks were not then very common, and the cathedral bells, rung at the different hours and heard at a great distance, furnished citizens and scholars with their ordinary mode of reckoning time. At the last stroke the scholars were supposed to be all assembled; seated on trusses of hay or straw, which supplied the place of benches, they listened to the lecture of the master, delivered after the manner of a spoken harangue, and took such notes as they were able. The method of dictation, which had been in use in the earlier schools, appears to have been dropped, or to have been retained only in the more elementary schools. The *vivâ voce* lecture was, in fact, the speciality of the university system; and to its use may, in great part, be attributed that enthusiasm which animated the scholars of some popular master, who contrived to infuse the charm of his personal grace and eloquence into the hard syllogisms with which he dealt. "The act of instruction *vivâ voce*," says one, himself a master, "has I know not what hidden energy, and sounds more forcibly in the ears of a disciple, when it passes from the master's lips, than the written word can do." Hence these dry logicians of the Middle Ages were possessed with as ardent an enthusiasm for their own pursuits as that which kindled the armies of the Crusaders; nay, when we read of the mad devotion of Abelard's followers, or the resistless impetuosity of those crowds who mustered in the Place Maubert to listen to the great Albert as he lectured on the Sentences, we need to bear in mind that the age was that of generous impulse; keenly susceptible to personal influence, capable of being roused to great enterprises by some strong word spoken to the heart, and ready to cast itself on the shores of Palestine, or to swell the ranks of a mendicant order, according to the deep emotions called forth by some eloquent tongue.

The history of the university, indeed, is not without its chapters of romance. At one time we may wander in imagination out into the green meadows of St. Germains, and watch a group of young scholars, John, the Englishman, and William Scot, with another John, of Provençal blood, and his Italian fellow-student, the young Lothairius Conti, as they join together in familiar talk, little thinking of the changes which a few short years are to make in the destinies of each; when the Provençal will have become the founder of the Trinitarian Order, and his old companions, John and William, shall have flung away their doctors' caps, to assume the blue and crimson cross, and it shall be from Lothaire himself, now seated in the chair of St. Peter as Pope Innocent III., that he is to receive its first formal confirmation.

Or, shall we gaze for a moment on that poor ragged boy, begging his bread in the streets of Paris, where like a rustic simpleton, he has come in hopes of finding the way to fame and fortune? Yet, a simpleton he is not;—he struggles on ill fed, ill-lodged, but, thanks to pious alms, just able to scrape together the means of study. He passes from one grade to another; and in time Paris learns to be proud of her great doctor, Maurice of Sully, and forgets that he owes his surname to the lordly territory where his fathers cultivated the soil. At last his fame reaches his native place, and his old mother who is still living, resolves to go and find out her boy, whom she always knew would make his fortune. So taking staff in hand, she found her way to the great city, and asked the first fine ladies whom she met in the streets, if they could tell her where she could find the Doctor Maurice. The good ladies, taking pity on her, took her to their house, gave her refreshment, and throwing a better kind of mantle over the coarse woollen petticoat which she wore, after the fashion of French peasants, led her to Maurice, and introduced her to him as his mother. "Not so," said Maurice, "my mother is a poor peasant woman, she wears no fine clothes like these; I will not believe it is her unless I see her in her woollen petticoat." Then she threw off her cloak, and seeing her in her own garb he embraced her, and introduced her to the great people who stood about him, saying, "This is indeed my mother." "And the thing spread through the city," says the chronicler, "and did good honour to the master, who afterwards became Bishop of Paris;" in which office he did many notable things, and among others built the present Cathedral of Notre Dame.[173]

I might ask my readers, in like manner, to glance at other scenes, no less characteristic; to look into that same cathedral where crowds have assembled to hear the preaching of the famous doctor, John of St. Quentin. He has chosen the subject of holy poverty, and he seems inspired by some unwonted strain of eloquence as he speaks of the snares, the emptiness, and the vanity of the world. At last he stops, and descends the pulpit stairs. Is his discourse finished, or what is he about to do? the crowd moves hither and thither with curiosity, and sees him kneeling at the feet of the Dominican Prior of St. James, of whose Order little was then known, save that its members were mendicants, and owed their lodging in the city to the bounty of this very John. But now the white habit is thrown over his doctor's gown, the black mantle, the garb of poverty and humility is added, and he returns to finish his discourse, exhibiting to his wondering audience that he can teach not by words only, but by example. Or, once more let us wander into that old church of St. Mery, which even to this day retains a certain air of quaint antiquity; where the long lancet windows, and the Ladye chapel with its carved wooden reredos, black with age, and adorned with silver statuettes, and its walls frescoed with the figures of saints, carry us back to mediæval times; and the cool air with its sweet fragrance of incense, and the silence broken only by a passing footstep on the worn and broken pavement, soothe and tranquillise us as though we had passed out of the busy streets into the atmosphere of another world. In that church, and before that Ladye altar, you might nightly have seen an English scholar, who had passed over to Paris whilst still a mere boy to study his course of arts. Every night he comes hither to assist at Matins, and remains there till daybreak, kneeling absorbed in heavenly contemplation till the hour strikes which is the signal for him to betake himself to the schools. Against those very pillars, perhaps, he leant his weary head; that dusty and shattered pavement was once watered with his tears; and who is there that loves and venerates the memory of St. Edmund of Canterbury, who will not, for his sake, be glad to escape from the thoroughfares of the brilliant capital to spend an hour of pilgrimage in the church of St. Mery?[174]

Pictures such as these, embodying the legends of an age, the daily life of which was fraught with poetry, might be multiplied to any extent; but I prefer to fix the reader's attention on one which tells more of the university life of Paris at this precise epoch, than could be conveyed by many a laboured description. It was then about the year 1199, just when the princes of Europe were deliberating on a fifth crusade, that there lived at Neuilly-sur-Marne, halfway between Paris and Lagny, a simple country Curé, named Fulk, unlearned in worldly and even in divine science, but full of holy zeal, governing his parish with all diligence, and preaching with a certain rude eloquence—not sparing of his reproofs, but ready at all times to speak the truth boldly and freely alike to rich and poor. He who, of old, chose unlettered fishermen to be the heralds of His Word, made choice of this poor priest to reform the follies of those vain scholars who, to use the words of James of Vitry, "intent on vain wranglings and questions of words, cared not to break the Bread of Life to little ones." Feeling his own want of knowledge, and specially his ignorance of the Holy Scriptures, Fulk determined, old as he was, to commence a regular course of study in the schools, and began to go regularly into the city, attending the theological lectures of Peter the Chanter. How the gay scholars stared and wondered at the sight of the rustic Curé, in his coarse frock and grey hairs, humbly entering the school, with his note-book in his hand, wherein he entered only a few phrases, such as his poor capacity was able to gather from the lips of the speaker. He understood little and cared less for all the terms of art which the dialecticians of those days so lavishly dispensed to their hearers; and if his companions had glanced over his shoulder, they would have read on the parchment page nothing but some scattered texts of Scripture, sprinkled here and there with trite and practical maxims. Yet these were enough for Fulk: they were the seed falling into good ground, watered with prayer and meditation, and bringing forth the hundredfold. Often did he read and ponder over his little book, and commit its maxims to his memory, and on Sundays and Festival days, returning to his own parish, he gave forth to his flock what he had thus carefully gathered in the schools. His master, observing the zeal and fervour of his new disciple, and penetrating through that rough exterior which concealed a richly-gifted soul, required of him at last that he should preach in the Church of St. Severinus before himself and a great number of the students. Fulk obeyed with his accustomed simplicity, and lo! "the Lord gave to His servant such grace and power that it seemed as if the Holy Spirit spoke by his mouth; and from that day masters and scholars began to flock to his rude and simple preaching. They would invite one another, saying, 'Come and hear the priest Fulk—he is another Paul.'"

One day a vast multitude were assembled to hear him in the Place de Champeaux, for the churches were not large enough to contain those who gathered to the preaching; and he spoke with such eloquence that hundreds, pierced to the very heart, fell at his feet, and, presenting him with rods, besought him to chastise them for their sins, and guide them in the way of penance. He embraced them all, giving thanks to God, and to each one he gave some suitable words of advice. He had something appropriate to say to all, to usurers and public sinners, fine gentlemen, men-at-arms, and scholars. He admonished the masters to give more pithy, wholesome, and profitable lectures in the fear of God; he bade the dialecticians put away what was unprofitable in their art, and retain only that which bore fruit; the canonists he reproved for their long and wearisome disquisitions; the theologians for their tediousness and over-subtlety; and so, in like manner, he fearlessly rebuked and admonished the teachers of other arts, and called on them to leave their vain babblings, and apply themselves to what was profitable to salvation.

The tide had now fairly turned, and those who, awhile before, were ready to turn the poor Curé into ridicule, gladly changed places with him, and brought their note-books to *his* preaching, that they might take down the words from his mouth. Many even entreated him to accept them as his followers, and missions began to be preached through all the neighbouring towns and villages by the company of learned doctors, who put themselves under the direction of the Curé of Neuilly. Among these were Peter the Chanter, his former master; Alberic de Laon, afterwards Archbishop of Rheims; Robert de Courçon, of whom we have already spoken; and our own Stephen Langton.

Fulk and his followers preached throughout France, Burgundy, Flanders, and a great part of Germany. Their missions were followed by a great reform of manners, and the sanctity of Fulk is said to have been attested by miracles. He had a vein of pleasantry in him, and sometimes treated his audience with a somewhat rough familiarity; and, if he could obtain silence by no other means, would freely use his stick over the shoulders of the disorderly. But the people esteemed his very blows a blessing; wherever he appeared, they pressed around him to tear away morsels of his habit. One day he was nearly suffocated, and owed his deliverance to an ingenious device—"My habit is not blessed," he cried, "to what purpose, then, would you carry it away? But I will bless the clothes of yonder man, and you may take as much as you choose." The individual whom he indicated was at once surrounded, and thought himself happy to escape with the loss of his mantle.

These scenes were of daily occurrence when Fulk, having himself assumed the Cross, began to preach the Holy War; and, in fact, the throngs who joined the Fifth Crusade from France and Flanders were chiefly induced to do so by his eloquence. He chanced, on one occasion, to hear that Count Thibault of Champagne had proclaimed a magnificent tournament, which was to take place at the Château d'Ecris, in the forest of Ardennes. All the chivalry of France and England were gathered there; but amid the tossing plumes and glittering pennons appeared the figure of Fulk of Neuilly, who bade them first hear him, and painted to them the higher glory which they might acquire in the sacred wars, instead of wasting their time and strength on the mock combats of a tournament. A fiery ardour kindled the brilliant throng, and Thibault himself, with his noble guest, Simon de Montfort, and the two brothers, Walter and John de Brienne, the latter of whom was destined to wear the crown of Jerusalem, and five of the house of Joinville, and that heroic knight, Sir Matthew de Montmorency, whose valour was so renowned that Richard of England reckoned it his greatest deed of prowess to have overcome him in single combat:—all these, and many more, hastened to receive the Cross from the hands of the preacher, and to prepare for that expedition which was to terminate with the Conquest, not of Jerusalem, but of Constantinople.

It is not my intention, however, to speak further of the crusading career of Fulk de Neuilly, and I have only introduced him here as an illustration of the spirit which then animated all classes, whether knights or doctors, easily swayed as they were to good or evil by the words of a powerful leader; and to show, moreover, in what light the subtle dialectics of the Paris schools were regarded by the Apostle of his times.

We must now turn our attention to some of the other European universities, and first to that of Bologna, the *Mater Studiorum*, as it was called, of Italy, which vied with Paris in point of antiquity as in renown. The revival of the study of Roman jurisprudence, which took place in this city under Irnerius, has already been noticed; when a chair of civil law was first erected in the High School, which had existed in Bologna from very early times. It is unnecessary to enter into the vexed question of the so-called discovery of the Pandects[175] at Amalfi in 1137, which, according to Sigonius, was the origin of a total change in the Italian jurisprudence. Tiraboschi calls the whole story in question, and represents that the Pandects had really never been lost, and that the revival of law studies must be traced to the efforts made about that time by the Italian cities to free themselves from the Imperial yoke, and appoint their own judges and magistrates. However that may be, the fame of Bologna as the first law school in Europe was fairly established by the end of the twelfth century, and there is not an Italian writer of that period who has not something to say of the science of *docta Bononia*. By the middle of the same century the study of canon law had been added to that of civil jurisprudence, chiefly, as has been before said, after the publication of the Decretals of Gratian. This prodigious work, executed by a simple Benedictine monk of Chiusi, was a summary of the decrees of the Popes, and of 150 councils, with selections from various royal codes, and extracts from the Fathers and other ecclesiastical writers, all methodically arranged so as to facilitate its use in the schools. Its compilation incessantly occupied the author for the space of twenty-five years. Many errors found their way into the work, which contained some false quotations, and cited as authorities certain decrees and synodical acts which have since been proved to be spurious, and are known as the False Decretals. But whatever were its shortcomings, it gave a facility to the study of canon law which had not before existed, and the two branches of jurisprudence were immediately professed side by side in the schools of Bologna. Almost at the same time the students obtained some important privileges, which encouraged foreigners to resort to a university where they were secure of protection from the civil power. In 1158, when the Emperor Frederick Barbarossa held his great diet on the plains of Roncaglia, for the purpose of publishing a code of laws which should secure his own power in Italy, four professors were summoned from Bologna to assist in the deliberations. He treated them with much distinction, and with good reason, as they fully supported the Imperial claims. They did, however, better service to their university by obtaining from the emperor those celebrated ordinances known as the *Habita*, which, though originally promulgated in favour of Bologna, came to be recognised as establishing similar rights in other European universities. In them he extends his protection in a special manner to the masters and scholars. "It is our duty to protect all our subjects," he says, "but specially those whose science enlightens the world, and who teach our people the obligation of obeying God and us, the ministers of His Divine power. Who will not have compassion," he continues, "on those precious exiles, whom the love of learning has banished from their own countries, who have exposed themselves to a thousand dangers, and, far from their friends and families, live here without defence, in poverty and peril?" He therefore directs that all foreign students shall have safe-conduct both for themselves and their messengers, both for coming, going, and reading at the university, and that if anything be taken from them, the magistrates of the city shall be bound to restore it fourfold. Moreover, he exempts them from the ordinary civil jurisdiction, and grants the right of being judged by the master of the school to which they belong, or by the bishop.

The grant of these privileges at once raised the Bolognese university to a position which ranked it on a level with that of Paris, and whilst a tide of scholars from beyond the Alps, as well as from the other Italian cities, flowed in, eager to take advantage of these imperial favours, the Roman pontiffs began to extend their protection to the rising institute. The first of these was Alexander III., who had a particular interest in the university, having taught theology there for some years before his elevation to the purple.

Among the more famous Bolognese scholars were St. Thomas of Canterbury; Lotharius Conti, afterwards Pope Innocent III., both of whom read canon law here after finishing their theology at Paris; Vacarius, afterwards law professor at Oxford; and the troubadour chronicler, Geoffrey de Vinesauf, who, though an Englishman by birth, seems to have been rather ashamed of the barbarism of his mother country, and declares that to go from England to Rome was like going from darkness to light, and passing from earth into heaven.

He was the author of the *Ars Poetica*, and of another learned work entitled *Ars Dictaminis*, written for the use of his Bolognese pupils; but he is chiefly remembered as the companion and historian of Richard Cœur de Lion, in the Second Crusade.

Before the end of the twelfth century, Bologna numbered 10,000 students, and in the following generation the influence exercised in the schools by the Dominican Order, which made its headquarters in Bologna, still further extended its fame. At this time, besides the law lecturers, there were professors of moral and natural philosophy; but it is somewhat singular that this flourishing university does not appear to have had any regular chair of theology before 1362, in which year a Bull for the erection of the theological faculty was issued by Innocent VI. But we are not to suppose that the study of theology was therefore neglected, for the want was supplied by the schools attached to the monastic houses, specially the monasteries of St. Felix and St. Proculus, and those of the two orders of Friars. It was in one of these schools that Rolando Bandinelli, afterwards Pope Alexander III., must have taught, as he professed theology at Bologna at the same time that Gratian taught canon law, when certainly no other theological schools existed in the university. Nor was this state of things peculiar to Bologna. In Padua likewise, the students appear to have been for some time dependent on the monastic schools for the means of following their theological studies; so that in 1280 we find the Abbot Engelbert, after completing his course of philosophy in the university, removing to the convent of the Friar Preachers to study theology. Afterwards, when the Emperor Frederic II. drove the Friars out of his dominions, the university had recourse to the Benedictines of Monte Cassino, who sent thither the monk Erasmus to open a theological school. We also find honourable mention in this century of a certain Florentine physician named Taddeo, a professor of the university, of whom the Bolognese were so proud that they granted his scholars the privilege of law students. The common physician's fee at this time was a load of hay for his horse; but Taddeo, if summoned to a distance, demanded fifty gold scudi, and a safe-conduct out and home. This is one of the earliest instances on record in which medicine takes its place among the other learned faculties. The pay of all these professors seems to have been extremely small, and never exceeding the sum of 200 *lire*, about £40.

The university of Padua appears to have owed its erection to a quarrel among the Bolognese professors, some of whom migrated in a body, about the year 1222, and opened schools which soon attracted the notice of the learned. The new university was specially distinguished by its excellent school of arts; these, as we have seen, were sinking into neglect at Paris; but under the genial sky of Italy, and in a country where Latin was still so completely regarded as the native and living tongue, that as yet no one had thought of using the vernacular Italian for literary purposes, it was impossible that the names of Cicero and Virgil should be suffered to drop into oblivion. Hence we find that the scholars of Padua *il Dotto* cultivated a taste for the profane poets and the great writers of antiquity; and it has been observed that Albert the Great, who studied in her schools for at least ten years, was so imbued with the classic literature, that his very sermons often present us with a tissue of philosophic maxims, drawn from the writings of Virgil, Juvenal, and Cicero, the latter of whom he styles affectionately *noster Tullius*. A love of the classics, in fact, survived in most of the Italian schools, and Hasse tells us that the Mantuans went so far as to give their capital the title of the "Virgilian city," in honour of the great bard, whose statue they erected in their market-place, and on the 15th of October (which was supposed to be his birthday) danced around it, crowned with laurel, and singing verses in his praise.

Tiraboschi observes that in none of these universities does there appear to have been erected anything like a library for the use of the students. Copyists seem to have been employed to furnish them with books, at a given price, and in Bologna, women were employed on this work, a fact to which P. Sarti ungallantly attributes the frequent errors found in many MSS. of the time. The rich collections of books which had formerly been found in the cathedral and monastic libraries, had been for the most part dispersed during the wars which had ravaged Italy for so many centuries, and the scanty catalogues which are preserved, generally present us with no more than the names of a few books on canon or civil law.

In addition to the Italian universities already named, must be noticed that of Naples, which owed its foundation, in 1224, to the Emperor Frederic II. That monarch, irritated at the opposition which he met with from the citizens of Bologna, who warmly embraced the cause of the Popes, and refused to receive the emperor within their walls, conceived, in revenge, the plan of ruining the university of the refractory city, by establishing a rival institution in his own Sicilian states. For this purpose he chose the city of Naples, and used every effort to attract scholars, by the grant of extraordinary privileges; and masters, by the promise of rare pecuniary advantages. As regarded his own subjects he did not allow much liberty of choice, but absolutely forbade them, under penalties, to study either at Bologna or Paris, or anywhere but at the Imperial academy. No cost was spared to put it on an equal footing with the institutions with which it was to compete; an immense sum was expended in the collection of Latin, Greek, Arabic, and Hebrew books, many of those in the last three tongues being translated at the royal expense. The works of Aristotle are said to have been translated into Latin by the famous Michael Scott, who at that time filled the office of astrologer to the emperor. The professor of philosophy was the almost equally celebrated Peter the Irishman, grammar and rhetoric being taught by another Peter, an Italian by birth. In short, ample provision was made for the intellectual profit of the students, but further than this little could be expected from a founder of Frederic's character.

Touron, in his life of St. Thomas, has given us a frightful picture of the state of morals prevailing in the Ghibbeline university, and says that there was a common proverb at that time current in Italy, to the effect that Naples was an earthly paradise inhabited by demons. Frederic was indeed a splendid patron of learning, and is said to have been well skilled in the German, French, Latin, Greek, and Arabic tongues. His book on birds is praised by Humboldt,[176] as displaying a knowledge of natural history which at that time was truly extraordinary. He was also reckoned, like all the princes of his house, to be a good poet, and a somewhat freethinking philosopher. Much of his literary and scientific tastes he owed to the influence of his celebrated chancellor, Peter delle Vigne, who had studied at Bologna, and was considered one of the most learned men of his time. But his learning was steeped in the infidelity peculiar to the age; and common belief attributed to him and to his Imperial master the authorship of a blasphemous work, entitled "The Three Impostors," though the truth of this is warmly disputed. Suspected of treachery by the emperor, Peter delle Vigne was at last deprived of his eyes, and imprisoned in a monastery, where, in 1245, he miserably put an end to his own life by dashing out his brains against a wall.[177]

So much has been said by historians of the protection afforded to letters by Frederic and his successors on the throne of Sicily, that we might almost be led to suppose that the Ghibbeline monarchs had none to share their fame in this respect. But in point of fact the Popes in this, as in all times, were the true nursing fathers of Christian science. To Innocent III., himself one of the most learned men of his age, the university of Paris was indebted for that body of laws of which we have already spoken; he also granted large privileges to the university of Bologna, and it was he who ordained in the Fourth Lateran Council that provision should be made for the maintenance of Christian studies, by the appointment in every cathedral church of a master in grammar for the instruction of the younger clerics, as well as of a theologian. His successor, Honorius III., directed the chapters to send certain of the younger canons to study at the universities, and granted them a dispensation from the obligation of residence; and we are told he once removed a bishop on finding him grossly ignorant of grammar. Benedict XII. confirmed the decrees of his predecessors, and required not only cathedrals, but also monasteries and priories, to provide a master to instruct the younger monks in grammar, logic and philosophy.

Gregory IX. who, according to Muratori, was profoundly skilled in the liberal arts, and whom he calls "a river of Tullian eloquence," drew up five books of decretals, and was so firm a friend to the university of Paris, that, to use the expression of Crevier "it had no other support during the troubles with which it was vexed in the thirteenth century, than in this Pope." Innocent IV. erected public schools of law at Rome, and founded the university of Piacenza, besides which, as Crevier acknowledges, he surpassed all his predecessors in the benefits which he heaped on the university of Paris, and the singular protection he afforded it. Such was the zeal of this pontiff in promoting learning, that wherever he was, he established in his palace a little university. Thus, being at Lyons in the second year of his pontificate, he opened a *studium generale* at his court for the study of theology and canon law; and did the same at Naples, where he died; and at the Council of Lyons in 1245, he enforced the decrees of previous pontiffs regarding the establishment of cathedral grammar schools for the gratuitous education of poor children.

It was Gregory X. who, among the other acts of his glorious pontificate, moved the King of Sicily to restore the schools which had fallen into decay in his dominions. His letter is printed in the collection of Martene. God, he says, has willed that man fallen into barbarism should be taught and civilised by the culture of the arts and sciences. It is study which confers on man the grace of a cultivated education, as a heavenly gift; and the king who uses his power to continue a generation of wise and learned men, and to provide the Church with worthy ministers, performs an act most honourable and pleasing to God.

To Urban IV. belongs the glory of having revived the study of philosophy in Italy. He is known to have commanded St. Thomas to comment on the works of Aristotle; and so great was his love of this branch of learning, that he always had at his table certain professors whom he would afterwards cause to sit at his feet and engage in erudite disputations among themselves, he himself presiding over their trial of wits, and deciding to whom the victory was due. It was to his noble encouragement that the world owed the mathematical works of Campano of Novara, whom he appointed his chaplain, and who wrote a learned commentary on Euclid. In one of the mathematical treatises of this philosopher, is to be found a dedication to Urban, in which he eulogises the magnificent support afforded by that pontiff to philosophical studies, which, owing to his encouragement, after having long languished in the dust, were once more loved and cultivated. The university of Montpellier was founded by Nicholas IV., and that of Cracow by Urban V.

We also find that, besides the universities, a vast number of public schools were opened in Italy during the twelfth and thirteenth centuries, most of them by authority of the Sovereign Pontiffs; those founded in Rome by Innocent IV. were at first exclusively intended for the study of law, but in 1303 Boniface VIII. erected these schools into a university for every faculty. Other schools of grammar, medicine, and law arose at Modena, Reggio and Parma, and at Milan there were no fewer than eighty schoolmasters instructing youth in the year 1288. The college of the Sapienza, at Perugia, was founded by Innocent IV. out of his private purse, for the education of forty boys, as the Gregorian college was raised somewhat later at Bologna by Pope Gregory XI. And of Urban V. we read that he supported more than a thousand scholars at different academies at his own expense, and supplied them with the books necessary for prosecuting their studies.

Enough has, perhaps, been said to show that the Roman Pontiffs of this period were not altogether indifferent to the interests of learning. Owing partly to their encouragement, and partly to the excessive popularity then attaching to the study of law, the number of universities continued, during the thirteenth and fourteenth centuries, to multiply in a manner which makes it difficult to conjecture how students could have been found to people so many academies. Thus, in France alone, we find the universities of Toulouse,[178] Montpellier, Orleans, Lyons, Avignon, Poictiers, Angers, Bourdeaux, Bourges, Cahors, Nantes, Rheims, Caen, Valence, and Grenoble; in Italy, there were those of Ravenna, Salerno, Arezzo, Ferrara, Perugia, Piacenza, Siena, Treviso, Vercelli, Pavia, and Vicenza; in Spain, the two great universities of Salamanca, and Valladolid, besides twenty-four smaller ones; in Poland, of Cracow; in Germany, of Vienna, Prague, Heidelberg, Cologne, and Erfurt, besides others of rather later date. Sixty-six such institutions altogether are reckoned as having been founded in various European countries before the period of the Reformation. The numbers of students who repaired to these academies was certainly very great. At Bologna, in the thirteenth century, we find mention of ten thousand scholars; at Paris, of forty thousand; at Bourdeaux, a single college boasted of upwards of two thousand scholars; and Oxford, in Henry III.'s time, is said to have contained thirty thousand. These universities had each their own distinctive character— Paris excelled in theology, Montpellier and Salerno in medicine, Pavia in the arts, Bologna, Bourges, and Orleans in jurisprudence. Caen, an English foundation was particularly favoured by the monastic students, and a great number of abbeys had here their own colleges, the abbots being accustomed to assemble and assist at the yearly opening of the schools. Of the English universities we will speak more at length in another chapter, but it remains for us to say a few words here on the general character and tendency of all these institutions, and of the revolution which their establishment brought about in the system of education.

To form something like an accurate judgment on this matter, we must glance back at some of the facts elicited in the foregoing pages. From what has been already said, it will appear that the germ of all Christian schools is to be found in the episcopal seminaries—those seminaries which, in ancient times, formed a part of the bishop's own household, and in which he himself personally directed the studies of his younger clergy, and trained them to the duties of the ecclesiastical state. The cathedral or canonical schools were but the expansion of these early seminaries, over which the bishop still presided, the office of scholasticus being conferred on one of the canons, though, as we have seen, masters were often invited to direct the studies from other dioceses. The monastic schools were formed on the model of these episcopal schools, the abbot doing for his own monks what the bishop did for the clergy of his diocese. The constitution of all these schools was most strictly ecclesiastical, and though seculars were admitted to share in their advantages, they were primarily intended for the education of the clergy. The strong religious character that must have been impressed on the education given in such academies was perfectly in harmony with the spirit of the early ages, when, as Balmez remarks, the intellectual development of Europe had a distinctly theological bias. Religion in those days was the preponderating element, it ruled the family and the state, as well as the individual: and in days when the laws were drawn up in the spirit and the language of ecclesiastical canons, there was nothing at all out of place in the sons of knights and nobles being set to study church chant, the Psalter, and the Fathers. That their studies were by no means *exclusively* theological has, I think, been amply shown; nevertheless, it is undeniable that, in the ecclesiastical schools, the liberal arts were chiefly cultivated in their relation to the things of faith, and that every branch of learning was more or less tinged with the theological element.

It was not to be expected that such a state of things could continue without large modification. Nations, like individuals, pursue an inevitable course of mental development, and the time necessarily came when the human mind, growing from childhood into maturity, demanded a wider and freer expansion. Hence ensued that remarkable change observable at the opening of the eleventh century, when the European intellect seemed to be passing out of a long winter into a sudden spring, and burst into a vigorous activity, accompanied, naturally enough, by many excesses. Schools and teachers were indefinitely multiplied; the office of teaching was no longer confined to ecclesiastics, and, falling into the hands of lay professors, unavoidably assumed a new character. But it is remarkable that the main principles of the former system still remained in force. Education was recognised to be a religious work, and one which, as such, fell under the jurisdiction of the bishop. As chief pastor in his own diocese, he was supreme in all things appertaining to the spiritual interests of his flock, and the office of teaching was acknowledged to be one that fell under his pastoral charge.[179] The new scholastics, therefore, were not entirely exempted from episcopal jurisdiction; and in the eleventh century we find the system generally established, according to which the *scholasticus* of the cathedral, or bishop's school, exercised a certain control over all the schools in the diocese, no professor being suffered to open any private school without a license from him.[180] I do not know whether we can affirm that there were episcopal inspectors, but there were certainly certificated masters in the days of St. Anselm. The office of cathedral *scholasticus* belonged properly to the archdeacon of the diocese, who might appoint a substitute to direct the school, but with whom the power of granting licenses always remained. In many churches it was also identical with the office of chancellor.[181]

And here one observation irresistibly presents itself. How striking a contrast does not this system offer to that which finds favour in our own times! Here we see it formally and distinctly recognised that the office of teacher was one of those that fell directly under episcopal supervision. The bishop of the diocese exercised jurisdiction over schools, as he did over churches, in virtue of his pastoral office, and his license was the necessary certificate of moral and intellectual fitness. But, according to the principles accepted by most countries which rejoice in a National system of education, the authority formerly exercised by the bishop is transferred to a Board. We make over to a minister of public instruction, or a committee of privy council, or some other secular organ of an unspiritual state, what our fathers regarded as an integral portion of the pastoral office, an incongruity which, little as it now startles us, is, we may say without exaggeration, scarcely less opposed to the

Christian order than if the crown should assume the power of granting faculties to preach. What wonder that the result of such a change should be the gradual, but most sure, unchristianising of the popular mind, and that infidelity has found no more efficient allies than the multitudinous and plausible codes of state education which have sprung up since the destruction of the ancient system!

That the control thus recognised as belonging to the bishop through his officers was not merely nominal is quite clear. In 1132, we find Stephen de Senlis, Bishop of Paris, through his chancellor, interdicting a certain professor, named Galon, from continuing to teach. Galon persisted, in defiance of the bishop; and, his pupils deserting his school through fear of incurring ecclesiastical censures, he was at last put to silence. However, he appealed to the Pope, and this, says Crevier, "is the first occasion in which the authority of the Court of Rome appears as interfering in the affairs of the university." He adds that it was also the beginning of those disputes which the university of Paris maintained for long years against the bishop and chancellor of Notre Dame, arising out of the claims of the latter to exercise jurisdiction over the schools, and the vigorous resistance of the academic authorities. It is clear that the episcopal rights were never totally and completely revoked; nevertheless, they were reduced to a *minimum*, and the universities, to all practical purposes, established their independence. And the change thus introduced was the more portentous from the fact that, with the rise of the universities, we date the disappearance of the episcopal seminaries. "The institution of seminaries," says Theiner, "disappeared throughout Christendom after the twelfth century." The universities became the great seats of learning, human and divine, and though the cathedral schools continued to exist, their students passed from them at an early age to finish their education in theology and canon law in Paris, Oxford, and Bologna; whilst, in many cases, the cathedral schools themselves were absorbed in the new universities of which they formed the nucleus. The bishops, unable to stem the tide, were forced to yield to it, and to witness the education of their clergy passing out of their own control into the hands of newly-constituted bodies which jealously disputed their authority, which were often enough infected with an infidel philosophy, which did not at first supply their members with any spiritual or moral discipline, and which were not necessarily impressed with an ecclesiastical character. For, what is a university? "It consists," says a writer in the "Analecta Juris Pontificii,"[182] "of an aggregation of schools, governed by a body of doctors, who divide among themselves the several branches of instruction which, in the public schools, are united under one master." "A university," says Crevier, "is a body composed of masters teaching and disciples who are taught." And the writer first quoted goes on to examine whether it would have been possible or desirable for the universities to have established the collegiate discipline of the ancient schools with a view to protect the piety and morals of the students, and decides that such an attempt would have been a chimera. The universities, he says, were intended for seculars as well as clerics, and it was, therefore, unfitting that the rule of clerical schools should be enforced in them. But it is at least obvious that a prodigious and calamitous revolution was being effected in the education of the clergy when young clerics were trained in academies wherein such rules were avowedly *not* enforced. The difference was this, that in old time they had received secular students into their seminaries, and then the education of laymen was tinged with an ecclesiastical character. Now the world received clerics into her academies, and the education of the future clergy of Europe became necessarily, in a certain sense, secularised. Nor is this said as in any way depreciating the universities, or representing them in an unfavourable light. They will lose nothing by being represented as what they truly are, academies of science, schools of worldly training, learned corporations in which degrees are granted for intellectual proficiency in liberal studies, and in which a man acquires knowledge, refinement, and all that can fit him for taking his place in society, and filling it with credit. Yet, all this does not make them substitutes for ecclesiastical seminaries. They are doubtless capable of being employed in the service of religion, and have often been so employed: they have been established and encouraged by the bulls of Popes, and, in more than one instance, founded with the direct view of furnishing bulwarks against the spread of heresy. Yet, it is evident that, as places of education for the clergy, the universities were at a disadvantage. They could not give the young clerics that training in the ecclesiastical spirit which they had hitherto enjoyed. Even granting that the establishment of colleges afforded the benefits of regular life to their students, it could not give them the watchful protection of their bishop's eye. That close and paternal tie which had grown up between the chief pastor and his future clergy was altogether lost, except, indeed, in so far as the evil results of the system were counteracted by the personal efforts of the bishop. And here, happily, some of the habits of feudal society came to his aid, and enabled him to receive into the enormous household then maintained by every lord, whether spiritual or temporal, a number of young clerks, who, after their university career was over, thus passed under the immediate rule of their bishop, and received a certain sort of ecclesiastical training at his hands.

Fleury speaks of this custom as universal throughout the Church in the Middle Ages; and says that each bishop took special care of the instruction of his clergy, particularly of those young clerics who were continually about his person, serving him in the capacity of lectors or secretaries, carrying his letters and transmitting his orders. These episcopal households, however, could not do the work of a seminary, still less could they undo the work of a university in the souls of those who had been subjected for a course of years to its social and intellectual training. The idea of the seminary, and the episcopal or monastic school, is pre-eminently that of preservation; it takes the soul in the freshness of youth, and hedges round with thorns the garden that is to be consecrated to God. But according to the mediæval university system, a lad began his studies at Oxford or Paris at the age of twelve or fourteen, and seldom spent less than nine, sometimes twelve, years in native or foreign academies, so that the whole of his most impressible years were spent in the midst of secular fellow-students, thus opening upon him a flood of evils that scarcely require to be pointed out. The dissolute manners which prevailed, specially in the Italian universities, which were, perhaps, next to that of Paris, the most frequented, are depicted by successive Pontiffs as a sort of moral contagion. In many there prevailed a tone of philosophic scepticism, even yet more gravely injurious. False opinions were supported by the example and eloquence of fine scholars and great intellects, and few could enter such an atmosphere, and be subjected to such an influence, without at least losing some of the instincts of faith. The habits of expense, rendered fashionable by wealthy students, brought poverty, the scholar's ancient and honourable badge, into disrepute, and encouraged an eagerness for offices and benefices. The office of teaching itself lost something of its ancient nobility when made a means of ministering to cupidity and ambition; for it must be owned there were few Wolfgangs to be found at Paris or Bologna. And as avarice and sensuality became the predominant vices of those out of whose ranks the future clergy were to be formed, what wonder that the two centuries which followed the rise of these brilliant and captivating academies should be filled with complaints of clerical corruption; that the salt of the earth should have lost its savour, and that abuses accumulated which cried loudly for reform?

But besides all this the universities had a spirit of their own. In most cases they were creations of the State, and betrayed their origin in the principles which they advocated. We shall have occasion hereafter to refer to the part taken by Paris university during the struggle between Philip le Bel and Boniface VIII. That Pontiff had been prodigal of his favours to the French schools, and had done more than any preceding Pope to extend their privileges; yet at the bidding of the crown the Paris doctors did not hesitate to give their sanction to the monstrous charges by which Philip sought to blacken the reputation of the man he had resolved to destroy. They certified to the truth of accusations drawn up at the king's direction, representing the Sovereign Pontiff as having a familiar demon, and as blaspheming the doctrine of the real Presence. Crevier says one cannot but smile at these articles, which were notoriously destitute of a shadow of foundation, and in which not one man who signed them for a moment believed. Yet, he adds, the university of Paris gave in its adhesion to this act, and her example was followed by that of Toulouse, *because they deemed it proper to support the authority of the Crown.* His own comments on these facts are not less startling than the facts themselves. "It was an act," he says, "of great consequence, and the university has constantly adhered to this *sound* doctrine, and made it her greatest glory that, owing all her privileges to the power of the Popes, she has never sought to extend their power beyond its just limits, but on the contrary, has ever been the scourge of theologians and canonists flattering to the court of Rome."[183] In the preface to his work he lays down this *sound doctrine* of the university in very plain terms, which we commend to the attentive study of the reader, as indicating the inevitable bias of State institutions. "The university of Paris is intimately united to the State, of which it forms a part. It finds in the public power that protection which it requires, and acquits itself of all its duties towards the State by inspiring with all possible care into the disciples whom it trains the sentiments of citizens and Frenchmen. This is one of the chief characteristics, I may say, the peculiar glory, of our university. Its first object is God and religion. But it knows that God Himself commands us to regard *as the first of duties those which refer to our country and our sovereign,* who resumes all the rights of the nation in his own person. Hence that enlightened and courageous zeal which has always animated the university of Paris for the defence of our precious maxims on the independence of the Crown, the distinction of the two powers, the legitimate rights of the Head of the Church, and the respective rights of the Church herself, *as opposed to her Head.* These maxims, so important to the tranquillity of Church and State, have always had adversaries, and our university shares with the Parliament the glory of having ever faithfully maintained them."

These words were written in the beginning of the reign of Louis XVI. Who can regret that an institution, the character of which is thus depicted by one of its own professors, should have been doomed to extinction in the midst of that storm which overthrew both state and monarchy, and taught the terrible lesson how little stability is to be looked for in any civil power which seeks to base itself on the "precious maxims" of State supremacy? Yet, this spirit was not confined to the university of Paris alone; her doctors put it forth, perhaps, with peculiar boldness and precision, but it was shared by almost all her sister academies, as may be seen by the part which the universities of Europe took in the contest between Henry VIII. and the Holy See, and the active support which he obtained from their professors. And there is no doubt that this is in great part to be attributed to the excessive predominance of the study of the Roman law, which rendered popular a certain Cæsarism in politics, which eventually proved as destructive to civil, as it did to religious, liberty.

So far, our observations apply to the universities at all periods of their existence. But, in the beginning of the thirteenth century, there existed some dangers peculiar to the time. The new academies threatened to prove no less hostile to the purity of doctrine than to the purity of manners. Aggregations of schools incorporated by royal charters are not the appointed guardians of the deposit of faith, nor has the promise of infallibility been given to doctors and theological professors. The monastic scholars had, for the most part, been secured from error by their reverence for tradition, and from the fact of their naturally contemplating truth, rather through the heart, than through the reason. But the new scholastics contemplated it through the metaphysics of Aristotle, and, what is more, through Aristotle as he was rendered by Arabic interpreters, who added to the errors of the pagan philosophers a pantheistic system of their own. At the head of these was Averrhoes, the son of an Arabian physician, whose religion it would be hard to determine, as he scoffed alike at Christianity, Judaism, and Mahometanism. His commentaries on Aristotle found such favour in the eyes of the free-thinking students of the day that they commonly spoke of him as "the Commentator." His grand doctrine was that which averred all mankind to possess but one common intellect. All after death were to be united to what the modern Germans would call the *Over-Soul*, and hence the dogma of reward and punishment, according to individual merit, crumbled away, and there was no difference between saint and sinner—between St. Peter and Mahomet. These doctrines were propagated by wandering minstrels, and supported by imperial scholars. Frederic II. entertained at his court the two sons of Averrhoes, whose religious views, in the main, coincided with his own. He patronised the Arabian schoolmen, partly out of a love of the natural sciences which they cultivated, and partly from a sympathy with their sceptical philosophy; and his support helped to set the fashion. Soon the new philosophy linked itself to those Manichean doctrines, the poison of which was always lurking somewhere within the fold. Secret societies were formed, the members of which were bound together by oaths, and were to be found in most of the great universities; and Bulæus tells us that an organisation existed for disseminating their opinions among the people by agents disguised as pedlars. A new translation of Aristotle's Metaphysics appeared in 1167, and, says Crevier, "men's minds became wholly filled with them." Many fell into open unbelief, and he relates the well-known story of Simon of Tournai, who, after explaining all the doctrines of religion with great applause, blasphemously boasted that it was as easy for him to disprove, as to prove the existence of God. He offered to do so on the following day, but, in the midst of his impious speech, he was struck with apoplexy, and the event was regarded as a manifestation of the Divine displeasure.

Another of the Paris professors, Amauri de Bene, was regent of arts about the same time with Simon. He was remarked as being fond of singular opinions; and as having a way of thinking on most subjects peculiar to himself, but in his own lifetime the real truth was never suspected. But after his death startling discoveries were made. He was found to have been the head of one of the Albigensian sects who preserved the name of Christianity, while rejecting all its dogmas. The doctrine of the sacraments was swept away; a new religion was announced to the initiated as the work of the Spirit, which was to replace that which had been introduced by the Son; and this second gospel was associated with hideous immorality. All this had been cautiously propagated among disciples bound to secrecy by oath. On investigation it proved that the greater number of the Paris professors were infected with this poison, and the university found itself compelled to limit the number of its doctors in theology to eight. A council being called at Paris in 1210, it was resolved to strike at the evil in its head by prohibiting the study of Aristotle's Philosophy in the schools. It was in consequence of this decree that Robert de Courçon in his statutes interdicted the reading of Aristotle's Physics and Metaphysics. In 1231 Gregory IX. rendered the prohibition less absolute, but before the end of the century a recurrence of the old disorders rendered it once more necessary to condemn a whole system of pagan errors taught by the Parisian masters.[184] "Even those who did not push the abuse to such extremes," says Crevier, "altered, at least in part, the purity of Christian dogma, by interpretations more conformable to the principles of Aristotle than of the Fathers." And it was this that caused Gregory IX., true friend to ancient learning as he was, to fulminate a bull against the Paris professors, charging them with presumptuous arrogance, and forbidding them to mingle their philosophic opinions with the truths of revelation.

Decrees of this nature were, however, insufficient to meet the evil. The intellect of Europe, as it flowed into these academies, was trembling on the brink of infidelity, and so long as the schools of philosophy were in the enemy's hands, it was vain to expect to put down error by the simple voice of authority. What power, then, was to be evoked in defence of Christian dogma? Where were the champions to be found to meet the teachers of error on their own ground, and beat them with their own weapons? The monastic orders had ever proved the militia of the Church at such crises, but in the present case their position seemed to preclude their taking a prominent part in the contest. Though they were beginning to make use of the universities for the education of their younger members, yet this was felt by many to be a straining of their rule, and a very general prejudice against the practice prevailed among the monks themselves. Certainly it would never have been tolerated for them to have aspired to the professor's chair, yet the battle, it was plain, would have to be fought in the arena of the schools. Something seemed required in which the spirit of the schools and of the cloister should be combined; in which all the science of the one should be united to all the unworldly self-devotedness of the other. A new institute seemed called for in the Church, and at the moment that it was called for, it appeared. The

Divine Householder, bringing out of His treasure-house things new as well as old, had in His providence prepared the shield which was to cast back the weapons of the new scholasticism on those who wielded them; to Christianise the schools, and press philosophy into the service of the faith. And this gigantic work was to be wrought by the ministry of doctors indeed, but of men who were not merely doctors, but saints. But of them and of their triumphs we must speak in a separate chapter.

CHAPTER XIV.

THE DOMINICANS AND THE UNIVERSITIES.

A.D. 1215-1300.

IN the very same year which witnessed the publication of the Paris Statutes by Robert de Courçon, the city of Toulouse was being electrified by the lectures of a certain professor of theology named Alexander, who was held in great esteem throughout the south of France. One autumn day in the year 1215, having risen at a very early hour to pursue his studies, he fell asleep in his chair, and in his sleep he had a dream. He thought that seven stars appeared before him, small at first, but gradually increasing in size, and at last illuminating the whole world with their splendour. Starting from his slumber, he found that the hour had come for him to open his school, and hastening thither, seven men presented themselves to him as he entered, and informed him that they were about to preach in the country round about Toulouse, and desired, before doing so, to attend his lectures. They wore the usual dress of the Canons Regular of St. Augustine, namely, a white serge tunic covered with a linen surplice, and over that a black mantle; and they were headed by one on whose brow the master seemed to recognise the starry splendour which he had seen in his late vision: they were Dominic Guzman, prior of Prouille and Canon of Osma, and his first six followers.

The Order of Preachers was at this time but just founded, but even before its holy patriarch had given it a rule, and obtained for it the Apostolic confirmation, he directed its first steps to the schools. The institute, of which he had conceived the plan, was expressly designed for the purpose of teaching and preaching, and hence the culture of sacred science formed, from the first moment of its existence, one of its primary and essential duties. Having, therefore, established his followers at Toulouse to pursue their studies under the direction of Alexander, St. Dominic hastened to Rome to lay his plans before Pope Innocent III., then presiding over the Fourth Lateran Council. The Fathers of that Council had already formally recognised the grand evils of the age, which cried for a remedy, to be the want of sound religious instruction among the people and of theological science among the clergy. And a decree had been passed directing the bishops in each diocese to choose persons capable of preaching and instructing the people who were to be employed in this office; and requiring that certain learned men should be appointed in all churches, whether cathedral or conventual, to assist the bishops in preaching the Word of God and administering the Sacraments. Thus the outline of a teaching and preaching order had been sketched by the Lateran Fathers even before its perfect design had been submitted to the Pope by its founder. No wonder, therefore, that it was readily approved; it appeared as though raised up by God to supply a want at the very moment when the existence of that want had been distinctly acknowledged. And as if to mark the fact that, from the first moment of its formal existence, the Order of Preachers was expressly intended to teach and cultivate sacred science, Honorius III., when confirming the rule in the year following, bestowed upon St. Dominic the office of Master of the Sacred Palace, which may be briefly defined as that of the Pope's theologian. This office became hereditary in the Order, and distinguished the sons of St. Dominic as the chosen theologians of the Church.

To form a just idea of the solicitude of the holy founder, and of those who immediately succeeded him, in establishing a perfect system of studies, we must turn to the Constitutions of the Order. It was at the first general chapter held at Bologna in 1220, and presided over by the saint himself, that an ordinance passed declaring that as the principal end of the Order is preaching, the brethren should concern themselves rather with books and studies than with the singing of Responsories and Antiphons, provided, however, that prayer be vigilantly attended to.[185] And elsewhere the pursuit of sacred learning is declared to be "most congruous to the design of the Order," both because the Order professes the contemplative life, and the study of sacred things is necessary to this end, and because it is also designed for teaching others the Divine knowledge which its members have acquired by learning.[186] Schools were therefore to be opened in every convent, under a Master of Studies, which differed from the old monastic schools in being exclusively intended as theological seminaries, and not as academies of the arts. The study of arts was not indeed absolutely prohibited, but it was to be pursued under limitations, and too much time was not to be given to secular branches of learning.[187] It was, however, required that in all convents the brethren should study the languages of the neighbouring countries;[188] and early in the fourteenth century the study of the Greek, Hebrew, and Arabic tongues was likewise enjoined. Still later, in 1553, it was ordained that in all convents where there were younger brethren, there should be a lector appointed to teach them grammar and the arts, according to their capacity. But the studies chiefly contemplated by the rule were those of philosophy and theology. Three years were to be devoted to the study of philosophy, before the commencement of the theological course. The length of time devoted to theological studies may be gathered from the rule which enjoined that in each of the chief houses of studies there should be a Regent of Studies, a certain number of Bachelors and Lectors, and a Master of Studies; but no one could be appointed Regent till he had publicly taught theology for twelve years, and the Bachelor or Lector, ten years; and all these must have maintained at least five public disputations in the schools before the assembled doctors and scholars. Moreover, before any one could present himself for the examination required in order to become a Master of Studies, it was necessary to have completed the course of arts, and another four years' course of theology.[189]

During the year of religious probation which preceded profession, the novices were exclusively to occupy themselves in acquiring a knowledge of their rule and the duties of their state, and were exercised in chanting the Divine Office and studying the Ceremonies of the Order. During this time they were not allowed to engage in any study except that of languages. After their profession their scholastic course began, during which time every facility was to be afforded them for pursuing their philosophical and theological course. They were to have suitable cells in which they might read, write, and even sit up at night with a light. There was to be some place in which the Master of Studies could assemble them to propose doubts and questions, in discussing which good order and courtesy were to be observed. Every student was to be provided with three books; a Bible, a copy of the Sentences, and a book of histories.[190] The studies began with a course of philosophy, then the Scriptures were explained, and no one could be sent to a *Studium Generale*, a house of general studies, until he had passed at least one year under a professor of the Sacred Scriptures. After this came the explanation of the Sentences, which formed the theological text-book, until the works of St. Thomas were substituted in their place. In the schools the Lector was forbidden to use any written manuscript; he might have the text of Aristotle and of the Sentences, but no gloss. The pupils might take written notes if they chose, and if they were able to do so, though, as they sat on bundles of straw, or at best on benches without desks, this was not always easy. Most were content to trust to their memory, and assist it afterwards by repetitions of the master's lesson among themselves. Classes were held every day, and there were weekly and yearly examinations. At first there was but one *Studium Generale*, that, namely, of St. James's Convent in Paris, but in 1248 four others were established at Cologne, Oxford, Montpelier, and Bologna, in all of which the students were able to take the same degrees as in Paris. The number of these houses was afterwards greatly multiplied, one being provided for each province. Certain scholars of remarkable capacity were selected by their superiors and sent to those houses. From the *Studium Generale* the students passed on to graduate at some university, unless, as was often the case, the house was itself aggregated to a university, as at Paris and Bologna. The order observed at Paris in advancing to the degree of Doctor, is given by Fleury in his "Fifth Discourse," and was as follows. He who was named *Bachelor* by the General of the Order, or by the Chapter, began by explaining the Sentences in the school of some doctor, for the space of a year, at the end of which time the prior of the convent, with the other doctors then professing, presented him to the Chancellor of the Church of Paris, and affirmed on oath that they judged him worthy of obtaining a license to open a school of his own and teach as a doctor; after going through certain examinations, he taught the second year in his own school, and the third year was allowed to have a bachelor under him, whom at the end of that year he presented for his license. Thus, the doctor's course lasted three years, and no one could be raised to the degree of Doctor of Divinity or Master of Sacred Theology, who had not thus publicly taught.[191] The teaching of the Friar Preachers, however, was not exclusively given in the pulpit or the professor's chair. It was their aim to ingraft in men's minds a knowledge and love of the truth, to protect them from heresy by informing them with the spirit of the Church, that spirit which finds expression, not in her creeds alone, but her Liturgy and sacred ceremonies. In our own day we have become accustomed to the idea that institutes founded for the purpose of teaching must necessarily lay aside something of the monastic character. The long offices, the solemn ceremonial, the austerities and ritual observances which take up so large a portion of cloistered life, are, it is thought, difficult, if not impossible, to associate with the active work of the Apostolate. But in the thirteenth century men were still deeply penetrated with the Liturgical spirit which animated the Church in earlier times; it was held that no words could be so fit to convey her teaching as her own, and not words alone but acts, the exact performance of her beautiful rites, made familiar to the eye and heart of the worshipper; her office, her music, the beauty of her sanctuary, and the silent eloquence of her sacred art. All these, therefore, were embraced by the Dominican rule and used as instruments of popular instruction, and it is probable that the Friars cherished those privileges which threw open their churches to the people, and encouraged them to assist at their public offices, almost equally with those that secured to them the free possession of the professor's chair.

How thoroughly the newly-constituted order was fitted to supply the intellectual wants of the times is proved by the fact, that in the first period of its existence it was chiefly recruited from the ranks of university scholars and professors. Among the names that figure in its early annals those of the Blessed Reginald of Orleans, and St. Peter Martyr, Jordan of Saxony, and his friend Henry of Cologne, the Englishman, John of St. Giles, and the Parisian, Vincent of Beauvais, the three Bolognese doctors Roland, Conrad, and Moneta, Cardinal Hugh de St. Cher, and his disciple the Blessed Humbert, with the Spanish canonist St. Raymund Pennafort, were all taken from this class.

The chief extension of the Order, especially among the students of Paris and Bologna, took place under the generalship of Blessed Jordan, who had a remarkable gift of drawing to himself the affection and confidence of the young. His influence was naturally enough most powerfully felt among his own countrymen. The convent of Cologne had already been founded by his old fellow-student and bosom friend Henry of Utrecht; and a namesake of his, Henry the German, who had begun life as a student, then assumed the cross, and finally taking the religious habit, became its first theological professor. And there in 1230 arrived the young Swabian, Albert of Lauingen, who had been drawn to the Order by B. Jordan, whilst pursuing his studies at Padua. Albert during his student-life had been remarkable for his love of the old classic literature and his enthusiastic admiration for Aristotle; and had already displayed a singular attraction to those physical sciences which he afterwards so profoundly studied. He had examined various natural phenomena, such as earthquakes, the mephitic vapours issuing from a long closed well, and some curious marks in a block of marble, which he explained in a manner which betrays an acquaintance with some of the chemical theories of modern geology.[192] After going through his theological course at Bologna, he was appointed to fill the vacant post of professor at Cologne, where he taught sacred and human science for some years, and lectured moreover at Hildesheim, Strasburg, Friburg, and Ratisbonn, in which last city an old hall is shown which still bears the title of "Albert's School." Converted into a chapel by one of his successors and ardent admirers, it may be supposed to exhibit the same form and arrangement as that which it bore five centuries ago. Round the walls are disposed ancient wooden seats, for the accommodation of the hearers, and fixed against the middle of the wall is an oak chair, or rather pulpit, covered with carvings of a later date, representing St. Vincent Ferrer delivering a lecture, and a novice in the attitude of attention. The chair is of double construction, containing two seats, in one of which sat the master, and in the other the bachelor, who explained under him the Book of the Sentences. All around are texts from the Holy Scriptures, fitly chosen to remind the student in what spirit he should apply himself to the pursuit of sacred letters. *Ama scientiam Scripturarum, et vitia carnis non amabis. Qui addit scientiam addit et laborem. Bonitatem et disciplinam et scientiam doce me. Qui fecerit et docuerit, hic magnus vocabitur in regno cælorum. Videte ne quis vos decipiat per philosophiam, secundum elementa mundi, et non secundum Christum.*

In such a hall as this we may picture to ourselves the Blessed Albert the Great lecturing at Cologne in 1245, where he first received among his pupils that illustrious disciple whose renown, if it eclipsed his own, at the same time constitutes his greatest glory. There are few readers who are not familiar with the student life of St. Thomas of Aquin, the silent habits which exposed him to the witticisms of his companions, who thought the young Sicilian a dull sort of importation, and nicknamed him "the dumb ox;" the obliging compassion which moved a fellow-student to offer him his assistance in explaining the lessons of the master, and the modesty and humility with which this greatest of Christian scholars veiled his mighty intellect, and with the instinct of the saints, rejoiced to be counted the least among his brethren. But the day came which was to make him known in his true character. His notes and replies to a difficult question proposed by Albert from the writings of St. Denys, fell into the hands of his master, who reading them with wonder and delight, commanded him on the following day to take part in the scholastic disputation. St. Thomas obeyed, and the audience knew not whether most to admire his eloquence or his erudition. At last Albert, unable to restrain his astonishment, broke out into the memorable words, "You call this the dumb ox, but I tell you his roaring will be heard throughout the whole world." From that day St. Thomas became the object of his most solicitous care; he assigned him a cell adjoining his own, and when in the course of the same year he removed to Paris, to govern the school of St. James for three years, in order afterwards to graduate as doctor, he took his favourite scholar with him.

The position which the Friars at that time occupied in Paris requires a few words of explanation. In the year 1228, a tavern brawl, which terminated in a disgraceful riot, had brought on a collision between the civic and academic authorities; and the indiscriminating severity with which the excesses of the students had been punished, had determined all the masters to desert the city, and open their schools elsewhere. This quarrel, which threatened the entire break-up of the university, lasted three years, and was only finally adjusted by the interference of the Pope. During the absence of the masters, the archbishop and chancellor of Paris conferred one of the vacant chairs of theology on the Friars Preachers, and shortly afterwards erected a second chair in their favour, Roland of Cremona and John of St. Giles being named the two first university professors of the order.

When the masters returned to Paris they affected to regard this as an infringement of their rights, and a warm controversy arose, which lasted with ever-increasing violence for forty years, and was at its height when the two saints made their first appearance in the Parisian schools. It did not, however, prevent Albert from winning his doctor's cap, together with the reputation of having illuminated every branch of science, and of knowing everything that was to be known.[193]

His doctor's triennium had scarcely expired when he was recalled to Cologne to take the Regency of the *Studium Generale*, newly erected in that city; and St. Thomas accompanied him to teach, as licentiate or bachelor, in the school which proved the germ of a future university. This epoch of Albert's life appears to have been that in which most of his philosophic writings were produced. They consist chiefly of his "Commentary on Aristotle," in which, after collating the different translations of that author with extraordinary care, he aims at presenting the entire body of his philosophy in a popular as well as a Christian form; a commentary on the Book of the Sentences; other commentaries on the Gospels, and on the works of St. Denys, all of which are preserved; and a devout paraphrase of the Book of the Sentences cast into the form of prayers, which has been lost. His published works alone fill twenty one folio volumes, and it is said that a great number of other treatises exist in manuscript. Fleury, who is pleased to say that he knows nothing great about this writer except his volumes, takes in very bad part the labour he has expended on the study of natural science. The course of the stars; the structure of the universe; the nature of plants, animals, and minerals, appear to him unsuitable subjects for the investigation of a religious man; and he hints that the seculars who paid for the support of such students by their liberal alms expected them to spend their time on more profitable studies. The reader need not be reminded that Albert was not singular in directing his attention to these subjects, and that the scientific labours of our own Venerable Bede have ever been considered as among his best titles to admiration as a scholar. But more than this, it is surely a narrow and illiberal view to regard the cultivation of science as foreign to the purposes of religion. At the time of which we are now speaking, as in our own, physical science was unhappily too often made an instrument for doing good service to the cause of infidelity. It was chiefly, if not exclusively, in the hands of the Arabian philosophers, who had drawn great part of their errors from the physics of Aristotle. Schlegel, indeed, considers that the extraordinary popularity of Aristotle in the Middle Ages did not so much arise from the love of the mediæval schoolmen for his rationalistic philosophy, as from the attraction they felt to some great and mysterious knowledge of nature. His works seemed to give promise of unlocking to them those vast intellectual treasures reserved for the scrutiny of our own age, but of the existence of which they possessed a kind of dim half-consciousness. Hence the teachers of the thirteenth century could hardly do more effective service to the cause of truth than by handling these subjects according to a Christian method, and proving that faith and science were in no sense opposed to one another. Hallam affects to grieve over the evil inflicted on Europe by the credit which Albert's influence gave to the study of astrology, alchemy, and magic. The author of Cosmos, however, passes a very different verdict on the nature of his scientific writings, and one which our readers will be disposed to receive as more worthy of attention. "Albertus Magnus," he says, "was equally active and influential in promoting the study of natural science, and of the Aristotelian philosophy.... His works contain some exceedingly acute remarks on the organic structure and physiology of plants. One of his works, bearing the title of *Liber Cosmographicus de Natura Locorum*, is a species of physical geography. I have found in it considerations on the dependence of temperature concurrently on latitude and elevation, and on the effect of different angles of incidence of the sun's rays in heating the ground, which have excited my surprise."[194] Jourdain, another modern critic, says, "Whether we consider him as a theologian or a philosopher, Albert was undoubtedly one of the most extraordinary men of his age; I might say, one of the most wonderful men of genius who has appeared in past times."

It may be of interest to notice here a few of the scientific views of Albert, which show how much he owed to his own sagacious observation of natural phenomena, and how far he was in advance of his age. He decides that the Milky Way is nothing but a vast assemblage of stars, but supposes, naturally enough, that they occupy the orbit which receives the light of the sun. The figures visible on the moon's disk are not, he says, as has hitherto been supposed, reflections of the seas and mountains of the earth, but configurations of her own surface. He notices, in order to correct it, the assertion of Aristotle that lunar rainbows appear only twice in fifty years; "I myself," he says, "have observed two in a single year." He has something to say on the refraction of the solar ray, notices certain crystals which have a power of refraction, and remarks that none of the ancients, and few moderns, were acquainted with the properties of mirrors. In his tenth book, wherein he catalogues and describes all the trees, plants, and herbs known in his time, he observes, "all that is here set down is the result of our own experience, or has been borrowed from authors, whom we know to have written what their personal experience has confirmed: for in these matters experience alone can give certainty." (*Experimentum solum certificat talibus.*) Such an expression, which might have proceeded from the pen of Bacon, argues in itself a prodigious scientific progress, and shows that the mediæval friar was on the track so successfully pursued by modern natural philosophy. He had fairly shaken off the shackles which had hitherto tied up discovery, and was the slave neither of Pliny nor of Aristotle.

He treats as fabulous the commonly-received idea, in which Bede had acquiesced, that the region of the earth south of the equator was uninhabitable, and considers that, from the equator to the south pole, the earth was not only habitable, but, in all probability, actually inhabited, except directly at the poles, where he imagines the cold to be excessive. If there are any animals there, he says, they must have very thick skins to defend them from the rigour of the climate, and are probably of a *white colour*. The intensity of cold is, however, tempered by the action of the sea. He describes the antipodes and the countries they comprise, and divides the climate of the earth into seven zones. He smiles with a scholar's freedom at the simplicity of those who suppose that persons living at the opposite region of the earth must fall off—an opinion which can only arise out of the grossest ignorance, "for, when we speak of the *lower* hemisphere this must be understood merely as relatively to ourselves." It is as a geographer that Albert's superiority to the writers of his own time chiefly appears. Bearing in mind the astonishing ignorance which then prevailed on this subject, it is truly admirable to find him correctly tracing the chief mountain chains of Europe, with the rivers which take their source in each, remarking on portions of coast which have in later times been submerged by the ocean, and islands which have been raised, by volcanic action, above the level of the sea, noticing the modification of climate caused by mountains, seas, and forests; and the divisions of the human race, whose differences he ascribes to the effect of the countries they inhabit. In speaking of the British Isles, he alludes to the commonly-received idea that another distant island, called Tile or Thule, existed far in the Western Ocean, uninhabitable by reason of its frightful climate, but which, he says, has perhaps not yet been visited by man. He was acquainted with the sleep of plants, with the periodical opening and closing of blossoms, with the diminution of sap during evaporation from the cuticle of the leaves, and with the influence of the distribution of the bundles of vessels on the folial indentations.[195] His minute observations on the forms and variety of plants intimate an exquisite sense of floral beauty. He distinguishes the star from the bell flower, tells us that a red rose will turn white when submitted to the vapour of sulphur, and makes some very sagacious observations on the subject of germination. The extraordinary erudition and originality of this treatise has drawn from M. Meyer the following comment:—"No botanist who lived before Albert can be compared to him, unless it be Theophrastus, with whom he was not acquainted; and after him none has painted nature in such living colours, or studied it so profoundly, until the time of Conrad, Gesner, and Cesalpini. All honour, then, to the man who made such astonishing progress in the science of nature as to find no one, I will not say to surpass, but even to equal him for the space of three centuries."

In the Treatise on Animals which Jourdain particularly praises, nineteen books are a paraphrase of Michael Scott's translation of Aristotle, but the remaining seven books are Albert's own, and form, says Jourdain a precious link between ancient and modern science. It was not extraordinary that one who had so deeply studied nature, and had mastered so many of her secrets, should by his wondering contemporaries have been judged to have owed his marvellous knowledge to a supernatural source, or that his mechanical contrivances,[196] his knowledge of the power of mirrors, and his production of a winter garden, or hothouse, where, on the feast of the Epiphany 1249, he exhibited to William of Holland, king of the Romans, plants and fruit-trees in full blossom, should have subjected him in the mind of the vulgar to the suspicion of sorcery. But it is certainly surprising that such charges should be reproduced by modern critics, who, it might have been thought, would have condemned the very belief in witchcraft as a mediæval superstition. The more so as Albert devotes no inconsiderable portion of his pages to the exposure and refutation of those forbidden arts, which he will not allow to be reckoned among the sciences, such as geomancy, chiromancy, and a formidable list of other branches of magic.

During the time that Albert was engaged in these labours, his daily life was one which might rather have seemed that of a contemplative than of a student of physical science. "I have seen, and know of a truth," says his disciple Thomas of Cantimpré, "that the venerable Albert, whilst for many years he daily lectured on theology, yet watched day and night in prayer, daily recited the entire Psalter, and at the conclusion of every lesson and disputation gave himself up to Divine contemplation." His skill as a master drew an incredible number of students to Cologne, whom he not only inspired with his own love of science, but directed in the spiritual life. Among these were the blessed Ambrose of Siena, and Ulrich of Engelbrecht, who afterwards became provincial of Germany, and made use of the mechanical and scientific lore he had acquired from his master in the construction of the great organ in Strasburg cathedral.

But the fame of all the other pupils of Albert pales like his own before that of St. Thomas of Aquin, who claims our notice in these pages less in his character of saint and theologian than in that of Regent of schools. From the period of his promotion to the doctorate to the day of his death, he was incessantly engaged in the work of teaching, as a very brief outline of his life will show. After lecturing for four years in Cologne, he was recalled to Paris in order to take his degrees, and though under the accustomed age, for he was then but twenty-five, no opposition was offered on the part of the university to his being received as Bachelor, and lecturing as such in the public schools. But at the end of the year, when he should, by right, have proceeded to the degree of Doctor, the quarrel which had already broken out between the Seculars and Regulars was fanned into a flame by the calumnies of William de St. Amour, and the secular Regents persisted in refusing to admit the friars to any of the theological chairs. The dispute being at last referred to Rome, St. Thomas was summoned thither, and by his eloquent defence procured the condemnation of St. Amour's book on "The Perils of the Latter Times," in which the religious orders were attacked in scandalous terms. Not only were the deputies of the university obliged to subscribe this condemnation, but also to promise on oath, in presence of the cardinals, to receive members of the two mendicant orders to their academic degrees, and especially St. Bonaventure and St. Thomas, who had hitherto been unable to obtain their Doctor's caps. The publication of the Pope's bull, and the authority of St. Louis, finally brought this vexatious dispute to a close, but the university authorities, though forced to yield, contrived to give expression to their ill-will by an act which provided that the Dominicans should always hold the last place, not only after the secular regents, but after those of every other religious body.[197]

On the 23rd of October, 1257, the two saints were received to their Doctor's degree. St. Thomas, who had no small difficulty in overcoming the scruples of his humility, and who only yielded at last to the orders of his superiors, chose for the text of his "Act of Theology," not as it would appear without a divine inspiration, the words of the Psalmist, "Thou waterest the hills from Thy upper rooms; the earth shall be filled with the fruit of Thy works;"[198] words which he interpreted to refer to Jesus Christ, who, as the Head of men and angels, waters the heavenly mountains with the torrent of His graces, and fills the Church with the fruit of His works, in the Sacraments which convey to us the merits of His Passion. But as Père Croiset observes, the event gave to this text the character of a prophecy regarding his own future career.

Having taken his Doctor's degree, he now, according to custom, taught in his own school, having under him a bachelor, who appears to have been either Annibal Annibali, his particular friend, and afterwards cardinal, or Peter Tarantasio, afterwards Pope Innocent V. Many of his theological works were composed during the time he was teaching at Paris, and among the rest his "Summa against the Gentiles," written at the particular request of St. Raymond Pennafort. Father Nicholas Marsillac, one of his disciples, who gave evidence at the process of his canonisation, speaking of his extreme love of poverty, declared that when he was composing this work, he was often in want of paper to write it on. Nor were his charity and humility less remarkable than his spirit of detachment. In the arena of disputation, where the desire to be right, and the shame of appearing wrong, are apt enough to elicit warm feelings and sharp words, those who watched him the most closely never saw his tranquillity for one moment disturbed;[199] master of himself and of his passions, he possessed his soul in meekness and patience.

On the death of Alexander IV., in 1261, his successor, Urban IV., summoned St. Thomas to Rome, where he continued to discharge the same functions as at Paris, and composed a great number of his theological treatises. It was also during this period of his life that he visited England, being present as Definitor to the General Chapter, held at the Blackfriars in London, in the year 1263. Immediately on his return he was called to Orvieto, and charged by Urban to draw up an office for the newly-appointed Feast of Corpus Christi. "What chiefly strikes us in this office," says Dom Guéranger,[200] "is the grand scholastic form which it presents. Each of the Responsories at Matins is composed of two sentences, one drawn from the Old, and the other from the New Testament, which are thus made to render their united testimony to the great mystery which is the object of the Feast. This idea, which has in it something truly great, was unknown to St. Gregory and the other authors of the ancient liturgy. But St. Thomas possessed the genius not only of a theologian, but of a poet. In his prose *Lauda Sion*, as the same writer observes, he has found means to unite scholastic precision to poetry, and even to rhyme. For," he adds, "every sentiment of order necessarily resolves itself into harmony, and hence, St. Thomas, the most perfect scholastic of the thirteenth century, is on that very account its most sublime poet." About the same time he appears to have composed his Treatise on the "Unity of the Intellect," against the errors of Averrhoes; at least it is known to have been written during the pontificate of Urban IV., who died in 1264.

Clement IV., who succeeded him, showed himself no less sensible of the merits of the great doctor than his predecessor had been. He wished to have raised him to the archbishopric of Naples, and even published a Bull conferring that dignity on him, but the prayer of the saint induced him to suppress it, being unwilling, by persisting in his design, to afflict one so dear to him. St. Thomas was therefore left in peace, and he used his liberty to commence his great work, "The Summa of Theology," of which John XXII. is reported to have said, that if the author had worked no other miracle, he might be deemed to have worked as many as there were articles in the book. Tolomeo of Lucca says, that it was begun in the year 1265, and that the saint devoted to it the remaining nine years of his life, during which time, however, he never ceased to preach and teach publicly both at Rome, Bologna, and Naples. At Bologna, in particular, his lectures caused a sort of revival of learning in that city, and drew thither a great number of foreigners. He remained there for three years, at the end of which time he was called to Paris to attend the General Chapter of his order, and, according to Echard, was again raised to the professor's chair in that university, which he filled for two years. On his return to Bologna, in 1271, the publication of the second part of his "Summa" produced such an excitement that all the universities of Europe disputed which should gain possession of him. Naples won the preference, and thither the saint repaired, passing on his way through Rome, where he began the third part of his "Summa" and lectured in public according to his custom. A contemporary writer, quoted by the Bollandists, affirms that being engaged in explaining the mystery of the Holy Trinity, the waxlight, which he held in his fingers, burnt down and scorched them without his being conscious of the pain, so entirely was he absorbed in the greatness of his subject.

At Naples he found a very different state of things from that which had prevailed there when he had studied as a youth in the Ghibbeline university of Frederic II. The rule and the race of that emperor had passed away like a dream, and the kingdom of the Two Sicilies was now held by Charles of Anjou, the brother of St. Louis, and the faithful supporter of the rights of the Holy See. He reckoned it among the glories of his reign to have drawn to his capital the greatest doctor of the Church; and an inscription engraved on marble was long to be seen at the entrance of the school of the Dominican Convent at Naples, bidding the visitor, before entering, do reverence to the chair whence St. Thomas had taught an infinite number of disciples, King

Charles I. having procured this happiness for his kingdom and assigned an ounce of gold per month for the support of the said doctor. During the year and a half that he resided at Naples, St. Thomas continued his accustomed labours; only during the three last months of his life did he lay aside his pen, and cease to write or dictate.

It appeared as though he were conscious of his approaching end, for which God was preparing him by astonishing revelations. Often he was rapt in ecstasies at the altar, concerning which, when questioned, he could only answer, "So great are the things that have been revealed to me, that all I have hitherto taught and written seems to me as nothing." Yet he was able, before his death, to complete the third part of the Summa, which he left in the state in which we still possess it, and besides this to compose several other lesser treatises. On his deathbed, as is well known, his humility yielded to the entreaties of the religious who surrounded him, and he consented to explain to them the Canticle of canticles. His dying words, as they are reported by the Bollandists, are precious as the last instruction of the greatest of Christian scholars. When he beheld the Sacred Host in the hands of the priest who was about to administer to him the last sacraments, he made his profession of faith according to the accustomed form. Then he added, "I have written much, and have often disputed on the mysteries of Thy law, O my God! Thou knowest I have desired to teach nothing save what I have learnt from Thee. If what I have written be true, accept it as a homage to Thine Infinite Majesty; if it be false, pardon my ignorance. I consecrate all I have ever done to Thee, and submit all to the infallible judgment of Thy Holy Roman Church, in whose obedience I am about to depart this life."

It will be seen that the career of St. Thomas was exclusively that of a scholastic professor, and the anecdotes left us by his biographers prove with what a hearty and genuine earnestness he devoted himself to the cause of sacred learning. His prodigious powers of mind were accompanied with a childlike simplicity of character, which has been recognised by every writer of his life, and which, no less than the purity of his doctrine, won him the title of the Angelic Doctor. In the schools he was known as the sweetest and most charitable, as well as the most learned, of masters; no harsh word was ever heard to pass his lips, and the youngest of his scholars could reckon on commanding his whole attention. He had no thoughts apart from his religious duties and his books; and the splendours of the courts of France and Naples, in both of which he was received with such distinguished honour, had no power to dazzle him. Seated at the table of St. Louis, he was absorbed in a convincing argument against the Manicheans, and became wholly forgetful of the royal presence; and at Naples his student-like absence of mind was not less conspicuous. When the cardinal legate and the Archbishop of Capua came to visit him, he descended into the cloister to receive them; but on the way, revolving in his mind the solution of a theological difficulty, became so absorbed in his subject that by the time he reached the cloister he had forgotten all about the business and the visitors that had called him thither, and stood like one in a dream. The archbishop, who had formerly been his pupil, persuaded the cardinal to leave him alone till he should have recovered himself, and assured him that these reveries were perfectly well understood by those familiar with his habits.

F. Daniel d'Agusta once pressed him to say what he considered the greatest grace he had ever received from God, sanctifying grace, of course, excepted. He replied, after a few moments' reflection, "I think, that of having understood whatever I have read." St. Antoninus says, in his life, that no doubt was ever proposed to him that he did not solve, and that he remembered everything he had once heard, so that his mind was like a huge library. He often wrote, dictating at the same time on other subjects to three or four secretaries. Erveo Britto, one of these secretaries, declared that on one occasion the saint becoming weary, closed his eyes and appeared to have fallen asleep, but that in this state he nevertheless continued to dictate as before.

There are few saints, in fact, of whose daily life and habits we know more than St. Thomas. He is familiar to us as one of ourselves. We seem to see him enjoying his ordinary recreation of walking up and down the cloister of his convent, occasionally dragged off by his brethren to take a breath of fresh air in the garden, but sure in such cases to be found before long in some remote corner, absorbed in cogitation. Or we behold him contentedly following a lay brother through the markets of Bologna, who, ignorant of the rank of the new guest in the convent, had summoned him to be his companion on the quest, and charged him with the bag, which he carried all day on his shoulder, with undisturbed good-humour. His clothes were always the poorest in the whole convent, and his love of poverty was so great, that we are told that he wrote his "Summa against the Gentiles" on old letters and other scraps of paper. He ate but once in the day, and his total indifference to comfort or convenience, seemed to indicate that he had been heard, in what is said to have been his daily prayer for detachment: *Da mihi, Domine, cor nobile, quod nulla deorsum trahat terrena affectio.* And with these homely anecdotes are mingled others which exhibit him to us in ecstasy before his crucifix, preparing himself for his daily celebration of Mass by penance, confession, and meditation, and making his thanksgiving by humbly serving another, feeding his devotion by acts of charity, and binding himself by a law never to admit into his soul a single thought that should not be directed to God.[201]

In the last chapter we have seen something of the ravages caused by that pagan philosophy which had gradually established itself in the schools, and without some knowledge of which it is impossible to appreciate the work accomplished by St. Thomas. The university professors of the thirteenth century regarded Aristotle much as the masters of Carthage had done, of whom St. Augustine says that they spoke of the Categories of that philosopher with their cheek bursting with pride, as of something altogether divine. To displace a system which had obtained so firm a hold of the European mind, would probably have been a hopeless enterprise, and St. Thomas therefore achieved his triumph in another way. He humbled the proud Agar, Reason, under the hand of her mistress, Faith, and presented the truths of Revelation in the language of philosophy. In the five volumes which he devoted to his Commentaries on Aristotle he purged the text of the pagan philosopher from everything opposed to the truths of Christianity, and in his Summa of Theology he used the Aristotelian system of reasoning to combine those truths in one vast and harmonious whole.[202] Far from depreciating the office of the understanding, he vindicated its rights, by proving how close an alliance existed between Faith and Reason, and drove from the field the pantheistic dreams of Averrhoes by defining the nature and powers of the individual intellect.

The Arabian philosopher had attempted to explain the existence of universal ideas as found alike in all minds, by the hypothesis that mankind had but one common intellect, and that their ideas were therefore the creation not of many intellects, but of one. His view was embraced by many of the schoolmen, and carried to its extremest consequences, so that it was not uncommon to hear it asserted that after death all souls were merged in one, and thus that all distinction of rewards and punishments would be impossible.

"St. Thomas fought the new sceptical school with their own weapons; with the Conceptualists he admitted the axiom that the mind is the creator of its own objects:[203] by its own powers it forms its ideas of external things; yet its ideas are no false representations of the external world, for the matter of these ideas has been furnished from without by the senses.[204] There was, therefore, no necessity for imagining such a oneness of intellect as Averrhoes held, in order to give objective certainty to human knowledge. The intellect of each man has its own powers, and is the image of the Everlasting Wisdom; and its ideas are shadows of the archetypal ideas of the Divine mind, according to which the world was created. Limited as are its powers, by looking on itself it can form a notion of God, which, though feeble and inadequate, is capable of being developed by the Church on earth, and more perfectly still in heaven. The Pantheism of Averrhoes was nothing but the perversion of a great truth. There is, indeed, one Light 'which lighteneth every man who cometh into the world,' but the intellect of each man is a substantive thing with its own powers and operations. Moreover, Averrhoes had removed the intellect utterly out of the control of the conscience; according to him and his disciples the doctrines of faith and the conclusions of reason were the direct contradictory to each other; nevertheless, both might exist together in the mind without the necessity of coming to any conclusion. In other words, they believed in nothing whatever; and truth was a mere matter of words. St. Thomas, therefore, set himself to place faith and reason in right relations to each other. The intellect, he said, was a sacred gift of God, and could never be really contrary to the truth.[205] In its own sphere it was perfect, but the field of faith was a vast system lying beyond the sphere of the intellect. It was out of the jurisdiction of the reason which could pronounce nothing on the matter. Yet though powerless as an organ for the discovery of the faith, it may serve as an expression of the doctrines of revelation. Faith no more excludes reason than grace excludes nature,[206] and Divine truths when received into the human mind, must take the shape of human ideas and human words. Therefore it was that St. Thomas conceived it possible that the great truths of revelation might be expressed in terms of reason, and that the faith might be systematised and presented as one vast whole. And to effect this he chose the terms of Aristotle's philosophy, as the most scientific classification of the ideas of the human mind."[207]

The mind of Europe, which had been fast lapsing into infidelity, found itself at last in possession of a system of Christian philosophy wherein the Aristotelian dialectics were employed to defend the Catholic dogmas. "In the Summa of Theology was presented," says Ozanam, "a vast synthesis of the moral sciences, in which was unfolded all that could be known of God, of man, and of their mutual relations,—a truly Catholic philosophy." The value of such a gift, at such a time, was at once apprehended, and so instantaneously was the doctrine of St. Thomas accepted in the schools of his own order, that only four years after his death we find a decree of the general chapter of Milan directing that certain English friars should be severely punished for having departed from his teaching, and having had the temerity to call in question some of his propositions. Before the end of the century decrees were passed[208] expressly requiring all the brethren to adhere to the doctrine which he taught, without allowing the least departure from it, and this even before his canonisation. But it was not his own order alone which thus adopted his teaching, and bore witness to his position as a Doctor of the Church. That very university of Paris, which in 1255 had refused him his Doctor's cap in 1259, agreed to refer to his sole decision a theological question of deep interest, regarding the Sacramental species which then agitated the schools; and in 1274 addressed a letter to the Chapter-General of the Order, in which it speaks of the consternation into which the schools of the metropolis have been cast by the news of his death. They know not where to find expressions honourable enough by which to designate him; he is the morning star, the luminous sun, the light of the whole Church. They remind the Fathers how vehemently they had desired to have him restored to them, and beg that they may now at least be permitted to have his ashes. Two years after his canonisation, certain students in arts having revived some of the philosophical errors refuted by St. Thomas, Stephen, Bishop of Paris, immediately issued a letter, condemning every article which seemed to affect "the doctrine of that most excellent Doctor, the Blessed Thomas," whom he calls "the great luminary of the Catholic Church, the precious stone of the priesthood, the flower of Doctors, and the bright mirror of the university of Paris." The universities of Bologna, Padua, Naples, Toulouse, Salamanca, Alcala, and Louvain, at various times and in various ways formally declared their adhesion to his doctrine, as did also a great number of the religious orders, enumerated by Touron in his life of the saint.[209] And even during the lifetime of the saint, as Echard remarks,[210] the numerous disciples whom he had trained in his school, carried his teaching into the universities of Oxford, Cambridge, Bologna, Rome, and Cologne, for so great was the authority which his name enjoyed, that they seldom made use of any other commentaries than those of their master.

The character of St. Thomas is commonly regarded as presenting us with the perfect model of a Christian doctor. The ideal of such a character has been sketched by his own pen in that commentary on St. Matthew's Gospel, wherein he reminds the reader that it is not enough for the scholar to study the truths of religion, if he does not draw near to God in his life. For God is the source of light, whom if we approach by faith and charity we shall be truly illuminated, and it is by a holy life rather than by subtlety of reasoning that we must seek for a knowledge of the truth. There is a light which men may gain by study, but it suffices not to fill the soul; and there is a light which God pours out on those who sanctify study with prayer, and this is the true wisdom; according to the words of the Wise Man—"I called upon God, and the spirit of wisdom came upon me." The perfect Doctor, therefore, he continues, is he whose life, as well as whose doctrine, is light. Three things are necessary to him: stability, that he may never deviate from the truth; clearness, that he may teach without obscurity; and purity of intention, that he may seek God's glory, and not his own.[211] The life and the writings of St Thomas verified his own words. "The most learned of the saints," said Cardinal Bessarion, "he was also the holiest among the learned." He has himself expressed the guiding principle of his scholastic career in a passage which we may be permitted to quote here for the edification of all scholars. It occurs in his Summa against the Gentiles, wherein he attempts to define the office of the true philosopher, and shows that, even according to Aristotle, the only real philosophy is the science of truth. But, if truth is to be held, error must be refuted; hence, the office of the wise man is twofold— to meditate on the divine truths, and to combat all errors opposed to them.

"Encouraged, therefore, by the divine goodness to undertake this office, albeit the enterprise is far beyond my powers, my intention is, according to my scanty measure, to manifest the truth professed by the Catholic faith, and to eliminate the contrary errors; for to use the words of St. Hilary, I feel and am persuaded that the chief duty of my life which I owe to God is, in all my words, as in all my thoughts, to speak His praise."[212]

What an earnest loyalty to God breathes forth in these words! What a deep conviction of the oneness of philosophy with divine dogma! What a majesty of resolve in his determination to make the manifestation of Catholic truth the "duty of his life," and how rare a picture of lifelong purpose nobly achieved when we compare these expressions with his dying words!—"*Sumo Te pretium redemptionis animæ meæ, sumo Te viaticum peregrinationis animæ meæ; pro cujus amore studui, vigilavi et laboravi, prædicavi et docui; nihil unquam contra Te dixi; sed si quid dixi ignorans, non sum pertinax in sensu meo. Totum relinquô correctioni Sanctæ Romanæ Ecclesiæ, in cujus obedientia nunc transeo ex hac vita.*"[213]

The reconciliation of revealed truth and philosophy to which St. Thomas devoted his life must doubtless be regarded as the great intellectual triumph of the thirteenth century; and when we contemplate the group of illustrious men who took part in that work, it is impossible not to render homage to the good providence of God, who, in the hour of need, supplies His Church with fit instruments with which to effect His own purposes. The Friar Minors shared with the Friar Preachers the toils and glory of this great enterprise. Their order had not, indeed, been founded with the same express view of cultivating sacred science; but they were required to labour for the salvation of souls, and as souls could only be saved at this crisis by the vigorous defence of Catholic dogma, the humble sons of St. Francis scrupled not to enter the university schools, and soon gave to the Church a long line of doctors. The seraphic St. Bonaventure was bound to St. Thomas in the ties of friendship, and intimately associated with him in his work; and his teaching regarding the office of the human intellect, and the source of its illumination, is homogeneous with his. "All illumination descends to man," he says, "from God, the Fontal Light: all human science emanates, as from its source, from the Divine light." This light, he goes on to say, is fourfold—there is the inferior, the exterior, the interior, and the superior light. The first gives us the knowledge of those things manifested by the senses. The second illuminates us in respect of artificial forms, and includes a knowledge of the useful and ornamental arts, even those of the loom and the needle.[214] The third is the light of philosophical knowledge, and its object is intelligible truth; and this is threefold, for there are three kinds of verities—truth of language, truth of things, and truth of morals. Lastly, superior truth is that of grace and holy Scripture, and illuminates us in respect of saving truth. "Thus, the fourfold light descending from above has yet six differences, which set forth so many degrees of human science. There is the light of sensitive knowledge, the light of the mechanical arts, the light of rational philosophy, of natural philosophy, and of moral philosophy, and lastly, the light of grace and holy Scripture. And so there are six illuminations in this life of ours, and they have a setting, because all this knowledge shall be destroyed. And therefore there succeedeth to them the seventh day of rest, which hath no setting, and that is the illumination of glory."[215]

It is obviously beyond our present purpose to attempt anything like an account of the Dominican theologians who succeeded St. Thomas, and were formed in his school; and I shall content myself, therefore, with noticing a few of those friars of the thirteenth century, whose influence may be said to have told on education rather than on theology. And the first who claims our attention as having distinguished himself in this line, is, naturally, the librarian of the good king St. Louis, and the tutor of his children, Vincent of Beauvais. He devoted a great part of his life to a gigantic undertaking, the very conception of which attests the colossal scale on which men of those days thought and laboured for futurity. He desired to facilitate the pursuit of learning by collecting into one work everything useful to be known. The plan was not a new one; many such Encyclopædias had already been produced, as that of St. Isidore, and their value was great in an age when the scarcity of books rendered it next to impossible for any ordinary student to procure all the authors he would require to consult, if he desired to perfect himself in various sciences. But it is also possible that a more profound motive than that of mere convenience induced so many of the Christian writers to spend their labours on these encyclopædiac collections. They desired to present to the student the idea of knowledge as a whole, the parts of which were intimately connected, and could not be dissevered from one another without mutual injury. By philosophy, they understood a knowledge of truth in all its parts; and hence the student, according to the old established system, was steadily led through his trivium and quadrivium, those seven liberal arts selected as representing the chief divisions of philosophy, properly so called. The scholastics of Abelard's stamp had revolutionised this system, and, as we have seen, had all but banished the arts from the school, and made philosophy to consist in little more than the science of reasoning. And this was one point on which Hugo of St. Victor attacked them. Bred up in the old school of monastic students, he contended that their philosophy was no philosophy at all, and that the seven liberal arts cohered one with another, so that, if one were wanting, philosophy, which consisted in a comprehensive knowledge of all science,—rational, physical, and moral,—must necessarily be imperfect.[216] The same teaching is implied in the passage from St. Bonaventure, quoted above; and it seems probable that this sound view of the intimate connection of all parts of human knowledge flowing, as separate streams, from One Fontal source, prompted Vincent of Beauvais to undertake his gigantic work, that so the great edifice of science should be once more presented with all its halls and porticoes forming one harmonious whole, *domed* over, if we may so express ourselves, with Theology, and surmounted by the Cross.

He had some special facilities for carrying out his design which were not at the command of ordinary students. He was able to make free use of that noble library collected by St. Louis, and attached by him to the Sainte Chapelle. It was thence that he drew the materials of his work, and nature had endowed him with exactly the kind of genius which his task demanded. Antoine Poissevin says of him that he was a man who was never tired of reading, writing, teaching, and learning; the most gigantic labours did not alarm him; neither work, watching, nor fasting was ever known to cause him fatigue; and after devoting one-half of his life to reading the royal library, and every other collection of books that came within his reach, he did not shrink from employing the other in producing a compendium of all he had read. He limited himself to no one subject, or section of subjects; but resolved to embrace all arts and all sciences, whatever he found that was beautiful and true in the physical or in the moral world; whatever could make known the wonders of nature, or the yet greater wonders of grace; all that poets, philosophers, historians, or divines had said that was worth remembering— all this he determined to set before his reader in orderly arrangement; and undismayed at the magnitude of his enterprise, he laboured at it day and night till it was accomplished. "The Great Mirror," as he calls his work, is divided into three parts, in which are treated separately, Nature, Doctrine, and History. All his scientific and philosophic views are not, of course, original, for he proposed rather to give to the world the cream of other men's thoughts than of his own. But for this very reason the statements contained in his book are of greater value, as they show the shallowness of those charges so continually brought against the science of the Middle Ages, by writers who have probably concerned themselves very little to ascertain in what that science consisted. Vincent did not write to support new theories or explain away vulgar errors; he aimed only at presenting, in a compendious form, the commonly-received views of his own time, and of times anterior to his own, occasionally illustrating his subject with a sagacious remark, derived from reflection or personal observation. And what a host of misconceptions and traditional calumnies fall to pieces, as we glance through such an analysis of his pages as is given by Rohrbacher![217] How then, we exclaim, did not the mediæval *savants* oscillate between the opinion that the earth was a flat plane, and that other equally luminous view, that it was a cube? Is it possible that they knew anything of the principle of the attraction of gravitation, and stranger still, that they explained the spherical form of the earth by reasoning drawn from that very principle? Are we to believe our eyes when we read that Vincent of Beauvais illustrates this part of his subject by reminding us of the globular form of the rain drops, which he says, in language which reads like an anticipation of the verses of Montgomery, are so formed by the very same law as that which regulates the shape of the earth?

And who would expect to find the librarian of St. Louis putting forth the argument which still does good service in our popular class-books, wherein the spherical form of the earth is demonstrated by the gradual disappearance below the horizon of the hull and sails of a receding ship, and their as gradual reappearance in a contrary order, on its approach towards us? Yet there it is, together with yet more learned things; such as the method for measuring an arc of the meridian as a means of obtaining the circumference of the earth, quoted from the writings of Gerbert. His treatment of the metaphysical questions which occupied so much attention at the time at which he wrote, is no less remarkable than his natural philosophy, and Rohrbacher, comparing his explanation of *universal ideas* with that of Bossuet, gives the preference in point of profundity to the mediæval friar. "Thus, then," he continues, "by the middle of the thirteenth century, the religious of St. Dominic and St. Francis had resumed all Christian doctrine, the teaching of the Scriptures, the Fathers, and the Councils into a sum of theology; St. Thomas had examined in detail the pagan philosophy, had corrected it, and reconciled it with Christian truth. Roger Bacon, the Franciscan, not content with the ancient sciences catalogued by Aristotle, had begun to penetrate deeper into the secrets of nature, and the Dominican, Vincent of Beauvais, presented in his 'Mirror' an epitome of all that man, up to that time, knew in nature, science, art, philosophy, and history."[218]

Even had the benefits conferred by the friars on the world of letters stopped here, they would have done very much to counteract that narrowing tendency which has been noticed in the last chapter and to restore the broader and truer theory of education which in the twelfth century had been gradually pushed out of place. But to complete our idea of the work achieved by the Dominicans, we must add that they largely encouraged the cultivation of Biblical studies, and of the Greek and Oriental tongues. The Cardinal Hugh de St. Cher claims the gratitude of students as the author of the first Biblical Concordance, a work which he commenced in the year 1236. The Chapter-General of the Order, which was that year held in Paris, entered with large liberality into so useful a design, and appointed a great number of the brethren to labour at it under his direction. Martene, in his *Thesaurus Anecdotorum*, gives an ordinance of the Chapter of Paris, directing that all copies of the Sacred Scriptures used in the Order should be revised, corrected, and punctuated according to the correction of the body of religious thus employed. This great work was begun under the generalship, and with the hearty concurrence, of Blessed Jordan of Saxony; his successor

St. Raymund Pennafort, whose election had been mainly brought about through the exertions of Hugh de St. Cher, made yet more important provision for the encouragement of the Scriptural sciences. With a view of promoting the critical study of the Scriptures, and arming his brethren with weapons of controversy against the Jews and Mahometans, whose influence in this century was far more powerfully felt among Christians than it now is, he established Arabic and Hebrew studies in all the convents of Spain. Not content with this, he founded two colleges more expressly intended for the same purpose, attached to convents of the Order, one at Murcia, and the other at Tunis, filling them with religious whom he selected as best qualified to devote themselves to these pursuits. One of these was his celebrated namesake, Raymund Martin, the author of the *Pugio Fidei*, whom a learned French academician, M. Houtteville, has, by a singular blunder, numbered among the literary stars of the sixteenth century, unable, as it would seem, to credit the fact that so erudite a scholar could have flourished before the age of Francis the First. He was, however, a contemporary of St. Raymund, and is declared to have been as familiar with the Arabic, Hebrew, and Chaldaic tongues, as he was with Latin. The two last parts of his book are written in Hebrew, and he employed his last years in teaching the same language to a number of disciples, as well secular as religious.[219] The value of St Raymund's labours in founding these schools, which won him the title of the Restorer of Oriental Studies, was publicly acknowledged in a Bull of Clement VIII., who declares that the revival of the Eastern languages in the Dominican schools has contributed to the glory both of Spain and of the entire Church, and has been the proximate cause of a vast number of conversions.[220] Ten thousand Saracens had already been won to the faith before the year 1236.

Nevertheless, no charge is more commonly brought against the scholars of the Middle Ages, than that of neglecting the study of the Greek and Oriental languages. Hallam, in his "Literary History," with a great show of candour and painstaking research, notices certain examples of authors belonging to the twelfth, thirteenth, and fourteenth centuries, who, he says, appear to have known a few words of Greek. Greek books, he admits, were to be found in the libraries of the eleventh century, and Greek lexicons were compiled by Benedictine abbots, which seems an odd waste of labour if no one ever dreamed of using them. In the "Philobiblon" of Richard of Bury, written in the fourteenth century, he gravely informs us that he has counted five words of Greek. As to the statement made in the same book to the effect that the learned author had caused Greek and Hebrew grammars to be drawn up for the use of students, he dismisses the passage with the comment that no other record of such grammars is to be found. Nor does the decree of the Council of Vienne, passed in 1311, ordering the establishment of Greek, Hebrew, Arabic, and Chaldaic professorships in the universities of Paris, Oxford,

Bologna, and Salamanca, strike him as offering any evidence that these languages were really cultivated. The decree, he says (though he brings no authority in support of his words), *"remained a dead letter."* He accounts for the occasional phenomenon which is to be met with, of a scholar acquainted with five words of Greek, by attributing it to the assistance of Greek priests who found their way into Europe; and observes, that after all, supposing anybody did really know the language, he only used it to read "some petty treatise of the Fathers, or apocryphal legend." One is tempted to criticise the accuracy of a writer who begins by denying that any mediæval scholars in the West were acquainted with Greek, and then goes on to tell us what they did, and what they did not, read in that language. But there is a more serious fault in these statements than their bad logic. Having made an assertion of this nature on a subject which is certainly of no mean importance in the history of literature, he was bound to take some pains in investigating it. And it is difficult to understand how he can really have examined the literary history of the thirteenth century, without coming across some incidental proof of the ardour with which the Greek and Oriental languages were being at that time pursued in the Dominican schools. It was a fact of such world-wide notoriety that the motive which induced the university of Oxford to assign the Jews' quarter of the town to the Friars Preachers, was their known familiarity with the learned tongues, by means of which it was hoped they might become efficient instruments for the conversion of their Jewish neighbours. General after General added to the ordinances made by his predecessors for keeping up these studies. Humbert de Romanis, the fifth General of the Order, to whom St. Raymund had communicated the success of his own efforts in Spain, at once determined to extend the ordinance, which had hitherto been partial in its operation, to all the convents of the order; and in 1256 he addressed a circular letter to the brethren, in which he invites all who feel themselves inspired by the grace of God to devote themselves to the study of Greek, Hebrew, and Arabic, to communicate with him, because the knowledge of these languages is most necessary in order to extend the light of the Gospel among the Greek schismatics and Moorish infidels.[221] F. Penna, auditor of the Rota to Clement VIII., assures us that it was the success of the colleges established by the Friars Preachers, and specially in Spain, that moved the Council of Vienne to issue the decree already quoted, and the same is repeated by other writers. The acts of that council are, however, by others attributed to the influence of the celebrated Franciscan Raymund Lully, the Illuminated Doctor, as he was called, who devoted many years and much labour to the endeavour to obtain the foundation of colleges for the study of these languages, in order to provide missionaries qualified to labour among the infidels. He himself was a profound Orientalist, and the legendary tales which multiplied in connection with his extraordinary life, represent the tree under which he constructed his mountain hut, as bearing on its very leaves the Greek, Arabic, and Chaldaic characters. At last he persuaded King James of Arragon to found a college in the island of Miraman for thirteen Franciscans who were to be given up to the study of the learned tongues. Pope Honorius IV. entered warmly into his views, but died before he was able to forward them; Philip le Bel acceded so far as to endow a college at Paris, and the Council of Vienne passed its decree confirming the erection of that college, and directing that similar establishments should be formed in the other chief European universities. Hallam, as we have seen, boldly asserts that the decree remained "a dead letter." How generally it was carried out, or how long its provisions remained in force, may not be easy to determine; but there are precise documents to prove that it was at least put in force at Paris and Oxford. A letter is preserved, written in 1325, by Pope John XXII., to his legate in Paris, recommending him to watch the holders of the new professorships very closely, lest, under colour of the study of the Oriental tongues, they introduce any of the pernicious philosophical doctrines already condemned, and gathered out of the Gentile books.[222] The historic evidence of the *bonâ fide* existence of the professorships at Oxford is yet more circumstantial, and is thus referred to by Ayliffe in his history of that university. "I pass on," he says, "to speak of the lectures founded by Pope Clement V. for the teaching of the Hebrew, Chaldaic, Arabic, and Greek languages, among which lectures John de Bristol, a converted Jew, read the Hebrew for many years at Oxford with great applause; and this year (1318), received a stipend settled on him by Walter Reynolds, Archbishop of Canterbury, and a tax of an halfpenny per mark from every ecclesiastical benefice throughout his province. This money was collected at the beginning of every Lent, and was lodged with the prior of the Holy Trinity."[223] He goes on to notice some frauds committed in the collection of this tax in 1327, which, he says, is the last notice he finds concerning it. It is very probable that the professorships afterwards fell into abeyance, but the assertion that they were never founded is manifestly one of those made by a writer who draws his bow at a venture, and never cares to inquire into the fact.

Among those who took part in the deliberations of the Council of Vienne was Aymeric of Placentia, twelfth General of the Order of Preachers, who in the previous year had established a house of studies in every Province for the Greek and Oriental languages, requiring the Provincials to provide very learned teachers of the same, and if none such were to be found among the brethren, they were to engage the services of secular professors, to be paid out of the revenues of the Province,[224] a provision which certainly seems to imply that such professors were there to be found. This Aymeric, whom the chronicle of the Masters-General call "a learned man, and a great lover of letters," did much also to promote the study of the Scriptures at other chapters of his Order. Echard tells us of the magnificent present bestowed by him on the convent of Bologna, in the shape of a Hebrew Pentateuch, which Bernard of Montfauçon describes as having himself seen. It contained an inscription, declaring the book to be the identical copy written by Esdras the scribe after the return from Babylon, and which he read in the ears of the people. After being preserved in various Jewish synagogues with the utmost veneration, Aymeric had obtained possession of it, and its authenticity was attested by several learned Jews. Though Echard hesitates to yield full credit to the tradition, he admits that the antiquity of the copy was not to be doubted.

The culture of Greek in the Order is no less distinctly proved than that of the Oriental tongues. William de Moerbeka made a number of translations from Plato, Galen, and Proclus of Tyre; and his translation of Aristotle was made directly from the original, at the request of St. Thomas, who himself understood the language well enough to criticise his friend's version. Moerbeka was appointed Archbishop of Corinth in 1277, after being several times despatched as apostolic missionary to the East. Another fellow-student and intimate friend of St. Thomas, the cardinal Annibal Annibaldi,[225] is declared to have been learned both in Greek and Arabic philosophy. These examples of the linguistic erudition of the friars are but few out of many that might be given, and it is clear that their Greek reading was not limited to Apocryphal legends and petty treatises of the Fathers. It certainly included the Greek philosophy, both Plato and Aristotle having found translators among the Friars Preachers of the thirteenth century. But it is more than probable that the poets and historians of Greece were little known or cultivated, for the object of these studies was less literary than practical. The Friars had to contend with a false philosophy, drawn out of the books of the Gentiles, and to maintain controversies with Greek schismatics and Jewish and Moorish unbelievers; and they studied to arm themselves for the work in which they were engaged. Practical views predominated very generally in that wonderful thirteenth century, which we are so disposed to contemplate through a poetic medium; and so we may safely admit the likelihood that the Greek poetry was not much studied before the period of classic renaissance.

The influence of the Dominicans meanwhile extended to other universities besides those of Paris, Cologne, and Bologna, to which they were first affiliated. At Toulouse, the nursery of their Order, they naturally held a forward position, and led the struggle against the Albigensian errors, for the suppression of which the university had been mainly founded. At Orleans their convent was used as the place of assembly for the doctors, and the establishment of the university being for some reason regarded with disfavour by the citizens, they directed their spleen against the friars, regarding them as the main prop of the unpopular institution, and did their best to level the convent with the ground. But they always held their ground at Orleans, and their larger theories on the subject of education may have had something to do with the character which distinguished that university, for Orleans opposed itself to the rage for logic, and always upheld the study of the arts.

One other foundation must be named, which, though it in no way shares the brilliant historic fame of so many sister academies, is too illustrative of the position held by the Dominicans in the mediæval schools to be passed over in this place.

The ancient university of Dublin was founded in 1320 by Archbishop Bicknor, in virtue of a Bull from Pope Clement V., confirmed by Pope John XXII.; one of its first masters and doctors being an Irish Dominican, William De Hardite.[226] This university was established in connection with St. Patrick's Cathedral, but from the troubles of the times and the want of funds, it very soon declined, and in the following century became all but extinct. To supply the means of academic education to the youth of Ireland, therefore, the Dominicans of Dublin made a noble effort. In 1428 they opened a gymnasium, or high school, on Usher's Island, dedicated to St. Thomas Aquinas, in which all branches of knowledge were taught, from grammar to theology, and to which all classes of students, whether ecclesiastical or secular, were admitted. Hither a great number of young men flocked to pursue their course of philosophy and theology. As the convent was on one side of the river, and the house of studies on the other, the friars, with that munificence which characterised the ancient regular orders, erected a stone bridge of four arches at their own expense, long known as the "Old Bridge," which was not destroyed till 1802, and which for two centuries was the only bridge of the kind in Dublin. With the consent of the common council, a Dominican lay brother received the tolls paid by carriage passengers over the bridge, and sprinkled the passers-by from a font for holy water, which was erected there. "It is an interesting fact in the history of education in Ireland," says Mr. Wyse,[227] "that the only stone bridge in the capital of the kingdom was built by one of the monastic orders as a communication between a convent and its college, a thoroughfare thrown across a dangerous river for teachers and scholars to frequent halls of learning, where the whole range of the sciences of the day *was taught gratuitously*." But even this noble foundation did not satisfy the Irish Dominicans. In 1475, the four mendicant Orders, headed by the Friars Preachers, presented a memorial to Pope Sixtus IV., praying for canonical authority to erect their schools in Dublin into a university for the liberal arts and theology, which petition was granted, and a Brief[228] was issued the same year to that effect, granting the new academy the same rights and privileges that were enjoyed by the members of the university of Oxford. It appears certain that the proposed scheme was really carried into effect, for Campion, in his History of Ireland, written in 1570, before his conversion to the Catholic faith, declares that before the subversion of the monasteries, "divines were cherished" in them, "and open exercise maintained." But whatever were the success or the failure of the scheme, it is equally worthy of our admiration that four mendicant Orders should thus unite, under the leadership of the children of St. Dominic, to supply an academic education to the youth of their country solely out of their own resources. They asked neither for royal charters nor state endowments, but, content with the authority of the Papal Brief, they offered to their countrymen, with more than princely munificence, a gratuitous university education.

The result of the Christian philosophy established in the schools by the labours of St. Thomas, and propagated by the brethren of his Order, spread far beyond the academic circles. That philosophy appeared in an age which was full of the force and passion of youth, and ready to find utterance in the language of the heart and the imagination. It spoke, not in the Summa alone, but in the poetry of Dante, in the paintings of Cimabue and Giotto, and in the minsters of Salisbury or Cologne. For in each and all of these we see in various ways the reflection of Christian dogma. If we may credit the voice of tradition, it was to the geometrical science, united to the profound Christian mysticism of Albert the Great, that the German architects were indebted for many of the secrets of their art. He is known to have consecrated, and is believed to have designed, more than one of those superb cathedrals which date their existence from the same century which witnessed the rise of the universities; and the choir of the Dominican convent at Cologne, which Rodolph tells us was rebuilt by the great master "according to the rules of geometry, and as a most skilful architect," is said to have served as the model on which the cathedral itself was designed. Almost at the same time the two Dominican artists, Fra Sisto, and Fra Ristoro, were initiating an architectural reform in Italy, and it was the Greek paintings that decorated their beautiful church of Sta. Maria Novella, at Florence, that gave the first impulse to the genius of Cimabue. That great man, the father of Italian art, was a pupil of the Florentine Dominicans. The friars, "in order to carry out that portion of their rule which commands them to be useful," says Marchese, "had opened a grammar school for the instruction of the Florentine youth, as well as for their own novices. The grammar master was sometimes one of the friars, and sometimes a secular; and in the latter case he received a fixed salary of a florin a month, with board and lodging." At this time the office happened to be filled by an uncle of Cimabue, who numbered his own nephew among his scholars. The boy often escaped from his books in order to watch the painters at work in the church; and in school, instead of attending to his lessons, would sometimes employ himself in making rude pen-and-ink sketches. His masters discerned his rare gifts, and instead of punishing him for preferring his pencil to his grammar, they wisely determined to encourage his genius, and placed him under the tuition of the Greek artists, whom he soon surpassed, as he was himself surpassed by his own pupil Giotto. The latter also was largely indebted to the Dominican Order, for his first patron was Pope Benedict XI., a Friar Preacher, and a disciple of St. Thomas, who was gifted with that love of art which has ever been hereditary in the order. Giotto was the friend of Dante, and, like him, steeped in the essentially Christian ideas of the age. The hero of his pencil was St. Francis, and he has left his poems in honour of that hero painted on the walls of the church of Assisi.

We may judge how very powerfully the Christian philosophy of the thirteenth and fourteenth centuries told on the restoration of art by a glance at such documents as the statutes drawn up for the corporation of Siennese painters, in 1335. "We are called by the grace of God," they say, "to manifest to rude and ignorant men who cannot read the miraculous things operated by the power of the holy faith. Now our faith chiefly consists in believing and adoring one eternal God—a God of infinite power, immense wisdom, and boundless love and goodness; and we are persuaded that nothing, however small it may be, can be begun or finished without three things—namely, power, wisdom, and will, with love."[229] Who drew up these statutes, and whence were such ideas of art derived? We know not; yet the theological cast of the phraseology leads us to infer that their author must have been perfectly familiar with the writings of St. Thomas.[230]

To speak broadly, then, we may say that the victory achieved in the thirteenth century, through the labours of the scholastic theologians, was that which established the supremacy of dogma in the schools, and which made its power indirectly felt in every province of thought, art, and literature. The immediate result may be stated in the words wherein Rohrbacher sums up the ecclesiastical history of this period. "During the whole of this time," he says, "in spite of the prodigious activity which we have seen taking possession of men's minds in the West, moving them to embrace and examine every question of theology, philosophy, and other sciences, as well in general as in detail, *not a single new heresy arose*."[231] Order had been introduced into the wild chaos of opinion, and the Christian schoolmen assumed the position as masters of thought, which had hitherto been held by pagans.

Before closing this chapter, we will anticipate an objection which has probably suggested itself to some who have accompanied us through the foregoing studies. Whilst freely acknowledging the services rendered to the faith by the scholastic theologians, they may be disposed to fear lest something of the elder tone of spirituality was lost when the lecture halls of university professors were substituted for the claustral schools of the Benedictines. There was doubtless more accurate science; but was there the old contemplative wisdom that fed itself in silent communing on God? Had the heart kept pace with the intellect, or had not the schools become more rich in dogma, and less full of love? And this kind of doubt as to the possibility of uniting things apparently so little in harmony as philosophic acuteness and unction of heart, is the more natural and excusable as we find that it actually prevailed to a very considerable extent among the religious students of the period, and gave rise to not a few disputes. Hence, in the early days of the order of Preachers, conscientious scruples were entertained by some among the friars themselves as to the lawfulness of cultivating philosophy and the liberal arts; and we find a decree passed, in consequence, at one of the first Chapters-General, declaring the use and necessity of such studies. So powerful, however, was the impulse felt in the order towards the contemplative life during the first century of its existence, that some still felt uneasiness lest the too great application to scholastic science should leave the heart dry and barren. But Humbert de Romanis severely condemned such scruples, comparing those who entertained them to the Philistines, who deprived the children of Israel of all smiths' tools;[232] and declared the study of philosophy to be necessary on the part of Christian scholars, inasmuch as it was now employed by unbelievers as a weapon with which to attack the dogmas of the Church.

Dryness and spiritual barrenness, in fact, were the last faults which could be charged against the dogmatic theologians of the thirteenth century. It is remarkable that the Dominican convent most noted as a house of studies north of the Alps, and which was the nursery of all the greatest doctors of the order, was precisely that in which the brethren most eagerly devoted themselves to the contemplative life. All the first friars of Cologne, including Brother Henry, the first prior, distinguished themselves as contemplative writers.[233] Albert the Great—the greatest star of the Cologne school—displayed in his later writings the germs of that tender mysticism which afterwards appeared in the writings of Tauler and Suso. In the distinction he draws between Christian and pagan philosophy, he clearly shows that the studies then pursued in the order, whilst they illuminated the intellect, were far from drying up the heart. "The contemplation of the Catholic Christian is one thing," he said, "and that of a pagan philosopher is another. The philosopher meditates for his own utility alone—his end is merely to learn and to know. But the Christian contemplates out of love for Him whom he contemplates—that is, God. Hence, not only has he a more perfect knowledge for his end, *but he passes from knowledge into love.*" And the very last of his works, written in his old age, and, as his biographer says, with the view of refreshing his mind when weary with the fatigues of teaching, bears the title *De Adhærendo Deo*, and opens with these touching words:—"Having desired to write something, in order, as far as possible, to end well our labours in this region of exile, we have proposed to ourselves to inquire how a man may best detach himself from all below, in order to attach himself solely, freely, and purely, to our Lord God. For the end of Christian perfection is love, and it is by love that we adhere to God."[234]

To the same effect are the words of St. Thomas: "In the perfect contemplative life, divine truth is not merely *seen*, but *loved*."[235] The soul, plunging itself in the contemplation of the Divine greatness, acquires a knowledge of God, not so much by means of light and cognition, as by an experimental union with Him; so that, through the affections thence derived, it knows and it contemplates. "Hence it comes to pass," he continues, "that He is loved more than He is known, because He can be perfectly loved, even although He be not perfectly known."[236]

His life corresponded to his teaching. Though not exhibiting to the ordinary observer that miraculous and extraordinary character which attaches to many of the saints, all his biographers agree in asserting that his union with God became at last wholly uninterrupted. "So entirely was his mind intent upon God," says Flaminius, "that nothing was able to separate him from this contemplation." "I have learnt more by prayer than by study," were his own words to his familiar companion, Brother Reginald, and he often repeated the warning that, Wisdom being the gift of God, a man ought not to endeavour or hope to acquire it by dint of study, without humbly asking for it in prayer. From none of the writings of the saints could there be collected maxims of more tender piety than from St. Thomas; it was he who said that the measure of our love of God was to love Him without measure,[237] who called the Holy Scriptures *the Heart of Christ*,[238] and who confessed to one of his friends that there were two things he did not understand: how a religious could ever think or speak of anything, but God, and how a man who had committed mortal sin could ever smile. Divine science took in him its most attractive form, and, to use his own words in describing the truly wise man, it lifted him into a world beyond the moon where he enjoyed a perpetual serenity.[239] The violence and injustice to which he was exposed in the long and vexatious controversy with the Parisian doctors never had power to disturb him; and this sweet serenity of heart was so apparent on his countenance that he is said to have had a peculiar power of imparting the gift of spiritual joy to all who conversed with him.

When he preached the Lent to the people of Naples, he appeared in the pulpit like one rapt in ecstacy, with his eyes closed and his face turned towards heaven, as though he were contemplating another world. Even at table he was always ruminating divine things, and St. Antoninus tells us that, when he was asleep, he was often heard to pray aloud. It is clear that he fully recognised the possibility of a life of study drying up the fountains of devotion, for he gave as his reason for daily reading the Collations of Cassian, after the example of his holy patriarch St. Dominic, that he might draw thence devotion, and that by means of devotion his understanding might be raised to sublimer things.[240] And it was the same principle which made him, like Bede, inflexible with himself in never absenting himself from assisting in choir, both by day and night, frequently telling his religious that a student must by all means keep open the wells of devotion, so that the work of the head may never cause the heart to grow dry and tepid.

Some particular instances are recorded of his special love for the Divine Office, and the singular relish he took in the Sacred Psalmody. Flaminius speaks of the frequent raptures and devout tears which certain portions of it elicited from him, such as the versicle "*Ne projicias me in tempore senectutis,*" which recurs so frequently in the time of Lent. It may also be observed that all his biographers notice the unction which attached to his preaching, for he possessed an extraordinary power of moving the hearts of his hearers, and exciting compunction and amendment of life. He was frequently called upon to preach the Lent both at Rome and Naples, and on one of these occasions, when preaching in St. Peter's to an immense audience on Good Friday, all the people who heard him were moved to tears, and ceased not to weep until Easter day, when his Paschal sermon filled them with holy jubilation.

Massoulié, one of the greatest commentators on St. Thomas, has remarked the erroneous impression entertained by many who believe that great doctor to have been "so completely occupied with the speculations of the intellect as not to have applied himself equally to excite the emotions of the heart.... It is, however, certain," he continues, "that, if we attentively read his works, we shall find his love to have been equal to his knowledge, for they contain all the secrets of the mystical life, and the sublimest and most divine operations of grace in the hearts of those consecrated to God. In fact, there is nothing really important in all the states to which a soul can be raised in the spiritual life, and in all God's secret communications with holy souls, which he has not explained in the second part of his *Summa*; whilst in his smaller works he has given his heart full liberty to expand itself.... Hence," he adds, "we must not suppose that St. Thomas received the name of the Angelic Doctor only on account of his profound arguments and vast knowledge of the truths of faith; but still more justly on account of those ecstacies which made him enter into the society of the blessed Spirits."[241] So far, indeed, was the Angel of the Schools from being all intellect and no heart, that even the more human side of his character exhibits him to us as peculiarly accessible to the tenderness of Christian friendship. He described it with his pen, he felt it in his heart, and he failed not to excite corresponding sentiments in others. The tie which existed between him and St. Bonaventure is well known, nor was that which bound him to Blessed Albert less close and enduring. After the death of St. Thomas, Albert was never able to speak of his great pupil without shedding tears, a circumstance which is even alluded to in the process of canonisation. His brethren wondered at it, and feared lest this excessive weeping should arise from some weakness of the head. But his tears flowed only out of the abundance of his love. The very name of his beloved disciple sufficed to draw from him these tokens of affection, and he never wearied in repeating to those around him that they had lost "the flower and ornament of the world."

The stem that produced that flower did not lose its fertility when its fairest blossom was transplanted to Paradise. The "Order of Truth," as it was called, continued to bud forth a long succession of philosophers and theologians, the bare enumeration of whose names would fill a volume, for according to a moderate computation they number about 5000. When St. Dominic and his six disciples first entered the school of Alexander of Toulouse, who could have anticipated the mighty stream that was to flow from that seemingly humble source? Yet now "the brook had become a river," and the river had swelled into a sea, and the doctrine of his sons "shone forth as the morning light," and was poured out to "all those who sought the Truth."[242]

CHAPTER XV.

ENGLISH SCHOOLS AND UNIVERSITIES.

A.D. 1149 TO 1170.

THE paramount importance attaching to the schools of Paris has too long detained us from following the history of scholarship in our own island; and we shall now have to retrace our steps some two hundred years, in order, before speaking of the Oxford schools and scholars of the thirteenth century, to say something of the origin of the university, and to notice the other English schools existing at the same period. It would be little less than audacious to pretend to give any authentic account of the rise of Oxford University, and we may as well at once admit the fact that one of our great national institutions, alive and vigorous in the nineteenth century, dates its beginning from ages whose traditions are purely mythical. However far we go back in the history of Oxford, we are always referred to some date that is yet earlier. From the reign of the Confessor, we glance back to the days of the great Alfred, who allotted one-eighth of his revenue to the support of her schools, and is popularly regarded as her founder. But even Alfred cannot claim to have done more than restore the schools which had existed there before his time, and the history of St. Frideswide carries us back to the eighth century, and tells us how in the reign of her father, Didan, King of Mercia, certain inns were constructed in the vicinity of St. Mary's Church, *diversoria religioni aptissima*, which were used as places of education, and grew into a religious house, afterwards dedicated to St. Frideswide. This famous priory was the real nucleus of the university. In 1049 Harold, then Earl of Oxford, placed canons here; then came the Norman Conquest, and in the reign of Henry the Scholar, who had received his early education from the monks of Abingdon, the king handed the priory over to his favourite chaplain Guimond, who established therein a community of Norman canons, and set about building, as none but a Norman prior knew how to build.

From St. Frideswide's priory let us now turn to the old residence of the Mercian kings, in which Offa resided, which Alfred made a "king's house," which had Saxon towers, deemed to be ancient in the days of the Confessor, and which, eight years after the Conquest, was granted to Robert D'Oyley, who added the great keep and other buildings. Within the castle of Oxford thus founded, he and his sworn brother in arms, Robert D'Ivery, raised a church dedicated to St. George, and served by secular canons. This was the second foundation stone of the university; and in 1149 his nephew, Robert D'Oyley the Second, transferred the foundation to his priory of Austin Canons at Osney. I cannot withhold from the curious reader the legend of the foundation of Osney, as it is quaintly related by Leland. After telling us that Robert D'Oyley had married a wife named Edith, and founded a priory of black canons "at Oseney by Oxford, among the isles that Isis river ther makyth," he continues: "Sum write that this was the occasion of the making of it. Edithe usid to walke out of the Castelle with her gentlewomen to solace, and oftentimes wher yn a certen place in a tre, as often as she cam, a certen Pyes usid to gither to it, and ther to chattre, and as it were, to speke on to her. Edithe much mervelyng at this matter, and was sometyme sore ferid as by a wondre, whereupon she sent for one Radulphe, a Chanon of S. Frediswide's, a man of a vertuous lyfe, and her confessour, askyng hym counsell: to whom he answerid aftir he had sene the faschion of the Pyes chatteryng only at *her* cummyng, that she shulde bilde sum chirche or monasterie in that place. Then she entreated her husband to bilde a priorie, which he did, makyng Radulphe first prior of it. The cummynge of Edithe to Oseney, and Radulphe waiting on her, and the tre with the chatteryng Pyes be payntid in the waulle of the arch over Edith's tumbe in Oseney Priorie."[243]

The two priories of Osney and St. Frideswide became both of them great houses of study, but the little church of St. George had also its share in the same work. The apartments in the castle formerly occupied by the canons were, after their removal to Osney, made over to certain poor scholars, known as "the wardens and scholars of St. George, within the castle of Oxford." They formed perhaps the earliest collegiate establishment of the university, being governed by a body of statutes, wherein mention is made of a warden, fellows, scholars, and commoners. The warden was always one of the Osney canons, who came once or twice in the week to see that good order was preserved, and in his absence governed through his deputy. Tanner gives some curious particulars of the customs in use among the fellows, and the ceremonies of their installation, and tells us that Henry V. had intended to have enlarged this college into a splendid royal foundation, but was prevented by death from carrying out his design.

Other inns and halls of a *quasi* collegiate character gradually clustered round these religious houses. No fewer than forty-two *hospitia*, or inns for scholars, were inhabited in Robert D'Oyley's time. So early as 1175, the Benedictines of Winchcombe Abbey had established a *studium generale* at Oxford, for the use of their monks, and a great number of schools, some attached to religious and collegiate houses, and others presided over by independent masters, very early gave their name to "School Street." In these buildings there was no attempt at architectural grandeur. They were only distinguished from those devoted to "base mechanic uses" by quaint devices and inscriptions over their doors. Both halls and schools before 1170 were built of timber and thatched with straw, when a great fire destroyed the greater part of the city, and the inhabitants were induced to erect a few stone and slated edifices, the "stramina," or thatched houses, still appearing in many localities. The schools of Osney Abbey were only rooms over certain shops, and the lectures were read by the masters in their own chambers. The effect of the "Aularian" system, as it has been called, was certainly to multiply the *number* of the scholars; for many were able to pursue their studies in the wretched accommodation thus afforded them, who could find no place in the richer colleges of later times. To the thousands of native scholars were added those who, after the fashion of the times, resorted to Oxford from other countries, no man being then content with studying at a single academy, or thinking he had qualified himself for the post of doctor till he had passed some years in foreign schools. It was no easy matter to preserve discipline in such a motley society; the chancellor was the only recognised authority, and when his single arm proved insufficient for the task of government, he was assisted by an officer named the Hebdomadarius, now represented by the Hebdomadal Board. The disorders which prevailed here, as at Paris, finally led to the establishment of colleges with regular statutes of discipline; but this change, which had the immediate effect of diminishing the number of students, was not even begun before the reign of Henry III.

Previous to that date, it would not be easy to determine with any exactness the system of discipline or of studies that prevailed. We know, however, that in 1133, when Robert Pulleyne came over from Paris and opened his school in Oxford, he found sacred letters had for some years fallen into neglect, and, to restore them, not only read lectures on the Scriptures gratuitously, but obtained the services of other professors at his own expense. He also preached every Sunday to the people, and left no stone unturned to instruct the students in the learned languages. In 1142 he was summoned to Rome by Innocent II., and, becoming Cardinal and Chancellor of the Roman Church, obtained large privileges for the Oxford scholars. In 1149, the very date of the Osney foundation, when England was in the thick of the disturbances of Stephen's reign, Vacarius, a Bolognese professor, began to deliver lectures on civil law at Oxford, and that with so much success as to throw the schools of arts and theology into the shade. Before the end of the century, the study of canon law was added, and about the same time the lectures on medicine began to attract so much attention that the authorities felt a reasonable alarm lest their university should altogether cease to be a seat of liberal learning. "Physic brings men riches," they said, "and law leads to honour, while logic is forced to go a-foot." All the divines of the day, both at home and abroad, agreed in condemning the preference given to law over theology. "What is this?" exclaims St. Bernard, "from morning till night we litigate and hear litigation: day after day uttereth strife, and night after night indicateth malice." And in the same spirit Stephen Langton reproves his fellow-ecclesiastics for "leaving the true field of Booz, the study of Holy Scripture, in order that they may win the poor honour of being called decretalists." Arts, indeed, always continued to be regarded *theoretically* as the proper subject of Oxford University studies, but in their eagerness to acquire the more lucrative branches of learning, the students were too often content with a smattering of polite letters. Hence, according to Wood, they came to be divided into three classes, the Shallow, the Patchy, and the Solid. The first did not study arts at all, the second crammed from convenient abstracts, and the third, a very small minority, laid a good foundation, and thereon built a tolerable superstructure.

The troubles which affected the English Church in the reign of Henry II. affected the university very unfavourably. The persecution directed against St. Thomas and his adherents, created such a general feeling of insecurity that, in 1169, a great number of the Oxford students emigrated in a body to Paris, where they were well received by Louis VII. Indeed, at this time there was no European country in which some English scholars might not be found, who preferred a voluntary exile to the dangers to which they thought themselves exposed at home from the hands of the royal tyrant. This crisis hastened the decay of liberal studies at Oxford. Daniel Merlac, who, about the close of Henry's reign, travelled into Spain to collect books and perfect himself in mathematics, declares, in the preface to his treatise *De Rerum Naturis*, that it was his knowledge of the neglect of good learning which prevailed in his own country which induced him to remain so long in exile. He passes a very severe criticism on the ignorance of the professors, not only at Oxford, but at Paris also, agreeing pretty much with the strictures passed by John of Salisbury on the "Cornificians." In particular, he describes with great disgust the conduct of certain "beasts," as he calls them, whom he saw occupying seats at the latter university with an air of great importance, having desks set out before them, with huge books adorned with golden letters, wherein, from time to time, they solemnly jotted down a word or two. It was all very well, so long as they kept silence, but as soon as they opened their mouths they betrayed their ignorance. Wood, who complains bitterly of the decay of humane learning caused by the reign of law at Oxford, and of logic in France says that polite letters would never have fallen into such neglect had the monastic schools retained their ascendancy. As it was, he says, "purity of speech decayed, philosophy was neglected, and nothing but Parisian quirks prevailed."

Oxford revived a little during the reign of the Lion-hearted Richard, who loved the city as his birthplace, and, moreover, was inclined to favour the university, were it only to emulate his great rival, Philip Augustus, who had declared himself the protector of the Paris scholars. His brother John seemed at first disposed to follow his example, and granted the students their first charter, exempting them from the jurisdiction of the Ordinary; but he soon counterbalanced this favour by hanging three clerks—an act so deeply resented by the ecclesiastical authorities that the city was laid under an interdict, and the scholars dispersed to Cambridge, Reading, and Maidstone.

Better days dawned on the Church on the accession of Henry III. The arrival of the mendicant orders in England gave an immense stimulus to the schools, and in 1229 the king took occasion of the quarrel just then raging between the civil and academic authorities at Paris, to invite the discontented masters and scholars over to England. This immigration from France raised Oxford to a high degree of prosperity. The number of her students is said to have risen to 30,000, though Wood admits that the company was not always the most select. "Among these," he says, "were a set of varlets, who pretended to be scholars, shuffling themselves in, and doing much villany in the university by thieving, quarrelling, &c. They lived under no discipline and had no tutors, but, only for fashion's sake, would sometimes thrust themselves into the schools at ordinary lectures; and when they went to perform any mischief, then would they be accounted scholars, that so they might free themselves from the jurisdiction of the burghers."

The presence of so many "varlets" will perhaps account for the frequency of unseemly brawls which disturbed the peace of the city, and brought sad discredit on the university. One instance will suffice to show the semibarbarous state of society in the city of letters at the beginning of the thirteenth century. Cardinal Otho, the cardinal legate, coming to Oxford in 1238, was honourably entertained at Osney Abbey. The scholars sent him a handsome present for his table, and a deputation of them came after dinner to pay their respects. The Italian porter, however, not only refused them admission, but, through the half-open door, loaded them with abuse. This, of course, was not to be endured; the door was forced in a moment, and a lively contest ensued between the English and the Italians. The cardinal's steward, stung with the derisive epithets lavished on him by the scholars, threw some dirty water in the face of a poor Irish priest, who was patiently waiting at the door for some broken victuals. This was the signal for a call to arms, and one of the party, seizing a bow, shot the unhappy steward dead on the spot. The legate took refuge in the church tower, whence, escaping by night, he joined the king and demanded justice. Thirty scholars were accordingly arrested, the city was laid under another interdict, and all the university exercises suspended. Nor was tranquillity restored till ample satisfaction had been offered by the English bishops, who, says Matthew Paris, were ready to make any sacrifice necessary to preserve "the second school of the Church."

Brawls of this sort make up a very large portion of early Oxford history. Here, as at Paris, the division of "nations" was a fruitful source of squabbling. Northerns and Southerns, Welshmen, Englishmen, and Irishmen, fought pitched battles, one with another, on all available opportunities; and the Jews, whose audacity reached an incredible height, did their best to add another element of discord by disturbing the scholars at their prayers. We need not enter into the history of these strange disturbances. The Irish seem to have exhibited the greatest pugnacity, and obliged the magistrates to pass many wholesome laws for their correction and conversion to "more civil walking," though, as it would seem, with very small success. The chief occasions on which the king's peace was wont to be broken were the national festivals celebrated in honour of St. George, St. Patrick, and St. David; and at length it became necessary to forbid popular demonstrations on these days, under pain of the greater excommunication.

In this early period of the university history, the schools frequented by the scholars were of two kinds,—the secular schools ruled by masters who rented rooms in the houses and over the shops of the burghers, and the claustral schools, held in the various religious houses. As a general rule, the students were expected to know grammar before matriculating at the university, but in case they entered very young, or that their early education had been neglected, they could make up their deficiencies in the grammar schools, some of which were afterwards attached to colleges, for the benefit of the clerks and choristers connected with those institutions. Wood gives some interesting particulars about these grammar schools. He says they were placed by the chancellor under the supervision of some master of arts, to whom the grammar master promised obedience. He moreover engaged to read nothing with his scholars without license from the chancellor, to instruct them in Latin authors, and make them construe in French as well as English, and not to read certain portions of the Latin poets, which might be considered injurious to good morals. Degrees were at that time granted in grammar, as in other faculties. Thus, in the reign of Edward I., we find Maurice Byrchensaw graduating as bachelor of grammar and rhetoric, and composing, as his customary exercise on that occasion, a hundred verses in praise of the university, and thereupon having his head solemnly crowned with laurel.

Some of the illustrations which Wood has collected as to the state of studies at Oxford in ancient times, are sufficiently amusing. It seems that Lent was generally a time unfavourable to peace, by reason of the unusual amount of logical disputation, indulged in at that season by the scholars who were preparing for their degrees. Hence the king's peace was very often broken over the discussion of quiddities, and the grammar students showed themselves equally pugnacious over the niceties of Latin syntax. Musical degrees were very often granted, the candidates being required to read the musical books of Boëthius, and on the day of inception to present a mass of their own composition, which was to be sung on the occasion, together with certain antiphons. The masses and antiphons were generally composed in two parts, up to the time of Henry VIII., who, being exceedingly skilful in musical science, was able, not only to sing his part sure, but to compose masses in four, five, and even six parts, which more complicated style of composition thus came into fashion at the university.

The Oxford scholars often complained of the grievance of having to attend the schools on festival days, and presented more than one poetical petition to the ruling powers that they might have a little breathing space, at least on the greater feasts. And certainly, if we may take the account given us at a considerably later period as furnishing any notion of the life of a poor scholar of the thirteenth century, it was one of hard work and little comfort. It occurs in a sermon preached at Cambridge in the middle of the sixteenth century, by Thomas Lever, Fellow of St John's, and has been preserved by the historian Strype. There is every reason to suppose that the picture which he gives would apply as well to the reign of the First as to that of the Sixth Edward; substituting the hearing of Mass for the attendance of common prayer. "There be divers which rise daily about four or five of the clock in the morning, and from five to six use common prayer in a common chapel; and from six till ten of the clock use ever either private study or common lectures. At ten of the clock they go to dinner, whereat they be content with a penny piece of beef among four, having a few pottage made of the broth of the said beef, with salt and oatmeal, and nothing else. After this slender diet they be either teaching or learning until five of the clock in the evening; whereat they have a supper not much better than their dinner. Immediately after which they go either to reasoning in problems or to some other study until it be nine or ten o'clock; and then, being without fires, they are fain to walk, or run up and down half an hour, to get a heat on their feet when they go to bed."

At the opening of the thirteenth century, then, we find England possessed of schools and universities, the value of which was felt both at home and abroad, and which had already produced several men of eminence. Among these was Giraldus Cambrensis, the Welsh historian, who received his early education in the school of his uncle, the Bishop of St. David's; after which he passed on to Paris, which city he twice revisited and lectured there on polite literature. Giraldus was one of those who deeply deplored the preference then given to law and logic over classical studies, and laboured hard to keep alive a better taste among his contemporaries. The second time he went to Paris he assures us the doctors and scholars were never weary of listening to him, being thoroughly bewitched by the sweetness of his voice and the elegance of his language. Henry II. summoned him to court, and appointed him his chaplain and tutor to Prince John, with whom he travelled into Ireland, the result of which expedition was seen in his two works, the "Topography" and the "Conquest" of Ireland. Then he accompanied Archbishop Baldwin in his progress through Wales and the western counties of England, preaching the Crusade, and has given a description of this journey also in his "Itinerary." It was performed on foot, and its difficulties are described with a graphic, and, sometimes, a poetic pen. We see the weary travellers making their way through the mountain ravines near Bangor, till the poor archbishop is forced at last to sit down and rest on an oak tree torn up by the winds and lying by the wayside. As he converses with his followers, the sweet notes of a bird are heard from an adjoining thicket. Is it a thrush or a nightingale? "The nightingale is never heard in Wales," observes one. "Is she not? Then she has followed wise counsel never to come into Wales," replies the archbishop, "whilst we, following unwise counsel, are going right through it." What an exquisite picture is that which he gives of the Vale of Llanthony, where the monks, as they sit in the cloister of their abbey, have but to raise their eyes from their books in order to behold the pleasant prospect of mountains ascending on all sides to a great height, and may watch the deer peacefully grazing on the verdant slopes. In old times, he adds, a hermitage stood on this spot, with no other ornament than green moss and ivy. One sees in passages like these that artistic love of beauty which is one of the marked characteristics of our early writers.[244] In 1179 we find Giraldus at Oxford, where he recited his "Topography" before the university, dividing it into three parts and assigning a separate day to each. On each day there was a great feast—the first day for the poor, the second for the doctors, the third for the scholars and burghers. The entertainment, he says, was worthy of classic times, and its like had never before been seen in England.

By far the greater number of the literary men, however, who flourished in England at this time were monks, and the pupils of monks. Such were the historians William of Malmsbury, Florence of Worcester, Simeon of Durham, Roger Wendover, Matthew of Westminster, Eadmer of Canterbury, and many more. Some of them indeed had graduated at the universities before assuming the monk's cowl, like Simeon of Durham, who lectured on natural philosophy at Oxford, "diving into the hidden recesses of nature," during the reign of Stephen. In England, as elsewhere, not a few of those who in early life had won their doctor's cap in the schools, grew weary of the vanity which they found there, and took refuge in the cloister. It seems idle to speak of men whose names are now known only to the curious, yet, in their own day, who was more thought of than Robert de Bertune, "the Oxford clerk," as Gervase calls him, who died Bishop of Hereford, and whose sanctity of life caused some steps to be taken to procure his canonisation? Or Thomas of Marleberg, who, after teaching canon law at

Oxford, Paris, and Exeter, retired to Evesham, bringing with him all the books he had used in the schools, and became first prior and then abbot of his monastery. His doctor's library included one book of Democritus, the Gradual of Constantine, St. Isidore's Offices, several of the works of Cicero, Lucan, and Juvenal, together with a valuable collection of MS. notes, sermons, and questions on theology. There were, besides, other notes and rules on the art of grammar, and a book concerning accents. During his government he caused a great number of useful books to be copied out and bound, and bought a fine collection of the books of Scripture, with their accompanying gloss. Evesham always retained its character for learning, and there, as well as at Reading, St. Alban's, Ramsey, and Glastonbury, a great number of excellent scholars were reared. There can be no doubt that the monastic schools of England continued to cultivate humane letters long after they had fallen into neglect at the universities. The Latin poets who flourished in England in the twelfth century are noticed with respect by all critics; and the epic poem of "Antiocheis," composed by Joseph of Exeter, after his return from the Holy Land, whither he accompanied King Richard I., is declared by Warton to be "a miracle of classic composition." He also praises the elegant versification of Henry of Huntingdon, Robert of Dunstable, Lawrence of Durham, and others, all of whom were monks. None of these English Latinists condescended to the barbarism of Leonine rhymes, which they probably regarded with much the same feeling that Bede expressed for the "songs of vulgar poets." One and all did their utmost to uphold the rules of prosody, and rejoiced in the solemn protest put forth by their countryman, Geoffrey de Vinsauf, against the corruption of pure Latinity.

Henry of Huntingdon, named above among our Latin poets, and equally distinguished as an historian, was altogether a scholar of monastic training. He received his education in the school of Ramsey, a monastery which enjoyed the reputation of having none but learned men for its abbots. The library collected by them was the richest in the kingdom. The catalogue may still be seen among the Cottonian MSS., and contains, besides books of more ordinary occurrence, the works of Aristotle, Plato, Sallust, Terrence, Martial, Ovid, Lucan, Horace, Virgil, and Prudentius. There was also a Hebrew Bible, and Hebraic literature was cultivated by many of the monks. When the Jews were banished from England, a great number of their books were sold, and the monks largely possessed themselves of these treasures. A great sale of Rabbinical MSS. took place at Huntingdon and Stamford, when Geoffrey, prior of Ramsey, made large purchases, and used the books he thus procured to such good purpose as to become a great adept in the Hebrew language, and communicate similar tastes to many of his brethren. Even down to the middle of the thirteenth century, notices occur of Hebrew scholars among the monks and librarians of Ramsey, and one of them, Lawrence Holbech by name, is spoken of as compiling a Hebrew Lexicon.

Great work at this time went on in the English scriptoria, and a pleasant sort of barter was practised among the different abbeys, by means of which each was supplied with the goods most to their liking. Thus brother Henry, of Hyde Abbey, wrote out with his own hand the works of Boëthius, Suetonius, Terence, and Claudian, which he exchanged with a prior of St Swithin's, who had a more classical taste than himself, for four missals and a copy of St. Gregory on the pastoral care. All the monks of Hyde Abbey were good writers and illuminators, and were taught to bind their books with much care. In 1240 the library of Glastonbury contained four hundred books, and among them were the chief Latin classics. At Edmondsbury the scriptorium was endowed with two mills, and at Ely the revenues of two churches were granted to the monks "for the making of books." At Peterborough Abbey the library at the time of the dissolution contained 1700 manuscripts. And at Tavistock, besides the ordinary school and library, there existed another school in which the Anglo Saxon language was taught, for the purpose of enabling the monks to decipher their own ancient charters. But Tavistock was not the only religious house in which the old English tongue continued to be studied. In the library of Trinity College, Cambridge, is still preserved a Latin Psalter after two versions, each version written in a separate column. Over the lines of one column runs an Anglo-Saxon translation, and over those of the other one in Anglo-Norman. The writing is exquisite, and the whole manuscript is richly illuminated, containing several historical paintings, together with the portrait of Eadmer, the monk of Canterbury, who wrote it out in the reign of Stephen. He holds in his hand a metal pen, and an inscription over his head records his caligraphic skill. He is, moreover, found worthy to be noted in the library catalogue as mighty in the art of transcription, and from his name is considered to have been of Saxon lineage.

Some of the larger of our English abbeys had not only schools within their own precincts, but others dependent on them in the neighbouring towns. Thus the school of Dunstable was dependent on the abbey of St. Alban's, and in 1180 was governed by a pupil of that abbey, who in every way deserves mention as one of the most remarkable scholars of his time. Alexander Neckham was foster-brother to Richard I., and educated in the claustral school of St. Alban's. Being appointed regent of the Dunstable school, he taught there for some time with considerable success, and thence proceeded to Paris, where he studied and professed for seven years. At the end of that time he returned to England, and resumed his former functions at Dunstable. At last, wishing to enter the monastic state, he is said to have applied for admission to the abbot of St. Alban's, in an epistle commencing with the words, "Si vis, veniam," to which the abbot, who loved a joke, replied, "Si bonus es, venias,—si *nequam nequaquam.*" The pun on his name (Neckam) appears to have disgusted him; at any rate, instead of a Benedictine, he became an Augustinian, and took the habit in the priory of Cirencester, about the year 1187. He was a universal scholar, a proficient in canon law, medicine, and theology, the best Latin poet of his age, and remarkable for the purity of his style. Like a true scholastic, he was a great lover of grammar, and wrote several works on the subject, which are still preserved in MS., some at Oxford, some at Cambridge, and some in the British Museum. He was also the author of a set of tracts, common enough in later times, for teaching scholars the Latin names of different articles by connecting them in a sort of descriptive narrative. To this work he gives the title of *De nominibus Utensilibus*, in which he describes every apartment of a house, from the kitchen to the bedrooms, with the furniture, dress, &c., in use in the twelfth century. An interlinear version is given in French, and at the end are grammatical notes and comments. He has also left a poem on the monastic character, another on science, in which he treats with some sublimity of the creation of the angels, stars, and elements; of the birds, fishes, rivers, and principal towns in England; of the earth, with her metals, plants, fruits, and animals; and of the seven liberal arts. His remarks on natural history are original and sagacious, specially those contained in his treatise *De Rerum Naturis.* In his poems he praises his country with its pastures, cornfields, and running streams, and celebrates the good qualities of its sons. "The feathered birds of Lybia, and pheasants," he says, "often enrich thy tables, O Anglia. Nowhere are there more joyous countenances at the festive board, more gracious hosts, more profuse hospitality. The adornment of the table could not be more exquisite, or the service more prompt and cheerful. The Englishman, by nature and from his boyhood, gives gifts worthy to be given; and no age is too old to give." After adding much on the liberality of his countrymen, he observes, that they are fond of hunting, and that they have a very subtle genius for mechanics, as well as for the liberal arts.

The character here bestowed on our countrymen corresponds well enough with the more satirical portraiture of Nigel Wireker, who, in his *Speculum Stultorum*, whilst lashing the follies of the world in general, and the universities in particular, describes the English students at Paris, as "noble in look and manner, full of strong sense brightened with wit, lavish with their money, and haters of everything sordid, whilst their tables groan with dishes, and the drinking knows no laws."

The students who frequented the English seminaries were seldom of the nobler class. So late as the reign of Henry II., the Anglo-Norman barons preferred sending their sons to French schools and universities, out of a nervous dread lest their Norman speech should be barbarised by any admixture of the English accent. Even in the English schools for the higher orders, the native tongue was never used. Children were taught the French tongue from their cradle; and this custom, introduced at the Conquest, continued to prevail down to the reign of Edward III. However, it was not easy to preserve the Norman dialect pure from Saxon adulteration in a Saxon land, and hence the sly allusions which Chaucer throws out to the difference between the French of Paris and that of the school of "Stratford atte Bowe." Robert of Gloucester, who felt the absurdity of the system, and was one of the first writers after the Conquest who ventured to use the English language for literary purposes, after telling us that the Norman spoke nothing but French, and "their children did teche," observes that, unless a man know French, men talk of him but little, and that none but "low men" now hold to their national speech—a thing not to be found in any other country. "But I wot well," he continues, "that it is well to know both, for the more a man knoweth, the more worth he is."

Besides the great monastic and cathedral schools, there existed in London and other large towns certain public schools, of which Fitz Stephen has given a lively description, doubtless familiar to the reader. "On holidays," he says, "it is usual for these schools to hold public assemblies in the church, in which the scholars engage in logical disputations, some using enthymems, and others perfect syllogisms; some aiming at nothing but to gain the victory, and make an ostentatious display of their acuteness; while others have in view the investigation of truth. Artful sophists on these occasions acquire great applause, some by a prodigious inundation of words, and others by their specious but fallacious arguments. After the disputation, other scholars deliver rhetorical declamations, in which they observe all the rules of art, and neglect no topic of persuasion. Even the younger boys in the different schools contend against each other about the principles of grammar, and the preterites and supines of verbs. There are some who, in epigrams, rhymes, and verses, use that trivial raillery so much practised by the ancients, freely attacking their companions with Fescennine license, but suppressing the names, touching with Socratic wit the failings of their school-fellows, or even of greater personages, or biting them more keenly with a Theonine tooth."[245] It was in one of these London schools that St. Thomas of Canterbury received his early education, after leaving the school of the Canons Regular at Merton, and before proceeding to the university. The masters were generally some of those professors whom Oxford and Paris sent forth at this time in such abundance that not only cities, but villages also, had their learned teachers, as Roger Bacon testifies. They were, of course, skilled in the disputatious sciences of the day, and extremely well fitted to train a generation of "artful sophists."

There was one private school of this period of which we must give a more particular notice, associated as it is with the history of St. Gilbert of Sempringham, the founder of the only religious order which we can claim as strictly of English growth. He was the son of a Norman knight of Lincolnshire and a Saxon mother, inheriting more of the Saxon than the Norman temperament. In youth he showed no taste for the chase or the tilt-yard, and gave no promise of intellectual superiority to make up for his deficiency in manly accomplishments. But as he grew in years a studious disposition began to manifest itself, in consequence of which his father sent him to study at Paris, where he remained until he had received his master's degree, and, with it, license to open a school. The school of Sempringham very soon became famous. It received pupils of both sexes, who were trained not merely in the rudiments of learning, but also in a holy life; for, says the biographer of the Saint, the scholars, though they wore a secular garb, lived under a kind of monastic discipline. They were not allowed to play and wander about like other children, but were obliged to keep silence in the church and in the dormitory, where the boys all slept together, and were only supposed to speak in certain appointed places. They had, moreover, set hours for study and prayer, and, in a word, were trained in the rules of strict discipline. "For, from his childish years, it had been the one thought of Gilbert how he could best win souls to God, and profit them by word and example; wherefore, keeping himself unspotted from the world, he occupied himself incessantly in holy and spiritual things."

After a time, two churches were founded on his father's manor, and Gilbert was instituted rector of the parishes of Sempringham and Torington; although, not being at that time in holy orders, he was obliged to appoint a chaplain to serve the church in his stead. However, he acted as rector in so far as regarded the government of his parish and his school. He catechised and instructed his parishioners, and that with such success that we are told the greater number of those who heard him served God as if under regular monastic discipline, although remaining seculars: he was earnest in his endeavours to withdraw them from the revelries so attractive to their class, and to accustom them to the practice of the works of mercy; he particularly made it his aim to instruct them in the ritual and ceremonies of the Church; and at length it came to be said that you might tell a parishioner of Sempringham by his way of entering church, the humility of his attitude, and the devotion he exhibited in prayer.

The young rector himself resided in a little house which he built for himself in the churchyard, and spent most of his day in the church. After a time, however, his reputation reaching the ears of Robert Bloet, Bishop of Lincoln, he was summoned to the Episcopal Palace, and, having received minor orders, was appointed to an office in the bishop's household, which he retained under his successor, Alexander. By the latter he was ordained priest, and promoted to the post of Penitentiary to the diocese. Greater dignities were offered to him; but Gilbert longed to return to his rustic parishioners, and, in 1130, he escaped from his court life, and with a glad heart made his way back to Sempringham. He had conceived the idea of attaching a religious house of some sort to his church, and among his former pupils he selected seven young women, for whom he built a small monastery adjoining the north wall of the church of St. Andrew. We are told that the nuns retained the learned tastes they had acquired in the founder's school, so that at last it was found necessary to forbid them to speak Latin to one another, unless occasion should oblige them. A very considerable portion of their time was given to reading and meditation, and minute rules were given as to their manner of behaving as they read in the cloister, where they were to sit one behind another, and all looking one way, unless two chanced to be reading out of the same book. The same rule enjoined that they should ever preserve a sweet and cheerful countenance, and never exhibit signs of anger. To provide for the temporal necessities of his nuns, Gilbert appointed first a community of lay sisters, and then of lay brothers, and he conceived the idea of establishing a certain sort of religious rule among all the labourers on his paternal estate, to which, by the death of his father, he had now succeeded, and making his various farms dependent, in some sort, on the monastery, at the same time that they supplied the temporal necessities of the nuns.

Gilbert's aim in this singular experiment was the amelioration of the lower orders; for the expressions used in speaking of those whom he selected show that they were of the very humblest class. Some were those whom he had known from childhood, the hinds and peasants attached to the manor; others were runaway serfs, for whom he obtained freedom by giving them the religious habit; and others, again, were very poor beggars. In fact, like the servant in the Gospel, he went out into the highways and hedges, and wherever he found the poor and the despised, he invited them into the house of the Lord. He did not attempt to teach these lay brethren letters, only requiring them to learn the Pater, Credo, and Miserere in Latin, but he trained them in obedience, humility, and temperance. They had constitutions of their own, admirably fitted for their state, and for giving religious discipline to a community made up of shepherds, herdsmen, and farm-labourers, who were to discharge the humble duties of their several callings under the religious garb. Some of the rules show plainly enough the kind of men for whom Gilbert was legislating; they were Saxon rustics, whose besetting sin was a love of the alehouse, and whom Gilbert accordingly forbids to drink wine, unless it be well watered, and prohibits, under any pretext, from selling anything to seculars, or from opening any house for the sale of liquor, *seu, ut lingua Teutonica dicitur, tappam*. It was a strange experiment this, of converting a gross rustic population into a religious community, and for a time it seemed blessed with perfect success. The institute spread rapidly, till at last Gilbert felt the necessity of providing for its more regular government, and for this purpose he applied to the Cistercians, in order that it might be grafted into their family. The request was, however, declined, and Gilbert had no other course open than to found another order of canons, who might take the spiritual direction of his convents of nuns. The foundation of this third branch of the institute did not take place till nearly twenty years after the establishment of the first convent. The first canons, like the first nuns, were chosen from Gilbert's own scholars; seven were attached to every priory of the religious sisters, besides which, some houses were founded exclusively for the canons, and before he died Gilbert saw himself the spiritual father of fifteen hundred nuns and seven hundred canons, besides a vast number of lay brethren, whom he had rescued from their life of abject serfdom, but from whose turbulent conduct he had unhappily much to suffer. The order, in fact, declined rapidly after the death of its founder, who lived to extreme old age, being upwards of a hundred at the time of his death. Its weak point was the attempt made to unite so many forms of religious life under one government, and perhaps the hope of long preserving an austere religious discipline among an association of rural labourers savoured somewhat of a scholar's Utopian dream.

The Gilbertine canons, however, continued for many years to cherish a love of letters, and had the chief part in the foundation of that pseudo-university of Stamford which threatened at one time to draw away the north country students from Oxford, the Stamford schools taking their rise in a Gilbertine house of studies. Among the first writers who condescended to make use of the English vernacular tongue was a Gilbertine canon named Robert Manning, who, about the beginning of the thirteenth century, considering in his heart that the "lewd," as well as the "learned," ought to know something of the history of their own country, and to be familiar with the deeds of kings,

Whilk did wrong and whilk did right,

And whilk mayntened pees or fight,

composed his metrical chronicle, in which, desiring to lay a good foundation, and to begin from the beginning, he commences his story,

"gre by gre,

Since the tyme of Sir Noe."

In the reign of Henry II., however, the English tongue (as distinguished from the Anglo-Saxon) had not yet assumed a literary shape. In all higher schools, public or private, the French and Latin languages were exclusively used. The Saxon or Teutonic dialect, referred to in the Gilbertine rule, was considered only fit for peasants, and even they had a certain comprehension of Latin. This is clear from many circumstances. Thus, Giraldus tells us that when Archbishop Baldwin journeyed through Wales for the purpose of preaching the Crusade, he was never so successful as when he preached in Latin. The populace, as we know, do not always measure their appreciation of a discourse by the degree in which they understand it, yet it is difficult to think that these effective sermons can have been delivered in an altogether unknown tongue. But the fact is that, in one respect, the rude ignorant peasantry of the Middle Ages were a great deal more learned than the pupils of our model schools. In a certain sort of way, every child was rendered familiar with the language of the Church. From infancy they were taught to recite their prayers, the antiphons, and many parts of the ritual of the Church, in Latin, and to understand the meaning of what they learnt, and hence they became familiar with a great number of Latin words; so that a Latin discourse would sound far less strange in their ears than in those of a more educated audience of the same class in the present day.

In many cases, indeed, the children who were taught in the priest's, or parochial school, learnt grammar, that is, the Latin language; but all were required to learn the Church chant and a considerable number of Latin prayers, and hymns, and psalms. This point of poor school education deserves more than a passing notice. Its result was, that the lower classes were able thoroughly to understand, and heartily to take part in, the rites and offices of Holy Church. The faith rooted itself in their hearts with a tenacity which was not easily destroyed, even by penal laws, because they imbibed it from its fountain source—the Church herself. She taught her children out of her own ritual and by her own voice, and made them believers after a different fashion from those much more highly educated Catholics of the same class who, in our day, often grow up almost as much strangers to the liturgical language of the Church as the mass of unbelievers outside the fold. Can there be any incongruity more grievous than to enter a Catholic school, rich in every appliance of education, and to find that, in spite of the time, money, and method lavished on its support, its pupils are unable to understand and recite the Church offices, and are untrained to take part in Church Psalmody? The language of the Church has, therefore, in a very literal sense, become a dead language to them, and it is from other, and far inferior, sources that they derive their religious instruction. Thus they are ignorant of a large branch of school education, in which the children of a ruder and darker age were thoroughly trained; no doubt, on the other hand, they know a great many things of which children in the Middle Ages were altogether ignorant, and the question is simply to determine which method of instruction has most practical utility in it. Without dogmatising on this point, we may be permitted to regret that through any defect in the system of our parochial schools, Catholic congregations should in our own days be deprived of the solemn and thorough celebration of those sacred offices which in themselves comprise a body of unequalled religious instruction; and that in an age which makes so much of the theory of education, we should have to confess our inability to teach our children to pray and sing the prayers of the Church, as the children of Catholic peasants prayed and sang them six hundred years ago.[246]

The English schools of that period enjoyed the benefit of no other inspection than that of the parish priest and the archdeacon, "the eye of the bishop," as he was called; and if their pupils knew little about "monocotyledons," the "crustacea," or grammatical analysis, they were able to recite their *Alma Redemptoris* and their *Dixit Dominus* with hearty, intelligent devotion. They knew the order of the Church service, and could sing its psalms and antiphons in the language of the Church, and to her ancient tones; and so they did not, through their ignorance, oblige their pastors to lay aside, as obsolete, the use of that office so truly called Divine, in order to substitute in its place English hymns and devotions from any less inspired source. On this point we hold their education, therefore, to have been immeasurably superior to our own, nor are we to suppose that because they learnt Latin prayers and the Church chant, they learnt nothing besides. Reading and grammar are often named as taught in parochial schools; and among the humblest class of pupils a good deal of instruction, both devotional and practical, was conveyed in English verse, which the pupils committed to memory, much as some among ourselves have, ere now, learnt to remember the number of days in each month by means of doggerel rhymes. The traditions of the Saxon schools, wherein so much use was made of these versified instructions, was kept up so late as the fifteenth century, when we shall have occasion to quote some of the methods in popular use for teaching children the succession of the English kings, the names of towns and villages, the four quarters of the globe, and the outline of the Latin accidence. The Commandments of God and the Church, the Creed, Our Father, and Hail Mary, and other similar portions of Christian doctrine, were also taught in verse, as they may still be seen in most French elementary books of religious instruction; and specimens of the English language, as it existed in the thirteenth, fourteenth, and fifteenth centuries, might very fairly be selected from the different versified forms of the Hail Mary in use at these periods. I will give but one, which is supposed to belong to the early part of the thirteenth century:—

Mary ful off grace, weel thou be,

God of heven be with the,

Over all wimmen bliscedd thou be,

So be the bairn that is boren of the.

It is needless to observe, that in all times a very special importance has been attached by Catholic teachers to the instruction of the people in their prayers. In those early times, when the laws of the State recognised that the people had souls as well as bodies and purses, this was even made a matter of legislation, as in the canons of King Edgar the Peaceable, and the statutes of Canute, wherein every father was commanded to teach his children the Creed and the Our Father, and every man was required to know them, "if he desired to be laid in a hallowed grave, or to be thought worthy of Holy Housel." The familiar explanation of these prayers, and of the Sunday Gospels, formed the ordinary subjects of the parish priest's sermon; and in almost every collection of Synodal decrees we find injunctions calling on Christian men and women to learn their prayers, and say them seven times a day. The Hail Mary was enjoined, in addition, about the beginning of the thirteenth century, as we find in the constitutions of St. Richard of Chichester.

Some of the very earliest known specimens of the English, as distinguished from the Anglo-Saxon language, are fragments of hymns which appear to have been in popular use in our poor schools. One of these is commonly known as St. Godric's hymm, and runs as follows:—

Seinte Marie, clene Virgine

Moder Jhesu Christe Nazarene,

Onfoll, scild, help thin godrich,

Onfangen bring hœle width the in godes riche.

Seinte Marie, Christes bour,

Meiden's clenhed, Modere's flour,

Dilie mine sennen, reyne in min mod,

Bring me to winne wit the selfe God.[247]

To understand whence St. Godric derived his poetical inspiration, we must briefly glance at his history. He lived in the reigns of Stephen and Henry II., and began life as a Norfolk pedlar, getting his living by travelling about the country and selling smallwares in the villages through which he passed. We may fancy him such a one as Wordsworth's Wanderer, concealing under a humble speech and garb a sublime philosophy. Wanderers of the twelfth century, however, had one advantage over our modern pedlars; they visited not only fairs and cities, but holy shrines and places of pilgrimage; nay, generally speaking, the fairs which they attended were assembled round some holy spot, and took their origin in the devout celebration of a martyr's or a founder's festival. Godric, as he plodded on through the north country on his way from Scotland, whither he had gone by sea on a trading expedition, visited Lindisfarne and Durham, and the Isle of Farne, made sacred by the hermit-life of St. Cuthbert. These pilgrimages awoke his soul to a new life, and abandoning his trade, he repaired to Jerusalem, and on his way back visited the holy shrine of Compostella.

Returning to England, he took service in the family of a Suffolk gentleman, but disgusted with the profligacy of his fellow-servants, once more left his country and went to visit the holy places of Rome. Nevertheless, the scenes where first his heart had been touched by God drew him back to them by a sweet, irresistible attraction; and after some years more spent in these devout wanderings, Godric felt himself moved to return to the north of England, and there seek out some solitude where he might lead the life of an anchorite. He entered Durham, therefore, a way worn, ragged pilgrim, and desiring, before he utterly retired from the world, to acquire a knowledge of such psalms and devotions as might enable him to sing the praises of God in his cell, he repaired for that purpose to the school which, as was often the case, was held, in default of a schoolhouse, within the church of St. Mary's.[248] In this school, says Reginald of Durham, children were taught the first elements of letters, and here Godric learnt many things of which he was before ignorant, but which he now acquired "by hearing, reading, and chanting them." And those things which he heard the children frequently repeat became tenaciously fixed in his memory. In a very brief space of time, therefore, he learnt as many psalms, hymns, and prayers as sufficed for his purpose, and retired to a lonesome wilderness north of Carlisle, which he afterwards exchanged for that of Finchdale, where he died, about the year 1170. William of Newbridge, who often visited him, describes him as one whose body seemed already dead, but whose tongue was ever repeating the names of the Three Divine Persons. The similarity of some of the expressions occurring in St. Godric's hymn, to productions of the same kind in popular use in the following centuries, leads us to believe that it may have been one of the school hymns he had learnt at Durham, unless indeed we accept as literally true the legend which represents it as having been taught him by Our Lady herself. The whole notice of this Durham school is exceedingly interesting, and not only confirms what has been said as to the teaching of the Church chant and office, but shows us that the poor children likewise learnt their letters, and were taught *to read*—a fact greatly at variance with the vulgar notion of mediæval ignorance. For that this was only a poor school is certain, from the fact of the ragged and penniless vagrant being able to find admission into it. And having begun to speak of the Durham poor schools, I may take this opportunity of remarking that the city of St. Cuthbert was remarkably well supplied with them. For besides her parochial schools, she possessed an excellent monastic poor school, which continued to flourish down to the time of the Reformation. The usages of monastic bodies underwent so little alteration in the lapse of centuries that the description of this school, as it existed at the time of its suppression, probably gives us a sufficiently accurate notion of its condition in far earlier times. "There were certain poor children, called the children of the almery, who were educated in learning, and relieved with the alms and benevolence of the whole house, having their meat and drink in a loft on the north side of the abbey gates. This loft had a long slated porch over the stairhead, and at each side of the porch were stairs to go up to the loft, with a stable underneath.... The children went to school at the Infirmary School, without the abbey gates, which was founded by the priors of the abbey at the charge of the house. The meat and drink that the children had was what the monks and novices had left. It was carried in at a door adjoining the great kitchen window, into a little vault at the west end of the Frater House, like a pantry, called the *covie*, kept by a man. Within it was a window, at which some of the children received the meat from the said man (who was called the clerk of the covie) out of the covie window, and carried it to the loft. This clerk waited on them at every meal to preserve order." The description given of the Song school attached to Durham monastery, which, according to the same authority, was built "many years without memory of man, before the suppression of the house," is worth quoting, as showing that the material comfort of the pupils was not uncared for. It was "very finely boarded round about, a man's height about the walls, and had a long desk from one end of the school to the other for the books to lie on; and all the floor was boarded under foot *for warmness*, and long forms set in the ground for the children to sit on. And the place where the master sat and taught was all close boarded both behind and on either side, *for warmness*."[249]

Similar schools for poor scholars were attached to all the great abbeys, and were of a higher order with respect to learning than the parochial schools. The pupils reared in them, though of the humblest origin, often rose to high dignities in Church and State. John of Peckham, Archbishop of Canterbury, born of a peasant's family, received his early education in the poor school of the Cluniac monks of Lewes, where, many years later, Dudley, the son of a poor travelling carpenter, was also received, and sent to Oxford by his charitable patrons, who little foresaw the kind of renown which their *protégé* would achieve, or the evil which his descendants would bring upon the Church. Alexander of Hales, "the Irrefragable Doctor," as he was called, was in like manner a pupil of the Cistercians, who, says his biographer, "had the heroic charity to teach youth;" and it is well known that the facilities afforded by the religious houses to poor scholars were so great as to be regarded with much jealousy by the feudal lords, whose pride revolted at the promotion to ecclesiastical dignities of men who had risen from the lowest grades.

There will be occasion to examine our English poor schools more closely in a future chapter, but at present we must return to Oxford, where the collegiate system was gradually developing in its grandest form, and the influx of the mendicant orders was introducing a splendid era for the schools.

CHAPTER XVI.

OLD OXFORD.

A.D. 1200 TO 1300.

THERE are probably few prospects which unite so many forms of beauty and interest as the distant view of a great city; and none in which the reality is more thoroughly idealised in the eye of the spectator. As he gazes at some fair assemblage of ancient towers gleaming aloft through a framework of green boughs, and hears their far-off chimes mingling with the nearer music of the thrush's note, he forgets "the loud stunning tide of human crime" which surges at their base, and is ready to cheat himself into the pleasant fancy that he beholds a sacred city full of venerable shrines. But if this character of solemn beauty attaches even to our busiest capitals when seen from a distance, much more does it belong to Oxford, the ancient "Bellositum," which finds no rival to compete with her in the marvellous aspect of her

Majestic towers

Lifting their varied shapes o'er verdant bowers.

Gardens, churches, and palaces shining through a vista of stately forest trees, surrounded by green meadows and reflected in the waters of a noble river, make up a picture which may well arrest the eye of the artist or the poet, and suggest a dream which, if it find no substantial reality, is yet a form of beauty evoked from the ancient worship, carrying our thoughts to days when the sanctuaries of Oxford were first raised for cloistered students, and when St. Edmund and St. Richard were teaching in her schools.

Yet, if we were suddenly transported back to the beginning of the thirteenth century, very little of this architectural beauty would meet our eye. There was the castle indeed, and the spire of St Frideswide's priory, but they were surrounded, not as now with graceful colleges, but with the humble straw-thatched houses of the citizens, and with those equally humble inns and halls of which we have already spoken. A great oak forest separated the city from the village of Abingdon, and was inhabited by wolves and wild boars; and tradition preserves the story of a certain student who was met in his walk by a ferocious boar, which he overcame by thrusting Aristotle down the beast's throat. The boar, having no taste for such logic, was choked by it; and his head, borne home in triumph, was no doubt honourably served up at table with a sprig of rosemary in its mouth. The stately abbey of Osney, second to none in the kingdom, would have been seen in those islet meadows, where at present not a stone remains to mark its former site; and its two grand towers rose among the trees, musical with the bells which now ring out their tuneful chimes from the cathedral spire. There were to be seen the stately quadrangle and the abbot's house, so often the resort of kings and papal legates; and pleasant walks under the elm trees wound along the waterside overlooking the stream which separated the abbey lands from those other islets where the two orders of mendicant friars had just established themselves.

The scholars were fond of such shady walks, and had laid out a certain plot of ground which bore the name of *Campus Martius*, and was divided into several portions, according to the scholastic degrees. One of the walks was *non ultra* walk, and led to a little hill called Rome, wherein was a cave and a meander, or winding path, and at the top thereof a cross of stone. Two clear springs were seen at either end of this scholastic garden, appropriately bearing the names of Plato and Aristotle. There were many other such wells in the city, one of which was called Holy Well, over which was raised a stately cross. Its waters were pure and intensely cold, and were esteemed for the many cures which were wrought by them on pious pilgrims. For Oxford drew pilgrims as well as scholars to her holy shrines. Not only was the tomb of St. Frideswide visited by thousands, but also her image in that little country church of Binsey, which she is said to have founded, and which in early days was surrounded by hawthorn woods, and was a place of recreation for the nuns of her convent. There you may still see, not the image, but the empty niche where it formerly stood, and the stone pavement worn away with many feet and many knees, a relic in itself, which we may stoop and reverently kiss; for here St. Edmund was wont to pray; and here on certain festivals the scholars came out with cross and banners, and wound their way among the flowering hawthorn woods to pay their homage to the patron saint of Oxford.

There was another well in St. Clement's parish, near the old hospital of St. Bartholomew, which claimed to have been founded by Henry the Scholar, which was also held in much esteem. It was one of those spots which our ancestors were wont to designate "Gospel places," where, on the Rogation Days, it was the custom to read portions of the Gospel, by way of invoking a blessing on the corn-fields, and the streams, and the fountains of water, that they might not be infected by the power of wicked spirits. The well was in a grove hard by St. Bartholomew's chapel; and here came out the students, young and old, carrying poles adorned with flowers, and singing the canticle *Benedicite*, wherein they called on the fountains and all the green things of the earth to bless the Lord. The poor folk of the hospital made ready for them by strewing the ground with flowers, and adorning the well itself with green boughs and garlands. Then the Gospel was read, and the well was blessed, and in later times an anthem, in three or more parts, was sung by the scholars.

The meadows that lie around the city, through which, to use the words of brave old Stowe, "the river passeth on to London with a marvellous quiet course," were then, as now, highly prized by the scholars as places of recreation, and are as frequently alluded to in the university histories, as the famous "Pré aux Clercs" at Paris. But let us enter within the walls, and take a glance at the streets with their quaint designations. "School Street" and "Logic Lane" speak for themselves, but what can have been the origin of the "Street of the seven deadly Sins"? Here is a very important turning which leads to the *Schedeyerde*, or *Vicus schediasticorum*. You shudder perhaps, at the sound of such barbarous Latin; yet had you been an Oxford scholar of good King Henry's days, you would very often have bent your steps hitherward: for here abode the sellers of parchment, the *schedes* or sheets of which gave their name to the locality, and here the transcribers and book merchants carried on their traffic; and here scholars with long purses obtained their literary wares, and those with empty ones were fain to look and long. You can tell the schools by their pithy inscriptions, *Ama scientiam, imposturas fuge, litteras disce*, and the like, but you will look in vain for public schools, or congregation house, or library, or observatory, or collegiate piles. Churches, indeed, there are in plenty, and if the tower of St. Martin's strikes your eye by its strength and height, you may be surprised to learn that the citizens use it as a fortalice, and on occasion of quarrels with the students retire there to shoot at them with stones, and bows, on which account it was afterwards cut down to its present dumpy proportions by Edward III. In truth, it must be confessed, the state of things in old Oxford was anything but orderly. Not only did the northern and southern men embrace different sides both in philosophy and politics, and fight out their differences in the public streets, but the townsmen and the gownsmen stood on much the same terms as those which existed of old time between Athens and Sparta; there might be a truce between them, but there was never a peace. The students lived, as yet subject to no statutes and very little law, and committed many villanies; and, on the other hand, the burghers preyed on them, provoked them, and sometimes burnt their books.

We have now to watch the gradual growth into form and order of these chaotic elements, and will pass over to the other side of the great oak forest, and make our way to the village of Abingdon, where the abbey which we saw founded by good St. Ethelwold had been rebuilt by his Norman successors, and in the early days of the reign of Henry III. was flourishing in great splendour. In the village that had gathered round its walls there lived, at that time, a widow, named Mabel Rich, the mother of four children, whom she brought up in all holy living. Her husband, before his death, had put on the monk's cowl in the neighbouring abbey of Eynsham, whither his eldest son had followed him; another son retired to the priory of Boxley in Kent, whilst Mabel, in heart also a religious, remained in the world to educate her remaining children. Growing up under the shadow of the old cloister, by the side of a mother who trained him in the austere practices of ancient piety, Edmund Rich was steeped from childhood in the spirit of Catholic devotion. He assisted with Mabel at the midnight office in the abbey, he learnt the Psalter from her lips; and his soul gradually received that beautiful mould which we have again and again admired in the scholars of old time, and which perhaps found in him its most perfect realisation. At twelve years old he went to Oxford, and it is his own brother, Robert Rich, who tells us how, at that time, going out into the meadows in order to withdraw himself from the boisterous play of his companions, the Child Jesus appeared to him, and saluted him with the words "Hail, beloved one!" And he, wondering at the beauty of the Child, replied, "Who are you, for to me you are certainly unknown?" Then said the Child, "How comes it that I am unknown to thee, seeing that I sit by thy side at school, and wherever thou art, there also do I accompany thee? Look in My face and see what is there written." Edmund looked and saw the words, "Jesus of Nazareth, King of the Jews." "This is My name," said the Child, "write it on thy forehead every night, and it shall protect thee from sudden death." Then He disappeared, on Whom the Angels desire to look, leaving the other with a sweetness in his heart passing that of honey.

From Oxford Edmund proceeded to Paris, where we have already seen something of his manner of life. He seems to have studied more than once at both universities, and also at Merton abbey, then a great seat of learning. As soon as he had taken his master's degree, he opened a school of his own on the spot now occupied by St. Edmund's Hall. The favourite maxim he was accustomed to give to his pupils, was this: "Study as if you were to live for ever, live as if you were to die to-morrow." For himself, he heard Mass daily, attended matins in the nearest parish church, and recited the canonical hours before beginning his lectures. And to satisfy his devotion with the greater convenience, he spent part of his slender patrimony in the erection of a Lady chapel attached to St. Peter's church, where he and his pupils regularly recited the Divine office. It must be remembered, that at this period Oxford possessed none of those colleges and collegiate chapels, in which the Church office was afterwards celebrated with so much splendour; but the custom, introduced for the first time by St. Edmund, was soon followed by other students. Those who love the memory of the holy scholar may still visit his chapel, which looks desolate enough, with its once delicate lancet windows walled up; yet it is something to know the spots where saints have prayed.

Did we know St. Edmund only by the records left us of his tender piety, his singular devotion to our Blessed Lady, and his manifold austerities, we might picture him as some contemplative saint, whose thoughts were wholly withdrawn from the world, and fixed on unseen things. Yet he was a scholar and a teacher; a close logician, and a great lover of mathematics. Wood says that he was the first who publicly read some of Aristotle's Treatises at Oxford, and for six years after the opening of his school he continued to lecture on arts. The circumstance which led to his exchanging these studies for that of theology is thus told by his biographer: "After he had taught the liberal arts for six years, and was reading geometry with his pupils, his mother one night appeared to him as he slept, saying: 'What is it, my son, that you read and teach, and what are those figures over which you are poring so intently?' He replied, that they were the figures of geometry, on which she took his hand in hers, and drew thereon three circles, at the same time naming the three Divine Persons—Father, Son, and Holy Ghost. Then she added, 'These are the figures which you must henceforth study.'" From that time he applied himself exclusively to the sacred sciences, and that with greater ardour than he had hitherto bestowed on secular learning. He hardly gave himself time for sleep and refreshment, but studied night and day. An ivory crucifix, with the mysteries of our redemption carved round it, was always on his table when he read, and to it from time to time he directed his eyes, feeding his heart the while with pious ejaculations. He never went to bed, but took his scanty rest on the floor, or in his chair, and was at his books again as soon as the morning dawned. Does this intense application seem excessive? and does any reader conceive a distrust of such absorbing studies? Let them learn that at this very time St. Edmund sold all his books, to supply the wants of some poor scholars whom he had no other means of relieving, and seems to have been indebted to a charitable friend for the gift of a Bible, which afterwards formed his principal study.

After some years, having taken his doctor's degree, he once more began to teach; and strange and beautiful were the scenes in that saintly lecture-room, where the master was often rapt in ecstasy, and the scholars were fain to shut up their note-books, being too much blinded with their tears to use them. Wood mentions the tradition, common at Oxford, that an angel, in the form of a beautiful youth, was often seen standing by his side while he spoke, a legend which at least shows in what sort of esteem he was held by his scholars. Among them were St. Sewall, afterwards Archbishop of York, St. Richard of Chichester, Stephen Lexington, and Robert Grosteste, all of whom took part in the great intellectual movement shortly afterwards set on foot at Oxford by the mendicant friars. He did not make much profit out of his school, for the money he received from his pupils was either spent in charity, or suffered to lie loose on his window sill, where he would strew it over with ashes, saying, "Ashes to ashes, dust to dust." Any one might take it who chose, and his friends did so sometimes, to see what he would say; but he asked no account of it, and no persuasion would ever induce him to keep it under lock and key. He was not the mere professor, whose care of his pupils ceased when they left his lecture-room. He nursed them when they were sick, and relieved them when they were in want; and they in their turn loved to gather up each trait of their beloved master, and handed down to those who came after them the portraiture of the saint, with his beautiful countenance, the pallor of which became of a fair shining red when he spoke of God or holy things, in his grey scholar's gown, which was poor without meanness, for he was wont to say that a clerk should remember that his state was an honourable one, and that his appearance, if simple, should never be abject.

St. Edmund had a real love for the work of teaching, and several times when he had been persuaded to accept of benefices, he resigned them in order to return to Oxford. At last, however, we find him treasurer of Salisbury; and with his habits, a very strange treasurer he must have made. And in 1234 he became Archbishop of Canterbury. We need not follow the history of his troublous primacy; he fared the usual fate of English primates who resisted the tyranny of Plantagenet kings; and six years later was an exile at Pontigny, living among the Cistercian monks as one of themselves, writing his "Mirror of the Church," and preparing for his end. He did not die at Pontigny, however, but at Soissy, whither they brought him in hopes that the cooler air might revive his exhausted strength. His last days were spent in giving alms to the poor pilgrims who passed that way, and when he was too feeble to rise from his chair and go to the gate, he made one of his chaplains take his place, and give to all who came. His last words are preserved, the words he pronounced with outstretched hands, when about to receive the Holy Viaticum:—"Lord, thou art He in whom I have believed, whom I have preached, whom I have truly taught: and Thou art my witness that while I have been on earth, I have sought nothing else besides Thee. And as Thou knowest that I will only what Thou willest, so now I say, Thy will be done." "All the rest of that day," says his biographer, "he was joyful and even gay; you would not have thought he was suffering from sickness; and many wondered to see him thus. The tears of devotion were indeed in his eyes, but his beautiful countenance manifested the serenity that filled his heart. There was no sign of approaching death; and at the last moment, neither sigh nor death-rattle was heard; he did not even sink back on his bed, as dying persons are wont to do, but remained sitting, and so gently expired, leaning his head upon his hand." Pontigny keeps his dust as her most precious treasure, and even in our own day, such a strange attractive power is possessed by the sacred relics of the saints, that a newly-founded religious congregation has selected its desolate church for the site of their mother house, with the view of obtaining for their apostolic work the blessing of *Saint Edmé*.

Meanwhile, if England had cast out her holy primate, Oxford had not forgotten her doctor. The work he had begun in his schools was carried on by the band of scholars whom he had trained and left behind him. Five years before he left the university, the two orders of mendicant friars had been established in the town. The first colony of the Franciscans was sent thither in 1220, by Brother Agnellus, who soon after came himself, and caused a decent school to be built, in which he induced Master Robert Grosteste to deliver his lectures. Grosteste was at that time the most illustrious doctor of the university, and soon brought the Franciscan schools into high repute. Agnellus, though himself unlearned, was most desirous that the studies of his brethren should be amply provided for, and often visited the schools to watch their progress. One day, to his great surprise, he found them disputing on the thesis, "Whether there be a God." Whereon he cried out in great distress, "Alas, alas! simple friars penetrate the heavens, while the learned are disputing if there be a God." With these words he left the school "in a chafe," says Wood, "to think he had built it for such debates," but, becoming a little calmer, sent the sum of ten marks to Rome to buy a correct copy of the Decretals, charging his friars to apply themselves wholly to the study thereof, and to lay aside questions of sophistry and foolish babbling.

It must not be supposed from this story that the learning encouraged at the university by Grosteste was entirely of that disputatious and empty kind which had become fashionable in the schools since the time of Abelard. Grosteste, if he exercised the friars in such scholastic disputations, was himself a decided advocate of the older learning, and may be regarded as, in the main, a disciple of the school of St. Victor. When chancellor of the university, he used his influence to promote the study of positive theology, and of that Biblical learning in which he was himself a proficient. One of his modern biographers has candidly admitted that "his wonderful knowledge of Scripture might probably be worthy of remark in our day, though in his own not more than was possessed by all theological students." But Grosteste had largeness of mind enough to appreciate the value of the scholastic method at the same time that he laboured to prevent the study of the Scriptures and the liberal arts from falling into decay; and he probably found means of satisfying Brother Agnellus on this point, for whatever use was made of the copy of the Decretals, it is quite certain that the friars did not "apply themselves wholly" to them, or lay aside their scholastic exercises. On the contrary, Fuller tells us that they soon beat all their competitors in school divinity, "out of all distance;" and Wood adds to his narrative as given above, that Grosteste was not superficial in his performances, and that under him the friars made extraordinary advances both in disputation and preaching.

The great esteem in which Grosteste held the Franciscans led him, not only to teach in their schools, but to persuade other first-rate regents to do the same; besides which, he induced several of his own personal friends to enter the order, among whom was Adam Marsh, the parish priest of Wearmouth, better known by his Italian name of Adam de Marisco, who is reckoned as the first regular professor of the order at Oxford, and was known as "the Illustrious Doctor," and Roger Bacon, the wonder of his age, and the greatest natural philosopher who appeared in England before the time of Newton. Besides these, the Franciscans were joined by a crowd of other illustrious novices, such as John Wallis, surnamed the "Tree of Life," Alexander of Hales, Haymo of Feversham, and more than one Benedictine and Augustinian abbot, which latter circumstance has greatly excited the spleen of Matthew Paris.

Grosteste, after for some time filling the office of chancellor, became Bishop of Lincoln in 1235, in which capacity he was still *ex officio* head of the university, and continued to keep up an active interest in its affairs. Among his letters is one addressed to the regents of Oxford, in which he gives them much useful advice as to the regulation of their studies. "Let the foundation-stones be well laid," he says, "on them the whole building rests. The morning is the best time for study, and the good old Paris custom should be observed of reserving those early hours for the lectures on Scripture, giving the later part of the day to other subjects." Even when treating of questions altogether unconnected with natural science, his love of it peeps out in spite of himself, as in the passage where he gracefully compares the difference between direct and delegated authority to the different powers of the sun's rays when falling direct, or reflected from a mirror. He was undoubtedly one of the greatest men of his time, a universal genius, and revered by his countrymen as a saint. After his death, the university united with the king in petitioning for his canonisation, and sent a document to Rome, in which it is declared "that the said Robert never left undone any good action pertaining to his state and office for fear of any man, but was rather prepared for martyrdom should the sword of the assassin have fallen upon him. Likewise, the university certifieth of his splendid learning, and that he most admirably governed Oxford, in his degree of doctor of holy theology, and was illustrious for many miracles after his death, wherefore he is named by the mouth of all men, 'Holy Robert.'" He may, in fact, be regarded as, in his own time, the representative of the university, and hence it is of particular importance to ascertain what the studies were which he followed and promoted. As a theologian, he belonged rather to the mystic than the speculative school, and as a scholar he was a warm upholder of the liberal arts, doing his utmost to encourage the study, not only of the Latin classics, but also of Greek and Hebrew. He translated the works of St. Dionysius the Areopagite, and, to facilitate the study of Greek, is also said to have translated the Lexicon of Suidas. He promoted two ecclesiastics who are likewise known to have been Greek scholars: John Basing, archdeacon of St. Alban's, who in 1240 returned from Athens laden with Greek manuscripts, and Nicholas, chaplain to the abbot of St. Alban's, surnamed *Græcus*, who assisted the bishop in some of his translations. He is also said to have been acquainted with Hebrew. But his skill in the learned tongues formed but a small part of Grosteste's acquirements. He was a mathematician, a poet, a musician, and a philosopher. Among the two hundred treatises of various kinds which he left behind him are to be found, besides his theological writings, works on the sphere, on physical science, husbandry, political economy, medicine, and music; commentaries on Aristotle and Boëthius, and Norman-French poems. Of these last, one is entitled the "Château d'Amour," a name he bestows on the Blessed Virgin, and consists of a religious romance on the fall and redemption of man. This, together with his "Manuel des Péchés," was translated in the following reign into English verse, by Robert Manning, who, in the prologue to his poem, alludes to the bishop's well-known love of music, and tells us that—.

He loved moche to here the harpe,

For mannys witte yt maketh sharpe.

Next his chaumber besyde hys stody

Hys harper's chaumber was fast thereby

And many tymes by nyghtes and dayys

He had solace of notes and layys.

Most readers are aware that Grosteste is commonly represented as an enemy to papal supremacy, and is rather favourably treated, in consequence, by some historians who find great consolation in the thought that he died excommunicate. That he opposed the nomination of foreigners to English benefices, and that in very bold language, is quite certain, but the rest of the story belongs to our mediæval myths. It is supposed to have been conjured out of the anathemas attached to the Bull of provisors, the execution of which he resisted. It is scarcely necessary to observe that petitions would hardly have been presented to the Holy See in the next reign for the canonisation of one who had died under the censures of the Church, and in these petitions there is not to be found the smallest allusion to his having even incurred any sort of disgrace. More than this, Wood tells us that just before the death of Innocent IV., that Pontiff granted to the university four new Bulls containing great privileges, which had been procured *through the interest of Grosteste*. In point of fact, however bold and uncompromising he may have been in resisting what he deemed a practical abuse, there was no English Divine who ever expressed himself with more hearty loyalty towards the chair of St. Peter than "Holy Robert." He plainly declared that to refuse obedience to the Supreme Pastor was "as the sin of witchcraft and idolatry," and even Mr. Berington is forced to allow that his language regarding the authority of the Holy See is so "adulatory," that the attempt to rank him among its enemies must be deemed a total failure.

It would carry us too far to attempt anything like a particular account of the Franciscan scholars, who flourished at Oxford during the time of Grosteste. One among them, it need hardly be said, towers above all the rest, his celebrity having survived undiminished to our own day. Roger Bacon, a west countryman by birth, and a pupil of St. Edmund's, had passed from Oxford to Paris, where he received his doctor's degree, and then returning to the English university, spent forty years of his life in studying and lecturing upon the sciences. He had acquired the Greek, Hebrew, and Oriental languages in Paris, and wrote grammars of the two first-named tongues which are said to be preserved in MS. at St. Peter's College, Cambridge. But it was as a natural philosopher that he chiefly distinguished himself above his contemporaries, and anticipated the discoveries of later science. At this time the physical sciences were chiefly cultivated by the Arabians, who presented them in a mystic and fanciful shape, which did not render them less acceptable to mediæval students. The study of physics was understood to include mathematics, alchemy, astrology, medicine, and mechanics, each of which received its own colouring of romance. Thus a certain Arabian physician put forth the theory that medicines could only be properly mixed according to the principles of music, and no one ventured to doubt the connection of astronomy with the medical science. Bacon was certainly not less credulous than his contemporaries, but he was more experimental, and hence, though he does not seem to have done much towards establishing truer scientific principles, he obtained many brilliant results. The long list of his writings includes treatises on Optics (then called Perspective), Mathematics, Chemistry, Arithmetic, Astronomy, the Tides, and the Reformation of the Calendar; and, as is well known, he was familiar with the properties of mirrors, and appears to have been acquainted with the principle both of the microscope and the telescope, and with the powers of steam and of gunpowder. It is not to be doubted that he was greatly in advance of his age in scientific knowledge, and it was probably his skill in the use of optical and mechanical instruments, which earned for him the vulgar reputation of dealing in magic. Charges of this sort are commonly enough explained as arising out of the ignorance of the multitudes, who thought every man who could read Greek to be possessed of unlawful knowledge. But besides the awe with which a semibarbarous age naturally regarded one possessed of secrets not revealed to the vulgar herd, it must be remembered that Bacon's science sometimes clothed itself in very suspicious language. He declared that his wonderful tube possessed the power of beholding, not *distant objects* only, but *future events*; and his enthusiastic language in praise of his favourite science may read to us as simple nonsense, but was understood in his own day to imply something very like a magic art. He was not a whit less disposed than his contemporaries to credit the wildest theories of the alchemists, but believed in the possibility of contriving lamps that should burn for ever, magic crystals, the elixir of life, and the philosopher's stone, and wrote treatises on the two last-named subjects. It is plain, indeed, that he only expected to realise these schemes by an application of the secret powers of nature, and not by any forbidden arts. Yet it sounded startling to simple ears to hear of schemes whereby one man might draw a thousand to himself, might raise himself into the air and fly, or manage a ship with his single arm; not to speak of his boastful offer to teach any man Hebrew in three days, Greek in another three, and the whole course of arithmetic and geometry in a week.[250] Unfavourable rumours having reached the ears of Jerome of Ascoli, then general of his order, he was prohibited from teaching, and for a time imprisoned; but in 1264, Cardinal Fulcodi, formerly legate in England, becoming Pope under the title of Clement IV., Bacon despatched to Rome his favourite disciple, John of London, who placed in the Pontiff's hands all his master's books and instruments, an examination of which appears to have justified him in the opinion of his judges. Clement bestowed great marks of favour both on the master and scholar, and it was at his suggestion that Bacon made that collection of his chief philosophical views which is known as the *Opus Majus*. When Jerome of Ascoli himself became Pope Nicholas IV., Bacon was again imprisoned, but as Wood shows, the assertion that he died in confinement during the pontificate of Nicholas is clearly an error, for his death did not take place till 1292, he having survived the Pope four years, and having before his death recovered his liberty, and published several theological works.

The only other Oxford Franciscan who must be mentioned in this place, is Nicholas de Lyra, whose claim to be regarded as a native of this country is not, indeed, undisputed, though it rests on the respectable authority of Trithemius, Sixtus of Sienna, and a majority of writers. The Flemings assert that he was born at Lyre in Brabant, the French as peremptorily declare him a native of Lyra in Normandy, and the English author of the *Collectanea Anglo-Minoritica*, will have it that his real name was *Harper*, Latinised after the fashion of the day into *Lyra*. Equal uncertainty rests on the point whether he were by birth a Christian or a Jew, the common belief inclining to the view that he was the son of Jewish parents, though this fact is hard to reconcile with the assertion of his biographers, that he only began the study of Hebrew at an advanced age. But whatever doubt hangs over his origin, none exists as to the position he held among the scholars of the day. Biblical learning and the study of the Scriptural tongues had not quite fallen into decay, when the age could produce the author of the "Scholastic Postils," a commentary upon every part of the Sacred Volume, which was the first commentary on the

Scripture ever printed. Nicholas de Lyra had studied at the Universities of Paris and Oxford, and if it be true, as is asserted, that he did not apply himself to Greek and Hebrew learning until after his entrance into the Franciscan Order, we must allow his erudition to have been gained in the university schools. Whether himself a Jewish convert or not, his labours are said to have been undertaken in the first instance with a view to the conversion of that unhappy people, a work which, in the thirteenth century, engaged the attention of the most illustrious divines. By his writings, disputations, and sermons, Nicholas is said to have converted six thousand Jews to the faith. But his great work was far from being exclusively intended for their instruction; it became the Text Book of Biblical students, an indispensable part of every cathedral and monastic library, and laid down rules for the safe interpretation of Scripture based upon the right intelligence of the literal sense. It must be added, to the honour of English scholarship, that this important work, which fills five folio volumes, was first published at the expense of a private London citizen, and that the money paid for copying it amounted to 670 florins. Its composition occupied the author thirty-seven years, for, as he himself declares, it was begun in 1293, and not completed until 1330.

Let us now turn to an Oxford scholar of a different stamp, whose name, inseparably united to that of St. Edmund, almost closes the catalogue of our English Saints. Born of respectable parents, who owned the lands of Burford, near the little town of Wyche, in Worcestershire, Richard had very early given evidence of a scholar's tastes, and the first fact which his biographer, Ralph Bocking,[251] records regarding him, is his determined refusal to be drawn away from his books to join in any of the village dances and revelries. But a hard fortune left him little hopes of being able to devote his life to books and learning. The death of his father, and the mismanagement of the guardians to whose care he and his brothers were consigned, reduced the family to extreme poverty. And Richard, with generous self-devotion, gave up all his own cherished plans, and entered his elder brother's service in order, by a life of vigorous labour, to put the affairs of the family on a better footing. "He served him," says Bocking, "in poverty and abjection, and that for many years; working, now with the plough and now with the cart, and enduring many other kinds of hard and humble toil, patiently and modestly." Richard's memory was long preserved and revered in his native place, and even down to the time of the great Rebellion, the Droitwich peasantry put on their best clothes on St. Richard's day, and went to decorate with boughs and flowers a certain well dedicated to the Worcestershire saint. Aubrey, who notices this circumstance,[252] informs us that St. Richard was a person of good estate, and "a brisk young fellow that would ride over hedge and ditch;" a description which, quaint as it is, expresses well enough one feature in his thoroughly English character. He was not a dreamer or a bookworm; he did nothing by halves, and his strong, manly nature loved the practical side of everything. As a Worcestershire farmer he was just as ready to ride over hedge and ditch when that was needed, as he was, when bishop, to do his pastoral work in the guise of a poor beggar. The future chancellor of Oxford began life, in short, as a simple yeoman. His energy and perseverance had their reward, and in a few years his brother's lands, well tilled and managed, began to yield an ample revenue. But when a prosperous fortune seemed opening before him, he refused every offer made him by his kinsfolk, and as soon as his self-imposed task was over, he bade farewell to his Worcestershire home, and betook himself to Oxford, whence, after a time, he passed on to Paris. In both universities he led the hard and mortified life of a poor scholar. For it must be remembered that this was before the time of colleges; it was the golden age when Oxford numbered her thirty thousand scholars, most of whom had scanty means of subsistence. Some were supported by the alms of private individuals, others by the great abbeys of Eynsham and Osney, which on certain festival days, bound themselves to regale the poor scholars with "honest refection." Others went about begging and singing the "Salve Regina" at the doors of the citizens, well content to receive by way of payment a dish of broken meat from the rich man's table. Every one will remember the picture drawn, many years later, by Chaucer, who describes the clerke of Oxenforde in his threadbare doublet, who would rather have

At his beddes hed

Twenty bokes clothed in blake or red

Of Aristotle and his philosophie

Than robes riche, fidel or sautrie,

For al be that he was a philosopher

Yet hadde he but litel gold in coffor,

And all that he might of his frendes hente

On bokes and on learning he it spente,

And besily gan for the soules praie

Of them that gave him wherewith to scholaie.

The account that Bocking gives of St. Richard's student life is hardly less graphic. Like the poor Cambridge scholar before spoken of, who had to run about to keep his feet warm, Richard never saw a fire. But, unlike him, he was seldom able to afford himself the luxury of *beef* or even *mutton*, then reckoned as ordinary "scholar's fare." "So entirely," says Bocking, "was he carried away with the love of learning, that he gave but little thought to the necessities of the body. For, as he used afterwards to relate, having two companions with him in his poor chamber, the three had but one tunic each, and one hooded gown between them. One of them at a time, therefore, put on the gown and went to hear the lectures, leaving the other two in their lodgings, after which they in their turn put on the gown and so went to lecture. Their food was bread, with a very little wine, and salad, or other such poor sort of viands. For then poverty did not allow them to eat flesh or fish except on Sundays and high days, or when any friends were their guests. Nevertheless, the saint was wont to affirm that no period of his life had ever been more joyful and delightful." His love of Oxford induced him to return thither a second time, instead of taking his master's degree at Paris; and for some years after graduating at the English university he taught in his own school, "liberally dispensing to others what he had himself acquired." After a while he repaired to Bologna, and there spent seven years in the study of the canon law. And in 1235 we find him once more at Oxford, where he was unanimously chosen Chancellor of the University. He does not seem to have filled this office for any great length of time, for Robert Grosteste and St. Edmund of Canterbury were both anxious to draw him to their respective dioceses, St. Edmund succeeded, and appointed him his chancellor, and a close friendship sprang up between the two saints, which is thus eloquently described by Bocking:—"In all things," he says, "Richard had an eye to the peace and quiet of his lord and archbishop, who, as he knew, had chosen Mary's better part. And the archbishop exceedingly rejoiced that by the discreet affection and loving discretion of his chancellor he was saved from the tumult of outward business; while the chancellor was in like manner glad to learn from the holy and heavenly conversation of his prelate. Each leaned on each, the saint on the saint, the master on the disciple, the disciple on the master, the father on the son, and the son on the father. To one who looked on them religiously, they seemed like the two cherubim stretching their wings over the ark of the Lord—the church of Canterbury; each with holy eye gazing on the other, and touching each other with the wings of holy love; their faces, that is, their wills, ever turned towards the Mercy-seat."

Richard followed his friend into exile, and was with him both at Pontigny and at Soissy, where he died. Up to that time St. Richard had not given much time to the study of theology, and had only received minor orders on his appointment to the Chancellorship of Canterbury. He had made himself known rather as a man of practical sense than of profound intellect, and the tie that bound him to St. Edmund drew something of its strength from the very contrast of their natural characters. But the snapping of that bond was the heart wound destined to draw St. Richard to yet more excellent things.

The tree must be pierced to give out its most precious balm, the leaf must be bruised to yield its fragrant odours. The strong, manly heart of the Worcestershire yeoman was bowed in anguish over Edmund's grave; but the anguish softened, refined, and elevated his nature; it drew heaven nearer to him, and him nearer to heaven; so that, conceiving a distaste for all secular studies, he retired to Orleans, and set himself to study theology in the convent of Dominican Friars.

This was not his first acquaintance with the Friar Preachers, who had established themselves in the Jews' quarter of Oxford before St. Richard's residence there as Chancellor. The excellence of their theological schools was therefore well known to him; and after studying with them for two or three years, and receiving ordination as a priest from the hands of the Bishop of Orleans, he returned to England, and for some time exercised the office of parish priest of Deal. Boniface of Savoy, the successor of St. Edmund in the primacy, soon found him out, and compelled him to resume the office of chancellor; but, before doing so, Richard, whose desire was to lead a poor and apostolic life, took a vow to join the Dominican Order, trusting that such an obligation would stand in the way of his retaining any public dignity. He was never able actually to fulfil this vow; yet, as Bocking remarks, the after circumstances of his life may be regarded as a sort of virtual accomplishment of it, "inasmuch as for many years he led the life of a true Friar Preacher, preaching Jesus Christ in poverty, and labouring for the salvation of souls, stripped of all worldly possessions."

In 1244 the unwelcome news reached him that he was elected Bishop of Chichester; but king Henry III., enraged that the canons had rejected his own unworthy minister and nominee, Robert Passelew, revenged himself by seizing the temporalities of the see; and when an appeal to Rome resulted in the confirmation of St. Richard's election, the new bishop, compelled by obedience to accept the weighty charge, and consecrated at Rome by the Pope's own hand, returned to England to find his manors confiscated and an edict published forbidding any man to assist him even with a loan. This may be taken as a fair specimen of the system steadily pursued by the English kings against the Church, from the Conquest to the Reformation; and if such examples may be adduced from the policy of him who was avowedly the most pious and least ferocious of the Plantagenets, we may judge what sort of measure was dealt to English prelates by sovereigns of more tyrannic temper. In his younger days St. Richard might probably have repelled the royal injustice with the bold courage of St. Thomas; he preferred now to meet it in the spirit of patient endurance, and taking up his residence with a poor priest of his diocese, gave England an example no less sublime than that of her martyred primate. Utterly penniless, and as dependent on the alms of the faithful as the poorest beggar, St. Richard did not on that account neglect his flock. Like a true apostle he journeyed on foot over the downs of Sussex, visiting in turns every remote village, and exercising the Pastoral office with a vigorous hand that stood in no need of courtly splendour to enforce its authority. A poor priest of Ferring, named Simon, gave him hospitality, and there, in the intervals of his toilsome journeys the bishop recreated himself with gardening, and displayed the skill in budding and grafting which he had acquired during his yeoman's life in Worcestershire. Simon regarded the plants which the bishop tended as sacred relics, and was greatly distressed when one of the grafts was destroyed by a beast which broke through the garden fence. The next time that Richard visited Ferring he good-naturedly consoled his host by putting in another graft, which that same year bore flowers and fruit. It was during this time of outlawry and humiliation that he published his Constitutions for the reform of his diocese, in which he made special provision for the instruction of the poor. At last, about 1247, king Henry was forced by the threat of excommunication, to restore the temporalities, and Richard was joyfully welcomed to his Cathedral city. But his private habits underwent no change. He adhered to his old Oxford fare of bread and a little wine; he seldom touched flesh, and if delicacies, such as lambs or young chickens were placed on his table, would exclaim, "Poor innocents; what have ye done to deserve death! Could ye but speak, ye would surely blame our gluttony!" He rose with the lark, to say his office in the silent early hours; and if it so fell out that the birds had begun their matin-song before him, it mortified him: "Shame on me!" he would say, "that I have allowed these irrational creatures to be beforehand with me in singing God's praises!" His hand was ever open to poor scholars, and he would take the silver goblets off his table to supply their needs. His whole life presents us with a succession of beautiful, homely, and pathetic scenes, which display to us a character wherein pastoral firmness, scholarlike acuteness, and rustic simplicity are blended together, all bound and beautified by the spirit of patience, humility, and prayer. At one time we find him baptizing a Jew whom he has converted by his learning; at another, preaching the Crusade on the Sussex sea-coast to the rough sailors who flock to hear his simple, energetic eloquence. It was whilst engaged in this last work that he was called to his reward. He died in 1252 at St. Mary's Hospital at Dover, where he had just consecrated a church in honour of St. Edmund. In his last moments his thoughts wandered back to the Convent of Orleans, and with his parting breath he repeated the invocation, which he had so often heard repeated by the white-robed Friars:

Maria, Mater gratiæ,

Mater misericordiæ,

Tu nos ab hoste protege,

Et hora mortis suscipe.

Of the English Friar Preachers, to whom St. Richard in heart at least may be said to have belonged, and of their position in the university, something must now be said. It was on the feast of the Assumption 1221, that they first arrived at Oxford, and obtained from the canons of St. Frideswide a settlement in the Jews' quarter of the town, where it was hoped that their learning and their preaching might win many converts. From Elizabeth Vere, countess of Oxford, they obtained a piece of ground on which they erected their first schools, known as St. Edward's schools, where the first lecturers were the two friends Robert Bacon and Richard Fishacre, both of them old pupils of St. Edmund, of whom Matthew Paris says that England had no greater men living. The resort of scholars soon obliged them to choose some more commodious site and in 1259 they removed to St. Ebbe's island in the south suburb, another adjoining island being occupied by the Franciscans. The extraordinary popularity enjoyed by the Dominican Order during the first century of its establishment in England is attested by every historical document. The lower classes loved them for taking the popular side in politics, while the nobles were no less forward in appreciating their merits. It became a coveted privilege to be buried in their churches, and Wood says that even in his day skeletons and hearts encased in lead were continually being disinterred from the ground formerly occupied at Oxford by the Dominican convent, supposed to be those of devout clients of the order. However, in spite of all this, they had their enemies, especially among the secular regents, who were jealous of their privileges, their popularity, and possibly also of their learning. In 1360 Richard, afterwards Archbishop of Armagh, being elected Chancellor of Oxford, was despatched by a certain party of the Oxford doctors to Rome, to lay a formal complaint before the Pope of the alleged delinquencies of the friars. One of his complaints was, oddly enough, their perseverance in collecting libraries; if he was to be believed, no one could now procure any books at Oxford on canon law, arts, or theology; they were all bought up by these insatiable friars, a charge which at least sets them in the light of being favourers of learning. The chancellor's mission proved utterly fruitless, a result which Ayliffe attributes to the fact that "they had money wherewith to purchase the Pope's protection." This last-named writer, in common with most of the Post-Reformation writers, labours hard to affix the stigma of ignorance on the mendicant orders, which he denominates as locusts and caterpillars, who devoured the vital parts of learning, and involved the Oxford students in a fog of darkness but partly dispelled by "the daybreak of Wickliffe's doctrine." Even their vast libraries were collected, he assures us, only to lock up the treasures of knowledge from other men, and to become the food of moths and worms. And here is perhaps the place to notice the grave accusations brought against the

Christian schoolmen in general, and the mendicants in particular, of bringing in a reign of literary barbarism. Fleury devotes a considerable part of his fifth discourse to this subject, and the German critics, especially Meiners, can never find enough to say condemnatory of the scholastic jargon. Hallam adopts the same line, and assures us that "the return of ignorance was chiefly owing to those worse vermin, the mendicant friars, who filled all Europe with stupid superstition." Whether this is the best specimen that a man of letters could give of refined and polished diction may be questioned, but he goes on to remark (in a sentence which, considering the zeal of its writer for grammatical accuracy, exhibits a rather remarkable confusion of tenses),— "the writers of the thirteenth century display an incredible ignorance, not only of pure idiom, but of the common grammatical rules. Those who *attempted* to write verse *have lost* all prosody, and *relapse* into Leonine rhymes and barbarous acrostics. The historians use a hybrid jargon intermixed with modern words. The scholastic philosophers wholly neglected their style, and thought it no wrong to enrich the Latin, as in some degree a living language, with terms that seemed to express their meaning.... Duns Scotus and his followers in the next century carried this much further, and introduced a most barbarous and unintelligible terminology, by which the school metaphysics were rendered ridiculous in the revival of literature."

That the thirteenth century witnessed a great decay of Latinity is not to be denied, though, as has been before shown, this decay and the neglect of classical studies had set in before the rise of the mendicant orders and is in no way to be attributed to them. Oxford enjoyed the reputation of talking the very worst Latin in Europe, whence arose the proverb, *Oxoniensis loquendi mos.* Certainly, if the grammatical errors condemned in the visitation articles of John of Peckham, as reported by Wood, were common in the schools, there is not much to be said in their defence. The prevalence of law studies, too, helped on the decline of rhetoric, for the diction of the jurists was, if possible, worse than that of the scholastics; and the inferiority, apparent during the reign of Edward II., in the schools of divinity, philosophy, and arts, is attributed by the learned Dominican, Holcot, to the over-abundance of law lectures. Granting, however, a full share in the corruption of Latinity to have been the work of the schoolmen, it is difficult to understand how they can be said to have committed a "wrong" by "enriching the Latin with terms which seemed to convey their meaning." It is usually supposed to be the object of language to convey one's thoughts, and writers who had to express the nice distinctions of Christian theology would have been puzzled had they been bound to confine themselves to the Ciceronian phraseology. They did, therefore, what Cicero himself had done before them, and coined words and idioms to express ideas which were not current in the Augustan age. The writings of the scholastics must be regarded as in some sort scientific works, in which the object was not elegance of style, but accuracy of sense. We are not, therefore, necessarily to conclude that the Latin of Duns Scotus was an example of the best that the age could produce; on the contrary, many instances might be cited to prove that even this unfortunate thirteenth century possessed scholars whose Latin was at least as pure as the English of some of their critics. Thus the Bull of Gregory X. for the canonisation of St. Louis, is cited by M. Artaud, the biographer of Dante, as "a very model of pure Latinity." Cicero's Rhetoric was so far from being devoured by the moths, that it was almost the very first work chosen for translation into Italian prose, and appeared in the vulgar idiom in 1257, the translator being Galeotto, the professor of grammar at the university of Bologna. But, putting aside all exceptional cases of those who still studied and imitated the classics, may we not reasonably complain of the narrowness of that criticism which stigmatises as barbarous everything which does not belong to one style, or reflect the phraseology of one arbitrarily chosen period? "It is strange," observes Rohrbacher, "that every one supposes and repeats that the scholastics and the cloisters of the Middle Ages produced no book capable of pleasing the world and becoming popular; and yet, for centuries past, the world has read and delighted in a book of scholastic morality, composed in the Middle Ages by a monkish superior for the use of his novices, and that this book which has been read, known, and admired by everybody, is especially a popular book; and has been translated into every language, and gone through thousands of editions." He is speaking of the *Following of Christ*, which, according to very probable conjectures, appears to have been composed in the thirteenth century, by John Gersen of Cabanaco, abbot of the Benedictine abbey of St. Stephen, at Vercelli.[253]

Again: among the writers who displayed such incredible ignorance as to write Leonine verse were the authors of a sacred poetic literature which will defy all the attacks of time, and which no classic revival can ever render obsolete. The "Dies Iræ," the "Ave Maris Stella," the "Stabat Mater," the "Veni Sancte Spiritus," the "Hymns of the Blessed Sacrament," and those innumerable sequences so familiar to every Christian ear, owe nothing of their inspiration to classic sources. It is even possible that they may set at defiance the rules of Latin prosody; but all sense of harmony must be destroyed before we can designate the language in which they are composed as a "hybrid jargon." And who were the writers of these exquisite compositions, which gave a voice to popular Christian devotion, and still preserve, like some choice balm, not merely the dogmas of the faith, but the very unction of a believing age? They were, for the most part, monks, schoolmen, and friars, the very men who stand charged with a conspiracy against literature and common sense. St. Peter Damian, Adam of St. Victor, Pope Innocent III., the Franciscan Jacopone, the Dominican St. Thomas, and we may add, the gifted and unfortunate Abelard, the very type and representative of the earlier scholastics—these are the barbarians to whom we are indebted for that mediæval lyric poetry, much of which has been incorporated into the office of the Church. In the seventeenth century France grew ashamed of her ancient hymnology, and committed the task of liturgical reform to Santeuil, the half-scholar, half-buffoon, to the Jansenist Coffin, and the Deist De Brienne. The hymns of Fortunatus and St. Ambrose were then exchanged for studied imitations of Horace, from the pen of a writer who boasted that he was ready to be hung up at a lamp-post if he were detected in writing a single bad verse, though one of his Jesuit critics has cruelly enumerated no fewer than a hundred and eight. But whatever be the merit of his poetry, the Catholic sense has long since passed its verdict on the question, and declared the unction of the ancient lyrics to be worth the pure Latinity of a thousand such writers as Jean Baptiste Santeuil.[254]

Both orders of Mendicant Friars gave to the English Church great prelates as well as great scholars; Kilwarby the Dominican and Peckham the Franciscan, two of the grandest of our English primates, may be taken as fair representatives of their respective orders. In the first we see the Oxford and Paris doctor, learned in scriptural and patristic lore, the "great clerk," as Godwin calls him, who "disputed excellently in divers exercises," and who, as primate, distinguished himself by his bold, uncompromising resistance to the tyranny of powerful nobles, and his efforts for the advancement of learning and the correction of public morals. After filling the see of Canterbury for six years, "he was obliged to fly from the king's anger," says Harpsfield, and, retiring to Rome, resigned the English primacy and became Cardinal Bishop of Porto.[255] His successor was the Franciscan, John of Peckham, appointed like himself by papal provision. How little was there of a worldly spirit in these appointments, so loudly and captiously condemned, when a Pope could put aside so powerful a personage as Robert Burnel, the chancellor of the greatest king of England who had reigned since the Conquest, in order to promote one, by birth a poor Sussex peasant, whose only recommendations were his exquisite scholarship and his saintly life! Peckham's learned reputation was not indeed of an ordinary kind. He was a doctor both of Paris and Oxford, and a pupil at the latter university of St. Bonaventure; he had made the tour of all the Italian universities, and in the Pope's own palace had lectured on sacred letters to a crowd of bishops and cardinals, who were proud to call themselves his pupils, and who every day as he passed through their ranks to his pulpit arose from their seats to show him reverence. Wadding speaks of his singularly noble countenance and graceful demeanour, and adds that, besides his other learned acquirements, he was an excellent poet.

His appointment to the primacy being, strange to say, unopposed by the Crown, he began his administration by calling a Provincial Synod, among the acts of which is that memorable one which enjoins every parish priest to explain to his flock the fundamentals of the Faith, laying aside all the niceties of school distinction, and which draws out in admirable and lucid terms what may be called an abridgment of Christian doctrine, under the heads of the Creed, the Ten Commandments, the Two Evangelical Precepts, the Seven Works of Mercy, the Seven Deadly Sins, and those that proceed from them, the Seven Contrary Virtues, and the Seven Sacraments.[256] Moreover, we find him appointing parochial schoolmasters in holy Orders for teaching the children of the poor.

Peckham not only visited his whole diocese, but travelled over the greater part of England, informing himself of the exact state of cathedrals, monasteries, clergy, and people, and making war on pluralism, and every other abuse which be discovered. He also showed himself very active in reforming the disorders that had crept into the universities, and at his visitation, held at Oxford in 1283, condemned a considerable number of false propositions, as well in theology, as in grammar, philosophy, and logic. His fearless independence of character did not shrink from presenting a remonstrance against the tyranny of Edward I., and administering a rebuke to the great Earl of Warren for allowing his deer and cattle to trample down a poor man's field of corn. The immense list of his works, as given by Pitseus, shows that he was not of the number of those who neglected the arts. Besides his "Concordance of the Scriptures," and his theological and scholastic works, there are poems, treatises on geometry, optics, and astronomy, others on mystical divinity, others on the pastoral office intended for the use of the parochial clergy, and some apparently drawn up to facilitate the instruction of the poor. Yet this illustrious man, undoubtedly one of the greatest of our English primates, was never in private life anything but the simple Friar Minor. "He was stately in gesture, gait, and outward show," says Harpsfield, "yet of an exceeding meek, facile, and liberal temper." At his own table sumptuously furnished for his guests, he ate only the coarsest viands, always travelled on foot, and chose to perform the humblest offices in his cathedral church, such as lighting the waxen tapers on the altar. It is a significant fact, that he always retained a prebend attached to the see of Lyons, in case he might at any time be forced to fly from England; and Godwin tells us, that after his time this benefice continued annexed to the see of Canterbury, in order to provide against the case of the more than probable exile of the Primates.

Our last specimen of an Oxford Don of the thirteenth century shall be taken from a different class; no Worcestershire yeoman, or Sussex peasant boy, but the son of the greatest and noblest of the English barons, Cantilupe, Earl of

Pembroke, marshal and protector of the realm during the stormy minority of Henry III. Thomas Cantilupe, his eldest son, was educated first at court, and then at the universities of Oxford, Paris, and Orleans; and whether at court or in the schools, he displayed the same piety and delicacy of conscience. Deeply learned both in canon and civil law, he was raised by king Henry to the post of Lord Chancellor, and was also elected Chancellor of the University of Oxford. But on the accession of Edward I. he obtained leave to resign his dignities, and retired to Oxford, where he trusted he might spend the rest of his life in the practice of study and devotion. He took his degree of Doctor of Divinity in the church of the Dominicans, on which occasion his old master and spiritual director, Robert Kilwarby, then Archbishop of Canterbury, was present, and scrupled not publicly to declare his belief that he had never forfeited his baptismal innocence. He was then fifty-four years of age. "So help me God," were the archbishop's words, "I believe him to be this day as pure from all actual sin as on the day of his birth. And if any man ask, let him know that from his childhood I have heard his confessions, and read his life and conscience as clearly as a man may read an open book."[257]

After attending the second Council of Lyons, he was elected Bishop of Hereford, and in the government of his diocese found himself, singularly enough, opposed to his saintly metropolitan, John of Peckham, who, as he conceived, overstrained his authority as Primate. Yet though he staunchly defended the rights of his Church, and was constantly engaged in vexatious disputes with some of the great barons, no one ever dreamt of charging him with a haughty or ambitious spirit. The speciality of his sanctity was charity, and it was said of him that he was never seen angry, save when a whisper of detraction met his ear.

Such were some of the Oxford doctors and chancellors of this period, and such the prelates chosen from their ranks. Not indeed that we would be thought desirous of representing our ancient universities as exclusively schools of saints; the slightest acquaintance with the academic annals suffices to show that they were disgraced by many scandals, and were too often the scenes of lawless outrages and contentions, which, in our days of higher civilisation, must naturally excite both wonder and disgust. Moreover, the halls of Oxford were haunted by a spirit very different from that which pervaded the cloisters of Jarrow. The world had entered there, with all its false maxims, and scholars were not ashamed to squabble for benefices, and often, on the motive of self-interest, to take part with the Crown against the Church. Still, when all has been said that impartial candour demands, we cannot doubt that many precious traditions must have been preserved in the university schools, and that they moulded many a poor scholar in the old saintly and beautiful type. Moreover, we are approaching the time when the most flagrant evils of the universities were about to receive a partial remedy by the establishment of the collegiate system, which soon became tacitly accepted as *the* educational system of England. It aimed, and to a great degree successfully, at combining the discipline of the old monastic schools with the larger intellectual advantages of the universities. The reputed priority is ordinarily assigned to University College, which, on the ground of its supposed foundation by Alfred, claims to be the first in point of antiquity of the Oxford foundations. But its real existence as a college dates only from the time of William, Archdeacon of Durham, by whose will a sum of money was assigned for the maintenance of a body of masters, who, in 1280, were required to live together in one house, and receive a body of statutes. But Merton College had already received its royal charter in 1264, and one year previously to that date, John Baliol, father to the unfortunate Scottish King, had taken some steps towards the foundation of the college which bears his name. His intentions were carried into effect by his widow, the Lady Devorgilla, who, at the instigation of her Franciscan confessor, Richard Stickbury, founded the college in honour of the Holy Trinity, Our Lady, and St. Catherine the Martyr. It would be pleasant to present to the reader the heiress of the ancient princes of Galloway, as she appears in semi-monastic costume, in her Oxford portrait, or to reproduce those exquisitely engrossed statutes, which provide that the students of Baliol shall be present at the divine offices on Sundays and holidays, and shall on other days frequent the schools; that they shall always speak Latin in common, and if they neglect to do so, shall be served last at table; that a sophism shall be disputed among them once a week, and that they be allowed a penny a day for their sustenance, and two pence on Sundays! But as our object is only to notice those collegiate foundations which in a marked way influenced the system of education, we shall pass on to Merton, avowedly the first English college incorporated by charter, and the model on which most of the subsequent foundations, both of Oxford and Cambridge were raised. Its founder, Walter de Merton, Bishop of Rochester and Chancellor of the realm, may be, in fact regarded as the originator of the collegiate system, and is designated in his monumental inscription *unius exemplo, omnium quotquot extant collegiorum Fundator, maximorumque Europæ totius ingeniorum felicissimus parens*. The immense evils of the university system, which was practically no system at all, early attracted his attention, and determined him on making the experiment of gathering a certain number of scholars from the halls and hostels where they now congregated subject to a merely nominal discipline, and placing them under the control of masters and tutors in a spacious building under semi-monastic rules. What was designed with so much sagacity was executed with corresponding magnificence, and the *Domus Scholarium de Merton* became the curiosity of its age. Architectural splendour was not at first considered any necessary part of a collegiate foundation, but the various tenements purchased by Bishop Merton were reduced to a regular quadrangular form, and a college chapel was included in the original design, two chaplains being appointed for "the ministration of Divine service." In 1265, the parish church of St. John Baptist was made over to the founder by the monks of Reading, and granted to the perpetual use of the scholars. Their studies appear to have differed in no way from those of the other Oxonians, but Wood considers the appointment of a grammar-master to indicate that Bishop Merton designed to put some check on the decay of arts.

Among the early benefactresses to this college was one who might almost be called its co-foundress, Ella Longspée, Countess of Warwick, and daughter to that other Ella, Countess of Salisbury, who had obtained the conversion of her ferocious husband, Longspée, through the instrumentality of St. Edmund.[258] The friendship of the elder Ella with the saintly archbishop appears to have inspired both her daughters with a singular goodwill towards Oxford, and Ella in particular made large donations of lands and endowments to the Merton scholars. Such was the success of the new foundation that the king himself recommended it to Hugh de Balsham, Bishop of Ely, as a model for his proposed Cambridge College of Peterhouse; and the example once set, was soon taken up by others. The Benedictines had possessed houses of studies in Oxford from a very early period, but the proposal was now made to found a regular college, intended, in the first instance, exclusively for students from Gloucester Abbey, but the benefits of which were afterwards extended to those of St. Alban's, Glastonbury, Tavistock, Chertsey, Coventry, Evesham, St. Edmundsbury, Winchcombe, and Malmsbury, all of which contributed to the expense of rearing the necessary buildings. The real founder of Gloucester College, however, was not an abbot, but a baron, John Giffard, Lord of Brimesfield, and husband of Maud Longspée, whose persuasions doubtless had great share in promoting his munificence. In 1291, a general chapter was held at Abingdon of the monks of the province of Canterbury, and a tax imposed on all the Benedictine houses of the province, to raise the necessary funds.

The result was the erection of a grand and commodious pile of buildings, some of which remain to this day, and form a part of the modern Worcester College. The apartments occupied by the students of the different religious houses were separate one from another, and distinguished by their arms or rebusses. Thus, we see the cross-keys for St. Peter's of Gloucester, a comb and a ton, with the letter W, for Winchcombe, and so of the rest. Each abbey sent a certain number of students at a time, who were governed by a prior, elected by themselves, called the "Prior Studentium," and who had a rule adapted to suit their peculiar requirements. They were enjoined not to mix familiarly with the secular students, to have divinity disputations once a week, and to practise preaching, both in Latin and English. A chair of theology was afterwards founded for their special instruction. In short, Gloucester College was a true religious seminary, and continued to enjoy a high character for learning down to the time of the general suppression of religious houses. Wood gives many interesting particulars of the college, and the good scholars whom it produced. Whethamstede, abbot of St. Alban's in the reign of Henry VI., of whom we shall have hereafter to speak more at length, was at one time the "Prior Studentium," and afterwards bestowed such large benefactions on the house as to be called its second founder. He put in the five painted windows of the chapel, built a vestiary and a library, and presented many books. Moreover, he adorned the images of the Crucifix and the Saints with "deprecatory rhymes." His dear and learned friend, Humphrey of Gloucester, likewise enriched the library with several valuable manuscripts. The first Benedictine of this college who took his doctor's degree was William Brok, who graduated in divinity in 1298. The inception of a university doctor was in those days a stately ceremony, and on this occasion the Benedictines thought it well to celebrate the auspicious event with more than ordinary splendour. Six abbots of the order, therefore, attended the customary procession on horseback, besides "monks, priors, obedientiaries, and claustral clerks, a hundred noblemen and esquires," and most of the Benedictine bishops of the province of Canterbury. The Durham monks were not long before they provided themselves with a similar seminary, and in 1286 obtained lands for the erection of their college from Dame Mabel Wafte, abbess of Godstow. The endowments of this establishment were intended half for lay and half for religious students. They also had their "Prior Studentium," and the good repute of their learning induced Richard of Bury, the celebrated Bishop of Durham, to leave them his magnificent library of books. The site of this foundation is now occupied by the more modern Trinity College.

These religious establishments, it is not to be doubted, had a considerable share in promoting the extension of the collegiate system now fairly introduced into Oxford. The Merton scholars soon attracted notice; of whom the most famous was Duns Scotus, who after leaving the university entered among the Franciscan friars of Newcastle, and returning to Oxford to study a second time under the doctors of his own order, won perhaps the highest renown which attaches to the name of any English divine since the days of Bede.[259] The reign of Edward II. witnessed the foundation of two more colleges. Oriel claims as its founder that unfortunate monarch himself, who, whatever may have been his faults, was an undoubted patron of letters. It is probable, however, that he had little more than a nominal share in the foundation, which was the real work of his almoner, Adam de Brom. Exeter owes its name to its founder, Walter Stapleton, Bishop of Exeter, and both these were, more or less, in their statutes and general spirit, copies of Merton. The effects of the changes thus introduced into the university system are differently estimated by different writers. By many the diminution in the number of students which became apparent in the fourteenth century, is attributed to the increase of colleges. These of course could only accommodate a limited number, whereas any amount of students might swarm in the hostels and lodging-houses which were formerly their only resort. However, if the old adage, that quality is to be preferred to quantity, is to be held of any force, this can hardly be said to be a disadvantage. Six thousand students living under regular discipline were perhaps better than thirty thousand, containing a large proportion of "varlets;" and although in our days the collegiate system may be regarded as having a tendency to aristocratical exclusiveness, this was far from being its intention or result in the early period of its institution. The endowments were for poor scholars, and by poor scholars they were mostly enjoyed. It appears probable also that the successive pestilences which desolated Oxford in the reign of Edward III., and the troubles occasioned by Wickliffe and his followers, had a great deal to do with the decrease of the scholars. Besides which, it must be borne in mind that the rage for scholastic learning which characterised the thirteenth century, gave place in England during the fourteenth to a rage for French conquests. So completely did the brilliant successes achieved by the two Edwards root this passion in the English mind, that the cultivation of letters was little regarded, and perhaps after Wickliffe's time it was looked on by some with a not unnatural suspicion. Many of the colleges had become tainted with Lollardism, and remained under a cloud; the tide of popular favour had set in for the showy chivalry of the day, and clerks and scholars went somewhat out of fashion. The close tie which had hitherto knit together the schools of Oxford and Paris was henceforth totally sundered, nor is it easy to estimate the injury thus accruing to the English university, which in the thirteenth century enjoyed the freest intercommunion with the French and Italian academies. The narrow insular spirit which thus sprang up, and which was nourished by the anti-Roman tendencies of English legislation, was fatal to intellectual progress. Hence the learned renown of our universities certainly declined, but so far was this from being the result of the collegiate system that it is evident the noble foundations of Wykeham, Waynflete, Fleming, Chicheley, and Henry VI., were undertaken with the view of supplying a remedy to the existing evils, and as a means of effecting a revival of learning among the English clergy.

The history of these foundations belongs however to a later date. For the present we must leave our semibarbarous island (for so, under favour, must baronial England doubtless have been regarded by dwellers south of the Alps), and see what kind of scholarship was flourishing in the more classic atmosphere of Italy at the very time when the first stones were being laid of our ancient Oxford cloisters.

CHAPTER XVII.

DANTE AND PETRARCH.

A.D. 1300 TO 1400.

IN what has hitherto been said of the universities, which in the thirteenth century had fairly established themselves as the great organs of education, it has not been possible to convey any just or satisfactory notion of the exact nature of those studies fostered within their schools. The reader will perhaps have gathered a general idea that a great change had been gradually effected since the days of St. Anselm; that humane letters were becoming neglected, and that scholastic philosophy and canon law had even threatened at one time to discourage the cultivation of Scriptural and patristic studies; that theology, on the other hand, had become digested into a scientific system by the great scholastic doctors, who had reinstated the study of the Scriptures and the Biblical tongues, but who had not done much to restore polite letters; and finally, that the physical sciences had made a certain sensible advance. This general statement has in it a fair amount of truth; nevertheless, general statements are such unsatisfactory things, that the desire rises to one's mind that some scholar of our old universities could be put on his examination before a Royal Commission, and tell us with his own lips what he did, and what he did not, learn from his mediæval teachers. The wish is not so extravagant as it might appear. Fortunately for our purpose, one scholar existed who gathered in himself the learning of Padua, Bologna, Paris, and Oxford Universities, for he studied successively at them all, and has left the result in writings, which for six centuries have been submitted to close critical examination, and are still in our hands. A glance through their pages promises, therefore, to give us some information on the point in question.

It was probably some time in the reign of Edward I., that among the 30,000 students who crowded the inns and hostels of old Oxford, there appeared an Italian of middle age, of whose previous career at other universities we know no more, than that at Padua and Bologna he had addicted himself to moral and natural philosophy; that at Paris he was held to be a first-rate theologian; and that returning thither a second time, after political troubles had driven him into exile, he had held a disputation against fourteen opponents, had taken his bachelor's degree, and was only prevented by an empty purse from graduating as master; and finally, that both at Paris and elsewhere he had evinced a marked predilection for the mystical interpretation of the Holy Scriptures. These are all the traces that he has left behind him in the schools, and yet how well we know him! The countenances of Shakespeare or Byron, or Sir Walter Scott, are not more familiar to us than the grand and melancholy features of Dante Alighieri, whom we claim as an

Oxford student, on the authority of John de Serraville, Bishop of Fermo, a writer who, as he lived only a century later than the poet, may be supposed to have derived his information from contemporary sources.[260] Plain in dress, temperate in his habits, polished and dignified in his manners, which were, however, dashed with more than a touch of sarcasm,—a man of few words, given to long fits of abstraction, his form a little stooping, his sight early impaired by excessive application to his books; something of an artist, and such a lover of music that, as he tells us, it had power to soothe him even in the worst of times, an exquisite caligrapher, as they attest who have seen his writing, and describe it as *magra e lunga, e molto corretta*, a close and curious observer of nature, and above all, of the phenomena of the starry heavens, a perfect scholar, yet, withal, a soldier too, well skilled in all the martial exercises that became his rank—such was he whom we have ventured to select as the representative man of the Catholic universities as they existed before that new era of taste and literature which was ushered in by his countryman Petrarch.

Dante is acknowledged by all critics to have been the most learned of the poets, not excepting Milton, the character of whose genius so closely resembles his own. His learning was characteristic of his age: the extraordinary prominence given in his poem to the scholastic theology and philosophy tells us at once in what century it was composed. Aristotle, Christianised and interpreted by St. Thomas, is the master whom he follows;[261] yet perhaps he is not quite so exclusive an Aristotelian as most scholastics of his time, for it is evident that he had studied Plato with almost equal attention, specially the Timæus of that philosopher, to which he frequently refers. He, however, invariably gives the preference to Aristotle, whom he calls, "the master among the wise;" whereas Petrarch assigns the first place to Plato. But "Dante the Theologian," as he is called in his epitaph, had other masters besides the Greeks. He who had won his bachelor's degree in fair fight against fourteen opponents, a reminiscence to which he refers in his poem, had to be furnished with arms from the scholastic arsenal. Accordingly, when he describes himself as undergoing the questioning of the Apostles on the subject of Faith, Hope, and Charity, he gives his answers in the language of the Master of the Sentences, as well as of St. Denys the Areopagite, and St. Augustine. His diction is thickly sown with the phraseology of the schools, with "quiddities," "syllogisms," "propositions," "demonstrations," and the like; yet when he comes to make his profession of faith, how sublimely does he rise above these technicalities, and declare that his belief rests neither on physical nor metaphysical proof, but on the testimony of the Holy Ghost, on Moses, the Prophets, the Psalms, and the Gospels.[262] Elsewhere he appeals to the teaching of St. Jerome, St. Isidore, St. Gregory, St. Bernard, and most of the other Latin Fathers, and names with loving reverence not a few of those monastics and schoolmen with whom we have made acquaintance in the foregoing pages, such as Bede and Rabanus, St. Peter Damian, Peter Comestor, Hugh and Richard of St. Victor, and Albert the Great. But above all these appear St. Thomas and St. Buonaventura, the former of whom is, beyond all doubt, the guide of Dante in philosophy and theology, and whom he introduces in the thirteenth canto of the Paradiso, speaking in his own person, and using the scientific phraseology of the schools.

The political opinions set forth by Dante are no less characteristic of the mediæval university student than his theological views. Born of a family attached to a party of the Guelphs, he himself kept aloof for some time from either faction, and, as Chief Prior of Florence, aimed at holding an even balance between them. This line of conduct gave little satisfaction to the Neri, as the Florentine Guelphs were called; and they accused him, as it would seem not without cause, of concealing, under the show of impartiality, a secret leaning towards the Ghibellines. On occasion of a popular insurrection, the Priors agreed to banish the leaders of both parties; on this the Guelphs leagued to call in the assistance of Charles of Valois, Captain-General to Pope Boniface VIII. This appeal to the protection of the hated lilies of France moved Dante to an act of severity which proved his own ruin. The banished chiefs of the Bianchi were recalled, while those of the Neri remained in exile. Driven to extremity, the Guelphs despatched an envoy to Rome, entreating the Pope to put the pacification of Florence into the hands of Charles of Valois. Dante hastened to Rome to oppose this demand, but in his absence another popular *émeute* broke out, the Neri triumphed, their exiles were recalled, and in their turn decreed banishment and loss of goods against their enemies. The original document is still preserved, in which, to the sentence of confiscation is added that of *burning alive*, decreed against Dante and fourteen other citizens, should they ever again set foot in Florence.[263]

It must be admitted that if the writings of Dante exhibit after this time all the bitterness of "Ghibelline bile," there was some excuse to be made for him. Almost against his own will he had been thrown from his position of theoretic impartiality into the arms of the Ghibelline faction. Not that he ever entirely embraced their cause; he had good sense enough to admit that truth is seldom to be found in the ranks of party, and owned in after years that it was hard to say whether Guelph or Ghibelline were most to be blamed for the evils which their animosities had brought upon Italy.[264] He felt for the sufferings of his country scarcely less than for his own; and the only remedy which he saw for the miseries resulting from the rage of factions was the establishment of a firm monarchical government, such as was presented in the theory of the Holy Roman Empire. This fancy he dwelt on and idealised till he came to believe that Empire a thing of divine institution, applying to it the words of the Apostle, "There is laid up for me a crown of righteousness." The extravagances into which he suffered himself to be led on this subject are not entirely to be referred to the influence of his university studies, yet it is certain that the principles current in all the great academies offered nothing to correct the absolutism of his political creed. Bologna had received her "Habita" from the Emperor Frederic II., in reward for the good services which her lawyers had rendered him in supporting his claims against the Italian Communi. Paris was on the very eve of supporting the sacrilegious enormities of Philip le Bel. At Oxford, the greatest law school north of the Alps, the imperial jurisprudence formed the favourite study; and though, with that happy *inconsequence* which is the national characteristic, the English would none of it for practical purposes, yet they learnt enough from their law studies to induce them to support a course of legislation, the ultimate result of which was the establishment of a royal supremacy.

In all these academies the supremacy of the temporal power was, in one form or other, the favourite political dogma, and the tendency of their teaching was, perhaps, more directly anti-Papal than that of the Italian poet, for Dante's Ghibellinism, bitter and resentful as it was, never clouded the instincts of his faith. He regarded Boniface VIII. as his personal enemy, and attributed to his intervention the revolution that had driven him into exile. With the terrible anger of his silent nature which suppressed every outward demonstration of passion, he pursued and made war upon him with his pen; yet the hatred he felt for the man never blinded him as to the character of his office. When he comes to speak of the outrages committed against him at the instigation of Philip le Bel, he forgets that it is his enemy who is being thus dealt with, and gives expression to the deep religious sense of a child of Holy Church in lines for ever memorable. He beholds Christ once more mocked and derided in the person of His Vicar, he sees the gall and vinegar renewed, execrates the cruelty of the new Pilate and the new thieves, and weeps over the sufferings of the Church, whose woes are now, he says, the theme of every prayer.[265] Indeed, in all save his politics, Dante reflects the spirit of the ages of faith. The grim grotesqueness which mingles with his most terrible pictures breathes the identical character to be found in the illuminations and sculptures of the same period, evincing an intense sense of certain grave realities which the mediæval artists never shrank from picturing to the mind and eye. The liturgical spirit, too, is there, reminding us almost at every page that we are reading the words of one who lived when the office of the Church was still the Prayer Book of the faithful, and when university students, like St. Edmund, or Jordan of Saxony, were accustomed to rise at midnight and attend the singing of Matins in their parish church.[266] Some of the most exquisite passages of his poem owe their beauty to the skill with which he has woven into his verse passages and phrases from the Psalms, the Breviary Hymns, and other devotions of the Church. Yet Dante was very far from being exclusively a theologian and a scholastic. His writings offer sufficient evidence that the scholars of the thirteenth century were familiar with other Latin than that of Duns Scotus. He had closely studied all the Latin poets, and sometimes translates or paraphrases entire lines from Virgil. His mind was so steeped in the history and mythology of the ancients, that many of his pages, if translated, might be taken for quotations from Milton; for like him he possessed the art of stringing together a series of classic names and allusions, the melody of which makes us willing to pardon their pedantry. One example may suffice, which shall be given in its English dress, the better to convey the resemblance which it bears to kindred Miltonic passages. It is the poet Virgil who is speaking to Statius, and describing the state of the good heathen in limbo:—

There oft times,

We of that mount hold converse, on whose top

For aye our nurses live. We have the bard

Of Pella, and the Teian; Agatho,

Simonides, and many a Grecian else

Ingarlanded with laurel. Of thy train

Antigone is there, and Deïphile,

Argia, and, as sorrowful as erst,

Ismene, and who showed Langia's wave;

Deidamia with her sisters there,

And blind Tiresias' daughter, and the bride,

Sea-born of Peleus.[267]

Every one of the names here named are Greek, and it is clear that Dante was well acquainted with the stories of the Greek poets; but was he also acquainted with their language? This is a question fiercely debated by his commentators, and considered to be still an unresolved problem. In his prose work, the "Convito," he has criticised an erroneous translation from Aristotle, and in one of the finest passages of the "Purgatorio" introduces a Greek word, which alone has furnished matter for a voluminous controversy.[268] These and other passages have led many to give him credit for being possessed of Greek scholarship. The point is not decided, but the probability appears to be that his knowledge of the language was at any rate not very profound. In the same way he may be said to have been not totally unacquainted with Hebrew and Arabic, for several explanations of Hebrew words occur in his works, and the mysterious words which he places with so tremendous and dramatic an effect in the mouth of Nimrod,[269] are declared by one critic to be Arabic, and by another to be Syriac; but are more probably, as Bianchi observes, a jumble of sounds chosen from the Oriental dialects, and intended to convey a notion of the confusion of tongues, and to startle the ear with their uncouth cabalistic sound. Without claiming for our poet the merit of Hebrew and Oriental learning, we may at least gather from such passages that he had studied in schools where these tongues were not entirely unknown, where the decree of Clement V. was probably carried out, and professors were to be found who could furnish him with enough of Eastern erudition to serve his purpose. On other points his acquirements were, however, far less superficial. The trivium and quadrivium in all their branches are easy enough to be traced through his writings. He is known to have been a proficient in music. He refers to the quadrature of the circle and other problems of geometry, but astronomy was evidently his science of predilection, and occupies a very considerable place in his poem. He wrote at a time when the Pythagorean system was the only accepted theory, and his scientific allusions can of course only be explained according to its supposed laws. But he did not draw all his ideas from the books of the ancients. In his "Convito," after giving the various explanations of the Milky-way furnished by Pythagoras, Anaxagoras, and others, some of them sufficiently absurd, he decides in favour of the opinion that there is a multitude of fixed stars in that part of the heavens, so small (or, as we should now say, so distant), that we cannot separately distinguish them, but which cause the appearance of whiteness. The other views, he observes, seem devoid of reason. The astronomer, Ideler, was the first to point out that Dante's description in the opening canto of the "Purgatorio" of the four stars,[270] which he makes symbolic of the four cardinal virtues, betrays a knowledge of the constellation of the Southern Cross, of which he may have heard from the Genoese and Pisan mariners who had visited Cape Comorin, and which he may even have seen depicted on that curious globe constructed by the Arabs in 1225, where it was distinctly marked. He had attentively studied geography, and notices many such points as find a place in our manuals of the globes, such as the intersection of the great circles, as they are exhibited on the armillary sphere; and reminds us that within the torrid zone at certain seasons no shadows fall, on account of the sun being then directly overhead.[271] Tiraboschi gives him credit for anticipating a supposed discovery of Galileo's, that wine is nothing but the heat of the sun mingled with the juice of the grape; and Maffei comments on the "marvellous felicity" with which he expresses his scientific ideas. The theory of the attraction of gravitation[272] is stated as distinctly in his pages as in those of Vincent de Beauvais; and his allusions to the nature of plants and the habits of animals, and particularly of birds, seem to evince, not merely a familiarity with the works of Albert the Great, but the observant eye of a real naturalist.[273] His artistic feeling appears in a thousand passages, which were afterwards given a visible shape by Orcagna, and so many other painters of the early Florentine school; as well as in some wonderful landscape-painting in words, which, as Humboldt says, "manifest profound sensibility to the aspect of external nature." Such is his description, imitated by so many later Italian poets, of the birds beginning their morning songs in the pine forest of Chiassi, of the dawning light trembling on the distant sea, of the goatherd watching his flocks among the hills, and of the flowery meadow illuminated by a sudden ray of sunlight darting through the broken clouds.[274] He never directly alludes to those grand creations of Christian art, the cathedrals, most of which were coeval in their rise with the European universities. Yet he continually reminds us that he lived when religious artists were carving the sacred sculptures on their walls, or filling their windows with a mystic splendour, and that he had felt the power of those vaulted aisles, which he had, perhaps, visited as a pilgrim.[275]

Enough has been said to indicate the nature of Dante's learning, which was undoubtedly the learning of his time. It differed from that of his contemporaries in degree, but not in kind. When Mr. Berington gives expression to his delight at having at last found a man who could admire Virgil, he shows not only a very imperfect appreciation of the acquirements of mediæval scholars, but even of the poet whom he condescends to praise. Dante's aim was avowedly to write a *popular* poem; he desired to be read, not merely by the learned, but by the mass of his countrymen; and it was with this object that he sacrificed his first intention of writing in Latin verse, and chose the rude Italian vernacular, not without a certain regret, but with the design of being more widely intelligible, for, to use his own words, "we must not give meat to sucklings." We may safely dare to affirm that had not the Latin classics been freely admitted into the Christian schools of the thirteenth century, Dante would never have ventured to have chosen Virgil as his representative of Moral Philosophy. And if the world to which he addressed himself had not known something—perhaps a good deal—of classical history and poetry, his poem could not have achieved the popularity at which he successfully aimed. But it is probable that on this point things were not greatly changed from what they had been in the days of his ancestor Cacciaguida, when, as he tells us, the ladies of Florence, as they sat with their maidens,

Drawing off

The tresses from the distaff, lectured them

Old tales of Troy, and Fesole, and Rome.[276]

Certain it is that the erudition of the "Divina Commedia" proved no obstacle to its popularity. There is nothing in the history of literature that can be at all compared with the instantaneous conquest which it achieved over the Italian public. Within thirty years of the poet's death an Archbishop of Milan appointed a carefully-chosen commission of learned men to write a commentary on the poem; Florence, which had cast him out of her walls when living, now founded a public lecture to explain his works; and in 1373, called on Bocaccio to deliver this lecture in the Church of St. Stefano, at the annual salary of a hundred florins.

We are not, however, concerned with the literary history of Dante, who is only here spoken of as the representative scholar of his times. His profound learning has never been disputed; yet it is worthy of remark that if it be good criticism to measure a man's scholarship solely by the style of his Latin compositions, we should have to number the author of the "Divina Commedia" among the other writers whose "incredible ignorance" disgraced their age. His prose treatises, *De Monarchia* and *De Vulgari Eloquio*, in substance learned and full of acute observation, are declared to be rude and unclassical in style; a fact which suggests doubts how far this standard of criticism is a just one. It was fortunate indeed that he abandoned his first purpose of writing his poem in the Latin tongue, and chose rather that vernacular idiom which he raised to the dignity of a language. How he dealt with it is the real marvel; he built up his verse, much as the Athenians constructed their walls in the days of Themistocles, laying hold of any material that came in his way, quarrying words and phrases out of the Latin at his pleasure, filling up chinks and vacancies with verbs and adjectives which, whatever may have been their plebeian origin, became ennobled by his use; and creating many a good strong word of mighty meaning which it would have been well if his countrymen could have persuaded themselves to retain. After his time the formation of the Italian language rapidly developed, and the majestic mass which had been hewn into shape by Dante, received a finer and softer polish from Bocaccio and Petrarch.

Of the latter poet we now have to speak; for any sketch of mediæval scholarship would be imperfect without some notice of him who is commonly regarded as the restorer of polite letters. The father of Petrarch had been banished from Florence at the same time with Dante; and when a child, he himself had once beheld the great poet, whose fame he was in some respects destined to surpass. When he was nine years old his parents removed to Avignon in France, where the establishment of the papal court drew many Italians. There for four years he learnt as much grammar, logic, and rhetoric as the schools of Avignon and Carpentras could teach, and that does not appear to have been much. However, even at this age his classic tastes betrayed themselves. Whilst his comrades were still reading Æsop's fables and the verses of Prosper, he studied the works of Cicero, which delighted his ear long before he understood their sense. Then came another four years at Montpelier, after which he went to Bologna, and there studied civil law for three years more. But as soon as he found himself removed from his father's watchful eye the study of jurisprudence somewhat languished. "It was thus," he says, "that I spent, or rather wasted, seven years; and if I must say the truth, disgusted with my legal studies, I spent my time mostly in reading Cicero, Virgil, and the other poets. My father learnt this, and one day he unexpectedly appeared before me. Guessing at once the object of his coming, I hastily hid the great Latins, but he drew them from their hiding-place, and threw them into the fire, as if they had been books of heresy. At this sight I cried out as though I myself had been burnt. My father, seeing my affliction, drew out two volumes half-scorched with the flames, and holding one in his left and the other in his right hand, he said, "Here, this is Virgil, take it, and it will comfort your soul a little—and here is Cicero, you may have him too, for he will teach you how to plead." Somewhat consoled by this, I ceased my lamentations."

But a lawyer Petrarch was determined never to become. In 1327, having lost both his parents, he returned to Avignon, put on the ecclesiastical dress, and received the tonsure; but he had no more serious intention of following the clerical than the legal profession. He cared only for a life of literary ease, and the "graceful indolence" which has been declared to form one of the charms of his verses, was the predominant feature in his character. It was at this time that he formed that attachment to Laura de Sade which inspired the 400 sonnets, and other "Rime," which have made the celebrity of their author. At once to soothe his grief and to satisfy his curiosity, he undertook a voyage through France and Germany. He visited Paris, and describes its University as "a basket filled with the rarest fruits of every land." The French, he says, are "gay of humour, fond of society, and pleasant in conversation; they make war on care by diversion, singing, laughing, eating, and drinking." He visited Toulouse, and was introduced to the famous academy of the *Gaie Science*, established in 1324, of which Laura de Sade was herself a member. Seven poets, with a chancellor at their head, held their meetings in a palace surrounded by beautiful gardens, and solemnly granted the degrees of bachelor or doctor to the candidates for Parnassian honours, the prize for the best poem produced at the floral games of the month of May being a golden violet. At last he returned to Avignon, and, retiring to a country house in the solitude of Vaucluse, composed, amid its woods and fountains, some of his sweetest Italian sonnets, some Latin prose treatises, and his heroic Latin poem of "Africa," on which he bestowed immense labour. Great, indeed, would have been his own surprise could he have foreseen that posterity would have cared nothing at all for the classical imitations which procured him his laurel crown from the hands of the Roman Senate, and that his immortality as a poet would rest on those careless rhymes which he calls the unpremeditated songs of his juvenile sorrows, and which, being written in the despised vernacular tongue, he counted as of little merit. It was as a Latin writer that he desired to be remembered, and it was the fame of his "Africa" that induced the Senate of Rome and the University of Paris to offer him their honours on the same day. Petrarch's classic predilections, and his intense love of his native country, determined him to give the preference to Rome; and after a three days' examination, which was presided over by the learned King Robert of Naples, he was crowned on the Capitol, on Easter-day, 1341, and hung up his laurel wreath in the Basilica of the Apostles.

The rest of his life was chiefly spent in Italy, where the reigning princes of the Visconti, the Este, the Scaligeri, and the Gonzaga vied one with another in doing him honour. He devoted himself with a sort of passionate eagerness to the enterprise of seeking out copies of the neglected classics, and his correspondents in all parts of Europe assisted him in his labours. Cicero was his literary idol, and when the strangers who crowded round him asked him what presents they could send him from their distant lands, his reply was ever, "Nothing but the works of Cicero." He rescued from oblivion some of the epistles of his favourite author, and was once possessed of a copy of his treatise *De Gloria*, now lost to the world. He had almost an equal zeal in collecting and preserving medals and ancient monuments of art, and severely reprehended the practice, so common among the Romans, of destroying the venerable remains of antiquity, in order to procure building materials at an easy rate. Though never able to master the Greek language, he had the consolation of witnessing the first steps which ushered in the revival of that study. In 1339, Barlaam, a Calabrian monk who had for many years been a resident in Greece, was despatched to Avignon on a mission to Pope Benedict XII., from the Emperor Cantacuzenus. Petrarch took some lessons in Greek from him, but had too little perseverance to profit much from his master's lessons. Barlaam is declared by Bocaccio to have been a treasury of every kind of learning, and superior to any other scholar of the time. He wrote on theology, astronomy, and mathematics, and was well acquainted with the ancient Greek poetry. And so, after all, the Greek literature was restored to Europe through the instrumentality of a *monk*! For it was one of Barlaam's disciples, by name Leontius Pilate, also a Calabrian, who afterwards visited Petrarch at Venice, and from whom Bocaccio acquired a knowledge of Greek. The latter scholar persuaded the Florentine magistrates to appoint Leontius Greek professor in their city, and in 1361 the first Greek chair was erected in the West, and curious crowds flocked to listen to lectures on the "Iliad" and the "Odyssey," delivered from the lips of one whose outward appearance was that of an uncouth savage. He wore the philosopher's, or rather the beggar's, mantle, his countenance was hideous, his beard long and uncombed, his manners rude, and his temper gloomy. He remained at Florence three years, and then returned to the East to search for manuscripts; but such was his overbearing insolence that, in spite of his treasures of classic erudition, Petrarch would have nothing to say to him when he proposed a second visit to Italy. Leontius, however, embarked on board a vessel with the intention of returning to Florence, but was overtaken by a tempest, and struck dead by lightning. Petrarch was concerned at his loss, and yet more so by the fear that his books had perished with him. "Inquire, I beseech you," he wrote to Bocaccio, "whether there were not a Euripides or a Sophocles among them, or some other of the books he promised to bring me." He had already procured from Nicholas Sigeros a Greek Homer, which he prized, though unable to read it. "Your Homer," he writes, "is dumb to me, and I am deaf to it; nevertheless, the sight of it consoles me, and I often kiss its cover. I beg of you send me Hesiod, send me Euripides."

It was not only by the Italian dukes and princes that Petrarch was cherished; the Popes—Benedict XII., Clement VI., and Urban V.—all testified their sense of his merit, and enriched him with many benefices, and Urban is said to have been somewhat influenced in his determination to revisit Rome by the arguments of the poet. For whilst Petrarch allowed his pen the most unwarrantable freedoms in censuring the conduct of the papal court, he had nothing more at heart than the restoration of the Popes to their ancient capital, and on this point he shared the sentiments of Dante. Neither were the middle and lower classes at all behind their betters in the enthusiasm with which they regarded the great scholar. A certain grammar-master who had grown half-blind and wholly crippled, hearing that Petrarch was at Naples, determined to go thither to see him, and made his son carry him there on his shoulders. By the time they arrived the poet had departed for Rome. However, the old man declared himself ready to journey to the Indies if he could only come up with the object of his search, so they took the road to Rome; again too late, they proceeded to Parma, and there, to the inexpressible consolation of the venerable grammarian, he saw "his Petrarch," and causing his son to lift him up, he reverently kissed the head that had conceived so many noble thoughts, and the hand that had written so much good Latin.[277] In one of his familiar epistles, Petrarch relates the story of a certain goldsmith of Bergamo who, having exchanged the pursuits of trade for those of literature, was possessed with such a passing great admiration of the author of the "Rime," that he declared he should not die content unless he were once suffered to receive him in his house. Petrarch gave him that satisfaction but the delight of the goldsmith was so excessive, that his servants feared he would go mad with joy, and his guest had some difficulty in freeing himself from his troublesome attendance. Petrarch affected to treat these demonstrations of popular homage with studied contempt, but whilst he talked and wrote of the charms of solitude, it was evident that he was not a little intoxicated with the vapours of gratified vanity. Whatever pains he took to express his indifference to the world, he lost no opportunity of letting his friends know that the world was not indifferent to him. "Whenever I leave my house," he wrote from Milan, "a thing that happens very rarely, I bow right and left, and stop to speak to no one. I am more esteemed here than I deserve, and far more than suits my taste for quiet. Not only do the prince and his court love and honour me, but the people respect me far beyond my merits, and love me without so much as seeing me, for I rarely appear in public." His letters are filled with passages of this kind, which sufficiently betray that the would-be philosopher, who had written long treatises on the Solitary Life, and on Contempt of the World, was secretly devoured by a hungry egotism. His notions of the joys of Solitude attained to nothing more sublime than lying under a tree with a book in one's hand, and no one would have been less pleased than he, if his admirers had taken him at his word and ceased to pester him. Yet the homage of the world had no power to soothe the restlessness that devoured him, and in the midst of all his outward successes, fortune failed not to deal him many a cruel blow. The great plague of 1348, which desolated all Europe, and which was so powerfully described by the pen of Bocaccio, carried off Laura de Sade among its first victims, and Petrarch recorded his sorrow on the blank leaves of his Virgil. Other losses followed, and in the midst of these private griefs, Petrarch, who had given his confidence to the celebrated Rienzi and had dedicated a noble sonnet to one whom he fondly trusted would have been the restorer of his country's greatness, felt the fall of the great Tribune as a personal misfortune. "Some," he exclaimed, "can still rejoice in riches, some in intellect, and some in health; but for me, I see not what anything in the world can henceforth give me, save tears." A sad avowal for the greatest scholar of his age, but a scholar whose character, whatever may be said of his genius, was utterly hollow and superficial. The mere man of letters—and whatever may have been his sincere regret for the graver irregularities of his youth,—we must add, the unworthy ecclesiastic, ever sensible in the midst of his literary triumphs of a want and a weariness, is a poor exchange indeed, with all his erudition, for the race of Christian scholars with whom we have hitherto been engaged. His last residence was fixed at Arqua, near Padua; and there, on the 18th of July 1374, he was found dead in his study, with his head leaning on an open book. He had been struck by epilepsy, and so, as has been said, passed from the quiet of his library to the quiet of the grave. He had been the first to inaugurate a vast intellectual revolution, and the restoration of classical studies, begun by him, was carried on in the following century by Poggio and his contemporaries. For Italy, at least, the age of mediæval darkness, had passed away for ever, and with it passed away also not a few of the old Christian traditions of thought, art, and taste. The mind of the coming generations was to be formed on pagan models, and from this time, as Hallam remarks, it became the main, if not the exclusive, object of an educated man, to write Latin correctly, to understand the allusions of the best classic authors, and to learn at least the rudiments of Greek. That the revived taste for ancient letters did eventually bring about a certain anti-Christian reaction in art and literature cannot be denied; and the character of many of those who became distinguished among the leaders of the Renaissance was such as scarcely entitled them to be numbered among "Christian Scholars." Yet it would be most unfair to include under any sweeping censure all those who originated, or took part in, the classical revival, or to suppose that the movement was exclusively favoured by an irreligious party. The Augustinian friars and the Camaldolese monks of Florence were among the first encouragers of the new studies; and one of the earliest institutions of the nature of a literary academy, was that established in the Augustinian convent of the Holy Spirit at Florence. This convent adjoined the house where Giannozzo Manetti, then a mere boy, resided; and he contrived to make a door through the partition wall, by means of which he was able to enter the convent whenever he liked, and attend the conferences on literary subjects held among the brethren; the subjects of which were every day posted up in some conspicuous part of the cloister. Among the Camaldolese the same studies were introduced even before the death of Petrarch, and the monks of St. Mary of the Angels had among them men like Zenobio Tantino, who corresponded with all the *literati* of the day in poetical epistles. So heartily did they take part in the literary movements of their times that Ambrose Traversari, of whom Roscoe says that he had the best pretensions of any man of his age to the character of a polite scholar, was exclusively given up by his superiors to learned pursuits for the space of thirty years. Some, indeed, were to be found who dreaded the possible effects of reviving the study of Gentile writers, and it was scruples such as these which drew forth a graceful reply from Coluccio Salutati, the friend of Petrarch and the learned chancellor of Florence, whose achievements as a Latin poet won him the laurel wreath which was placed, not on his brow, but on his coffin, and whose unblemished life secured him a yet nobler reward in the friendship of St. Antoninus of Florence. He justly protested against the narrowness of supposing that a man could not be walking in the ways of God because he read the poets, and argued that in literature, as in all besides, we may find God, because all Truth and all Beauty is from Him, and to Him alone are they to be referred. That the restoration of good models, those same models which, as the historian Socrates informs us,[278] had been studied by Christians from the very first centuries of the Church for the sake of grace of elocution and the culture of the mind, was in itself lawful and desirable, does not appear a point requiring proof. Nevertheless, it is evident that the revolution effected in the studies of Christendom by the introduction of this new element, was one which demanded very powerful safeguards both on the side of faith and morals; and falling, as it did, under the direction of a race of captious and greedy professors, it resulted at last in grievous excesses which threatened little short of an extinction of Christian ideas altogether.

Already we begin to see the tide of learning dividing its waters into two streams, running in contrary directions. The close of the fourteenth century was illustrated, it is true, by a crowd of saintly men, who endeavoured to establish schools of sacred art and literature in the convents which they established or reformed. At Fiesole, St. Antoninus of Florence passed through his noviciate, in company with Beato Angelico, whilst, contemporary with them were St. Bernardine of Sienna, and St. John Capestran, the two Franciscan apostles, the former of whom drew half the Florentine grammar-masters to listen to his eloquence, while the latter terrified the fashionable ladies who thronged to his sermons into sacrificing their perfumes, dice, and false hair, of which he had the satisfaction of making several bonfires. An attentive study of the monuments, as well as of the literary history of the times, will, however, reveal significant tokens of the existence of a very different element from that which appears in the paintings of Angelico. It is remarkable that he formed no school, and found none to inherit his ideas. After his time, Christian art, the faithful exponent of the popular mind, daily lost something of the chaste severity of former times; there was a growing disposition in favour of more florid ornamentation in architecture, of a freer naturalism in painting, and of a capricious effeminacy even in sacred music, which destroyed the solemn religious character of the ancient chant. This latter abuse was severely reprehended by Pope John XXII. in his Bull, entitled *Docta Sanctorum*, wherein he complains of the innovations introduced by "certain disciples of a new school, who, employing their whole attention in marking time, endeavour, by new notes, to express airs of their own invention to the prejudice of the ancient chants." In this, as in everything else, the mischief was chiefly effected by the professors, who were gradually assuming a sort of dictatorship in literature and the arts, and who, whether they lectured, sang, or painted, sought as their main object, not the solid instruction of their hearers, or the symbolism of divine truths, but merely the display of their own talents.

The literary movement did not at first extend itself very rapidly beyond the Alps, and in France particularly many circumstances combined to check for a time the progress of letters. King Charles V. had indeed a taste for the sciences, and founded a royal library at the Louvre containing 900 volumes, and forming what his accomplished biographer, Christine de Pisa, calls "une

belle assemblée de notables livres moult bien escripts, et richement adornés."
She was the daughter of his Venetian astronomer, the authoress of fifteen
volumes in prose and verse, and was, as Tiraboschi affirms, well acquainted
with Greek. The king, however, found few among his courtiers to share his
learned tastes. The knights and nobles who fought at Creçy piqued
themselves on their ignorance of letters as a sign of their gentle blood, and it
is no uncommon thing to find a formula like the following attached to public
deeds of the fourteenth century:—"Lequel a déclaré ne savoir signer, attendu
sa qualité de gentilhomme." Eustache Deschamps, who wrote during the
reigns of John and Charles V., bitterly complains of the ignorance of the
upper classes as contrasted with those of an earlier generation. Formerly, he
says, nobles studied the liberal arts until their twentieth year, before receiving
knighthood; now they begin their education on horseback, abandon learning
to men of meaner birth, and give themselves up to gaming and profligacy.
He praises the older days of chivalry, when knights loved truth, virtue, and
loyal love, and were not ashamed of being thought clerks, "car meilleur temps
fut le temps ancien." Alain Chartier, another writer of the same period, makes
similar complaints. "Gentlemen live now," he says, "as if they were only
made to eat and drink; and everywhere you hear the ridiculous saying that it
is unbecoming for a nobleman to know how to read and write. It used not
so to be in the days when men held an ignorant king to be a crowned ass."
Nor are the accounts of the actual state of the University of Paris much more
satisfactory. The schools were filled with teachers who introduced both
philosophical and theological errors, and the Latinity of the Parisians is said
to have been worse than that of their English neighbours. Discipline too was
beginning to flag, and in 1366 the Faculty of Arts had to publish a decree of
reformation, from which it appears that the regents had begun to open their
schools at a later hour, and to introduce the hitherto unknown luxury of
benches in place of the time-honoured bundles of straw. With the exception
of a few great names, such as those of Gerson and Nicholas Oresme, this
period is a dreary and barren one in the literary annals of France. And the
sterility of her schools at this precise epoch is a remarkable and significant
fact. It was exactly the period when the peculiar political doctrines of the
Paris doctors appeared to have won their triumph. Adapting the principles
of the old imperial jurisprudence to the circumstances of Christian Europe,
if they did not actually identify the offices of Emperor and Pontiff, they yet
put forth doctrines which virtually implied a species of royal supremacy.
Gerson's teaching on the same subject, if less absolute, was not more
orthodox, and tended to make men regard the Pontifical dignity as a human
thing which could be legislated for according to principles of human policy.
National vanity came in to swell the pretensions of the Parisian doctors.
France was the centre of Christendom, and the heart of France was the
University. "Not Rome, but France," said Nicholas Oresme, in his oration

to Urban V., "is the country beloved by God. Charlemagne transplanted the liberal sciences from Rome to Paris, whose doctors may be compared to the stars of the firmament and the voice of many thunders; and on that *holy soil*, therefore, and not at Rome, ought the Pope to reside." This sort of eloquence was continually reproduced in the treatises on the temporal and spiritual powers which poured forth from the pens of the Paris legists, who were the first to adhere to the Antipope, Clement VII., thus involving France in the guilt of the Great Schism, and whose influence, fifty years later, at the Schismatical Council of Basle, obtained the pretended deposition of Eugenius IV., and the election of another Antipope, Felix V. Nay, so thoroughly was the University of Paris in love with schism, that when, in 1438, King Charles VIII. ordered all his subjects to acknowledge the authority of Eugenius, she alone refused to obey: the Antipope had been a creature of her own fabrication, and she obstinately clung to his fortunes.

On schools which had thus deliberately cut themselves off from the source of benediction the blessing of fertility could not rest.[279] No dew fell on them, and it was as if the clouds had been commanded that they should rain no rain upon them. Moreover, the frightful wars that desolated France for 150 years were adverse to the spread of letters. In them even Protestant historians have recognised the marked and terrible retribution of sacrilegious crime. The long struggle between Philip le Bel and Pope Boniface VIII. terminated, in 1303, in what seemed the complete triumph of the Crown. Not only had Philip firmly asserted the independence of the temporal power, but to secure his victory he had calumniated the Vicar of Christ by accusing him before all Europe as a sorcerer, a heretic, an infidel, and a simonist. His two infamous satellites, William de Nogaret and Sciarra Colonna, had entered Anagni with the banner of France displayed, crying aloud, "Death to the Pope, and long live the King of France!" They seized the venerable old man of eighty-six, as he sat awaiting them, with passive courage, on his throne, with the cross in his hand and the tiara on his brow, and treated him with indignities which hastened, if they did not actually cause, his death. And then the seat of the Popes was transferred from Rome to Avignon, a calamitous event which weakened their independent power, and eventually plunged the Church into schism. Respect for the authority of the Sovereign Pontiff declined apace in the schools of France, and it became fashionable for her lawyers and doctors to discuss the question how far that authority extended, and to affix limits to it of their own devising. All this was doubtless a great victory, and seemed to be something very like the triumph of the secular over the spiritual power. But it was a triumph terribly avenged. At the time when these fancied successes crowned the daring policy of Philip le Bel, he was in the flower of his age, surrounded by his three sons, all inheritors of their father's beauty, and promising to carry on the glories of his race to distant generations. But the King, in the forty-seventh year of his age, was killed by a wild boar; his sons, one by one, followed each other, heirless, to the tomb; at one and the same time the disgraceful crimes of their three wives were published to the world; and the crown passed from his family—and *to whom?* To the son of Charles de Valois, the friend and captain-general of Boniface VIII., who had refused to take part in his brother's crimes, and always remained loyal to the injured Pontiff. But this was not all. A daughter of Philip le Bel still survived, the she-wolf of France, who, after dyeing her hands in the blood of her husband, King Edward II. of England, left to her son, Edward III., those fatal claims which brought upon France the outpouring of the cup of vengeance. Those golden fleurs-de-lys, which Dante had beheld borne in triumph through the gates of Anagni, were rolled and trampled in the dust for a century and a half by English descendants of that very king who had fondly thought to establish his royal power on the humiliation of the Vicar of Christ. France was brought to the very lowest abyss of ignominy, and had to witness the coronation in her capital of an English conqueror, who quartered those same dishonoured lilies on his shield. What more need be said? History teaches many lessons, but there is one which she repeats through all ages with unvarying fidelity. It is vain for the kings of the earth to stand up against the Lord and against His Christ. It is idle for them in their mad presumption to dash themselves against the Rock of Peter; for "whoso falls on that Rock shall be broken, but on whomsoever it shall fall, it shall grind him to powder."

CHAPTER XVIII.

ENGLISH EDUCATION IN THE FOURTEENTH CENTURY.

A.D. 1300 TO 1400.

ALTHOUGH the French wars were hardly less injurious to the cause of polite learning in England than in France, the reigns of Edward III. and his successors are not without a peculiar interest in the history of our popular education. One after another those magnificent foundations were rising at the universities, the commencement of which has been noticed in a previous chapter; and the English collegiate system was taking root and attaining maturity. The threefold pestilence of Lollardism, the Black Death, and a rage for military glory, offered, it is true, some serious checks to the progress of letters; yet in spite of every such disadvantage, this epoch, so brilliant in the annals of chivalry, was hardly less important in those of English literature, which in Chaucer and Mandeville produced its first writers in prose and verse. And, indeed, if the reign of Edward III. was not a splendid literary era the fault is not to be charged to the deficient education of the sovereign. His great natural powers had been cultivated with extraordinary care under the direction of Richard Angervyle, or, as he is commonly called, Richard of Bury. The most learned scholar of his age, Richard was also a very great man as far as dignities could make him so: Archdeacon of Northampton, Prebendary of Lincoln, Salisbury, and Lichfield, Dean of Wells, and finally Bishop of Durham; Lord High Chancellor and Treasurer of the Kingdom, and Envoy Plenipotentiary for concluding the peace with France. Posterity, however, has forgotten his honours, and remembers him rather as the patron of learning, the correspondent of Petrarch, the founder of the Angervyle library at Oxford, and the author of the *Philobiblion*, a book in the compilation of which he was largely assisted by the learned Dominican Robert Holkot, and in which he gives full expression to that devouring passion for books, wherewith, says Harpsfield, "he was mightily carried away." His library was the first public one ever founded in England. He bestowed it on Durham college, which he completed and partly endowed, and made the inheritor of his books, of which, says Wood, he had more than all the other bishops of England put together. All his palaces were crammed with them, and the floor of the room where he sat was so strewn with them that it was no easy thing to approach him. He kept three collectors constantly employed for him in France, Germany, and Italy. In his palace a staff of writers, illuminators, and binders were constantly at work under his own eye, and he gives ample details in his work of the incredible pains and expense he was at to complete his collection. It was undertaken in no light or capricious mood, but as a serious and solemn duty. "Moved," he says, "by Him who alone granteth and perfecteth a good will to man, I diligently inquired what, among all the offices of piety, would most please the Almighty, and most profit the Church militant. Then before the eyes of our mind there came a flock of chosen scholars in whom God, the artificer, and His handmaid Nature, had indeed planted the roots of the best manners and sciences, but whom penury so oppressed that they were dried up and watered by no dew; and so they who might have grown up strong columns of the Church were obliged to renounce their studies. Deprived of the writings and helps of contemplation they return, for the sake of bread, to base mechanical arts. And the result of our meditation was pity for this humble race of men, and the resolution to help them, not only with the means of sustenance, but also with books for the prosecution of their studies; and to this end our intention ever watched before the Lord. And this ecstatic love so moved us that, renouncing all other earthly things, we applied ourselves to collect books."

In his bibliographical researches the still unplundered monasteries afforded him an inexhaustible mine of literary treasures. Whenever he visited towns where there existed religious houses, his first visit was paid to their libraries; and he was not slow in examining their chests and other repositories where books might lie concealed. Often amid the greatest poverty he found the rarest stores; and the richest in this kind of wealth, as well as the most liberal in dispensing the use of it, were the Friars Preachers. Sometimes, however, he had complaints to make of the carelessness and indifference of those possessed of books, which he often found "turned out of their interior chambers and secure depositories, and given over to destruction for the sake of dogs, birds, and those two-legged beasts called women."

No catalogue of the Angervyle collection now exists, and at the Reformation it was dispersed, and in great measure destroyed by the Protestant plunderers, who saw a vision of Popery in every illuminated manuscript. But there can be little doubt that it was rich in works of high literary value. For the good bishop was one of those who esteemed the liberal arts above the study of law, and he expressly tells us that he provided his students with Greek and Hebrew grammars. He gave them also very quaint and pithy directions how to use his books. They were to take care how they opened and shut them, not to mark them with their nails, or write alphabets on the margin of the leaves. He criticises the bad habits of indolent and careless youths, who lean both their elbows on their books, put straws and flowers to keep their places, and eat fruit and cheese over the open pages; and he exhorts those into whose hands his treasures may fall, to wash their hands before reading, and to take a little more care of their books than they would of an old shoe.

Several other prelates imitated the laudable example of Richard of Bury, and endeavoured to make provision for the wants of poor scholars by the foundation of public libraries. It is probable, however, that most of these collections were extremely limited in their range. The English universities were at this time almost exclusively resorted to by lawyers and ecclesiastics, or, in other words, by those who had chosen the calling of *clerks*. They were not, as they afterwards became, and as they continue to be in our day, places of liberal education for the sons of the gentry; and hence the education given in them had a certain professional narrowness; a defect which was further increased at this particular period, by the presence among the students of a very large proportion of beneficed clergymen, who having been appointed from an inferior class to fill up the vacancies caused by the ravages of the Black Death, were often found so ignorant as to render it necessary for their diocesans to require their spending a certain time at the universities, in order to acquire just so much learning as was actually indispensable for their office. Men of this sort, of course, spent little time on polite literature, and the influence of such a class of students was, naturally enough, to pull down the academical studies to a very low standard.

It will occur to every reader to inquire where the sons of the gentry received their education, if they were not as yet in the habit of frequenting the universities and public schools. And to furnish a reply, we must call to mind the habits which prevailed in feudal society, according to which every great baron or prelate presided over a huge household, including, besides his domestic servants and chaplains, a crowd of knights, esquires, and pages, among the last of whom a certain number of noble youths were always admitted, in order to receive the training suited to their rank. Chivalry, it will be remembered, was not an accident, but an institution, and one which was furnished with a rigorous system of graduation. A man who aspired to the profession of arms, had to be trained for it according to fixed rules, and to go through each successive degree with as much precision as the bachelors and masters in the schools. Indeed, the feudal castles may not unfitly be called schools of chivalry, and in them alone could the future knight be instructed in the duties of his state. As page in a baronial household, a youth was able to acquire an education far more suited to his future position in the world, than he could possibly have received at the universities. There he would have been chiefly called on to attend lectures on the Sentences, or on civil and canon law; but as page to a great lord, spiritual or temporal, he learnt how to serve and carve at table, to fly a hawk, manage and dress a horse, bear himself in the tilt-yard, and handle his arms. Noble youths generally began their education at the age of seven, when they were admitted to the service of the ladies of the family, and were styled *Damoiseaux*. They were under the immediate control of the lady of the house, and learnt from her at once their Christian doctrine and the laws of courtesy.[280] I say, the *laws*, for the teaching of this virtue was reduced to a science, and had a literature of its own. By the fair virtue of courtesy our forefathers understood something more than the mere outside polish of worldly refinement. The author of the "Lytylle childrene's lytylle boke" informs us that according to cunning clerks—

"Curtesye from hevyn come,

Whan Gabryelle our Ladye greete,

And Elizabeth with Mary mette."

"Alle vertues are closide yn curteseye," he says, "and alle vices in vyllonie;" and he goes on to teach his pupils that they must love God and their neighbours, speak the truth, keep their word, and neither swear, quarrel, nor be idle. They are not to be proud or to scorn the poor, and are to speak honestly whether it be to the lord or to his servants. If his directions how to behave at table are somewhat homely, it cannot be denied that they are much to the point, and Dame Curtesye forgets not to remind her scholars that before eating they should think of the poor, because a full stomach wots little what the hungry ails.

As the boy grew older he came under the training of the seneschal and the chaplain. The first, who was generally some old veteran knight, taught him his martial duties, while the other imbued him with a reasonable amount of book-learning in Latin and Norman-French. The ignorance of French knights in Du Guesclin's time must not be held to disprove this latter statement, for it is plain that ignorance was opposed to the older traditions of chivalry, and was commented upon as a sign of decay by writers of the time. Knights were certainly expected to know how to read and write, for the youthful aspirant to chivalric honours, who, in the twelfth century, wandered from land to land seeking goodly adventures, was always required to carry tablets, and note down the deeds which he witnessed most worthy of remembrance and imitation. He was required to know something of the tuneful art, whether the plain song of the Church, or the lays of the troubadours, and, as a matter of course, every well bred man was well instructed in the abstruse science of heraldry. Chaucer, in describing his squire, takes care to let us know that besides sitting his horse, carving at table, and jousting in the lists, he could sing, write songs, dance, "and wel pourtraie and write." The education of his mind, then, was not entirely neglected, and still less was that of his manners. He was "courteous, lowlie, and serviceable;" and elsewhere the same authority informs us, that the young squire was often charged to be wise and equitable, godly in word, and reasonable, to be courteous in salute, and to abstain from all words of ribaldry, "and fro all pride to keep him well." The last words are worthy of notice, for this eschewing of pride is greatly insisted on by all chivalric writers as one of the special characteristics of a gentleman. It is a point on which Chaucer constantly loves to dwell:—

But understand to thine intent,

That this is not mine intendment,

To clepen no wight in no age,

Only gentyl for his lineage;

But whoso that is virtuous,

And in his port not outrageous:

When such one thou seest thee beforne

Tho he be not gentyl yborne,

Thou mayst wel seem in sooth,

That he is gentyl because he doth

As longeth to a gentyl man,

Of him, none other, deme I can.[281]

Exactly in the same spirit does the good king Perceforest in the old romance instruct his knights: "Si me souvient d'une parolle que ung hermite me dist une fois pour moy chastier. Car il me dist que si j'avois autant de possessions comme avoit le roy Alexandre, de sens comme le sage Salomon, et de bravoure comme le preux Hector de Troy, seul orgueil, s'il regnoit en moy, destruieroit tout." And in a book of instructions on the duties of Chivalry, we find the following: "Louange est reputée blâme en la bouche de celluy qui se loe, mais elle exaulce celluy qui ne se attribue point de louange, mais à Dieu. Si l'ecuyer a vaine gloire de ce qu'il a fait, il n'est pas digne d'être chevalier, car vaine gloire est un vice qui destruit les merites de chevalerie."[282] In the same Treatise the virtues of chivalry are declared to be the three theological and the four cardinal virtues, and a good knight will hold the opposite vices in horror; he must keep himself from villanous thoughts, and be unstained within and without, and must withal be modest, "the first to strike on the battle-field, but the last to speak in the hall."

Schools in which maxims such as these prevailed, and in which the duties of religion were strictly enforced, must be admitted to fill an important place in the system of Christian education. It may be doubted, too, whether Eton or Rugby could bestow a more careful polish than was inculcated by that minute etiquette which chivalric usage demanded. The grace and manliness, the "pluck" and spirit which Englishmen prize so highly, and purchase at so dear a rate, were certainly not disregarded; but they were tempered with a certain admixture of lowliness which has not retained an equal place in our esteem.

Despite all the extravagances of Chivalry, and the exaggerated and injurious effect of some of its maxims, such as those which inculcated a heathenish sensitiveness on the point of honour, it enforced a law of self-restraint, a polite diction and etiquette, and a government of the exterior man, in all which the education of our own day is fatally defective. "One of the essential principles of chivalry," says Godwin, speaking of the education bestowed on noble youths in these baronial households, "was, that no office was sordid that was performed in aid of a proper object. It was the pride of the candidate for knighthood to attend upon his superiors, and perform for them the most menial services. The dignity of the person assisted raised the employment, and the generous spirit in which it was performed gave it lustre and grace. It was the office of a page or an esquire to spread the table, to carve the meat, to wait upon the guests, to bring them water to wash, and conduct them to their bed-chamber. They cleaned and kept in order the arms of their lord, and assisted him in equipping himself for the field. There is an exquisite beauty in offices like these, not the growth of servitude, not rendered with unwillingness and constraint, but the spontaneous acts of reverence and affection performed by a servant of mind not less free and noble than the honoured master whom he serves."[283] The truth and justice of this observation will be readily admitted, and we stop and ask ourselves what substitute has our increased civilisation furnished for this beautiful element in the education of the Middle Ages? Where, except among the fags below the fifth form, does a noble youth of our day learn anything of these "lowly and serviceable" courtesies; and are they there performed in that spirit of "spontaneous reverence and affection," which renders them not sordid, but illustrious? We must leave it to our public schoolmen to reply.

Such an education as has been described above, taught exactly what a secular youth of good birth now goes to the universities to acquire—it taught him to be a gentleman. And it is probable that in these chivalric households he received the culture suited to his position with more safeguards to faith and morals than would have been found in the schools of Paris or Oxford. In those days the government of the family was the active, earnest business of the lord and lady; noble rank was not held to dispense a baron and a baron's wife from seeing to very homely details with their own eyes; and the everyday habits of their retainers were regulated by them in a way which put into their hands a vast parental power. Doubtless this "wondrous middle age" had plenty of barbarous violence, and was disgraced by much gross immorality; nor do we aim at painting it other than it was. But, whatever were its failings, it had one merit,—the Family Life was then a reality and not a name.[284] Most readers are familiar with the beautiful picture of the household of Sir Thomas More, which all his biographers agree in holding up as a model and pattern, though possibly an exceptional form of excellence. It was exceptional, however, only in its extraordinary cultivation of letters; in every other respect it did but present the old Catholic type, of which we might adduce innumerable specimens both in earlier and later times. Let us see what sort of rules were drawn up by a French earl of the fourteenth century for the regulation of his household, just premising that this is not an exceptional case, but that any acquaintance with mediæval literature will convince the reader that Elzear de Sabran ruled his family as many a good knight of France and England besides him were doing at the same period. Elzear had the greatest of all blessings, a good mother, whose piety and charity had earned her the golden title of "The Good Countess." When he was born she took him in her arms and offered him to God, and had him educated by his uncle in the abbey of St. Victor's at Marseilles. But he did not become a monk or a clerk: on the contrary, he lived as a great baron, fought as a brave soldier, administered justice to his feudal retainers, and was employed as ambassador from the King of Naples to the court of France. He was at the head of the State Council of Naples, and fought two pitched battles against the Emperor Henry VII., so that I think we need have no mistaken notion as to his being a mere pious recluse. Like other nobles of the time, he received a number of youths into his house, among whom was the eldest son of King Robert himself: Duke Charles of Calabria, a circumstance which induces us to think that a certain instruction in letters must have been given to the pages, for this King Robert was the same who acted as examiner to Petrarch, and was used to say that if he must choose between his crown and his studies, the latter should have the preference. Surius tells us that Elzear took great pains with the duke's education, explaining to him the principles of piety, justice, and clemency, making him frequent the Sacraments, and advising him to keep flatterers at a distance. His wife, Delphina of Glandeves, was worthy of directing a Christian household; she looked to all things with her own eye, banished brawls and tale-bearing, and was honoured by her servants as a mother and a saint. When first they began to keep house at Puy-Michel, in Provençe, Elzear drew up rules for the regulation of his family, of which the following is a short abridgment:—

"Every one in my family shall daily hear Mass. Let no one curse, swear, or blaspheme, under pain of chastisement. Let all persons honour chastity, for no impure word or deed shall go unpunished in the house of Elzear. The men and women shall confess their sins every week, and communicate every month, or at the least at the chief festivals, namely, Christmas, Easter, and Pentecost, and on the feasts of our Lady. No one shall be idle, but in the morning, after prayers, let all go to their work, the men abroad, the women at home. The life of the pious woman is not merely to pray, but to ply her work, and take care of her household. Therefore, the ladies shall read and pray in the mornings, and afterwards spend their time in useful work of some kind. Every evening all my family shall assemble for a pious conference, in which they shall hear something said for the salvation of their souls. And let none be absent on pretence of attending to my affairs. I have no affairs so near my heart as the salvation of those who serve me. I will have no playing at dice or games of hazard; there are plenty of innocent diversions, and time passes soon enough without being thrown away: yet I do not wish my castle to be a cloister, nor my people hermits. Therefore, let them be merry, but without offending God. If any quarrel fall out, let not the sun set before it be appeased. And I strictly command all under my jurisdiction to hurt no man in goods, honour, or reputation. I will not have my coffers filled by the emptying of others; we shall be wealthy enough if we fear God."

The nobles educated in such households are often spoken of in after-life as evincing a certain love of polite letters, such as Count Capranica, whom Petrarch describes as living in his feudal castle, "governing his vassals with justice and love, cultivating the Muses, and seeking the society of the learned." Ordinarily speaking, however, the merits of the mediæval system of education for the upper ranks lay less in its intellectual than in its moral training. It is true indeed that all great barons and their wives were not Elzears and Delphinas, but it is probable that the families usually chosen as homes for the young were those which were held in highest repute as virtuous and well-ordered. And in such families we are justified in saying that, as a general rule, the grand Christian traditions were certainly upheld; that children were taught to be subject to parents and governors, and parents were held bound personally to superintend the education of their children; that there was a real parental rule, that priests were had in worshipful honour, the poor regarded as the members of Christ, women treated with respect and courtesy, and elders had in reverence. The domestic virtues were taught after another fashion than among ourselves, and whilst the education of a gentleman aimed at making him brave, clement, courteous, and devout, a high-born lady was trained to a life of vigorous practical utility. She learnt to fill the responsible office of head of the family, which demanded in those days no small capacity of government. She was instructed in a hundred details of domestic life, which ladies are now-a-days content to entrust to their servants. No great variety of accomplishments was of course expected of her; and the author of the "Advice to Ladies," written in 1371, enumerates reading, church music, embroidery, confectionery, and surgery as among the most useful branches of female education. As to writing, he considers it superfluous, and thinks it better if women "can nought of it."

In the same spirit the good housewife is addressed in the "Menagier de Paris," and exhorted to take both pains and pleasure in her household duties. She is expected to know something about gardening and tillage, to be able to choose grooms, porters, and other servants, and look after labourers, pastrycooks, bakers, shoemakers, and chambermaids; to see that the sheep and horses are taken care of, and the wines kept clear. Moreover, she must know what to order for dinner and supper, and must understand how to make all manner of ragôuts, and pottages for the sick. Much account was made of early rising in all the books of instruction addressed to ladies. The "Menagier" humorously complains of those sluggards whose Matins are, "I must sleep a little longer," and their Lauds, "Is breakfast ready yet?" But in general it was the habit to rise with the lark, and give the early hours, as in Elzear's household, to prayer and reading. Thus an old French poet describes it—

Le matin se donne à l'estude,

Chacun demeure en solitude,

Après avoir dedans les cieux

Fait monter l'offre de ses vœux.

Such homely duties as those enumerated above might seem to leave but little room for cultivation of letters. Probably the writers of these treatises made the most of their subject, but it is quite clear that the "Valiant women" of olden time were not mere homely housewives, innocent of intellectual culture, and with no ideas beyond their distaffs and their confectioneries; on the contrary, many of them were learned in their way, like the saintly Isabel of France, sister to St. Louis, who was an excellent spinster, but was also well read in St. Augustine. Froissart incidentally lets us know that many of the noble ladies he names in his Chronicle were lovers of learning; such as Mary de Bohun, the first wife of Henry Bolingbroke, who, as he tells us, was well skilled in Latin and Church Divinity. And the character of not a few of those grand heroic women, whose names so beautify the page of history, might be summed up in the words with which Gabrielle de Bourbon is described by the biographer of Bayard. "She was," he says, "devout, religious, chaste, and charitable; grave without haughtiness, magnanimous without pride, and not ignorant of letters, specially delighting in reading and hearing read the Sacred Scriptures." The considerable part taken in the foundation of the English Colleges by noble ladies of the fourteenth century shows that they were, at any rate, not indifferent to learning. I have already spoken of Ella Longspée and the Lady Devorgilla, and in the following century their noble example was followed by Philippa of Hainault, the foundress of Queen's College, Oxford, and Mary de St. Pol, the widowed countess of Pembroke, who founded Pembroke College, Cambridge, and was chosen on account of her virtue and learning to direct the education of Queen Philippa's daughters. No one can study the histories of those times without being frequently struck by the superiority which appears in the characters of their illustrious women. Their education, however slender it may have been in a merely literary sense (and, if less showy, it was perhaps quite as solid as what finds favour among ourselves), evidently fitted them to take an active and intelligent part in domestic and social life. The old chroniclers often allude to the happy influence exerted over their lords by such queens as Eleanor of Castile, and the Good Queen Maud. Not a few English countesses merited the praises bestowed on Ildegard by the historian Donizzo, who calls her *docta, gubernatrix, prudens, proba, consiliatrix.* The practical mind of Philippa of Hainault was employed in introducing useful arts into England, just as, a few years later, the intelligence and commanding powers of Margaret, "the Great Countess" of Ormonde, were similarly exercised in Ireland, where she planted weavers and other artisans, built schoolhouses, and "was ever showing herself liberal, bountiful, and devout." They who would understand the character of a true Catholic household, presided over by a wise and intelligent mistress, may find it depicted in countless beautiful pictures, both of history and romance. Thus, in one of the works translated by Caxton, the Knight of the Tower holds up for the imitation of his daughters the example of the Lady Cecily of Balleville, whose daily ordinance was to rise early and say matins with her chaplains, and then to hear High Mass and two low Masses, "saying her service full devoutly." Then she walked in her garden, and finished her other morning devotions, and betimes she dined. After dinner she visited sick folk, and caused her best meat to be brought to them, and spent her day in other charitable and useful works. After hearing vespers she went to supper, and betimes to bed, making great abstinence, and wearing haircloth on all Wednesdays and Fridays. In the same volume we find that the maxims of courtesy and humility which found place in the training of a gentleman were equally inculcated on noble ladies. The Knight of the Tower reminds his daughters that courtesy is to be shown to persons of low degree as well as those of gentle blood, and even more scrupulously, and he gives his reasons. "Courtesy shewn to those of low estate," he says, "is more honourable than that shewn to the great, because it the more evidently proceedeth from a frank and gentle heart." He cites the example of a certain great lady whom he once saw in company with some fine knights and ladies, and who humbled herself to curtsey, as she passed, to a poor tinker; and when her gay companions asked her why she did so, she replied, "I would rather miss shewing such courtesy to a gentleman than to him." And this, he says, is what all understand and practise who know the laws of true courtesy.

What has been said of the character of domestic life in the Middle Ages will doubtless seem a partial view to those who consider that we ought to gather our notions of the state of society then prevailing from the debased literature of the jongleurs and troubadours, which is universally acknowledged to have been exceedingly bad. It will be remembered, however, that the "goliardi," as they were called, were a distinct class in society, the dead branches of the universities, men who followed no profession save that of buffoonery, and had gathered just so much education in school as enabled them to give point to a licentious song or story. They wandered about from city to city and from castle to castle; and in days when no places of public amusement existed, there were plenty of knights and nobles ready to receive such guests, and to while away the dulness of a winter's evening by listening to their narratives. The appetite for recreation in an unregenerate world is hardly less clamorous in its demands than the appetite for food, and the goods which are produced to supply such a demand, are seldom, even in our own more refined age, of the choicest description. But to take the offensive literature produced by a corrupt and excommunicated class, for such the "goliardi" really were,[285] and draw thence any conclusions respecting the manners of the higher classes in ancient times, is about as fair as it would be to judge of the state of society among ourselves by the plot of a "sensation" novel or a French vaudeville. Even allowing the character of their fictions to be taken as evidence of the existence of widespread scandals, at least equal weight must be attached to the *bonâ fide* historical descriptions of households such as those of Elzear or Charles the Wise, of whom Christine de Pisa says that he suffered no pernicious book to remain in his palace for a single day; nor any person whose language was not pure and innocent. Mr. Wright expresses his surprise at the inconceivable corruption of a society which could endure the goliardic tales to be recited in its presence. But it would be easy to match the instances which he brings forward with others which show us the domestic circle amusing itself in a very different manner, like that in the castle of Count Charles of Flanders, who entertained three monks, doctors of theology, that they might daily, after supper, read and explain the Scriptures to his family; or like that again, of the good king named above, who always kept readers in his palace to relieve the winter evenings by reading aloud "les belles ystoires de la sainct Escripture, ou des fais des Romains, ou moralitées de philosophes, et d'autres sciences;" and examples of this sort are by no means exceptional.

What, however, we are chiefly concerned with, is not so much the practice of this or that individual, as the character of the education by which they were trained. Our inquiry is what were the principles and the standard of morals enforced in the chivalric system of education. And the fact that this standard was far higher than what exists among ourselves, has been acknowledged by writers whose sympathies are all in another direction. Thus, M. Guizot, whose study of European civilisation has certainly not been superficial, expresses his admiration at "the moral notions, so delicate, so elevated, and above all so humane, and so invariably stamped with a religious character," which are to be found in the oaths and obligations imposed by the laws of chivalry. "Crimes and disorders abounded in the Middle Ages," he says, "yet men evidently had in their minds lofty desires and pure ideas. Their principles were better than their acts. A certain high moral ideal always soars above the stormy element." He goes on to remark that this pure tone of morality which prevails in the laws of chivalry must be traced to the influence of the clergy, who, though they did not invent that institution, made it an instrument for civilising society and introducing "a more enlarged and vigorous system of morality in domestic life." Expressions like these, which are abundantly confirmed by a study of the ancient monuments, justify us in claiming for the mediæval system of education the merit of at least presenting to the world a lofty standard of right and wrong. That the acts of the pupils often fell far below their principles, is saying no more than that they were men. But it cannot be supposed that society could be permeated with a high moral ideal, and that the strict obligations of that class to which every man of gentle blood belonged, should be redolent of a spirit at once "delicate, scrupulous, and humane," without effecting some practical results. The young were trained to reverence a whole class of virtues which popular writers declare must be regarded in our own day as "dead." The system of education which prevailed, presented them with a high ideal of moral excellence, a lofty standard of thoughts and desires, precisely that, the loss of which among ourselves is so bitterly deplored. And what is all education but the formation of such an interior standard? A teacher can do little more than grave on the soul principles which may survive many practical shortcomings, and may eventually recall a wanderer to better things. This is a point which non-Catholic writers can hardly be expected to appreciate as it deserves, bound up as it is with a class of ideas, and even of dogmas, to which they are necessarily strangers. But whilst acknowledging the contrast too frequently observable between the profession and the practice of Christians in the Middle Ages, another remarkable feature in those extraordinary times ought not to be overlooked,—I mean those numerous episodes in history which exhibit its great criminals in the light of great penitents. There had been early impressed on those fierce hearts a fear of God, a sense of sin, and a living faith in the possibility of obtaining pardon; nay, we will add, a certain capacity of self-humiliation, which evoked grand heroic acts of contrition from many whose previous lives had been a tissue of enormities; and thus a man like William Longspée needed but the look and the word of a saint to feel all the old teaching reawaken in his soul, and with a rope about his neck "to abhor himself in dust and ashes."

To return from this digression, which is yet intimately connected with our subject, let us proceed to examine a little more closely the actual schools for rich and poor existing in England in the fourteenth century. Besides the universities and monastic schools, there were, as we have already seen, others presided over by independent masters. Schools of greater or less pretension were attached to most parish churches, and the scholars assembled either in the church, or the porch, or "parvis." Thus in 1300 we read of children being taught to sing and read in the "parvis" of St. Martin's, Norwich. Endowed schools in connection with hospitals and colleges were also springing up, of which we shall speak more fully in another chapter, and in all these schools, as well as in the universities, the studies, up to the latter part of the reign of Edward III., were carried on in Latin and French. Ralph Higden, a monk of Chester, who wrote his *Polychronicon* somewhere about the year 1357, informs us that in his day French was the only language which schoolboys were allowed to use, except Latin. The passage as translated by John de Trevisa in 1387 is as follows: "Children in scoles agenst the usage and maner of all other nations beeth compelled for to leve thir own language, and for to construe thir lessons and thinges in Frenche. Also gentylmen children beeth taught to speke Frenche, from the time that they beeth rokked in thir cradel. And uplondish men (*i.e.* country people) will lyken hymself to gentylmen and soundeth with gret besynesse for to speke Frenche to be told of." When Ralph was protesting against this custom its knell was about to sound. In 1362 the celebrated statute was passed which ordained that all pleadings in the Royal courts should now be made in English instead of French, a change for which we stand indebted to the spirit of nationality called forth by the continental wars. By the time therefore that John of Trevisa wrote his translation of the *Polychronicon*, a great revolution had taken place, so that he thought it necessary to introduce this correction into the body of his work: "This maner (the use of the French language) is now som dele ychaungide: for John Cornwaile, a maister of gramer, chaungide the lore in gramer scole and construction of Frensch, into Englisch, and Richard Pencriche lerned that maner of teching of him, and other men of Pencriche; so that now the yere of oure Lord a thousand thre hundred foure score and fyve, of the secunde king Rychard after the conquest, in alle the gramer scoles of England, children leveth Frensch, and construeth and lerneth in Englisch, and haveth therby avauntage in one side and desavauntage in another. Ther avauntage is, that thei lerneth ther gramer in lasse tyme than children were wont to do; desavauntage is, that now children of gramer scole knoweth no more Frensch than knows thir left heele; and that is harm to them, if thei schul passe the see and travaile in strange londes, and in many other places also: also gentylmen haveth now myche ylefte for to teche thir children Frensch." It is evident that John of Cornwaile and Richard Pencriche, were, like the author himself, Cornish men. John of Trevisa was a Cornish priest, one of the earliest students at Exeter College, or, as it was called at that time, Stapleton Hall, Canon of Westbury in Wiltshire, and Vicar of Berkeley. His translation of the *Polychronicon* was undertaken at the request of his Patron, Thomas Lord Berkeley, and was afterwards modernised and continued by Caxton. At the request of the same noble friend he is said to have undertaken an English translation of the Old and New Testaments. Warton, and after him Craik, have stated that no account of this work is known to exist, and doubts have even been raised whether it were ever really written. One antiquarian, quoted by Lewis in his History of the Translations of the Bible, assures a "learned friend" that Trevisa translated no more of the Scriptures than certain sentences painted on the walls of Berkeley Castle, which sentences turn out to have been painted in Latin and French. But the existence of the translation is uniformly alluded to by early writers as a well-known fact, and Dr. Ingram informs us in a note appended to his *Memorials of Oxford* that in 1808 he was actually presented with a copy of the work.[286]

There was the less excuse for the English gentry having eschewed the use of the national tongue, from the fact that the language had long since been redeemed from the character of a barbarous idiom by the labours of the monks. Their rhyming chronicles and a vast quantity of beautiful and pathetic poetry, attributed by critics to the thirteenth and fourteenth centuries, must be regarded as the real first-fruits of English literature; and the adherence to what Chaucer lets us know was exceedingly bad French, in preference to good English, was simply a remnant of Anglo-Norman pride. Chaucer himself had to apologise for his use of the vulgar idiom, and in the prologue to one of his prose treatises, he protests against the speaking of "poesy matter" in French which, in the ears of Frenchmen, is about as agreeable as a Frenchman's English. "Let Frenchmen endite their quaint terms in French," he says, "for it is kindly to their mouths; but let us show our fantasies in such words as we learned of our dames' tongues." His example, of course, had great influence; yet such was the force of this sentiment of gentility, that at the universities the Oxonian and Cantabrian French (which was not much better than that spoken at "Stratford-atte-Bowe") held its ground for some years; but in the primary schools the English tongue asserted its supremacy, and primers and grammars began to be divested of their foreign clothing. A great many fragments of English school literature exist belonging to the fourteenth century, some of which may furnish amusement to the reader. All perhaps may not have a very clear idea of what an ancient *Primer* really was. It was something very different from the school books to which we ordinarily give the name. For in the dames schools, of which Chaucer speaks, children were provided with few literary luxuries and had to learn their letters off a scrap of parchment nailed on a board, and in most cases covered with a thin transparent sheet of horn to protect the precious manuscript. Hence the term "horn-book" applied to the elementary books in use by children. Prefixed to the alphabet, of course, was the holy sign of the Cross; and so firm a hold does an old custom get on the popular mind that down to the commencement of the present century alphabets continued to preserve their ancient heading, and derived from this circumstance their customary appellation of "the Christ-cross row," a term so thoroughly established as still to find its place in our dictionaries. The mediæval primer is, however, best described in the language of the fourteenth century itself. The following passage occurs in the introduction to a MS.

poem of 300 lines, still preserved in the British Museum, each portion of which begins with a separate letter of the alphabet:—

In place as men may se

When a childe to schole shal sette be

A Bok is hym ybrought,

Naylyd on a bord of tre,

That men cal an A, B, C,

Wrought is on the bok without.

V paraffys grete and stoute,

Rolyd in rose red.

That is set, withouten doute,

In token of Christes ded.

Red letter in parchymyn,

Makyth a childe good and fyn

Lettres to loke and see,

By this bok men may devyne,

That Christe's body was ful of pyne,

That dyed on wod tree.

After the difficulties of the primer had been overcome, a great deal of elementary knowledge was taught to the children, as in Saxon times, through the vehicle of verse. For instance, we find a versified geography of the fourteenth century, of which the two following verses may serve as a specimen, though it must be owned the second is not very creditable to our mediæval geographers:—

This world is delyd (divided), al on thre,

Asie, Affrike, and Eu-ro-pe.

Wol ye now here of A-si-e,

How mony londes ther inne be?

The lond of Macedonie,

Egypte the lesse and Ethiope,

Syria, and the land Judia,
These ben all in Asya.

The following grammar rules are of rather later date, and belong to the fifteenth century:—

Mi lefe chyld, I kownsel the

To forme thi vi tens, thou avise the,

And have mind of thi clensoune

Both of noune and of pronoun,

And ilk case in plurele

How thou sal end, avise the well;

And the participyls forget thou not,

And the comparison be in thi thought,

The ablative case be in thi minde,

That he be saved in hys kind, &c.

There is something in this last fragment very suggestive of the rod. What would have been the fate of the unhappy grammarian, if in spite of this solemn counsel he had failed to have his ablative case in his mind, we dare not conjecture. Our forefathers had strict views on the subject of sparing the rod and spoiling the child. Thus one old writer observes of children in general:—

To thir pleyntes mak no grete credence,

A rodd reformeth thir insolence;

In thir corage no anger doth abyde,

Who spareth the rodd all virtue sette asyde

Yet the strictness was mingled, as of old, with paternal tenderness, and children appear to have treated their masters with a singular mixture of familiarity and reverence. And it is pleasant to find among the same collection of school fragments a little distich which speaks of peacemaking:—

Wrath of children son be over gon.

With an apple parties be made at one.

There is good reason for believing that schoolboys of the fourteenth century were much what they are in the nineteenth, and fully possessed of that love of robbing orchards, which seems peculiar to the race. Chaucer has something to say on this head, but Lydgate's confessions are exceedingly pitiful:—

Ran into gardens, applys there I stol,

To gadre frutys sparyd kegg nor wall,

To plukke grapys in other mennys vynes,

Was more ready than for to seyne matynes,

Rediere chir stooney (cherry stones) for to tell,

Than gon to chirche or heere the sacry belle.

I must, however, add a few school pictures of a graver and sweeter character. Chaucer, who painted English society as he saw it with his own eyes, has not forgotten to describe the village school where "an hepe of children comen of Christen blood," acquired as much learning as was suitable to their age and condition:—

That is to sey, to singen and to rede,

As smal children do in thir childhede.

And among these children he describes one, "a widewe's lytel sone," whom his pious mother had taught whenever he saw an image of Christ's Mother, to kneel down and say an Ave Maria; and he goes on to tell us how

This lytel childe, his litel boke lerning,

As he sate in the scole at his primere,

He Alma Redemptoris herde sing,

As children lerned the Antiphonere;

And as he derst, he drew him nere and nere

And herkened ay the wordes, and eke the note

Til he the first verse coulde al by rote.

He was too young, however, to understand the meaning of the words, though, be it observed, his elder schoolfellows were more erudite than himself:—

Nought wist he what this Latin was to say,

For he so yong and tender was of age,

But on a day his felow gan to pray,

To expounden him this song in his langage,

Or tell him why this song was in usage.

And when "his felow which elder was than he," had expounded the sense of the words, and made him understand that it was sung in reverence of Christ's Mother, the little scholar makes known his resolve to do his diligence to con it all by Christmas, in honour of Our Lady.

In these parochial schools, as we have elsewhere seen, children of the lower orders, even from St Dunstan's time, were taught grammar and church music gratuitously. It has been very constantly affirmed that the education here spoken of was exclusively given to those intended for the monastic and ecclesiastical states. But there is direct evidence, that the parochial schools were frequented by the children of the peasantry indiscriminately, and by those of the very lowest and poorest condition. The proof of this is to be found in the statutes of the realm. About the year 1406 a law was passed, wherein, after complaint being made that in opposition to certain ancient statutes, a vast number of the children of husbandmen, *who laboured with cart and plough and had no lands*, were apprenticed to handicraft trades, and thereby induced a great scarcity of husbandmen and labourers in many parts of the country, it was enacted that henceforth no one should be allowed so to apprentice his child to any trade, unless he rented land to the annual value of twenty shillings. The object of this blundering and tyrannical piece of legislation was, of course, to keep down the lower orders from endeavouring to raise themselves in the scale of society, and to oppose that upward movement which had been one of the results of the enfranchisement of so large a number of feudal serfs in the reign of Edward III. But whilst decreeing that day-labourers *with the cart and plough* should thus be kept back from advancing, or helping their children to advance, in point of station and wealth, the very same statute encourages them to *send their children to school*. "Every man or woman, of whatever state or condition they be, shall be at liberty to send their son or daughter to take learning in any kind of school that pleaseth them within the realm." This clause seems to have had reference to a petition which had been presented to parliament by certain lords in the reign of Richard II., to the effect that children of serfs and the lower sort might not be sent to school, and particularly to the schools of monasteries, wherein many were trained as ecclesiastics, and thence rose to dignities in the State. The statute aimed at appeasing the jealous pride of the nobles, who regarded with dismay the prospect of bondsmen and husbandmen emerging from their state of servitude; whilst at the same time, the influence of the ecclesiastical body was strong enough to preserve for the lower classes their hitherto undisputed right of receiving such education as circumstances placed within their reach. I need not pause to comment on the light which such a passage of history sheds on the supposed solicitude of monks and clergy to check the spread of learning for the furtherance of selfish ends. But it is clear that the permission formally granted by this statute would have been a simple mockery, unless schools existed adapted to the class in question; and it may satisfy us of the fact that village schools, in Chaucer's time, were really frequented by much the same class of scholars as in our own; and that not merely in special and more populated localities, but in remote rural districts. William Caxton, who was born about the time of the passing of this statute, tells us that he learned his English in the Weald of Kent, a tract of country which, fertile as it now is, was, even a century later than Caxton's time, a waste wilderness, thinly inhabited, save by herds of deer and hogs, and a few adventurous men who undertook to clear the forest and break up the land with the plough.[287] Yet in this wild country Caxton learnt his English, "a broad and rude English, as is anywhere spoken in England." And in after-life, apologising to his readers for the plain unadorned style which his "simple cunning" uses, he speaks of his early education, "whereof I humbly and heartily thank God, and am bounden to pray for my father's and mother's souls, who in my youth sent me to school." His education, we know, was carried on in London at a later date, but it must have been begun in some very primitive parochial school of Kent, where his companions could only have been rustics. The teaching in such schools was, doubtless, simple enough, but however small may have been the amount of secular learning acquired by the scholars, all received instruction in Christian doctrine, and learnt their prayers; the duty of providing such instruction for the poorer members of their flocks being earnestly pressed on the parish priests in the visitation articles and synodal decrees of John of Peckham and other English prelates.

Prayers and instructions, both secular and religious, were often taught to those who could not read, in a versified form, as had been the custom in Saxon times. Thus there is a curious poem of this period addressed to "Those who gete their lyvynge by the onest craft of masonry," in which the young mason is instructed, rather minutely, how to behave himself when he comes to the house of God. Wherever he works, he is to come to Mass when he hears the bell. Before entering church he must take holy water, and is to understand that in doing so devoutly, he quenches venial sin. Then he must put back his hood, that is, uncover his head, and as he enters the church, look to the great Rood, and kneeling down on both knees "pull up his herte to Christe anon!" He must stand and bless himself at the Gospel, and avoid

carelessly leaning against the wall; and when he hears the bell ring for the
"holy sakerynge,"—

Knele ye most both ynge and olde,

And both yer hondes fayr upholde,

And say thenne yn thys manere,

Fayre and softe withouten bere;

Jhesu, Lord, welcome Thou be

Yn forme of bred as y The se;

Now Jhesu for Thyn holy name,

Schulde Thou me from synne and schame.

Schryff and hosel, grant me bo,

Ere that y schall hennus go.

Versified instructions of this kind were capable of being remembered by
many who never learnt to read, and were evidently in very common use. We
find them in all languages and on all subjects. Thus the old French treatise
entitled "*Stans puer ad mensam*," selected by Caxton for one of his translations,
and another called "*Les contenances de la table*," which exists in a great variety
of forms, give excellent rules for behaving at table and saying grace:—

A viande melz main ne mette,

Jusques la beneisson soit faitte,

Enfant, dy benedicite

Et fait le signe de la croix.

After dinner he is reminded to pray for the dead:—

Prie Dieu pour les trespassez,

Et te souviengne en pitié

Qui de ce monde sont passez,

Ainsi que tu es obleigez,

Prier Dieu pour les trespassez

And the child is thus gently warned against the bad habit of noisy disputes at
table:—

Enfant, soyes toujours paisible,

Doulx, courtois, bening, aimable,

Entre ceulx qui sierront à table,

Et te garde d'estre noysible.

Il est conseillé en la Bible

Entre les gens estre paisible.

Teaching of some sort the peasantry certainly received, whatever means may have been used to convey it; they probably knew little of grammatical analysis, or the relative lengths of the European rivers, but it may be doubted whether, with all our cumbrous machinery of State education, we have hit on any system which is likely to form the Christian character so successfully in the hearts of our people as that which existed in the days of St. Anselm or Chaucer. "The majority of husbandmen are saved," writes the former, "because they live with simplicity, and feed the people of God with their hands; and therefore they are blessed."[288] And the poet who never paints a fancy picture, thus portrays from the life the character of his poor ploughman:—

A true worker and a good was he,

Living in peace and perfect charity;

God loved he best, and that with alle his herte,

At alle times, were it gain or smart;

And then his neighbour right as himselve.

He wolde thresh, and thereto dyke and delve

For Christe's sake, for every poor wight

Withouten hire, if it lay in his might.

His tithes paid he full fair and well,

Both of his proper work, and his cattel.

Have we not a right to say that such a character had somewhere and by some means received a thoroughly Christian education, even though he may never have learnt to read or write, and were wholly innocent of grammar?

I must not be tempted to enter on the endless theme of school sports and customs. But it is proper to mention that English schoolboys had their patron saints, of whom St. Gregory the Great was one. So we learn from the—shall I call it poetry?—of the Puritan, Barnaby Googe, who tells us that

St. Gregory lookes to little boyes to teach their a, b, c,

And make them for to love their bookes, and schollers good to be.

On his feast the boys were called into school by certain songs; presents were distributed, to make them love their school, and one of their number was made to represent the bishop. But a yet more universally acknowledged patron was St. Nicholas of Myra, in honour of whom schoolboys of all ranks and conditions elected their boy-bishop, and played pranks in which jest and earnest were strangely blended together. The "childe bishope" preached a sermon, and afterwards received welcome offerings of pence. And this custom was one of those to which the people clung with the greatest tenacity, so that it continued to survive down to the close of Elizabeth's reign.

The character of the studies followed at this time in the higher English academies, may perhaps be best gathered from an examination of the kind of learning displayed by the poet already so often quoted. If Chaucer is to be taken as in any way a fair representative of an educated Englishman of his time, it is plain that there was, in a certain sense, no want of learning in the English schools, though his critics acknowledged that however varied and extensive his reading may have been, it was loose and inaccurate. In this respect the English were far behind the Italians. I am not aware that Dante has ever been convicted of a blunder in his classical allusions, but in Chaucer such solecisms abound. "All through the poem," says Craik, in his critical examination of the *House of Fame*, "there runs the spirit of the strange, barbarous, classical scholarship of the Middle Ages. The Æneid is not wholly unknown to the author, but it may be questioned if his actual acquaintance with the work extended much beyond the opening lines. An abridgment, indeed, of the story of Æneas follows, but that might have been got at second-hand. The same mixture of the Gothic and the classic occurs throughout that is found in all the poetry of the period, whether French, English, or Italian." He proceeds to quote lines, in which "the harper *Orion*" is made to do duty for *Arion*; Mount Cithæron is supposed to figure as the individual "Dan Citherus;" the musician Marsyas, who was flayed alive, appears as "Mersia, that lost *her* skin," and so on. However, it is agreed that Chaucer was, in a certain inaccurate way, familiar with the stories of the Latin classics, and possessed of whatever learning was to be acquired in the schools of London and the universities of Oxford, Cambridge, and Paris, in all of which, according to Leland, he had "gained great glory."[289] At the universities, moreover he had learned men for his cronies; his two most familiar college friends were John Gower and Randolph Strode, both of whom, like himself, afterwards attained poetic fame. It is to them that he dedicated his *Troilus and Creseide*, addressing them as "the philosophical Strode" and "the moral Gower." The name of Gower is too well known to require any comment, but all readers may not be equally familiar with that of Strode, so we will briefly state that he was a Scotchman by birth, a fellow of Merton, afterwards a pilgrim to the Holy Land, and the author of a poem in the vernacular, entitled "Phantasma," which critics scruple not to place on a level with Chaucer's verse. He finally entered the Dominican Order, and greatly distinguished himself in the controversy against Wickliffe, thereby earning the distinguished honour of some very coarse abuse from the pen of Bale.

Chaucer was educated for the law, and Speght records the doubtful tradition that he was at one time a member of the Inner Temple, at which period of his career he is said to have been fined two shillings for beating a Franciscan friar in Fleet Street. At any rate, his education was that of a "clerk," and the office he eventually filled under the Crown was that of Comptroller of the Customs and Subsidies of wool, skins, and tanned hides in the port of London—an office about as suitable to him as that of gauger was to Robert Burns. He seems to have felt its incongruity with a poet's sensitiveness, and its necessary "reckonings" are often alluded to in his verses as sad trials of patience. He was perfectly at home in the French tongue, and his familiarity with Italian is stoutly maintained by some, and as vehemently denied by others. Lydgate says that he translated Dante, but no fragment of such a work is known to exist. He was an incessant reader, as he is never weary of letting us know. When he had done his "reckonings," his manner was to go home to his house and sit at his books, "as dumb as any stone," and read till he was half blind. Once, he tells us, he spent a whole day reading Cicero's *Somnium Scipionis*, from the Commentary of Macrobius. He had a great liking for old books, and expresses it sweetly enough—

For out of old fields as men sayth,

Cometh all this new corn from yere to yere,

And out of old books, in good faith,

Cometh all this new lore that men lere.

He seems to have had a decided taste for mathematical and scientific pursuits. The writings and example of Roger Bacon had given a great stimulus to these pursuits in England, and Hallam mentions the names of several Englishmen of the fourteenth century who distinguished themselves as mathematicians, such as Archbishop Bradwardine, the profound Doctor, as he was called. Among Chaucer's prose works is a Treatise on the Astrolabe, written for the instruction of his youngest son, Lewis, who was studying at Oxford under a tutor. He dedicates the work to his boy in the following words:—

"Lytel Lewis, my sonne, I perceive well by certaine evidences thine abilitie to learne sciences touching numbers and proportions, and also wel consider I thy busie prayer in especiall to learne the Treatise of the Astrolabie ... therefore I have given thee a sufficient Astrolabie for an orizont, compounded after the latitude of Oxenford." He has compiled it, he adds, because the charts of the Astrolabe that he has seen were "too hard for thy tender age of ten yeares to conceive," and he has written it in English, "for Latine ne canst thou nat yet but smal, my lytel sonne."

In one of his poems he gives an exposition of the theory of gravitation, and appeals to Aristotle and "Dan Plato" in confirmation of his philosophy. He also explains the propagation of sound, which he declares to be produced by a series of undulations of air like those that appear when you throw a stone into the water. He was familiar with the jargon of the astrologers and alchemists, and his commentators assure us that he displays a very considerable knowledge of the real science of chemistry as well as of its quackery, which last does not escape his lash. For quacks of all sorts indeed he has no indulgence, and spends his humour on the doctor of physic, whom he describes as "well grounded in astronomy," able to help his patients by his knowledge of magic, no great reader of his Bible, which was not a very fashionable study with the followers of Averrhoes and Avicenna, but on excellent terms with his apothecary, and ready to help him to get rid of plenty of drugs and electuaries. It will be remembered that at the time when Chaucer wrote, the "Doctor of Physic," though a graduate of the universities, and a very important person in his way, had no great claims to the character of a man of science. John Gaddesden, a fellow of Merton, and court physician to Edward, wrote a book called the "Rosa Anglica," on his great and successful method of treating patients for the smallpox, which consisted in hanging their rooms and enveloping their persons in *scarlet cloth*! He informs us that, with the blessing of God, he purposes writing another book on Chiromancy, or fortune-telling by the hand, condescends to give directions to the court ladies for preparing their perfumes, washes, and hair-dyes, and interlards his quack recipes with scraps of original verse.

In his treatment of religious subjects Chaucer represents the tone of feeling which prevailed among a very large class of Englishmen in his day. He was a political partisan of John of Gaunt, and therefore gave the Lollards a certain kind of support. To a man of free life and coarse humour it was both tempting and easy to exercise his wit on fat monks and lazy friars, and to grumble like a true Englishman at their demands on his purse. Doubtless there were plenty of unworthy representatives of both professions to stand as the originals of his poetical caricatures, and broadly enough did he paint their unseemly features. But that was all; and his biographer, Godwin, admits that, so far from sharing any of the heretical opinions of the Lollards, his poems unmistakably prove his adherence to the Catholic dogmas, especially those which they most malignantly attacked, namely, the Sacraments of Penance and the Holy Eucharist; while his devotion to the Blessed Virgin is expressed in a thousand passages, such as the following:—

Lady, when men pray to the,

Thou goest before of thy benignitie,

And getest us the light of thi prayere

To giden us to thi Sonne so dere.

Occleve, his disciple, himself no mean poet, bears testimony to the fact that his lamented master was a devout client of the Queen of Heaven:—

As thou wel knowest, O blessed Virgyne,

With lovynge hert and high devocion,

In thyne honour he wroot many a lyne,

For he thi servant was, mayden Marie,

And let his love floure and fructifie.

Contemporary with Chaucer, the father of our poetry, was Sir John Mandeville, who commonly enjoys the credit of being the father of English prose, and whose travels let into the popular mind a glimmering light as to the whereabouts of Tartary, Persia, Armenia, Lybia, Chaldea, and Ethiopia, all which he visited, besides some Eastern lands that he calls by the name of "Amazoyn," "Ind the Less and the More," and "many isles that be abouten Ind." In his "Itinerary" he describes his visit to Jerusalem and the Holy Land, apologising for possible inaccuracies by reminding the indulgent reader that "thynges passed out of long time from a man's mynd turnen soon into forgetting; because that the mynd of man ne may not be comprehended ne withholden for the freelty of mankind." The "Itinerary" was written in Latin, and translated by the author first into French, and from thence into English, and enjoyed great popularity. And the publication of these travels, together with those of Marco Polo, stimulated an interest in the study of geography, so that we begin to find more frequent mention in the catalogues of monastic libraries of maps and charts. The whole science of map-drawing, it may be observed, had developed in the cloister; the German monks showing themselves indefatigable in improving this branch of science. About the year 1370 Prior Nicholas Hereford of Evesham Abbey, after collecting a fine assortment of books, caused a great map of the world to be executed, at the cost of six marks, for the use of his convent. And a certain Camaldolese monk, named Fra Mauro, made use of the information derived from the writings of Marco Polo, and produced a grand Mappamondo, wherein he depicts the sea rolling round the southern extremity of Africa. On the margin of his map appear some learned notes, referring the phenomena of the tides to the moon's attraction—a piece of natural philosophy, however, which, as we have seen, was not unknown to Bede.

It has been already said that during the reign of Edward III. the English universities had to sustain the twofold attack of Lollardism and the Black Death, by the united effects of which they were reduced to so low a condition, as at one time to have ceased to be regarded as seats of learning. Nine tenths of the English clergy are said to have been swept away by the terrible plague, together with the population of entire cities, and the necessity of the case obliged the bishops to fill the vacant benefices with men of inferior education, a practice which for the moment told severely on the state of the schools. But the effects of the pestilence were less fatally disastrous than those caused by the heresy of Wickliffe. When in 1361, that celebrated man, then master of Baliol College, Oxford, first made himself notorious by his attacks on the mendicant orders, he seems to have done little more than repeat the old threadbare calumnies of William de St. Amour and Richard Fitz Ralph. His views were of course exceedingly relished by the secular doctors, and his reputed talents induced the primate, Simon Islip, to offer him the wardenship of Canterbury Hall, then newly founded, partly for secular and partly for monastic students. In order to make room for him, the former warden, Woodhal, a Canterbury monk, had to retire, and three other monastic students who held scholarships in the college were at the same time removed. Langham, the successor of Islip, pronounced these proceedings irregular, and restored Woodhal to his post. The matter was referred to the decision of Pope Urban V., who decided in favour of Woodhal, and from that day Wickliffe became the deadly enemy of the papal power. The university, or rather the secular regents of the university, immediately took part with him against the Pope and the Friars, and in 1372, to mark their adherence to his cause, elected him Professor of Divinity. He succeeded, moreover, in obtaining the powerful support of John of Gaunt, and on occasion of a congress, held at Bruges, to settle various points in dispute between the English Government and the Holy See, the name of John Wickliffe appears in the list of Royal Commissioners. All this time there had been no whisper of heresy, nor was it until after his return to England, when he was promoted to a prebend in the collegiate church of Westbury, and a little later was presented by John of Gaunt to the rectory of Lutterworth, that he began to disseminate his pernicious doctrines. Besides his peculiar views regarding the possession of property, he had started views on the subject of predestination, analogous to those afterwards embraced by Calvin, and attacked the supremacy of the Pope, and the doctrines of penance, indulgences, the worship of the saints and of holy images, and prayer for the dead. He and his followers propagated their opinions by a sort of popular preaching suited to the tastes of the common people, and accompanied by a certain low buffoonery, in all ages specially attractive to rude audiences of the Anglo-Saxon race. The coarse invectives levelled against the clergy found eager reception among such hearers; for there is perhaps to most men an irresistible fascination in doctrines which aim at bringing down any dominant class of society to a lower level. The English commons were at this period seething in a chronic state of insurrection, and the Lollard denunciations of the priests and land-holders were extremely to the taste of the Socialists of the fourteenth century. It is therefore quite easy to understand how it was that Hob Miller and Colin Lout should have thought it an excellent joke to ridicule and despise their betters; but that Wickliffe should have found warm supporters in the university of Oxford is a fact that may well surprise and startle us. But Lollardism had a double aspect, its theological heresies were at first as little relished at Oxford as at Rome, but its enmity to the religious orders happened to chime in with the views of the secular faction, and therefore they gave it their support. An appeal had already been made, not to Rome, but to Parliament, for a law to prohibit any member of the university joining a religious order before his eighteenth year, and the Oxonian divines were not ashamed to accept, together with the desired statute, a prohibition to carry the matter to Rome. They next established the rule that no religious, whether monk or friar, should be admitted to graduate in arts, while at the same time, by the university statutes, no one could fill a theological professorship without so graduating. The monks appealed to the Holy See, and obtained a dispensation from this unjust law, and thus increased the ill-will of their thwarted and malicious adversaries. The struggle was at its height when Wickliffe raised his cry against the mendicant orders, whom he declared to be Antichrist, and proctors of Satan; and he at once found plenty of grave divines who were willing to regard him as a useful ally, and forgive both his heresies and his nonsense for the support he furnished to their side of the quarrel. Hence, in 1377, when Gregory XI. sent Bulls to the Archbishop of Canterbury the Bishop of London, and the university of Oxford, calling on them to take active measures for the condemnation of the heresiarch, we are assured by Walsingham that the heads of the university deliberated whether or no they should receive the Bull, nor does it appear certain that it ever was received. At last, however, in 1381, Wickliffe startled even his Oxford allies by his attack on the doctrine of the Holy Eucharist, and a decree was drawn up, and signed by William de Burton, the chancellor, and twelve of the chief divines, condemning his errors, and forbidding them to be promulgated in the university. Hereupon Wickliffe scrupled not to appeal to the Crown and Parliament, but the English people were not yet quite prepared for such a step, and the act caused general scandal. Even John of Gaunt, who had hitherto, from political motives, given him his countenance, now withdrew his protection, and declared his teaching on the Sacrament of the Altar to be a "doctrine of devils."

Oxford, however, had not yet entirely given up his cause. In 1382, when Courtenay, Archbishop of Canterbury, set on foot vigorous measures for the eradication of the new heresies, he met with stout resistance from Rigge, who had succeeded De Burton in the office of chancellor of the university, and who flatly refused to silence a Lollard professor. Courtenay at last obtained a royal mandate, in virtue of which Wickliffe and his most obstinate adherents were expelled the university, a good number of professors purchasing immunity, however by a ready recantation of their errors, for few evinced any desire of becoming martyrs in the cause.

The steps taken by Courtenay vindicated the authority of the Church but they were far from being sufficient to purge the university from the heretical leaven, or remedy the evils caused by these internal troubles. So far is Ayliffe's statement that the Wickliffites restored sound learning at Oxford, from possessing a shadow of truth, that the period when this heresy was rampant among her doctors was precisely that when her schools had confessedly sunk to their very lowest state of decay. The authorities were themselves perfectly aware of the fact, and represented it as one of the unhappy effects produced by papal provisions. But the statutes of Provisors, passed in the reign of Edward III., by which all such provisions were forbidden under severe penalties, instead of applying a remedy to this evil, only hastened the decline of learning. It was found that the Crown was far less disposed to promote men of learning than the Popes had been; and, to quote the words of Lingard, "experience showed that the statutes in question operated to the depression of learning and the deterioration of the universities." Accordingly in the year 1399 petitions were presented to Convocation from Oxford and Cambridge, setting forth that *while the Popes were permitted to bestow benefices by provision, the preference had always been given to men of talent and industry*, and that the effect of such preference had been to quicken the application and increase the number of the students; but that since the passing of the Act against Provisors, their members had been neglected by the patrons of livings, the *students had disappeared*, and the schools were nearly abandoned.[290] Sixteen years later the House of Commons awoke to a sense of the suicidal character of their own policy, and petitioned King Henry V. that, *to save the universities from destruction*, he would suffer the statutes against

Provisors to be repealed. The King referred the matter to the bishops, who, however, had no wish at all to interfere with the existing legislation, and contented themselves with passing a law in convocation obliging every patron of a benefice for the next ten years to present a graduate of one of the universities.

These facts may serve as sufficient reply to the vaunted "restoration of learning" achieved by the Lollards. The effect of their influence in the universities, coupled with that of an anti-Roman course of legislation, had been to bring those institutions to the very verge of ruin, and that in spite of the extraordinary efforts which were being made by private munificence to enlarge and perfect the collegiate system of education. Indeed, though Wickliffe himself was a man of undoubted ability, the attempt to convert him into a restorer of humane letters, savours of the absurd.[291] His learning was precisely the same which, when found in the possession of friars and other scholastics, earns for them such bitter taunts and gibes as "locusts," who devoured all the green things in the land, and darkened it with bad Latin and captious logic. Wickliffe's Latin was not better than that of his adversaries, and his logic was of that true Oxonian temper which Wood qualifies as "frivolous sophistry whereby scholars could at any time be for or against anything proposed." The well-known ballad in which an Oxford student puzzles his simple-minded parent by proving a pigeon and an eel pie to be convertible terms, seems hardly a caricature when we read the shifts, or, as Wood terms them, the "screws" by which the Lollard chief sought to prove that he meant the precise contrary of what he had been convicted of saying. "He so qualified his doctrines with conditions," says Lingard, "and explained them away by distinctions, as to give an appearance of innocence to tenets the most mischievous. On the subject of the Holy Eucharist he intrenched himself behind unintelligible distinctions, the meaning of which it would have puzzled the most acute logician to detect."[292] And Rohrbacher observes that instead of appealing to the Scriptures explained by the Fathers, he took refuge in "arguments and dialectic subtleties, wrapped up in an obscure and barbarous phraseology;" in other words, he exhibited precisely the same description of learning, the display of which has earned so many hard epithets for the academic "locusts."

Wickliffe's literary fame rests chiefly on his translation of the Bible into the vulgar tongue, often incorrectly spoken of as the earliest English version. It is not clear that he himself ever translated more than the Gospels, for of the various manuscripts which bear his name, some are now admitted to have been the production of later Lollard writers. His English is declared by Mr. Craik to be "coarse and slovenly," and far more harsh and obscure than that of Mandeville or Chaucer. His version was made the vehicle for conveying his peculiar tenets, by means of corruptions of the Sacred Text, and was accompanied by certain Prologues or Glosses, explaining it in an heretical sense. On this account it was enacted by Archbishop Arundel, in a Provincial Synod held in 1408, that "no one should hereafter translate any text of Holy Scripture into English by way of a book, and that no such book, *composed lately, in the time of Wickliffe, or since his death*, shall be read." This decree has been erroneously interpreted as a prohibition to the laity to read the Scriptures. But its real meaning is very clearly explained by the Canonist Lyndwood,[293] a contemporary of Arundel's, as being, first, a prohibition to any private person to translate the Scriptures into English without authority; and secondly, a prohibition to use or read any such unauthorised and incorrect versions. And he expressly adds that from the terms "newly composed, in the time of Wickliffe, or since his death," it is evident that the Lollard versions only are prohibited, but that every one is still at liberty to read those formerly translated from the text of Scripture into English or any other modern idiom. Lyndwood died in 1446, and was living when the decree in question was first published. His testimony as to its meaning as then understood and interpreted, as well as to the fact that other earlier versions did exist at that time, cannot therefore be called in question. Moreover, Fox the Protestant martyrologist, tells us, on the authority of Polydore Vergil, that this same Archbishop Arundel, who is so often accused of prohibiting the reading of the Scriptures, preached the funeral sermon of Queen Anne of Bohemia, and mentioned among other things in her praise that she was a diligent reader of the Four Gospels written in Bohemian, English, and Latin, with divers expositions, which book she had sent to him to be viewed and examined.

If this account be correct, it equally vindicates Arundel from the charge of prohibiting the Scriptures, and Queen Anne from that of Lollardism on the ground of reading them, for it will be observed the copy she used had been first submitted to the archbishop's approval, and his formal permission had been obtained. We have also another interesting testimony to the existence of these earlier versions, and an explanation of the decree against those of the Lollards, in the words of Sir Thomas More, who, in his Dialogue, notices the prohibitory Constitution of Arundel in the following terms:—

"Ye shall understand that the great arch-heretic, Wickliffe (whereas the Holy Bible was long before his time by virtuous and well-learned men translated into the English tongue, and by good and godly people, with devotion and soberness, well and reverently read) took upon him, of a malicious purpose, to translate it anew. In which translation he purposely corrupted the Holy Text, maliciously planting therein such words as might in the reader's ears serve to the proof of such heresies as he went about to sow; which he not only set forth in his own translation of the Bible, but also in certain prologues or glosses, which he made hereupon. So that after it was perceived what harm the people took by the translations, prologues, and glosses of Wickliffe's, and also of some others who after him helped to set forth his sect, then, for that cause, it was at a council holden at Oxford provided, upon great pain, that no man should henceforth translate the Scriptures into the English tongue *upon his own authority* by way of book or treatise, nor no man should read such books as were newly made in the time of Wickliffe, or since, or that should be made any time after, *till the same translation were by the Diocesan or Provincial Council approved.* But that it neither forbade the translations to be read that were already well done of old before Wickliffe's time, nor condemned his because it was *new*, but because it was *naught*, nor prohibited new to be made, but only provided that they shall not be read if they be made amiss, till by good examination they be amended; except they be such translations as those of Wickliffe and Tindal, which the malicious mind of the translator hath so handled that it were lost labour to go about to mend them."

He goes on to say that he has seen, and, if necessary, could show, copies of English Bibles, "fair and old," approved by the Diocesans, which have been left with lay men and women, and used by Catholic folk with soberness and devotion, and that the clergy never kept any Bibles from the laity save those that were "naught," and not so approved; that is, those in which heretical corruptions of the text had been introduced, or to which were attached the pernicious Lollard glosses. And he explains how it was that no printer had yet ventured to print an English Bible, a great and expensive undertaking, which might, after all, have been unsaleable, through the question which might have been raised whether it were printed from a version made before or since the days of Wickliffe. The whole passage is sufficiently explicit, both as to the fact of approved English versions of the Scriptures existing before the time of Wickliffe, and also as to the received interpretation of Arundel's decree. We have the very explicit testimony of Cranmer to the same effect. "It is not much above a hundred years," he writes, "since Scripture hath not been accustomed to be read in the vulgar tongue within this realm; many hundred years before that it was translated and read in the Saxon tongue, and when that language waxed old and out of common usage, because folks should not lack the fruit of reading it, it was translated again into the newer language."[294] It is, however, by no means easy in all cases to distinguish these early versions from their later imitations. All the translations of the Scriptures preserved in manuscript in the Oxford libraries have been commonly assigned to Wickliffe, although Dr. Thomas James is of opinion that a close examination of some of them would show them to be of much more ancient date. He is also disposed to think that one of the prologues ordinarily assigned to one of Wickliffe's disciples belongs to an earlier translation. Lewis, in his "History of the English Translations of the Bible," supposes this prologue to have been written in 1396 by John Purvey, one of Wickliffe's most learned followers; but its allusions to the care taken to consult St.

Jerome, and the gloss of Nicholas de Lyra, do not seem to harmonise very well with this theory. Dr. James considers that the copies preserved in the Bodleian Library, and in Christ Church Library, are of ancient Catholic versions, that in Queen's College Library alone being properly assigned to Wickliffe. Lewis opposes this view, yet he admits that the Bodleian and Queen's College versions are different from that of Christ Church. Warton claims one of these for John of Trevisa, and Weever assigns one to the Venerable Richard of Hampole, an Austin hermit, who lived about the year 1349, near the Monastery of Hampole in Yorkshire, and, according to Camden, wrote many books full of "heavenly unction," and whose translation of the Psalter is still preserved. Whatever may be the real history of these three versions (and it is evident that critics are by no means unanimous as to their authorship), several fragments exist of different books of Scripture which are admitted to be of ancient date. In the library of Bennet College, Cambridge, a translation is preserved of two of the Gospels and St. Paul's Epistles, with a gloss, written in the English spoken after the Conquest. In Sydney Sussex College are portions of the Old Testament commented on in like manner. A translation of the Psalter, with a gloss, is in the Harleian Library, besides the Psalter of Richard of Hampole, mentioned above, to which is prefixed a prologue, in which the author explains that he has sought no strange English, but only that which was commonest and easiest, and has been careful to consult the holy doctors. There are also, according to Lewis, other translations extant of the Psalter, the New Testament, and the Church Lessons and Hymns, all made before the time of Wickliffe. It must be borne in mind that the manuscripts preserved in our libraries are mere fragments accidentally saved from destruction, and can scarcely be taken as evidence of what existed in England before the Reformation. The pious visitors of Edward VI., in their zeal to purify the university of Popish service books, destroyed every manuscript they could lay hands on, which exhibited illuminations or other ornaments, without the slightest reference to its contents. Whole libraries were then sold for waste paper, and bought by bakers to feed their ovens, or for other base purposes. But among the scanty relics that escaped the hands of these worse than Vandals, stray leaves are to be found of sermons, treatises, and mutilated hymns, many of which are in the vernacular English of the thirteenth and fourteenth centuries. One of these interesting fragments has been printed by Messrs Wright and Halliwell in the *Reliquiæ Antiquæ*, and is assigned by them to the fourteenth century. The preacher appears to have been familiar with some English version of the Canticle of Canticles, and introduces a passage which may be quoted as a beautiful specimen of our ancient English idiom:—
"Behold my derlyng speketh to me; arys, come nerre my beautiful, now wynter is passid; that is, the coulde wynd of worldly covertise that mad me hard y-froze as yse: the floures scheweth them on erth, the voys of the tortel

is herd in our herber; that is, the soule that the kyng of heven has y-lad to his vyne celler, syngeth chast songes of mornyng for hir sinnes and for deth of Christ hir mate: she will no more sette on grene bows lovynge worldlye things, bote fedeth hir with love of Christ, the clene white corne, and fleeth up to the holes of His five woundes, lookyng with sympel eyne into the cler waters of holie writ."

From what has been said, it may be gathered that before the time of Wickliffe, the Scriptures were in no sense shut up from the laity; that considerable portions of them were rendered into English, and are known to have been actually in the possession of lay persons, and that it was not until the corrupt versions and glosses of the Lollards were made instruments of disseminating pernicious errors, that any decrees were made on the subject. Even then the restrictions were not prohibitions: the laity were still allowed to read approved Catholic versions: though it is very probable, that at a time when so large a portion of the population was infected with Lollardism, and when there was a disposition to make the Sacred Text, interpreted by each man's whim, the rule of each man's belief, the private reading of the English Scriptures by lay persons was not greatly encouraged. In fact, prohibitions or restrictions of this sort were never promulgated by the ecclesiastical authorities, until rendered necessary by the perverse misuse of the Sacred Volume by heretics. Thus, in France no such restrictions existed until 1229 when the extravagant doctrines which the Albigenses pretended to adduce from Scripture, obliged the Council of Toulouse to forbid the translation of the Sacred Books, the use of which had, up to that time, been freely permitted. In no case was the *Latin* Bible withdrawn from the laity,[295] and it must be remembered that in those days the majority of those who could read at all, could read Latin. Lewis, indeed, would have us believe that before Wickliffe's time, even the Latin Bible was not allowed in common use; and gravely assures us, that the monks and friars collected copies and laid them up in their libraries, not (as one might suppose) for the obvious purpose of reading them, but "to imprison them from the curates and secular priests, and so prevent them from preaching the Word of God to the people." Nonsense of this sort is scarcely worth refuting, though it finds a place in very grave writers, and by certain readers is often enough believed. Bibles were, of course, comparatively rare and expensive books, and not within reach of every poor curate's purse. But so far from any conspiracy existing to make them rarer, it was a common devotion among those who possessed such a treasure, to bequeath it by will to some public church, there to be set up and chained, *ad usum communem*. This practice is often supposed to have originated with the Reformers, and a modern artist has depicted, with great skill, the grey-haired peasant approaching the chained Bible set forth by order of his sacred majesty king Edward VI., and turning over its pages with pious awe. It was, however, a good thought stolen from the ancients, as there is abundant evidence to show. Thus, in 1378 a Bible and Concordance were left by will by Thomas Farnylaw, to be set up and chained in the north aisle of St. Nicholas' Church, Newcastle; and in 1385, a Bible and Concordance were to be found chained in St. George's Chapel, Windsor.

These Bibles were, of course, copies of the Latin Vulgate, for it is not pretended that any effort was made to place a version of the Scriptures, in the vulgar tongue, at the command of the unlettered laity. The Catholic system of education did not aim at enabling every poor man to read his Bible, but rather at making him know his faith. Nevertheless, so true is it that a strong Scriptural element has always predominated in the teaching of the Church, that the first attempts to provide the poor with cheap literature of any sort were called *Biblia Pauperum*, or the Bibles of the poor. They were rude engravings of Scriptural subjects, or stories of the saints, taken off carved wooden blocks, and accompanied with texts of Scripture, or pious verses. These were known as block-books, and were reproduced at a much cheaper rate than books written out by hand. Of course they were not Bibles, but they show that even in the age most tainted by the Lollard heresy, there was a disposition on the part of Catholic teachers to supply the people with instruction into which a certain Biblical element had been infused. The block-books were likewise used to strike off small school manuals of grammar, and a book of this sort was technically called a "Donatus." If the grammars were welcome boons to schoolboys, the Bibles of the poor were not less convenient for the use of preachers, who could not carry so cumbrous a volume as a whole Bible into the pulpit, and were often glad to help their memory by a selection of suitable texts. Specimens of these block-books are preserved as curiosities by modern bibliopolists, and the contrivance seems to have been the immediate forerunner of the more important invention of printing. But in mentioning them we are somewhat departing from the order of time, as they can hardly be assigned an earlier date than the beginning of the fifteenth century.

CHAPTER XIX.

THE RED AND WHITE ROSES.

A.D. 1386 TO 1494.

THE close of the fourteenth century witnessed the establishment in England of two new schools, the importance of which caused them to be regarded as models for all subsequent foundations of a similar kind in this country. These were William of Wykeham's twin colleges at Oxford and Winchester the first of which, opened in 1386, may be said to have perfected the collegiate system of our universities, while the second, which was not completed till seven years later, laid the foundation of another system, more peculiarly national— that of our English public schools. The object of these two institutions was to furnish a complete course of free education to two hundred scholars, who were to be led from the lowest class of grammatical learning, to the highest degrees of the various faculties. And at the same time that their intellectual training was thus amply provided for, they were subjected to a strict rule of discipline, and the religious element of education was given a much larger development than it had received in any collegiate foundations which had yet appeared. Chapels had, indeed, in some cases been attached to colleges before the time of Wykeham, though they do not seem to have been regarded as any essential portion of such institutions; but now the choral office and the magnificent celebration of ecclesiastical rites were provided for with no less scrupulous care than the advancement of studies; and thus the founder set his seal to one great principle of the earlier monastic education, namely, that habits of devotion, and those too of a certain liturgical character, ought to be infused into the training which is given to the children of Holy Church. And in many ways these foundations reflected the spirit of more ancient times, in what regarded discipline. When the universities began to be frequented in place of those monastic and cathedral schools, which up to the twelfth century had been the chief academies resorted to by students, clerical or lay, no provision at all had been made for the government of the scholars; a fact which sufficiently explains the scandals and disorders which fill up the early history of Paris and Oxford. Nor need the want of such provision excite any surprise, if we bear in mind that the first universities were not institutions, founded at any particular period according to some sagacious scheme; but that they sprang up of themselves out of small beginnings, and developed, like the grain of mustard seed, into a mighty tree. Scholars and professors came first, and it was not till they had insensibly grown into a population, and had committed the excesses of which most lawless populations would be guilty, that authority stepped in with statutes and decrees, and endeavoured to give shape and method to the unwieldy mass. The collegiate system, as we have seen, semi-monastic in its character, and undoubtedly formed in partial imitation of the religious houses of study, was called into being in order to struggle with the monster evils which had arisen out of the university system; it was an attempt to return, in some measure, to the ancient paths, and to reassert the principle that intellectual education, when separated from moral and religious training, is no education at all. Wykeham adopted this principle in all its fulness, and herein lay the special value of his work. But with an admirable discretion he contrived so to adapt it to the wants, the feelings, and the habits of his age, that it assumed the appearance, not of a retrogression but of an advance: nay more, he managed so thoroughly to root his system in the English mind that it stood the brunt of many revolutions, and even in our own day obtains a traditionary kind of honour, encrusted as our old foundations have become with the overgrowth of three Protestant centuries.

The Wykehamist colleges were not only the most splendid academies of learning founded at this time, but they opened the way to other foundations of a similar description; and a kind of fashion set in for founding schools and colleges, which, during the reigns of our Lancastrian kings, multiplied over the land. The alarm excited by the spread of Lollardism had something to do with this movement, and it is remarkable that one Oxford college, that of Lincoln, was founded by a prelate, Richard Fleming, who at an earlier period had taken part with Wickliffe, but who, thoroughly startled out of his partisanship, hastened to make amends for his fault by raising what he hoped would become a nursery of learned divines, who should confute the errors of the wily heresiarch. That Fleming was thoroughly in earnest in his change of views was manifested at the Council of Constance, when we find him distinguishing himself by a very able opposition to the Hussites.[296] His kinsman, Robert Fleming, travelled into Italy, and there studied in the school of the young Guarini. He was one of the earliest English scholars who took part in the revival of classical learning, and during his foreign travels collected great store of books for Lincoln College, some of which he transcribed and illuminated with his own hand, being in fact a very skilful limner. He was the author of a Greek and Latin dictionary, as well as of a Latin poem entitled, "Lucubrationes Tiburtinæ." In 1438, Chichele, Archbishop of Canterbury, who had already shown himself a patron of learning by the erection of a free school at Higham Ferrars, and of St. Bernard's College at Oxford for the use of the Cistercian students, laid the foundation of his noble college of All Souls, most liberally endowed, and furnished with books, chapel furniture, and every requisite for the use of the students. And in 1448 William of Waynflete, Bishop of Winchester, obtained the royal grant empowering him to erect his college of Magdalene, in which the collegiate system was more perfectly carried out than in any previous or subsequent foundation.

Besides these Oxford colleges, those of Eton, and King's at Cambridge, owed their foundation to the zeal of Henry VI., being in avowed imitation of the plan, already adopted by Wykeham, of uniting a public school to a house of higher studies at the university, thus providing an entire course of instruction for elder and younger scholars.

Having elsewhere[297] given a more particular account than space will here admit of the foundations of Wykeham, Waynflete, and Henry VI., so important in the history of English education, it will not be necessary to dwell on them more at length in this place; but it should be remembered that these, if the most splendid, were very far from being the only educational institutions of the period. Our ancient school-system had ramifications which extended into every grade of society and we are, generally speaking, but little familiar with the method by which that system was worked, because we are equally unaccustomed to study the grand system of our ancient Catholic charities. A class of magnificent foundations formerly existed in England, of which there only remain such scanty ruins as escaped the rapacity of Henry VIII. and the Protector, Somerset, but the multitude and real nature of which is hardly appreciated. I refer, of course, to the hospitals and collegiate establishments, which administered a vast revenue, voluntarily made over by private charity, for the discharge of all the works of mercy.

Some amongst my readers may be able to look back to early days, whose first associations are blended with the thought of a venerable pile, which seemed altogether out of proportion in size and magnificence to the purposes of a simple parish church. On Sunday afternoons when the psalm has been unusually long, or the preacher unusually drowsy, their childish fancies have, it may be, been busy, among the bosses of the fretted roof, speculating as to the possible meaning of its wondrous embellishments, and perplexed to account for the fact that they should be summoned week after week to worship in what had the outward grandeur of a cathedral, whereas the town or village clustered round the minster walls seemed wholly undeserving of such a dignity. Attached to the church there is probably a school, as at Ottery, or Southwell, or Crediton, or Doncaster, or Shrewsbury; and if tourists come that way to inspect the encaustic pavement, or to take rubbings of the fine old brasses, and wonder to find so huge a building in so insignificant a locality, they are content to receive the information given them by their guide book, that "the church was once collegiate." How vast a meaning may be enclosed in a simple phrase! "The church was once collegiate!" Yes: it was attached to one of those creations of Catholic piety which did the work of almshouse, schoolhouse, workhouse, hospital, and parish church, or rather, which did a great deal more than any or all of those put together, and did it with a magnificent profuseness of liberality, which strikes one dumb with astonishment and admiration. Thus, the great Lancastrian College at

Leicester, known as the Newark, or College of St. Mary's the Greater, the remains of which still cover many acres of ground, was originally founded for a dean, twelve secular canons, twelve vicars, three clerks, six choristers, fifty poor men, as many poor women, ten nurses, and other officers and attendants, all plentifully provided for. It had, according to Leland, an exceedingly fair "college church, large and fair cloisters, some pretty houses for the prebendaries in the college area, and stately walls and gates," much of all which is still standing. That of St. Cross at Winchester was founded by Henry de Blois, Bishop of Winchester, for the maintenance of thirteen poor men, and the daily feeding of a hundred others, who were to enjoy their loaf of good wheaten bread, weighing three pounds, their three quarts of good small beer, and two messes either of fish or flesh, as the day should require, in the Hundred-mennes-hall; and as the allowance was more than any ordinary capacity could dispose of at table, the statutes judiciously permitted them to carry home what they could not eat. Cardinal Beaufort enlarged this noble foundation by providing for the maintenance of thirty-five additional brethren, and appointing three religious sisters to attend the sick, and bestowed on it the beautiful title of the "Almshouse of Noble Poverty." Here, too, we find a grand collegiate church, with a warden, four chaplains, thirteen clerks, and seven choristers, for whose instruction provision was made by keeping up a school. Sometimes the school appears as the chief object of the foundation, as in the College of Ottery St. Mary's in Devonshire, which Bishop Grandison erected in 1337, for a warden, eight prebendaries, ten vicars, a master of music, a grammar-master, two parish priests, eight secondaries, eight choristers, and two clerks. Sometimes the corporal and spiritual works of mercy were blended together, as at the hospital of St. Leonard's at York, which maintained a master, thirteen poor brethren, four secular priests, eight sisters, thirty choristers, two schoolmasters, two hundred and six bedesmen, and six servitors. The whole was governed by semi-monastic statutes under the rule of St. Austin. Most of the smaller hospitals of York had likewise schools attached to them.

Sometimes, again, as at Beverley and Ripon, the magnificent collegiate establishments seem principally designed for the celebration of the divine offices with a splendour which could not be carried out in parochial churches; and the schools and other charities attached to these foundations were not the primary idea. The same seems to have been the case in the great college of Stoke-by-Clare, the statutes of which are so very precise and rigorous as to the quality of the plain chant to be sung in choir; but here, too, there was a school in which boys were to be taught "grammar, singing, and good manners." The endowments are not always on so sumptuous a scale as in these last-named colleges; yet often in very remote villages and rural parishes we find a modest hospital designed for the support of a few bedesmen of honest life, and a grammar-school, wherein, as in St. Gabriel's

Hospital at Brough, in Westmoreland, the chaplain was required to teach grammar and singing to the children of the place. Thus, too, at Ewelme, in Oxfordshire, De la Pole and his duchess had founded an almshouse, called God's House, wherein a priest was appointed as schoolmaster to teach their grammar to the children of the Ewelme tenantry; and a very similar foundation existed at Bentley, in Derbyshire, where the family of Mountjoy erected a small college for seven old servants of the lordship, who were to have pasture for seven cows, wood from the lord's manor, and a new gown and hood every third year, on condition of their saying our Lady's Psalter twice a day for the founder in the chapel of the hospital. This last item in the constitutions sealed its fate at the time of the Reformation, and it was abolished, as being mixed up with "superstitious observances." In foundations of this sort, which were exceedingly numerous, the great proprietors educated the children of their own tenantry at the same time that they provided for their superannuated servants.

There is much in the character of these ancient institutions that is suggestive and instructive to ourselves. What a vast machinery, what an enormous disbursement for, comparatively speaking, small results! Surely thirteen poor brethren could be fed and clothed without its being necessary for Dame Isabel Penbridge to found that great college of Tonge, in Shropshire, with its establishment of clerks, and chaplains, and choristers, and to supply them with that body of solemn statutes which regulates their community life and choral office with the exactness of a religious rule! Turn again to St. Giles' Hospital at Norwich, and reckon what endowments it must have taken[298] to support a master, deacon, and subdeacon, eight chaplains, wearing the habit of St. Austin's canons, four lay brothers, and seven choristers, who were to be scholars likewise; together with four religious sisters, in order to take care of eight infirm folk and a few poor superannuated priests, and daily to entertain thirteen non-resident poor at the common table. A liberal foundation, it may be said, for a few insignificant paupers; but it is clear the founder had in his mind the celebration of High Mass and the choral office; and that providing for the celebration of holy rites with becoming solemnity was reckoned then a good work as pleasing to God as the feeding of the poor.

Again, in what a beautiful light were the poor themselves regarded. They were not "paupers," but "brethren." They were not kept alive with water gruel, but fed with meat and ale, and good "mostrell."[299] They were not assigned a narrow bench in a distant corner of those grand collegiate churches, but often enough had stalls like so many canons. Such stalls are still to be seen, or at least were so a few years since, in St. Mary's Hospital, Chichester, and, I am glad to say, were still occupied by their lawful owners— the thirteen poor brethren. The church was *their* church; its numerous staff of clerks and choristers were assembled there to sing the divine office for *them*; they were honoured, not despised; and in their turn they felt an honest pride in wearing that reverend garb—the black gown or overcoat, with its red, white, or silver cross—such as may still be seen in the hospitals of Winchester or Worcester.

And, as to the schools attached to such foundations, what must have been the effect produced on the mind of the scholars whose earliest and most abiding lesson was, that nothing was too great or too good to give to God or the poor! For God, the stately minister, the magnificent vestments, and the solemn chant, which made up the daily business of a whole college of priests, clerks, and choristers.

And for the poor, a home in their old age, the care of religious women in time of sickness, generous maintenance, kindness, honour, and respect. What a prodigious amount of moral and religious education was conveyed in schools for the young, annexed to such hospitals and colleges, wherein the two duties of prayer and almsdeeds made up a portion of the daily life, and in which the instincts of reverence must have become a sort of second nature!

In the fifteenth century we find these foundations rapidly multiplying, and their scholastic character assuming a larger development. To the masters of grammar and singing is now frequently added a third for *writing*; the grammar-master is not unfrequently provided with an usher, which seems to argue that the scholars were becoming more numerous, and the salary of the masters is fixed higher than that of the other priests. In the College of Bradgate in Kent no chaplain was to be admitted who had not three qualifications—*bene legere, bene construere, et bene cantare*. The great English prelates had a special love for founding colleges of this description in the places of their birth. Thus Thomas Scott, Archbishop of York, founded the college and school of Rotherham; and Kempe, Archbishop of York, and cardinal, who was a poor husbandman's son, converted the parish church of Wye, his native place, into a college for the education of youth, and for perpetual prayer to be made therein "for the sowles of them that set hym to schole." And Chichele of Canterbury, as has been already said, founded the college of Higham Ferrars in Northamptonshire. This formerly occupied a grand quadrangle with two great wings. The schoolhouse, in the florid style of Gothic architecture, is, I believe, still standing; but the remainder of the stately and beautiful buildings were a few years since laid waste by the steward of a noble earl, and the site occupied by barns and hunting stables. Choral schools appear moreover to have been attached to the private chapels of great households. Thus there was a "Maister of the childer" among the officers of the Earl of Northumberland's chapel, and the eight children belonging to King Edward IV.'s chapel had likewise their "Maister" who was to draw them not only to the study of prictsong, but also to that of their *facet* or grammar, "and suche other vertuous things." Moreover his household accounts contain the pay and livery of the "Scholmaster's teaching, given in the house." Besides this choral school the same king maintained a sort of Palatine Academy at his court, formed of six or more young gentlemen, or *henxmen*, as they are called, whose master was to teach them "to read clenely and surely, to learn them their harness;" and moreover to teach them *"sundry languages*, and other vertuous learnings, such as to harp, to pipe, to sing and to dance, each to be trained to that kind of vertue that he is most apt to learn, with remembrance dayly of Goddes Service."

Another proof of the increasing interest which was being felt in the work of education, is the occasional transformation of charitable, into educational, institutions. Reading school was originally one of those numerous hospitals which the lordly abbots had established in their town. It was designed for certain poor women serving God day and night, who prayed for the king's estate and the soul of the founder, the good abbot, Hugh. They had a fair chapel for divine service, bread, meat, and drink from the abbey, and an annual sum of money and outfit of clothing. The sisters were widows of respectable persons in the town who had fallen into poverty; they had a *quasi* religious character, and the formulary of their admission included prayer, sprinkling of holy water, the blessing of the veil and mantle, and the giving of the kiss of peace. In 1446, Abbot Thorne suppressed this hospice, though as he applied its revenues to the use of the almoner, we will hope that they were expended in charity. "On a tyme, however," says an anonymous and rather discontented writer, "Kyng Edward IV. cam through Redyng to Woodstock," and expressed himself much displeased that "Saint Johny's House," as well as another house for lazars, had been diverted from its original purpose. He commanded Beauchamp, Bishop of Salisbury, to institute a reform, but he was unable to do so, and departed "ful ylle content." However, some years later, at the suggestion of Henry VII., the hospital was re-endowed as "a fre scole," and although when the nameless author, above quoted, wrote, there was as yet "neither scole, nor man, nor woman, nor chyld, relieved there," yet in due time the master and usher were appointed, and the school attained no inconsiderable renown as a place of learning. It is remarkable that among the privileges of the abbots of Reading was that of granting school licenses. No one was permitted to open a school of any description in the town without the approbation of the Abbot and Convent, who exercised within certain limits the same authority as a diocesan chancellor.

At Bury, again, the abbots had so early as 1193 founded in the town a free school for forty poor boys. The building was near the present shire house whence the street still retains the name of School Street. This school was still flourishing in the reign of Henry VI., for we find a letter addressed by Abbot Curteys, a great friend of that amiable and scholar-loving king, to Master William Farceaux, graduate in grammar and arts, and master of the School of Bury. And not to weary the reader with the enumeration of names and places, I will only add that all the large abbeys appear to have maintained not one, but several of these endowed free schools in various parts of their domains.

The greater variety of seminaries now existing was gradually introducing a greater separation of classes; hitherto students of all ranks had mingled under the same master, but now aristocratic distinctions began to be made. Eton soon became the favourite resort of the sons of the gentry, though not a few continued to be prepared for the universities at the monastic schools, especially at Glastonbury and Pollesworth. The latter was found in an admirable state of discipline at the time of the suppression, when the commissioners testified to the fact that the town which had sprung up round the monastery was almost entirely peopled, by "artifycers, laborers, and vitellers, that lyve by the said house, and the repayre and resorte that ys made to the *gentylmennes children and studiounts* that doo ther lif to the numbre of xxx. or xl. and moo, that ther be right vertuously brought upp." At Hyde Abbey eight noble youths were received as students, who always ate at the abbot's table. Winchcombe likewise retained its character for learning, and Abbot Kidderminster, by his wise government and encouragement of good letters, is said to have made his school flourish so much that it became equal to a little university.

If we put together the different classes of schools enumerated above, it will, I think, appear that in the fifteenth century England was quite as amply provided with the means of education for rich and poor as she is in the present day. There were, it seems, two large public schools for the gentry, other schools for the upper classes attached to monasteries and the larger colleges; monastic and collegiate schools for the middle classes, and other endowed free schools of a similar grade, and schools attached to smaller hospitals, evidently for a yet humbler class, such as the children of the neighbouring villages, or the tenantry of the founder; and lastly, there were the priests' or parish schools, usually governed by a dame.

A more general interest was being felt in the work of education among all classes, and an attentive study of the household accounts of noble families of this period will discover among the items of expenditure a more frequent mention of "pennes," "ynke," and "bokes." Hallam notices that the Paston letters, all written by members of a private family during the reigns of Henry VI., Edward IV., and Richard III., are not only grammatical, but fluent and elegant in their style, and he remarks that it is a proof how unfairly we should measure the refinement and education of an age merely by its published literature. England in the fifteenth century was in too troublous a state for men to have much leisure for writing books; and hence though there was evidently an increased relish for literary pursuits under our Lancastrian princes, we are not surprised to find few additions to our national literature during this period. Yet some writers there were, such as the poets Occleve and Lydgate; the former a disciple of Chaucer, and author of a poem on the education of princes; whilst Lydgate, the monk of Bury, enjoyed an immense reputation in his own day, and in ours has been equally undervalued. He was educated at Oxford, and was a man of varied learning, familiar with the literature of France and Italy, both which countries he had visited, a mathematician and a classical scholar, and altogether well qualified to fill the post of professor in his own abbey. Here he taught the sons of the nobility "the art of versification, *elegancies*, poetry, rhetoric, geometry, astronomy, and theology." He was equally esteemed by the pious king Henry VI., who visited him in his monastic cell, and by the London goldsmiths and citizens, who employed him in writing verses, and contriving quaint devices for their May games and city pageants. Of his two hundred and fifty poems none have been judged worthy to find a place in the various collections of the British poets, published during the last century. Halliwell has published a selection of his minor pieces, but his "Court of Sapience," a noble poem extending to several hundred stanzas, remains still in MS., or in the early Caxton editions. The student of English literature is often perplexed to understand the principles which appear to have directed the choice of our modern editors. With the exception of Chaucer and Gower, whose claims were too great to be disallowed, no ante-reformation poets are admitted into the collections of Southey or Chalmers, with the exception of Hawes and Skelton, whose doggerel is tolerated, possibly on account of its scurrility. Even Occleve, though but a second-rate versifier, is better than these, but Lydgate's "Court of Sapience" is incomparably superior to anything that appeared between the times of Chaucer and Spenser. Its tone, however, is essentially Catholic, and even theological, and this, together with the monkish titles of some of his works, such as *the Lyf of our Ladye, and the Legende of St. Edmund,* seem to have occasioned his exclusion by collectors, who have not been ashamed to rake together all the rubbish, and worse than rubbish, of our Restoration and Georgian periods. If the ancient religious poetry of this country should ever find an editor, readers who are accustomed to suppose that intelligible English dates from the time of Spenser, would be amazed at the power and pathos possessed by earlier writers. When we examine such poetical fragments as are still preserved, the wonder perhaps ceases, that they should have found small favour from modern editors. For the most part they are devoted to celebrate the glories of the Blessed Virgin, or the Mysteries of the Passion. The first subject has, of course, no chance of indulgence from a Protestant public, and the second is hardly more popular when treated precisely in the same spirit as it is presented to us in the prayers of St. Bridget, or the devout productions of antique Christian art. To Catholics, however, it is a joy and a solace to look back into past centuries, and remember that there were days when our poets drank of a purer fount than that of Castaly; and made it their pride to celebrate in their verse, not Dian, nor Proserpine, but the Immaculate Queen of Heaven. Of Chaucer's devotion to this theme I have already spoken, but other poets before his time delighted in dedicating their verses to her who, as she has inspired the most exquisite designs of the artist's pencil, has also claimed not the least beautiful productions of the poet's pen. Thus, one sings of her as "Dame Lyfe," and describes how

As she came by the bankes, the boughs eche one,

Lowked to the Ladye, and layd forth their branches,

Blossoms and burgens (new shoots) breathed ful swete,

Floures bloomed in the path where she forth stepped,

And the gras that was dry greened belive.

Others, according to their quaint fashion, mixed up English and Latin rhymes in a style which, barbarous as it is, is certainly not deficient in harmony. One little poem, ascribed to a writer in the reign of Henry III., commences thus:—

Of all that is so fayr and bright,

Velut maris Stella;

Brighter than the day is light,

Parens et puella.

I crie to The, Thou se to me,

Levedy, preye the Sone for me,

Tam pia,

That Ich mote come to The,

Maria.

Another class of poems is dedicated to the sorrows of Mary; from one of which, apparently of the fourteenth century, entitled "The Lamentation of the Blessed Virgin," I extract but two verses, the exceeding pathos of which can hardly be surpassed. Our Ladye is supposed to be addressing her complaint to some happy mother, and drawing a contrast between *her* joys and her own sorrows:

O woman, a chaplet chosen thou hast

Thi childe to wear it does the gret likynge,

Thou settest it on with great solas,

And I sit with my Sone sore wepynge,

His chaplet is thornys sore prickynge,

His mouth I kis with a sorrowful cheer,

I sith wepynge, and thou sit synnynge,

For now lies ded my dere Sone dere.

Thou hast thi sone ful whole and sounde

And myn is ded upon my kne,

Thi childe is lose, and myn is bounde,

Thy childe is lyf, and myn—ded is He!

Whi was this, doghter, but for the?

For my Childe trespast never here;

Me think ye be holden to wepe with me,

For now lies ded my dere Sone dere.

The mystery, entitled "The Wepynge of the Thre Maries," is a dramatic paraphrase of the Gospel history, told in the same homely and pathetic strain. It is thus that St. Mary Magdalene describes Our Ladye at the foot of the Cross:—

When she herd Hym for His enmyse preye,

And promesid the thefe the blissis aye,

And to hirself no worde wolde saye,

She sighed, be ye sure;

The Sonne hynge, and the Mother stode,

And ever she kissid the drops of Blode

That so fast ran down.

And when after the Resurrection she runs joyfully to tell the holy women that she has seen her risen Lord, and the second Mary asks

But have ye seen our Lord, Sister, are ye sure?

Her reply is from the heart:—

Sister, I have sene mi gretest tresure,

He callit me Mary by my name,

And spake with me homlye.

Warton, in his "History of English Poetry," has published a few fragments of poems on the Passion, which he ascribes to the reigns of Henry III. and Edward I. There is a harmony in the versification of the following that one scarcely looks for at so early a date:—

Jhesu for thi muckle might

Thou gif us of Thi grace,

That we may day and night

Thinken of Thi face:

In myn herte it doth me gode

Whan y thinke on Jhesu blod,

That ran down bi ys syde;

Fro ys herte don to ys fot,

For us he spradde ys hertis blod,

His wondes wer so wyde.

Ever and aye He haveth us in thought,

He will not lose that He so dearly bought.

And again:—

Now sprinketh[300] rose and lylie flour

That whilen ber that swete savour,

In somer, that swete tyde:

Ne is no queen so stark and stour,

Ne is no Ladye so bright in bower,

That ded ne schal by glyde:

Whoso wot flesh lust forgo, and heven's blysse abyde

On Jhesu, be is thought anon, that therled[301] was in ys syde.

I will give but one fragment more, which is taken from a sort of dialogue between our Lord on the Cross and the devout soul:—

Behold mi side

Mi woundes spred so wide

Restless I ride,

Lok on me, and put fro ye pride:

Dear Man, my love,

For my love sinne no more.

Jhesu Christe, mi lemman swete,

That for me deyedis on rood tree,

With al myn herte I The biseke

For Thi woundes two and thre;

That so fast in my herte

Thi love rooted might be,

As was the spere in Thi side

When Thou suffredst deth for me.

A great number of the Church hymns and other devotions are also to be found translated in a versified form for the use of the laity, such as the *Veni Creator*, the *Popule mi, quid feci?* and other portions of the Holy Week office. These fragments, which are mere indications of the rich stores of religious literature possessed by our ancestors, must not be lost sight of when studying the subject of popular education. Were we to credit the majority of writers on ancient manners, the poetry of the Middle Ages was exclusively furnished by the profane and licentious *jongleurs*, whose productions have been very diligently sought out and republished for the edification of the curious, whilst the very existence of a vast body of popular religious poetry is systematically ignored. Yet the one class of writings is surely as characteristic of the age to which it belongs as the other; and we are bound not to condemn the morals of our forefathers from the study of that portion of their literature which is corrupt and reprehensible, without also receiving the evidence furnished by poetry of a totally opposite description.

We must not conclude our notice of the English writers of the Lancastrian period without briefly noticing the names of two learned monks. The first was John Capgrave, author of the *Legenda Sanctorum Angliæ*, which Leland says was chiefly derived from an earlier collection of saints' lives by John of Tynemouth, a monk of St. Alban's, who died in 1370. Capgrave also produced other learned works, a MS. copy of one of which, a commentary on the Book of Genesis, is preserved in the library of Oriel College, and contains in its initial letter a portrait of the author presenting his book to Duke Humphrey, whose autograph is at the end of the volume. The other religious writer was Walter Hilton, a Carthusian monk of Shene. His "Scale of Perfection," an invaluable spiritual treatise, which formed the favourite study of Sir Thomas More, has been reprinted, but a considerable number of his other spiritual works exist in manuscript in the British Museum, and yet await an editor.

If the English did not compose many books at this period, they bought and transcribed them with great diligence. More books were copied during the first half of the fifteenth century than during any previous century and a half. Book collectors were enterprising enough to take journeys into Italy, and returned laden with literary treasures; among whom, besides Fleming, already noticed, were Tiptoft, Earl of Worcester, the friend of Pius II.; John Free, a British ecclesiastic, afterwards Bishop of Worcester; Millyng, Abbot of Westminster; and Sellynge, Prior of Canterbury; all of whom had studied the classical literature at Padua, or in Guarini's Florentine school. In the household accounts of Sir John Howard, founder of the house of Norfolk, is a bill for the transcribing, illuminating, and "flourishing" of books. Enormous sums were spent by literary dandies on bookbinding. Edward IV. is said to have spent as much on binding a book as was then the price of an ox, and "caused thereafter to be delivered to his binder six yards of velvet, ditto of silk, besides laces, tassels, and gilt nails." The Lancastrian princes were all patrons of letters: Henry V., as we know, was a scholar of Queen's, though, judging from his life after leaving the university, we can hardly suppose him to have been at that time much of a reading man. At a later period, however, he seems to have had literary tastes, and in order to gratify them he did not always return the books he borrowed. After his death, petitions were presented from the Countess of Westmoreland and the Prior of Christchurch, praying that certain books borrowed of them by the King might be restored. Those lent by the Prior consisted of the works of St. Gregory. His son, Henry VI., was the very type of a scholar; whilst his uncle

Beaufort, Cardinal and Bishop of Winchester, and his two brothers, the Regent, Duke of Bedford, and Humphrey, Duke of Gloucester, were all distinguished as men of learning. Duke Humphrey was beyond all doubt the most munificent patron of letters that had yet appeared in England, and did his best to redeem her schools from the charge of barbarism brought against them by Poggio and the other classic scholars of Italy. He was a great book collector, and the copies he caused to be transcribed were all of the most costly and splendid description, written on vellum and adorned with illuminations: 129 such manuscripts[302] were bequeathed by him to the University of Oxford, of which *one*, and one alone, remains. All the others were destroyed by the pious visitors of Edward VI., who considered that everything that was enriched with illuminations must be a popish missal, and therefore only fit to be cast to the flames. The solitary survivor is a copy of *Valerius Maximus*, the index to which is written by the hand of Humphrey's dear and learned friend Whethamstede, Abbot of St. Alban's.

Humphrey's patronage was not confined to English scholars. Heeren prints a Latin epistle, addressed by him to the Italian Decembrio, who had presented him with a translation of Plato *De Republica*. He employed several learned French and Italian translators, and to him Leonard Aretino dedicated his version of Aristotle, the presentation copy of which is preserved in the Bodleian. Pope Pius II., in a letter written about the middle of the century, mentions the fact that the duke had sent into Italy and procured several professors to explain the Latin poets and orators in his own country. And Vossius speaks of a certain master from Ferrara, to whom he gives the name of Titus Livius, and who, he says, came into England by the invitation of the Duke of Gloucester, and while there wrote a life of Henry V., and dedicated it to his son Henry VI. This life has been republished by Heeren. The real name of the author is unknown, and he probably assumed that of the Latin historian to indicate that he imitated his style.

Duke Humphrey's chief assistant, however, in his literary labours was the learned abbot named above, John Whethamstede of St. Alban's. He was originally a monk of Tynemouth, in Northumberland (which was a cell of St. Alban's), whence he removed to Gloucester Abbey; then he was made prior of Gloucester College at Oxford, in which office he had every opportunity for indulging his taste for study and his equally characteristic liberality; for he spent a considerable sum in the erection of a new library, on which he bestowed many books prefixed with verses, warning off the fingers of pilferers. He also adorned the college with painted windows, set up inscriptions under the Crucifix and other holy images, and poured out so many other benefactions on the house that he was formally declared to be its second founder.

He was elected Abbot of St. Alban's for the first time in 1420, and having resigned his office in 1440, was elected a second time in 1451. It would be no easy matter to catalogue all his good deeds, for Whethamstede was a great reformer and builder, and setter to rights of decayed offices. In fact, he united in a very uncommon degree the literary and the practical gifts, and while busy with his books and libraries, did not forget the repairing of brew-houses and enclosing of kitchen gardens; in spite of which services, the monks very unjustly accused him of neglecting their affairs, and giving all his time to study. Weever enumerates all the multifarious decorations in the shape of painted windows, gilded and illuminated verses, and other ornaments which he set up in his abbey. "Our Lady's Chapel," he says, "was very curiously trimmed and depicted, and letters dispersed therein in gold." The north part of the abbey church being somewhat dark, he made it glorious with new windows, introducing, with taste more classical than suitable, the figures of such heathen philosophers as had testified of Christ. He also expended great sums in books for the abbey library, "as well for the use of the brethren of the cloister as for the scholars;" an expression which shows that the monastic school was still kept up. These books exceeded eighty-seven in number, besides which he caused to be begun the copying of Nicholas de Lyra's great commentary on the Bible, and employed Lydgate to translate the metrical life of St. Alban into English verse. He also added many of his own compositions, such as his *Granarium*, a sort of theological commonplace book, in five volumes, dedicated to Duke Humphrey. The duke was fond of visiting the abbey, to which he was a great benefactor, and employed Whethamstede in collecting books for him; and after his death, St. Alban's was very fitly chosen as the place of his interment.

We must now for a time leave the company of princes and abbots, and take our way through the streets of London—a city which, even in the days of Henry II., was thickly populated with schoolboys, and which, thanks to his pious namesake Henry VI., kept up its name as a place of good learning in the fifteenth century. We have already seen something of the university and domestic education of Old England, but we have yet to make ourselves acquainted with the schools and scholars of the middle class. The English Commons were at this precise period fast rising in wealth and importance, and the number among them who sought a good education for their children was every year on the increase. The London citizens particularly were men of intelligence and enterprise, fully conscious of the weighty position they held in the State, and perfectly well qualified to fill it. Nor let the fastidious reader scorn the idea of scholarship as associated with that of a community of mercers and fishmongers; for it is a fact of which England has no cause to be ashamed, that many of her greatest public men, and not a few of her best scholars, have risen from the mercantile and working classes. Lord mayors and aldermen have not unfrequently spent the wealth they have amassed by trade in foundations of charity or learning. Thus, Elsing Spittal, at Cripplegate, was founded in 1329, by a London mercer, for the sustentation of a hundred blind men; St. Lawrence's College, in 1332, by Lord Mayor Poulteney; St. Michael's College, by Sir William Walworth, of Wat Tyler-slaying celebrity; and Leadenhall College, by Sir Simon Eyre, another lord mayor and draper, who provided that a school should be attached to his college under the care of three schoolmasters and an usher. His wishes do not seem to have been carried out, but in 1446 his beautiful chapel was given over to the newly-established confraternity of the Holy Trinity; and some of the priests belonging to this society, says Stowe, celebrated divine service in this chapel every market day for the market people.

So again in 1418, William of Sevenoaks, who from a foundling had made his way to civic honours, built and endowed a college in his native place, and a free school for the townsmen's children; and, not to multiply examples, the renowned Sir Richard Whittington, mercer and Lord Mayor of London, after founding his noble College and Hospital of St. Michael's Royal, and repairing St. Bartholomew's Hospital, built at his own expense the great library of the Grey Friars, and expended a considerable sum in furnishing it with reading pews, and causing to be transcribed a fair copy of Nicholas de Lyra for the friars' use. Men of this stamp were solicitous to see their city provided with good schools, and in 1446 we find a petition presented to Parliament by four city priests, begging the honourable Commons to take into consideration the great number of grammar-schools that had formerly existed in the metropolis, and the fact that many of them had lately fallen into decay. The petitioners go on to say that many persons now resort to London to be informed of grammar, through lack of good schoolmasters in the provinces, "wherefore it were expedient that in London were a sufficient number of scholes and good informers in grammar; for where there is gret number of lerners, and few techers, the maisters wax rich of money, and the lerners poorer in cunning, agenst all virtue and order of weal publik." They entreat therefore that schools may be opened in each of their parishes, and persons learned in grammar set over them "there to teach to all that will learn." In compliance with this petition, we find the good king Henry VI. founding no fewer than eight grammar-schools in this and the following year. And Mercers' School was likewise established in connection with the Mercers' Company.

Stowe describes the grammatical disputations kept up between the scholars of these academies even in his time, and lets us know that the scholars of St. Paul's were wont to call those of St. Anthony's "Antonie pigs," by reason that St. Anthony is usually figured with a pig following him; and that they in their turn retaliated on their rivals the sobriquet of "pigeons," many such birds being wont to make their haunt in the spire of St. Paul's church. And it was their custom when they met one another in the street to provoke one another to disputation with the words *Salve tu quoque; placetne disputare?* To which, if the answer were *Placet*, they fell to words, and soon to blows also, the satchels full of grammars serving as convenient weapons, which oftentimes bursting in the fray, the books were scattered about in heaps to the great trouble of the passers-by. The least admirable thing recorded of the London schoolboys, however, is their taste for cock-fighting. On Shrove Tuesday every schoolboy in London brought a cock to his master, and the whole of that forenoon, says Fitz Stephen, "is spent by them in seeing the cocks fight in their schoolroom." No wonder that Colet, among other retrenchments, prohibited his scholars of St. Paul's from taking part in these Shrovetide cock-fightings, as a description of sport eminently fitted to foster in the boyish nature those brutal tendencies which are perhaps indigenous to the soil. That a taste for learning and a generous disposition to encourage it were to be found among not a few of the London citizens of this period is sufficiently clear; and among many names that might be given of founders of schools and lovers of letters, that of John Carpenter, town clerk of London in the reigns of Henry V. and Henry VI., must not be omitted. He was executor to Whittington, and the personal friend of two at least of those four priests above named who had petitioned Parliament for the establishment of more schools. These were Thomas Neel, Master of the Hospital of St. Thomas de Acon, and Incumbent of St. Mary, Colechurch; and William Lichfield, Rector of Allhallows the Great. Lichfield was a considerable writer both in prose and verse, whom Stowe calls "a great student and a famous preacher." These two excellent ecclesiastics took part in many good works with John Carpenter, and probably assisted him in making that collection of books, afterwards mentioned in his will. Carpenter seems also to have had a taste for the arts; for the famous Dance of Death painted in the cloisters of old St. Paul's, was placed there at his expense, with accompanying verses from the pen of Lydgate. It is, however, as an encourager of liberal education that he claims a place in these pages, and the benefaction by which he left certain tenements in the city "for finding and bringing up four poor men's children with meat, drink, apparel, and learning, at the schools in the universities, for ever," was the foundation which has since grown into the City of London School.[303]

But after all, the mind is trained by other things than schools and pedagogues; and the London apprentice, no less than the university undergraduate, drew in no small part of his education from the scenes and daily life that went on around him. Old London, no less than old Oxford, had a teaching of her own; she was not altogether that place of smoke and trade and unceasing business which we think of now when we name "the City:" she had a fairer,—I had almost said a poetic—side, and her old historians grow eloquent when they describe it. Who would suppose that it is the great Babylon that Fitz Stephen is speaking of when he praises the picturesque beauty of the suburbs, "with the citizens' gardens and orchards planted with trees tall and sightly, and adjoining together. On the north side," he continues, "are pastures and meadows, with brooks running through them, turning water-mills with a pleasant noise. Not far off is a great forest and a well-wooded chase, having good covert for harts, does, boars, and wild bulls. The cornfields are not of a hungry, sandy mould, but as the fruitful fields of Asia, yielding plentiful increase, and filling the barns with corn. And there are near London abundance of wells, sweet, wholesome, and clear, such as Holy-well, Clerken-well, and St. Clement's-well, much frequented by scholars and youth of the city in summer evenings when they walk forth to take the air." Stowe likewise speaks of these pleasant walks in the suburbs, and adds a feature of touching beauty to the picture:—"Near a fair field in Houndsditch, belonging to the Prior of the Holy Trinity, were some cottages and little garden-plots for poor bed-rid people, built by some prior of that house; and in my youth I remember devout persons were accustomed, specially on Fridays, to walk that way to bestow their alms on the poor, who lay in their beds near the window, that opened low, and on it was spread a fair linen cloth and a pair of beads, to show that there lay a bed-rid person unable but to pray only." Within the walls were 130 churches, besides convents, priories, and hospitals innumerable. In Westcheap, near the north door of St. Paul's, stood the great Crucifix surrounded by figures of saints, where the choristers of St. Paul's had a goodly exhibition for singing on certain days the responsory, *Sancte Deus fortis*, and thither on all feasts of St. Paul's came the chapter in embroidered vestments and wearing rose garlands on their heads. This last ornament was very commonly worn in English processions, specially on the summer festivals of Whit-Sunday and Corpus Christi, and not only by canons and choristers, but also by young scholars, as we learn from Matthew Paris. There were city companies then as now, and there were guilds and confraternities, which gave to their members "gret commodyte and surety of lyvyng," and which recreated the citizens with their gorgeous processions, while they provided support for their poor brethren during life, and after death, burial, prayers, and masses. On the feast of the patron saint, the guild brethren had a dinner, of course, and generally an interlude or sacred drama; and Fitz Stephen assures us that the citizens of his time preferred those which were from sacred subjects, such as the Passion, or the martyrdom of a saint. Clerkenwell received its name from the Fraternity of Parish Clerks, who yearly assembled there to play "some large history of Holy Scripture," and in the reign of Henry IV. enacted one which lasted *eight days*, and was "of matter from the creation of the world."

But, to use the words of our old historian, "a city should not only be commodious and serious, but also merry and sportful," and London had nothing to blame herself for on this head. During the Easter holidays there were sham fights on the river, with leaping, dancing, shooting, and cock-fighting, and great twisted trees were brought in from the woods to adorn the house of every man of worship. The great May-pole hung in Westcheap, and on May morning every citizen went forth early into the country to seek the May. All through the summer months bonfires were kept up on the eves of great festivals, and tables set out in the streets with meat and drink plentifully provided by the wealthy householders, who invited the neighbours and passers-by to eat and be merry with them with great familiarity, and so thank God for His benefits. And Rome herself never witnessed a more graceful celebration of the feasts of St. John Baptist and the Holy Apostles than that which used to be held in the streets of London, where "every man's door was shadowed with green birch, fennel, and St. John's-wort, together with white lilies and such like, and garnished with garlands of beautiful flowers, among which lamps of glass burnt all the night;"[304] while some hung out huge branches of iron, curiously wrought, whence hung hundreds of lamps at once, and this was particularly the custom in New Fish-street. At Christmas, of course, the houses and conduits were decked with a profusion of evergreens, and the Christmas revels must be left to the imagination of the reader.

When the holidays were over, came sports and contentions of another sort. The masters of the different schools held solemn meetings in the London churches, and their scholars disputed logically, grammatically, and demonstratively. The disciples of rival academies "*capped* or *potted* verses one with another, nipping and quipping their fellows with pleasant rhymes, which caused much laughter." The poets sometimes addressed their fun and their verses to their masters, expending their wit in hopes to obtain a holiday. And, however it may be explained, I find more notices of versifiers among the London scholars than elsewhere. Indeed, we must fain suppose that the citizens had a naturally poetic vein when we read of their gorgeous and fanciful devices. Chaucer tells us that the good shopkeepers of the Cheap had weary work with their apprentices, who, when there were any "ridings" or royal entries, would leap out of the shop, and not return till they had seen all the sight, and had a good dance into the bargain. And really, when we read how the fifth Harry rode into London with little birds fluttering round his helmet, green boughs cast in his way, priests, with gilded copes, swinging censers, and every street exhibiting a castle, or a giant, or a legend of some saint, we cannot wonder that it was sometimes a difficult matter to keep the 'prentices behind the counter.

Surely too there must have been scholars among the citizens to devise such scenes as were exhibited at the entry of Henry VI., when a tabernacle of curious work arose on Cornhill, wherein Dame Sapience appeared, surrounded by the seven liberal arts; and when divers wells poured forth goodly wine to the passers-by, appropriately named the Well of Mercy, of Grace, or of Pity. But, in fact, most of such pageants were designed by men of letters, and no one was more frequently called on for this purpose than the monk of Bury. He was exceedingly popular with the London citizens, and whether a disguising was intended by the company of goldsmiths, a May game for the sheriffs, or a carol for the Coronation, it was generally Lydgate who supplied the poetry. And he, in his turn, loved the citizens, and ever spoke well of them in his verse:—

Of seaven things I prayse this citty,

Of true meaning and faithful observance,

Of righteousness, truth, and equity,

Of stableness aye kept in legiance.

A testimony to which we must add that delivered two hundred years earlier by Fitz Stephen. "I do not think," he says, "that there is any city to be found wherein are better customs in frequenting the churches, in serving God, in keeping holidays, in giving alms, in entertaining strangers, in solemnising marriages, in furnishing banquets, celebrating funerals, and burying dead bodies." He adds, however, that London had some "inconveniences," such as the immoderate drinking of some foolish persons, and the frequent fires.

Such then were some of the scenes in the midst of which the young citizen grew up, and which supplied him with many ideas beyond those of his shop wares and his reckonings. Sometimes he passed over to France or Flanders to procure his stores of silks and velvets, or fine Paris thread; and on such occasions, book collectors, like Duke Humphrey, or Tiptoft of Worcester, did not disdain to employ the services of an intelligent merchant to procure them choice copies of foreign works. Treaties of commerce were generally negotiated by merchants, who were thus brought into contact with courtiers and politicians, and not unfrequently the commercial treaty was but the veil to conceal more profound political intrigues. We need not, therefore, be surprised to find a commission issued by Edward IV., in 1464, to Richard Whitehill and William Caxton, conferring on them the quality of ambassadors at the court of Burgundy, to reopen the trade with that country, which had been suspended in consequence of certain prohibitive decrees issued by Philip the Good. All that we know of Caxton up to this time was, that he had begun his education in a poor school of the weald of Kent, and had probably perfected it in some one of the London grammar-schools; that he had been apprenticed to Master Robert Large, a mercer of Cheapside, who became Lord Mayor in 1440, and dying the next year, left the sum of twenty marks to his *servant* William Caxton. Then he appears as a travelling agent of the London mercers in Brabant, and Holland, and Flanders, in which countries he spent thirty years of his life, and at last we find him at the court of Burgundy, to which the Flemish provinces were then subject. When his mission was ended, he continued to reside at the court, and was at Bruges in 1468, when the marriage took place between Duke Charles the Bold and Margaret Plantagenet, sister to Edward IV. He probably received some office in the household of the Duchess, but he seems to have had little to do, and to fill up his time the English mercer took to literary pursuits; considering, as he says, that every man is bounden by the counsel of the wise man to eschew sloth and idleness. He therefore resolved to translate into English the "Recuyell of the Historyes of Troye," by Raoul de Fevre, wherein he had great delight, both for the novelty of the same, and the fair language of the French; and having concluded to begin this work, he forthwith took pen and ink, and set to work; but after writing five or six quires, fell into despair over his task and put it aside. Duchess Margaret, however, at this juncture came to his aid: she had heard of his proposed translation, and required the quires to be brought to her for inspection; praised them, found fault with the English here and there, and finally commanded the translator to continue and make an end.

"I might not disobey her dreadful command," says Caxton, "seeing that I was a servant of her Grace, and received of her yearly fee." Dibdin, in his "Typographical Antiquities," endeavours to prove that Caxton had *printed* the original French book before *translating* it into English; but this is mere conjecture, and there seem no satisfactory grounds for supposing him to have turned his attention to the new art of printing before the year 1471, when his English translation of the "Recuyell of the Historyes of Troye" was printed by him at Cologne. We are not told how he acquired a knowledge of the art, which had then been in operation for about twenty years, but the motive which led to his first applying himself to it was, as he tells us, the desire to multiply copies of his book, which was in request with divers gentlemen. Three years later he returned to England and set up the first English printing-press in the Almonry of Westminster Abbey, the learned abbot Millyng being his first patron, and evincing a lively interest in his success. Caxton's earliest works were mostly his own translations; "The Game and Play of Chess" was the first production of his Westminster press, and its second edition was adorned with woodcuts. Another was "The Doctrine of Sapience," also translated by him from the French, and intended "for the use of parish priests, and for the erudition of simple people." "The Dictes and Sayings of Philosophers" was a translation from the pen of his accomplished friend Anthony Woodville, Lord Rivers, who had so high an opinion of his printer's literary powers that he permitted him to overlook and correct the sheets. This accomplished nobleman, the chosen "champion" of the English ladies, the best scholar, the best poet, and the best jouster of King Edward's court, helped to set the types with his own hand, and afterwards presented both the book and the printer to his royal brother-in-law.

Caxton did not altogether pursue his art in the spirit of a tradesman. He evidently had it much at heart to provide his countrymen with good and useful books, and took considerable pains in their selection. In spite of Gibbon's sneer at the number of saints' legends[305] and romances that issued from his press, we have every reason to admire the variety of subjects to be found in the sixty-four works which he lived to publish. They embrace religion history, poetry, law, ritual, and romance. No original work of the Latin classics appears on the list, which does not argue much for the scholarship of the English reading public at that time, and offers a striking contrast to the state of things in Italy, where the first works printed at the Subiaco press were "Lactantius," St. Augustine's "City of God," and Cicero's "Rhetoric;" and these were followed a little later by twenty-three editions of ancient Latin authors. But in England, though a few individuals had shown an interest in the classic revival, the nation at large was, at this time, wholly indifferent to the subject, and Caxton had to consult their taste, at the same time that he attempted to raise and refine it. He himself was no classical scholar; nevertheless, he chose a certain number of French versions of ancient authors for translation into English, such as the Treatise "De Senectute" of Cicero, Ovid's "Metamorphoses,"[306] Boethius' "De Consolatione," the "Fables of Æsop," and Cato's "Morals." The last he recommended as the best book that could be used by children in schools. He likewise translated a French narrative of Virgil's "Æneid;" and contemptible as this sort of literature may appear to scholars, it helped to give his readers a certain acquaintance with the names and subjects of classical authors, and prepared the way for the study of the originals.

On the other hand, the number of English works which he produced, and the care he expended on presenting them to his readers in clear and simple language, "casting away the chaff of superfluity, and showing the picked gram of sentence," gave a powerful stimulus to his native literature. His own favourite author was Chaucer, in printing whose works he grudged neither care nor expense: and he incidentally gives us to understand that the English gentry of that period had, like himself, a marvellous love for their great poet. He had no slight difficulty in getting a correct MS. to print from, and his first edition of Chaucer's poems was, therefore, full of inaccuracies. A young gentleman criticised its defects, and offered, if he would print another edition, to supply him with a certain very correct copy, which was in the possession of his father, who loved it much, and would not willingly part with it. Caxton agreed to the proposal, by which, of course, he lost considerably as a tradesman, but gained in the esteem of the learned: and one is glad to find that the young gentleman, in fulfilment of his part of the bargain, did not purloin the book from his father but "got it from him full gently," and delivered it to the careful custody of the honest printer.

Not content with the labour of printing and translating, which he carried on with so much eagerness that, as he tells us, his eyes were half blinded with continual looking at the white paper, the indefatigable old man undertook, at the age of seventy, to compose his "Chronicles of England," and "Description of Britain," which books he intended to convey to English readers a certain amount of information about the history and geography of their own country. He had plenty of critics while engaged on these works; some wanted him to use only "old and homely" terms; others, who were finer clerks, begged him to write the most *curious* words he could find. Caxton good humouredly complains of the difficulty he found in pleasing everybody, and remarks on the variable character of the English language, which gives ground for supposing that the English people must be born under the domination of the moon, never steadfast, but ever wavering. His own good sense, however, decided that the best English for any writer to use is that common phraseology which is more readily understood than what is antique or curious. He never assumed the airs of a scholar, and in his preface to a modernised version of Higden's "Polychronicon," calls himself "William Caxton, a simple person," and modestly apologises for his attempt to render the rude old English of his author into more intelligible language.

One of his translations from the French, entitled "The Mirror of the World," gives an outline of as much natural philosophy as was at that time known. This book was printed at the request, and at the cost, of Hugh Brice, a London alderman, and the choice speaks well for the intelligence of that worthy citizen. Caxton seems to have taken considerable pains over it, and says he has made it so plain, that every *reasonable* man may understand it, and begs his readers' indulgence if there be found any fault in the measurements of the sun, moon, or firmament. To assist the intelligence of his "reasonable" readers, he added twenty-seven diagrams explanatory of scientific principles, and woodcuts representing the seven liberal arts. In these woodcuts we observe that the schoolmaster generally appears seated, while his scholars kneel before him. The grammar-master is furnished with a rod, which need not cause dismay, for perhaps it was but the ferule, part of the academic insignia of a master of arts. The logician's book rests on a reading-desk, and he is expounding its contents to his kneeling pupils.

Dibdin calculates that Caxton's translations alone would fill twenty-five octavo volumes, and that they extend to over 5000 closely-printed pages. His biographer Lewis bears witness to the fact that in his original writings he constantly expresses himself as "a man who lived in the fear of God, and desired much to promote His honour and glory." But he thinks it necessary to regret that he should have been carried away by the superstitions of his times so far as to print saints' legends, advocate pilgrimages to the Holy Land, and proclaim himself an enthusiastic admirer of the Crusades. Mercer and printer as he was, Caxton was indeed thoroughly informed with the spirit of chivalry. It was this that directed his choice of "The History of Godfrey de Bouillon," "The Book of Chivalry," and the "Histories of King Arthur." In his preface to the first, the venerable printer makes an appeal to all Christian princes to establish peace and amity one with another and unite for the recovery of the Holy City, where our Blessed Saviour Jesus Christ redeemed us with His Precious Blood; to encourage them to which "he emprised to translate his book." In the second he utters a lament for the good days when the knights of England were really knights, "when each man knew his horse, and his horse knew him." And in the third he confesses his conviction that Arthur was no fabulous character, but a real man; and exhorts his readers to study his noble deeds, "for herein may be seen noble chivalry, courtesy, humanity, friendliness, hardiness, love, friendship, cowardice, murder, hate, virtue, and sin. Do after the good, and leave the evil undone, and it shall bring you good fame and honour."

Lewis informs us that the progress of printing terribly alarmed the ignorant and illiterate monks, who saw in the advancement of learning their own impending ruin. If so, they took a very strange way of expressing their alarm, for they were the first to patronise the new invention; so that in a very few years after Caxton had set up his press in Westminster Abbey, other printing-presses were at work in the monasteries of St. Alban's, Worcester, Bury, and others. The monk who first introduced printing at St. Alban's was the schoolmaster; his name is not known, though Sir H. Chauncey styles him "Insomuch." Bale and Pits tell us that he was a reader in history, and say that he had collected materials for a history of England, but died before it was completed, that his papers fell into Caxton's hands, who printed them under his own name. But this is evidently incorrect. The St. Alban's printer was still working his press in 1486; and Caxton's chronicles were printed six years earlier. Before the death of Caxton, several other printers, both English and foreign, were established in London, and among the latter was the celebrated Fleming Wynkyn de Worde. An Oxford press was at work so early as 1478, and seven years later the Latin translation of the Epistles of Phalaris issued from the press, to which is affixed a Latin couplet, boasting that the English who had been wont in former times to be indebted to the Venetians for their books, now themselves exported books to foreign countries:—

Celatos, Veneti, nobis transmittere libros

Cedite; nos aliis vendimus, O Veneti.

However, I have no intention here of tracing the history of English printers, and have only said thus much of Caxton, because he presents us with an admirable example of an intelligent Englishman of the middle class—a practical persevering man, full of the healthy energy which belongs to a life of labour; a vigorous, homely writer who desired, in his day, to serve his country in so far as he had the needful "cunning;" whose plain broad sense is illumined by a ray of piety, and warmed into a touch of generous enthusiasm, which makes his name more dear and venerable to us than that of many a profounder scholar. Is it fancy or partiality which makes one detect in the fair large type that he uses, so clear and readable, a reflection of his own simple and genuine character; a character which, making allowance for the difference of station, reminds us of that of the great Alfred, to whose written language also that of Caxton bears a remarkable resemblance.

He died in the year 1492, at the age of eighty, having two years previously completed his translation of "The Craft how to Die Well," from which the following is an extract:—"When it is so, that what a man maketh or doeth, it is made to come to some end, and if the thing be good and well made, it must needs come to good end; then, by better and greater reason, every man ought to intend in such wise to live in this world in keeping the commandments of God that he may come to a good end. And then out of this world, full of wretchedness and tribulation, he may go to heaven unto God and His saints, into joy perdurable."

Two years after writing these lines he was laid to rest in the Church of St. Margaret's, Westminster, not far from the spot where for eighteen years he had carried on his noble and useful labours.

CHAPTER XX.

THE RENAISSANCE AT FLORENCE.

A.D. 1400 TO 1492.

EASTERN travellers tell us of certain richly-irrigated soils in tropical lands, whereon the seeds that are cast spring up in a single night, covering, as if by magic, vasts plains, which before appeared barren wastes, with a mantle of tender green. Something like this was the rapid fertilisation exhibited in the world of letters after the death of Petrarch. More than a century, indeed, had to elapse before Italy could produce any names fit to compete with those of Dante, Petrarch, or Bocaccio; but the freshly-awakened enthusiasm for ancient learning, to which the writings of the two latter had so largely contributed, gave birth to a generation of scholars whose labours communicated a new direction to European studies. They did not leave behind them, as monuments of their genius, epic poems or philosophical discoveries, but they disinterred forgotten manuscripts, restored their corrupted texts, revived the study of Greek, and at the same time made known to Western Christendom the works of the great Greek authors by means of their own laborious Latin translations. They were, in short, a generation of grammarians, critics, and pedagogues, and were the instruments of achieving an intellectual revolution hardly less momentous than the religious and political revolutions which were to follow in after years.

The watered soil and the fruitful seed did not fail to be cherished by the sun of princely favour. The fifteenth century was not more remarkable for its learned men, than for its noble patrons of learning. In Naples there was Alphonsus of Arragon, who, in the midst of his warlike campaigns, had the Commentaries of Cæsar read to him daily, and whose displeasure against the Florentine Republic was appeased by the timely present of a copy of Livy. When Gianozzo Manetti was sent to him as ambassador from Florence, and delivered to him his opening oration, the king, out of respect to so great a scholar, would not so much as raise his hand to brush away a troublesome fly; and on one occasion, when Manetti had joined in a dispute which Alphonsus was carrying on with certain learned men of his court on the subject of the Holy Trinity, he so won the royal heart by his skill and eloquence that the king exclaimed, "Had I but a single loaf, I would divide it with Gianozzo!" He was one of the greatest book collectors of his time, and loved to surround himself with scholars, such as Antony of Palermo, commonly known as Panormita, who is said to have cured his royal master of a fever by reading to him the Life of Alexander, by Quintus Curtius. Perhaps it was after his recovery that Alphonsus despatched Panormita to Venice for the singular purpose of begging from the Venetian senators *an arm* of the Roman historian, with which classical relic he triumphantly returned to Naples. Most of the other men of letters who then flourished in Italy, such as Poggio, Filelfo, Valla, and George of Trebizond, were at one time or other attached to his court, and magnificently rewarded for their literary labours; and Pius II., in his "Description of Europe," numbers Alphonsus himself among the philosophers of the day, and says that he could discourse both learnedly and gracefully on the most abstruse theological questions.

At Ferrara, Nicholas of Este not only refounded the university of that city, but succeeded in gaining possession of two great teachers, Guarino the Elder, and John Aurispa, who directed the education of his son Lionel, and whose schools were frequented by students from every European land. Lionel repaid their care by himself becoming an elegant scholar, and establishing at his court an academy of poetry; and his brother Borso, who succeeded him, proved, perhaps, a yet more splendid patron of letters, though he had not himself received a learned education. A new poem of Leonardi, a map of the world, or a correct copy of Ptolemy's geography, were treasures which won from Duke Borso many a golden florin for the scholar fortunate enough to present them; and the archives of Ferrara and Modena became crowded with decrees for the protection of scholars, which Tiraboschi assures us are no less remarkable for the elegant Latinity in which they are drawn up, than for the munificent spirit in which they are conceived.

The Gonzaghi held rule at Mantua, and there an academy flourished under the princely patronage of the Marquis John Francis, concerning which I must speak a little more particularly, as its master in some respects stands alone among the pedagogues of the Renaissance. Who has not heard of Victorino da Feltre, and the "Casa Giojosa," in which he taught his crowd of princely pupils, contriving to mingle in their ranks not a few poor scholars, the perpetual objects of his generous solicitude; whose fame was so widely spread, and whose blameless character was so respected, that in those days of bitter scholastic jealousies all the greatest masters of Italy offered him their gratuitous services, and counted it an honour to direct a class in the "Joyous House" of Mantua? The house derived its name from the beauty of its situation, and the care which Gonzaga had taken to adorn it with everything that could contribute to the pleasure or instruction of its inmates. It contained galleries and arcades, all painted with pictures of children at prayer, at study, or at play; around it stretched delicious gardens and woods well stored with game, and the graver lectures of the master were relieved by lessons in riding, dancing, fencing, and every other graceful accomplishment suitable for noble youth. Victorino, on assuming the direction of the academy, did not entirely discountenance these pleasant pastimes, nor did he turn the Joyous House into a Castle Dismal; he contented himself with introducing such reforms as banished habits of self-indulgence, and prepared his pupils, not only to become elegant gentlemen, but hardy soldiers. He reduced the princely banquets to a reasonable limit, confiscated sweetmeats, and showed himself pitiless upon all coxcombry in dress. It is remarkable, that though he left not a line behind him as a monument of his scholarship, his celebrity has survived to our own day, and certainly equals that of the greatest of his contemporaries, resting as it does solely on his merits as a teacher of youth. Not merely was he distinguished as a lecturer in Greek, Latin, and mathematics (though even in that capacity he had few equals), but as one who trained the heart, formed the manners, and established, as the basis of all education, a strict observance of religious duties, victory over the passions, and the mortification of pride, selfishness, and sensuality.

A no less passionate admirer of the ancient authors than his friend Guarino, who often assisted him in his school, Victorino was careful to guard his pupils from the paganising tendencies which he discerned in the spirit of the age. Along with the Greek and Latin classics, therefore, he presented to their study the Fathers of the Church, and the Divine Scriptures, and when lecturing on the heathen poets and historians, he was wont, in a few luminous words, to lay before his hearers the grand Christian principles which were never to be effaced from the soul by Gentile sophistries and eloquence. Those principles he taught yet more by example than by precept. Two hours before his classes opened, Victorino might have been found in the hospitals and prisons of Mantua, relieving and comforting every form of distress. He founded among his noble pupils an association of charity, for enabling poor scholars to pursue their studies with greater facility, and this he did, not merely as a means of carrying out his favourite work of charity, but yet more with the view of training the sons of the Italian *noblesse* from their earliest years to care for the inferior classes, and to give to the poor out of their abundance. His whole life was marked by a total disregard of his own private interests. The good Marchioness, Paula Gonzaga, never made but one complaint of him, and that was, that often as she tried to furnish him with a better wardrobe, he frustrated her charitable attempts; for so soon as he found himself possessed of two coats, one went to clothe a poorer man than himself. It may be added, that though a simple layman, he embraced a stricter rule of life than was followed by many an ecclesiastic of the time. In an age when the practice of frequent communion was far from common, he approached the holy table twice every week, and encouraged his pupils to communicate every Sunday. It is said that in the early part of his scholastic career, his intercourse with St. John Capistran and St. Bernardine of Siena had awakened in his soul a strong desire to enter the cloister, from which he was deterred by the arguments of his learned friend Ambrose Traversari, who assured him that his vocation was to remain in the world, and there train souls for heaven. And as a divine vocation he embraced it; and cast over the scholastic profession a grace, a dignity and a beauty of holiness which made Eugenius IV. exclaim, when he was presented to him at Florence, "If my rank as Supreme Pontiff permitted it, I would rise from my seat to show honour to so great a man!"

However, it must not be supposed that Victorino was a mere devotee, or that his school was of a retrograde class, excluding the new lights of classical literature. He was the friend and correspondent of all the scholars of his day, and the pupils of the "Casa Giojosa" were no whit behind their countrymen in classical acquirements. Ambrose Traversari, who was considered to equal Leonard of Arezzo as a Latinist, and to surpass him in his knowledge of Greek, has left an account, in his "Hodœporicon" and in his epistles, of a visit which he paid to the school of Victorino, and a kind of friendly examination to which he subjected its pupils. "I reached Mantua," he writes, "where I was welcomed with singular kindness by Victorino, the best of men, and my very dear friend. He is with me as much as his serious occupations allow; and not he alone, but the greater part of his disciples. Some of them are so well advanced in Greek, that they translate it into Latin. He teaches Greek to the sons and daughters of the prince, and they all write in that language." Again, "Yesterday Victorino presented to me Gian Lucido, the youngest son of the prince of Mantua, a youth of about fourteen. He recited to me 200 Latin verses of his own composition, in which he described the pomp with which the Emperor Sigismund had been received at Mantua. The little poem was very beautiful, and rendered more so by the grace and correctness of its delivery. Then he showed me two theorems which the boy had added to the geometry of Euclid. There was also one of his sisters at the academy who, though only ten years old, writes Greek so well, that I am ashamed to say many of my own scholars cannot show anything to equal it." This last-named pupil was Cecilia Gonzaga, whose learning afterwards became renowned throughout Italy. Her sister Margaret, also a pupil of Victorino, became the wife of Lionel of Este, but she herself consecrated her talents to God, and entered a convent of poor Clares, founded by her mother in the city of Mantua.[307]

While the smaller potentates of Italy were vying one with another in their encouragement of letters and learned men, the Sovereign Pontiffs were setting them the example on a yet more magnificent scale. From 1447 to 1455 the chair of St. Peter was filled by Nicholas V., who to extreme simplicity of manners united immense learning, and a mind capable of vast and magnificent designs. Whilst he was restoring peace to Italy putting an end to the schism which had sprung out of the Council of Basle, planning a fresh crusade, and laying plans for the rebuilding of Rome, on a plan realised only in the pages of Vasari, his agents were busy, all over the world, collecting, collating, or translating manuscripts, and giving to the world, in versions undertaken at his sole expense, those long-forgotten works of classical antiquity, the "History of Diodorus Siculus," the "Cyropedia" of Xenophon, the histories of Polybius, Thucydides, and Herodotus, the "Iliad" of Homer, the geography of Strabo, many of the works of Plato, and the Greek Fathers of the Church. Most of the scholars of whom we shall have to speak in the following pages were employed by him as translators and secretaries, and were amply recompensed for their work. Poggio was thus enabled to complete his version of Diodorus. Lorenzo Valla received 500 gold scudi for his translation of Thucydides; 10,000 scudi, a house and estate, were promised to Filelfo for his translation of Homer, and when giving Perotti 500 scudi for his Latin Polybius, the Pontiff condescended to apologise for the smallness of the sum, which he owned was below the value of the book. He is known to have offered 5000 scudi for a Hebrew version of St. Matthew's Gospel, which, however, was never found. In his early years he had often given utterance to the promise that if he ever found himself in the possession of riches, he would employ them in the multiplication of good books. He nobly kept his word; and, when he died, left, as his bequest to his successor, the Vatican library, furnished, through his munificence, with 5000 precious manuscripts.

The accession to the pontifical chair of Eneas Sylvius Piccolomini, who became Pope in 1458, under the title of Pius II., seemed to promise much for the world of letters. He had already acquired a European fame as a poet and historian, and had received the laurel crown from the hands of Frederic III. But his short pontificate was almost entirely absorbed in preparations for the projected crusade, which he had resolved to undertake for the recovery of the Eastern Empire, and death alone prevented his carrying out his grand designs, and accompanying the army into the East in order to encourage the soldiers with his presence. Meanwhile a flood of Greek refugees poured into Europe, contributing very largely to encourage the restoration of ancient learning, though they certainly had not given the movement its first impulse. Even before the fall of Constantinople in 1453, many Greek scholars had judged it prudent to pass over into Italy in order to escape the ruin impending over their country. Others, again, had been attracted thither by the Council of Florence, held in 1441, for the extinction of the Greek schism. Among the latter was the celebrated Bessarion, Archbishop of Nice, who, convinced of the fallacy of the Greek claims by the arguments of the Latin prelates, urged his countrymen to acknowledge the supremacy of the Holy See, and thereby incurred so much odium among them as to be forced to remain in exile. He was raised to the purple by Pope Eugenius IV., and employed in several important legations, but it was as a man of letters that he chiefly distinguished himself. His house at Rome became a sort of academy, and in it he trained a number of scholars, both Greek and Latin, not only in learning, but in piety and good manners; for Bessarion was as remarkable for his courtesy and virtue as for his erudition. His great library, collected at a cost of 30,000 golden scudi, was presented to the Republic of Venice, in return for the affection with which he had been received in that city; and though he only acquired a knowledge of the Latin tongue after his removal to Italy, he produced several works in that language, among which was a "Defence" of his favourite philosopher Plato.

But neither Rome nor Naples was destined to be the Athens of modern Europe, but a city, still proud of her republican institutions, though on the point of surrendering all but the name of sovereignty into the hands of a successful family of merchant princes. Many circumstances had combined to render Florence the focus of the great literary movement then in progress, and thither chiefly resorted the exiled Greek scholars—such as Argyrophilus, George of Trebizond, Theodore of Gaza, and Gemistus. Schools had been opened in this city so early as 1393 by Emmanuel Chrysoloras, which may be said to have given the first impulse to the revival of Greek studies. Emmanuel came over to Italy, in the first instance, in the quality of ambassador from Constantinople, to seek for aid against the Turkish arms among the princes of the West. But he found it more to his taste, and possibly also to his profit, to exchange his diplomatic functions for those of a professor of letters, and soon reckoned among his disciples a group of scholars who were in their turn promoted to chairs of Greek rhetoric in the universities of Venice, Ferrara, Bologna, and Naples. One of these, Guarino, had been formerly acquainted with Chrysoloras at Constantinople, whither he had travelled in 1388 in search of manuscripts. Guarino was at that time only eighteen years of age, and after acquiring the Greek language, he set out on his return to Italy, bearing with him two great chests filled with the treasures which he had collected. A storm overtook the vessel, and in his dismay the captain ordered the whole cargo on board the ship to be cast into the sea. In vain did Guarino throw himself at his feet, and conjure him to spare his precious volumes; they were ruthlessly hurled to the fishes, and when morning dawned the poor scholar's raven locks were discovered to have turned as white as snow, such had been the anguish which his loss had caused him. However, if he had lost his books, he had not lost his learned gifts, and on reaching Italy, he became professor of rhetoric, first at Florence, and afterwards at Venice and Ferrara. John Aurispa was more fortunate in his researches, and succeeded, in 1423, in bringing back to Italy 238 Greek manuscripts. We have already spoken of him as lecturing at Ferrara under the patronage of the Este. He was secretary both to Eugenius IV. and Nicholas V., and before settling at Ferrara had also taught both at Bologna and Florence. He was succeeded in the chair of rhetoric in the latter city by the celebrated Filelfo, who had likewise made the grand tour of the East, and brought home a magnificent Greek library. This last-named scholar had studied at Constantinople under John Chrysoloras, brother to Emmanuel, whose daughter Theodora he married, a circumstance which swelled his already preposterous vanity, and which he never lost any opportunity of trumpeting to the Greek-loving world.

Filelfo, on returning to Italy, first selected Bologna as the happy spot which was to be blessed with his erudite presence. He entered the city in a sort of triumph, the enthusiastic populace giving him the welcome ordinarily reserved for sovereign princes, and erecting a chair of Moral Philosophy and eloquence for his express occupation, with the handsome annual salary of 450 gold scudi. Every day saw some new festa invented to do honour to the great Professor and his charming "Chrysolorine," as he somewhat affectedly designated his Greek spouse; and for a brief space Filelfo declared himself satisfied with the amount of homage offered to his genius. "Bologna is a charming city," he writes in one of his epistles; "the inhabitants are courteous, and not insensible to letters; and what specially pleases me is the consideration and affection which they display towards *me*." In 1428, however, a popular revolution dissipated all these pleasing prospects; Filelfo, in company with the Papal Legate, had to fly for his life, and while the cities of Italy scrambled which should obtain possession of so rare a scholar, the coveted prize fell to the share of Florence, where Cosmo de' Medici and his rival, Philip Strozzi, were just then struggling which should outshine the other in acts of princely munificence. The vanity of Filelfo was once more for a time amply gratified for the Florentines yielded him their hearty applause, and if we are to credit his own words, made him the great lion of their city. "All Florence runs after me" he writes in his letters; "everybody loves me; everybody honours me and lauds me to the skies; my name is in everybody's mouth. Not only the first men of the city, but the noble ladies also give place when they meet me, and show me so much respect that I am really ashamed. I have every day 400 hearers, or more, and all of them persons of rank and importance."

And it must be owned that Filelfo worked hard to gain their applause. The routine of his everyday work involved an amount of labour to voice and brain, under which any one but a professor of the fifteenth century must have succumbed. About daybreak he began by lecturing to a crowded audience on Cicero, Livy, or the Iliad. His explanations of Cicero were considered his greatest successes and by his ready and brilliant eloquence he seemed to reproduce the Roman orator to the eyes and ears of his hearers. Returning home, he gave audience to the favoured few who were happy enough to be on his list of private pupils; and at mid-day he was again in the public chair, commenting on Terence, or the Greek historians, Xenophon and Thucydides. Every evening there were literary reunions and learned academies to be attended, or private assemblies, in which Filelfo was, or, at any rate, considered himself to be, the great centre of attraction, and nurtured his good opinion of himself with the homage of an obsequious crowd. Even Sunday was no day of rest to him, for then, in the Church of Sta. Maria dei Fiori, he lectured and commented on Dante.

The fascination of such a life, however, had a make-weight of mortification. Filelfo was possessed with one of those bitter and malignant dispositions that turn the very sweets of life into poison. His very jokes were malignant, as, when disputing with another grammarian on the quantity of a Greek syllable, he offered to pay him 200 scudi if he were proved wrong, on condition that, if right, he might have the satisfaction of shaving off his adversary's beard. The poor grammarian lost his wager, and, in spite of all his entreaties, Filelfo gratified his revenge in the true spirit of a literary Shylock. It was quite enough for any other scholar to be praised and honoured for him to become at once the mark for Filelfo's spite. "What does Guarino know, of which Filelfo is ignorant?" he exclaims in one of his letters, his bile being excited by the fact that Guarino's name was just then in everybody's mouth. This intolerable presumption raised him enemies in every city; and, indeed, in those days it seems to have been the habit of literary men to spend the greater part of their time in biting and devouring one another. Filelfo, perhaps, may be regarded as the most venomous disputant of them all. He who talked so much of being "loved" by everybody, hated and made himself hated by the entire world. He hated the men of learning who shared with him the favour of the Florentines, because he regarded them as his rivals. He hated the great Cosmo, the Pericles of the New Athens, because his benefits were not exclusively showered on himself. He hated the good and honest citizen Niccoli, the founder of St. Mark's public library, because he was a friend of the Medici. And he hated the very populace who gaped and wondered at his erudition, because his appetite for flattery growing as it was ministered to, they could not always satisfy its cravings, and at such times Filelfo was ready to denounce them all in that malignant language of which the elegant commentator on Tully was an accomplished master. He poured out his venom on Cosmo in a series of villanous libels, accusing him of attempting his life by poison and the dagger; yet, at the very time when he was inventing these calumnies against a man who had loaded him with favours, he was himself hiring assassins to attack his rival, Carlo Marsuppini, in the streets of Florence—a crime for which the Republic afterwards condemned him to have his tongue cut out, should he ever set foot again upon their territory.

To his other vices Filelfo added that of a grasping avarice: he was continually appealing to the different princes of Italy for larger money advances, and loading them with abuse if they did not satisfy his demands. He threatened Pius II. to turn Turk, if the pension granted by that Pontiff were not more regularly paid; and his contemporary scholars continually complained that, after promising them books, he would afterwards withdraw from his bargain, and demand back again from them what was not really his own property. But, in candour, it must be confessed that, in this last-named matter, Filelfo appears to have been more sinned against than sinning. A very bad habit prevailed at that time among literary men of borrowing books and never returning them. Francesco Barbaro is accused of keeping a chest of Filelfo's books for thirty years; and similar peccadilloes are charged to the account of Aurispa and Giustiniani. Possibly, observes Tiraboschi, they regarded book thefts in the same light as monks had been used occasionally to regard the pilfering of holy relics. Anyhow, the injury was sensibly felt by the unfortunate owner, and did not improve the asperity of his temper.

Whatever infamy attaches to the character of Filelfo, he met with his match in one of the literary rivals whom he encountered at Florence. Poggio Bracciolini had received his education in his native city, and to a perfect knowledge of Latin and Greek literature added the rarer merit of being a good Hebrew scholar. For thirty-four years of his life he held the office of apostolic secretary under successive Pontiffs, and during all that time he never spent an entire year in any one city. He was present in his official capacity at the Council of Constance, and to while away the hours that hung heavy on his hands, made an excursion to the neighbouring abbey of St. Gall, and disinterred from a damp tower the mouldering manuscript of Quinctilian's "Institutes." From thence he passed over to England to pursue his researches in the monastic libraries of this country, but declares that they were full of nothing but "modern doctors, whom *we* should not think worthy so much as to be heard." By his discoveries of classic authors, and his own critical and historical writings, he contributed more than any other scholar of his time to the revival of learning, so that some writers have gone so far as to confer on the first half of the fifteenth century the title of "the age of Poggio." But his glory was sadly clouded by the furious quarrels in which he engaged with all his contemporaries, and the foul and disgraceful language which he poured out against every one who was unhappy enough to come into collision with him. Among the works of this great champion of classic Latinity are four "Invectives" against Filelfo, and five against Lorenzo Valla. The latter were written in revenge for certain criticisms which Valla had published of his Epistles, and are, says Tiraboschi, "a disgraceful monument to the memory of a writer who observes neither rule nor measure, but defiles his pen with every hideous abomination which malice could suggest against his adversaries." Valla, who was a scholar of precisely the same temper, replied in his "Antidotes to Poggio," and Filelfo in his "Satires"—all of which are said to be conceived in the same rabid and malignant strain. Nor was it only against such men as these that Poggio directed his venom. Guarino was made the subject of another ferocious onslaught, for no worse misdemeanour than having differed from Poggio in preferring the character of Cæsar to that of Scipio! George of Trebizond, a man of like temper to his own, was another of his opponents, and on one occasion the two disputants, after publicly giving each other the lie, came to blows, and were with difficulty separated by their hearers. And at last this detestable spirit grew on him to such a degree that, no longer content with attacking individuals, he published libels, if we may so say, on the literary world at large, and did his best in his "Dialogue against Hypocrites," to slaughter the reputation of every man of virtue and celebrity in the world of letters, such as the Blessed John Dominic, Ambrose Traversari, Cardinal Luca Manzuoli, and the entire Franciscan Order. With all this, Poggio probably held the first place among the scholars of his time, unless the superiority be given to his adversary, Lorenzo Valla, who is generally held to have surpassed him in grammatical erudition. Erasmus, indeed, treated the merits of Poggio very lightly. "Poggio was possessed of so little real learning," he says, "that, even if his books were less full of abominations than they are, they would not repay perusal; as it is, were he even the most erudite of writers, all good men must regard him with horror." Nor can a much better character be given to Valla; in arrogance and vanity he equalled Filelfo; and in his famous "Treatise on the Elegance of the Latin Tongue," gave the world to understand that he was about to explain a language which before his time had been understood by none. "These books," he says, "*will contain nothing that has ever been said by anybody else.* For many ages past, not only has no one been able to speak Latin, but none have understood the Latin they read, the philosophers have had no comprehension of the philosophers, the advocates of the orators, the lawyers of the jurists," and so of the rest. This kind of self confidence is, however, so universal among scholars of the age as hardly to call for special notice; but it was the least fault of which Valla stands charged. Passing over grosser accusations brought against him by adversaries whose habits of calumny render their testimony of little value, there was a taint of ingratitude in Valla's character which is particularly offensive. Having, in his "Declamation against the Donation of Constantine," attacked the claims of the Holy See in terms which Hallam himself admits could not be excused, he retired from Rome, and found a warm welcome at the court of Naples. Here, however, he soon got involved in difficulties with the Inquisition, in consequence of certain impieties to which he gave utterance on the subject of the Holy Trinity and other fundamental dogmas of the faith. He was only released from prison through the friendly interference of Panormita. Yet as soon as he recovered his liberty he engaged in a furious quarrel with his benefactor, and spared no calumnies by which he could bring discredit on his name and character. He treated it as a crime for any one to differ from him in any point of taste and criticism, and punished all such transgressions by blackening the fair fame of his opponents. Nevertheless, he met with far gentler treatment than he deserved, for it was after he had established his renown as the best Latinist, and, next to Poggio, the most malignant calumniator of his day, that Nicholas

V. invited him back to Rome, made him a canon of St. John Lateran, and employed him in numerous translations, all of which were liberally paid for. Valla accepted the dignities and the money offered him by the Pope, and took advantage of his favourable turn of fortune to complete that attack on the papal sovereignty which he had before left unfinished; and he did so in a style which, Hallam informs us, rather resembles the violence of Luther than what might have been expected from a Roman official of the fifteenth century. The clemency shown him by the Pope was perhaps excessive, for he was suffered to live at Rome unmolested, and retained the office and pension of apostolic secretary to the day of his death.

It must be owned that the portrait gallery through which we are passing, has thus far been anything but pleasing, nor can it be denied that in their main features of malice and presumption, most of the scholars of the age exhibit a family resemblance to those noted above. Hallam observes that the inferior renown enjoyed by Giannozzo Manetti, is probably owing to the greater mildness of his character, which involved him in fewer of those altercations to which Poggio and Valla owed a great part of their celebrity. And Tiraboschi apologises to his readers for leaving some portions of his history somewhat obscure, on the ground that the calumnies and misrepresentations indulged in by almost all writers of the period, render it nearly impossible to rely on any of their statements, and to accept as facts anything which they may say unfavourable of one another.

Some noble exceptions, however, are to be found, and among them may be quoted the example of Leonard Bruni, or, as he is more frequently styled from the place of his birth, Leonard Aretino. Whilst Chancellor of Florence he one day engaged in a public philosophic dispute with Giannozzo Manetti, in which the latter gained the advantage over him. Stung with annoyance, Leonard let fall some injurious words, to which, however, Giannozzo replied with his customary good temper, and both returned to their respective homes. But Leonard was so pursued by remorse for his fault that he could not close his eyes all night, and so soon as morning dawned, he hastened to the house of Giannozzo, who was greatly surprised to see the first magistrate of Florence at his door at such an early hour. Leonard, however, only bade him follow him into the city, and conducting him to the great bridge over the Arno, then the most frequented thoroughfare, he publicly asked his pardon, and acknowledged he had had no rest since he had spoken injuriously of so noble an adversary. Giannozzo received his apology with a modesty which was equally admirable, and the friendship which from that day sprung up between these two great men, remained unbroken to the death of Leonard, on which occasion the funeral oration was spoken over his body by Giannozzo.

From the scholars of Florence let us now turn to her Mecænas, the merchant prince, who, for thirty years, held the first rank in the Republic, and deserved to obtain from his grateful fellow citizens the title of "Father of his country." Cosmo de' Medici was beyond all question the greatest of his illustrious race. Machiavel calls him the most magnificent and most generous of men, and Flavio declares that he surpassed all his contemporaries in wisdom, humanity, and liberality. His political career seems to have been for the most part free from the vice of selfish ambition; whilst as a patron of letters, even in that age of splendid patrons, he had no equal. In Florence alone he founded three public libraries, expending 36,000 ducats on that of St. Mark's, which he enriched with 400 Latin and Greek manuscripts, whilst he appointed as librarian Thomas di Sarzana, afterwards Pope Nicholas V. A few years later he rebuilt the library, and added a collection of Hebrew, Arabic, Sanscrit, and Chaldaic books, collected at enormous cost. His love of literature was so genuine, and so superior to the selfishness of a mere bibliopolist, that even when in temporary exile at Venice, he could not help opening his purse-strings in favour of the Venetian library of St. George, and employed his fellow exile, the architect Michelozzi, in providing it with reading benches and other conveniences, presenting it also with many books. It was his wish to draw to Florence all the learned men of the day. He it was who invited thither the Greek Professor Argyrophilus, to the end that he might instruct the Florentine youth in the philosophy of Aristotle. A vast number of Greek exiles received from him a princely welcome, to say nothing of the crowd of native scholars who thronged his palace. Pages might be filled with the mere enumeration of the convents, churches, and hospitals which he built or endowed, not merely at Florence, but even at Jerusalem, where he founded a large hospital for poor pilgrims. He had stewards and administrators in every part of Europe, who helped him to dispense his treasures on worthy objects. Yet with all this, his own establishment was always conducted on the most modest scale, and he who enriched scores of Florentine families, never assumed a more brilliant appearance than that of an ordinary citizen. His liberality was altogether free from ostentation, and appears to have flowed from the purest and most Christian motives. "Never yet," he complained to one of his friends, "have I been able to spend in God's honour the sums for which, when I look over my ledger, I find myself indebted to Him."

It was in the year 1438, whilst Pope Eugenius IV. was residing at Florence, and the Council was still sitting which had for its object the extinction of the Greek schism, that a certain Greek, named George Gemistus, arrived in the city, and one day entered the palace of Cosmo with a copy of Plato under his arm. This celebrated scholar had received the surname of *Pletho*, in consequence of his enthusiastic admiration of the academic philosopher, and is more commonly known by this sobriquet than by his patronymic. Pletho, as we shall therefore call him, read a few pages of his book to the enraptured ears of Cosmo, and very soon communicated to him a portion of his own enthusiasm. Until then Cosmo had been a stranger to all save the Peripatetic philosophy, and the ideas which now presented themselves to his mind seemed like the opening of some new world. In his delight he conceived the plan of establishing a Platonic academy at Florence, a design which was put into execution without delay. Platonism, however, was then so new in the schools of the West, that Cosmo could find no professor who seemed capable of filling the chair of philosophy to be attached to this academy; and he resolved to educate for that purpose a child whose talents had already attracted his notice. Marsilius Ficinus was the son of his physician; his tiny frame and delicate constitution seemed incapable of making head against the host of maladies with which he had been beset from the cradle. But Cosmo's quick eye discerned the indications of early genius. "This boy," he said, "is destined to cure, not the maladies of the body, but those of the soul."

With his customary bounty, he became a second father to his future professor, and under his direction, Ficinus received a thoroughly Platonic education. He was carefully reared in the maxims and philosophy of the great master, to the end that having early imbibed the principles of Platonism as a kind of second nature, he might be qualified afterwards to become the head preceptor of the new academy. The whole scheme had something visionary about it, and no less so was the character of the man chosen to carry it out. From his boyhood he was a poet and a dreamer. He loved to wander at early daybreak by the banks of the Arno, and recite aloud to the woods and the stream the verses of Virgil's "Georgics." Light and country air were his two necessaries; he seemed to live in the sunshine, and on those rare occasions when the fair sky of Florence was overspread with clouds, he could neither write nor study. His work as a composer was exclusively carried on in the early morning hours; then it was that his genius seemed to wake with the sunrise; and if he also spent long night hours over his manuscripts, he only then applied himself to the labour of revision. Cosmo gave him a little lamp, which was often found burning when daylight dawned in the east; he also provided him with books, and specially with manuscripts of Plato procured from Venice at an enormous cost, and to these Ficinus applied himself with such incessant application, that his health almost entirely gave way; in fact, his life seemed always hanging by a single thread, and was preserved only by such extraordinary precautions as are bestowed on some exotic plant. At the age of twenty-three, the young student considered himself ready to read to a learned assembly, presided over by Cosmo, the first pages of his "Platonic Institutions." When the lecture was over, his patron smiled and gently shook his head. Ficinus understood the gesture, but was not discouraged; he prepared for a fresh course of studies, and placed himself under the historian Platina, more illustrious for his Greek erudition than for his orthodoxy, but the latter condition was not greatly cared for by the young Platonist. In a few months he found that he had made such rapid progress, that, remodelling his work, he submitted it to the judgment of Marcus Musurus, the Greek professor of Venice, and the first editor of Aristophanes. He found Musurus sitting at his writing-table, and having engaged him to give an impartial opinion, began the reading of his manuscript. As the professor listened, he amused himself with turning over the various implements before him. Ficinus at last paused, and asked him what he thought of it.

"I think *this*," said Musurus, and taking the ink bottle, he shook it over the open manuscript as if it had been sand. Ficinus betrayed no impatience, which is saying something for his philosophy; and retiring to the country house which Cosmo had presented to him, devoted himself to the task of a third revision. Before it was completed his great patron died leaving his son Pietro and his grandson Lorenzo de Medici to succeed him in his pre-eminence, both in the literary and political world. Pietro and Lorenzo showed themselves as eager to encourage the Platonic academy as its first founder had been; and their enthusiasm was shared by their contemporaries. All the scholars of Italy aspired to the honour of membership; Landino, Alberti, and John Picus of Mirandola, these met together, and contended for the silver laurel wreath, which was the prize of merit; and one of Pietro's first acts was to establish a professorship, the chair of which was immediately bestowed on Ficinus. In the meetings of this academy the honours bestowed on Plato came very near to idolatry. Its festivals were the anniversaries of his birth and death, a lamp was burnt in his honour, and the professor, in lecturing to his fellow academicians, addressed them, not as "my brethren in Christ," but as "my brethren in Plato." It was, perhaps, unfortunate that Ficinus did not rest content with his professor's chair and his academic reputation. In such a position his Platonic enthusiasm might have been productive of little injury, but at the age of forty-two he entered the priesthood, became canon of Florence, and took up the study of theology. Plato, however, was not laid aside for St. Paul. On whatever subject he wrote or spoke, says Tiraboschi, he seemed unable to refrain from tinging it with the doctrines of the academy. Gemistus, his first master, had been an avowed disciple of the Alexandrian school, and in the furious controversy then raging between the Platonists and the Aristotelians, had highly lauded not only the writings of the Greek philosopher, but those of Hermes and Zoroaster. In fact, as Hallam cautiously expresses it, "there were some grounds for ascribing to him a rejection of Christianity." Ficinus cannot be charged with similar scepticism, though his lectures seem to have sown the seeds of religious doubt in the minds of some of his hearers. He believed the Gospels, but they were the Gospels *Platonised*. He went so far as to desire that his favourite author should be read in the Christian churches, and published eighteen books of what he called "Platonic Theology." Hallam calls this work "a beautiful, but visionary and hypothetical system of Theism." He did not attack the Christian dogmas, but he treated them as a philosopher rather than as a theologian. He was not content with gathering up and giving to the world the profound maxims of his illustrious master; but he undertook to harmonise the teaching of Plato and the teaching of Scripture, and attempted to prove that all the most prominent Christian mysteries were to be found in the *Criton*, which he regarded almost as a second Gospel.[308]

The extravagances in which Ficinus indulged were equally maintained in other learned academies. That which flourished at Rome under the direction of Pomponius Lœtus drew on its members the hostility of Paul II., who has been repeatedly charged with "persecuting the learned," out of that natural antipathy to learning, of which Popes and cardinals are sometimes imagined to possess a kind of monopoly. The historian who originated the charge, however, is no other than Platina, the former master of Ficinus, whom Paul II. had made an enemy by suppressing the college of the *Abbreviatori* to which he belonged. He was himself a member of the Roman academy, the suppression of which has been differently related by different historians, but it appears certain that the alleged crime of the members was, not their learning, but a real or supposed plot against the Government and certain impious and anti-Christian tenets which they were reported to hold. Tiraboschi considers that their innocence of the charges brought against them may be deduced from the fact that, after a year's imprisonment, they were all set at liberty, and that Platina in particular was afterwards honourably employed by Sixtus IV., who made him librarian of the Vatican Library. Possibly the impieties of which they were guilty might rather have sprung from the foolish conceit of pedants than any positive unbelief; yet still it must be owned that some of their acts had a suspicious character, and could not but have appeared reprehensible in the eyes of the Pontiff. Michael Canensius declares they were wont to affirm that the Christian religion rested on no sufficient evidence, but only on the testimony of a few weak-headed saints: that they laid aside the use of their Christian names, and adopted others chosen from the great heathens of antiquity; that they were in the habit of swearing by the heathen gods and goddesses; that they disputed concerning the immortality of the soul, and maintained many Platonic errors, that Pomponius disdained the Scriptures, and was wont to say that Christianity was only fit for barbarians, and that, in his enthusiasm for ancient Rome, he even raised and decorated altars to the god Romulus. Some of these charges the accused did not deny; but though examined under the torture, it does not seem that anything transpired which offered satisfactory proofs of the existence of a conspiracy.[309] Paul contented himself, therefore, with suppressing the academy, and thereby earned for himself immense obloquy, and the character of being an enemy of letters; a most undeserved reproach, for, besides maintaining a number of poor scholars in his palace, and being an eager collector of ancient manuscripts and monuments, his biographer tells us that he was accustomed to spend many hours of the night reading the ancient authors, and "that he loved all learned men, *provided* that to their learning were joined good manners." This last condition was not always thought equally essential by patrons of letters of this period, who seem, as a general rule, to have cared but little what a man's life was, provided he knew Greek. Filelfo, however, adds his testimony (which, in this instance, may perhaps be regarded as trustworthy), that Paul II. "was ever a favourer of learned men."

We must not, however, suppose that the scholars of the Renaissance were exclusively made up of captious grammarians and philosophic sceptics. The movement had its fairer side; it was bewitching in its promise of literary excellence, and was not even devoid of its character of romance. Chivalry was not yet entirely extinct, and among the masters and scholars of the Italian schools some took up the cause of learning in a truly chivalrous spirit, and without a thought of self-interest, devoted themselves to study and teaching, as to a work by which they might benefit their kind. Their enthusiasm for their favourite pursuits appears sometimes in a more amiable character than that which it assumed in the hands of Poggio and his adversaries. Among the grammar professors enumerated by Tiraboschi we find the name of Piattino de' Piatti, a noble youth brought up as a page in the household of Galeazzo Sforza, who for a very small offence caused him to be imprisoned for fifteen months in a frightful dungeon. We next find him figuring at a splendid tournament at the court of Ferrara, where he bore away the prize, and at the same time struck up an ardent friendship with the poet Strozza, who addressed some verses to him, praising him for knowing how to blend together the merits of the soldier and the scholar. For several years he bore arms under the Duke of Urbino, but his warlike occupations did not hinder him from cultivating the Muses, and he published a volume of Latin poems, which was one of the earliest works printed in Italy. Disappointed at not receiving the promotion he expected from the French kings Charles VIII. and Louis XII., he abandoned the profession of arms, and embraced that of schoolmaster in the little village of Garlasco, opening his humble academy with as much solemnity as if it had been a university, with a learned Latin oration. And we are assured that the number of good scholars then to be found in Italy was so great that many other villages besides Garlasco could boast of possessing as their schoolmasters first-rate professors of eloquence.

But the palm of Christian scholarship belongs, at this time, beyond all question, to John Picus, Prince of Mirandola, whose brief life closed in his thirty-second year, and whose acquirements probably surpassed those recorded of any other scholar. Whilst still a child he evinced so retentive a memory as to be able at once to repeat any verses recited in his presence, and displayed a sort of natural predisposition to the study of the *belles-lettres*. His mother, however, who wished him to embrace the ecclesiastical state, sent him to Bologna, to read canon law, at the age of fourteen, and after spending two years there, he proceeded to study philosophy in the principal schools of France and Italy. Besides a knowledge of the scholastic writers, he acquired during the next six years the Latin, Greek, Hebrew, Arabic, and Chaldaic tongues; but his enthusiastic and imaginative disposition led him to explore with eagerness the mysteries of the Jewish Cabala, a mass of mystic doctrine attributed to Esdras; on which idle fallacies, says Corniani, Mirandola expended a genius which was fitted to reach the most elevated truths of philosophy.

In his twenty-third year the young scholar appeared at Rome, and astonished the learned world by offering publicly to defend nine hundred theses on questions logical, ethical, mathematical, physical, metaphysical, theological, magical, and cabalistic; in short, *de omni re scibili*. Four hundred of these propositions were taken from Latin, Greek, Jewish, and Arabic doctors; the rest were announced to be his own opinions, which he was prepared to defend, subject to the judgment of the Church. There was a dash of vanity in all this, excusable perhaps in so young a scholar, who could not but be conscious of his superiority, and who in his anxiety to display it, offered to pay the expenses of any learned man who might come to oppose him from the utmost parts of the earth. His propositions were meanwhile examined by order of Innocent VIII., and thirteen of them pronounced unsound; whereupon he published an "Apology," explaining in what sense they were put forth, but wholly submitting to the judgment passed on them by authority. The Holy Father, therefore, while condemning the theses, forbade their author to be in any way molested, and when some of his enemies revived these accusations on the death of Innocent, his successor, Alexander VI., appointed a commission, which declared his innocence of the charge of heresy. He next appeared at Florence, the most brilliant of all the brilliant throng that was gathered in the court of Lorenzo de' Medici, and was admitted to the closest friendship of that prince, and his favourite scholars Ficinus and Politian. Young, gifted in mind and person, and possessed of all the fairy favours of rank, wealth, and an honourable fame, Picus of Mirandola yielded at first to the fascinations of the world, which perhaps never assumed a more bewitching guise than in the court of the Medici. His ardent poetic temperament was sensitively alive to the seductions of pleasure, when pleasure came hand in hand with all that was graceful in art and polished in literature. But a few years of such life sufficed to withdraw the veil from his eyes; the pursuit after worldly honours and delights seemed after all, to use his own words, but a child's chase after painted soap-bubbles; and the day came when, flinging all his lighter poetry into the flames, he prostrated before the altar of the Blessed Virgin, and vowed to dedicate the remainder of his life to the service of God alone. From that time he became as remarkable for his admirable virtues, as he had been before for his learning; his charities to the poor were dispensed on a princely scale, and so great a horror did he conceive for the vain glory into which he had been once betrayed, that he only allowed his writings to appear under the name of some other author. He refused every solicitation to engage in public disputations, and spent the remainder of his days in mingled prayer and study, to which latter exercise, says Paul Cortese, he generally devoted twelve hours a day.

It is remarkable that Picus of Mirandola, though so thoroughly imbued with the literary tastes of the Renaissance, was very far from sharing in that contempt for the elder Christian schoolmen, in which the scholars of the fifteenth century commonly indulged. When Hermolaus Barbarus, in one of his letters, gave vent to his sentiments of scorn for men who could write such bad Latin, Picus replied in an epistle, which Hallam quotes as affording a favourable example of the ease and elegance of his own style, and in which he puts a very good defence in the mouth of those despised barbarians; and Hermolaus had nothing better to say in return than that they would certainly have disowned their advocate for defending them in such classical language.

But we must now enter the school of another Florentine canon, who had the merit not only of being learned in Greek and Latin, but of possessing some of that original and poetic genius which, since the days of Petrarch, had been rare in Italy, overlaid, it may be, by the superincumbent weight of grammar learning. Angelo Politian had first made himself known to the world of letters by a graceful poem, composed when a mere youth on the occasion of a tournament, at which Julian and Lorenzo, the two sons of Pietro de' Medici, appeared in the lists. The young poet, scarce fifteen years of age, was at once received into the Medici Palace, and astonished his tutors, Landino, Argyrophilus, and Ficinus, with his Latin epigrams. He was not much older when he undertook to translate Homer into Latin verse, and at twenty-nine we find him filling the chair of rhetoric at Florence, a distinction of which he was abundantly vain. Vanity was, in fact, his prevailing fault, and it raised him a swarm of enemies who could not forgive his airs of superiority, and those biting sarcasms which he knew how to clothe in the most elegant Latin. But even his enemies admitted that, as a professor of eloquence, he stood without a rival. Equally at home in Greek, Latin, or Hebrew eloquence, in the Platonic or the Peripatetic philosophy, in rhetoric or in jurisprudence, he amazed his hearers by the multiplicity of his acquirements, no less than by the facility of his style. No wonder that a lecturer of this stamp should succeed in drawing around him all the great intellects of that wonderful age. On the benches beneath that chair you might see the young prince Picus of Mirandola, and the grey-headed men who had been Politian's own masters; a crowd of foreigners, too, such as the Englishmen Grocyn and Linacre, who were destined to carry back the seeds of polite letters to their own barbaric land, and other pilgrims from France, Germany, and Portugal, besides native scholars from all the cities of Italy. Lorenzo, who in 1469 had succeeded to his father's wealth and dignities, would also join the learned throng, and hang on the honied words of the young professor. As every one knows, the Muses are not always so happy as to carry the Graces in their train, and Politian's portrait has been drawn by Jovius in no very flattering terms. On first beholding him, he says, it was impossible to avoid an involuntary movement of surprise and disgust; his huge, unsightly nose, squinting eye, and awkward stoop, inspired no favourable impression; but no sooner had he begun to speak, than your senses were fairly taken captive, and closing your eyes, you willingly gave yourself up to the power of that graceful eloquence and the exquisite music of that voice, which very soon made you indifferent to the defect of other natural advantages in the speaker. "Yes," you might have said to yourself as you listened, "this is indeed rhetoric; hitherto in that chair I have listened to grammarians and critics, but the Muses have at last taken pity on our grammar-beladen ears, and sent us one who can feel the sentiment of Virgil and Homer, as well as explain their syntax."

It was, in fact, the possession of that inexplicable gift, the poetic sensibility, which raised Politian to an eminence differing so very widely from that of the Poggios and Vallas who had preceded him, and which made him more charming as a lecturer, and perhaps more amiable as a man. Instead of wrangling over verbs and cases, he loved to picture to his own and his hearers' imagination, the rural scenes which Virgil painted; and seizing some happy phrase of the Latin poet, to expand, to colour, to revivify it till you wandered under the shade of the beech trees, and heard the very hum of the bees among the odorous limes. At such moments, laying down his book, with the skill of an Improvisatore, he would take you to the woods and fields, and make you listen to "the soft and soul-like sounds" of the wind, as it sighed among the pines, to the rustling of the oak leaves in Vallombrosa, to the merry chattering of the tiny brook over its bed of pebbles, and the lowing of the herds in the rich Tuscan pastures. All this, to the ears of the Florentines, so long condemned to a sort of intellectual aridity, was like fresh showers on a thirsty soil. To none was it more delightful than to Lorenzo, himself a poet of no mean ability, and keenly alive to the charm of rural sights and rural sounds; and after listening to such a lecture, he would wait in the hall, and taking the professor by the arm, would lead him out to that fair villa at Fiesole, which looked over the dome and towers of Florence, and over a varied landscape of mountains, woods, and gardens, all glittering in the sunset glories of a Tuscan sky. There were gathered day after day the choicest intellects and the most erudite minds, men of all nations and of all gifts: critics, artists, poets, antiquarians; Lorenzo had a welcome for each, and was as ready to reward the happy presentee of an ancient medal or a classic vase, as he was to add to his library a Greek manuscript brought from the farther end of Europe by Lascaris,[310] or a new treatise from the pen of Landino. Every day some fresh treasure was displayed to the admiration of his illustrious friends, some *chef d'œuvre* of ancient sculpture, or a heap of Eastern manuscripts, sold to him by a Jewish merchant for their weight in gold. "I love these books so dearly," he once said, "that I would give my whole princely wardrobe to purchase them." The arts were not forgotten. Perugino was among the honoured guests of Fiesole; and among the pupils of Politian was the young sculptor Michael Angelo Buonarotti, whom Lorenzo lodged in his palace, and treated as his own son. The Platonic academicians, too, found a warm supporter in the grandson of their founder, and Ficinus gratified to the full his thirst for sunshine, and his dreamy poetic tastes in that little chamber, where morning after morning he loved to throw open the windows, and listen to the song of the birds as they greeted the dawn, and drink in the fragrance of the hawthorn and the honeysuckle, and the thousand exotic plants which blossomed on the parterres and terraces. There, to use the exquisite similitude of the English philosopher, "the breath of the flowers in the open air came and went like the warbling of music;"[311] there the fountains threw up their graceful jets, and made a pleasant murmur to the ear, and the sensitive and highly-wrought organisation of the Platonic scholar was soothed and invigorated by contact with all that was beautiful to the eye and ear in nature or in art.

All this was delightful enough, nor is it to be wondered at that the grace and fascination of such scenes blinded the eyes of those who took part in them, and the judgment of those who have been their historians. But, in truth, there was another side to the picture. The revival of classic taste at Florence was a revival of practical Paganism. It was not a mere return to those principles which had been admitted in the Christian schools before the rise of Scholasticism, when the Latin poets were freely studied even in ecclesiastical seminaries, and the Greek learning of the monks of St. Gall earned for some among them the title of the *Frati Ellenici*. It was a great deal more than this. It not only restored the study of the classic writers, but also their habits of thought, and their gross sensuality. It revived the Pagan, and excluded the Christian ideas; Christ was no longer recognised as "the One Teacher of man;" on the contrary, even from the pulpit you heard quotations from Virgil and Juvenal quite as often as from the Gospels. A style of speaking had become fashionable, according to which a certain sort of barbarism was associated with the idea of Christianity, as though it were something Gothic and transmontane. The Saints and Fathers of the Church gradually disappeared from the schools; the touching representations of Christian mysteries were withdrawn from the public eye; and society, instead of being permeated, as in former centuries, with an atmosphere of the faith, was now redolent of heathenism. Christianity was looked on as unworthy of furnishing subjects to the pen or pencil of the scholar. In those trellised gardens where the wits of Florence assembled to listen to the graceful eloquence of Politian, were grouped fragments of ancient art or the copies of modern sculptors, the eager students of the new school of naturalism. Here it was an undraped Venus, there a Satyr or a Bacchanal. Sometimes Lorenzo appeared among the brilliant throng, and condescended to assign to the artists whom he entertained a new subject for their genius. To Pollajuolo he gave the twelve labours of Hercules, to Ghirlandajo the misfortunes of Vulcan, to Luca Signorelli all the gods and goddesses of Olympus, whose stories were to be represented with little of that reserve demanded by Christian modesty. Yet artists might have been found at that time whose genius was impressed with a more religious character, but they received no encouragement at Florence, where the school most in favour was that which substituted sensual for mystic beauty; and this debased heathenised taste equally pervaded the Florentine literature and schools.

The books admitted as class-books into the new academies were precisely those authors which have been in all ages proscribed as the most dangerous, but which were now placed in the hands of the young without restriction of any sort. And, indeed, what kind of moral safeguards were likely to be supplied by professors such as Filelfo, Poggio, and Valla, whose licentious language was unhappily rather the rule than the exception among the teachers of the day? The study of the Scriptures, which in earlier times had filled so large a place in the scholastic course, was now all but entirely laid aside; and we are assured that some would even ask, with astonishing simplicity, what use could be derived from the knowledge of events that had happened so many ages ago? As to that liturgical element which had hitherto mingled so largely in the scheme of Christian education, it had little chance of being preserved in an age when not lay professors alone, but even ecclesiastics, were so besotted with their devotion to Pagan models, as to show themselves ashamed of the language of the Church formularies. Whilst some escaped from the misery of reciting their Latin breviaries by obtaining permission to use a Greek or Hebrew version, others gave up reading the Epistles of St. Paul through fear of accustoming their ears to so unclassical a style; and numerous proposals were set on foot for what was called a reform of the Liturgy, which should have for its object the correction of its style and its adaptation to classical forms. But even these were not the worst excesses. Tiraboschi assures us that scepticism and open unbelief were becoming frightfully common among men of letters, and specially in the Italian universities which were declared in the following century to be hot-beds of infidelity. Yet so innate in the human soul is the craving for some kind of mysticism, that at the very time that faith in the Christian mysteries was being rejected, many were entangling themselves in the absurdities of the Jewish Cabala; and not a few addicted themselves to magical studies, practising rites and incantations of most shocking impiety. Even where these grosser disorders did not exist, the combined influence of heathenism and sensuality produced a certain irreligious and intensely worldly tone, more difficult, perhaps, to combat than open vice or infidelity; and it was of this that Savonarola complained when from the pulpit of St. Mark's he first addressed the Florentines with his fervid Biblical eloquence, but found his glowing words fall, as he expressed it, upon hearts as hard and as cold as marble.

In other respects, also, the age of the Medici resembled but too closely that of Augustus. It was an age when a people were being cajoled to surrender their freedom into the hands of an absolute ruler, who used as his instrument for undermining republican institutions weapons far more deadly than the sword. Lorenzo had read Tacitus to some purpose, and thoroughly understood his maxim, that the easiest way to enslave a nation is first to corrupt it. He scrupled not to secure his political ascendancy in Florence by ministering to the baser passions of the populace. He amused them with shows and dances, carnival masquerades, and midnight processions, in which the flood-gates of license were freely opened, and heathen fables were represented in all their most unseemly crudeness; and in return they let him steal away their independence, and appropriate to himself the authority of the sovereign of Florence under the title of her First Citizen. Magnificent orgies were held by torchlight, wherein the triumph of Bacchus and Ariadne, or some other such subject, was enacted by bands of superbly-dressed masquers, singing those celebrated carnival songs composed by Lorenzo, which were, we are told, for the most part, immoral and indecent, expressing, not the graceful Platonism of a classical academy, but a mythological burlesque, flavoured for the grosser tastes of the populace.

It was against this flood of iniquity in the schools, the palace, and the public streets, that the bold eloquence of Savonarola was at this time directed, creating a moral reaction, which proved, however fallacious in its brilliant promise of reform. Taking the Scriptures as his weapon of warfare, he dealt rude and terrible blows at those who were sapping the very foundations of Christianity with their elegant Paganism. He complained that priests and doctors now thought of nothing but rhetoric. They studied Horace and Cicero to prepare themselves for the cure of souls. They gave up the study of the Scriptures in order to preach Plato from the pulpit. The very art and music which they encouraged were instruments of demoralisation rather than of popular instruction. Most terrible was the eloquence with which he attacked the authors of such abuses. "How have *you* renounced the Devil and his pomps?" he exclaimed in one of his sermons—"you, who every day do his works, and attend not to the law of Christ, but the literature of the Gentiles; declaring the Scriptures to contain only food fit for women, and demanding in their place the eloquence of Tully and the sounding words of the poets to be preached to you!" On no subject were his strictures more unsparing than on the education of the young. He built his hopes of reform not on his grown-up hearers and converts; but on the children, for whose benefit he sought to introduce a system of studies, the principles of which in the main coincided with those of the ancient Christian schools. He did not propose the exclusion of the heathen poets and philosophers, but demanded that no lesson in Pagan literature should be given without a simultaneous one from Christian sources; that the Scriptures should be ever in the hand of the professor; that St. Jerome and St. Augustine should be studied together with Homer and Cicero; that no book of immoral tendency should be tolerated in the schools; and that teachers should not fail to point out to their pupils the folly and impiety of the heathen fables.

Savonarola had the satisfaction of effecting not a few conversions among the men of letters who gathered round his pulpit. Ficinus became his warm apologist, and after listening to his sermons declared his intention of devoting the rest of his life to religion. Nicholas of Schomberg and Zenobius Acciajoli abandoned the world, and assumed the Dominican habit. Picus Mirandola sold all his estates and distributed the price to the poor, and even Politian on his death-bed received the habit of religion from the hand of one of his friars. But whatever were the success gained by the preacher among the Florentine courtiers, his eloquence was powerless over the mind of their master. Lorenzo and Savonarola each tried to gain the other, and each was doomed to suffer defeat. Lorenzo vainly tried to corrupt or silence an orator who was equally indifferent to threats or bribes; and when the prince lay on his death-bed, Savonarola, as vainly, strove to wring from him a promise to restore her liberties to Florence. After his death, indeed, which took place in 1492, a brilliant triumph seemed to crown the hopes of the popular friar, and under his leadership, Florence, having expelled the Medici, seemed about to exchange her debased republicanism for a theocracy, and her free life of pleasure for an almost puritanic severity of manners. But the tide of social corruption which had for a moment been thus forcibly dammed up, soon burst the barrier that opposed it, and swept away all traces of the seeming reform, the reformer himself being the first victim of its fury. Those very streets of Florence which had witnessed the Medicean carnival shows, and where a little later the Florentines, under the direction of their republican chief, had made solemn acts of reparation for past license, now saw the reformer himself borne to ignominious execution amid the howls and blasphemies of an infuriated populace.

The expulsion of the Medici from Florence in no way checked the progress of the classical Renaissance, which only attained its full growth in the following generation. To the age of Lorenzo the Magnificent succeeded that of his son Pope Leo X., under whose princely rule Rome drew to herself the literary throngs who had before illuminated the Tuscan court, and rejoiced in the questionable glories of a second Augustan age. But of Rome and her Pontiffs, her garish splendour and her true reform, we shall speak in another chapter. Before doing so we must first look across the Alps, and see what has been going on in the world of letters in the colder climate of the North.

CHAPTER XXI.

DEVENTER, LOUVAIN, AND ALCALA.

A.D. 1360 TO 1517.

IT is not to be supposed that the development which had been taken by the universities, and which we have been engaged in tracing in the foregoing chapters, the perils to which their younger members were exposed, and the yet graver results that might be expected to ensue to faith and morals if their influence continued without some salutary check, could fail, even in their own day, of attracting the attention of thoughtful men; and much curious illustration might be drawn from the literature of the fourteenth century, tending to show how questionable a place the great academies of learning at that time held in popular estimation. The most racy legends of mediæval *diablerie* generally introduce us to some student of Paris or Salamanca, who has made a compact with the enemy of souls; while the graver histories of the saints are crowded with examples of those who fled into the cloister to escape the contagion of the schools.

The danger to which the scholastic convertites seem to have been most sensitively alive was not one, perhaps, which, to modern notions, would seem the most appalling. It was not the licentious manners, nor even precisely the heterodox opinions of the schools, which chiefly terrified them, but the subtle perils of intellectual vanity. It has been before remarked that, among the old monastic scholars, the existence of this danger was hardly recognised. The obligations of their state for the most part protected them from its attacks. "What they learnt without guile they communicated without envy,"[312] and they believed and practically set forth the doctrine which, as one of modern times has beautifully expressed it, acknowledges "humility, the basis of morals, to be also the foundation of reason." So entirely did the rules of holy living purge the pursuit of science from the leaven of pride, that it is quite common to find ancient writers speaking of learning as though it were almost a virtue. Things had sadly changed in this respect since the close of the tenth century, and the warnings which St. Bernard addressed to the scholars of his day had to be repeated by the ascetics of each successive age with ever-increasing earnestness. He sorrowfully lamented that those who pursued learning were daily more and more losing sight of its right *order*, its right *motive*, and its right *end*. The order of true knowledge, he said, is to set in the first rank the things that concern salvation; its motive should be charity, and its end, neither curiosity nor vain-glory, but our own or our neighbour's edification. And he failed not to remind the would-be philosophers whom he addressed, and whose chief object seemed to be to make themselves talked about, that the "biting tooth" of the Latin satirist had long before drawn their portraits, and ridiculed those who only care to know in order that somebody else may know that they know.[313] The evils he complained of had certainly not abated with time; nevertheless, the old Christian morality, which was so based on intellectual lowliness as to be hardly capable of realising a fear of the opposite vice until it arose before the eye in all its deformity, was too deeply rooted in Christendom to be eradicated by one or two generations of professors; and its influence may be traced in the horror which good men felt and expressed for what they regarded as a more radical poison than the grosser temptations of an undisciplined life. And we who have witnessed the later issues of that great Revolt of Reason which took its beginnings in the pride of intellect, and which will find its end in the reign of Antichrist, are bound to bear witness that they judged aright, and to applaud a sagacity which originated less perhaps in any very quick-sighted intelligence than in the undulled instincts of the Christian sense.

When, therefore, we represent to ourselves the learned world of the Middle Ages crowding to the universities that were starting up in almost every provincial capital of France, Germany, Italy, and Spain, we must not forget that a quiet undercurrent was always flowing in an opposite direction, though it had no power to overcome the strong full tide of fashion. Thus, the life of the Blessed Peter Jeremias, of the Order of Preachers, presents us with the picture of the student of Bologna about to read for his doctor's degree, when, one night as he sits at his books, the window of his room is dashed in, and the voice of one of his fellow-students, recently departed, warns him in terrible accents to renounce those academic honours, in the greedy pursuit of which he had lost his immortal soul. Peter, pierced to the soul by this voice from beyond the grave, abandons his intention of reading for honours, and presents himself the next morning at the gates of the Dominican Convent to implore admission among the friars. And it was to another conversion of this sort, somewhat less pictorial in its colouring, that we owe the foundation of a very remarkable religious institute, too closely associated with the history of education to be left unnoticed here.

Somewhere about the year 1360 there appeared at Paris a young Flemish student named Gerard, a native of the town of Deventer, whose success in every branch of study acquired him no mean fame in academic circles, and inflated him with a corresponding degree of vanity. He took his master's degree in his eighteenth year, received several rich benefices, began a very pompous and expensive way of life, and at last removed to Cologne, less to study than to display and enjoy himself. There, however, he found his fate awaiting him. It was the precise period when a great spiritual reaction was going on in Rhenish Germany: not twenty years before Cologne had witnessed the conversion of the celebrated John Tauler, whose pride of learning had yielded to the simple word of a nameless unlettered layman, and who spent the rest of his life in preaching those doctrines of self-abnegation on which he built the edifice of the spiritual life. Ruysbroek, the greatest contemplative of his time, was still living in the Green Valley of the forest of Soignies, and training many a fervid soul in the mystic science which aimed at uniting man to God by utterly separating him from creatures. It was probably one of these disciples of Ruysbroek, a religious solitary, whose name, like that of Tauler's "layman," has not been preserved, who determined to undertake the conversion of the gay young canon, in whom, despite his vanity and his love of the world, he detected the promise of more excellent things.

The biographer of Gerard has told the story of his conversion briefly enough, and compressed the arguments of the orator into one brief sentence, *Quid hic stas, vanis intentus? Alius homo fieri debes.* And another man Gerard indeed became. He flung the world behind his back, and entered on a life of penance with no less ardour than that with which he had applied himself awhile before to the business of the schools. For three years he retired among the Carthusians and wholly disappeared from the world; and when he returned there was little of the old Gerard about him. He at once devoted himself to the work of preaching, and generally preached twice a day, his sermons being seldom less than three hours in length. But it was difficult to weary a German congregation of that enthusiastic period, and no complaints appear to have been made of Gerard's prolixity. During his retirement he had placed himself under the direction of Ruysbroek, and appears to have caught much of his tone and spirit. He had made the Scriptures his only study, and these, expounded with simple eloquence from earnest lips, drew him crowds of hearers, "clergy and laity, men and women, little and great, learned and unlearned, lawyers and magistrates, bond and free, rich and poor, beggars and pilgrims." He laid the axe to the root of the tree, and like St. John Baptist, called on all men to do worthy works of penance. In short, he gave the age what it wanted, and though he met with many contradictions, he also effected many practical reforms.

Gerard the Great, as he was called, soon reckoned a considerable number of disciples, whom he made it his chief object to ground in the spiritual life; and in spite of his renown as one of the most learned doctors of his time, he thoroughly inculcated the lesson of intellectual humility. Out of the ranks of his followers was gradually formed a sort of fraternity or congregation; and he had conceived the design of founding for their reception certain monasteries under the rule of the Canons Regular, in which purpose he was greatly encouraged by Ruysbroek. Gerard died before he was able to put his plans into execution, but they were carried out by his disciples, and specially by Master Florentius Radewyns, a canon of Utrecht, a former student at the university of Prague. The new religious assumed the title of "Brethren of the Common Life;" their mother house was at Deventer, they lived like monks, though without at first taking the religious vows, and their employment was the correction and transcription of books, which formed their principal source of revenue. Gerard, in the rule he had drawn up for his own guidance, had prohibited all profane studies. He desired that his children should exclusively addict themselves to the reading of the Scriptures and the Fathers, not wasting their time over "such vanities as geometry, arithmetic, rhetoric, logic, grammar, lyric poetry, and judicial astrology." In the rigorism of these views we detect the spirit of one who has tasted of a poisoned cup, and knows no other security than a rule of total abstinence. He specially forbids all gainful studies, which obscure and obliquify the human reason, and do not tend to God; and he roundly asserts that very few persons who follow the pursuits of law or medicine are ever found who live a just, honest, and quiet life. No doubt his principles were extreme, and it is some consolation to find that he admitted of certain dispensations. The wiser of the Gentile philosophers, such as Plato and Socrates, might, he admitted, be read with profit. Seneca also was to be tolerated, and with an amiable inconsistency we find him, even in his rule of life, slipping in, half unconsciously, a quotation from Virgil.

All this was exactly what might have been expected from a converted man of the world; but Florentius had gone through a different kind of experience, and one which made his views less austere and exclusive. He had passed the ordeal of a university career unscathed, and his biographer expends an entire chapter in bringing forward proofs why the name he bore was specially appropriate to one whose life from childhood had been so holy and unspotted. Not only was he himself a flower of all perfection, but he was also destined to make the houses he governed flower-beds from which spiritual bees were to suck the honey of wisdom; his brethren were to give out to a naughty world the sweet odour of virtue, according to that of the Spouse in the Canticles, "The flowers have appeared in our land." Florentius was the model of a good scholar, kind to his equals, respectful to his superiors, a proficient in the liberal arts, but keeping his heart for the Divine law, which he loved and studied far more diligently than he did the book of the Gentiles.

Under his superiority the labours of the brethren were made to embrace a larger sphere of usefulness, and to include the education of youth. The prohibition against profane learning speedily disappeared, and the schools of Deventer attained high celebrity; and there, in 1393, a little scholar, Thomas Hammerlein by name, was admitted under the roof of Florentius, becoming afterwards the biographer of his revered master, and the reputed author of the "Following of Christ."

Not to enter into the vexed question whether he were indeed the author, or only the transcriber, of that first of uninspired books, it is yet satisfactory to know that the Thomas à Kempis, whom from infancy we have been used to revere, is not reduced by the investigations of ruthless critics to a mere mythical existence. He really lived, wrote, taught, and prayed. In the college of Deventer he studied grammar and plain-chant under Florentius, and tells us how, when present in choir with his schoolfellows, he loved stealthily to watch his master, because of his devout aspect, being cautious, however, that his pious curiosity was not perceived, inasmuch as the good rector could make himself feared as well as loved. He takes us into the school, too, and shows us the master setting copies, and praising the flexible fingers of a little disciple, whom, with the blessing of God, he hopes to form into a good writer. Or we enter the cell of the devout brother, Gerard of Zutphen, whose whole consolation lay in holy books, and who was liable to get so absorbed in the study of them, that a charitable brother had to come and warn him when the bell had rung for dinner. He was the librarian, and had a passing great care for his books; but as for himself and his corporeal wants, if superiors and companions had not seen to them better than he did himself, he would have fared but poorly. He thought so highly of the benefits to be derived from useful reading, that he lent his books to ecclesiastics out of doors, to win them from idle and frivolous amusements. "Books," he would say, "preach better than we can do." And therefore he held them in great reverence, read them lovingly, and copied them with the utmost diligence. Nor must we omit to mention the pious cook, John Ketel, the saint of the community, as all, by common consent, seem to have regarded him. Florentius knew his merit, and to increase it never gave him a civil word; but his humility and sweetness were proof against every trial. Or that devout clerk, Arnold Schoonhove, a schoolfellow of Thomas, who never played in the streets with other idle boys, and when he sat in school with them heeded not their childish pranks, but steadily wrote down the master's words on paper, and got a chosen comrade (who was probably Thomas himself) to read over the lesson to him, or hear him repeat it. "It was God whom he chiefly sought in his studies," says his friend, "and what he liked best was to get into a quiet corner and pray." After seven years' study among the Brethren of Common Life, Thomas took the habit of the Canons Regular in the monastery of St. Agnes, at Zwoll, where he lived till his ninety-second year, engaged in useful labours, transcribing and composing pious books, which earned for him the sobriquet of the Hammer of Hearts. He has left us memorials of his monastery and his college-life, written with a sweet simplicity which reminds us of Bede. Of his own life we know but little, yet that little has a character of its own. His world was his cell; he was never quite happy out of it, and if sometimes induced by his brethren to go abroad and take a little air, he would soon contrive to get away, with the transparent excuse, that "Some one was waiting for him in his chamber." The others would smile, knowing well Who He was of Whom he spoke, even the Beloved, of Whom it is written that He stands at the door and knocks. In all the books that he transcribed he wrote his favourite motto, "Everywhere I sought for rest, but I found it nowhere save in a little corner, with a little book." And a certain old and much-defaced picture was long preserved, which represented his effigies surrounded with the legend, which must here be added in its original phraseology:—"In omnibus requiem quæsivi, sed non inveni, *nisi in Hoexkins ende Boexkins.*"

In process of time the Brethren of Common Life spread over Flanders, France, and Germany, and the schools they founded multiplied and flourished. They were introduced into the University of Paris by John Standonch, a doctor of the Sorbonne, who gave into their direction the College de Montaigu, of which he was the principal, and established them in Cambray, Valenciennes, Mechlin, and Louvain. He drew up statutes for their use, which are supposed by Du Boulay to have furnished St. Ignatius with the first notions of his rule, an idea which receives some corroboration from the fact that the saint studied at the College de Montaigu during his residence at the University of Paris. Standonch himself received the habit of the Poor Clerks, as they were now often called, and had the satisfaction of seeing more than 300 good scholars issue from his schools, many of whom undertook the direction or reform of other academies. In 1430 the Institute numbered forty-five houses, and thirty years later the numbers were increased threefold. The Deventer brethren were far from being mere mystics and transcribers of books. The aim of their foundation was doubtless to supply a system of education which should revive something of the old monastic discipline, but they cultivated all the higher branches of learning, and their schools were among the first of those north of the Alps which introduced the revived study of classical literature. One of their most illustrious scholars was Nicholas of Cusa, or Cusanus, the son of a poor fisherman, who won his doctor's cap at Padua, and became renowned for his Greek, Hebrew, and mathematical learning. Eugenius IV. appointed him his legate, and Nicholas V. created him Cardinal and Bishop of Brixen, in the Tyrol. His personal character won him the veneration of his people, but, according to Tennemann, his love of mathematics led him into many theological extravagances. He was strongly inclined to the views of the Neo-Platonists; he considered, moreover, that all human knowledge was contained in the ideas of numbers, and attempted to explain the mystery of the Holy Trinity on mathematical principles. He was undoubtedly a distinguished man of science, and was the first among moderns to revive the Pythagorean hypothesis of the motion of the earth round the sun. Cusanus had studied at most of the great universities, but held none of them in great esteem, for he professed a sovereign contempt for the scholastic philosophy which still held its ground in those academies. At his death he left his wealth to an hospital which he had founded in his native village, and to which he attached a magnificent library. Deventer could boast indeed of being the fruitful mother of great scholars, such as Hegius, Langius, and Dringeberg, all of whom afterwards took part in the restoration of letters. The brethren, moreover, displayed extraordinary zeal in promoting the new art of printing, and one of the earliest Flemish presses was set up in their college. And in 1475, when Alexander Hegius became rector of the schools, he made the first bold experiment of printing Greek.

It is not to be supposed that such a revolution as that which was brought about in the world of letters by the new invention could fail of producing events of a mixed character of good and evil. Whatever was fermenting in the minds of the people now found expression through the press, and Hallam notices "the incredible host of popular religious tracts poured forth" before the close of the fifteenth century, most of them of a character hostile to the faith. The first censorship of printed books appears to have been established in 1480, by Berthold, Archbishop of Mentz, who explained his reasons for taking this step in a mandate, wherein he complains of the abuse of the "divine art" of printing, whereby perverse men have turned that to the injury of mankind which was designed for their instruction. Specially he alludes to those unauthorised and faulty translations into the vulgar tongue of the Scriptures, and even the canons of the Church, wherein men of no learning or experience have taken on them to invent new words or use old ones in erroneous senses, in order to express the meaning of the original, "a thing most dangerous in the Sacred Scriptures." He therefore forbids any such translations to be thenceforward published without being approved by four doctors, under pain of excommunication, desiring that the art which was first of all discovered in his city, "not without divine aid," should be maintained in all its honour.

This mandate was only directed against the faulty translations of the Holy Scriptures. No opposition was offered to the multiplication of correct versions, both of the Latin Vulgate and its various translations. The Cologne Bible, printed in 1479, had before this appeared, with the formal approbation of the university. The very first book printed by Gutenburg and Fust in 1453, was the Latin Bible, and among the twenty-four books printed in Germany before the year 1470 we find five Latin and two German editions of the Bible. Translations of the Holy Scriptures into various modern tongues were among the very first books issued from the press; as the Bohemian version in 1475, Italian in 1471—which ran through eleven editions before the close of the century, the Dutch in 1477, and the French in the same year. The admirers of Luther have therefore fallen into a strange error, when they represent him as the first to unlock the Scriptures to the people, for twenty-four editions of the German Bible alone had been printed and published before his time.

It was in the year 1476 that a little choir-boy of Utrecht entered the college of Deventer, and gave such signs of genius and industry as to draw from his masters the prediction that he would one day be the light of his age. He was a namesake of the founder, but, after the fashion of the day, adopted a Latin and Greek version of his Flemish name of Gerard, and was to be known to posterity as Desiderius Erasmus. Like Thomas à Kempis, he passed from the schools of Deventer to the cloisters of the Canons Regular, a step which, he assures us, was forced on him by his guardians, and never had his own assent. A happy accident enabled him to visit Rome in the suite of the Bishop of Cambray and once released from the wearisome discipline of convent life, he never returned to it, but spent the rest of his life wandering from one to another of the capitals of France, Italy, and England, teaching for a livelihood, courted by all the literary and religious parties of the day, and satirising them all by turns, indisputably the literary Coryphæus of his age, but penetrated through and through with its scoffing and presumptuous spirit. It was an age fruitful in pedants and humanists, whose destiny it was to help on the revolution in faith by a revolution in letters. Schools and professors multiplied throughout Germany. At the very time when Hegius was teaching the elements of Greek to Erasmus, his old comrades Langius and Dringeberg were presiding over the schools of Munster and Schelstadt. Rodolph Langius exerted himself strenuously in the cause of polite letters, and whilst superintending his classes occupied spare moments in correcting the text of almost every Latin work which at that time issued from the press, and in making deadly war on the scholastic philosophy. His rejection of the old-fashioned school-books and his innovations on time-honoured abuses raised against him the friars of Cologne, and a controversy ensued in which Langius won so much success as enabled him to affix the stigma of barbarism on his opponents. His friend and namesake Rodolph Agricola, who had studied at Ferrara under Theodore of Gaza, and was held by his admirers superior in erudition to Politian himself, at this time presided over the school of Groningen. Besides his skill in the learned tongues he was a poet, a painter, a musician, an orator, and a philosopher. Such a multitude of accomplishments won him an invitation to the court of the Elector Palatine at Heidelberg, where a certain learned academy had been founded, called the Rhenish Society, for the encouragement of Greek and Hebrew literature, the members of which, says Hallam, "did not scorn to relax their minds with feasting and dancing, not forgetting the ancient German attachment to the flowing cup." This is a polite way of rendering a very ugly passage, which in the original tells us plainly that the Rhenish academicians were addicted to excessive inebriety and other disgraceful vices. It is somewhat remarkable, however, that Agricola, who died three years after his removal to Heidelberg, received on his death-bed the habit of those very friars whom, during life, he and his friend Langius had done their best to hold up to popular contempt.

About the same time Reuchlin was studying at Paris, where, in 1458, Gregory of Tiferno had been appointed Greek professor. Reuchlin visited Rome, and translated a passage from Thucydides in the presence of Argyrophilus, with such success that the Greek exclaimed, in a transport of delight (and possibly of surprise, at such an achievement on the part of a Northern barbarian), "Our banished Greece has flown beyond the Alps!" Reuchlin was a Hebrew scholar, a circumstance which, in the end, proved his ruin; for, embracing the Cabalistic philosophy, he abandoned classics and good sense in the pursuit of that absurd mysticism. In this strange infatuation he had many companions. Not a few of those who had shown themselves foremost in deriding the scholastic philosophy, ended by substituting in its place either open scepticism or the philosophy of magic. A few years later, the wild theories of Cornelius Agrippa, Paracelsus, and Jerome Cardan, found eager adherents among those who conceived it a proof of good scholarship to despise St. Thomas as a Goth. Reuchlin, whilst pouring forth his bitter satires against the old theologians, was printing his treatise on the Cabala, entitled *De Verbo Mirifico*, wherein magic is declared to be the perfection of philosophy, which work was formally condemned at Rome. However, all the French savants of the Renaissance were not Cabalists, nor did all, when they introduced the study of Greek, forget that it was the language of the Gospels. The real restoration of Greek studies in France must be ascribed to Budæus, who made up, by the piety and indefatigable studies of his later years, for a youth of wild irregularity. He had studied under Lascaris, and though he had reached a very mature age before he devoted himself to letters, he soon became as familiar with the learned tongues as with his native idiom. His treatise on the Ancient Money first rendered his name famous, and secured him the friendship of Francis I. He profited from the favour shown him by that monarch, to solicit from him the foundation of the Royal College of France, for the cultivation of the three learned tongues, and thus fairly introduced the "Cecropian Muse" into the University of Paris. If we may credit the authority of a grave rector of that university, this momentous change was advantageous, not merely to the minds but also to the morals of her students. St. Jerome, as we know, imposed upon himself the study of Hebrew as an efficacious means of taming the passions; and Rollin affirms that many who, in former years, had been nothing but idle men of pleasure, when once they began to read the Greek authors flung their vices and follies to the winds, and led the simple and austere manner of life that becomes a scholar. He quotes a passage from the manuscript Memoirs of Henry de Mesmes, which gives a pleasant picture of the college life of those days, and may be taken as an example of the sort of labour imposed on a hard-working law student of the sixteenth century:—"My father," he says, "gave me for a tutor John Maludan of Limoges, a pupil of the learned Durat, who was chosen for the innocence of his life and his suitable age to preside over my early years, till I should be old enough to govern myself. With him and my brother, John James de Mesmes, I was sent to the college of Burgundy, and was put into the third class and I afterwards spent almost a year in the first. My father said he had two motives for thus sending me to the college: the one was the cheerful and innocent conversation of the boys, and the other was the school discipline, by which he trusted that we should be weaned from the over-fondness that had been shown us at home, and purified, as it were, in fresh water. Those eighteen months I passed at college were of great service to me. I learnt to recite, to dispute, and to speak in public; and I became acquainted with several excellent men, many of whom are still living. I learned, moreover, the frugality of the scholar's life, and how to portion out my day to advantage; so that, by the time I left, I had repeated, in public, abundance of Latin, and two thousand Greek verses, which I had written after the fashion of boys of my age, and I could repeat Homer from one end to the other. I was thus well received by the chief men of my time, to some of whom my tutor introduced me. In 1545, I was sent to Toulouse with my tutor and brother, to study law under an old grey-haired professor, who had travelled half over the world. There we remained for three years, studying severely, and under such strict rules as I fancy few persons nowadays would care to comply with. We rose at four, and, having said our prayers, went to lectures at five, with our great books under our arms, and our inkhorns and candlesticks in our hands. We attended all the lectures until ten o'clock, without intermission; then we went to dinner, after having hastily collated during half an hour what our master had written down. After dinner, by way of diversion, we read Sophocles, or Aristophanes, or Euripides, and sometimes Demosthenes, Tully, Virgil, and Horace. At one we were at our studies again, returning home at five to repeat and turn to the places quoted in our books till past six. Then came supper, after which we read some Greek or Latin author. On feast days we heard mass and vespers, and the rest of the day we were allowed a little music and walking. Sometimes we went to see our friends, who invited us much oftener than we were permitted to go. The rest of the day we spent in reading, and we generally had with us some learned men of that time."

We have the satisfaction of knowing that the frugal and laborious training of Henry's early life was the means of forming a manly and Christian character. Nor is the portrait less pleasing which the biographer of Budæus has left us of the domestic life of that great man, who, though he had visited the court of Leo X., in quality of ambassador of France, and was the chief lion of the French world of letters, retained to his dying day those simple tastes and habits, which we are assured resulted from no affectation of laconic manners, but a certain genuine sentiment of humility.[314] His secretary and constant fellow-labourer was his wife, who sat in his study, found out passages in his books of reference, copied his papers, and withal did not forget his domestic comfort. Budæus needed some such good angel by his side, for he belonged to that class of scholars who are more familiar with the Latin *As* than with the value of louis d'ors. His mind was in his books, and whilst busy with the doings of the Greeks and Romans he could not always call home his absent thoughts. It is to be regretted, that with a character in many respects so amiable, Budæus should have permitted his love of Greek to lead him to take part with the Humanists in the ferocious onslaughts which they directed against the adherents of the mediæval learning. It was surely possible to revive the study of Homer and Cicero with rejecting the philosophy of St. Thomas, nor did there seem any reason why the lovers of polite literature should seek to establish their fame as scholars by savage and unseemly pasquinades on their literary rivals. And here it may be remarked that the title of *Humanists*, applied to the rising school, was one of their own choosing. By it they intended at one and the same time to indicate themselves as the only cultivators of "humane" letters, and to imply that the professors of the old school were barbarians. They were not content with advocating good Latin, and reviving the study of Greek; no one could join their camp who was not ready to rail at monks and schoolmen as offensive idiots. The former, in the choice vocabulary of Luther, were "locusts, caterpillars, frogs, and lice," the latter, in the more polished phraseology of Budæus, "prating sophists," and "divines of the Sorbonian Lake," "Monks," says Erasmus (himself an apostate canon[315]), "are only acceptable to silly women, bigots, and blockheads." The Dominicans had the audacity to protest against the freedoms he had taken with the Latin Vulgate, and to complain of his version as that of a poet and orator rather than of a divine. "Most men who know anything of the value of a poet," replies Erasmus, "think *you* to be swine rather than men, when they hear your stupid raving. Poetry is so little known to you, that you cannot even spell its name;[316] but let me tell you, it would be easier to cut two *Thomists* out of a log of wood, than one tolerable orator." No matter what were a man's talents, or how reasonable were his arguments, the moment he opened his mouth in opposition to these writers, he was placarded as a dunce. Erasmus, in his new Version of the Greek Testament, had given just cause of complaint by his use of a phraseology more elegant than theological. A certain Franciscan friar ventured to object in particular to his rendering of the Magnificat, whereupon Erasmus vented his spleen in a Colloquy, and branded the critic as "a pig and a donkey; more of a donkey than all donkeys put together;" and proceeded to justify his translation by quoting the comedies of Terence. Standish, Bishop of St. Asaph, took exception to another blot in the new version, the substitution, namely, of the word *Sermo*, for that of *Verbum*, in the first chapter of St. John's Gospel; and Erasmus and his friends considered that they sufficiently vindicated their good Latin by nicknaming the objector, the *Bishop of St. Ass.* In the same style of wit, Vincent the Dominican was *Bucentum* the ox-driver, and the Carmelites were commonly designated the *Camelites.* "I have hopes of Cochlæus," writes Luther, speaking of some of his adversaries, "he is only an idiot; as for the other two, they belong to the devil." This was the ordinary style of the humanist controversialists; their puns and sarcasms being, in most cases, accompanied with a shower of mud.

With these, however, we need not more particularly concern ourselves, but turn our glance on Louvain, where, in the early part of the century, a new university had arisen, under Duke John of Brabant, which received its first diploma from Pope Martin V. in 1425, the theological faculty being erected six years later by Eugenius IV. The latter Pontiff had the satisfaction of receiving the firmest support from the Louvain doctors during the troublous times of the Council of Basle; and during the following century Louvain continued to be not merely the chief seat of learning in Flanders, but one of the soundest nurseries of the faith. She held stoutly to scholasticism, and was distinguished by her resolute opposition to the Lutheran heretics; yet it was in vain that her enemies attempted to charge her with retrogression, for even Erasmus owns in his letters, that the schools of Louvain were considered second only to those of Paris.

It is not difficult to explain the hostility which the Louvain scholars had to encounter on the part of the partisans of the new learning. Louvain, from the first, consecrated herself to the defence of the scholastic theology. Immediately on the erection of the theological faculty in 1431, the Dominicans arrived at Louvain, and opened a school whence they sent forth fourteen doctors in the space of twenty years. In 1447 they were formally admitted to all the rights of the university, and obtained chairs of theology, and the other privileges formerly granted to them at Paris and Bologna. Their brethren were frequently aggregated to the college of the strict faculty, and one of their order was always a member of the council *strictæ facultatis.* From this period the *studium generale* of the order at Louvain ranked as one of the highest character in the order, and the influence of the Dominican doctors made itself powerfully felt throughout the whole university. St. Thomas of Aquin was *the* doctor, *par excellence*, of the Louvain schools, and in 1637 was chosen by the faculty of theology their perpetual patron and protector. It is needless to say that this determined *Thomism* was not more agreeable to the humanists and their partisans than the *Scotism* of the Paris theologians; and they sought, with very poor success, to squib down the university by representing it as nothing but a nest of friars.

The University of Louvain enjoyed some advantages in which the more ancient academies had been wanting. Not having grown up out of accidental circumstances, like so many of her elder sisters, but having been begun at a time when the principles necessary for governing such institutions had been made manifest by long experience, her founders were careful to provide her, from the first, with a body of statutes sagaciously drawn up, so as to ensure the preservation of regular discipline; and a well-organised collegiate system protected the students from those disorders which had disgraced the beginnings of Paris and Oxford.

In course of time separate schools and colleges were established for the different faculties, one for medicine, eight for arts, and eight for mixed studies. Among the latter was Standonch's college of poor scholars, and the celebrated *Collegium Trilingue* founded in 1516 by Jerome Busleiden, the friend of More and Erasmus, for the study of Greek, Latin, and Hebrew. The idea of this academy had been suggested to the founder by a visit to Alcala, where Cardinal Ximenes was then completing the establishment of his university. Hallam tells us that its foundation was fiercely opposed by the monks and friars, "those unbeaten enemies of learning," and it is true that the old professors did at first regard the new institution with some jealousy. They had been used to write and speak mediæval Latin, and grumbled sorely when required to turn Ciceronians. The college happened to be first opened in the fish-market, and hence arose the favourite bon-mot of the Louvain Conservatives, "*We* do not talk *Fish-Market* Latin." In time, however, the fish-market Latin established its supremacy, and Louvain grew proud of her classical professors, such as Louis Vives and Conrad Goclen. The colleges gradually multiplied in number, and even at the present day the city is filled with splendid buildings, all of which owe their existence to the university of which they once formed part.

It was at Louvain that Pope Adrian VI. received his education, and from a poor scholar rose to fill the posts of professor and rector of the university. The son of a boat-builder of Utrecht, he was admitted among a certain number of poor boys whom the university bound itself to educate gratuitously, and endured rather more than his share of the hardships and privations to which scholars of that class are usually exposed. Seldom able to provide himself with the luxury of a lamp or a candle, he was accustomed to prosecute his studies after dark in the porch of some church, where a lamp was then usually suspended, or at the street corner, which supplied him with a feeble light. However, he seems sometimes to have been able to procure himself a better sort of light, for we read that, one cold winter's night, Margaret, the widow of Duke Charles of Burgundy, then governess of the Netherlands, remarked a tiny ray that issued from one of the college windows at a very late hour, and bidding her chamberlain find out which of the students sat up so late in such intense cold, she was told that it was only "little Florentius" over his books. With a woman's instinct of compassion, she sent him the next day three hundred florins for the purchase of books and firewood.

When he was afterwards raised to the head of the university, he exhibited the same zeal for the promotion of ecclesiastical discipline which afterwards won him so much unpopularity from his Roman subjects. In spite of their contemptuous strictures on his supposed barbarism, Adrian was revered in Louvain as a generous patron of letters. He erected and endowed one of the most magnificent colleges of which Louvain could boast, and in it was deposited the autograph copy of his works, which is still preserved in the great seminary of Mechlin.

A considerable number of other new universities sprang up in Germany about the beginning of the sixteenth century, all more or less stamped with the literary character of the age. Of these the most famous was Wittemberg, marked out by an evil destiny as the cradle of the Lutheran apostasy. It was founded in 1502 by Frederic, elector of Saxony, who commissioned Staupitz, the provincial of the Augustinians, to seek out men of learning and ability to fill its vacant professorships. Luther was invited hither in 1508 to teach the Aristotelian logic, and, four years later, after his return from Rome, received his doctor's cap, and took the customary oaths to defend the faith against heresy to the last drop of his blood. In 1516 the professor was to be found waging open war against the philosophy he was engaged to teach, and drawing up ninety-nine theses against the scholastic theology, in which is clearly laid down the fundamental dogma of Lutheranism—the denial of free-will. They were published many years later with a preface by Melancthon, declaring them to contain the veritable sum of the reformed religion, which had thus been reduced to system a year before that quarrel with Tetzel, usually represented as the origin of Luther's revolt.

Melancthon was given the chair of Greek in 1518, on the recommendation of his master Reuchlin, and was introduced to Wittemberg at the moment when Luther's quarrel had been taken up by the students and professors. In him Luther gained a disciple whose learning and natural moderation of character were worthy of better things than to become the author of the Confession of Augsburg, and the colleague of Bucer. That horrible apostate, a renegade Dominican, who condescended to every one of the rival schools of heresy, provided only he was suffered to enjoy the license which first tempted him to abjure the faith, filled for twenty years the theological chair at Strasburg. Everywhere the reins of power had fallen into the hands of the pedagogues, and the Lutheran army was to be seen officered by humanists and university professors. The facilities offered by the numerous academies that had sprung up since the beginning of the century encouraged a rage for learning among all classes, and many a poor artisan's son, like Wolfgang Musculus, or the notorious Henry Bullinger, scraped together a scanty pittance by street singing, which they afterwards spent in procuring the means of study at one or other of the universities. Musculus, indeed, found charitable patrons in the person of some Benedictine monks, who educated him, and gave him the habit; but he soon abandoned the cloister, and after a wild adventurous life, during which we find him working as a mason, and, during the scanty moments he could snatch from his toil, studying the Hebrew grammar, he became "Minister" of Strasburg, and theological professor in the Protestant University of Berne. About the same time the Greek professorship of Calvin's college at Geneva was filled with another of these strange itinerant scholars, Sebastian Castillon, a native of Dauphiny, who studied the Oriental tongues in the early morning hours, before he went to his day labour in the fields. He afterwards quarrelled with Calvin, who accused him of theft, and went to teach Greek and Hebrew at Basle. Here he produced a Latin and French version of the Scriptures, and endeavoured to render the sacred books into the classical diction of profane authors. We can scarcely form any correct idea of the period of the Reformation without a glimpse at men of this stamp, who then swarmed in every part of Germany; restless, self-sufficient, often more than half self-taught, their minds untrained with the healthy discipline of the schools, disposed to run after every novelty, and to overvalue themselves and their attainments, they inevitably fell into the extravagances to which vanity commonly betrays her victims.

From this class of men the German professorships were chiefly recruited, and little foresight was needed to anticipate the consequences which must ensue when the work of education had passed into such hands. The state of the German universities during the century subsequent to the Lutheran revolution, has been described by the Protestant historian Menzel, from whom Rohrbacher has quoted some remarkable passages. "The colleges where the future ministers of the Lutheran religion spent six or seven years, were the abode of a ferocity and licentiousness from which our moral sensibility shrinks aghast. In the German schools and universities, the elder students obliged new-comers to go about in ragged garments, filled their mouths with 'soup' made of mud and broken bits of earthenware, compelled them to clean their boots and shoes, and by way of salary, to imitate the barking of dogs and the mewing of cats, and to lick up the filth from under the table. In vain did the princes endeavour to banish these savage customs; they held their ground in spite of ordinances and edicts."[317] At the University of Jena, the younger students were robbed of their money, their clothes, and their books by their elder companions, and compelled to discharge the most disgraceful services. Those who had received what was called "absolution," treated new-comers in the same way; and these outrages were often committed in the streets, and even in the churches during the preaching, when the poor victims were pulled and knocked about, and otherwise maltreated by their persecutors. And that no one might escape, a particular part of the church was devoted to the reception of "freshmen," who were installed there with these edifying ceremonies. Hence, during the whole time of divine service, one incessant clamour went on, made up of the trampling, the cries, the murmurs, and coarse laughter of the combatants.

If such were the manners of the future pastors, those of their flocks may be imagined. Any one who tried to lead a good life, observes Menzel, was stigmatised as an enthusiast, a Schwenkfeldian, an Anabaptist, and a hypocrite; Luther's dogma of justification by faith only having brought good works into actual discredit. It was dangerous at that time for a preacher to exhort his people to keep the commandments—as if they were able to do so—it was quite sufficient to render him a suspected person.[318] But we have no heart to dwell on this subject, or to realise the degradation of those old German dioceses and schools, the names of which are so linked in our hearts with the memory of St. Boniface and St. Wilibald, St. Bernward and St. Anscharius. So we will turn our back on Germany and seek on Catholic soil for some more consoling spectacle. We shall hardly find it in France: there, indeed, a revival of letters is going on, under the splendid patronage of Francis I.; and Budæus, the prodigy of his country, as Erasmus called him, is writing his learned treatise on Ancient Money, and persuading the king to found the College Royal. There perhaps the greatest scholar of his time, though known to posterity chiefly by his artistic fame, Leonardo da Vinci, is expiring at Fontainebleau in the arms of the king. But the French Renaissance school is mostly remarkable for its poets, by whom, indeed, the revival of letters was first set on foot. Much edification was not to be anticipated from a movement that reckoned as its originator Villon, whose verses were as infamous as his life, and who found a worthy successor in Clement Marot. The French kings, who by their Pragmatic Sanctions[319] had condemned the Papal provision of benefices as a crying abuse, used their royal patronage of the same as a convenient mode of rewarding Court poets. Thus Octavien de St. Gelais, the translator of Terence, obtained the bishopric of Angoulême from Charles VIII.; and his son, Melin de St. Gelais, surnamed the French Ovid, was rewarded by Francis I. for his "Epigrams" with an abbey. Ronsard, formally proclaimed "the Poet of France, *par excellence*," who was born on the same day as the defeat of Pavia—as though (to make use of the king's words) "Heaven would make up to France, by his birth, for the disgrace sustained by her arms"—who was the literary idol of his time, had statues erected to his honour, and silver images of the goddess Minerva presented to him by learned academies, to whom Elizabeth sent a rich diamond, and Mary Stuart presented a gilded model of Parnassus—the most appropriate present that could be offered to the new Apollo—Ronsard, the vainest of men, as he might well be, for assuredly he was the most flattered, died, literally overwhelmed under the weight of his laurels and his priories. I will not attempt the enumeration of his benefices, and perhaps he would hardly have undertaken the task himself, for the prince of poets enjoyed the revenues of half the royal monasteries of France. It would be unbecoming to notice any writer of less renown, after so very illustrious a personage, and the bare name of Rabelais will probably content most readers. These were the stars of the French Renaissance, well worthy of the monarch who patronised them, and the Court over which he presided. Warton has thought good to praise the enlightened wisdom which induced this prince to purge his Court from the monkish precision of old-fashioned times, and enliven it with a larger admixture of ladies' society. There was certainly not much to be complained of on the score of precision in the coteries of Fontainebleau; yet it is curious that the fair dames who graced the royal circle were chosen by the grim disciples of Calvin as the likeliest agents for disseminating their views. The ladies of the Court of Francis I. were the first Huguenot apostles, and it was in this school that Anne Boleyn, in her quality of maid of honour to Queen Claude, acquired, together with her inimitable skill in dancing, that "gospel light" which, the poet informs us, first shone on England and her king "from Boleyn's eyes."

Let us rather direct our steps across the Pyrenees, and watch the erection of a Catholic university on the orthodox soil of Spain. Up to this time the education which prevailed in the peninsula appears to have been thoroughly of the old school. The Spanish universities had indeed some peculiarities arising from their proximity to the Moorish schools, and appear to have cultivated the geometrical sciences and the Eastern tongues more generally than was elsewhere the practice. But the prevailing tone was scholastic and ecclesiastical. The monasteries still maintained those public schools, which served as feeders to the universities, and in these a discipline was kept up differing very little from that of Fulda and St Gall. At Montserrat, peasants and nobles were received together, and each wore a little black habit, and, in church, a surplice. They sang every day at the Mass, and recited the Office of Our Lady, eating always in the refectory of the brethren, and sleeping in a common dormitory. Every month they went to confession, as well as on all festivals, and their studies were of the monastic stamp, with plenty of Latin and plain chant, and also instrumental music. A number of the bravest Spanish knights had their education in these monastery schools, and one of them, John of Cardonna, who commanded the galleys of Sicily, and relieved Malta when besieged by the Turks, chose as his patroness, in memory of his school days, Our Lady of Montserrat, and bore her banner into battle. He used to call himself Our Lady's page, and said he valued the privilege of having been brought up in her house more than his rank as admiral.

But these are old-fashioned memories, and must give place to something more in accordance with the requirements of the age. The Renaissance was making its way even into the Spanish schools, and the literary movement had been fortunate enough to find a nursing mother in the person of Isabella the Catholic. German printers and Italian professors were invited into her kingdom, and Spanish students sent to gather up the treasures of learning in foreign academies. Among these was Antonio de Lebrija, whom Hallam calls the restorer of classical literature in Spain. Italian masters directed the education of the royal children, and from them the Princess Catherine, doomed to be the hapless Queen of Henry VIII., received those learned tastes which won the admiration of Erasmus. A Palatine school was attached to the Court, in imitation of that of Charlemagne, and was placed under the direction of Peter Martyr,[320] whose letters are filled with accounts of the noble pupils who thronged his school, won from frivolous pastimes by the charm of letters. In 1488 he appeared at Salamanca to deliver lectures on Juvenal, and writes word that the audience who came to hear him so blocked up the entrance to the hall, that he had to be carried to his place over the heads of the students, "like a victor in the Olympic games." The rage for learning went on at such a pace that the proudest grandees of Castile thought it not beneath them to ascend the professor's chair, and even noble ladies delivered lectures on classical learning in the halls of universities.[321] The queen's noble encouragement of learning had been fostered by her confessor, F. Francis Ximenes; and when, in 1495, the Franciscan friar became Archbishop of Toledo and Primate of Spain, one of his first thoughts was the erection of a model university, to which he resolved to devote the immense revenues of his see.

It has been said that seats of learning require the accessories of a fine air, and even the charms of natural scenery; and we might quote one of the most exquisite pieces of word-painting to be found in any language,[322] which is written to show the special gift enjoyed by Athens, rendering her worthy to be the capital of mind. It was the clear elastic air of Attica which communicated something of its own sunniness and elasticity to the intellect of her citizens, just as it imparted a golden colouring even to the marble dug out of that favoured soil. So it had been with Paris, the Athens of the Middle Ages, where students from the foggy shores of Britain conceived themselves endowed with some new faculty when relieved from the oppression of their native atmosphere. And even Louvain, though less favoured than these by nature, had been chosen in preference to other Flemish cities, chiefly on account of her purer air and her pleasant *entourage* of copses and meadows, with their abundant store of "corn, apples, sheep, oxen, and chirping birds."

It is not surprising, therefore, that Ximenes, when seeking the fittest spot in which to plant his academy, took very gravely into consideration the question of scenery and climate. The clear atmosphere of Alcala, and the tranquil landscapes on the banks of the Henares, so soothing to the meditative eye, had their share in determining him to fix his foundation at the ancient Complutum. In its grammar schools he had made his early studies, and old boyish recollections attached him to the spot, the ancient traditions of which rendered it dear to Christian scholars.[323] There, then, in the year 1500 he laid the foundation of his first college, which he dedicated to his saintly predecessor, St. Ildefonsus. This was intended to be the head college of the university, to which all the others were in a manner to be subordinate. It consisted of thirty-three professors, in honour of the years of our Lord's earthly life, and twelve priests or chaplains, in honour of the twelve Apostles. These latter had nothing to do with the education of the students, but were to recite the divine office in common, and carry out the rites of the Church with becoming solemnity. The professors, who were all to be theologians, were distinguished by their dress, a long red robe, which, being flung over their left shoulder, hung to the ground in large and graceful folds. The colleges of St. Balbina and St. Catherine were intended for students in philosophy, each containing forty-eight students. There was a small college, dedicated to Our Lady, for poor students in theology and medicine; and a larger one, used for the reception of the sick. The college of SS. Peter and Paul was exclusively for Franciscan scholars, corresponding in character to the monastic colleges or houses of study at Oxford. There were also two classical schools for young students, forty-two of whom received a free education for three years; these were severally dedicated to St. Eugenius and St. Isidore. And lastly, there was the college of St. Jerome for the three languages, in which ten scholars studied Latin, ten Greek, and ten Hebrew; a foundation which, as we have seen, formed the model on which the *Collegium Trilingue* at Louvain was afterwards established.[324] I will say nothing of the libraries, refectories, and chapels, all of which were finished with great splendour; and the whole city was restored and beautified, so as to make it more worthy of being the site of so magnificent a seat of learning. Other houses of study soon sprang up in connection with the different religious orders, all of which were anxious to secure for their members advantages which were nowhere else to be found in such abundance. For though Ximenes was a mighty builder, and thereby exposed himself to many bad puns from Court wits, who made much of the *"edification"* he gave when he superintended his workmen rule in hand, he certainly did not neglect the spiritual for the material building. Eight years after he had solemnly laid the foundation stone of his first college, the university was opened, and a brilliant staff of professors—in all forty-two in number—were gathered round the Cardinal primate to receive their respective offices from his hands. The government of the university was vested in the hands of a chancellor, rector, and senate. The system of graduation was copied from that of Paris, except that the theological degrees were given a pre-eminence over the others, and made both more honourable and more difficult to attain. The professorships were distributed as follows:—Six for theology; six for canon law; four for medicine; one, anatomy; one, surgery; nine, philosophy; one, mathematics; four, Greek and Hebrew; four, rhetoric; and six, grammar. There was no chair of civil law, as this faculty was excellently taught at the other Spanish universities, and Ximenes had no liking for it, and did not wish to introduce it at Alcala, probably fearing lest it might prevent that predominance of the theological faculty which he desired should be the characteristic of his university. Provision was made for the support of the aged and infirm professors; and on this point the Cardinal consulted his former colleague in the regency of Castile, Adrian of Utrecht, and established similar regulations to those which existed at Louvain. The system of studies and rule of college discipline were drawn up by himself, the former being in a great degree borrowed from that established at Paris. Frequent disputations and examinations quickened the application of the students, and at these Ximenes loved to preside, and encourage the emulation of his scholars with his presence. In the choice of his professors he considered nothing but the merit of the candidates, and set at nought all the narrowness of mere nationality. Spain was by this time, however, able to furnish humanists and philologists equal to those of Italy or Germany. And most of the first professors were of native birth. Among them was Antonio de Lebrija, and though he afterwards accepted a chair at Salamanca, yet he finally returned to Alcala, and rendered invaluable aid to Ximenes in the philological labours in which he was about to engage, and which shed an additional lustre over the new academy.

Ximenes had always manifested a peculiar predilection for the cultivation of Biblical literature. In his earlier years his love of the Holy Scriptures had induced him to devote himself to the study of Hebrew and Chaldaic, and he had often been heard to say that he would willingly give up all his knowledge of jurisprudence to be able to explain a single verse of the Bible. He considered a thorough revival of biblical studies the surest means of defeating the new heretics, and in the midst of Court engagements and political toils, he at length conceived the plan of his great Polyglot Bible, in which the sacred text was to appear in the four learned languages, after the most correct versions that could be obtained. This great work, which was to serve as the model for all subsequent attempts of a similar kind, was no sooner designed than he set about its execution, and secured the co-operation of a number of skilful scholars, fixing on Alcala as the scene of their labours. Immense sums were expended in obtaining Latin, Greek, Hebrew, and Chaldaic manuscripts; and in his dedication, Ximenes acknowledges the invaluable assistance which he received from Pope Leo X. The plan was exactly one sure to engage the sympathies of that generous

Pontiff, who accordingly placed at his command all the treasures of the Vatican Library. The costly work when complete presented the Hebrew text of the Old Testament, the Greek version of the Septuagint, the Latin version of St. Jerome, and the Chaldaic paraphrase of the Pentateuch, together with certain letters, prefaces, and dissertations to assist the study of the Sacred Books. The work was commenced in 1502, and the last volume was published in 1517. The same energy which had succeeded, in the brief space of eight years, in raising a university which received the title of "the eighth wonder of the world," was able, in fifteen years, to bring to a happy conclusion a literary undertaking which might well have occupied thrice that space of time. Ximenes, who felt his end approaching, desired to leave all his great works complete, and urged on his scholars with frequent admonitions on the shortness of human life. If *they* lost *him* as their patron, or if *he* were to lose *their* labours, the whole design might fall to the ground. On the 10th of July 1517 the last sheet of the great Complutensian Polyglot was printed, and the young son of the printer, Bocario, putting on his holiday garments, ran at once to present it to the Cardinal. Ximenes received it with a solemn emotion of gratitude and joy. "I thank Thee, O Lord Christ," he said, "that Thou hast brought this work to a desired end." It was as though he had been permitted this as his last earthly consolation, for four months later he closed his great and useful career, being in the eighty-second year of his age.

Louvain and Alcala, the two great Catholic creations of the age of the Renaissance, both fell under the hammer of Revolution. The memory of Ximenes has not prevailed to preserve his university from destruction at the hands of the Spanish Progressistas, and we can but hope that its restoration may be reserved for another generation. That of Louvain has been witnessed even in our own time. Swept away in 1797 by the decree of the French Republic, which at the same time suppressed all the great ecclesiastical seminaries, it was not restored by the Nassau sovereigns who, in 1814, became masters of the Catholic Netherlands. William of Holland, so far from showing his Catholic subjects any larger degree of favour than they had enjoyed under French rule, did his best to render their position worse than it had been under the Revolution. He put down all the little seminaries, and proposed to supply the place of the ancient university of Louvain by a grand royal philosophical college, through which all ecclesiastical students were to be compelled to pass before being received into the great seminaries. This was in the June of 1825; in the January of 1830 the determined resistance of the Belgian Catholics obliged him to suppress his college, which had proved a total failure. The August following witnessed the expulsion of his dynasty and the establishment of Belgian independence; events which were followed in 1834 by the erection at Louvain of a new university, in virtue of an Apostolic brief of Pope Gregory XVI.

Planted on the Belgian soil, which has so long and so successfully resisted the inroads of heresy, and which appears destined in our own day to become the battle-ground of a yet deadlier struggle with open unbelief, the Catholic university of Louvain has already merited to be declared by illustrious lips "the glory of Belgium and of the Church." She has been presented by the Sovereign Pontiff to the Catholics of these islands, as the model on which our own academic restorations may fitly be formed; and at this very moment her example is understood to have encouraged the prelates of Germany to attempt a similar foundation in that land. May their generous efforts be crowned with ample success, and may such institutions, wherein Faith and Science will never be divorced, multiply in the Church, supported by the prayers and good wishes of every Catholic heart.

CHAPTER XXII.

THE RENAISSANCE IN ROME.

A.D. 1513 TO 1528.

ON the morning of the 11th of April 1513 the streets of Rome were thronged with a joyous and expectant crowd, assembled to witness the public procession of the newly-elected Pontiff, Leo X., on occasion of his taking possession of the Basilica of St. John Lateran. Many circumstances combined to render the accession of Leo welcome to his new subjects: they had already felt the charm of his courteous manners, springing partly from careful culture, and partly from an innate kindness of heart; and whilst the Roman citizens, who were heartily tired of the wars and war-taxes of Julius II., rejoiced at the prospect of peace and plenty, the artists and professors, who made up a population by themselves, regarded the election of a Medici as a sufficient guarantee for the protection of their personal interests. The son of Lorenzo, and the pupil of Politian, of Chalcondylus, and of Bernard Dovizi, he had imbibed a love of art and poetry in the gardens of Florence and the villas of Fiesole. Created a Cardinal at the age of fourteen, he was but thirty-seven at the period of his election to the Papal chair, and during his residence at Rome under the two preceding Pontificates had acquired a character which his friends condensed into a motto, and exhibited in golden letters on the canopy under which he was enthroned, *Litteratorum præsidium ac bonitatis fautor.* If an ancient statue had been disinterred in the baths of Titus, the Cardinal de' Medici had been the first to celebrate the auspicious event in graceful iambics improvised to the music of his lyre; his house had been the *rendezvous* of artists, poets, and, above all, of musicians; and whilst men of this stamp loudly proclaimed the taste and munificence of the new Pontiff, the unblemished name which he had preserved in the midst of a society the corruptions of which were matter of public notoriety, put to silence the busy tongue of scandal.

It was truly, therefore, a festa-day which his subjects were now celebrating; and as he rode on his white charger through the brilliant streets, men contrasted his mild and *débonnaire* countenance, his gay smile, and affable address; with the imperious bearing of his predecessor, the warlike Julius; and the contrast was all to his advantage. What a scene it was through which he was now passing! Rome had been all but rebuilt under the four last Pontiffs, and from the Vatican to the Coliseum the way was marked with monuments of their munificence and of the genius of their artists. Domes, amphitheatres, arcades, and fountains had risen during the last seventy years with magnificent profusion; the old Basilica of the Apostles had disappeared, and was in process of being replaced by a pile worthy of the vast conceptions of its founders and its architects. And now the splendid city had decked herself in gala costume, and amid velvet tapestries and flowery wreaths, triumphal arches, and private houses, with their facades improvised into heathen temples, appeared a strange medley of saints and mythological characters, in which the statues of Mars, Apollo, Minerva, and Venus, were exhibited in close proximity to those of SS. Peter and Paul. On the whole, however, the classic element predominated, and the characters chosen at each resting-place to harangue the new Pontiff were the Muses, the Seasons, and their attendant nymphs.

The hopes and expectations of the Roman populace on that day were abundantly fulfilled. Leo did his best to restore peace to Italy, and raised Rome to the dignity of a great capital. Few princes have ever been more richly endowed than he with the qualities which make princedom popular; a liberality which bordered on profuseness, a generous readiness to reward merit, and a charming urbanity of manners, which made every one who approached his person believe himself the object of the Pope's particular regard. Erasmus felt the magical influence of his presence, and wrote to his friends, saying, that Leo was as far superior to the rest of men, as men are superior, to beasts. "He has the genius and the virtues of all the Leos who have preceded him, and to perfect goodness of heart," he continues, "he unites an incredible strength of soul." In the church all beholders admired the majesty with which he officiated at the sacred ceremonies; and his temperate habits in private have been praised by all his biographers. He was not only a passionate lover of literature and science, but was firmly persuaded that the cultivation of letters, rightly regarded, is ever friendly to the faith. "I have always loved learned men and good letters," he wrote to Henry VIII. "This attraction was born with me, and it has only increased with years; for I always see that those who cultivate literature are most firmly attached to the dogmas of the faith, and form the glory of the Christian Church." His patronage of arts and letters, therefore, was hearty and munificent enough to satisfy even the requirements of the learned world around him. He restored the Roman University, and appointed a brilliant staff of professors, men not only of the first ability, but of exemplary life. In his Bull addressed to the students, he failed not to warn them against substituting Plato and the poets for more serious studies, and reminded the preceptors that they were called on to defend the faith as well as to teach good letters. His own tastes, however, had the character which might have been anticipated from his education: they inclined almost exclusively to the *belles-lettres*. In many cases the classic acquirements of those who were now promoted to canonries and Cardinals' hats were more regarded than their personal merits. Bernard Dovizi, who, as tutor to the young Medici, had studiously and successfully laboured to confer on his manners that exquisite polish which was his greatest charm, was now raised to the purple, and, as Cardinal Bibiena, endeavoured to surround the Pontifical palace with every attraction of a secular Court. The literary public of those days was not easily scandalised, but it was at least taken by surprise by the first production which came from the new Cardinal's pen, his comedy of "Calandra," written as a carnival piece for the amusement of a noble lady, and acted in the private apartments of the Vatican.[325] Ariosto was also welcomed at Court, and even the infamous Aretino received marks of favour, whilst Bembo and Sadolet, the two first Latinists of their day, were appointed the Pope's secretaries.

The patronage of Leo was not limited to any one kind of literary excellence. He was as ready to reward a scientific treatise as an imitation of Horace, and whilst encouraging the study of the Eastern tongues, and publishing at his own expense a magnificent edition of Tacitus from the unique manuscript obtained from the abbey of Old Corby, he was accepting the dedication of Italian tragedies and causing the "Rosamunda" of Ruccellai to be acted in his presence. Almost his first act after his accession to the Papal dignity was to summon Lascaris to Rome, and establish him in a palace on the Esquiline, where, in concert with Musurus, he superintended a Greek academy and printing press. Zenobius Acciajoli, the most learned Orientalist of his day, who had shone among the stars of Lorenzo's Court, and had afterwards assumed the Dominican habit and dedicated his genius to sacred studies, now became Prefect of the Vatican Library; whilst another Oriental scholar of the same order, the celebrated Sanctes Pagninus, found generous encouragement to undertake his Latin translation of the Scriptures from the original tongues.

But whilst extending his splendid patronage to every department of literature, the personal predilections of Leo were undoubtedly for poetry and the arts. Like a true Medici he loved the sunny side of life, and delighted in surrounding himself with poets, wits, and musicians, he himself being the gayest wit and best musician of the party. The Court was crowded with professional improvisatori who enlivened the suppers at the Vatican with their jests and pastimes. In the mornings there were literary assemblies in which the great men of the day recited their poems or epigrams, or more learned works. Now it was Vida, whom Leo had engaged to undertake the composition of his "Christiad," and who beguiled his lighter hours by setting forth the mysteries of the game of chess in Latin hexameters; or Paulus Jovius,[326] the Italian Livy, who came to read a chapter of his history; or "the divine Accolti," as he was called, who recited his poems surrounded by a guard of honour, and who in return for his lyric productions was raised to the dukedom of Nepi and a bishopric.

Under such a *régime* the arts flourished, and men of letters were promoted to wealth and dignities; Rome grew daily more luxurious and more splendid, but, alas! it must be said, her moral atmosphere was a pestilence. The historian Mariana declares that at the opening of the sixteenth century greater disorders existed there than were to be witnessed in any other European capital. Even Bembo, whose own life at this time was a disgrace to the ecclesiastical habit, admits the charge, and owns that he who desired to lead a holy life would do well to fly from Rome.[327] What else could be anticipated of a society made up of artists and professors, paganised to the very core in its literature, its language, and its every maxim? And when we say *paganised*, let it not be supposed that the simple restoration of classical studies is here intended, or that the abuses complained of consisted only of the extravagances of a few learned pedants. In Italian literary circles, if we may credit historians of the time, the Christian ideas were slowly becoming obliterated. It had grown fashionable in certain coteries to scoff at all the Christian dogmas as obsolete and barbarous; and Antonio Bandino complains that you were no longer regarded as a man of education unless you could jest at the Scriptures and indulge in some witty piece of scepticism. Many of the Italian schools were deeply infected with infidelity, particularly the University of Padua, which for more than a century had been notorious as the focus of atheism. Pomponatus,[328] one of the Paduan professors, published a treatise on the immortality of the soul, during the reign of Leo X., in which he endeavoured to show that the doctrine was not held by Aristotle, that it rested *only* on the authority of Scripture and the Church, and was plainly opposed to reason. A great number of professors taught similar errors, and pretended that though contrary to revelation they might yet be taught as *philosophically* true. These were condemned in 1513 by the Fifth Council of Lateran, which formally declared that "truth could not contradict truth;" and to counteract the dangerous spirit prevalent in the universities it was at the same time decreed that students aspiring to sacred orders should not follow the course of philosophy and poetry for more than five years, unless at the same time they studied theology and canon law.[329] But little or no fruit was produced by this decree, and as we shall see, at a somewhat later period the "great and pernicious abuses" which were admitted as loudly demanding reform, were formally declared by a commission of Cardinals to have arisen mainly from the impious teaching tolerated in the public schools.

In fact, Italy was at this time *professor-ridden*. Of all odious dogmatisms surely that of pedagogues is the most intolerable form of social tyranny, and under this the Transalpine world was then groaning. Armed with their pens and their tinsel eloquence the men of letters wrote down and talked down all opposition, and made so much noise in the world that they seemed for a time to occupy a much larger and more influential position than was really the case. They dictated their laws to the literary world, and every one who would not be pasquinaded as a barbarian was content to follow the fashion. So in the pulpit preachers called on their audience to contemplate the examples of Epaminondas or Socrates; parallels were drawn between the sacred events of the Passion, and the self-devotion of a Curtius or a Decius: our Divine Lord was commonly spoken of as a hero who had deserved well of his country, and not unfrequently allusions would be introduced to the thunders of Jupiter and the stories of heathen mythology.

The grand object of Italian scholars at this time was to attain a pure Ciceronian style, and in this none were more successful than the two papal secretaries, Sadolet and Bembo. The pains taken by the latter on his compositions at least deserved success. He is said to have kept forty portfolios, into each of which his sheets were successively entered, and only passed on to the one next in order after undergoing careful revision. The rejection of every phrase not absolutely Ciceronian led to very strange affectation when speaking of events of ordinary life, as well as to the more offensive fault of adopting heathen phraseology on matters relating to the Christian faith. Thus the accession of Leo was announced to foreign Courts as having taken place "through the favour of the Immortal Gods;" Divine grace was the *magnificentia divinitatis*; Our Lady was the *Dea Lauretana*, or the *Alma Parens*; and the Christian mysteries were described in terms taken from the sacrificial terminology of the Greeks. Erasmus had good sense enough to despise these extravagances, and he did his utmost to render them ridiculous.[330] He describes the Ciceronian spending a whole winter's night on the composition of a single sentence, compiling lexicons of Ciceronian words, tropes, locutions, and pleasantries, more bulky than the great orator's entire works, and struggling with the insuperable difficulties of rendering the wants and habits of a modern age into the colloquial phraseology of the ancients.

The poets and artists followed the example set them by the professors. They still occasionally condescended to choose Christian subjects, but in most cases it was to debase them by a pagan method of treatment. When Sannazar thought fit to employ his muse on so old-fashioned a theme as the birth of Our Lord, he converted it into a pagan fable, placed the prophecies of the Sibyls in the hands of the Blessed Virgin, and the words of Isaias in the mouth of Proteus, omitted the name of Jesus Christ throughout his entire poem, and surrounded the holy crib with nymphs, satyrs, and hamadryads. The very liturgy of the Church had a narrow escape of undergoing a classical reform, and a new *Hymnarium* appeared, drawn up by Zachario Ferreri, "according to the true rules of Latinity and metre," in which, says Dom Guéranger, "occur every image and allusion to pagan belief and customs which are to be met with in Horace." This work was undertaken by command of Leo X., but its use, though permitted by Clement VII., was happily never enjoined on the clergy.

Hand in hand with the paganism of literature advanced the paganism of morals. We are not here engaged in studying the history of the Church, and may therefore be spared the pain of contemplating her scandals—those scandals the existence of which, far from weakening our faith, may rather confirm it, when we remember that they were distinctly prophesied by her Divine Head as evils which "must needs be" accomplished. Our business is with schools and scholars, and, sooth to say, after wandering amid the dim religious light of the mediæval cloisters, the blaze of the Roman literary circles, after first dazzling our eyes, reveals such bewildering spectacles, that we look about for some retreat into which the Christian scholar may creep and hide himself.

Such, perhaps, was the feeling of many a student who, coming fresh from the schools of Louvain, or the cloisters of Winchester or Oxford, found himself suddenly dropped down upon a world which seemed to have broken loose from all time-honoured traditions of scholastic life. Perhaps he had been used to set before him the musty maxim of Philip the Almoner,[331] that "that is no true science which is not the companion of justice;" or he had learned from Hugh of St. Victor to regard humility as the foundation of wisdom; or he was familiar with the saying of the Angel of the schools, that the best way to make progress in philosophy was to keep the commandments of God. But if he had the gift of prudence, he would think twice before citing such authorities in the polite circles of the Roman *literati*. He would have been hooted at as a barbarian. The monks and schoolmen were never spoken of by the professors of the new learning save in terms of execration and contempt. They were, to use the language of Erasmus, wretched creatures, whose language was as uncouth as their apprehension was dull. In those days there was no greater reproach than to call a man a *Scotist*—it meant precisely a *dunce*[332]—and those who held communion with the Muses and the Graces would have judged it an affront to be required to treat with respect the memory of St. Thomas or St. Bonaventure. And truly their venerable names, and the maxims they had laid down for the guidance of Christian scholars, would have been sadly out of place in the sumptuous orgies of the Chigi palace, or those luxurious soirées where prelates, ambassadors, and men of letters did not refuse to appear as the guests of the most questionable characters. The Roman academy which had been suppressed by Paul II., and had revived under Julius II., was now at the height of its renown. Its members generally met in some delicious suburban garden, and there, under the shade of the thick foliage, in an atmosphere heavy with the perfume of the orange-flower, they recited poems, proposed philosophic questions, and whiled away with song and merriment long hours of the day and night. Amid scenes of such Epicurean enjoyment the stranger might have been forgiven had he imagined himself taking part in the revelries of pagan rather than of Christian Rome. On the walls of the luxurious banqueting-rooms, in which he assisted at those suppers of world-wide celebrity, he might see representations from the comedies of Plautus, reminding him how close a parallel was to be drawn between the manners described by the Latin poet and those of the sixteenth century. From the elegant revellers around him he might hear the authority of Pliny quoted to prove that the human soul differed in nothing from that of beasts; or, exchanging the philosophic for a lighter mood, he might perhaps be called on to assist at some macaronic exhibition, such as the crowning of Querno, the drunken buffoon, arch-poet of Rome; or be required to listen to the facetious improvisation of Folengo or Mariano Fetti,—the former a monk, the latter a friar,—both of whom had quitted their cloisters to ply the trade of professional jesters. Thankful enough he would be to escape from these polished circles and return to his own barbarous land and the society of those rude English, who, as Politian contemptuously remarked, "knew nothing of letters, and busied themselves with their sheep," and who perhaps might, in their turn, have thought with the Psalmist, that it was well with those who knew no literature, and were only mindful of justice.[333]

We are not left merely to conjecture the abuses which throve in such a soil. We have the grave avowal of the commission of Cardinals already referred to, that "in no city was there to be witnessed such corruption of manners as in this city, which should be an example to all." Vice, in fact, had ceased to wear a veil; it stalked abroad under the noonday sun, and too often found illustrious support. Yet, strange to say, the existing abuses, monstrous as they were, were more superficial than they seemed. The evil scum that rises to the surface of society must not always be taken as a test of what lies beneath; the gaudy charlock may toss its wanton head and blazon itself to the eye, but the good seed is quietly germinating below, and in the day of harvest its sheaves will not be wanting. The Church is happily not governed by professors and scholastics, and at the very time when the literary world of Rome was exhibiting the spectacles described above, the Fifth Council of Lateran was holding its sessions in that very city, and promulgating its decrees for the reform of the Universities, the College of Cardinals, and the Roman Court.[334] The Church, by the mouth of her episcopate, was solemnly exposing and condemning those very evils which thoughtless observers were perhaps laying to her charge. In the decree of the Council on the study of the Scriptures and the liberal arts, the Fathers, after setting forth the vital importance of the education of youth, go on to declare that schoolmasters and professors are bound not merely to teach their scholars grammar and rhetoric, but yet more to instruct them in their religion, and to make them study sacred hymns and psalms, and the lives of the saints; and forbid anything to be taught on Sundays and festival days save what refers in some way to religion or holy living. Decrees of this sort, if they plainly indicate the deplorable practical paganism which at that time prevailed in most public academies, show us also that the rulers of the Church were sensible of the evil, and earnestly desirous to apply a suitable remedy. And, as we shall see hereafter, this very city of Rome that seemed so corrupt, cherished in her bosom a principle of life and power, which eventually cast out the infection which had hung over her so long, and so accomplished her own purification. Long before Luther had uttered the word "Reform," it had rung through the halls of the Lateran. The Fathers of the Council spared nothing and dissimulated nothing; and at the opening of the ninth session, a remarkable oration was delivered by Antonio Pucci, clerk to the Apostolic Chamber, in which he called on the Pope to set about the work in earnest. "Holy Father!" he exclaimed, "you desire to restore peace to Christendom, and you do well in so desiring. But see first that you extinguish the intestine wars of our vices, and exterior peace will soon reappear. Behold the world! Behold the cloister! Behold the sanctuary! Everywhere there are abuses to reform, and it is with the house of God that we must begin."

Yet it can be no great matter of surprise that passing strangers did not always penetrate the distinction between the *Church* and the *City* of Rome, and that the undeniable corruption of the Roman literary circles brought ecclesiastical rulers into disrepute, and sapped in many minds the sentiment of loyalty to the Apostolic See. That both Erasmus and Luther carried with them from Rome fatal impressions, which, each in his own way, turned to the detriment of religion, is not to be doubted. Erasmus, indeed, had no cause to be scandalised by a state of society which was exactly to his taste. He was *fêted* and flattered by prelates and philosophers, and in his letters from Rome he wants words to express his raptures at those delicious hours which he spent among libraries and academies, in the reunions at the palace of the *divine* Cardinal San Giorgio, or the yet more charming assemblies in the Pope's private chambers. Yet, while enjoying the cup of pleasure to the full, his keen sarcastic eye was taking the measure of all he saw, and it was on his journey back to the north, that he beguiled his travelling fatigues with composing his "Praise of Folly," in which Cardinals, Popes, and Prelates are made the subject of his most caustic gibes and pleasantries. And this, after all, is the way of the world; it is a lynx-eyed critic, and has ever a rigorous standard for those who ought to be saints, and a ready condemnation for those who fall short of it. Erasmus, who was himself worldly to the heart's core, had yet sense enough to feel that worldliness, however delightful, was out of place on the threshold of the apostles, and he made other men feel it too, with all that biting irony of which he was the master.

Luther, a man of different mould, visited Rome in a widely different spirit. He was in the first fervour of what he considered his religious conversion, when in 1510 he came thither full of enthusiasm, and fell on his knees as he entered the city, to kiss the soil watered by the blood of martyrs; though he afterwards mocked at his own devotion and at the simplicity with which he ran about from church to church prepared to believe and venerate everything that he saw. He too carried away impressions that were never effaced. His coarse, strong Saxon nature had little taste for the arts and the *belles-lettres*, and was only repelled by the magnificence around him. The Olympic deities that met his eye at every street corner, the heathenish adornments of the very churches, where pictures and images of Christian mysteries were presented in the garb of paganism, and the yet worse heathenism which met his ears from the elegant literary crowds among whom he passed in his coarse friar's frock, all this sank into his soul to be reproduced on the day when he launched his imprecations against the seven-hilled city, and held her up to the scorn of his countrymen, as "the dwelling-place of dragons, the nest of bats and vultures, the resort of hobgoblins, weasels, gnomes, and demons."[335] Nor did it matter anything to his audience that the enormities he exposed were far surpassed by those which he committed, and that the apostle of reform had himself let loose on the world the reign of frenzied license; the scandals he propagated did the work which he intended, and indelibly fixed in the Saxon mind the tradition which identified Rome with Babylon.

We need not here concern ourselves with the history of that great revolution which history miscalls the Reformation. Before the death of Leo X., that which had been deemed in its beginning to be but "a squabble of friars," was ending in the apostasy of nations. The Roman academicians, however, were less moved at the tidings which reached them in 1520, that the Pope's Bull, the Decretals, and the Summa of St. Thomas, had all been burnt together by Luther in the public square of Wittemberg, and that the Pope himself had been declared by the same authority to be Antichrist, than at another piece of intelligence, which was communicated to them on February 9, 1522, and which startled them like a clap of thunder. Leo was dead, and the choice of the Cardinals had fallen on the Cardinal Adrian of Utrecht. The burning of St. Thomas in person would have been a light matter to them, in comparison with the election to the Papal dignity of a plain austere Louvain professor; already known to fame as the advocate of ecclesiastical discipline, the friend and colleague of Ximenes, and it was more than whispered, the supporter of scholasticism. He was a Fleming, a "Scotist," a Goth, and the enemy of letters. He had come into the city without pomp of any kind, and had ordered one of the half-finished triumphal arches, that was to have cost a thousand ducats, to be destroyed. He had discharged ninety out of the one hundred equerries kept by his predecessor. He had brought his old Louvain housekeeper with him to the Vatican, and was dismissing the improvisatori and whole troops of other Court idlers. They had taken him over the Museum attached to his palace, and he had been heard to mutter the words *Idola antiquorum*, when standing before the group of the Laocoon. Some of Sadolet's most elegant Latin epistles had been placed in his hands, and he had briefly commented on them as "the letters of a poet." "I verily believe," writes Jerome Negri, in terrible alarm, "that he will do as Pope Gregory did before him, make a clean sweep of our libraries, and perhaps grind up our statues to furnish mortar for building St. Peter's." The artists cried out that now they should all be starved; the professors bewailed the certain return of Gothic barbarism: Bembo set out at once for Venice, and Sadolet retired to his bishopric of Carpentras, where he displayed those noble qualities which had as yet found no room to expand in the artificial atmosphere of the Court.

Never was there a more undeserved reproach than that which stigmatised Pope Adrian as the enemy of learning. Erasmus, who had been defended by him from the attacks of some over-zealous scholastics, judged far otherwise, but the Romans could not forgive his indifference to ancient art, and his condemnation of those paganising scholars, whom he termed "Terentians." Still less could they forgive his plain speaking on the subject of reform. "Many abominations," he said, "have existed near this Holy Chair, abuses in spiritual matters, and evil everywhere. We pledge ourselves, on our part, to use our utmost endeavour to reform that Court which has, perhaps, been the source of the evils we deplore."

In his brief pontificate of twenty-two months he was unable to accomplish the work which lay so close to his heart. His death was regarded by the Roman literati as a kind of providence, a special grace from heaven which had averted the return of mediæval barbarism; and some of them went so far as to adorn with garlands the house of his physician, to whose want of skill the fatal termination of Adrian's illness was ascribed, hanging over his door the inscription—"To the Saviour of his country."

Yet those two-and-twenty months, which seemed so fruitless, witnessed the turning of the tide. The election of another Medici as successor to Adrian was the signal for extraordinary rejoicings, and for the return to Rome of many who had abandoned it after the accession of Adrian. Clement VII. had all the personal grace and refined intellect of his family; he had less taste for pleasure, and more aptitude for business than Leo, and was a true lover of learned men. He induced Sadolet to resume his functions as secretary, and did his best to engage Erasmus to devote his genius to the earnest defence of the Church.

The spirits of the Romans revived when they witnessed the splendid patronage of letters exercised by the new Pope and his kinsman, Cardinal Hyppolitus de' Medici, who entertained in his household no fewer than three hundred learned men. The artists and academicians confidently reckoned on a return of their golden age; and yet all were more or less conscious of a certain indefinable change which had stolen over the public mind, betokening that a reaction was setting in, and that a new era was at hand. The German revolt from the Church had by this time assumed proportions which it was impossible to ignore. The question of the English divorce was causing grave inquietudes, and whilst the shadow of new and unprecedented calamities hung heavy over the world, even the most indifferent minds felt perhaps that something more earnest was called for at that moment than the cultivation of the Muses. It cannot, indeed, be said that the tide of social corruption was checked; yet another and a better element was silently at work; and, hidden in the glittering crowd,

Some few there were who with pure hearts aspired

To lay their just hands on the golden key

That opes the palace of eternity.

Clement had summoned to his Court several illustrious ecclesiastics who, whilst inferior to none of their contemporaries in literary merit, were desirous above all things to provide a remedy for those grave domestic abuses which, they rightly felt, afflicted the Church more heavily than any attacks from her exterior foes. Among these were the Venetian, Gaspar Contarini, a profound scholar, and a man of fervent piety; Sadolet, who, now greatly weaned from the pursuits which had formerly absorbed him, desired to devote his remaining years to his pastoral duties; Matthew Ghiberti, the worthiest prelate of his time, whom Clement had admitted to his closest confidence, and raised to the dignity of Chancellor and the see of Verona; the Prothonotary, Cajetan of Thienna, and the Cardinal Caraffa, Archbishop of Theate, who afterwards became Pope under the title of Paul IV. The jubilee year 1525 also brought to Rome a number of devout and earnest pilgrims, among whom was our own great countryman Reginald Pole, then a student at Padua, whom Bembo called the most virtuous young man in Italy, and whose happiness it was to enter on his list of friends the name of almost every one of his contemporaries most illustrious for scholarship or piety. Men of this stamp felt the need, in the midst of that luxurious and enervating atmosphere, of some tie of Christian fellowship which might support and invigorate their spiritual life; and the result was the formation of a humble confraternity which met in the church of SS. Silvestro and Dorotea, and took the name of "the Oratory of Divine Love."

Similar associations were springing up in other cities of Italy, but that at Rome is remarkable as being the germ whence afterwards developed the order of the Theatines. A plan was concerted among the members of the confraternity for instituting an order of regular clerks, in which the ancient canonical mode of life should be revived; this being suggested as offering the surest means for effecting that reformation of manners among the clergy which all good men so earnestly desired to forward. This design was carried out with the approbation of the Pope; Caraffa and St. Cajetan being chosen the two first superiors. Of the latter it was commonly said that he desired to reform the world without letting the world know he was in it, and in the northern cities of Italy, where he had hitherto chiefly resided, he had the character of uniting in one person the seraphic gifts of a contemplative to the heroic virtues of an apostle. The rule adopted by the regular clerks was nearly the same as that of the ancient Canons Regular. It appears certain that their original design included the formation of ecclesiastical seminaries, and in all essential particulars the new foundation bore a striking resemblance to that set on foot in the eighth century, with a very similar purpose, by St. Chrodegang of Metz. And thus we see how saintly men, when they took in hand the work of ecclesiastical reform, found no better means for carrying out their views, than turning back into the old paths, and following the traditions bequeathed them by a golden antiquity.

The order of Theatines, however, whilst yet in its infancy, was threatened with extinction when that terrible calamity fell upon Rome, to describe which one needs to use the language of the inspired writers, when they detail the woes that were to chastise the guilty city, which was yet the chosen city of God. The political combinations which had closely allied the Roman Pontiff with the Court of France, exposed him to the hostility of the Emperor Charles V., whose armies entered Italy in the early part of the year 1527, and threatened to lay siege to Rome. On the 5th of May, the city was stormed by the ferocious bands of the Constable de Bourbon, consisting chiefly of German Lutherans, animated to frenzy by the thirst for plunder and a wild religious fanaticism. The Pope took refuge in the castle of St. Angelo, and from thence had the anguish of witnessing his capital given up to scenes of sacrilege and violence which find no equal in history. The sack of Rome by the barbarian Goths lasted but six days, but the Germans held possession of their prey for *nine months*, every hour of which witnessed some fresh abomination. The citizens were subjected to horrible tortures, to compel them to give up their hidden treasures; the churches were desecrated, and sacred relics tossed about the streets; troop-horses were stabled in the Pontifical chapel, and littered with Bulls and decretals; mock celebrations of holy rites were performed by drunken troopers, who, decked out with cardinals' dresses, pretended to hold a conclave, and proclaimed the election of Luther as Pope. Out of a population of 85,000, 50,000 citizens are calculated to have perished by torture and the sword, and the excesses of the soldiers at last brought a pestilence in their train, which all but annihilated, the conquerors themselves; so that the city, awhile before so brilliant and luxurious, became little better than a desolate and fetid tomb.

Amid the nameless horrors of that time it is needless to say that neither piety nor learning procured any mercy for their owners. St. Cajetan was scourged and tortured, and then compelled with his brethren to abandon the Roman territory and take refuge in Venice; where their modest house a few years later afforded hospitality to St. Ignatius and his first companions. As to the academicians, we are assured by Jerome Negri that the very few who escaped from the sword were dispersed into foreign lands, and that all subsequent efforts to restore their Society on its former footing proved an utter failure. In fact, when the city was at last delivered from the apostate hordes that possessed her, it was only to be exposed to the new scourges of famine, pestilence, and inundation, and during these calamities there reappeared in her streets, not the gay bands of artists and *literati*, but reformed Camaldolese and Capuchin friars, whose existence in the city, says one writer, was first made known to the Romans during the plague of 1528. Rome, indeed, recovered from her overwhelming disasters with astonishing rapidity, and it was not long before the Court of Clement VII. reassumed much of the brilliant character which it had borne under Leo X. But Roman society no longer groaned under the dictatorship of professors. The grave troubles of the Church drew to her capital men of earnest and exalted piety, who responded to the cry that came from every Catholic land for a General Council that should not only vindicate the doctrine of the Church against heretical innovators, but courageously enter on the reform of practical abuses. Delivered by her terrible chastisement from the meretricious splendour of a false prosperity, Rome prepared to put on her beautiful garments as of old, and to purify herself from the contagion which worldly men had brought into the very presence of the sanctuary. Even whilst her enemies were counting her among the dead, and rejoicing over her humiliation, she arose to a more beautiful and vigorous life than ever, so that many of those whose hearts had become estranged turned to her once more, and beholding her invested with the majesty of ancient discipline, recognised the seven-hilled city to be indeed "the city of truth, the mountain of the Lord of Hosts, the sanctified mountain."[336]

CHAPTER XXIII.

ENGLISH SCHOLARS OF THE RENAISSANCE.

A.D. 1473 TO 1550.

THE revival of polite letters in this country may be considered as dating from the foundation of Magdalen College, in 1473. Not only was it the most perfectly constituted college in the realm, but its great founder had amply provided for the cultivation of humane literature; and at the period of his death, Grocyn, the future restorer of Greek studies at Oxford, was Divinity Professor, and Wolsey and Colet were among his pupils. Oxford at this time presented a spectacle which seems to have struck the imagination of all her foreign visitors. Three hundred halls and grammar-schools, besides her noble colleges and religious houses, furnished means of education to a far larger number of students than resort thither at the present time. The English universities, though admitting the new learning, still adhered to the scholastic philosophy—a fact which formed the groundwork of those charges brought against them by some of their contemporaries, and re-echoed by Wood, of being behind their time. It is not very easy to determine what was the precise state of the English schools at the opening of the sixteenth century. On the one hand, it is clear that the revival of classical literature found plenty of enthusiastic supporters among English scholars; and, if we are to draw any conclusions as to the nature of English education of this time from Sir John Elyot's treatise of "The Governor," we should be disposed to think that children of the upper classes were then expected to begin their classical studies while still in their cradles. A nobleman's son, he says, should have none about him, not even his nurses, who cannot speak pure and eloquent Latin. At the very least, their English should be clean, polite, perfect, and articulately pronounced, omitting no letter or syllable. At seven, a boy is to begin his Greek and Latin grammars together; and at twelve he is supposed to have so completely made the Latin tongue his own that he need no more apply himself to its study, but confine his labours to Greek. The whole treatise, which is in many respects valuable and interesting, proves that the writer had imbibed that tiresome form of classical enthusiasm which wears you out with its illustrations from the ancients. Even the necessity of religion is supported by an appeal to the examples of Romulus and Numa Pompilius, though, accidentally, we are allowed to peep into the old Catholic nursery, and see the children "knelyng in thir games before ymages, and holdyng up thir litel white handes, movyng thir mouths as if they were praieing, or going and singyng, as it were in procession." This treatise, published in 1531, plainly infers that at that time a noble youth was expected to begin his studies very early, and to aim at something more than the name of a scholar. On the other hand, there was a certain prejudice in favour of foreign academies, which induced those who in all ages make it their business to follow the fashion, to undervalue Eton and Oxford, and to consider you a Goth or a rustic if you had not graduated in some Italian university. The mediæval spirit which still hung about the cloisters of Oxford was quite out of harmony with the prevailing tastes; and undoubtedly those same cloisters sheltered many worthy Conservatives of the old school who clung to Aristotle and Oxford Latin, and thought very little of the new-fangled Platonists.

Hence, those who desired to imbue themselves with classic literature generally found their way to Italy, and the rage for a foreign education had become so excessive that Barclay introduces an allusion to it in his "Ship of Fooles:"—

One runneth to Almayne, another to France,

To Paris, Padwy, Lombardy, or Spayne,

Another to Bonony, Rome, or Orleans;

To Caen, Toulouse, Athens or Colayne;

And at the last returneth home agayne

More ignorant.

The reproach conveyed in the last line was probably deserved by some whose foreign scholarship was only sought for fashion's sake; but it does not certainly apply to the knot of illustrious Englishmen whom we find studying in the Italian schools at the close of the fifteenth century. Among them was Richard Pace, who had been brought up in the household of Langton, Bishop of Winchester, and had been sent by his patron to study at Padua, where he had Latymer and Cuthbert Tonstall for his tutors; William Linacre, who had repaired to Florence and been received into the family of Lorenzo de' Medici, who, charmed with his modesty and talents, chose him for the companion of his son's studies: and the amiable and simple-hearted William Lily, whose Greek learning had been acquired at Rhodes, and who was then perfecting himself in Latin literature in the schools of Rome and Florence. Colet also made the tour of Italy, after taking his degree at Magdalen, and on coming back to England, he returned a second time to Oxford, where in 1497 he found Grocyn and Linacre delivering public lectures on Greek. Their audience was at first a small one, for the new learning was regarded with no little jealousy and suspicion in many quarters, and parties ran high between the Greeks and the Trojans, as the adherents of the opposite factions were commonly called. The Greeks expended their wit on the dulness of their adversaries, whom they represented as "sleepy, surly fellows, who talked bad Latin, and never said a smart or clever thing;" whilst the Trojans denounced their brilliant rivals as dangerous innovators. The truth lay pretty evenly between the two parties. The Oxford studies were possibly in some respects behind the time, and not merely profane, but sacred learning also appears, from Wood's account, to have been at a low ebb; and for this, as has been elsewhere shown, the lawyers and the logicians, the Lollards and the Anti-Roman party, must share the blame among them. Still, when we remember the enthusiasm with which men like More and Erasmus regarded the English universities, it is difficult to believe that sound and solid learning can have been entirely wanting at Oxford,[337] and considering what sort of clouds hung on the horizon, the "Scotists," perhaps, did not show themselves such dull fellows after all, when they warned their disciples to keep clear of foreign fashions, and set afloat the well-known proverb, "Let the Greeks beware of heresy."

Colet did not hesitate to join the party of the Greeks, and to this he was moved not merely by a love of polite literature, but by the contempt and aversion which he had conceived for the scholastic philosophy. At Florence he had not only attended the Greek lectures of Politian and Demetrius Chalycondylus, but he had listened to the preaching of Savonarola, from whom he had caught an enthusiasm for Scriptural studies, and a burning zeal for the reform of abuses. So soon, therefore, as he had been ordained deacon he flung aside the Master of the Sentences, and began to read public lectures on the Epistles of St. Paul, though with characteristic temper he had disdained to receive any degrees in Divinity, accounting the studies which he should have had to engage in for that purpose as wholly empty and unprofitable. His earnest eloquence and original mode of treatment drew him more hearers than the classic erudition of Grocyn had been able to command, and there was not a doctor of law or divinity in the whole university, but gladly came to hear the young preacher, bringing their books with them.

It was at this moment that Erasmus paid his first visit to England, having been invited over by Lord Mountjoy, his former pupil at Paris. Erasmus at this time supported himself partly by his tutorships, and partly by the pensions which he received from the sovereigns who sought to attach him to their Courts, and from the learned friends whose pecuniary assistance he availed himself of with considerable freedom. At Oxford he was received into St. Mary's Priory by the kind-hearted Prior Charnock, and in his letters expresses the singular delight which he felt at all he heard and all he saw. He soon made acquaintance with Colet, and was by him introduced to More, then studying at Magdalen, and to Wolsey, bursar of the same college; and in company with these new friends (he wrote to Mountjoy) he would be content to live all his days in the farthest extremity of Scythia. In short, he drew so brilliant a picture of the pleasant hours they spent in one another's company, that Mountjoy, who was but just married, could not resist the temptation of running down to Oxford, and beginning a fresh course of study under his old master.

The friendship that sprang up from that time between Erasmus and Colet was strong and enduring. Yet no two men could be more unlike in their real character, however much their literary tastes may have coincided. Colet was heart and soul in earnest, and herein lay the strength and nobleness of a disposition which, as his friend owns, had in it many a dash of human infirmity. "When he speaks," writes Erasmus, "you would think he was more than man: it is not with voice alone, but with eyes, and countenance, and with his whole demeanour." He was of a hot and haughty spirit, and impatient of the least affront, qualities which imparted a certain harshness and vehemence to all his words and actions. Yet he had (and who has not?) his softer side, and the stern and fiery orator, as rigid and severe to himself as he was to others, was a lover of children, and delighted to make himself little with little ones, whom he compared to the angels, though, as we shall presently see, his love even of them was somewhat lacking in tenderness. Erasmus himself was not likely to be led into the excesses to which a nature like Colet's easily betrays itself. There was no real earnestness about him. Had he not left his Epistles behind him, we might be amazed that one so deficient in every sterling quality of soul could have found a way to the hearts of all with whom he associated. But his letters explain the mystery. There was no resisting the charm of his wit, and his extraordinary gift of treating every subject on which he touched in the way that was most agreeable. After the lapse of three hundred years, the reader, who possesses nothing but the dead written letter of that graceful eloquence, feels its indescribable magic, the "certain Erasmianism," as Colet calls it, and is carried away against his will by the bewitching pleasantry of a writer whose whole life he knows to have been contemptible. There was, moreover, one most attractive quality which he shared with More: nothing was able to ruffle his temper; and he had the happiest ways of restraining the sallies of his more fiery companions, and preventing their table talk after dinner from ever ending in a quarrel. Thus, on one occasion, when a disputation had arisen upon the sin of Cain, Erasmus, who judged by Colet's sparkling eyes that the conversation had lasted long enough, and wished to end it, invented on the spot a story from some pretended ancient author, by which ingenious fraud the argument was broken off, and the company parted in the best of humours. He was moreover an advocate for moderation in all things, even in hostility to the scholastics, and once took up the defence of St. Thomas against the attacks of Colet, and represented that the Angelic doctor really did seem to have studied the Scriptures. But this time Colet bore him down, and could not contain his impatience at hearing a word said in favour of one whose dogmatic definitions of theology he hesitated not to accuse of arrogance. More held an equal place in the affections of both his friends; he had all the wit of Erasmus without his flippancy, and all the earnestness of Colet without his asperity of temper. He chose the latter as his director, and learnt from him a singular love for the inspired writings, and many precious secrets of self-mastery and mortification; but he had some spiritual instincts to which Colet was an utter stranger; and while the one was venting his annoyance at what he deemed the childish superstitions of the Canterbury pilgrims, as he watched them crowding to kiss the relics of St. Thomas à Becket, the other, with truer humility, thought it not beneath the character of a man of letters to feed his faith at the homely springs of popular devotion, and visited many an old English shrine on foot—a rare thing in those days, when even the common people went on horse-back.

We will pass over a few years, which brought their usual changes to the Oxford friends in all save the mutual regard which they bore for one another. The princely boy to whom Erasmus had first been introduced in his schoolroom, and who had won his heart by challenging him to reply to a Latin epistle, was now on the throne, "tall in body, and mighty in will," says Stow, "and so prosperous in his kingdom, that it was called 'The Golden Realm.'" Wolsey, whom we left a Demy of Magdalen, was now Cardinal, and had just succeeded Warham as chancellor, having the learned Richard Pace for his secretary. The European politics which he sought to guide had not made him neglect the cause of letters:—

"Witness for him

Those twins of learning which he raised in you,

Ipswich and Oxford!"

Good Bishop Fisher was hard at work introducing Greek studies at Cambridge, where Croke was delivering lectures, and where the new learning was better received than it had been at Oxford. The noble Countess of Richmond[338] had founded her two Cambridge colleges, her grammar-school at Wimbourne, and her "Lady Margaret" professorships; Fox, now Bishop of Winchester, was drawing up the statutes of Corpus Christi, that classical beehive, as he was pleased to term it, in which he provided for the study of Latin, Greek, and Hebrew, under the professors or "herbalists," who were for ever to drive all barbarism out of the bee-garden, and provide that the best classical authors should be read by his students. Linacre was now the royal physician and a man of importance; he had translated Galen, founded two lectureships at Oxford, and the College of Physicians, but at this moment he was contemplating whether it might not be well to give up professional fame and Court favour, in order to die a priest; and this design he afterwards executed. Grocyn, too, had ably maintained his scholar's reputation, and was universally respected as long as he lived, says Erasmus, for his chaste and holy life. In the judgment of that critic, however, his firm adherence to Catholic dogma was somewhat excessive, and bordered on superstition, and he considers it necessary to apologise for this weakness on the part of his friend, who, he says, had from childhood been trained in the scholastic theology, and was exceedingly learned in questions of ecclesiastical discipline. More, whose early inclination for the cloister had yielded to the persuasions of his director Colet, had married and embraced a professional career; he had written his Utopia, and was struggling hard to preserve his independence, and keep out of the royal service, into which others so eagerly sought admittance. He desired nothing better than to be suffered to enjoy in freedom his happy Chelsea home, where it was his delight to direct the education of his children, to gather around him his learned friends, and relieve the intervals of business with polite and Christian studies. In that family circle Erasmus always found a place during his visits to England, and it is to him that we owe the charming portraiture of a household, the venerable memory of which has sunk into the English heart and become almost the typical example of an English home. As to Erasmus himself, his course during the same period is easily told: he had published his Greek Testament and his learned editions of the Fathers, and had thereby earned a European reputation; he had flitted about from England to Paris, from Paris to Germany, from Germany back again to England, and thence to Rome. Courted, flattered, and admired by all, he was the great *bel-esprit* of the day, and the lighter productions of his pen were telling upon public opinion, much perhaps in the same sort of way that clever journalism affects it in our own day. He was directing his keen powers of ridicule against some real abuses, but at the same time his mocking wit was recklessly striking at sacred things and bringing them into popular contempt. In his "Praise of Folly," and his "Adages," he had hit hard at popes, cardinals, pilgrimages, devotions to the saints, and indulgences, but above all at monks and friars, whom he invariably holds up to execration, as something too pitiably vile and puerile to be endured by men of sense. In short, to use the oft-quoted saying, he had laid the egg which Luther was to hatch, and though he afterwards resented this charge, and was wont to say that he had laid a hen's egg, and Luther had hatched it a crow's, yet, as Hallam has shrewdly remarked, whatever were the bird, it pecked hard against the Church and her religious orders. His mode of warfare was to paint every one who opened his lips in defence of the old order of things as a half-witted ignoramus, and to bespatter his adversaries with epithets and witticisms, in an easy flowing style which everybody read and everybody laughed at; and when the laugh was once raised the victory was more than half won.

It remains to speak of Colet, now Dean of St. Paul's, who had steadily followed out the purpose to which he had devoted himself at Oxford, had given himself up heart and soul to the task of reviving the study of Scriptural Divinity, and was opposing himself like a rock to every form of practical corruption. At this distance of time it is not easy for us to satisfy ourselves as to the real character of one who has left nothing but his fame behind him, and whose views and teaching are to be gathered, not from his own writings but from the epistolary correspondence of Erasmus, whose narrative is naturally coloured by the bias of his own mind.[339] In those days of Court sycophancy, we cannot but admire the courageous independence of such a man, and the single-hearted fervour with which he set himself to reform his chapter, to expound the gospel to the people, and to urge upon his fellow clergy a strict observance of the canons. In his sermon preached before Convocation, in 1511, he chose for his text the words of St. Paul: "Be ye not conformed to this world;" and thundered out in plain, strong, and noble words his denunciation of those abuses which he called the "matter of the Church's reformation;" such as "the worldly lives of the prelates," "their hunting and hawking," and "their covetousness after high promotions." The reformation he said must begin with my "reverend Fathers the Lord Bishops," whom he prayed to excuse his boldness, for he spoke out of very zeal for Holy Church. In this famous sermon there is doubtless something too much of asperity, yet it does not seem to have been taken amiss. The single-hearted honesty of the speaker was understood and appreciated by his hearers; and it must be added that his own example added force to his words. Colet was a man of pure and blameless life, simple and austere in manners, and ready to spend himself for what he deemed the cause of Christ. His exhortations had extraordinary success; other ecclesiastics were animated to greater zeal in the discharge of their pastoral duties, and began to preach to their people on sermons and festival days. Divinity lectures, too, were delivered in the church of St. Paul, both by the Dean, and certain learned men whom he invited to assist him, and these lectures were no longer permitted to take the form of dry disputations, but were chiefly commentaries on the Scriptures, particularly on the Epistles of St. Paul, with which Colet was so enamoured, says Erasmus, that he seemed to be wholly wrapped up in them. With all his classical tastes he thought less of manner than of matter, in his public orations. Scriptural simplicity was what he aimed at; he wanted, to use his own rather uncourteous phrase, to "clear away the cobwebs of the schoolmen from the plain text of the Bible." He did not altogether neglect the study of style, and sometimes condescended to read Chaucer and other English poets for the purpose of improving his diction. But in general his thoughts came out too hot and molten for him to deliberate much in what words to utter them, and the careful polish which Erasmus bestowed on his writings was viewed by him as more worthy of a pedagogue than of a preacher, who has his heart full of big thoughts and is in haste to utter them.

How little there was of a courtier about him may be gathered from the sermon which he preached before the king at the time when he was preparing for his French war, in which, instead of offering that monarch the welcome incense of flattery, he very plainly expounded to his hearers the sin which Christian princes committed by wars of ambition, in which they fought, not under the banner of Christ, but under that of the devil.[340] Much of this was surely excellent; and had this been all, we should be ready to yield our hearty sympathy to Colet in spite of those "specks of human infirmity" which his best friends saw and regretted. A reformer has rough work to do, and in doing it has need of a certain fund of audacity which easily overpasses the just bounds of discretion, and can scarcely avoid wounding the susceptibilities of those whom he undertakes to amend. Yet such things are easily pardoned in them whom we know to be only "zealous for the Lord of Hosts," and who cannot "restrain their lips" when they declare His justice in the midst of the people. But there were other elements in the character of Colet from which we instinctively shrink, for the simple reason that they betray a mind out of harmony with the teachings of faith. We have already seen him bringing the charge of arrogance—himself surely with greater arrogance—against the Angelic doctor, unable to repress his intolerance of what he deemed his too strict definitions of doctrine; and betraying an angry contempt for the popular devotions sanctioned by the Church, but which *he* impeached of superstition. That practical abuses may easily have crept into many of these devotions is what no Catholic will think himself called on to deny, and that where they existed they deserved to be exposed and denounced is equally obvious; yet when we find that the only *fact* alluded to by Colet's biographer as having stirred the wrath of the reformer was the eagerness displayed by the Canterbury pilgrims to kiss the shoe of St. Thomas, preserved there as a relic, we are disposed to think that it was not merely these supposed abuses, but the devotions themselves which he regarded with dislike. And this judgment is confirmed when we find him betraying a similar want of sympathy with the spirit and practice of the Church in cases where there could be no question of superstition. He set very little store by the practice of daily hearing or saying Mass: he considered the recitation of the Divine Office in private by priests to be both a burdensome and a superfluous duty, and seems to have been, to say the least, indifferent to the value of prayer for the dead. All this we learn from the correspondence of Erasmus, who further informs us that there were a vast number of opinions received in the schools from which Colet strongly dissented, and that he not only read the works of heretical writers without scruple, but was accustomed to say that he often learned more out of them than he did from orthodox writers, who were content to be always running over a beaten track.[341] It can therefore be no great matter of surprise that Colet, before long, became involved in trouble. While some men regarded him as little short of a saint, others, alarmed at his bold views and the uncompromising language in which he expressed them, looked on him as an incipient heretic, and as such denounced him to his bishop. Articles were drawn up against him and laid before the Primate, but Warham dismissed the case as frivolous, and Colet was never afterwards interfered with on account of his liberty of speech.[342]

Erasmus, and after him Fox, tells us that the three articles of accusation referred to his manner of treating the worship of images, his preaching against the worldly lives of the clergy, and his complaints of those who read their sermons in a cold and formal manner; vague charges, which would be very justly designated as "frivolous." Tyndale, however, in his usual burlesque style, declares in his "Reply to More," that "the bishop would have made Colet a heretic for translating the Pater Noster into English," and this random shot has been gravely taken up and handed on from one author to another as a sober bit of history. "He *even* gave the people parts of the Bible in English," says a Scotch reviewer, "such as the Lord's Prayer!" Whilst Knight seriously assures his readers that not only were the English Scriptures at this time utterly unknown, but that "*there was scarce so much as a Latin Testament in any cathedral church in England.*"

Colet's friendship with More and Erasmus meanwhile remained unbroken, and in the intervals of graver duties the three friends were wont to meet at the house of Dame Christian Colet, the Dean's mother, in the (then) pleasant country suburb of Stepney, of which parish Colet was vicar. Erasmus has sketched the good old lady in her 90th year, with her countenance "still so fair and cheerful, you would think she had never shed a tear;" and Colet lets us know the pleasure which she found in receiving her son's guests, and in their agreeable and witty conversation. Stepney, with its green lanes, fresh country air, and rural population, would often picture itself to the eye of More when he grew weary of his life in town; and in his early married days, when his narrow means obliged him to content himself with a house in Bucklersbury, the hardworked lawyer was glad enough, like other cockneys, to run down to Stepney on Saturday afternoons, and refresh himself with the merry talk of his friends, as they sauntered in the trimly-kept gardens and admired the noble strawberries brought over from Holland, or the damask roses lately introduced into England by Linacre.

Not unfrequently the party included some of the learned foreigners who just then crowded the Tudor Court, such as Andreas Ammonius,[343] the king's Latin secretary, whom Erasmus praises as being "so noble and generous, so free from envy, and so full of great endowments," or their old Oxford crony, John Sixtine, a Frisian by birth, but now naturalised in England, and esteemed by all good scholars for his versatile genius. It seems strange to us in these days to associate the names of foreign canonists and divines with our country parish churches, of which, however, they not unfrequently enjoyed the revenues. Hidden in a sequestered valley of Devonshire, surrounded by woods that are dear to village children for the sweet-scented violets that grow there in such wild profusion, shut in by hills which they will not easily forget who have seen their sloping fields all bright with golden sheaves, made brighter with the intense sunshine that seems borrowed from a southern sky; the tourist may perhaps have stumbled on the little church of St. Blaze of Haccombe, with its quaint encaustic tiles and cross-legged effigies of the crusading lords of Haccombe, all as perfect as in the days of John Sixtine, the friend of More and Erasmus, who was arch-priest of the college formerly attached to this church by Sir Stephen de Haccombe, to the end that perpetual prayer might be made there for the souls of his ancestors. Dr. Sixtine had other more splendid and lucrative benefices, but the beauty of that little rural valley seems to have clung to his heart, and among the various bequests which he names in his will, appears the sum of fifteen pounds in honour of God and St. Blaze, towards the reparation of the church of Haccombe. Let the good deed be noted here, as well as the kind and homely feeling which induced him to direct that twenty pounds should be distributed among his parishioners at Eglescliffe, "to buy them instruments necessary for their country labours."

Both these distinguished men were frequent visitors to Stepney, and in the pleasant conferences which Colet held with the familiar coterie, one project of his must often have furnished them with a topic of conversation: it was his wish to found a school. Schools, indeed, there already were in rich abundance; during the last thirty years a very harvest of them had been springing up all over England, but none yet founded were quite to Colet's mind. He desired to see an academy in which there should be laid a solid foundation of learning, both sacred and profane. Classical, or what he termed "clene Latin," the fashionable study of Greek, and Scriptural divinity, would never, he argued, establish themselves in the universities until they were first taught in preparatory schools; and he pleased himself with the thought of attaching such a grammar-school to his own church of St Paul's, and bestowing his wealth and his study in bringing it to perfection. He hoped to raise a generation of scholars who should be trained to understand the true sense and spirit of the classical authors, so as to read, write, and speak the learned tongues with ease and elegance; and who, at the same time, should have gone through a careful course of religious instruction; a large-hearted design, which met the warm approval of his literary friends, and of none more than of Erasmus.

The school was accordingly commenced in 1509, at the east end of St. Paul's churchyard. The front next the church was finished in the year following, and bore this inscription:—*Schola catechizationis puerorum in Christi Opt. Max. fide et bonis literis, Anno Christi, MDX.* The endowments provided for the free education of one hundred and fifty-three scholars,[344] and for the maintenance of a master, usher, and chaplain. The school, when complete, was divided into four parts. First the porch, where those whom Colet called his catechumens were instructed in religion, no one being admitted who could not at least say the catechism and know how to read and write. Then came a room for the lower class taught by the usher, and a third for the higher class taught by the master. The captain of each form had a little desk to mark his pre-eminence, and the apartments were only divided by curtains. Lastly, there was a small chapel opening into the schoolroom, where Mass was said daily. The children, however, were not intended to *hear* Mass daily, for, according to Colet's views, this would have been a waste of time. Unlike Bede and Alfred, he was ignorant of what has been called the grand secret of education, "the way how to lose time wisely." Week-day Masses were in his eyes simple superfluities, and he judged the moments so consumed much better spent in study. In accordance with this principle, he himself only said Mass on Sundays and festivals, and argued that he spent the time thus saved more profitably in arranging the matter for his sermons! His scholars, indeed, had their Mass said *for* them every morning in the chapel; but the statutes enjoined that when the Sacring bell was heard, they should only prostrate until after the Elevation, and then rise and go on with their studies. What a revelation of character appears in traits like these, and how wide a distance separates such a tone of spirituality from that of the monastic scholars! How little of the spirit of faith was likely to be imbibed during this daily lesson of irreverence, and what could have been the theory which this much-vaunted director possessed of the spiritual life, when he practically taught his pupils by word and example to value work above prayer, and to save time for study by cutting short their Mass! Yet Colet designed this as a *Catechetical* school, and intended it to be a nursery of Christian piety. The image of the child Jesus stood on the master's seat in the attitude of teaching, with the apposite inscription, "Hear ye Him." The children were instructed to regard Him as the Master of the school, and as they went and came, to bow to His image and salute Him with a brief hymn. Thrice a day, moreover, they were to prostrate, and recite appointed prayers; in short, there were not wanting provisions of a religious character, only much of the true spirit of Catholic devotion had been pared away.

The statutes regarding recreation were drawn up with Puritanic rigorism. Old traditions on this head met with small indulgence at the hands of the reforming founder, and hardening his heart to all the infirmities of the schoolboy nature, he strictly forbade Shrovetide cock-fighting and the disputations of St. Bartholomew's day, which he denounced as "idle babbling." The abolition of cock-fighting was beyond all praise, but I grieve to add that there were absolutely no play days. Nay, so rigid was this rule, that the master was to forfeit forty shillings every time he broke it, unless at the request of an archbishop, bishop, or king. But, strange to say, there was a special provision for the due celebration of Childermas day, when they were all to repair to St. Paul's church, hear the child-bishop's sermon, assist at the High Mass, and offer his lordship a penny. The studies were to consist of good Greek and Latin authors, *especially Christian ones*, "for my intent is," writes the founder, "by this scole specially to increase the knowledge and worshipping of God and our Lord Jesus Christ, and good Christian life and manners in the children." But whilst giving this preference to Christian over Pagan authors he requires "the verrye Romayne eloquence" to be taught, and warming at the bare notion of Scholastic barbarism ever invading his seminary, "will utterly have banished and excluded all such abusion as the later blind world hath brought in, which is rather to be called *bloterature* than *literature*."

Colet had no difficulty in finding a master fully qualified to undertake the direction of this academy. William Lily, the god-son and pupil of Grocyn, and the fellow-student of More, the very ideal of a humble, devout, and unworldly scholar, who had never yet thought of making his learning a way to fortune, but was still plodding on as a poor London pedagogue, was at once promoted to the mastership of St. Paul's, with John Rightwyse for his usher. The next step was to draw up a little book for the use of his scholars containing the rudiments of grammar, and an abridgment of Christian doctrine; and this little book, commonly called Paul's Accidence, was dedicated by Colet to Lily. Herein we find the creed in Latin and English, the seven sacraments, brief explanations of the love of God, and our duty to ourselves and our neighbours, including precepts for the observance of appointed fasts and holy days, and some rules of holy living, with a beautiful Latin prayer to "the Child Jesus, Master of this school," and two others for daily use, one for parents, and another for the virtue of docility.

In his preface to his "Rudiments," Colet apologises for writing on a subject whereon so many had written before him, but explains his purpose to have been the putting things in a clear order for the use of young wits, out of compassion to the tenderness and small capacity of little minds. "I pray God," he continues, "that all may be to His honour and the erudition of children. Wherefore I pray you all, lytel babes, learn gladly this lytel treatise, and commende it dylygently unto your memorye, trusting that ye shall proceed and growe to perfyte literature, and come to be grete clerkes. And lyfte up your lytel whyte hands for me also, which prayeth for you to God."

Wolsey reprinted this little manual for the use of his Ipswich scholars, recommending it to the masters in an epistle from his own pen. In 1513 the indefatigable founder resolved on providing his boys with something more complete. Grammars, indeed, there were in plenty; there was the old Donatus, and the more modern "Lac puerorum" of good Master Holte,[345] and a host of others whose quaint names and flimsy contents have been whimsically criticised by Erasmus. But they did not satisfy the requirements of Colet, and he accordingly composed his treatise on the Eight Parts of Speech, which, with some alterations and considerable additions, forms the syntax of the grammar which afterwards bore the name of Lily's grammar. After Lily had revised and corrected the manuscript, Colet put it into the hands of Erasmus, who made so many alterations, that neither of them could in justice call the work his own, and in 1515 it was published, with an epistle from Erasmus. After its publication Lily drew up the rules, known as the *Propria quæ maribus*, and *As in præsenti*, his usher Rightwyse adding some finishing touches. About the same time Linacre was engaged on a somewhat similar work, but his "Compendium of Grammar," originally drawn up for the use of the Princess Mary, was judged by Colet rather too abstruse for the comprehension of beginners, and he did not, therefore, admit it into his school. This seems to have been resented by the sensitive grammarian, and Erasmus had to interpose to restore a good understanding between him and the dean.

Lily proved an excellent master, and among his first pupils were the famous antiquary Leland and Thomas Lupset, son to Colet's amanuensis, who was afterwards admitted to close intimacy by More and Reginald Pole. One fault, however, appeared in the management of the school, too common at that time, namely, the excessive severity of the discipline. This is perhaps to be charged partly to the account of Colet, whose views were as austere in what regarded the education of children, as they were in the direction of souls; and partly to the influence of Rightwyse, who was a scholar of Eton, and brought with him thence maxims of school government, which were exceedingly harsh, not to say cruel. In fact, since education had passed from the hands of the monastics into those of professional pedagogues, the paternal spirit which formerly presided over the Catholic schoolroom had been gradually fading away. It seemed agreed by all that the Greek grammar, and the "verrye Romayne eloquence," could not be attained without an unsparing use of the rod; for we find the same complaint of cruelty made of the French professors of the time. In England this unmerciful system kept its ground throughout the whole of the Tudor period, and we find Sir John Elyot advising his "governor" to provoke a child to study with a pleasant face, and deprecating "cruel and yrous masters, by whom the wits of children be dulled, whereof we need no better witness than daily experience." The Eton fashion was to flog a boy directly he appeared in the school, as a sort of entrance fee, of which old Tusser dolefully complains;[346] and something of this sort of discipline existed at St. Paul's, and was supported by the approval of Colet.

To the credit of Erasmus, it must be said that he strongly condemned such severity; he knew from his own experience that brutal tutors ruin many a hopeful lad, and advocated the milder system of teaching, which he himself followed with so much success. He was wont to quote the example of Spensippus, who would have pictures of joy and gladness to be set round his school: and in his tract on education, quotes with pleasure the story of an English gentleman, who seeing that his little son was very fond of archery, bought him a bow and arrows, and painted them with the letters of the Greek alphabet. The capitals were marked on the butt, and whenever the child had hit a letter and could tell the name of it, he was rewarded with a cherry.

This was not at all in Colet's way, and Erasmus tells a frightful story of the cruelty which he himself witnessed—practised under his direction. "I once knew a certain theologian," he says, "who must needs have masters who were zealous floggers. He esteemed this an excellent means for subduing all asperity of character, and mastering the wantonness of youth. Never did he sit down to a repast with his disciples, but at the end of the meal some one or other of them was brought out to be flogged; and his cruelty was sometimes exercised on the innocent, merely to accustom them to stripes. I was once standing by when he thus called out from dinner a boy of, I should think, ten years old, who had recently come to the school from his mother. He began by saying that his mother was a most pious woman, and had specially recommended the boy to his care, and then that he might have an opportunity of flogging him, he charged him with I know not what atrocity, and made a sign to the prefect of the school to give him a flogging. The latter at once knocked the boy down, and beat him as if he had committed a sacrilege. The doctor called out several times, 'Enough, enough,' but the savage went on with his barbarity, till the boy almost swooned. Then turning to us, the doctor quietly observed that he had not merited any punishment, but that it was done to humble his spirit. Who would treat his bondslave in such a way? nay, I may say, who would thus treat his ass?"[347] Though Colet is not named in this passage, yet he is generally believed to have been the "theologian" in question, the prefect of discipline being no other than his usher, Rightwyse.

We gather from Colet's letters to his friend, that on one point of opinion they greatly differed, namely, in the view they took of religious life. Erasmus, when he speaks of monks, forgets his usual politeness, and descends to a style of which Luther might have been proud. They are designated as "foul and noxious insects, which it is a sort of pollution to touch; creatures so detested and so detestable, that it is regarded as an ill omen to meet one in the street; dolts and idiots, who think it a mark of consummate piety not to be able to read; wretched beings, who are distinguished by a certain obstinate malignity of disposition, and who think that they are charming the ears of the saints when, with asinine voices, they bray out their psalms in choir." One is ashamed to transcribe such language, and to remember that the greatest scholar of his time considered it to be wit.

But Colet was of another mind. He condemned the relaxed life led in many religious houses; but there was a theory of monasticism which he loved and admired. It was hardly the Catholic theory of religious life, for Colet's dream seems to have been to have found some retreat where he could have spent the close of life with a few chosen friends of kindred tastes, living and conversing with them after the manner of the ancient philosophers. He even set on foot inquiries, to discover if any house suitable for his purpose existed in Italy or Germany; but finding none to his mind, he built himself a residence adjoining the Carthusian monastery at Shene, whither he often retired, and purposed withdrawing there altogether, and giving up all his public engagements that he might prepare in quiet for his end. In his last letter to Erasmus, we see that his old interests were fast losing their hold upon him as he felt the sands of life running out. His friend had sent him some of Reuchlin's Cabalistic works. "O Erasmus," he replies, "of books and knowledge there is no end. There is no better thing in this world than a holy life, and no other way to attain it than by the earnest love and imitation of Jesus. Wherefore, leaving all wandering paths, this, to the best of my ability, is what I long for." He made all his last dispositions, therefore, bestowing extraordinary care in drawing up his will, in which there occurs no word suggestive of suffrages for his soul; a fact which shows, that if he did not condemn the practice of praying for the dead, he at any rate attached no value to it. Death overtook him sooner than he anticipated, and in the year 1519 he expired at his favourite retreat, almost at the moment when Luther was making his mock submission to the Sovereign Pontiff.

What shall we say of the character of this celebrated man? a strong and earnest one it was, no doubt; one that loved justice and hated iniquity, and had a zeal for the interests of God. Erasmus somewhere speaks of his "passionate admiration for the wonderful majesty of Christ." Nor in judging him must we forget that he lived in an age when worldliness had infected the high places in the Church; and that, if his denunciation of abuses was often arrogant, there were plenty of abuses to denounce. Yet granting all this, our readers will long ago have agreed on their verdict. From such a type of Catholicism, they will say, in which we see piety without unction, austerity without sweetness, and an absence—if not of faith—at least of all its tenderest instincts; from such a form of godliness, over which the coming spectre of Lutheranism had already projected somewhat of its baneful shadow, may the schools and scholars of England be long preserved! Such characters, if we cannot impeach them of formal heresy, yet indicate a woful wane of faith, and fully explain the significance of those rules[348] left by St. Ignatius to his disciples, wherein he taught them how to conform their sentiments to the sentiments of the Catholic Church. He was not content with bidding them hold fast to her creeds, but would have them esteem and speak highly of all her minor practices of devotion. For these, in the judgment of one of the most sagacious among the saints, are the pulses by which we count the heart-beatings of the true believer; and in Colet these were silent. Though he died a Catholic, therefore, Protestants unanimously claim him as one of their precursors; and his panegyric, from which we gather all that is known of his life, was drawn up by Erasmus for the edification of his Lutheran friend, the notorious Dr. Jonas Jodocus.

The mention of Shene may fitly introduce a younger and more illustrious scholar, who had received his early education in that monastery, and who, at the time of Colet's death, was studying at Oxford, and was received as a frequent and welcome visitor in the family circle of Sir Thomas More. Reginald Pole was then a youth of nineteen, exhibiting both the comely dignity of his Plantagenet blood, and a promise of intellectual excellence that was not belied by his after career. From Shene he had passed on to Oxford, and at Corpus Christi College, under the tuition of Linacre and Latymer, had thrown himself heart and soul into classical studies. Though he afterwards in great part laid them aside, in order more exclusively to devote himself to sacred letters, yet he always retained the style of a polished Latinist, as all his writings testify. Young as he was, he had secured the friendship of More, and was often admitted into the family circle and the happy schoolroom of Chelsea. In a letter to his daughter Margaret, More speaks of the admiration he had expressed on reading one of his Latin epistles, and calls him "not so noble by birth as he is by learning and virtue;" while Pole, on his side, was wont in after years to boast of the friendship of More and Fisher as something he valued more highly than the familiarity of all the princes of Christendom.

The society at this time gathered round the English Court was extraordinarily brilliant. Besides a throng of native scholars, it included several illustrious foreigners, such as Ludovicus Vives, the Spanish Quinctilian, as he was called, who condescended to direct the education of the Princess Mary. Three queens graced the royal circle, one of them the consort of Henry, and the other two his widowed sisters of France and Scotland. The poets and pageant-makers of the time racked their fancies to find new ways of introducing the Tudor roses white and red and the rich pomegranates of Arragon (the devices of the royal dames), and to make the most of a Court illuminated by three crowned beauties. Erasmus is never weary of praising the king, the queen, the cardinal, and the bishops; they are all patrons of letters, the Court is the seat of the Muses, and might vie with Athens in the days of Pericles. The queen is as virtuous as she is learned; she daily reads the English Scriptures, spends six hours at her prayers and kneels all the time without a cushion. The king is a scholar and a musician; he is devout, moreover, writes very elaborate Masses in eight parts, and has gone on pilgrimage to Our Lady of Walsingham, walking barefoot from the town of Barsham; and Erasmus has gone there too, and has hung up a copy of verses as his offering at her altar. How artistically he paints the broad green way across the fields by which the pilgrims approach, and the little chapel built within the splendid church, in imitation of the Holy House of Loretto, wherein there is no light save from the tapers that burn with so delicious an odour, and the walls of which are blazing with gold and jewels!

Or we are introduced to the "solemn Christmas" kept by the Court at Richmond or Greenwich, with "revels, disguisings, and banquets royal, all with great nobleness;" and we observe how the quaint mummings which found favour at the beginning of the reign are gradually giving place to "masks, after the manner of Italy, a thing not seen before in England, with which some were content, but which others that knew the fashion of it,"[349] appear to have disapproved. Such scenes were well calculated to dazzle and fascinate a young courtier; but Pole was proof against them; he showed no hurry either to plunge into the amusements of his age, or to enter on the brilliant political career which fortune seemed to open before him, and had hardly appeared at Court before he solicited from the king a fresh leave of absence.

The six years he had spent at Oxford did not by any means satisfy his ardour for study, and, with the consent of the king, who had charged himself with the education of his young kinsman, he proceeded to Padua, which Erasmus styled the Athens of Europe, and where students from all countries were eager to resort. Here "the nobleman of England," as he was called by the Italians, soon won golden opinions—from some, for his singular modesty and virtue, from others, for the graceful acquirements that so well became his royal birth; and here he first became introduced to Bembo and Sadolet, with the latter of whom his acquaintance ripened into friendship. After the fashion of the times, he received a certain number of humbler scholars into his household, and among these were Longolius, who records his dislike for frivolous conversation, and Lupset, afterwards Greek Professor at Oxford. Erasmus, too, was often a welcome guest when the wanderings of that restless scholar led him to Padua, and his voluminous correspondence includes many letters to Pole, who, though totally opposed to his views on religious matters, was yet unable, like the rest of the world, to shut him out of his affections.

Meanwhile the breach between the reformers and the Church had terribly widened, and open war was being waged between the two parties. Henry VIII. had written his "Defence of the Seven Sacraments," and Luther had published his "Reply;" the scurrility of which had called both More and Fisher into the field as controversialists. But Erasmus still kept silence. He was on excellent terms with Luther and Melanchthon, the worthy Dr. Jonas, and the other Coryphæi of the Reform. He corresponded with them all, and did them every service in his power at the head of those German Humanists whose literary labours were directed against the old-fashioned theologians, while their political intrigues aimed at winning over the young emperor to their side, or at least at procuring his neutrality. It is true he regretted that Luther should openly have broken from the Church, and the excesses of the heretics offered fair mark for his satire; nevertheless with most of their views of reform he heartily sympathised. On the other hand, as he was not ashamed of avowing, he had no intention of dying a martyr for his principles, neither did he at all contemplate offending the Catholic sovereigns by whom he was petted and pensioned. He counted on his own address for enabling him to steer a middle course, to save both his head and his Court remittances, and earn a good name for moderation. But on this fair horizon clouds were now about to rise. He received an official hint from Cuthbert Tonstall that King Henry was surprised and offended at his silence, and that rumours were even afloat that he had assisted Luther in the composition of his "Reply." In vain did Erasmus protest his innocence; only one course would satisfy the king. Let him write against Luther, if he wished his sincerity to be believed; the whole Catholic world expected it of him, and was scandalised at his delay. But if this did not suit him, he could not be surprised if his pension from the Court of England were withdrawn. Thus sorely pressed, Erasmus prepared to obey. But meanwhile, a whisper of what was going on had reached Luther's ears, and he wrote at once, advising his quondam ally to be wise and preserve silence. Luther, at least, had the merit of being a plain speaker; "If you take up the cudgels against me," he says, "you will be beset on both sides, and must infallibly be worsted. Everybody knows that what you style moderation, is really duplicity. All I ask is, that you will stand quietly by and see the play, and not take part in it, and then I will leave you alone; but if not, you know very well what you have to expect." This letter by some means became public, and Erasmus felt that his last chance was gone. If *now* he held his tongue, he should be accused of collusion; so, in pure desperation, he plunged into the combat, and wrote his treatise on Free Will, copies of which he was careful to send to all the crowned heads of Europe. Wonderful credit he took to himself for this achievement, declaring that he had exposed himself to be stoned to death by the heretics, but that he gloried in suffering for so good a cause. At the same time his letters to Melanchthon are couched in the most pitiful and apologetic strain. He could not help himself; he was a lost man if he had held his peace; the *figuli Romanenses* had made the Catholic sovereigns believe he was a Lutheran; he would have been ruined if he had refused to write. To Vives he was more explicit. "I have written a treatise on Free Will," he says, "but to confess the truth I lost my own. There my heart dictated one thing, and my pen wrote another."[350] However, whether his attack were sham or earnest mattered little to Luther; it was a declaration of war, and as such he treated it, replying to it with his usual promptitude, and with more than his usual grossness. The other leaders of the Reform likewise gave tongue on the occasion, and denounced the unwilling controversialist as a Balaam who had been hired to curse Israel. Poor Erasmus had reaped the just reward of his shuffling policy, and felt himself in a sad quandary. He knew not whether to advance or retreat, and either way he had to wade through the mire. He pours out his vexation in a letter to Pole; in which, however, he is careful to keep up the tone of a sufferer for the faith. "Luther has written a huge volume against me," he says, "in a style one would not use in addressing the Turk; and so, from the partisan of peace and quiet which I would fain remain, I am forced to turn gladiator, and, what is worse, to fight with wild beasts in the arena."

On his return to England, Pole found a sad and ominous cloud hanging over the Court which he had left so prosperous and splendid. The question of the divorce had already been mooted, and the bad success of the negotiations with Rome had brought about the fall of Wolsey. Henry was anxious to secure the support of Pole, whose influence at Rome he foresaw would one day be powerful, and employed his new favourite, Cromwell, to sound and tempt him. That worthy minister commenced operations by putting a copy of Machiavel's works into the hands of Reginald, who returned it to him with disgust, and contrived to get leave to retire to Shene, where he took up his residence in Colet's old house. Here he remained for two years, carefully abstaining from taking any part in public affairs, and at the end of that time asked and obtained leave to proceed for another term of study to the University of Paris. He was not long suffered to remain there in peace. The notable scheme of consulting the European universities and divines, which had been originally proposed by Wolsey, was warmly taken up by his successors, and royal agents were now busy in every foreign country, seeking, by bribes and cajolery, to obtain opinions favourable to the king's divorce. To the credit of the English universities it must be said they opposed a stubborn resistance, and the affirmative declaration sent to the king never received the votes of the majority.[351] But foreign academies were found more pliant; it is true the charge for a professor's conscience was somewhat exorbitant, but still they had their price, and did not refuse to be bargained for. In Germany, indeed, Luther's influence was powerful enough to prevent his old adversary from receiving any assistance, but greater success was met with in France and Italy, and a commission was now sent to Pole, requiring him to gather up the suffrages of the Paris professors. He contrived to evade the odious office thus wilily thrust upon him, and was sickened to the heart by observing the eagerness with which the Humanists came forward in this disgraceful business. No one was a more active agent than Croke, the Greek orator, who wrote complacently to the king, detailing the success which attended his "honourable presents" to the Italian professors. Richard Pace, too, the successor of Colet, and the holder of several diplomatic offices, writes to say he has found a man ready to put the case *either for or against* the divorce, according to his Majesty's pleasure, so as all the divines of England shall not be able to reply. The facile casuist here alluded to was no other than Wakefield, the Hebrew professor at Oxford; and, in short, turn where we will, we find the pedagogues busily engaged in doing very dirty work at high wages.

Pole was next recalled to England to be tempted with caresses. The Archbishopric of York, it was hinted, was at his command, if he were willing to bend to the king's wishes. His own family were employed to move his determination, and at last, beset on all sides, he wavered, and consented to see the king. Henry received him graciously in the gallery at Whitehall; but when he tried to speak, conscience gained the day, and, with a faltering voice, instead of protesting his readiness to serve his Grace in his "secret matter," he plainly declared his conviction that the proposed divorce was utterly unlawful. Though Henry cut him short with a volley of reproaches, he treated him with more magnanimity than might have been expected. He did not order him to the Tower, and silenced the officious courtiers who expressed their disgust at Reginald's ingratitude, by the unexpected declaration that he loved him in spite of his obstinacy.[352] His pension was not withdrawn, and he was suffered once more to retire abroad; and in 1531 Pole withdrew to Italy, never again to set foot on the English shores till he landed there a Papal legate, to reconcile his country, for too brief a space, to the communion of the Catholic Church.

It is unnecessary to pursue the events of the great tragedy, save in so far as they affected the career of Pole. In his retreat at Padua, his heart was torn by the news of each successive step by which the infatuated king was plunging his country into schism; the rupture with Rome, the repudiation of Catherine, the marriage with Anne, and the formal establishment of the royal supremacy. The English Lords and Commons submitted to all this with wonderful docility, but to Henry's vexation he found that his proceedings were daily losing him the countenance of friends abroad. The Emperor of course, was his sworn enemy; Francis I. had refused to listen to the explanations of his ambassadors; Cochlæus, and other grave writers, had drawn the pen against him; and even Calvin made game of his new-fangled supremacy, and ridiculed the man who had delivered his country from the primacy of Peter to saddle it with the primacy of Henry. Erasmus, too, had withdrawn from a country where it was no longer safe for a man to have an opinion. He was just then directing his irony against the Protestants, who had disgusted him with their grossness, and whom he pronounces a sad set of hypocrites. "People talk of Lutheranism as a tragic business, but for my part I think it is a regular comedy, and, like other comedies, the piece always ends with a marriage." Elsewhere he says, "We have been stunned long enough with the cry of *Gospel, Gospel, Gospel.* What we want is Gospel manners. These Evangelicals love money and pleasure, and despise everything else." Henry's Acts of Parliament, too, seasoned as they were with axe and fagot, did not suit his notions of moderation; and, besides, just then Pope Paul III. was making him tempting offers, so that Erasmus was not at all disposed to take up the gauntlet on behalf of a prince, against whose conduct all the respectable part of Europe was protesting. Henry had, therefore, no one to look to out of his own kingdom save the small German princes and Protestant divines; and it was a sore humiliation to sue for support to the religionists whom it was his boast to have defeated in controversy. In this extremity, his thoughts turned to Pole, who owed him everything, and who, he could not believe, would ever openly take part against him. Cuthbert Tonstall, Reginald's dearest friend, had swallowed the new oath, and accepted the bishopric of Durham; why should Reginald's conscience be more tender? A messenger was, therefore, posted to Padua, with letters to Pole inviting him to accept the king's offers of favour, and write in defence of those royal claims which had been accepted as law by the English Parliament and Hierarchy.[353] Pole saw that the time was come to take his part openly and decidedly. He sat down and counted the cost, and then he took pen in hand and wrote, not an apology for the supremacy, but his celebrated treatise *De Unitate Ecclesiastica* in which he sums up all the acts by which England has been severed from Catholic communion, fearlessly condemns the sacrileges of the king, and calls on him to enter on the path of penance. Whilst thus engaged, terrible tidings reached him: the axe had fallen at last, and More and Fisher were numbered with the martyrs; and, with the tears blotting his paper, he gave vent to his sorrow in that magnificent apostrophe to the memory of his friends, which he introduces in his Third Book. The treatise was finished in four months, and despatched to England by a faithful messenger, who was charged to deliver it into the king's own hands; and then, fully aware of the consequences of his determination, Reginald set out for Rome, whither he had been invited by Paul III. almost immediately on his accession. His friends entreated him not openly to break with the king by accepting any preferment from the Pope. The two Houses of Parliament even sent him a common letter to the same effect; but before it reached him, Pole was at Rome, and had received from the new Pontiff the dignity of Cardinal.

Two months later he found himself charged with a dangerous and difficult mission. The fate of Anne Boleyn had, it was hoped, removed from the king his worst councillor, and the insurrection of the northern counties of England bore witness that the people themselves were still true to the faith. Hopes were, therefore, entertained that negotiations for a reconciliation might now be opened, and Pole was accordingly appointed legate north of the Alps, with instructions to proceed to Flanders, to bring about a peace between France and the Empire, to announce the Pope's resolve to call a General Council, and to seize any occasion that might present itself for confirming the English Catholics in their faith, and negotiating with the king's government. The legation, however, was an utter failure. Henry had proclaimed the Cardinal a traitor, and set a price on his head; he had offered to buy him of the Emperor in exchange for a force of four thousand men; he had so managed matters that the legate was warned to leave France as quickly as possible, and refused admission into the imperial territory; the English agents were everywhere busy endeavouring to procure either his open seizure or his secret assassination; and in the midst of these multiplied perils Pole had no support save his own great heart and dauntless courage. His chaplains and followers were perplexed and terrified. A legate in those days travelled in state, with his cross borne openly at the head of his train; but the attendant, whose duty it was to carry the cross, turned faint-hearted, and suggested the prudence of concealing these marks of dignity in a hostile country. The last of the Plantagenets, however, was not the man to quail in the presence of danger; he calmly took the cross from the hands of the bearer, and fixing its point firmly in his own stirrup, rode along, thinking perhaps of St. Thomas, and certainly as ready as he to face the assassins, and shed his life-blood in the cause of the Church.

A second legation in 1538 proved equally fruitless, and its only result was the slaughter of every one of Pole's family on whom Henry could lay his hands. The Cardinal meanwhile was recalled to Rome, and appointed to the government of Viterbo, where he heard, in 1541, of the murder of his aged mother, and gave thanks that she, too, had been deemed worthy to suffer for the faith. His political engagements had not weaned him from the love of letters, and, amid his many trials, he found his chief solace, after his exercises of piety, in the company of his learned friends. Pole entertained very strong views as to the necessity of restoring a more Christian system of studies, and laboured hard to bring those around him to the same mind. Sadolet had just published his "Treatise on Education," and Pole addressed him a letter which Erasmus calls worthy of Cicero, touchingly remonstrating with him for not giving a more prominent place to Christian theology. Sadolet defends himself by saying that theology is a part of philosophy, and the perfection of it; but Pole was not satisfied. It might do well enough, he says, if your pupil lived in the time of Plato or Aristotle, but a Christian scholar requires something more than philosophy. Their difference of opinion, however, was expressed on both sides with equal courtesy and moderation, and the correspondence between them offers a pleasing contrast to those acrimonious disputes, in which the scholars of the last generation had so frequently disgraced themselves.

This was not the only occasion when Pole exerted himself to give a more decidedly Christian direction to his friend's studies. Sadolet had two works on hand; one a treatise in praise of philosophy, the other a Commentary on St. Paul. He was doubting which to finish first, and Bembo of course advised the preference to be given to philosophy. Pole was as great a lover of classical antiquity as either of them, but at that grievous juncture, when a swarm of heretics were in the field, it seemed to him a kind of infidelity for the children of the Church to waste their time and genius on elegant trifling. His arguments decided Sadolet in favour of St. Paul, and he afterwards received his friend's hearty thanks for having thus determined his choice. "There were not wanting plenty," writes Sadolet, "who were ready to give me very different advice, but you counselled me to embrace studies, the emoluments of which extend to the other life, and your words have decided me henceforth to devote myself to sacred literature."

There was, however, nothing of the narrowness of a zealot in Pole's character; he and Contarini were advocates for a mild policy even with heretics; and his gentle persuasion had a happy success in recalling many who had been seduced by the new opinions, among others, the Latin poet Mark Anthony Flaminius. This celebrated man had been one of his early friends, but had suffered himself to be won over by the specious arguments of Valdes. Pole invited him to Viterbo, and, by dint of patience and kindness, restored him to a better mind, and it was in his house that he afterwards expired, as Beccadelli expresses it, "like a good Christian."[354] In the same spirit he received into his family Lazarus Bonamico, professor of humanity at Padua, saying that he was worth something better than the occupation of explaining Virgil, and that the study of theology which he wished him to embrace, required the whole man. He assisted Bembo also in his last moments, and his house was the refuge of all those English Catholics, who, like himself, preferred exile to apostasy.

Among these, one is glad to reckon George, the son of our old friend William Lily, whom he took under his protection, and who, after writing some learned works, and contributing to the history of Paulus Jovius, returned with Pole to England in Queen Mary's days, and died a prebendary of Canterbury. And so we will leave our great countryman for a time doing the work of an apostle among the scholars of his day, to find him again at the head of that momentous council, which owed to his influence not a few of its most important measures of reform. Before following him there, we have to take our farewell of the English schools, whose destinies from this time form a page in the history of sacrilege. The first royal visitation of the universities, held in virtue of King Henry's newly-claimed supremacy, took place in 1535, when the further study of scholastic philosophy and canon law were prohibited. For a brief space the attempt was made to fill up the hiatus with an extra quantity of Greek and profane studies, and then it was that Sir John Cheke achieved that celebrity at Cambridge which Milton has commemorated in a sonnet. All the Humanists indeed were not men of equally solid learning, for Saunders tells us the universities were filled with a multitude of young orators and poets, who, after celebrating the mock obsequies of Scotus and St. Thomas, tried, by means of unbecoming comedies, songs, and verses, to decoy the unwary into the errors of the sects, and immorality of life. On the whole, the attempt was a failure; English scholars were not yet sufficiently familiarised with the new learning to give it a very warm reception, and the exotic Greek studies, like plants that had been overforced, soon drooped and perished.[355] Canon law and theology, and, above all, the despised scholastic logic, were precisely the studies in which Catholic Oxford had most excelled; and their abolition was tantamount to the formal closing of her schools. And during the reign of Edward VI. the divinity school was actually closed, and in spite of every effort on the part of the Humanists, the decay became so universal that all the other schools, except two, were shut up, or let out to laundresses and glovers. "There, where Minerva formerly sat as regent," says Wood, "was nothing during all the reign of King Edward but wretched solitariness; nothing but a dead silence prevailed." The dissolution of the monasteries, moreover, had ruined upwards of a hundred flourishing academies, which served as feeders to the universities, the place of which was very imperfectly filled by King Edward's grammar-schools. Thus, a large proportion of those who had formerly followed the pursuit of learning, now betook themselves to mechanical trades, and the schools literally died out for want of scholars. In 1550 we find Roger Ascham, a strenuous adherent of the new worship, lamenting over the decay of the old grammar-schools, and predicting in consequence the speedy extinction of the universities: whilst Latimer about the same time is found declaring that there were at least ten thousand fewer students in the kingdom than might have been found twenty years previously.

The ruin of learning at the universities was completed by the bigotry of those foreign Protestant divines, who, in King Edward's time, were brought over from Germany and Switzerland to fill up the professorships which no English scholar could be found to accept under the new ecclesiastical régime. Among these the celebrated Peter Vermigli, better known by the name of Peter Martyr, was indeed a good scholar, but the greater number of his colleagues were not only without learning, but, following in the footsteps of Luther, they proclaimed war against it as "a human thing." They voted the academical degrees "Antichristian," and showed their horror of all the vain things fondly invented by Popery, not only by the breaking of images, but by the burning of libraries. Duke Humphrey's precious collection of classical authors was condemned to the flames; the exquisite illuminations of his costly volumes possibly suggesting the notion that they must be of the nature of Roman service books. When Sir Thomas Bodley took up his residence at Oxford, towards the end of Elizabeth's reign, he informs us that he found the libraries "in every part wasted and ruined," and it is well known that the splendid foundation which we owe to his munificence, was but a collection of such poor fragments as had accidentally escaped destruction.

Of the material sacrileges committed by King Edward's visitors it is unnecessary here to speak, and without necessity one would not willingly enter on the sorrowful tale. The shell of the universities was left, to be gradually informed with a new spirit, a new learning, a new life; which, as years rolled on, became no longer new, and so gradually grew to be regarded by Englishmen as venerable. Oxford, with her thousand Catholic memories, became in process of time the stronghold of Anglican Church Toryism; a pigmy destiny, indeed, for her who had been founded by the hands of saints, yet one with which, on the whole, she has showed herself amply satisfied. The Royal Supremacy, which had first cut down her fair proportions, clung to her like the poisoned garment of Nessus, but though it sometimes galled her, she made the most (as was fitting) of her solitary dogma, and, in a memorable moment of her history, proclaimed fidelity to it in its extremest form to be "the badge of the Church of England."

Here, then, we will bid farewell to Oxford; to those venerable walls round which there still hang shadows of the past, out of which alas! too many build up an unsubstantial cloudland, with the gorgeous beauty of which they rest content. The Catholic, while he feels the power which even such phantoms of the old faith exercise over the heart, knows well enough that he does but gaze on

The loveliness of death

That parts not quite with parting breath.

He reads her ancient motto, and can but pray that a beam of the True Light may one day again illuminate her, and that she, over whose beautiful places the fire has passed, may once more sing, according to the days of her youth, "*Dominus Illuminatio mea.*"

CHAPTER XXIV.

THE COUNCIL OF TRENT.

WHEN the conclave of October 13, 1534, announced the election of Cardinal Alexander Farnese as successor to Clement VII., few men probably anticipated what would be the character of the new pontificate. The antecedents of Paul III. appeared to link him with what may be called the Conservative party of the day. He had been a pupil of Pomponius Lætus, had been raised to the purple by Alexander VI., had grown up in the luxurious atmosphere of Leo's Court, and in his early youth, before he embraced the ecclesiastical state, had not escaped the worldly infection which clung to the literary circles among which he mixed. Men of letters indeed might naturally look for encouragement from the friend of Sadolet, the correspondent of Erasmus, and the elegant commentator on Cicero, but few expected to find in him the uncompromising champion of ecclesiastical reform. Yet such he soon proved himself. One fault alone was charged to his administration, the promotion of relatives whose subsequent misconduct brought scandal on the Church, and anguish to his own heart. But in other respects his favour was bestowed on precisely those who were best qualified to forward the interests of religion. He filled the sacred college with men worthy of the purple; Pole, Fisher, Caraffa, Contarini, Sadolet, Aleander, and Cortese, were all cardinals of his nomination. In his love of art and poetry he was hardly inferior to Leo X., but the thoughts that occupied his soul as Supreme Head of the Church had a higher and nobler aim than even the encouragement of letters. To restore peace between France and the Empire, to keep back the onward progress of the Turks, and to call a General Council for the purpose of healing the wounds of the Church, these were the objects he set before him as the work of his pontificate, and he never rested till he had accomplished them. Until Charles and Francis had laid down their arms, however, the Council so loudly demanded by men of all opinions was a simple impossibility, and ten weary years had to pass before these Christian princes could be brought to terms. If for a moment they suspended hostilities, it was only to renew them with greater animosity than before, and to give the French king an opportunity of covering himself with infamy by calling to his help the Turkish hordes, and inviting them to overrun Italy. Whilst Europe was involved in these broils, it was plain there could be no Council; but at least there could be the initiatives of reform, and in 1537 Paul III. proved his earnest desire to begin the work by naming a Commission of cardinals and other ecclesiastics, whom he charged with the delicate task of drawing up a statement of those abuses which, in their judgment, most loudly called for redress.

This Commission was composed of nine men, whose names were equally illustrious for integrity and learning. They were the cardinals Contarini, Caraffa, Sadolet, and Pole, together with five other prelates afterwards raised to the same dignity; namely, Fregoso, Archbishop of Salerno; Aleander, Archbishop of Brindisi; Ghiberti, Bishop of Verona; Gregory Cortese, Abbot of Lerins; and Father Thomas Badia, Master of the Sacred Palace.

Some of these have already been spoken of. Contarini and Aleander had distinguished themselves by their missions in Germany and their fruitless efforts to conciliate and win back the misguided Lutherans. Ghiberti had been associated with Pole in his legations, and was bound to him by close ties of friendship. He was regarded by St. Charles Borromeo as the ideal of a Christian bishop, and his portrait always hung in the saint's chamber, to urge him, as he said, to imitate his pastoral career. He was also profoundly learned, and had set up a printing-press in his episcopal palace, whence issued forth magnificent editions of the Greek Fathers. Cortese, a Benedictine abbot, had revived the fame of the old monastery of Lerins, and restored regular observance in a great number of other houses of his order. Tiraboschi calls him one of the most elegant writers of his age, and says that his theological works are free from the least tincture of scholastic barbarism. Frederic Fregoso was a Hebrew scholar, and Aleander a learned Orientalist. Not one, in short, of all the nine could be taunted as a disciple of the retrograde school, and all had in one way or other taken part in the revival of polite letters.

Out of the twenty-seven heads to which they reduced their statement of existing abuses, one only concerns our present subject. The whole report was indeed of great importance, and furnished the basis on which were framed many of the decrees of discipline subsequently promulgated by the Fathers of Trent. But it is the sixteenth article alone which touches on the subject of university education, which we will here reproduce as containing both a brief summary and a sufficient justification of much that has been put forward in the foregoing pages. After noticing the reforms urgently called for in the collation to ecclesiastical benefices, the Congregation of prelates proceed as follows:—

"It is a great and pernicious abuse that in the public schools, especially of Italy, many philosophers teach impiety. Even in the churches most impious disputations are held, and if some are of a pious nature, yet in them sacred things are treated before the people in a most irreverent manner. We think, therefore, that it should be pointed out to the bishops, in those places where public schools exist, that they admonish those who deliver lectures not to teach impiety to the young, but to manifest to them the weakness of natural reason in questions appertaining to God, to the recent origin or eternity of the world, and the like, and that they rather lead them to piety. Also, that they permit not public disputations to be held on questions of this nature, nor even on theological subjects, which certainly in this way lose much in vulgar esteem; but let disputations be held in private on these matters, and let the public disputations be on other questions of physics. And the same thing ought to be enjoined on all other bishops, specially of great cities where disputations of this sort are wont to be held. And the same care should be employed about the printing of books, and all princes should be written to, warning them not to allow books of all sorts to be printed everywhere in their dominions. And the care of the matter should be committed to the ordinaries. And whereas it is now customary to read to boys in the schools the 'Colloquies' of Erasmus,[356] in which there are many things which instil impiety into inexperienced minds, the reading of this book, and of others of a similar character, ought to be prohibited."[357]

This certainly is a most remarkable document. It proceeded not from a body of "Scotists" and "barbarians," but from elegant Humanists, all of them university scholars, whilst some, like Aleander, had themselves occupied Professors' chairs. It will be observed that the evils which they point out in the existing system of education, and which they indicate as lying at the root of so many prevailing corruptions, are precisely those the growth of which we have been watching from the time when the universities replaced the episcopal and monastic schools. The whole weakness of the Professorial system is here laid bare; its incitements to vanity, its tendency to substitute novelties that tickle the ears of a mixed audience for the teaching of solid truth; the system which had Berengarius and Abelard for its fittest representatives; which had already produced a goodly crop of heretics and false teachers, and which, while it extinguished the old ecclesiastical seminaries, supplied in place of them, nothing better for the training of the Christian priesthood, than universities which, in Italy, at least, had grown to be little else than academies of heathen philosophy. Such a grave and deliberate declaration, and from such authority, requires no commentary; it was a candid avowal from the choicest intellects of Christendom, that three centuries before, a false step had been taken; and a plain and solemn warning that if the evil results of that step were now to be remedied, it could only be by returning to the ancient paths.

It was precisely at this time that St. Ignatius and his companions first appeared in Rome, and submitted to the Holy See the plan for the foundation of their society. The education of youth[358] is set forth in the Formula of Approval granted by Paul III. in 1540 as the first duty embraced by the new Institute, and it is to be observed that the two patrons who most powerfully interested themselves in obtaining this approval were both of them members of the above-named commission, namely, Cardinal Gaspar Contarini, and the Dominican, Father Thomas Badia. Although the new religious were not at once able to begin the establishment of colleges, yet the plan of those afterwards founded was gradually ripening in the sagacious mind of St. Ignatius, who looked to these institutions as calculated to oppose the surest bulwarks against the progress of heresy. The first regular college of the Society was that established at Gandia in 1546, through the zeal of St. Francis Borgia, third General of the Society; and the regulations by which it was governed, and which were embodied in the constitutions, were extended to all the Jesuit colleges afterwards founded. The studies were to include theology, both positive and scholastic, as well as grammar, poetry, rhetoric, and philosophy. The course of philosophy was to last three years, that of theology four; and the Professors of Philosophy were enjoined to treat their subject in such a way as to dispose the mind for the study of theology, instead of setting up faith and reason in opposition to one another. The theology of St. Thomas, and the philosophy of Aristotle, were to be followed, except on those points where the teaching of the latter was opposed to the Catholic faith. Those points of metaphysics which involved questions depending for their demonstration on revealed truth, such as free-will, or the origin of evil, were not to be treated in the course of philosophy, but to be reserved for that of theology. No classical authors, whether Greek or Latin, wherein was to be found anything contrary to good morals, were to be read in the classes until first corrected, and the students were subjected to rules of discipline which aimed at forming in them habits of solid piety. It is clear that colleges thus constituted were exactly fitted to carry out those reforms which Pole and his colleagues had suggested as being so urgently called for, and that the system of education thus proposed effectually excluded the "impious philosophy" which had been nurtured in the academies of Italy.

Meanwhile the political horizon was gradually growing clearer, and on the 13th of December 1545, the first session of the long-expected Council was opened by the three legates nominated by the Pope. They were the Cardinals del Monte, Cervini, and Pole. The two first successively filled the chair of St. Peter after Paul III., under the titles of Julius III. and Marcellus II. Pole held his office only until the October of the following year, when the state of his health obliged him to retire from the legation. He nevertheless continued to be employed in affairs connected with the Council, and assisted in drawing up the Bull of Reform published by Julius III. in 1550. The exhortation addressed to the Fathers of the Council at the opening of the second session was composed by him, and the doctrinal decree on Justification, which defined the faith of the Church on the point most warmly controverted by the Lutherans, is believed to have been first sketched out by his pen,[359] and was certainly submitted by his colleagues to his approval in its complete shape before publication, he being then detained by sickness at Padua. In 1554 the accession of Queen Mary recalled him to England, where, for the four remaining years of his life, he was engaged in reconstructing the shattered constitution of the English Church, and was, of course, unable to take any active part in the affairs of the Council. But some of his Synodal Acts anticipated in so remarkable a manner the Tridentine decrees of discipline that they have been even supposed to have furnished the model on which the decrees were drawn up. At any rate, they evince how thoroughly Pole was himself imbued with the views and principles which guided the Fathers of the Council, and bear too closely on our subject to be omitted here.

The first act of his primacy, after the formal reconciliation of the nation to the Holy See, was to summon a Provincial Synod, which met in Henry VII.'s Chapel in Westminster Abbey, and continued to sit from the November of 1554 to the same month in the ensuing year. After regulations passed for the remedy of sundry abuses, such as pluralities and non-residence, and others which aimed at providing for the instruction of the people, by means of preaching, we come to the important decrees on the subject of Church seminaries. A return was made to the ancient ecclesiastical system, and the cathedral schools were put on a footing which should enable them to train the future clergy of the diocese. Every cathedral was to maintain, in its own school, a certain number of boys, in proportion to its revenues. Those only were to be chosen in whom there seemed to be tokens of a vocation to the priesthood; they were to be received about the age of eleven or twelve, rather from the ranks of the poor than the rich, and were required before admission to know at least how to read and write. All were to wear the tonsure and the ecclesiastical habit, to live in common, and to assist daily at the public office in the cathedral. They were gradually to be admitted to Holy Orders, at proper intervals. The school was to be placed under the superintendence of the Dean and Chapter. Other students might be admitted, who were required to follow the rules of the seminary in all things. Moreover, all the schools and schoolmasters of the diocese were placed under the jurisdiction of the Ordinary, and the books used in these schools were first to be approved by him.[360] The acts of this synod were sent to Rome, and formally approved by Pope Paul IV., and there is little doubt that they must have been in the hands of many of the prelates who assisted at the later sessions of the Council of Trent.

The next task which presented itself was the restoration of the universities, which, as we have seen, had sunk during the reign of Edward VI., into a state of utter decay. Here the Cardinal's efforts were nobly seconded by Queen Mary, who re-endowed the Colleges with such portions of their revenues as had been seized by the Crown, and at her own charges commenced the rebuilding of the schools. To restore the ancient theological studies, and place the universities on their former footing, Nicholas Ormanetti, formerly

Vicar-General to the good prelate Matthew Ghiberti, and now first Datary to the English Legation, was appointed visitor. The heretical professors were replaced with learned Catholics, both native and foreign, and among the latter number were the two Spanish Dominicans, Peter Soto and Bartholomew Carranza, both of whom had been present as theologians at some of the sittings of the Council of Trent. By their influence the scholastic theology was restored at Oxford—a circumstance which occasioned the charge of *obscurantism* to be very unsuitably brought against the Catholic professors, by those who had been engaged before them in crying down humane learning and burning Duke Humphrey's library. Pole certainly was not one to neglect the cultivation of humane literature, but the restoration of the Divinity schools of Oxford was just then of more urgent necessity than anything else, and we could not have blamed the Catholic prelates if, in their solicitude on this point, they had even allowed the polite letters to remain for a time uncared for. They did, however, the very reverse of this, and put such renewed life into the English schools as inspired Sir Thomas Pope with courage to propose a new Oxford foundation, for the express purpose of promoting classical studies. The statutes of Trinity College, Oxford, were submitted to the approval of Pole, who pleaded strongly for more Greek. Sir Thomas Pope is represented by some to have resisted this, but his own letters explain the true state of the case. "I like the purpose well," he says, "but I fear the times will not bear it now. I remember when I was a young scholar at Eton the Greek tongue was growing apace, but the study of it of late is much decayed." That is to say, that the real "obscurantism" had been occasioned, not by the Spanish Dominicans, but by the Genevese Reformers, who left it to Pole and his colleagues to undo their mischievous work. In consequence of the Cardinal's representations, a Greek lecturer was appointed at Trinity, and the buildings of old Durham College were given up to the new foundation, the present library being the very same originally built to receive the books deposited there by Richard of Bury.

The death of the queen in 1558, followed sixteen hours later by that of the Cardinal Primate, put an end to the work of restoration, and the curtain dropped heavily over the hopes of the English Catholics. And in what way, it may be asked, did the triumph of Protestantism affect the schools? "Duns, and his rabble of barbarous questionists" (to use the language of Ascham) were, of course, put to the rout; but what was substituted in their place during the golden reign of Queen Elizabeth? Five years after her accession, we learn from Wood, that there were only three divines in Oxford judged capable of preaching the university sermon. The established clergy were recruited from an illiterate class, who preached on Sundays, and worked at their trades on week days, some of them being hardly able to sign their names. Four years later, when Archbishop Parker founded three scholarships in Cambridge, for the best and ablest scholars to be elected from the chief schools of Kent and

Norfolk, it was found prudent to require no higher attainments from the candidates than a knowledge of grammar, "and, if it may be, that they should be able to make a verse." And three years later again, we find Horne, bishop of Winchester, requiring his minor canons every week to get by heart a chapter of St. Paul's Epistles in Latin, which task they had to repeat aloud at the public episcopal visitation. The universities revived in some degree towards the close of Elizabeth's reign, and yet more under the early Stuart princes, though it is remarkable how large a number of the best English scholars of this period, such as Campion and Crashaw, embraced the Catholic faith. But the free intercommunion with the mind of Europe, which had been the great intellectual advantage of these institutions in Catholic times, was now at an end. Whatever scholarship they fostered was henceforth stamped with a certain character of narrow nationality; their very Latinity became Anglicised in its pronunciation, and thus the Latin language ceased to be to English scholars what it was, and still is, to those of Catholic academies—a medium of intercourse between educated men. Among those Englishmen who have distinguished themselves in the ranks of science and literature since the Reformation, a very large proportion have not been university scholars, and our two philosophers of greatest note, Bacon and Locke, so far from acknowledging any obligations to their university training, avowedly despised, and set themselves to make others despise, the academic system of education.

It remains for us to speak of the decrees affecting the question of ecclesiastical education passed in the later sessions of the Council of Trent. The wars and political intrigues of that troublous time caused so many interruptions in the sittings of the Council that they were not finally closed until eighteen years from the date of their first opening.

Few, comparatively, of those who had taken part in the first sessions, assisted at the three last held in the year 1563, under the presidency of five cardinal legates.[361] Of the three who had presided at the opening of the Council, two had been successively raised to the Chair of St. Peter, and all had passed to a better life. Not one survived of those nine Cardinals who had sat in Paul III.'s Congregation of Reform. But the new generation which had arisen in their place were animated with the same spirit, or, if there were any difference to be noticed, it lay, perhaps, in the fact, that the deliberations of those eighteen years had supplied them with fuller light, and deepened their desire for the restoration of ecclesiastical discipline. The very troubles of the times had co-operated in the development of a strong Christian reaction against the Paganism of the last half century; and many prelates had not waited for the close of the Council before instituting a vigorous reform of abuses in their own dioceses. Thus the church of Verona under Matthew Ghiberti had become a model of discipline, and in Portugal the celebrated Bartholomew of the Martyrs, Archbishop of Braga, had set the example of exact observance of the canons, in the government of his large diocese. Among the other means he had adopted for the reform of his clergy, was the establishment of a sort of seminary in his own palace, which he endowed out of his episcopal revenues, appointing as scholasticus a religious of his order. The archbishop sat in the later sessions of the Council, and took a very prominent part in its deliberations. Again, the establishment of the Jesuit colleges, specially the German college in Rome, and the extraordinary success which had attended the labours of the Blessed Peter Canisius, in restoring Catholicism in Germany, had poured a flood of light on the whole subject of educational reform. Canisius assisted at the sittings of the Council in 1547 and again in 1562, and even when absent his opinion was continually consulted by Cardinal Hosius and the other legates. Reform was now not a theory, but a fact. In Aichstadt, the old diocese of St. Wilibald, where heresy and irreligion, had, as it seemed, firmly established themselves, the university was purged of the evil leaven, and the faith had revived in all its fervour. In Vienna, in spite of the protection of the Government, religion had so rapidly declined under the infection of the Lutheran doctrines, that for twenty years not a single candidate for holy orders had presented himself. Parishes were left without pastors, the sacraments were neglected, and through timidity and human respect the Catholic clergy opposed but a faint resistance to the encroachments of the heretics. But under the direction of Canisius the university was restored, a college was founded for the education of youth, and public catechisms were instituted, which effected a change little short of miraculous, and the same scenes were to be witnessed in the other cities of Germany.

The Fathers, therefore, who assembled at the twenty-seventh session of the Council of Trent had facts as well as principles before them, indicating a sound system of ecclesiastical education as the measure best calculated to remedy the evils which afflicted the Church. In earlier sessions the old canons had been confirmed requiring cathedrals to maintain a theologian and grammar-master for the instruction of the younger clergy, but this law fell very far short of what was needed, and its frequent renewal by former Councils does not appear to have been attended with much result. What the Church had possessed in former ages, and what she now desired to restore, were not mere theological classes, but rather nurseries, in which her clergy could be trained in ecclesiastical discipline as well as supplied with the learning proper to their state. Such seminaries had existed before the rise of the universities; they were now to reappear, and it was with unanimous consent, accompanied with an emotion of grateful joy not easy to express, that the Fathers passed that decree which has been called the practical *résumé* of the whole Council. It forms the eighteenth chapter of the twenty-seventh session, and its provisions are briefly as follows:—

Every cathedral or metropolitan church is bound, according to its means, to maintain a certain number of youths belonging to the city or diocese in some suitable college, who shall then be trained for the ecclesiastical state. They are to be at least twelve years old, and chosen from those who give hopes of their being eventually fit for the priesthood. The Holy Council desires that a "preference be given to the children of poor parents," though the rich are not to be excluded. The college, which is to be "a perpetual seminary for the service of God," is entirely under the direction of the bishop, who is to be assisted by two canons chosen by himself. The students, on their entrance, are to wear the tonsure and ecclesiastical habit; to learn grammar, church music, the ecclesiastical computation, and the other liberal arts; but they are specially to apply themselves to the study of the Scriptures, and all that appertains to the right administration of the Sacraments. The bishop, or the visitors whom he appoints, are to watch over the maintenance of good discipline among them, and to take all proper means for the encouragement of piety and virtue. The seminary is to be maintained by a tax on all the benefices in the diocese. If in any province the dioceses are too poor each to maintain its own seminary, the Provincial synod may establish one attached to the metropolitan church for the general use of all churches of the diocese; or, again, if a diocese be very large and populous, the bishop may, if necessary, establish in it more than one seminary. It belongs to the bishop to appoint or remove the scholasticus, and no person is to be appointed who is not a doctor or licentiate in theology or canon law. The bishop also has the right of prescribing what studies are to be pursued by the seminarists, according as he may think proper.[362]

So universal was the satisfaction caused by this decree, that many prelates hesitated not to declare, that if no other good were to result from the labours of the Council, this alone would compensate to them for all their fatigues and sacrifices. They regarded such a reform as was here provided, as the only efficacious means of restoring ecclesiastical discipline, well knowing that in every state and government, as are the heads, so are the members, and that the character of a people depends on that of their teachers.[363]

It will be observed that in this famous decree there is no allusion to the universities as in any way regarded as nurseries of the clergy. Canons for their reform were passed in the twenty-fifth session,[364] but not a word was said connecting them in any way with the proposed seminaries. It is not even recommended that seminaries should be established in the vicinity of universities where these already existed, though at that time universities were far more numerous than now, every province almost possessing one in its territory; but it is distinctly laid down, that they are to form a part of the cathedral establishment, and, where it can conveniently be done, that they be erected in the cathedral city of the diocese. The radical idea of the seminary is that of its being *the bishop's school*,[365] formed under his eye, and subject to his control—an idea which is manifestly totally inconsistent with the plan of a university. So strictly is this the case, that where colleges have since been founded (as at Rome) for ecclesiastical students of different nations, which of course could not be placed under the jurisdiction of their own bishops, these colleges are rarely given the name of seminaries, the nature of such institutions, properly so-called, requiring them to be subject to the canonical authority of their own Ordinary. Universities were not abolished or condemned, or even discountenanced, by the Fathers of Trent: they were reformed, indeed, and laws were passed requiring all masters and doctors to engage by oath, at the beginning of each year, to explain the Catholic faith according to the canons of the Council, and obliging visitors to institute the necessary corrections of discipline. But universities, when doing their own proper work, continued to receive the same encouragement as before; and even in our own time, we have witnessed new ones established, at the express recommendation of the Sovereign Pontiff, to the end that the Catholic youth of Belgium and Ireland might enjoy the same advantages for following a course of liberal studies as were at the command of the uncatholic world around them.[366] But other schools than those of the world were to be provided for those who were to minister divine things, that they might be "*wholly in them*, and that their profiting might be manifest to all."[367] Them the world was not to touch; the smell of the fire was not to pass on them; from childhood they were to be taken out of it, and fashioned after another model, signed and set apart as "holy to the Lord." Their consecration was not to be the change of a moment, but the formation of a life; and for ever they were to be preserved from what even the heathen poet bewailed as "the intolerable calamity of yielding to what is base," and to enjoy that which he declares should be the object of all men's prayers,—to dwell in those sacred temples where "nature and the law of the place should both conspire to present us in innocence to the Deity."[368]

Besides the important decrees already referred to, the reform of education was encouraged by other provisions of the Council of Trent, in which we recognise the same solicitude for restoring the Christian spirit, and abolishing the corrupt Paganism which had crept into its place. The Tridentine Fathers had something to say on the matter of art. The object of pictures and images, is, they remind us, to instruct the people, and recall to them the mysteries of the Faith; therefore everything profane and indecorous is to be avoided in the House of God, and the beauty that is represented must be that alone which savours of holiness. Nor was it to be supposed that they could be silent on the subject of that ecclesiastical chant, which from the very infancy of the Christian schools had taken its place by the side of grammar. The Gregorian chant had by this time all but disappeared in the greater number of churches, and had been replaced by orchestral music of the most profane and unsuitable description. Against this abuse, which had been growing for upwards of two centuries, Popes and Councils had uniformly protested, but with little fruit. The Fathers of Trent seriously contemplated prohibiting the use of instrumental music altogether, but at the earnest representations of the Emperor Ferdinand, they contented themselves with prescribing the abuses introduced by the musical professors,[369] and making the study of the plain-song of the Church one of the indispensable studies of the new seminaries. They number among the duties of those promoted to cathedral canonries that they should "reverently, distinctly, and devoutly praise the name of God in hymns and canticles in the choir appointed for psalmody;" and require the Provincial synods to regulate the proper way of singing and chanting the divine office. And the various Provincial councils and synods held to promulgate the Tridentine decrees, failed not to enforce the same salutary provisions, as that of Toledo, in 1566, which forbade those noisy exhibitions wherein the sense of the words is buried under the confusion of voices.[370]

The projected reforms had been very warmly urged on the Fathers by St. Charles Borromeo in his letters from Rome. The friend of Pole and of St Ignatius, he had watched with lively interest the success of the German college, and in his twenty-third year had already put his hand to the work of educational reform, by giving up the Borromeo palace at Pavia, for the purpose of a college which he founded out of his own revenues. When in the July of 1563, therefore, letters from Trent arrived in Rome notifying to the Holy Father the decree which had been passed, and soliciting his confirmation of the same, St. Charles earnestly supported the petition of the Legates, and had the happiness of conveying to them the warm approval of his Holiness, and his promise that the confirmation should be published with the least possible delay, and that he himself would be the first to carry it into execution. Accordingly, on the 18th of August following he convoked the Cardinals to deliberate with them on the subject. The foundation of seminaries in all the dioceses of the Roman State was at once determined on; 6000 scudi were assigned for the purpose by the Pope, and a Commission of Cardinals, of whom St. Charles was one, was appointed to carry the resolution into effect.

Thanks to the exertions of St. Charles, the solemn confirmation of the Canons of Trent was not long delayed. In a consistory held on the 30th of December, Pius IV, addressed a moving discourse to the assembled Cardinals, including several who had recently returned from the Council, in which, while declaring his firm resolve to enforce every one of the reforms which had been therein recommended, he took special notice of the decree on seminaries, which he praised as having been suggested by the "special inspiration of God,"[371] declaring again that he desired to be the first who should put his hand to so blessed a work. The confirmation of the Tridentine Canons followed on the 26th of January 1564, and on the 15th of April the same year, in a consistory which met in the Hall of Constantine, plans were proposed for the foundation of the Roman Seminary, the care of which was committed to the Fathers of the Society of Jesus.

Nor was it at Rome alone that the decree of the Council was thus eagerly and promptly carried out. The first act of Bartholomew of the Martyrs, on returning to his diocese, was to institute measures for the establishment of a seminary, in precise conformity to the prescribed canons. He accordingly summoned his chapter and laid before them the urgency of the business; giving them a noble example by his own munificent contribution to the necessary expenses. As it was an undertaking involving a question of finances, there were not wanting those who murmured at the idea of a compulsory taxation, but the prudence and moderation of the archbishop prevailed over every difficulty, and at the end of six months he had the satisfaction of seeing accommodation provided for sixty students, and of opening the first seminary founded in Portugal. This appears to have been in the year 1565. In the same year Daniel, the worthy successor of St. Boniface in the See of Mentz, commenced the foundation of the first episcopal seminary of Germany, which he appropriately dedicated to our great English apostle, and placed under the direction of the Jesuits. The Provincial Councils, held at Salzburg and Toledo in 1569, decreed the establishment of provincial seminaries, and, not to multiply examples, we have but to turn to the correspondence of St. Pius V. to see how rapidly this great work was taken up throughout every part of Christendom, and how energetically it was encouraged by the Sovereign Pontiff himself.

One Saint, however, and one diocese, stands out pre-eminent in the history of Church seminaries. St. Charles Borromeo had protected the design in its infancy, and he lived to give the Church a perfect model of its practical realisation. Appointed to the archbishopric of Milan when only in his twenty-second year, St. Charles found it impossible for several years to obtain leave from Pope Pius IV. to withdraw from Rome and devote himself to his pastoral cares. Nevertheless, he never ceased to occupy himself with plans for its benefit, and sought the counsel of every one whom he deemed best able to instruct him in the duties of government. One of the friends whose advice he most highly esteemed was Bartholomew of the Martyrs; another was one whose name, if less famous than that of the great Archbishop of Braga, has a peculiar interest to the English reader—it was the good priest, Nicholas Ormanetti. This saintly ecclesiastic had acted as Vicar-General to Matthew Ghiberti, and assisted in the reforms which that zealous prelate had instituted in his diocese. He had afterwards been appointed first Datary under Cardinal Pole to the English Legation, and as we have seen, had been named by him visitor of the English universities. He continued to act as confidential adviser to our last Archbishop of Canterbury up to the time of his death, when he left England and attended several sessions of the Council of Trent.[372] After this he retired to a humble country parish in the diocese of Verona, where he busied himself with his parochial duties as quietly and happily as if he had never exercised a more weighty charge. From this obscurity he was drawn by St. Charles, who conjured Navagerio, now Bishop of Verona, to send Ormanetti to him at Rome, that he might enjoy the benefit of his counsels. He received the humble Curé with extraordinary respect, and for weeks, to the amazement of the Roman courtiers, he was closeted day after day with a man whom nobody knew, and nobody thought worth knowing, and whose exterior was altogether poor and unpretending. In these long conferences every point of pastoral discipline was gravely and deliberately discussed, and the whole plan of the future government of Milan moulded, as it were, into shape. St. Charles listened eagerly to the account which Ormanetti gave of the views and methods of government which had been adopted by the two men whose example and maxims he most venerated, Ghiberti and Reginald Pole. They consulted together on the fittest method of executing the Tridentine decrees, and specially on the formation of seminaries, and the holding of diocesan synods. And these measures being thus concerted, Ormanetti was despatched to Milan to discharge the office of Vicar-General until St. Charles should himself be able to assume the government of his diocese. Poor Ormanetti, however, found his new dignity beset with thorns, and the contradictions he had to endure from the clergy who would not endure the name of reform, moved St. Charles to make such renewed entreaties that he might repair himself to his diocese, that he at last obtained from the Pope the desired permission, and set out for Milan in 1565, where he almost immediately held his first Provincial Synod. He commenced the visitation of his diocese in the following year, and in spite of the overwhelming labour which was thus imposed on him, found time to begin a series of educational establishments such as never before, we may confidently affirm, owed their existence to any single founder. "Reform education," said the sagacious Leibnitz, "and you will have reformed the world." And it was on this principle that St. Charles applied himself to the task of reforming, not the world indeed, but a vast province, in which doctrine and discipline had alike fallen into decay. To begin with his foundations for seculars, which were very numerous, the Borromeo College, dedicated to St. Justina, of which mention has been already made, had been planned by him while a student at Pavia, where his own observation of the disorders prevalent there moved him to make larger provision for the protection of his fellow-students. In 1572 he founded at Milan the College of St. Fidelis, in which Humane Literature and all the higher branches of study were taught, and which was more particularly intended for the benefit of poor scholars. A second college was in the following year attached to the church of St. John the Evangelist, for the education of noble youths. It was under the care of the Oblates of St. Ambrose, and was commonly known as the College of Nobles. St. Charles himself drew up the rules both for the masters and scholars. He marked the time to be assigned to prayer, reading, and study, and established such a discipline as was calculated to form a character of solid piety in the most influential classes of the laity. Next to virtue and learning he desired to see his noble scholars trained in habits of Christian courtesy, and was accustomed to insist much on the importance of good manners. He often visited the school in person, examined the boys at their tasks, and addressed them some brief religious instructions. Every year, at the close of the studies, he attended their public literary exercises, and distributed prizes with his own hand; and so solicitous was he to perfect this establishment, that he engaged Cardinal Sylvius Antonianus, his former secretary and a man of rare learning, to write a work on the education of the higher classes, for the guidance of those who taught in his College of Nobles. Besides these colleges, he founded others at Arona, Lucerne, and Fribourg, as well as the admirable Swiss college established at Milan, for the education of young Swiss ecclesiastics, which became afterwards the great means of upholding religion in the Catholic cantons.

For the clergy of his own province he founded no fewer than six seminaries—three in his cathedral city, and three in other parts of the diocese. It must be remembered that the giant evil with which St. Charles had to struggle was a slothful and corrupt clergy: the salt had lost its savour, and had to be salted anew. The whole face of the diocese had to be changed; and such a change demanded a body of skilful workmen. To create these was his first care, and with the sagacity of a mind illuminated with something higher than mere human prudence, he perceived at once that an undertaking so vast as the creation of a new body of clergy, and the reform of the old one, could only be grasped by division. He had to classify his work in order to master it, and in this lay the secret of his success.

His first and principal seminary was attached to his cathedral church, and was intended to receive 150 of the most promising candidates for the ecclesiastical state. In this greater seminary dedicated to St. John the Baptist, the students went through a regular course of philosophy, theology, and canon law.[373] But the second seminary, called the *Canonica*, which was intended for youths of less ability, who from their good dispositions, nevertheless promised to make useful parish priests, nothing more was required than a course of instruction on moral theology, Scripture, the Catechism of the Council of Trent, and the rubrics and ceremonies of the Church. A third seminary in the city was set apart to receive such priests as, either from ignorance or negligence, were found unfit to discharge their sacred duties, and were placed here for a time to renew their ecclesiastical spirit, and acquire the learning necessary for their state. These city seminaries received altogether about 300 students—a number quite inadequate to supply the wants of the diocese. Three others were, therefore, added in the different deaneries, and these were intended as nurseries to those at Milan. In them were received youths of all ages and ranks of society, principally those of the poorer classes, who, when properly prepared, were passed on into the higher schools, all being dependent on the great seminary of St. John the Baptist as their head.

At first the archbishop supported these establishments at his private charge, but he was at length obliged to have recourse to the plan of taxation laid down by the Council of Trent, though this was only continued until a permanent endowment had been secured. The rules for their government he drew up himself, placing the care of their temporal affairs in the hands of four of his clergy, chosen by himself.

Every student on entering was required to make a spiritual retreat under the director of the seminary, and a general retreat was made yearly by all before the opening of the classes. The great object aimed at in every regulation was to train the subjects in the spiritual life, and to supply them with both the learning and the habits proper to their state. The care and personal supervision which the archbishop bestowed on his seminarists, whom he used to call "the restorers of his diocese," were rather such as might have been expected from a father than a superior, and one whose time was never at his own command. There were few days that he did not visit the seminary, which occupied one side of his cathedral quadrangle; it was his wish to receive all new-comers in person, that he might examine their vocation himself; and when once he had seen and conversed with them, each one had a peculiar place in his memory, and became a separate object of his paternal care. Twice a year he made a visitation of his seminaries, and held an examination of all the classes. On such occasions he determined those who were to be promoted to higher classes, and when the course of study was finished, assigned them offices and benefices, according to the ability of each. These visitations lasted a fortnight, besides other shorter ones which he made in the course of the year. One result of the extreme solicitude he bestowed on the spiritual training of his disciples was not altogether such as he had anticipated: so many of his priests evinced an inclination to embrace the religious life, that he had to solicit from Pope Clement XIII. that some means might be adopted for keeping them for the service of the diocese;[374] for every religious order and every bishop were eager to obtain subjects who had been educated in a seminary of St. Charles. On the other hand, detractors were not wanting who busied themselves in representing these colleges as prisons, in which the unhappy students were worn to death by prayers, watchings, and austerities, by which means they succeeded in frightening away some who were about to enter. But the seminarists had but to show themselves in the streets of Milan to dispel these malicious rumours; their countenances and their whole deportment being marked with a certain character of peace and joy, that was recognised as the effect of that holy discipline under which the whole interior and exterior man was being formed anew.

St. Charles had now provided for the education of his clergy and seculars of the upper ranks, but he did not stop there; he had thought also for the children of the poor; and his plans on this point were formed when he was still at the Court of Rome, presiding over the brilliant academy of learned men which he had formed in the palace of the Pope, and taking part in the erudite conference of the *Noctes Vaticanæ*. Among the instructions which he gave to his Vicar-General, Ormanetti, the establishment of poor schools for teaching the Christian doctrine held a prominent place, and in his first Provincial Synod he made a special decree obliging his curates to assemble the children of each parish for catechism on Sundays and other festivals. By his exhortations he moved a greater number of pious persons, of both sexes, to interest themselves in the good work, so that at the appointed hour the churches of Milan were crowded with catechists and their classes, and it was the good archbishop's recreation, to go from one church to another, encouraging teachers and learners with his presence and his gracious words. Before he died there was not a parish in his diocese, however remote, which had not its school; and whereas before his time it was common enough to meet with persons of advanced age who scarcely knew the Our Father and the Hail Mary correctly, it was now as common to find children of ten or twelve perfectly instructed in their religion. The schools of the diocese were at last entirely placed under the care of the Oblates of St. Ambrose, that congregation which had been created by St. Charles, and which he employed as a kind of spiritual militia for carrying out all his charitable designs. The discipline established in the poor schools of Milan by their means was the admiration of every stranger, and the extent of their labours may be estimated from the fact, that at the death of the archbishop there existed in his diocese seven hundred and forty poor schools, two hundred and seventy-three superintending officers, and seventeen hundred and twenty-six others acting under their orders, having under their care no fewer than 40,098 scholars.

Here, then, we may fitly close our studies of the Christian schools. We have watched them in their infancy springing up under the shadow of the cloister, and having traced them through their varied fortunes of good and ill, we leave them at the moment when the episcopacy was recovering its ancient jurisdiction over the ecclesiastical seminaries, and when a vast majority of the secular schools of Catholic Christendom were passing into the hands of a great religious order, raised up, as it would seem, with the special design of consolidating anew a system of Christian education. Did we need a token that the reforms of the sixteenth century were truly the work of God, we should find it in that deadly hostility which the enemies of religion, and the rulers of the world, have never ceased to exhibit against the seminaries of the Church and the colleges of her religious orders. And this, not in Protestant countries alone, but under nominally Catholic Governments, where heretical impieties have been excluded, only, as it would seem, that there might be set up the odious idol of the State.

For two centuries at least, education has been the battle-ground of the Church, and the battle is not yet fought out and finished. In France, in Belgium, in Germany, and in Switzerland, infidelity has triumphed exactly in proportion as it has succeeded in substituting an Anti-Christian State system of education for the system of the Church, and has never done its work more surely than when its agents have been philosophic universities, and ministers of public instruction.

For us in England, who, by a strange anomaly enjoy a freedom denied to many a Catholic land, and who are called on in one way or other to take part in the reconstruction of so many of our shattered institutions, the educational annals of the past have imperative claims on our attention. It is not for a writer to point the moral of his own tale; we can but hope, therefore, that our story, however rambling and diffuse, may yet have been told with sufficient clearness for our readers to draw that moral for themselves, and to resolve that, in so far as they may be called on to lend their aid in the great work of education, they will take no lower models for their guidance than those that have been bequeathed them by the saints.

And what a calendar is that which belongs to the Christian schools! The profession of the teacher, which in our day falls, by choice or duty, on so vast a number, is irradiated by the light which streams from ten thousand saintly aureoles. If the work be often wearisome and seem to promise little hope; if the spirit flag, and, ignorant of those sweet secrets by which the saints kept fresh their springs of devotion in a thirsty soil, the teacher too often finds his heart grow dry with incessant labour of the head; if pressed on by a busy age, be he ever tempted to shorten prayer that he may double toil, forgetful of the example of those who with one hand only did the work, while with the other they held the sword;[375] if, in short, the spirit of the world steal in upon him and assault him with its manifold vexations, what can he do better than turn to those who have gone before him, and learn from their examples, and invoke their aid?

And what can we do better than commend these pages to the saints, under whose patronage they were first undertaken; but chiefly and above all to those,—too seldom venerated by us, too little loved,—the saints and martyrs of England? To St. Bede and St. Aldhelm, therefore, to St. Boniface, and St. Dunstan and St. Ethelwold; to St. Edmund and St. Richard, and all who with them have sanctified our cloisters with their prayers and studies,—for were not the studies of the saints themselves a prayer?—to them in whose ears the names of our own homes were once sweet household words, and who, as they listen to the eternal chimes, do not, as we fondly trust, forget those scenes where, in the days of their sojourning, they learnt at the springs of heavenly wisdom "the true knowledge of the things that are;" whose memory has been to us, wandering in the wilderness, "as the flower of roses in the days of spring, and as the lilies that grow upon the brink of the waters,"[376]— to our glorious English Saints we offer these pages as an act of homage due to them on a thousand grounds, and which, if unworthy of their greatness, may by its own littleness the better move them to shelter it with their aid, and may at least bear witness to the grateful love of the least and humblest of their clients!

FOOTNOTES:

[1] Fuit autem forma Beatissimi Marci hujusmodi: longo naso, subducto supercilio, pulcher oculis, recalvaster, prolixa barba, velox, habitudinis optimæ, canis aspersus, affectione continens, gratia Dei plenus.— Metaphrastes, *Vita S. Marci*, ap. Surium.

[2] Nahum iii. 8.

[3] Vita S. Marci.

[4] A faded copy of St. Mark's Gospel, preserved in St. Mark's Treasury at Venice, claims to have been written by his own hand. Montfauçon, who has described it in his *Iter Italicum*, considers that this claim cannot be supported, though he attests the great antiquity of the manuscript.

[5] The ecclesiastical chant took its first great development at Alexandria, and appears to have been brought thither from Rome by St. Mark. Philo the Jew, a native of Alexandria, who lived in the time of the Evangelist, describes the Christians passing their days in psalmody and prayer, and singing in alternate choirs (Euseb. lib. ii. c. 17). On the martyrdom of the Evangelist we read how certain just men buried him "singing prayers and psalms." (*Vita S. Marci*, Sim. Met.) The nature of the chant established at Alexandria in the time of St. Athanasius, is very precisely indicated by St. Augustine, in that passage of his Confessions (lib. x. c. 33) where, speaking of the *voluptates aurium*, he says that he sometimes desires even to banish from his ears the sweet tones to which the Psalms of David were generally sung in church; "and then that method seems to me more safe which I remember often to have heard of Athanasius, Bishop of Alexandria, who caused the lector to intone the Psalms with so slight an inflection of the voice, that it was more like reading than singing." Hippolytus, in his Book on Antichrist, declares that one effect of His coming at the end of the world will be the abolition of the Psalmody of the Church.

[6] Cassian, Inst. ii. c. 5; Coll. 18. 6.

[7] Euseb. Hist. l. v. c. 20.

[8] Durandus, Rational. lib. viii. c. 1. It is also frequently used to signify an elementary knowledge of arithmetic.

[9] In spite of the labours of recent critics, the history of St. Hyppolitus still remains obscure. It appears uncertain whether there were one or many saints of the name; whether the Hyppolitus celebrated by Prudentius was ever really Bishop of Porto, and lastly, whether he was, or was not, the author of the *Philosophumena*. The former opinion is maintained by Bunsen, Döllinger, and

the majority of German and English critics; the latter is generally supported by the Catholic writers of France.

[10] Acta S. Feliciani, ed. Boll.

[11] Fleury, l. xviii. 35.

[12] Breviary Lessons: Feb. 13, proper for Rome. Vignoli, Liber Pontificalis, tom. ii. c. 89.

[13] Cœpit vivere secundum regulam sub sanctis apostolis constitutam. (Office of St. Augustine.)

[14] Fleury, l. xx. 32.

[15] Fleury, l. xxxii. 22.

[16] Ruinart, Atti Sinceri, vol. ii. 367-381. Ed. Rom. 1777.

[17] S. Greg. Vita S. Benedicti.

[18] S. Aug. Conf. l. viii. c. 5.

[19] S. Basil. De Legendis Gentilium Libris, tom. ii. p. 245. Ed. Gaume.

[20] S. Joan. Chrys. tom. i. pp. 115-122. Ed. Gaume.

[21] The words of the Christian orator are almost identical with those of Quinctilian on the same subject. "Si studiis quidem scholas prodesse, moribus autem nocere constaret, potior mihi ratio vivendi honeste, quam vel optime dicendi videretur."—Lib. i. c. 3.

[22] *Regula S. Pachomii*, cap. i. cxl.

[23] Boll., Vit. S. Pach. c. 3, 4.

[24] Mabillon, Acta SS. Ord. Ben. Præf. in sec. iii.

[25] Reg. S. Basil. fus. tract. 15. Tom. 2, p. 498. Ed. Gaume.

[26] Omnes literas discant: omni tempore duabus horis, hoc est, a mane usque ad horam secundam, lectioni vacent.—S. Cæsarii Reg. ad Virg. cap. xvii.

[27] S. Leand. De Instit. Virg. cap. vi. et vii.

[28] There are, however, indications that at Alexandria at least young children took part in some of the exercises of the catechetical school. St. Clement's hymn to the Saviour appears to have been written for his younger disciples. "O Shepherd of the *lambs!*" he says, "assemble Thine innocent children, and let their stainless lips sing hymns to Christ, the guide of youth." And again: "Fed by the Divine milk of wisdom, that mother of grace has taught our

infant lips, and made them taste the dew of the Spirit. Let us then sing to Christ our King.... Let us celebrate the praises of the Almighty Child."

[29] 2 Tim. i. 5.

[30] Vit. S. Mac., cap. 2.

[31] Vita S. Fulgen., cap. i. ap. Surium.

[32] St. Hier., Ep. 96 (aliter 127, ed. Migne), ad Principiam.

[33] Gladstone, Studies on Homer.

[34] The works of Virgil the grammarian have been edited by Cardinal Mai (Auctores classici, tom. v.), who considers that the Toulouse Academy cannot be assigned a later date than the end of the sixth century.

[35] Mabillon, Acta SS. Ben. Præf. Secul. iii. 39.

[36] These are the words of Trithemius, who says that from the very beginning of the order the sons of nobles were educated in the Benedictine monasteries, "non solum in Scripturis Divinis, sed etiam in secularibus litteris."

[37] In allusion to the waxen tablets then used for writing.

[38] S. Ælred, Vit. S. Nin.

[39] *A solis ortus cardine* and *Hostis Herodes*, the latter of which stands in the Roman Breviary under a somewhat altered form. This Sedulius is to be distinguished from Sedulius the younger, who was also of Irish extraction, and was Bishop of Oreta in Spain, in the eighth century.

[40] Scripsit Abegetoria, ccclxv. Nenn. Camb. MS. c. 57.

[41] Acta SS. Boll. Mart.

[42] Columba had previously studied in the school of St. Finian of Maghbile and received deacon's orders, so that he could not have been a mere boy when he came to Clonard. But Adamnan tells us that he was still a youth, *adhuc juvenis*.

[43] Now Clonmacnois in King's County.

[44] I should not have thought it necessary to remind the reader that St. Columba, the founder of Iona in 563, is to be distinguished from St. Columbanus the founder of Luxeuil in 585, had not so considerable a writer as Thierry, in his history of the Norman Conquest, spoken of them as the same persons.

[45] Act. SS. Boll.

[46] Ara Multiscilus, *Schedæ de Islandia*, cap. 2, quoted by Haverty, who sums up the number of Irish saints known to have settled in different parts of Europe as follows: 150 in Germany, of whom 36 were martyrs; 45 in Gaul, 6 martyrs; 30 in Belgium; 44 in England; 13 in Italy; and 8 martyrs in Norway and Iceland. They founded 13 monasteries in Scotland, 12 in England, 40 in Gaul, 9 in Belgium, 16 in Bavaria, 15 in Switzerland, 6 in Italy, and others in different parts of Germany.

[47] It is first spoken of by John of Salisbury, a writer of the twelfth century, who quotes no authority for the statement. With regard to the reproof administered to Bishop Didier, it is not denied, for the passage is extant in one of St. Gregory's letters. But the real and authentic justification is given in the Gloss on the Canon Law, which explains that Didier's fault did not lie in his studying humane literature, but in his giving public lectures in his church on the profane poets, and substituting the same in the place of the Gospel lesson. "Recitabat *in ecclesia* fabulas Jovis, et eas moraliter exponebat in prædicatione sua." (*Decret.* pars i. dis. 86.) And again, "Beatus Gregorius quemdam episcopum *non reprehendit* quia litteras seculares didicerat; sed quia, contra episcopale officium, *pro lectione Evangelica*, grammaticam populo exponebat." (*Decret.* pars i. dis. 37, c. 8. ed. Antwerp., 1573, quoted by Landriot, *Recherches Historiques*, p. 212.)

[48] St. Ignatius is generally spoken of as a disciple of the Apostle St. John. But many writers call him a disciple of St. Peter also, and some even represent that Apostle as placing him in the see of Antioch (S. Chrys. Hom. in S. Ignat. t. ii. p. 712). Tillemont (t. ii. p. 87, ed. 1732) quotes St. Athanasius, Origen and Theodoret, to the same effect. The historian Socrates speaks of St. Ignatius as introducing into the ancient Church of Antioch the alternate chant of two choirs (Socrates, lib. vi. c. 8.). Theodoret says that it was used there, in the time of the Arians, as a powerful instrument to oppose their blasphemous heresies.

[49] Bede, lib. i. ch. 27.

[50] This expression requires some explanation, being an apparent contradiction of what has been said before as to the Roman origin of the Irish schools. It must be borne in mind that the error in the Irish manner of observing Easter was not that of the Eastern Quarto Decimans, as they are called, who kept it on the fourteenth day of the Jewish month Nisan, on whatever day of the week that might fall. This error was corrected at the Council of Nice, when it was commanded that the feast should always be celebrated on the Sunday after the fourteenth day of the moon; and the decree of the council was obeyed in Britain and Ireland as in Rome. But difficulties afterwards arose in the method of calculating Easter; the *Cycles*, or periods of years used for that purpose, were after a time found to be

incorrect, and the philosophers of Alexandria were applied to, to calculate the day and notify it each year to the Pope, who should publish it to the rest of the Church. Even this plan failed to secure uniformity, and in the fifth century Rome and Alexandria were to be found computing the time of Easter after different cycles, Rome using one of eighty-four years, and Alexandria one of nineteen, which caused the feast to be celebrated on different days. The old Roman cycle was that which had been introduced into Ireland, and the Irish clergy continued to use it after it had been reformed in the time of Pope Hilarion, by whose command the Alexandrian cycle was established as more correct, and the calendar was corrected by Victorinus of Aquitaine. Such was the disturbed date of the world at this time, however, that the British and Irish churches heard nothing of this change, and stuck to their old Roman cycle even after the arrival of St. Gregory's missionaries. The notion of the Irish having adopted the Eastern computation of the Quarto Decimans is very clearly disproved by reference to Bede, lib. iii. ch. 4. They at last adopted the Roman calendar at the Synod of Lene, held in 630, wherein it was agreed that "they should receive what was brought to them from *the fountain of their baptism and of their wisdom*, even the successors of the Apostles of Christ."

[51] By astrology and the calculation of horoscopes must not be here understood the practice of *judicial* astrology, which was regarded by all the Anglo-Saxon prelates as a forbidden art; but, as Lingard supposes, studies connected with the Zodiac, and the art of dialling, here called *horoscopii computatio*; an art much in vogue among early scholars, and which formed one of the scientific recreations of Boethius.

[52] Surtees, History of Durham.

[53] Bede, lib. iv. c, 18.

[54] Alc. Opera i. p. 282.

[55] Nec linguam Hebraicam ignoravit. (Breviary Lessons.)

[56] Among the authors quoted by Bede are Virgil, Horace, Terence, Ovid, Lucan, Lucretius, Prudentius, Juvencus, Macer, Varro, Cornelius, Severus, Fortunatus, Sedulius, and Pacuvius, besides the Latin Fathers. He also makes frequent references to Homer, which was not at that time translated into Latin, and which he can, therefore, only have known in its original Greek.

[57] See De Nat. Rerum, Op. tom. ii. p. 37.

[58] Iren. de Hær. l. iii. 4.

[59] Three, however, were preserved which expressed sounds not conveyed by the Roman alphabet, corresponding to w, th, and dh.

[60] The instruction of the people was not, however, to be limited to a knowledge of these prayers. "Let them be taught," he says, "by what works they may please God, and from what things they must abstain; with what sincerity they must believe in Him, and with what devotion they must pray; how diligently and frequently they must fortify themselves with the holy sign of the Cross; and how salutary for every class of Christian is the daily reception of the Lord's Body and Blood, which is, you know, the constant practice of the Church of Christ throughout Italy, Gaul, Africa, Greece, and the whole of the East." This is a most important testimony as to the existing practice of the Church in the eighth century, and Bede goes on to say that to his knowledge there are innumerable young persons, of both sexes, who might, beyond all question, be suffered to communicate, at least, on all Sundays and festivals.

[61] "Caras super omnia gazas." (De Pont. Ebor. Eccl.)

[62] Jamdiu optata adest dies. (Vita S. Bon. Acta SS. Ben.)

[63] "O felix collegium beatissimi Bonifacii!" exclaims the biographer of S. Sola.

[64] Dr. Campbell in his "Strictures on the Ecclesiastical History of Ireland," observes that "this great man was degraded by Pope Zachary on conviction of *being a mathematician.*" But perhaps the most remarkable reproduction of this oft-told tale occurs in Dr. Enfield's translation of Brucker's "History of Philosophy," which I give verbatim, as only to be paralleled in the "Art of Pluck." "Boniface," he says, "*the patron of ignorance and barbarism,* summoned *Polydore Virgil, bishop of Salisbury, to the Court of Inquisition* for maintaining the existence of the antipodes." (Vol. i, p. 363.) Would it be believed that a writer who is engaged in bewailing the *ignorance* of monkish philosophers should commit himself to a statement which confuses St. Feargil, or Virgil, bishop of Saltzburg, in the eighth century, with Polydore Vergil, archdeacon of Bath (for he was never bishop of Salisbury at all), in the fifteenth? And then the Inquisition! To make it complete he should have identified Virgil with the Latin poet, and convicted him of the Albigensian heresy. Yet these are the writers who find no terms contemptuous enough in which to speak of mediæval ignorance. "Among the scholastics," writes Dr. Enfield, in the very next sentence, "we find surprising proofs of weakness and ignorance." The scholastics, could they speak, might find something to retort on their accusers.

[65] The doctrines attributed to Virgil, and their condemnation by Pope Zachary, have been examined by Decker, a professor of Louvain, who shows very clearly that the error lay, not in their maintaining the existence of the antipodes, but in the notion of a race distinct from that of Adam. Feller, in the account he gives of the matter in his Historical Dictionary, refers to the

teaching of Bede, who, he declares, denied the spherical figure of the earth. But the work from which he quotes is not to be found among the writings of our English saint, whose real opinion on the subject may be seen from the following explicit passage: "We call the earth a globe, not that it is absolutely the perfect form of a globe, by reason of the unevenness of hills and plains, but because its whole compass, if comprehended within the circumference of lines, would make the figure of a globe."—*De Nat. Rer.* c. xlvi. 118.

[66] This question was resolved by Pope Zachary in favour of the validity of the baptism so administered.

[67] Vita S. Liob. ap. Surium.

[68] Tradition says that they stopped at Antwerp some days, and a grotto is still shown in the ancient church dedicated to St. Walburga, where she is said to have prayed.

[69] For the ingenious arguments by which certain writers have endeavoured to show that the Council of Cloveshoe *rejected* the authority of the Roman Pontiff (by whose command it was summoned), and for their able refutation, the reader is referred to "Lingard's Anglo-Saxon Antiquities," vol. i. Appendix, note G.

[70] Thorpe II. 414.

[71] Sid. Apol. Ep. iv. 3.

[72] Hist. Litt. t. iii. p. 22.

[73] Guizot, Hist. de Civil. vol. ii. lect. 22.

[74] Guizot, Hist. de Civil. vol. ii. lect. 22.

[75] According to Durandus, the circumstances under which Paul the Deacon wrote this hymn were as follows. Having to sing the blessing of the Paschal candle on Holy Saturday, he unfortunately lost his voice from hoarseness, and to recover it, invoked the aid of St. John Baptist, in whose honour he composed this hymn, in which he solicits him to restore him the use of his voice, and reminds him how at his nativity he had procured a like grace for his father Zachary. This anecdote explains the allusion in the opening lines. To avoid the tiresome confusion arising from the similarity of names, I will remind the reader that there were two persons designated as Paul the Deacon; one the contemporary of St. Gregory, and the other his historian; and moreover that he had another historian in the person of *John* the Deacon, who lived in the ninth century.

[76] The identical copy is still preserved in the Library of Sta. Maria in Vallicella at Rome, and bears on its fly-leaf the following inscription, which many suppose to be the autograph of Alcuin:—

Pro me quisque legas versus, orare memento.

Alcuine dicor; tu, sine fine, vale.

A folio Bible now in the British Museum, and formerly the property of M. de Speyer Passavant, has also its claims to be considered the original copy of Alcuin, though commonly held to have been written in the reign of Charles the Bald.

[77] Crevier, Hist. de L'Univ. de Paris, vol. i.

[78] Vita Caroli Mon. Engol. an. 787.

[79] Vita S. Greg. Joan. Diac. lib. ii. 7.

[80] Quatuor Evangelia Christi in ultimo ante obitus sui diem, cum Græcis et Syris optime correxerat. (Thegani, Vita Ludovici Pii, printed in Pertz, *Mon. Germ.* t ii.)

[81] Vita Karoli, Eginhard, cap. 22.

[82] See Patrologie Latine, vols. xcvii. and xcviii.

[83] The interior schools were known as *claustral*, and the exterior for secular students as *canonical*. Ekhehard, in his life of B. Notker, is the first who accurately distinguishes the two sorts of schools. "Traduntur post breve tempus Marcello *scholæ claustri* cum beato Notkero Balbulo et cæteris monachici habitus pueris: *exteriores* vero, *id est canonicæ*, Isoni cum Salomone et ejus comparibus." It is probable however that the law directing a total separation of the scholars under different masters, could not in all cases be carried out as rigidly as at the great abbey of St. Gall's, where the studium was, in Notker's time, the first in Europe; and in many monasteries both schools continued to be directed by the same scholasticus.

[84] Præfatio in IV. Sæculum, 184. Trithemius gives the names of sixteen monasteries containing these major schools; Mabillon adds eleven more, and the list might undoubtedly be yet further enlarged.

[85] He probably rested his statement on the petition presented by the Council of Paris in 829 to Louis le Débonnaire, in which they requested him, by his royal authority, to establish public schools *in three chief cities of his empire*, to the end that the troubles of the times might not quite destroy the good work set on foot by his father. But this was a suggestion and nothing more; the three cities were never named, and are merely spoken of as *in tribus*

congruentissimis imperii vestri locis; and the deposition of Louis, and the civil wars that raged between his sons, effectually prevented the suggestion from being carried out. The academy founded by Charlemagne at Pavia, which was directed by the Irish Dungal, was itself attached to a monastery. This is possibly the school alluded to by Bulæus, but there is certainly nothing in its history which claims for it the least pre-eminence over the monastic schools of France and Germany. The university historians have, in general, greatly misrepresented or misunderstood the character of the monastic schools. Du Boulay talks of the *public schools* of Charlemagne as if they were Etons or Harrows, and in one place likens them to universities. But, in fact, the term *public school* meant simply that they were not confined to the use of the monks of that monastery, but were open to all comers. We find in them rather the germ of the *collegiate* system, which was in some sense the counterpoise of the university idea. But Bulæus and Du Boulay always write with Paris University in their mind as the normal principle of education. They seem unable to conceive of any institution for teaching which was not either its copy or its anticipation.

[86] Mab. Vet. Analecta, i. 357.

[87] See his verses on the destruction of Lindisfarne (Acta SS. Ben.)

[88] At Aix-la-Chapelle his bones have been quite recently discovered and identified.—See *Die Eröffnung des Karlsschreines*, being No. 61 of the *Aachener Zeitung*, March 2, 1861.

[89] See Ampère, Hist. Lit. avant le xii. Siècle, t. ii.

[90] Matthew of Westminster represents him as taking refuge in England, where, according to the same authority, he was warmly received by King Alfred, and becoming scholasticus at Malmsbury abbey, was there stabbed to death by his scholars. This story was received as authentic, until Mabillon showed it to have been an incorrect version of the history of John of Saxony, who, when abbot of Ethelingay, was killed in a commotion with some of his monks. In spite of the pains taken by this writer to clear up the mistake, the narrative still finds its place in most works which treat of our old English schools, and will probably be as hard to dislodge as other traditions of the same genus. It appears certain, however, that Scotus Erigena returned to France and died there in peace, some time after the death of Charles the Bald.

[91] Many of these towns derive their names from the monks under whom the cells dependent on the abbey were first founded; thus we have Abrazell, Aichezell, Kerzell, and Edelcell, from Abraham, Haicho, Kero, and Edeling, all monks of Fulda.

[92] Nepotem meum et cum eo duo alios nobiles puerulos, quando, si Deus vult, nostro monasterio profuturos, propter Germanicæ linguæ nanciscendam scientiam, Vestræ Sanctitati mittere cupio. (Ep. xci.)

[93] He appears to have had some knowledge of Hebrew, and introduces a quotation from the Hebrew Scriptures in his Treatise *De Partu Virginis*.

[94] Rabanus, De Instit. Clericorum, lib. iii. c. 24.

[95] Tract. de Corpore Christi, printed in Martène, Vet. Script. t. 9.

[96]

Scandens et descendens inter montium confinia

Silvarum scrutando loca, valliumque concava.

(Hymn for the Procession of Relics. ap. Leibnitz.)

[97] Vita B. Notkeri. ch. ix. Acta SS. Ben.

[98] Archives of the Chapter of Rouen, ann. 1449.

[99] Spicilegium, t. ii. 311.

[100] Consuet. Clun. Spicileg. t. i. 687.

[101] Vita Ratgari. Acta S.S. Boll. t. i.

[102] D'Achery Spicileg. t. ii. p. 139.

[103] Hallam's Middle Ages, vol. iii. p. 330, and note.

[104] Guibert de Nogent refers to his school studies of Ovid and Virgil's Eclogues; and Peter de Blois names Suetonius and Q. Curtius, "besides the other books which are commonly used in schools." For a full and careful enumeration of the class-books used in the monastic schools, see Bahr: *Geschichte der Römischen Literatur*; and also Prof. Pauly's *Real Encyclopädie der Classischen Alterthumswissenschaft*.

[105] Acta SS. Ben. Præf. in Secul. iii.

[106] It is reprinted by Mai, Scrip. Vet. t. iii. p. 251.

[107] Hilduin, abbot of St. Denis in 814, was the chief supporter of this opinion. The letter addressed to him by the Emperor Louis, and his reply, are prefixed to the Areopagitica in Surius. t. v.

[108] Deut. vi. 7.

[109] In the preface to the metrical version of the Bible, executed by command of Louis le Debonnaire, we find the following passage:

"Præcepit namque uni de gente Saxonum qui apud suos non ignobilis vates habebatur ut Vetus ac Novum Testamentum in Germanicam Linguam poetice transferre studeret, quatenus *non solum litteratis verum etiam illiteratis* sacra divinorum præceptorum lectio panderetur."

[110] Martene: Thesaurus Anec. i. 489.

[111] Vos lumina; vos mea vita ... vos novella plantatio. (Vita Sanctæ Cæsariæ.)

[112] Si qua enim soror, reliquis in templo cantantibus, sonoræ vocis modulatione non congrueret, a pia illa matre objurgata, vel etiam in facie manibus cæsa, toto reliquæ vitæ spatio clara fuit et delectabili voce. (Vita S. Adehildæ: ap. Surium.)

[113] The whole document is to be found in D'Achery's "Spicilegium," vol. ii.

[114] Hallam, Middle Ages, iii. p. 332.

[115] This Saxon school became, afterwards, a great object of interest to Alfred; and Asser tells us, that at his request Pope Martin II. freed it from all taxes and tribute.

[116] Wise's Edition, Oxon. 1722.

[117] Asser (Wise's Ed.), p. 67.

[118] Among these homilies is that for the festival of Easter, commonly quoted in support of the audacious theory that the Anglo-Saxon divines knew nothing of the doctrine of Transubstantiation. The whole question is satisfactorily examined by Dr. Lingard, in his "History of the Anglo-Saxon Church," to which the reader is referred. But it may be observed, that whatever obscurity is to be found in Ælfric's language, that of other writers of his nation is singularly emphatic. The very term, *Transubstantiation*, is all but anticipated by Alcuin, who, in a letter to Paulinus, bids him remember his friend "at that time when thou shalt consecrate the bread and wine *into the substance* of the body and blood of Christ." And of two saints contemporary with Ælfric, viz. St. Odo and St. Oswald, their biographers record the fact, that while celebrating mass, the appearance of a bleeding Host in their hands removed the doubts of certain beholders. Yet, what doubts had to be removed if the doctrine were not then held?

[119] Hist. of Ramsey, ch. lxvii.

[120] In the first edition of this book allusion was made to the studies pursued in this century at Croyland abbey. But the chronicle of Ingulphus from which the narrative was quoted, is now generally admitted to be spurious, and the passage has therefore been omitted.

[121] Berington, Lit. Hist. book iii. 154.

[122] Hallam, Middle Ages, chap. ix. part 1. *passim.*

[123] Florus, Carmina Varia, Vet. Anal. 413.

[124] The battle of Fontenay was gained by Charles the Bald and Louis the German over their elder brother Lothaire. The latter was totally defeated, and the old Frankish or Teutonic nobility who supported him were all but entirely destroyed. From this time the Gallo-Roman element began to prevail in France over the German, and the treaty shortly afterwards renewed between Charles and Louis at Strasburg, is the first instance on record of the vernacular dialects being employed on any solemn occasion. Louis as king of the Germans, swore to the treaty in the Romance language, now formally recognised as the language of France while the French king took his oath in Tudesque, or German. On that day, France and Germany may be said to have first assumed their distinct nationalities. The Romance or Rustic Latin became the language of France, though this afterwards separated into two branches, that spoken in the northern provinces, which was more largely mingled with Germanic idioms, and which was known as the *Langue d'oyl*, or *d'oui* and the softer dialect of the south, which was called the *Langue d'oc*. Later on, the Italian Romance became distinct from either of these, and is sometimes spoken of as the *Langue de si.*

[125] Footnote: Hallam, Middle Ages, chap. i. part 1.

[126] Acta SS. Ben. Vita S. Anscharii.

[127] Odericus Vitalis, B. vi. ch. 10.

[128] Analect. tom. i. 426.

[129] Gesta Epis. Leod. cap. 25.

[130] Fleury observes that by the "Dialectics of St. Augustine" is supposed to be meant the treatise of the ten categories, attributed to St. Augustine from the time of Alcuin.

[131] D'Achery, Spic. t. i. 372.

[132]

Esuries Te, Christe Deus, sitis atque videndi

Jam modo carnales me vetat esse dapes.

Da mihi Te vesci, Te potum haurire salutis,

Unicus ignotæ Tu cibus esto viæ;

Et quem longa fames errantem ambedit in orbe

Hunc satia vultu, Patris Imago, Tuo.

[133] St. Maieul of Cluny always "refreshed his mind with reading" as he rode, and one day both horse and man fell into a quagmire. And Thierry, abbot of St. Hubert's, lost his way, and very nearly his life also, owing to his being so intent on the recitation of the Psalms that he did not see where his horse was going. Many examples of a similar nature are to be met with.

[134] Quando illi prandentes in angulis scholæ, dulcia obsonia magistro furantur.—*Vita S. Adalberti, Acta SS. Ben.*

[135] The following is his version of the "Our Father":—

Fater unser du in himele bist. Din na' mo vuerde geheiligot. Din riche chome. Din wille geskehe in erdo also in himele. Unser ta' golicha brot kib uns hinto-unde. Unsere sculde belak uns, also ouch wir bela' zend unsern sculdigen. Und in chorunga nit leitest du unsich. Nu belose unsich some ubele.

[136] I wish to be a Greek, lady, who am scarcely yet a Latin.

[137] I am altogether unable to compose worthy verses, for I am so confused by the caresses of the duchess.

[138] Oderic. Vit. B. vi. c. iv.

[139] Wis. vii. 17. 22-23.

[140] Richer's history is printed at length in Pertz's *Monumenta Germaniæ Historica*, Tom. iii.

[141] Gerbert taught his disciples the use of the monochord; a single string, which being struck at different intervals, gave out the different sounds of the gamut. These intervals were marked on the chord, and the words to be sung had written over them a cipher, showing to what interval on the monochord it corresponded. A person therefore could always set himself right by sounding the note he wanted, as we should use a pitch-key. A description of this instrument is given by the monk Odoramn, whose works have been discovered and published by Cardinal Mai, and whose musical treatises are said to be based on the scientific principles of Boëthius and Euclid.

[142] The Arabs received the knowledge of the Indian numerals in the ninth century. "But the profound and important historical investigations to which a distinguished mathematician, M. Chasles, was led by his correct interpretation of the so-called Pythagorean table in the geometry of Boëthius," says M. Humboldt, "render it more than probable that the Christians in the West were acquainted even earlier than the Arabians with the Indian system of numeration; the use of the nine figures, having their value determined by position, being known by them under the name of the

System of the Abacus." (*Cosmos*, vol. ii. p. 226, also note 358. See also M. Chasles, *Aperçu historique des méthodes en géométrie*, 464-472, and his papers in the *Comptes-rendus de l'Acad. des Sciences*.)

[143] The story has of course been taken up by the usual chorus of modern writers, but its fallacy is well exposed by Gretser, who shows that the tenth century knew nothing of the rumour, which entirely originated in the fertile brain of Benno.

[144] Meibomius, Scrip. Rerum German. t. i. 706.

[145] In the year 1867 a controversy arose in Germany concerning the authenticity of the works attributed to Hroswitha. Professor Aschbach, of the Imperial Academy of Vienna, in a paper printed that year in the Acts of the Academy, endeavoured to prove them audacious forgeries; and supposed the author of the fraud to have been one Conrad Celtes, a Humanist of the fifteenth century. The question was taken up on both sides. Several distinguished writers and their arguments and investigations appear to have successfully vindicated the genuine character of the works, and to have established Hroswitha's claim to be considered their real authoress. See B. Tenk, *Neber Roswitha Carmen de Gestis Oddonis*, Leipzig, 1876. R. Kœpke, *Ottonische Studien zur deutschen geschichte im 10ten jahrhundert*, II. *Hroswith von Gandersheim* (xv. s. 314.) *Die Aelteste deutsche Dichterin* (III. 127. S), Berlin, 1869. *Hroswitha, die helltönende Stimme von Gandersheim. In Westermann's Illustr. Monatsheften*, 1871, &c.

[146] Rohrbacher, Hist. de l'Eglise, vol. xiii. 540.

[147] Adelmann Rythmi Alphabetici. Vet. Anal. iv. 382.

[148] Analecta, t. iv. 385-387.

[149] Rémusat, St. Anselme de Cantorbéry, liv. ii. chap. iv. The various opinions in favour of and against this argument are given in chap. v.

[150] Fleury, lib. lxii. 1.

[151]

O'er wayward childhood wouldst thou hold firm rule,

And sun thee in the light of happy faces?

Love, Hope, and Patience, these must be thy graces,

And in thine own heart let them first keep school.

For, as old Atlas on his broad neck places

Heaven's starry globe, and there sustains it;—so

Do these upbear the little world below

Of education,—Patience, Love, and Hope.—*Coleridge.*

[152] So at least we conjecture from certain stage directions in the dramas of Hroswitha, which seem to infer a good deal of skill on the part of the stage manager.

[153] M. Delisle, in his Notice on the Life and Writings of Odericus, explains this expression to mean the Latin alphabet; Carmenta Nicostrata, the mother of the Arcadian Evander, being held by some to have first invented letters. He could not, however, have been five years learning his alphabet, so we may probably understand him to mean the ordinary elementary instruction in Latin.

[154] Now known as the *Priorata,* or Priory of St. John of Jerusalem.

[155] Rohrbacher, Hist. Ecc. tom. xiv. 48-60.

[156]

Essa è la luce eterna di Sigieri,

Che, leggendo nel Vico degli Strami,

Sillogizzò invidiosi veri.—*Parad.* x. 136.

[157] Pertz, Monumenta Germanica, tom. iv. 39.

[158] Chron. Clun. ap. Bib. Clun. 1645.

[159] It may be taken as tolerably well proved, however, that he was really an Irishman, and he is supposed to have been a monk of Clonard. Contemporary with him was another famous Irish historian, Tigernach, abbot of Clonmacnoise, who wrote his chronicle partly in Irish and partly in Latin, and is held to have been well acquainted with Greek. The Irish scholars highly distinguished themselves in this century. There was an Irish monastery at Erford, and another at Cologne, into which Helias, a monk of Monaghan, on returning from a visit to Rome, introduced the Roman chant (Lanigan, Ecc. Hist. c. xxiv.)

[160] Histoire Lit. tom. vii. 58, and tom. ix. 149. The same authority makes mention of other translations in French of the Four Gospels, the Epistles of St. Paul, the Psalms, and some books of the Old Testament, all made in the diocese of Metz in the twelfth century.

[161] Sicut rectus ordo exigit ut profunda Christianæ fidei credamus, priusquam ea præsumamus ratione discutere; ita negligentia mihi videtur si postquam confirmati sumus in fide, non studemus quod credimus intelligere.

Opp. S. Anselm, *de Fide Trinitatis et de Incarn.* Præf. et *Cur Deus homo?* c. i. et 2.

[162] Abelard is classed by John of Salisbury as belonging to the sect of the Nominalists. (*De Nugis Curialium*, 7, 12. *Metalog.* 2, 17.) His followers, however, disliked the name, and he is more commonly described as a *Conceptualist.*

[163] Jo. Saris. Ep. xxiv.

[164] A certain enemy of the poets in the days of Virgil.

[165] Except indeed we reckon St. Anselm as the first of the schoolmen. But though this would be, strictly speaking, correct, the formation of Scholastic Theology as a distinct science is not generally spoken of before the time of Peter Lombard.

[166] In his work entitled *De Nugis Curialium*, he is said to have quoted upwards of one hundred and twenty writers of antiquity.

[167] Metalogicon, lib. vii. c. 13.

[168] Jos. xv. 15.

[169] Jacob de Vitrag. Hist. Occ. c. 7. Fleury, Hist. Eccles. liv. 66. lix.

[170] Archi-Trenius, or the Chief Lamenter,—a name taken from the Greek title of the Book of Lamentations.

[171] Du Boulai. Hist. de l'Univ. t. iii. p. 31.

[172] Terra mota est, etenim cœli distillaverunt ... pluviam voluntariam segregabis Deus, hæreditati tuæ. Ps. lxvii. 10, 11.

"La main de Dieu, lorsqu'elle nous châtie, est comme celle du chirurgien qui ne blesse que pour guérir, et à la fin *les foudres se convertissent en pluies* que Dieu réserve pour l'heritage de ses élus." (Esprit de S. François de Sales.)

[173] Grandes Chroniques de France, ann. 1196.

[174] Lebœuf, Hist. du diocèse de Paris, i. 6.

[175] The collection of the Roman Imperial statutes, known as the *Justinian Code*, was published by order of Justinian in 529. Three years later appeared fifty books, containing the decisions of famous jurists, and this digest received the name of the *Pandects*. An introduction, to facilitate the study of the Pandects, with four additional books, make up the *Institutes*; and, lastly, certain new statutes added at the revision of the code made in 534, formed the *Novellæ*; the whole collection making up the body of the Roman or civil law.

[176] Cosmos (Sabine's Translation), vol. ii. note 331.

[177] His story is introduced by Dante into the Inferno, cant. xiii.

[178] The university of Toulouse was established in virtue of certain articles introduced into the treaty of peace between Count Raymund of Toulouse and St. Louis of France. The count agreed to pay 4000 marks for the maintenance of certain masters for ten years; namely, two doctors of theology, two canonists, six masters of liberal arts, and two of grammar. This foundation was made for the express purpose of combating the Albigensian heresy in its headquarters.

[179] The feudal lords in the eleventh century frequently claimed and exercised the right of appointing the scholasticus to certain churches where benefices were attached to the office. (See Martene, Ampl. Coll. t. ii. 974-979.) But even then the approval of the bishop or his chancellor was required, and he could claim the right of veto, when objections to the candidate existed on the score of faith or morals.

[180] Crevier, Hist. de l'Univ. vol. i. p. 256. The custom was made law by a decree of the Third Council of Lateran in 1179. But forty years earlier we find the Council of Westminster prohibiting cathedral scholastics from accepting payment for the licenses granted by them to schoolmasters in towns and villages.

[181] Thus we read that W. de Champeaux held the office of archdeacon of Paris, and governed the cathedral schools. "It had been the rule," says Crevier, "that all who wished to open a school should obtain a license from the scholasticus, *that is, the chancellor*, of the church in whose territory they wished to establish themselves." See also the statutes of Lichfield Cathedral. (Monas. Anglic. t. 3. p. 34.) "Officium Cancellarii est, sive residens sive non extiterit, lectiones legendas in ecclesia per se, vel per suum vicarium, auscultare, male legentes emendare, *scholas conferre*, &c." (Quoted by Du Cange.) The chancellor of St. Paul's, London, had jurisdiction over all the schools of the city. He was called the *Magister Scholarum*, and the master of the cathedral grammar school acted as his vice-chancellor. (Lib. Stat. Eccl. S. Pauli.) In the reign of Stephen we find an ordinance from the legate, Henry de Blois, to the effect that all schoolmasters teaching schools in London, without license from the cathedral scholasticus, should be excommunicated.

[182] Quoted in Catholic University Gazette, Oct. 26, 1854.

[183] Crevier, Hist. de l'Univ. vol. ii.

[184] For a summary of the errors condemned, see Martene, Thesaur. Anecdot. t. iv. col. 163, 164.

[185] Jasinski, Sum. Ordin. Cap. Gen. p. 403.

[186] Const. FF. Præd. dis. n. note *a.*

[187] Const. FF. Præd. dis. ii. note *b.*

[188] *Ibid.* Paris, 1236. De Studiis linguarum. S. (Const. Fontana, 1862.)

[189] Const. Dis. ii. De Student. iv. note *g.*

[190] Const. F. F. Præd. De Studentibus. This provision of the ancient Constitutions is commented on by the statutes of more modern addition, wherein we see the immense importance attached by the Order to the study of Church history. After speaking of the study of the Scriptures, it is said: "Another fount of theological science is ecclesiastical history, which is, as it were, the complement, and ever-living interpreter of Holy Scripture; so that these two are the *duo luminaria magna,* illuminating all the faithful in Christ, and manifesting without a cloud of error, all those truths revealed by God; for the history of the Church, rightly speaking, is nothing else than Christian doctrine in act, nor is there any better or more easy way of knowing the Catholic dogma; for it is nothing else than a series of battles and triumphs of our faith against the insurgent heresies, which the Church, by her doctors, martyrs, and decrees of Popes and Councils has successively pierced through and overcome; whence the certain interpretation of Scripture and the clear explanation of tradition and the authoritative definition of dogma, are all to be found in the History of the Church." Const. F. F. Præd. (Fontana, 1862.) De Studio, p. 458.

[191] Fleury, Histoire Eccl. Discours 5me.

The order of graduation, as it exists at present, is as follows: Eight years of study are required before any one can be admitted to the degree of Lector, and to obtain this a student must undergo an examination in Philosophy, Modern Controversy, Scripture, and the Summa of St. Thomas. The active or teaching course, required for the higher degrees of Bachelor and Doctor, remains nearly the same as in former days. Various modifications have from time to time been introduced into the legislation of the Order on this point, but the principle has always been retained of making a long course of teaching and repeated examinations the test of qualification. *Secular* students in a Dominican College, however, may be admitted to the degree of Doctor after only a three years' course of Theology, provided they stand an examination in the Summa; and by the Bull of Pope Clement XII., all such secular graduates of the Dominican schools hold the same position in every respect as though they had been promoted to the Doctorship in the Roman College of the Sapienza. (Fontana, p. 206.)

[192] His words are as follows: "When I was at Venice, being still a youth, they were sawing some stones for the repair of one of the churches, and it chanced that in one of these blocks there appeared the figure of a head; as

of a king, crowned with a long beard. The countenance had no other defect, save that the forehead was too high ascending towards the top of the head. All of us who examined it were satisfied that it was the work of nature. And I being questioned as to the cause of the disproportioned forehead, replied that this stone had been coagulated by the work of vapour, and that by means of a more powerful heat the vapour had arisen without order or measure." (Op. tom. 2 De Mineralibus. lib. 2, tract. 3, c. i.) The expressions here used are somewhat obscure, but they seem to imply that Albert knew something of those phenomena which geologists explain as the result of volcanic heat and the action of vapour. "Transformed, or metamorphic rocks," says Humboldt, "are those in which the texture and mode of stratification have been altered either by the contact or proximity of an irrupted volcanic rock, or, as is more frequently the case, by the *action of vapours* and *sublimations* which accompany the issue of certain masses in a state of igneous liquefaction." (Cosmos. vol. i. p. 236.)

[193] "Quia totum scibile scisti."—Jammy, Vita B. Alberti.

[194] The very remarkable passage here referred to by Humboldt is to be found in the Treatise, "De Cælo et Mundo."

[195] Humboldt, Cosmos, vol. ii. p. 247.

[196] Among these, besides the celebrated speaking head, the account of which is too legendary to be depended on, we must reckon the mode of rendering sensible the phenomena of an earthquake, which he describes in his book on meteors, and which finds a place in most modern works on popular science; his automata made to move by means of mercury according to the method of Chinese toys; and the so-called magic cup, which is still preserved in the Museum of Cologne.

[197] Rutebœuf, the celebrated crusading minstrel of the thirteenth century, whose reckless sarcasm spared no one, not even St. Louis himself, endeavoured to console the defeated seculars by directing his most cutting satire against their opponents, in a piece entitled "La descorde de l'université et des Jacobins." The poem contains many curious illustrations of the manners and studies of the Paris students, and it need hardly be said that the Jacobins fare but badly. When first the friars came into the world, he says, they took lodgings with humility, but now they are masters of Paris and Rome,

Et par leur grant chape roonde

Ont versé l'université.

[198] Ps. ciii. 13.

[199] Boll. Vita S. Thom. p. 712, n. 77.

[200] Institutions Liturgiques, tom. 1, 348.

[201] Frigerio, Vita di S. Tomaso, lib. ii. c. x.

[202] Sixtus of Sienna and Trithemius both declare that St. Thomas explained *all* the works of Aristotle, and that he was the first Latin Doctor who did so, but the Commentaries that are preserved treat only of fifty two books. This purgation of the pagan philosophy is alluded to in the Matins hymn for his office, as forming one of his chief glories:

Plusquam doctores cæteri

Purgans dogma Gentilium.

[203] Qu. 85, Act. 2, Ad. 3

[204] Qu. 84, 7.

[205] Contra Gen. 1, 7.

[206] Qu. i. Act. 8.

[207] Dalgairns, Introduction to the Life of St. Richard, pp. 36, 37.

[208] At Paris 1286, Bourdeaux 1287, and Lucca 1288.

[209] Vie de S. Thomas, livre v. ch. xi.

[210] Echard, de Script. Ord. t. i. 435.

[211] In c. 5. Matth. quoted by Touron, liv. 4, ch. 3.

[212] Lib. 1, contra Gentil. c. 2, quoted by Touron.

[213] Boll. p. 715, n. 80.

[214] This idea is doubtless little in accordance with our ordinary way of regarding the mechanical arts, but the reader will remember the words of Scripture, which tells us how the Lord called Beseleel the son of Uri, and filled him with the Spirit of God, with wisdom and understanding and all learning to work in gold and silver and carpenter's work; and how He put wisdom into the heart of every skilful man to know how to work artificially, and to the women that they might spin fine linen. (Exod. xxxi. 3; xxxv. 25, 35; xxxvi. 1.) How sublime is this view, which displays to us every part of human knowledge, the humblest as well as the most profound, as, alike, but sparks from the One Fontal Light,—the Illuminating Spirit of God!

[215] S. Bonaventure (quoted in the *Dublin Review*, Dec. 1851), from his small work called "The Reduction of the Arts to Theology."

[216] De Studio legendi, iii. 3-6, quoted in the Appendix to Newman's University Lectures.

[217] Eccl. Hist. vol. 18, p. 434-444.

[218] *Ibid.* vol. 18, p. 444.

[219] See Touron, *Vies des Hommes Illustres*, tom. i. 489-504; where are also to be found notices of F. Paul Christiani, and other Hebrew scholars of the order.

[220] These foundations are thought worthy of being named among his greatest works in the Breviary lessons for the Octave day of his feast: "Hebraicæ et Arabicæ linguæ publicas scholas in Ordine Prædicatorum impensis instituit."

[221] The letter is printed at length in Martene's Collection, Tom. iv. col. 1527.

[222] Crevier, Hist. de l'Univ. de Paris. Vol. ii. p. 227. There is incidental evidence that the Greek and Oriental tongues were occasionally studied even by members of the secular colleges of Paris, during this and the following century. Stephen Pasquier speaks of a certain youth of twenty, who in the year 1445 spoke very subtle Latin, Greek, Hebrew, Chaldaic, and Arabic, besides many other tongues; and winds up his account by saying that if an ordinary man had lived a hundred years without eating and sleeping he could not have learnt as much as this young prodigy. His learning, however, was evidently something rather uncommon, for, says the historian, it put all his fellow-students in fear lest he knew more than human nature ought to know, and might possibly be "a young Antichrist."

[223] Ayliffe; State of the University of Oxford, vol. i. p. 106.

[224] Fontana, Const. *De studio Linguarum.* g. p. 467; also Jasinsky, *Studium Linguarum.* lit. B.

[225] Annibaldi was a pupil of Albert the Great, and took his Doctor's degree in Paris, where he enjoyed a very brilliant reputation. Innocent IV. created him Master of the Sacred Palace. But being promoted to the purple in 1263 be solicited Urban IV. to name as his successor in that office a certain learned English Friar, F. William Bonderinensis, as he is called in the Catalogue of the Masters, who belonged to the Convent of London, and was the only one of our countrymen who ever filled that important post.

[226] Hibernia Dominicana, p. 191.

[227] Speech on the Extension of Academic Education in Ireland, delivered at Cork, Nov. 13, 1844; quoted in an article on the *Ancient Dominican Irish Schools*; Dublin Review, Sept. 1845.

[228] Hib. Dominicana, p. 193.

[229] Cantu, Histoire Universelle, vol. xi, p. 593.

[230] M. Cartier, in his introduction to the Life of Fra Angelico, has adduced many passages from St. Thomas, not only elucidating the philosophy of Christian art, but showing that he had a natural taste for such pursuits, and drew from them more than one graceful illustration. Thus he lays down the three conditions of beauty to consist in entireness, proportion, and clearness of colour. He also enunciates that broad principle which justifies us in requiring that one who aims at representing spiritual subjects should himself be holy in life, when he declares that "all inferior forms flow from the forms which are in the intellect." For how then, we may argue, can a spiritual form flow from a debased intellect? And among the maxims and sayings preserved by his biographers there occur more than one, the imagery of which seems to show even a practical acquaintance with the art of painting.

[231] Histoire Eccl., vol. xviii. p. 686.

[232] The image is taken from St. Gregory, who compares secular letters to the smiths' tools which were to be found in the hands, not of the Israelites, but of the Philistines. Nevertheless, he says, as the Israelites went down to the Philistines and borrowed their tools to sharpen their own instruments, so Christians may and ought to use the liberal arts in order to explain and defend the truths of religion. And those who seek to prohibit the faithful from the study of the liberal sciences are like the Philistines who did not suffer the children of Israel to have smiths among them, "lest they should make them swords or spears." (S. Greg. in 1 Reg. lib. v. c. iii. No. 30.)

[233] Greith; *Die Deutsche Mystik im Prediger-Orden*, pp 38, 39.

[234] Quoted by Sighart (French Trans.), p. 378.

[235] Summa, 2, 2, qu. 180, 1, ad 1 et 2.

[236] Ibid. 1. 2, qu. 27, a. 2, and 2.

[237] S. Thom. 2, 2, q. 27, a. 6.

[238] Sup. Psal. xxi.

[239] Sermon for the 23rd Sunday after Pentecost.

[240] S. Antoninus, Vita, § 6.

[241] Preface to his *Meditations from St. Thomas.*

[242] Eccles. xxiv. 43, 44, 47 (Lessons for the Common of Doctors).

[243] Leland.

[244] Nevertheless, oddly enough, the susceptibility to natural beauty and the power of describing it with the pen is often claimed as one of the good things restored to us by the Renaissance. The author of Cosmos, in that beautiful Introduction to his work in which he traces the history of the love of nature, observes that, "when the sudden intercourse with Greece caused a general revival of classical literature, we find as *the first example among prose writers* a charming description of nature from the pen of Cardinal Bembo." Had the writer opened any of the monastic Chronicles in which his own country is so rich, he would have found that the monks, whom Bembo would have regarded as barbarians, had been before him as landscape painters in words, by at least six centuries.

[245] Fescennia, a town of Etruria, was noted in the days of Horace for the rude extempore verses, full of coarse raillery, composed by its inhabitants, and commonly known as *Fescennina carmina* (Hor. Ep. ii. 1. 145). The *Theonine tooth* is likewise an expression derived from Horace (Ep. i. 18. 82); and seems to have been a proverbial expression derived from Theon, the name of a certain Roman freedman, well known for his malignant wit. (See Notes on Horace by Rev. A. J. Maclean.)

[246] If the suggestion to restore the teaching of the Latin prayers and the plain song of the Church in our parochial schools be deemed preposterous on the ground of its *difficulty*, we would simply beg objectors to try the experiment before passing judgment. A very short experience will prove that with ordinary perseverance nothing is easier than to make a class of boys recite fluently and chant correctly from note the Psalms of Vespers or Compline, or the *Credo, Gloria,* and other portions of the Mass; and we may add, that nothing seems more acceptable to the scholars themselves. What was possible in an age when the whole instruction must have been given orally, cannot have any insuperable difficulties about it in days when every child may be provided with a printed book. Possibly in a congregation thus trained there might be fewer complaints than there now are on the score of children behaving badly in church: for when children understand and take part in what is going on around them, they do not behave amiss. More valid objections can be conceived as arising from the difficulty of sparing the time when so many other subjects have to be taught. But what is more essential to teach Catholics than their Catholic prayers? and what branch of secular learning will prove a substitute for sound, genuine, and intelligent Catholic Faith?

[247] Many different versions exist of this hymn, which may be thus rendered into modern English: "Saint Mary, pure Virgin Mother of Jesus Christ of Nazareth, take, shield, help mine Godric, take, bring him safe with thee into the kingdom of God., Saint Mary, bower of Christ, purity of virgins, flower

of mothers, take away my sins, reign in my mind, and bring me to dwell with the only God."

[248] The custom was very general in poor parishes. Thus Reginald of Durham tells us of a certain scholar, Haldene by name, who was wont to attend the school which, "according to the known and accustomed usage," was held in the Church of St. Cuthbert, at Northam. One day Haldene, who did not know his lessons and was afraid of the rod, conceived the bright idea of getting hold of the key and throwing it into the Tweed, so that when the hour of Vespers came no key was to be found. The example, in far later times, of "Wonderful Walker," keeping school in his village church, was therefore but a surviving relic of the primitive manners.

[249] Antiquities of the Monastical Church of Durham, pp. 54, 77.

[250] Wood. Antiq. of Oxford, lib. i. p. 135.

[251] Ralph Bocking was a Dominican Friar and a native of Chichester, and wrote the life of the Saint (whose confessor he was) with great feeling and devotion.

[252] He adds that this decking of the well was prohibited by the Parliament, as a popish abomination, after which "the water shranke up." On this the rustics set the Parliament at defiance and revived the ancient custom, whereupon, to their inexpressible consolation the water recommenced flowing.

[253] For a statement of the arguments by which this opinion is supported, see Rohrbacher, Histoire Eccl. t. xviii. pp. 478-482.

[254] Fleury, who in his fifth Discourse has spoken with equal contempt of the theological and literary merits of the scholastics, winds up by reminding the reader that they wrote at a time when everything exhibited the same bad taste as was displayed in Gothic architecture, that absurd assemblage of petty ornaments *"which no architect would ever dream of imitating."* Nothing endurable in point of style or art was, according to him, to be seen in Europe from the fall of the Roman empire until the fifteenth century, that is, during the whole essentially Christian period. With what amazement would he have beheld the Christian Renaissance of our own days, and the reflux of taste into mediæval channels!

[255] Godwin, and some other writers, claim Kilwarby as a Franciscan. But the evidence in favour of his being a Dominican is irresistible. He was present at the general chapter of the Order of Preachers held at Barcelona in 1261; he attended the Provincial chapter of Montpelier in 1271, and is named in the acts of that council among other distinguished men of the Order then present. He was discharged from his office of Provincial in the General

Chapter held at Florence, 1272, but was re-elected by the Provincial Chapter of England the same year. He is described as a Friar Preacher in the Patent Rolls of Edward I., when the temporalities of Canterbury were restored; and Nicholas Trivet, the historian of the Order, who lived only fifty years after the archbishop, distinctly names him as a Dominican. Finally, his name does not occur in the Catalogue of English Franciscan Provincials.

[256] Collier, Eccl. History; vol. i. Book 5, p. 484.

[257] Nich. Trivet. *Annales regum Angliæ.*

[258] For the beautiful narrative of this event see the Life of St. Edmund, by the Abbé Massé.

[259] His name appears in the MS. Catalogue of Fellows of Merton under Edward II., preserved in the College Library.

[260] In his inedited commentary on the *Divina Commedia*, written whilst attending the Council of Constance, he says, "Anagogice dilexit theologiam sacrum in qua diu studuit tam in Oxoniis in regno Angliæ, quam Parisiis." And again: "Dante se in juventute dedit omnibus artibus liberalibus, studens eas Paduæ, Bononiæ, demum Oxoniis et Parisiis, ubi fecit multos actus mirabiles, intantum quod ab aliquibus dicebatur magnus philosophus, ab aliquibus magnus theologus, ab aliquibus magnus poëta." It is possible that his authority for this statement was drawn from English sources; for his own Latin translation of the poem was undertaken at the request of two English bishops present at the Council, Bubwith of Bath and Halam of Salisbury.

[261] Il *maestro vostro* ben vi scrive.—Par. canto viii.

[262] Par. xxiv. 130.

[263] It must not be supposed, from the mention of *burning*, that Dante was the object of religious persecution. A reference to the annals of Florence, Siena, or any of the other Italian republics, will show that this punishment was very commonly decreed by the dominant party against their political opponents. Thus Silvestro de' Medici, on gaining the upper hand in Florence, burnt several citizens of note, with their palaces. And these atrocious cruelties were perpetrated for no imaginable crime, but simply to get rid of hated rivals. In the Revolution of 1369 we read that Bruno da Renaldini had his head cut off, *senza cagione niuna.*

[264] Par. vi. 106.

[265] Purg. xx. 85.

[266] The celebrated Dominican, Durandus, Bishop of Mende, wrote his *Rationale Divinorum Officiorum* about the year 1290. He may be considered almost the last of the great liturgical writers of the Church, the catalogue of

whom includes the names of St. Isidore of Seville, Alcuin, Amalarius of Metz, Walafrid Strabo, Rabanus Maurus, Bruno of Asti, the Abbot Rupert, Honorius of Autun, and Pope Innocent III.

[267] Purgatorio, xxii. 101 (Carey's translation).

[268] Purg. x. 128.

[269]

Rafel maì amech zàbi almi,

Comincio a gridar la fiera bocca

Cui non si convenien più dolci salmi.—*Inferno,* xxxi. 70.

[270] Purg. i. 23.

[271] Par. i. 37; Purg. xxx. 89.

[272] Inferno, xxxiv. 110.

[273] See particularly the description of the falcon (Purg. xix. 63), the lark (Par. xx. 73), the rooks (Par. xxi. 34), the pigeon (Purg. ii. 118), the cranes (Purg. xxiv. 63), and of other birds (Par. xviii. 68, xxiii. 1).

[274] Purg. xxviii. 18, i. 113, and xxvii. 76; Par. xxxiii. 77.

[275] Purg. x. 37; Par. xx. 73, and xxxi. 40.

[276] Par. xv. 124 (Carey's translation).

[277] Tiraboschi, Istoria della Lit. Ital. v. 43.

[278] Soc. Hist. Eccl., l. 3, c. 16.

[279] "Pendant deux siècles, ni parmi les évêques, ni parmi les prêtres, ni parmi les moines français, on ne rencontre pas un seul personnage d'une vertu, d'une sainteté, d'une doctrine entièrement approuvées par l'Église. Cette expérience de deux siècles accuse dans le clergé français *une diminution de l'esprit de Dieu.*"—Rohrbacher, xxii. 462.

[280] St. Palaye, *Mémoires sur l'Ancienne Chevalerie,* part i. 7.

[281] Chaucer, *Romaunt of the Rose.* Eustache Deschamps is equally emphatic on this point:—

Vous qui voulez l'ordre de chevalier

Il vous convient mener nouvelle vie,

Devotement en oraison veillier,

Péché fuir, *orgueil* et villenie.

[282] Ordre de Chevalerie, fol. 10, 11.

[283] Godwin, *Life of Chaucer.*

[284] How significant are the words *famulus* and *famula*, by which the household servants are designated in the unclassical Latin of the Middle Ages! The *servus* of the Romans was, we know, nothing more than a slave; but the *famulus*, whether bond or free, was a member of the family, and a servant only in that sense in which his master owned himself the servant of Christ—*famulus Christi.*

[285] Innumerable decrees of provincial councils are to be found directed against these wandering clerks. And Edward II. issued a proclamation setting forth, "that whereas many idle and evil men, under colour of minstrelsy, get received into the houses of the rich to meat and drink, henceforth no great lord shall receive more than three or four minstrels of honour; and that none shall thrust themselves in unless they be sent for."

[286] Dibdin in his *Typographical Antiquities* (p. 142) examines the question whether Trevisa did or did not translate the Bible into English. To settle the question whether such a book was preserved at Berkeley Castle (where Trevisa was chaplain in 1387) Dibdin wrote to the Rev. J. Hughes, who filled the same office in 1807, and received the following reply:—

"I have the strongest reason for supposing that such a translation was made in the English language, and that it existed in the family so late as the time of James I. The book translated by Trevisa was given as a very precious gift by the Lord Berkeley of that time to the Prince of Wales, and I have read his letter thanking Lord Berkeley for the same. He does not positively say that the book was the Bible, but he says he hopes to make good use of so valuable a gift. This letter is still extant among the archives of the castle. Lord Berkeley has informed me that the book so given by his ancestor is at present in the Vatican Library. When he was at Rome several persons mentioned to him having seen there such a book, written by Trevisa; but as he had no opportunity of examining it, he cannot ascertain if it were the Bible."

[287] Lamberde's *Perambulations in Kent*, 1570.

[288] S. Anselmi Elucidarii, lib. ii. cap. 18.

[289] Chaucer's expansion of some of the Latin of Boëthius, in his English version of the "Consolation of Philosophie," has led some people to suppose that the poet translated from a French rendering of Boëthius, and not direct from the Latin. If he did so, the version he would have used was doubtless that of one of his known favourite authors, Jean de Méung, the continuator

of Guillaume de Lorris's "Romance of the Rose." A magnificent copy of Jean de Méung's Boëthius, printed in 1494, is in the British Museum. It is illuminated with miniatures, bound in velvet, and was presented to Henry VII. A chapter of this has lately been compared with Chaucer's translation and the original Boëthius, by Mr. Edward Bell, for the Early English Text Society; and the result is, that Chaucer's version was certainly not made from the French of Jean de Méung, but direct from Boëthius; though some phrases of the Latin are paraphrased rather than translated, in order to bring out their meaning more fully.

[290] Wilk. Con. iii, 242. Quoted by Lingard, v. ch. i.

[291] It appears that so far from being a friend to the classics, Wickliffe felt almost a superstitious intolerance for anything that savoured of ancient Rome. In one of his Prologues he condemns the ecclesiastics for their study of a *pagan* jurisprudence, meaning thereby the Roman law.

[292] See Lingard, iv. ch. 3, where he gives several examples of Wickliffe's system of non-natural interpretation of his own words.

[293] William Lyndwood, LL.D., was Bishop of St. David's, and a learned canonist. He was the author of a collection of constitutions of the English Primates, entitled, *Provinciale, seu Constitutiones Angliæ*, which were printed by Caxton.

[294] Strype's Cranmer, app. 242. We may compare this admission of the Protestant archbishop with the statute of his royal master (33 Henry VIII. c. 12), whereby it was enacted that "no women not of gentle birth, nor journeymen, artificers' apprentices, should read the Bible in English, either to themselves or others;" whilst another Act of the same monarch forbade the public reading of the Scriptures.

[295] A field of battle is perhaps the last place where one would expect to find a Bible; yet in the British Museum is still preserved the copy of the Scriptures found in the tent of King John of France after the battle of Poictiers. It may be remarked, that versions of the Scriptures seem to have appeared in all languages as soon as the vernacular idiom of any country assumed a literary form. Thus we see Queen Anne had her Bohemian Catholic translation; and in 1399 the Polish translation was made by command of the learned queen St. Hedwiges.

[296] The Lollard heresy had been imported from the University of Oxford into that of Prague by some Bohemian gentlemen, who had come over to England in the suite of Queen Anne during the height of the controversy. Prague University at that time numbered as many as 60,000 scholars, and was divided into several nations, and presided over by sixty deans. Only twelve of the deans were Bohemians, and the rest Germans. John Huss, the

rector of the university, who eagerly embraced the new opinions, endeavoured to destroy the German influence; and putting himself at the head of a national party obtained that in future the Bohemians should have two votes in all questions affecting the university and all the other nations united but one. In consequence of this change, which took place in 1409, the German students forsook the university, which from that time fell into decay. This *national* spirit, which was so largely mixed up with the origin and progress of the Hussite heresy, must be taken into account when studying the history of those social revolutions which followed in the track of the new Apostles.

[297] For an account of these foundations see *The Three Chancellors*. (Burns, 1860.)

[298] The present revenues amount to something like £4000 a year, and still afford relief to about 140 poor persons. But the beautiful collegiate church, the carved and gilded roof of which is still visible, is now converted to domestic purposes. The choir is occupied by the women's wards, and the nave by those of the men. This, however, is better than the fate which has awaited St. Paul's Hospital in the same city, which has been transformed into a Bridewell. Few English cities can have been richer in these charitable houses than Norwich, which contained, besides its great College, *seventeen* hospitals for the poor and the sick, by means of which it is probable that very sufficient relief was given to all in distress. For, in most cases, while only a limited number were received into the house, outdoor relief was very extensively granted, and at St. Giles' Hospital it was customary on the Feast of the Annunciation to distribute alms to 130 necessitous persons.

[299] *i.e.* bread and milk.

[300] Fadeth.

[301] Pierced.

[302] Warton says 600, but this possibly included the Angervyle Library, which was united to Gloucester's in 1480. The 129 volumes named above were valued at £1000. Possibly his collection included not a few of the 853 volumes sent over from Paris by his brother the Duke of Bedford.

[303] Carpenter's Life has been written by Brewer, and a statue to his memory, on the pedestal of which are engraved all his munificent deeds, has been erected by the Corporation of London. A catalogue of his books is given in the Appendix to his Life.

[304] Stowe.

[305] The Saints Lives printed by Caxton are *The Lyf of St. Katherin of Senis*, Bradshaw's *Lyf of St. Wenefryde*, and *The Golden Legende*, of which last he printed three editions.

[306] These he never lived to publish, but the autograph MS. of his translation from the French is preserved at Cambridge.

[307] Martene has published in his *Collectanea* an interesting letter addressed to Cecilia by Gregorio Corraro, an old schoolfellow of hers at the Joyous House, who then filled the office of Apostolic Notary, in which he affectionately encourages her in her vocation. Of her mother, Paula Gonzaga, we read that "she was a woman of singular virtue, the mirror of excellence to all Italy. She had a good knowledge of letters, always dressed with great modesty, and daily recited the Divine Office. It was enough to see her," adds her biographer, Vespasiano Bisticci, "to understand what she was."

[308] According to Echard, the dangerous tendency of his idolatry of Plato was pointed out to Ficinus by St. Antoninus, who engaged him to suspend his studies of the heathen philosopher till he had read the *Summa* against the Gentiles, of St. Thomas. And he was wont afterwards to acknowledge that if he had been saved from actual heresy, he owed it solely to the care of this good pastor.

[309] Some curious facts in connection with the proceedings of Pomponius and his associates have recently come to light. Among other discoveries made by the Cavaliere de Rossi in the Roman Catacombs, are certain inscriptions left there by the Academicians, who appear to have made use of these sacred excavations, which were at that time quite neglected by the literary world, as convenient places in which to hold their secret assemblies. One of the accusations brought against them by Paul II. was that they sought to make one of their own members *Pontifex Maximus*. In the Catacombs appear several inscriptions conferring this title on Pomponius: *Regnante Pom. Pont. Max.*, *Pomponius Pont. Max.*, &c.; and others, from which we gather that the *unanimes antiquitatis amatores*, as they called themselves, were lovers not merely of ancient names but of ancient manners; and that they saw no disgrace in thus perpetuating the dissolute habits of their members. It is remarkable that in none of their writings have any of the Academicians said one word about the Catacombs; for though they boasted of being the lovers of antiquity, it was only Pagan antiquity which they regarded worthy of their study: and the Catacombs were simply chosen by them for their convenient privacy. (See De Rossi, *Roma Sutterranea*, tom. i.)

[310] In his second journey into Greece, Lascaris brought back 200 manuscripts, of which eighty were, he informs us, of authors at that time unknown in Europe. The Medicean Library, however, was not destined long

to survive its noble collector. On the death of Lorenzo, his son Pietro having become odious to the Florentines in consequence of his intrigues with Charles VIII. of France, was compelled to fly, the Medici Palace was sacked, and the great library fell a little later into the hands of the French soldiery and the Florentine mob, by whom its vast treasures were soon dispersed. Such portions as could be recovered, however, were afterwards deposited in St. Mark's library.

[311] Bacon, Essay on Gardens.

[312] Wisd. vii. 13.

[313] St. Bernard, *Serm.* xxxvi. in Cantica Canticorum.

[314] Budæus did not escape the suspicion of heretical tendencies, but the charge appears to have been chiefly grounded on certain directions contained in his will for the performance of his funeral obsequies, which his biographers assure us arose from no indifference to religious ceremonial, but from a characteristic modesty and dislike of ostentation.

[315] Perhaps I am wrong in calling Erasmus an apostate canon, for though he quitted his monastery, he at times resumed his habit, whenever he found it convenient. He generally wore it in England, for old-fashioned ideas still held their ground at Oxford; and always appeared with it in Rome, until having been once mobbed by some ragamuffin boys, he applied to the Pope for a formal permission to lay it aside for ever.

[316] This was a hit at the monkish Latin, in which *poetria* sometimes does duty for *poeta*, and, as Erasmus seems to intimate, for the *ars poetica* itself.

[317] Menzel, t. 8, p. 455: t. 6, p. 6-10.

[318] Ibid. t. 6, p. 10-13.

[319] To do Francis I. justice, it must be admitted that he had in his concordat with Leo X. repealed the Pragmatic Sanction; but the same concordat abolished the right of election to benefices, on the plea that such a right was too often abused, and gave the Crown the nomination to all bishoprics, abbeys, and conventual priories within his dominions, with a few privileged exceptions.—See Gaillard, *Hist. de Francois I.* t. 6, p. 37.

[320] Not Peter Martyr Vermigli, the celebrated heretic who afterwards figured as Professor at Oxford, but Peter of Anghieria, a relation of the Borromeo family, who had come into Spain at the invitation of the Spanish Ambassador at Rome, and at the solicitation of Isabella, chose it for his adopted country.

[321] Prescott, Hist. of Ferd. and Isabella.

[322] See Newman's Lectures; "Athens, the fit site for a university."

[323] It was the scene of the martyrdom of the two scholars, Justus and Pastor. See Prudentius, Hymn 4.

[324] By the middle of the seventeenth century the ten colleges of the founder had increased to the number of thirty-five.

[325] This is generally spoken of as the first Italian comedy. The first dramatic composition of the Italian muse, however, was the Orpheus of Politian. Previous to this time the only scenic representations known in Italy were sacred mysteries drawn from Scripture. The questionable *glory* of introducing profane performances is due to Pomponius Lætus, who, along with his other revivals of ancient Roman manners, caused the comedies of Terence and Plautus to be acted in Rome, in which enterprise, says Maffei, he was greatly seconded by Cardinal Riario, who opened a theatre in his own private house. Jovius tells us that Cardinal Bibiena organised a staff of skilful players, and encouraged the youths of Rome to take part in his theatricals.

[326] Jovius, the first historian of his time, was accustomed frankly to avow that "he had two pens, one of gold and the other of iron, to write of princes according to the favours or slights which they bestowed." The Medicean princes were fortunate enough to secure the services of the golden pen, and Clement VII. rewarded his services with the bishopric of Nocera.

[327]

Vivere qui sancte vultis, discedite Roma:

Omnia hic esse licet, non licet esse probum.

[328] Pietro Pomponatus is by some writers erroneously confounded with Pomponius Lætus, the founder of the Roman academy, of whom mention has been made in a foregoing chapter. They resembled one another as in their philosophic errors, so also in their sincere conversion before their death. Pomponius died in 1495; Pomponatus, thirty years later.

[329] The following are the words of Pope Leo X. in the Bull, *Apostolici regiminis.*—"As truth cannot contradict truth, we declare every assertion contrary to the truth of Divine faith to be absolutely false, and strictly forbid any one to teach differently; we command that those who adhere to such assertions shall be avoided and punished, as men who seek to disseminate damnable heresies." Moreover, he rigorously prescribes to all and each of those who give public lessons of philosophy in the universities and elsewhere, that when they read or explain to their pupils the principles and conclusions of those philosophers who notoriously wander from the orthodox faith ... "they employ every effort to set before their eyes the truth

of the Christian religion, and persuade them to it with all their power, and use every care to refute and expose philosophic arguments of this kind, since there are none such which cannot be refuted."

[330] His critics, however, accuse him of often enough falling into the like absurdities. In his version of the New Testament he was accused of continually using pagan expressions, and even of adopting the word *fable* when speaking of the plan of Redemption, using it in the sense in which it is employed by the ancient dramatists to express the action which they portray.

[331] Also known as Philip of Having, or Philip de Bonne Espérance, from the name of the abbey which he governed in the twelfth century. He was the author of many learned works, and the good studies he established in his abbey continued to flourish down to the eighteenth century.

[332] A word first created by the Humanists, who made the name of *Duns* Scotus to stand for an ignoramus.

[333] Ps. lxx. 15.

[334] For the decrees of the Council on these heads, see Rohrbacher, vol. xxii. ch. v.

[335] Audin. Hist. de Luth., ch. viii.

[336] Zach. viii. 3.

[337] Knight, in his life of Colet, remarks that "the History and Antiquities of Oxford sufficiently confess that nothing was known there but Latin, and that in the most depraved style of the schoolmen." Yet two pages back he has quoted from Wood an account of Colet's university studies, which show that this statement, like many of a similar import, is grossly exaggerated. Colet, he says, was educated in grammaticals in London, and then, after spending seven years at Oxford in logicals and philosophicals, was licensed to proceed to arts, "in which he *became so exquisitely learned that all Tully's works were as familiar to him as his Epistles.*" He also read, conferred, and paralleled Plato and Plotinus (in Latin translations), and attained great eminence in mathematics. Erasmus, on occasion of his first visit to Oxford, writes thus to his friend Pisco:—"You ask, does our beloved England please me? Nothing ever pleased me so much. I have found here *classic erudition, and that not trite and shallow, but profound and accurate, both Latin and Greek*, so that I no longer sigh for Italy." In fact, his own Greek learning was chiefly acquired at Oxford, for previous to his coming thither, his knowledge of that language was very superficial. Elsewhere, he says, "I think, from my very soul, there is no country where abound so many men skilled in every kind of learning as there are here."

[338] "Right studious she was in books," says Bishop Fisher in his funeral sermon on this princess, "of which she had great number both in English, Latin, and French, and did translate divers matters of devotion out of French into English."

[339] Mr. Seebohm's interesting work on the "Oxford Reformers of 1498" has appeared since the publication of our first edition. His view of Colet's character is naturally a more favourable one than that here given; but in representing him as a sort of Broad Churchman of the sixteenth century, he sufficiently justifies our strictures on Colet as a Catholic divine.

[340] Knight, quoting from Antiq. Britan., speaks of his preaching a *second* sermon after his interview with Henry VIII., wherein, at the king's request, he spoke in *favour* of the French war. Of this Erasmus says nothing.

[341] To these free views, most Protestant writers, following the authority of Fox and Knight, have added that Colet was opposed to the practice of Auricular Confession. This charge is, however, distinctly disproved in his life. Not only did he bear witness to the comfort and help he himself found in the practice, but in his "Institution of a Christian Man," written for the use of his school, he expressly enjoins the frequent use of confession. 'Use oft tymes confessyon,' is one of his "Precepts of Lyvynge," besides other directions for the reception of the Sacraments of Penance and Houslynge, in sickness, and the hour of death. Colet's strictures, however free, were in fact never directed against the doctrines of the Church, but only against popular practices of devotion. The idea of his having set himself against the use of one of the sacraments, so very welcome to those who would fain claim him as a precursor of the Reformation, has arisen from a gross misconstruction put upon a passage in one of the Epistles of Erasmus. That writer, speaking of his deceased friend, says, among other things, "Ut confessionem secretam *vehementer probabat*, negans se ulla ex re capere tantundem consolationis ac boni spiritus; ita *anxiam ac subinde repetitam vehementer damnabat*" (Eras. Jod. Jon. Ep. 577). Knight, in his Life of Colet (p. 68), paraphrases this sentence in the following extraordinary manner: "Though he approved of private confession, receiving himself a great deal of comfort and inward satisfaction from the use of it, yet he could not but condemn the popular custom of the frequent repetitions of what they called *auricular confession*." The uninitiated Protestant reader is here given to understand that *private confession* was something quite distinct from *what they called auricular confession*, and that whilst Colet approved of the one, he vehemently condemned the other. The plain fact, of course, being that he approved, practised, and enjoined the right and proper use of the Sacrament of Penance, but condemned the indiscreet use which may be made of it by scrupulous and weak-headed penitents. And it is probable that most directors would be of the same opinion.

[342] Fox tells us that Colet sat with some others as judge on certain Lollards, who were burnt for heresy.

[343] In connection with the name of Ammonius, I cannot help noticing the ridiculous use which has been made of one of his familiar letters to Erasmus. A native of Lucca, he suffered much from the inclement English climate, and grumbles about it sadly, saying, moreover, that the burning of heretics has raised the price of wood. Erasmus replies in the same vein: "I am angry with the heretics for making wood so dear for us in this cold season." The jest was rather a heartless one, yet it was but a jest; twenty-three heretics had been induced to recant, but no more than *two* had suffered in England up to this date of Henry's reign: nevertheless, Knight, and some other writers, have made out from this passage the grave historic fact that such numbers were put to death at this time that *all the wood in London was spent in burning them*! The fact is, that Ammonius and Erasmus ceaselessly exercised their wits upon each other, and all their letters are couched in the same style of banter. Thus Erasmus professing to instruct his friend how to get on in England, says in the same merry strain: "First of all, my dear Ammonius, be impudent, thrust yourself into everybody's business, elbow every one who stands in your way, give nothing to anybody without a prospect of getting something better, and always consult your own advantage."

[344] This mystic number bore reference to the miraculous draught of fishes mentioned in St. John's Gospel: ch. xxi. 11.

[345] Holte was usher at Magdalen school, and published his grammar in 1497, under the patronage of Cardinal Morton. Among the grammars enumerated by Erasmus, was one entitled "Mammotrectus" (or "a boy taught by his grandmother"), a name which, as we shall see, was sadly out of place in the academies of the sixteenth century. Before Lily's time, says Wood, there were as many grammars as masters, and the rules of one were contradicted in another.

[346]

From Paul's I went, to Eton sent,

To learn straightway the Latin phrase,

Where fifty-three stripes given to me

At once I had;

For fault but small, or none at all,

It came to pass thus beat I was,

See, Udall, see, the mercy of thee

To me, poor lad.

The result of the Eton system was, that many boys ran away from the school to escape a beating, a circumstance which led Ascham to compose his "Schoolmaster," wherein, like Sir J. Elyot, he pleads for a more humane treatment of young scholars.

[347] Erasmus, de Pueris instituendis. Mr. Seebohm questions the fact of Colet being the "theologian" here referred to.

[348] Exercita Spiritualia. *Regulæ ad sentiendum vere cum Ecclesia.*

[349] Hall.

[350] Ep. 871.

[351] Wilkins, Con. iii. 736. Collier, ii. 52, 53.

[352] Pole had explained the motives of his conduct in a letter addressed to the king, of which Cranmer writes: "It is written with such eloquence, that if it were set forth and known to the common people, I suppose it were not possible to persuade them to the contrary."

[353] Pollina, lib. i. ch. xxix.

[354] As Flaminius is frequently made much of by Protestant writers as an adherent to their opinions, it may be as well to add that the passage touching his conversion by Pole, which appears in the original Italian life of Beccadelli, is omitted in Dudizio's Latin translation. Beccadelli was the personal friend both of Pole and Flaminius, and his testimony is above suspicion.

[355] This is admitted by Ascham, who after boasting in one letter that Homer, Thucydides, and Xenophon are now critically studied at Oxford, is to be found very soon afterwards complaining that these authors are being neglected for others of an inferior calibre. It was no better at Cambridge, where, after the departure of Sir John Cheke, the classical revival died a natural death, the study of divinity having expired long before. "It would pity a man's heart," says Latimer, "to hear what I hear of the state of Cambridge. There be few that study divinity, save those who must of necessity furnish the colleges."

[356] Erasmus died two years before the publication of this report. His "Colloquies" were intended as an educational work, and were written originally for the use of the son of his printer, Froben, their elegant Latinity having found them a ready admittance into the schools. He died in the Protestant city of Basle, unfortified by the sacraments of the Church. His friends erected a monument to his memory, which they surmounted with a bust of the God Terminus, and his fellow-citizens of Rotterdam raised his

statue in their great square, the bronze of which was obtained by melting down a large crucifix which had formerly stood there. The condemnation of his "Colloquies" by the congregation of cardinals, was confirmed by the judgment of the Council of Trent, which caused several of his works to be placed on the index.

[357] *Concilium delectorum cardinalium et aliorum Prælatorum de emendanda Ecclesia, S. D. N. D. Paulo III. ipso jubente conscriptum, et exhibitum, anno MDXXXVIII.*

[358] It is perhaps only fair to notice the earlier efforts made by St. Jerome Æmilian to establish religious colleges and seminaries for the clergy. He appears to have been greatly assisted by the advice of St. Cajetan, and as he died in 1537, must be reckoned as one of the first who organised any scheme for the reform of education. The regular clerks of Somascha continue to this day to carry on the work of their holy founder.

[359] It is stated by Phillips in his Life of Pole, that the rough draft of the decree was after his death found among his papers. Pallavicini tells us that during his absence at Padua, all important questions were communicated to him by his colleagues, *especially* the decree on Justification.

[360] Wilkins, Concilia, t. iv. p. 135.

[361] They were the Cardinals Moroni, Hosius, Gonzaga, D'Altemps, and Navagerio. Cardinals Simonetta and Seripando had also been joined in the Legation, but both died in the early part of 1563, and Cardinal Navagerio was appointed in room of Seripando.

[362] *Canons and Decrees of the Council of Trent, Sess. xxiii. ch. xviii. Pallavicini, lib. xxi. ch. xii. n. 8.* The prelate who most warmly supported the decree was Balduino Balduini, bishop of Aversa. See Martene, Coll. Vet. Scrip. tom. viii.

[363] Pallavicini, lib. xxi. ch. viii. n. 3.

[364] Pall., lib. xxiv. c. 7. n. 2.

[365] The words of M. Olier on this subject are worthy of quotation: "The true and only superior of the seminary is the bishop, who, containing in himself the plenitude of that grace and spirit which is to be shed over the diocese, can alone impart to it its spirit and its life. What the head is to the natural body, the bishop must be in the mystical body of his clergy, and we should labour in vain did we try any other means of sanctifying the ecclesiastical colleges. However excellent may be the sanctity possessed by those eminent and virtuous personages who are to be found scattered through the dioceses, not having that peculiar and essential grace, that spirit of headship (*cet esprit de chef*), which is attached to the sacred character of the episcopate, they cannot attain the fulness of spirit and of life which is capable of filling and vivifying the whole body of the clergy: for, according to St.

Paul, this must flow from the head to the members by means of those joints, veins, and nerves intended for the distribution and communication of life. And these channels communicating with the Fountain Head are nothing else than the priests united to their bishop, according to the primitive ordinance of Jesus Christ."—*Vie de M. Olier, t. 2. p.* 354.

[366] The Catholic university of Thonon was founded exactly with a similar purpose by Clement VIII., at the request of St. Francis of Sales, and the German bishops are said at one time to have contemplated the foundation of a university for the benefit of the Catholic youth of Germany.

[367] 1 Tim. iv. 15.

[368] Up to the present time, as we are informed by Dr. Döllinger, in his inaugural discourse to the University of Munich, the Italian clergy, the most numerous of Europe, make no use of the universities, but are content with the 217 Episcopal seminaries which they possess in their various dioceses.

[369] Ab Ecclesiis vero, musicas eas ubi, sive organo sive cantu, lascivum aut impurum aliquid miscetur, arceant Episcopi. Sess. xx. ch. ix.

[370] Caveant Episcopi ne strepitu incondito sensus sepeliatur.

[371] Pall., lib. xxiv. ch. ix. n. 6.

[372] Parvum gregem bonus Pastor, sancte quieteque pascebat. (Carol. Basc. in Vita S. Caroli. l. i. c. 6, p. 9.) It would seem as if this remarkable man were destined to take part in every good work set on foot during his lifetime, for in 1574 we find him in Spain, where as Apostolic Nuncio, he supported St. Theresa in her reforms. His love of strict discipline earned for him from the wits the nickname of "The World's Reformer."

[373] In the Acts of the Church of Milan (part 5, p. 948) are given the rules for study, drawn by St. Charles for the use of his seminarists. There was to be a grammar class, divided into two sections, which were to be exercised in the grammar of Emanuel Alvarez, the Jesuit, the Epistles of Cicero, and some of the works of Ovid and Virgil. The second class was to be that of the Humanities, also subdivided into two sections, in both of which the students were to practise an elegant Latin style, and to study Cicero *De Officiis*, his epistles to Atticus, and corrected editions of Virgil and Horace. The Greek grammar of Clenard, a celebrated professor of Louvain, was likewise to be explained three times in the week. In the Jesuit schools of Milan the Hebrew language was likewise taught.

[374] They did, in fact, after this take an engagement to serve the diocese for at least three years.

[375] 2 Esdras, iv. 17.

[376] Eccles. l. 8.

www.ingramcontent.com/pod-product-compliance
Ingram Content Group UK Ltd.
Pitfield, Milton Keynes, MK11 3LW, UK
UKHW040717280325
456847UK00002B/350